VANGUARD OF
THE REVOLUTION

VANGUARD OF THE REVOLUTION

The Global Idea of the
Communist Party

A. James McAdams

PRINCETON UNIVERSITY PRESS
Princeton & Oxford

Published by Princeton University Press, 41 William Street, Princeton, New Jersey 08540
In the United Kingdom: Princeton University Press, 6 Oxford Street, Woodstock,
    Oxfordshire OX20 1TR

press.princeton.edu

Jacket image: Vladimir Lenin, Leon Trotsky, and Lev Kamenev. Universal History
    Archive / UIG / Bridgeman Images

ISBN 978-0-691-16894-4

Library of Congress Control Number: 2017941546

British Library Cataloging-in-Publication Data is available

This book has been composed in Garamond Premier Pro, Goudy Trajan, and ITC
    Legacy Sans Std

Printed on acid-free paper. ∞

Printed in the United States of America

10 9 8 7 6 5 4 3 2 1

To Nancy

and

To our children and grandchildren

CONTENTS

What is—or was—the communist party? Political scientists and historians have produced a rich and extensive literature on individual parties. Thanks to this scholarship, we have both provocative theories and painstaking analyses covering the evolution and organization of nearly every communist party in the world. These studies range from such behemoths as the Communist Party of the Soviet Union and the Chinese Communist Party to much smaller, though no less interesting, parties such as the Albanian Party of Labor and the Mongolian People's Revolutionary Party. Yet, there are virtually no comprehensive studies of the communist party overall. This is surprising. In the twentieth century, the communist party was one of the two most influential party institutions in the world. It was the primary challenger to the liberal-democratic party. Communist leaders ruled huge parts of the globe and demanded the attention of hundreds of millions of people.

In this book, I seek to fill this gap through a systematic examination of this unique institution. I have two goals. The first is to provide an interpretive political history of the party's evolution over long periods and in vastly diverse settings. Despite the similarities in their names and shared beliefs, communist parties in countries like Germany, the United States, North Korea, and Cuba differed in fundamental ways. They also changed over time. My second goal is to offer a cohesive *argument* about why these parties took so many different forms. I contend that these differences were driven by their leaders' choices about a recurring theme: the relationship between the idea of the revolutionary party and the need for an effective party organization. Without compelling ideas, I argue, these parties would have had few followers, and without coherent organizations, they would have fallen apart.

In structuring my account, I have deliberately sought to speak to both scholars and general readers. I hope that political scientists and historians who specialize in one part of the world will find my analysis of the global evolution of the communist party useful for comparing their cases with those in other regions. Naturally, given the scope of my study, I have not been able to cover the cases of every party or every period in the communist era. Additionally, I hope that general readers will find this study to be a provocative introduction to one of the most significant political institutions of modern times. I have avoided jargon and limited endnotes to primary sources and statistical sources (wherever possible in English). Rather than providing an exhaustive bibliography, I have prepared a list of suggested English-language readings that should help the reader begin to explore my topic.

This book is the product of many years of studying, writing, and teaching about world communism. Many people have played a role in its gestation. In the early stages of my career, I was fortunate to encounter and be inspired by many of the foremost thinkers in the field that was then known as "comparative communism": Cyril Black, George Breslauer, Stephen Cohen, Gregory Grossman, Andrew Janos, Ken Jowitt, Richard Löwenthal, Norman Naimark, Robert Tucker, Richard Ullman, and Dale Vree.

In writing this book, I have benefited from the advice, generosity, and encouragement of numerous people. I am indebted to those who read and commented on significant segments of the manuscript: George Breslauer, Lowell Dittmer, Graeme Gill, Michel Hockx, Victoria Tin-bor Hui, Lionel Jensen, George Liber, Stephen Lovell, Semion Lyandres, Alex Martin, and Maria Rogacheva. I am also grateful to many others for their advice on individual chapters: Heinrich Bortfeldt, Shaojin Chai, Forrest Colburn, John Deak, Felipe Fernández-Armesto, Robert Fishman, Andy Gould, Ferenc Hörcher, Hrvoje Kekez, Elisabeth Köhler, Jeff Kopstein, Tom Kselman, Willem Melching, Balazs Mezei, Olivier Morel, Norman Naimark, Slawomir Nowosad, David O'Connor, Francesco Pitassio, Richard Rose, Wolfgang Seibel, Roman Setov, Ivette Sosa-Frutos, Ernesto Verdeja, Lynn White, and John Quangsheng Zhao. In addition, I thank the anonymous reviewers of this book for their excellent counsel. Finally, I express my gratitude to my graduate and undergraduate research assistants for their tireless work on my behalf: Joshua Bandoch, Michael Bocchino, Omar Coronel-Cuadros, Ellen Dahlby,

Juan Albarracín Dierolf, Helen Favorite, April Dan Feng, Laura Gamboa-Gutierrez, Brian Klein, Stephen Payne, Ana Petrova, Luis Schenoni, Gregory Siems, Flora Xiao Tang, Thomas White, and Kathy Wodolowski.

For more than two and a half decades, I have been fortunate to be a faculty member at the University of Notre Dame. In this unique intellectual community, I continue to be inspired by both my colleagues and my students, for their love of learning and their faith that scholarly pursuits should never be separated from their human context. For many years, I have been especially lucky to direct the Nanovic Institute for European Studies. Located within the Keough School for Global Affairs, the Nanovic Institute is an extraordinary home for interdisciplinary scholarship and conversation among all fields in the humanities, the arts, and the social sciences. I extend my heartfelt thanks to all of the Institute's staff members for their support. In particular, I am deeply grateful to Sharon Konopka. Over the past fifteen years, Sharon has helped me in countless ways to balance my multiple responsibilities at Notre Dame, and she has been an unflagging source of wisdom and good humor. In addition, I thank Cathy Bruckbauer, who has skillfully dissected my prose and been a much-needed source of insight and encouragement.

I am grateful to the Dr. William M. Scholl Foundation, which for many years has played a crucial role in making my scholarship possible. In 2012–2013, the Kulturwissenschaftliches Kolleg in Konstanz, Germany, afforded me an invaluable opportunity to conduct research while overlooking the Rhine River. I have been fortunate to publish this book with Princeton University Press. I am especially grateful to my editor, Eric Crahan, for his confidence, enthusiasm, advice, and patience. Also, I thank Kathleen Cioffi, John Donohue, and Hannah Zuckerman for their help in producing this book.

Finally, I dedicate this book with love to Nancy, without whose boundless understanding and devotion it would not exist, and to our children and grandchildren. In these politically tumultuous times, when liberal democracy is once again threatened by extremism and intolerance, I hope they will be inspired by public servants who are worthy of their intelligence, open-mindedness, and goodness.

NOTE

In writing a book that covers the histories of scores of parties over more than one and a half centuries, I have inevitably had to wrestle with word usage. As a rule, I have followed the conventions of a majority of scholars in matters of transliteration and abbreviation. For the transliteration of most Chinese words, I follow the Pinyin system. For example, I use "Mao Zedong" rather than "Mao Tse-tung" and "Guomindang" rather than "Kuomintang." In exceptional cases, I have followed the established practice of using the Wade-Giles system. Thus, I use "Chiang Kai-shek" instead of "Jiang Jieshi" and "Peking University" instead of "Beijing University." Russian transliterations can be even more complicated. I have used a hybrid model, one based on the ALA/LOC standard but also incorporating popularly accepted variants. For example, I use "Grigory Zinoviev" instead of "Grigorii Zinov'ev."

Abbreviations can be equally complicated. Some abbreviations, such as the names of political parties, are typically based upon their original language; others are based upon their English translations. Here, too, I have adhered to scholarly conventions. For example, I refer to the "Communist Party of the Soviet Union" (Kommunisticheskaya Partiya Sovetskogo Soyuza) as the "CPSU," whereas I use "PCF" in the case of the "French Communist Party" (Parti communiste français).

The hardest decision I have had to make was whether to use "Leninism" or "Marxism-Leninism" to refer to the set of principles identified with the communist party after Vladimir Ilyich Lenin's death. In general, I use "Leninism" because this is how the term was first rendered in formative works, such as in the title of Joseph Stalin's *Foundations of Leninism*. However, in those cases where this phenomenon is described in a rigidly doctrinal sense or when it arises in the speeches and publications of party leaders, I use "Marxism-Leninism."

ABBREVIATIONS

APC	Agricultural Producers' Cooperative
APL	Albanian Party of Labor
BCP	British Communist Party
BCP	Bulgarian Communist Party
BSP	British Socialist Party
CCP	Chinese Communist Party
CCP	Communist Party of Cuba (1925–1939)
CCRG	Central Cultural Revolution Group
CDR	Committees for the Defense of the Revolution
CGT	General Confederation of Labour
CNOC	Cuban National Labor Confederation
Cominform	Communist Information Bureau
Comintern	Communist International, Third International
CPC	Communist Party of Czechoslovakia
CPRF	Communist Party of the Russian Federation
CPSU	Communist Party of the Soviet Union
CPUSA	Communist Party of the United States
DC	Christian Democracy
ECCI	Executive Committee of the Communist International
FAR	Cuban Revolutionary Armed Forces
GDR	German Democratic Republic
GMD	Guomindang
GPCR	Great Proletarian Cultural Revolution
HCP	Hungarian Communist Party
HSP	Hungarian Socialist Party
HSWP	Hungarian Socialist Workers' Party
HWPP	Hungarian Working People's Party
ILP	Independent Labour Party
ISB	International Socialist Bureau
IWA	International Working Men's Association

Komsomol	Young Communist League
KPA	Korean People's Army
KPD	Communist Party of Germany
KPP	Communist Party of Poland
KWP	Korean Workers' Party
LCY	League of Communists of Yugoslavia
MPP	Mongolian People's Party
MPRP	Mongolian People's Revolutionary Party
NEP	New Economic Policy
NKVD	People's Commissariat for Internal Affairs
NRA	National Revolutionary Army
NSF	National Salvation Front
OGPU	Joint State Political Directorate
ORI	Integrated Revolutionary Organizations
PCC	Communist Party of Cuba (after 1965)
PCE	Spanish Communist Party
PCF	French Communist Party
PCI	Italian Communist Party
PLA	Party of Labor of Albania
PLA	People's Liberation Army
Politburo	Political Bureau
POUM	Workers' Party of Marxist Unification
POW	prisoner of war
PPR	Polish Workers' Party
PRC	Cuban Revolutionary Party
PRC	People's Republic of China
PS	Socialist Party
PSI	Italian Socialist Party
PSP	Popular Socialist Party
PUWP	Polish United Workers' Party
RCP	Romanian Communist Party
RCP(B)	Russian Communist Party (Bolsheviks)
RSDLP	Russian Social Democratic Labor Party
RWP	Romanian Workers' Party
SAPD	Socialist Workers' Party of Germany
SDAP	Social Democratic Workers' Party of Germany
SDP	Social Democratic Party of Hungary
SDRP	Social Democracy of the Republic of Poland
SED	Socialist Unity Party of Germany

SEM	Socialist Education Movement
SFIC	French Section of the Communist International
SFIO	French Section of the Workers' International
SLP	Socialist Labour Party
Sovnarkom	Council of People's Commissars
SPD	Social Democratic Party of Germany
SRs	Socialist Revolutionaries
TUC	Trades Union Congress
UIR	Insurrectionary Revolutionary Union
USPD	Independent Social Democratic Party of Germany
USSR	Union of Soviet Socialist Republics
WSF	Workers' Socialist Federation
YCP	Yugoslav Communist Party

VANGUARD OF
THE REVOLUTION

CHAPTER 1

Introduction

On March 14, 1990, a majority of the 2,250 members of the Soviet Union's one-year-old parliament, the Congress of People's Deputies, voted to amend Article VI of their country's constitution. The old article had been neat, compact, and to the point. It specified what had long seemed self-evident and nonnegotiable: the Communist Party of the Soviet Union (CPSU) was "the leading and guiding force of Soviet society and the nucleus of its political system and of all state organizations and social organizations." Furthermore, the CPSU was "armed with Marxist-Leninist doctrine." So equipped, the party's purpose was to impart to the Soviet people a "planned and scientifically-sound character to their struggle for the victory of communism."[1] In contrast, the delegates to the Congress of People's Deputies saw the CPSU quite differently. Their description of the party in the new version of Article VI could not have been more ambiguous. They voted to include the CPSU in the document, but only as one of various unspecified political parties, trade unions, public organizations, and mass movements. Unlike in decades past, its representatives would have to seek office in competition with other parties and, as in all political systems governed by the rule of law, they would be subject to the parliament's decisions. Most revealing, the revised article made no reference to the party's leading role.[2]

We cannot help looking back with astonishment at the decisiveness and finality of this change. Although two of the Soviet Union's allies, Hungary and Poland, had essentially cast aside the principle of single-party rule one year earlier in spring 1989, the significance of these events only became fully apparent when waves of protest and popular disaffection with communist rule resulted in the elimination of similar constitutional clauses in East Germany, Czechoslovakia, and Bulgaria.

In response, Soviet authorities struggled to prevent the contagion from spilling into their country. At the parliament's preceding session in mid-December 1989, CPSU general secretary Mikhail Gorbachev and his coleaders tried to keep Article VI off the agenda. When prominent deputies, like the poet Yevgeny Yevtushenko and the physicist-turned-human-rights-activist Andrei Sakharov, demanded that the party be divested of its sacrosanct character and forced to test its reputation at the voting booth, Gorbachev fought back. The Congress had more pressing topics to address, he insisted. "We don't need to act in this matter as if it were an emergency," the general secretary declared. "Why all this drama? We must approach the matter of constitutional changes with great responsibility."[3]

Nonetheless, this *was* an emergency, and Gorbachev knew it. His party's existence was in jeopardy. For more than a decade, the CPSU leadership had been painfully aware that many of its rank-and-file members no longer believed their organization was worth defending in its current form. Indeed, only a month earlier, when more than 200,000 protestors took their demands for multiparty elections into the streets of Moscow, one could easily find CPSU members among the marchers. Thus, if not by his words then by his actions, Gorbachev showed on the day after the amendment of Article VI that he recognized how much the world had changed. He allowed the People's Congress to elect him as the Soviet Union's first and—it would transpire—last president. When he delivered the CPSU's official report four months later at its Twenty-Eighth Congress in July 1990 in this new capacity, his position as general secretary of the party was no longer the primary source of his authority and his relationship with his longtime comrades was qualitatively different. One year later, following an abortive military coup, Gorbachev resigned from the CPSU leadership and, as president, ordered the abolition of all party posts in the government. For all intents and purposes, both in the Soviet Union and in a majority of countries like it, the party was finished.

An Idea before an Organization

What was the communist party? At first glance, the answer to this question seems straightforward. If we go by the doctrinal definition that the Soviets associated with the leader of the Bolshevik revolution, Vladimir Ilyich Lenin, and formulated under Joseph Stalin's rule, a communist party is a revolutionary organization committed to the forcible overthrow of capitalism. Its goal is to replace the rule of the bourgeoisie with a socialist dictatorship of the proletariat, which leads the way toward the attainment of a classless, communist society. Its "Leninist" or "Marxist-Leninist" members must be selfless individuals who care only about the common cause and adhere unquestioningly to the party's command. Equipped with the insights of revolutionary figures like Karl Marx, Friedrich Engels, and Lenin, they will bring truth to the proletariat and educate them about their real interests. With the vanguard's guidance, the working masses will fulfill their historical destiny by rising up and overthrowing their oppressors. Because these workers "have no country," a revolution in one part of the world will inevitably be followed in other countries once they have an advanced proletariat.

The parties that described themselves in these formal terms left an indelible mark in the twentieth century. When Gorbachev came to power in 1985, their members could legitimately count themselves as participants in a global institution. For more than a century, and long before the advent of the phenomena that we associate with globalization today—international currency flows, supranational corporations, the Internet, and social media—the communist party could be found everywhere. It reached across continents and into disparate countries, sprawling urban centers and tiny peasant villages, crowded factories and university discussion circles. Out of the 162 countries in the world in 1985, twenty-four were ruled by communist parties. This number compares favorably with the thirty-five countries that were governed by communism's primary global competitor, liberal democracy. At the same time, approximately 38 percent of the world's population lived under communist regimes (1.67 billion out of 4.4 billion). The CPSU's International Department officially recognized 95 ruling and nonruling communist parties. Overall, if one includes the 107 parties with significant memberships, there were approximately 82 million communist party members worldwide.[4]

Nevertheless, even someone with a casual acquaintance with the history of world communism will immediately recognize the challenge of sorting out the relationship between these figures and the revolutionary organs that people like Marx, Lenin, Mao Zedong, and Fidel Castro envisioned.[5] Unless they were imposed by an external force, few communist parties found their way to power as a result of the popular upheavals that the founders of the movement anticipated. In those cases when indigenous parties came to power, such as in China, Yugoslavia, and Vietnam, even fewer were based on the actions of the proletariat. A majority rose in developing countries and their success was heavily dependent on the engagement of nonworking-class strata, especially the peasantry. Furthermore, in both imposed and indigenous revolutions, the result was not a dictatorship by the formerly oppressed majority. It was a dictatorship of the party over the whole society.

This circumstance presents a puzzle to students of politics and history. How could an institution that made such a huge mark on the world have been significantly different from what its progenitors imagined—and still flourish? In this book, I shall argue that we can only resolve this question if we wean ourselves off the notion that the party should only—or, in many cases, even primarily—be understood as a formal organization. When we look back on the history of world communism, what stands out in many of the most prominent cases, including the Soviet Union and China, is that there were communists or left-wing radicals who would become affiliated with these movements long before the party acquired standardized rules and regulations. A majority had little or no experience with politics. They were not bound to the doctrinal conception of the communist party that I have sketched above. Instead, they were motivated by an evolving body of beliefs about what needed to be done to stage a successful revolution and what should come afterward. In fact, many of the communist parties that I shall consider in this book—in Russia, China, Italy, Germany, and others—were initially distinguished by their leaders' engagement in open deliberation and debate over their missions and tactics.

It is no accident that this fluid understanding of revolutionary leadership had enormous staying power. The idea of the communist party's leading role was born, nurtured, tested, and transformed in turbulent times. Between the second half of the nineteenth century and the first half of the twentieth century, one could find reasons for the wholesale rejection of the status quo everywhere. Establishment institutions failed to prevent human catastrophes that were occurring on a scale the world had never seen—world wars, civil wars, mass demonstrations, peasant uprisings, foreign invasions, and full-scale economic collapse. The youthful idealists, intellectuals, artisans, religious and ethnic minorities, and women's activists who threw themselves into revolutionary activity over these decades had many suitors—anarchists, syndicalists, populists, utopian socialists, terrorists, and fascists. But none could compete with the global appeal of the communist party. The idea of the vanguard simultaneously provided its adherents with three powerful reasons to follow its command: the confidence that they were part of a progressive movement that was destined to succeed, the satisfaction of serving a cause that was superior to themselves, and the pride of being associated with a drama of grand historical proportions.

Almost uniquely among modern political parties, the early conception of the communist party was based on the conviction of many revolutionaries that their victory was inevitable. In the party's embryonic period, the movement's foremost thinkers, Karl Marx and Friedrich Engels, outlined a theory of human relations that was tantalizingly simple. In their depiction, the coming revolution was preordained by an unresolvable contradiction between the interests of a minority class that controlled the means of production and a majority of workers whose labor was exploited in the never-ending pursuit of profit. Initially, the proletariat had no choice but to accept this condition. But eventually, the contradictions between these classes would become so unbearable that the working class would be propelled into overthrowing the existing system of production.

In fact, Marx and Engels's specific predictions were only realized, if at all, in a few isolated circumstances. Yet, this circumstance did not present communist leaders with an insurmountable dilemma. To the contrary, as I shall show throughout this book, the message they bequeathed about the ineluctable victory of an oppressed majority over an oppressive minority provided future generations of revolutionaries with a lasting resource. The "family resemblance" of this dichotomy to other, equally profound conflicts between majorities and minorities in their own countries, such as those between peasants and landowners, nationalist liberators and colonial administrations, and patriots and invaders, enabled those who called themselves "Marxists" to characterize their causes as worthy of support in the fight.[6] Their leaders did not always act on the possibilities afforded by these dichotomies. Still, they were available as lifeboats to carry their movements forward.

In addition, the idea of the communist party was attractive because it offered a sense of community and belonging in times when human relationships were fractured by social unrest and war. In return for the privilege of being a part of this community, party members were willing to sacrifice their individuality to the collective enterprise of discerning the path to a just society. The annals of communism are replete with evidence of the seriousness with which this holy "first communion" was taken.[7] Consider the words of Milovan Djilas, one of the preeminent figures in post–World War II Yugoslav politics and an equally influential dissident in later years, when he described the intoxicating impact of this shared agenda. "My own fate was of no account compared to the struggle being waged," he related, "and our disagreements were of no importance beside the obvious inevitability of the realization of our idea."[8]

The corollary to this moral obligation was the undeniable and often horrifying extent to which party members could consciously justify sacrificing their fellow believers in the name of the common cause. Two decades after Djilas's confession, Julia Minc, the former head of the Polish Press Agency and vice president of the State Employment Commission, defended this principle when asked about the execution of innocent party members: "If you have to choose between the party and an individual, you choose the party, because the party has a general aim, the good of many people, but one person is just one person."[9]

Finally, the party members' belief in the inevitability of the revolution and willingness to subordinate their private interests to the good of the whole were based upon the assumption that they would not abuse their positions. They had the privilege of leading this movement simply because they, more than others, were equipped to discern the interests of the people. "We communists," Joseph Stalin declared in 1926, "are people of a special mold. We are made of a special stuff.... There is nothing higher than being a member of the party whose founder and leader was comrade Lenin." At the same time, he admonished, each member was obliged to uphold Lenin's bequest "with honor."[10] To be sure, Stalin would vigorously violate this principle in later years. But the idea of the virtuous party would live on.

THE IDEA AND THE ORGANIZATION

The conception of the communist party as a revolutionary idea can account for the loyalties of its early members. But it cannot account for how these loyalties were sustained. In the face of this challenge, the greatest weakness of Marx's prophecies and those of other early communists is their foundation on a conception of time that placed the attainment of their dream at an unspecified future date. We can hardly fault nineteenth-century thinkers for this lack of specificity. Marx and his contemporaries' greatest contribution is the assertion that history marches according to a progressive logic. The fact, however, that the promised land lies in the distant future means that the leaders of parties that come later are particularly dependent on having the right conditions to convince their members that they should press ahead.

In times of turmoil, these parties' calls for sacrifice make sense. Their members have "nothing to lose but their chains" and "a world to gain."[11] The difficulties arise when adverse conditions abate. They not only test their leaders' skills in convincing their members that their ideals are worth the price of loyalty, they also force them to make a difficult choice. They can identify new reasons to demand ideological vigilance and a reinvigoration of the class struggle by invoking specters like the class enemy, hidden saboteurs, and imperialist aggressors. Or they can adjust the terms according to which the transition to a new society takes place.

These changing circumstances set up an unavoidable conflict between two conceptions of the party, one as an idea and the other as an organization. Those communists who emphasize the first conception maintain that the process of building socialism and making the eventual transition to communism will remain long and arduous. In their view, even parties that have successfully attained power will need to maintain revolutionary vigilance in the face of continuing threats from domestic and imperialist aggression. During this "state of simmering war, a state of military measures of struggle against the enemies of proletarian power," as Lenin observed in one of his last essays, the party is justified in doing whatever is necessary to defend its achievements.[12]

Conversely, those communists who emphasize the organizational features of the party contend that one cannot allow the focus on revolution to preclude the formation of established routines to hold their movement together, including meaningful membership requirements, regular meetings, and consistent standards of decision making. Moreover, they maintain that if the party is weak and threatened with obsolescence, its leaders may have to accommodate themselves to working with established institutions. Once these parties assume political responsibility, these tasks become even more important. After the devastating consequences of military conflict and social upheaval, leaders who suddenly find themselves in power must provide their followers with tangible signs that the self-imposed hardships of a revolutionary movement have been worth bearing. In these cases, they require the means to bring their broken economies back to good health and to restore an atmosphere of calm and stability.

In drawing this distinction between the idea of the revolutionary party and the organizational party, I do not mean to suggest that these two conceptions are destined to collide. Just as in any political movement, political leaders everywhere—although not always, as we shall see in the case of some revolutionaries—seek to minimize the degree to which their choices between the ideas and the practical demands of governance become mutually exclusive. In the communist world, a political order based solely on the idea of constantly revolutionizing society would explode; one based solely on organization would fail to inspire its followers and grind to a halt. Nonetheless, we can speak about competing tendencies on a spectrum of difficult choices. Historically, some rulers took their party's revolutionary ideals more deeply to heart in making their decisions, while others favored the stability and predictability afforded by clear rules and identifiable routines.

If communist parties were structured like those of their liberal-democratic adversaries, these choices would not be particularly consequential. When liberal-democratic institutions work effectively, strong legislatures, independent judiciaries, and regular elections impose meaningful constraints on the exercise of power. But in the case of communist parties, the difference is decisive. The primacy that these party regimes assign to centralized decision making and their insistence upon the disciplined observance of their commands leaves them open to corrosive tendencies that undermine their virtuous pretensions. Unlike parliamentary regimes, the absolute authority of single-party rule seriously limits the extent of personal accountability in the upper echelons of power. Under these circumstances, the party is vulnerable to being kidnapped by leaders who have the political savvy to build effective alliances and the charismatic vision to capture the imagination of a broad following. Indeed, it is a revealing indication of the party's susceptibility to such manipulation that we frequently associate the policies of these regimes with the thoughts, words, and deeds of single persons—a Lenin, a Stalin, a Mao, or a Fidel Castro—and not with their political institutions. In these cases, the idea that decision making is a collective enterprise evaporates and, in its wake, the leader's preferences take over.

One can only marvel at the ease with which dictators monopolized decision making. Stalin spoke the language of revolution, but he used repressive measures to guarantee that his rigid conception of the term drowned out all others. Manifesting his animosity toward opposing viewpoints, he listened from the corridors of the House of Unions as Soviet prosecutors induced his longtime Bolshevik comrades in arms to make preposterous confessions during the Moscow show trials. He often signed their death warrants. Mao casually made decisions from the comfort of his swimming pool that eviscerated his Central Committee and destroyed the lives of millions of people. Each figure was driven by the narcissistic belief that he alone was capable of solving the problems that confront humanity. The lack of institutional accountability provided them, as well as countless other despotic personalities, with the opportunity to steer the mechanisms of power to their use.

These factors also contributed to the all-around deformation of the idea of the virtuous vanguard. One cannot account for the greatest horrors in communist history—Stalin's purges, Mao's Great Leap Forward, and the unfathomable dimensions of Pol Pot and the Khmer Rouge's campaigns in the 1970s to "purify" Cambodian society— without recognizing the self-seeking and opportunistic motivations of midlevel party officials and cadres, as well as the secret police organs. Down the road, although in a far less violent way, these corrosive tendencies were evident in times of stability. In the 1970s and 1980s, in contradiction to official pronouncements that "communists have no special rights except the right always to be in the forefront where difficulties are the greatest," to quote CPSU chief Leonid Brezhnev in 1967, members frequently took advantage of their official positions to obtain benefits that were unavailable to ordinary citizens.[13] They had access to higher-quality consumer products, better apartments, and international travel, even if this privilege was confined to visiting fraternal allies like Mongolia, Angola, and Cuba. Some went further. Exchanging virtue for vice, they built personal fiefdoms, conducted business on the black market, and provided friends and family members with lucrative employment. In the 1990s and 2000s, Chinese and Vietnamese communists took the exploitation of personal privilege to new heights, even while denouncing the practice publicly.

In retrospect, one can easily understand why this cynical behavior eventually led to the erosion of popular support for these regimes. Yet significantly, this disillusionment was slow to take noticeable form in most socialist countries. In fact, given the benefits of holding office, party elites tacitly and perhaps even subconsciously colluded to maintain their privileges. In a culture of insiders, only the rare, wayward member chose to question these practices, even behind closed doors. Hence, notwithstanding occasional public expressions of discontent by nonparty members, a majority of these regimes had the appearance of relative stability.

An Idea in Motion

Thus far, I have provided reasons for the communist party's striking record of resilience and its members' commitment to maintaining its leading role. I have argued that single-party rule was, from the beginning, a compelling political idea. Even before it took organizational form, it garnered the loyalty of hopeful revolutionaries because it seemed to provide the solution to a multitude of different challenges—national liberation, economic modernization, cultural transformation—that went beyond the conventional Marxist focus on the class struggle over control of the means of production. Once in power, these parties evolved into viable organizations that, for the most part, proved up to the task of satisfying their members' political and personal desires. In some cases, such as during Stalin's socialist revolution from above, communist parties played crucial roles in transforming backward economies into industrial behemoths—albeit at the cost of unfathomable suffering. When these achievements lost their allure in the later stages of communist rule, they offered their supporters the less-than-virtuous comforts that come from sticking with the status quo.

If one were to stop at this point, as many scholars have done, one could easily leave the impression that the communist party's long life was based upon a coherent set of beliefs that gave it broad appeal in one era and then fizzled out when it could no longer satisfy its followers.[14] The shortcoming of this image, as I shall contend throughout this book, is that it does not capture the multiplicity of forms that the party assumed. Over long periods and across diverse regions, the definition of the party's leading role meant different things to different people. At some points, its leaders' interpretations of their responsibilities led to the elaboration of distinctive paths that determined their government's policies for decades. At others, the party's role as a meaningful revolutionary institution was minimal or, as it became after Stalin went to war with his longtime Bolshevik comrades in battle in the 1930s, simply nonexistent.

In contrast, other scholars have sought to account for the party's longevity by depicting it as an organization that provided its leaders with the flexibility to reflect upon their options and adapt to changing times and circumstances.[15] According to this perspective, party leaders were continually looking for ways to maximize their organization's attractiveness in diverse settings. Thus, parties that aspired to build followings in advanced industrial economies tailored their messages differently than those that sought to curry the favor of large peasant populations. Because working-class audiences were routinely exposed to the appeals of left-wing parties, such as moderate social democrats, communist agitators pragmatically set aside their prophecies of an imminent revolution and advanced policies that allowed for temporary accommodations with their competitors. In contrast, communist guerrilla fighters took different approaches because their survival depended on gaining the confidence of village communities. Rather than advancing policies that were geared to mobilizing urban workers or skilled professionals, they embraced broad populist appeals to win the hearts and minds of their audiences.

There is undeniable truth to both of these approaches. Without some common convictions, it is hard to imagine how the communist party would have spread to so many different parts of the world. Likewise, those parties that were unwilling to adapt to their circumstances quickly lost popular support. What these approaches lack, in my view, is an adequate way of accounting for change. The party's long history cannot be accurately described as a simple story of life and death. Nor did it represent a straightforward attempt to discern the right strategies from one stage of development to the next. Rather, in Europe, Asia, and the Americas, its story is a record of fits and starts, successes and failures, and steps that were neither forward nor backward. These developments cannot be reduced to a historical teleology. In this book, I shall argue that one can only make sense of the communist party's different forms by recognizing the decisive impact of the personalities who dominated it. These individuals' victory over other contenders for power and the prevalence of highly centralized institutions endowed them with the means to decide which aspects of the party's complex identity would be dominant. Additionally, they could determine the strategies that would be employed in pursuing its objectives. In short, they became the masters of the party idea.[16]

When we consider the party's long-term prospects, these dictators' overwhelming power had both advantageous and detrimental consequences for the character of the communist movement. On the positive side, as we shall see, Lenin's skillful portrayal of the Bolsheviks as a party that could serve the interests of multiple segments of the Russian population was an abiding contribution to the vitality of the international communist movement. Similarly, Mao's mastery of the idiom of peasant rebellion made foreign concepts intelligible and attractive to party members who might otherwise have been unresponsive to them.

On the negative side, the concentration of power in the hands of a single person or persons had recurrent tragic consequences. One of the most prominent features of communist rule in the twentieth century was the stubborn resistance of dictators like Stalin and Mao to modifying their policies in the face of perilous circumstances. Stalin obliterated his army's general command despite repeated indications of Germany's intention to go to war with the USSR. More broadly, his systematic assault on the old Bolshevik elite deprived the country of its single most credible source of legitimation, save for his own personality cult. As a consequence, when Stalin died he left his successors with the formidable challenge of rebuilding a viable party institution to defend their authority. Likewise, Mao's desire for total power and his refusal to heed the warnings of his advisers led him to champion the disastrous idea of a never-ending revolution during the Great Leap Forward of the late 1950s. When his deputies sought to promote more responsible policies in the wake of this debacle, Mao renewed his romantic focus on the party's purposes as a pretext to destroy it as a functioning organization. In the case of both despots, there was little those around them could have done to prevent these catastrophes from taking place.

Perhaps one can find a grain of solace in one aspect of the communist party's hypercentralized structure. One can imagine scenarios in which other figures could have risen to power. For every Stalin or Mao, there were equally influential personalities who were capable of offering alternate conceptions of party rule. As I shall suggest, it is conceivable that communists like Nikolai Bukharin in the Soviet Union and Liu Shaoqi in China would have instituted more benign forms of dictatorship if they had won the internal power struggles. Yet even if they had managed to get this far, their positions at the apex of decision making would have had the same, familiar drawback. They, too, had risen in a culture of revolutionary violence. Although one might hope otherwise, they could still have made the wrong choices.

The impact of personal despotism presents a nagging question about the party's longevity. Once power is monopolized by a single individual, how is it possible for the organization to adopt new policies when it needs to? One possibility is that a window of opportunity opens when a dictator either dies or is removed from office. In these instances, the record of reform is mixed at best. Whatever a new leader might profess in public, there is no guarantee that he will be any more responsible than his predecessors. As Soviet citizens found after Stalin's death, old dictatorial habits die hard. Although Stalin's successors mercifully broke free from the spiral of terror, Nikita Khrushchev's years in office demonstrated the abiding tendency to vacillate between adherence to stable routines and a return to the demagogic practices of old. In the same way, a dictator's removal from office is an equally unpredictable source of change. Until the 1980s, due to the concentration of power in these regimes, very few leaders lost their positions as a result of internal party struggles. In the exceptional cases when they were replaced, it was almost always the result of the intervention of a single external force—the Soviet Union. However, in these cases as well, new rulers did not necessarily mean new policies. These power holders not only had to want change, they also needed the wherewithal to build coalitions and, if they were fortunate, the support of an outside power, again the Soviet Union.

Ironically, many of the most profound changes in the understanding of communist party rule have come from circumstances in which the institution's role has been tangential. I have already described one of them. This is the "good luck" that comes from events that have been generated by political instability or the devastation of war. It is impossible to understand the longevity of the Bolshevik regime, virtually all of the Eastern European regimes that came into being after World War II, and the victory of the Chinese communists without taking into account the multiple tragedies that enabled them to force their way into power. In many cases, such as Castro's Cuba, one cannot account for these regimes' staying power without considering the impact of an external threat.

A final impetus to significant change comes from the "bad luck" of unintended consequences, when these leaders attempt to serve their interests by doing one thing and inadvertently create conditions that erode the chances of achieving their goals. An appreciation of this paradox is crucial for understanding the fortunes of dictatorships everywhere. If new policies can only come from those persons who monopolize power and these rulers will only take steps that they perceive to enhance their authority, it follows that major changes must derive from their misperceptions and mistakes. There is no better example of this unforgiving logic than the outcome of Mikhail Gorbachev's attempt to reform his party. It was no accident that Gorbachev's defense of the CPSU's leading role before the Congress of People's Deputies in spring 1990 was futile. He found himself in this position because he had idealistically attempted over the preceding five years to revitalize the reputation of a flagging institution. He never intended to raise doubts about the party's ruling authority. Quite the contrary, he was bent on restoring it. Yet, once he opened the legitimacy of the organ's vanguard functions to debate, he set forces in motion that culminated in the CPSU's loss of all credible reasons for existing. As a result, the entire edifice of communist rule came crashing down.

The Life and Death of the Party

This book is a postmortem on the long life and unexpected demise of a global institution. Looking back, there are manifold benefits to knowing how the life story of the communist party came out. We can ask pointed questions about the strengths and weaknesses of contending strategies and make informed judgments about leaders' choices in pursuing their ideals. Yet, we must steer clear of the trap of thinking deterministically about the party's history. The meanderings of the idea of the party's vanguard role over countries as diverse as England, Germany, the Soviet Union, China, and Yugoslavia were not predestined. After all, the people who were moved by this concept were living their lives forward. They were making choices about which types of political action had the best chance of realizing their dreams. They were acting on the basis of limited information under uncertain conditions. Despite their membership in a purportedly comradely association and their participation in an international movement, these figures were frequently caught up in internecine battles over both the minutiae of party doc-trine and the role of violence in pursuit of their revolutionary mission. They also had stubborn convictions. Some of their decisions redounded to the party's benefit. Others severely impaired its capacity to func-tion. Even in the worst times, however, both the ideas behind the party and the organization itself proved to be surprisingly resilient, that is, at least until those fateful days in 1989 and 1990 when these leaders' last sources of support vanished.

I shall begin this exploration of an institution that ruled significant segments of the globe with the common source of the communist move-ment, the prophecies of Karl Marx. As we shall see, when this nineteenth-century rebel contemplated the condition of the working class at the height of the Industrial Revolution, his idea of an inevitable revolution into socialism and communism made the adoption of the model of ru-dimentary party organization of his era seem unnecessary. As a result, he left the design of his party to later revolutionaries. Over the following decades, this bequest proved to be a priceless opportunity for revolu-tionaries who came to power by their own devices, people like Lenin, Mao, and Castro. As I shall show, the original idea of the party gave them tremendous flexibility in adapting Marx's view of history to spe-cific conditions in their own countries. Additionally, I shall demonstrate that other revolutionaries were not as lucky. Since a majority of the world's communist parties assumed power under the sway of the Soviet Union, they were forced to adopt conceptions of their mission that had little to do with the challenges they faced on their own soil.

Once I have set the stage for the communist party's rule, I will show how the party idea degenerated into a tool for personal despotism. As I have already indicated, I do not mean to suggest that all cults of per-sonality are alike. For example, I disagree with scholars who equate Stalin's and Mao's objectives.[17] Although the two despots were respon-sible for massive atrocities, they had fundamentally different ideas about the institution's proper functions. Nor will I contend that the descent into tyranny on such an unfathomable scale was preordained.[18] Once these personality cults were in place, however, the return to an understanding of party rule that was not based on a single individual's whim presented its advocates with a formidable obstacle. As I shall argue, they met the challenge to a greater, if far from inspiring, extent than many scholars have contended. By the 1970s, the Soviet regime and most of its Eastern European allies adopted a less exacting form of party dictatorship that gave them hope that they could renew their followers' faith in their decisions. In the 1980s, China's leaders pursued an even more aggressive legitimation strategy. Nonetheless, wherever one went in the communist world, the prospects for a reinvigorated conception of party leadership waned. The specific idea of an enlightened vanguard did not last beyond the twentieth century, even in purportedly outlying cases like China, Cuba, North Korea, Vietnam, and Laos. With a whimper and not a violent act of defiance, the communist party succumbed to its long-festering contradictions when its supporters lost both the will to fight for it and the conviction that it represented a morally defensible vehicle for securing the common good.

CHAPTER 2

A Revolutionary Idea

Karl Marx's *Manifesto of the Communist Party* begins with a puzzle so subtle that we barely notice it. He tells us virtually nothing about the communist party. In fact, after providing us with a title, Marx does not use the two words together again. Instead, he focuses on the coming of communism, which he treats as an incontrovertible fact. Communism, he declares, is a "specter haunting Europe." It is indisputable that this revolutionary spirit exists because every regressive force in Europe has entered into a "holy alliance" against it, from the pope to the tsar, German and French reactionary politicians, and their police spies. Now is the time for communists to repudiate the slanders against them by openly publishing their intentions.[1]

How can we explain this seeming omission of the organization that will be at the forefront of an impending revolution? One reason is that the first communist party was still in the process of formation at the time of the *Manifesto*'s publication on February 21, 1848. The *Manifesto* was commissioned by a rudimentary organization, the League of Communists, which brought together a handful of radical groups to pursue a variety of goals. With only a few hundred loosely affiliated members, the League had held two congresses, one in June 1847 and the next from November to December 1847. Yet it still lacked a formal declaration of principles to address the many differences among its members. Marx's fellow revolutionary, Friedrich Engels, was initially charged with writing the document, but Marx took over the task completely and finally delivered the finished manuscript of the *Manifesto* to the League in early February 1848.

An even more revealing explanation for the lack of attention to the party is that Marx seems to have taken it for granted that, whatever one did, the ruling class's exclusion of the working masses from political life was coming to an end. The entire document is a testament to the inevitability of the revolution. Thus, Marx tells his reader that the progressive logic of history is already churning forward. The irreconcilable contradictions between the bourgeoisie and the proletariat have reached a breaking point. The only conceivable outcome for humanity is a violent confrontation that will result in the overthrow of the old class structures and their replacement by proletarian rule. In this case, it seems, the communists will be the natural servants of the working class. They do not represent any special interests, Marx informs his reader. They speak for no one "separate and apart from the proletariat as a whole." They do not even espouse "sectarian principles of their own by which to shape and mold the proletarian movement." They are there to accompany the masses to victory.[2]

In these respects, Marx's communist party is about something much greater than a mere assembly of individuals. It is linked to an idea about revolutionary inevitability. As an expression of the looming specter of communism rather than a mundane organization, the party comes into being as a result of social and economic forces that transcend the interests of any specific person. It offers its members the privilege of riding atop an advancing wave of events. To be included in this community, Marx suggests, one must only decide to be on the right side of history and join the workers who are moving humanity forward.

Marx's prediction of a coming conflagration may seem far-fetched today, but it was entirely plausible at the time he was writing. At the end of the eighteenth century, the French Revolution had already demonstrated that the feudal institutions on which the European political order was based were far more fragile than either their defenders or their opponents assumed. In Great Britain, the appalling living and working conditions generated by the Industrial Revolution made a confrontation between the proletariat and the capitalist ruling class seem increasingly likely. As 1848 began and Marx finished his manuscript, he and the League's other members had good reason to think that their predictions of an imminent conflagration were on the verge of being confirmed. They were filled with anticipation at the outbreak of widespread unrest across Europe—urban riots, peasant uprisings, demands for universal suffrage and democratic representation, and virulent nationalism. In fact, within only a few months, their expectations appeared to be validated, if only for one glorious year, when scores of revolts and uprisings broke out across the continent.

In this light, when the "springtime of revolutions" of 1848 was snuffed out by autocratic governments and no further upsurge of popular revolt was on the horizon, Marx and other radicals were presented with a fundamental question. If it was unlikely that any sustained social upheaval, let alone one that followed Marx's strict prescriptions, would take place immediately, how should one hold the revolutionary movement together? A party based primarily on the confluence of historical forces may have had the advantage of encouraging like-minded insurrectionists to come together. But it could not survive if it failed to give them guidance about what they should do next. Complicating the situation, Marx and his fellow revolutionaries were not alone in making the case for a direct confrontation with the status quo. From Great Britain to France, Prussia, Spain, and the Italian states, myriad socialists, anarchists, labor organizers, and progressive reformers competed with them to win the support of the working class and other disaffected segments of society.

For these reasons, Marx and other European radicals had to make hard choices about the potential trade-off between revolutionary activity and political efficacy. Many founded formal organizations, including early political parties, to keep their goals alive. For some, this strategy appeared to bear fruit. Their influence was demonstrated in the first, self-described international working-class organizations, the First and, after Marx's death, Second Internationals. Moreover, they played significant roles in the formation of socialist mass parties, including the Social Democratic Party of Germany (SPD) and the British Labour Party. Yet in the view of other left-wing radicals, their parties' participation in these organizations led it to make unconscionable compromises on fundamental principles, such as the immediacy of the proletarian revolution and the prohibition on participation in bourgeois elections. By the turn of the twentieth century, their worst fears were confirmed. Following the outbreak of World War I, the mass parties of the Left swiftly abandoned their commitment to the international proletariat and devoted themselves to defending their respective nations.

This is not to say that Marx's conception of a unique association of revolutionaries passed away. To the contrary, I shall contend throughout this book that the political phenomenon that came to be known as "Marxism" was just taking off. While faith in the possibility of initiating a revolution became increasingly difficult to sustain in Europe, this idea would capture the imagination of radical movements on other continents. To understand this story, we must begin with the intractable political conditions in Marx's time, which made the idea of a unified body of communists appear attractive, necessary, and credible.

Gatekeepers of Change

At the beginning of the nineteenth century, European politics was dominated by two questions: What segments of society should take part in political life? And what could one do about those segments of the population that were not considered worthy of inclusion? At the time, the answer to the first question was straightforward. Politics was dominated by upper-class social and economic elites who acted as gatekeepers to the public realm. To defend their interests, they relied upon political parties of a far different order than those we associate with liberal democracy today. Loose alliances of nobles, gentleman-landowners, public officials, and merchants, these groupings, or "parties of notables," were based upon informal relationships, family ties, shared educational backgrounds, and business connections. Their electorates were small and largely limited to property holders. Accordingly, they could define the terms of engagement in public life by themselves.

Yet, these circumstances were about to change. Despite the appearance that the existing political landscape could be preserved, Europe in the early 1800s was significantly different than it had been a half century earlier. Above all, the French Revolution had challenged the accepted norms of political engagement. Its instigators' demands for constitutional guarantees of liberty and equality, contempt for aristocratic rule, and in the more extreme cases, pretense to absolute freedom threatened the principles on which the European order was based. Making the situation particularly frightening to these countries' traditional rulers was the Revolution's swift degeneration into violence, dictatorship, and war.

Moreover, both the events in France and the disruptive consequences of the Industrial Revolution created constituencies for change across all levels of society. Liberal politicians pressed for an expansion of the franchise to increase their influence within their parliaments. Burgeoning business elites pressed for a reduction in state involvement in their activities. Socialist activists, left-wing intellectuals, and utopian thinkers dreamed of ways to organize disaffected populations. Recurrent, though generally unconnected, instances of unrest in the cities and countryside demonstrated that demands for new political, social, and economic relations were present everywhere.

Of the three countries that interested Marx the most as potential centers of revolutionary activity—Great Britain, France, and Prussia— the British and French parties responded in significantly different ways to these pressures. With a long-established parliamentary tradition and ascendance over the powers of the monarchy, Britain's primary parties, the Tories and Whigs, generally agreed about how the issue of political inclusion should be handled. Especially in light of the French Revolution's consequences, change should be gradual and strictly limited to the upper strata of society. They differed primarily over policy. Until 1831, Tory governments had held the bounds of popular participation in check. But when the Whigs assumed control of the House of Commons, they passed the Reform Act of 1842, which broadened the franchise by lowering property ownership requirements for voting. This step not only won them additional seats in the House of Commons and added to their growing popularity in major urban centers, it also allowed them to cultivate support among the agglomeration of entrepreneurs, businessmen, and the modernizing gentry who constituted Britain's rising "middle class."

The Reform Act is equally significant, however, for what the Whigs did not seek to change. By retaining property ownership as a condition for voting, they upheld the consensus with the Tories that not everyone was qualified to participate in the political sphere. This was a bitter disappointment for artisan groups in particular, whose demonstrations had helped to lead the Whigs to victory. But the even more consequential feature of this decision was the Act's pointed exclusion of the masses of unskilled workers whose labors were a crucial element of their country's good fortune. Over the past century, hundreds of thousands of workers had moved from the countryside into the country's growing urban centers where they incurred the countless afflictions of migrants everywhere—poor wages, miserable working hours, unsafe factory conditions, and the ever-present threat of joblessness. An indignant twenty-five-year-old Friedrich Engels made the case for addressing their misfortune in a gripping description of an impoverished neighborhood in Manchester: "Everywhere heaps of *débris*, refuse, and offal; standing pools for gutters and a stench which alone would make it impossible for a human being in any degree civilized to live in such a district."[3] Yet rather than responding to these conditions with charity, the Whigs and Tories demanded that the poor work harder to prove their worth to society. Their enactment of the Poor Law Amendment Act of 1842 abrogated traditional forms of government relief and required the indigent to live and work at substandard wages in a centralized system of workhouses.

New thinking about the plight of the lower classes came from outside Parliament. Nonetheless, in these cases as well, the primary focus was on gradual reform, not radical change. Among the best-known reformers, Robert Owen, the Welsh philanthropist and early socialist, used the workforce of his own textile mill in New Lanark, Scotland, to undertake experiments in humanizing the modern factory system. He offered higher wages than his competitors, shortened the workday, imposed restrictions on the employment of children, and provided free education and medical services. Owen was joined by a proliferation of altruistic middle-class political associations. These leagues and societies were typically focused on specific causes, such as the creation of a national educational system and the abolition of the slave trade in the colonies. In response to the pressure of labor unrest following the passage of the Poor Law Amendment, Parliament opened the political realm slightly by revising draconian laws against the formation of workers' associations. Owen himself returned to the public stage to form one of England's first trade unions, the Grand National Consolidated Trades Union. Yet, in this case and others, the prospect of transforming society from above was limited by the lack of national organizations to hold such movements together.

In this context, the most serious challenge to the status quo came from below. In 1838, a committee composed of skilled workers and middle-class radicals and led by the English labor activist William Lovett published a People's Charter that sought to redress working-class grievances by pressing for electoral reform. The Charter demanded universal male suffrage, equal voting districts, the secret ballot, and annual parliamentary elections. The reformers never had a realistic chance of achieving these objectives, but the outpouring of popular support for the movement demonstrated that public discontent was rising. In 1839, Lovett and his supporters presented the House of Commons with a petition signed by more than 1 million people, most of them commoners. When this entreaty was rejected, the government could not prevent the mass meetings, demonstrations, and strikes that ensued, including an armed uprising by Chartist sympathizers in Newport. Three years later, the Chartists returned with a second petition with more than 3 million signatures. Once again, Parliament rebuffed their demands.[4]

Although the energy behind the Chartist movement had largely dissipated by the mid-1840s, its early success was revealing from multiple perspectives. For politicians in the established parties, the momentum behind the protests and the demonstrators' recourse to violence showed that the anger among the lower classes was more intensely felt than they had assumed. For the working-class population and its organizers, Chartism was a moment, albeit a fleeting one, in which it seemed possible to give voice to their views. The open question was whether these manifestations of mass discontent would have more than a passing impact on the disposition of the ruling classes.

In contrast to the otherwise gradual efforts to reform the British system, the prospects for political change in France were significantly hampered by the unhealed scars of the Revolution. When the Bourbon monarchy was restored in 1814 and 1815, the parties in the lower house of the National Assembly were weak and disorganized. But they already had one thing in common. They feared a resurgence of the lower classes who had taken their forebears to the guillotine. Although the Jacobin Constitution of 1793 had granted full suffrage to all adult males, the new parties guaranteed that this right would not be observed. One side, which initially dominated the National Assembly, was composed of extreme, right-wing monarchists who were deeply suspicious of representative institutions; the other was composed of liberal constitutionalists who favored modest checks on the power of the monarchy. In 1830, hopes for far-reaching change rose when Charles X and his supporters were pummeled by simultaneous backlashes from above and below. Liberal parliamentarians and their associated clubs and newspapers declared their unwillingness to cooperate any longer with the regime. For three days, enraged workers took their grievances over unemployment, exorbitant food prices, and urban poverty into the streets, engaging in open battles with the army. Yet, when the king was replaced by a new monarch from a different line of succession, the liberal constitutionalists showed that they too were unwilling to risk further instability. For the next eighteen years, neither the king nor his many different prime ministers were prepared to accede to popular demands for meaningful political and electoral reform.

The behavior of these parties' leaders was profoundly demoralizing to the regime's educated critics. With a greater sense of urgency than in Britain, left-wing intellectuals, journalists, and activists took up the cause of thoroughly transforming French society. But unlike in Great Britain, where the suffrage was broader and Parliament was strong enough to initiate moderate reforms, these dissenters lacked institutions of their own to express their grievances and put pressure on officials. Hence, their protests were diffuse and frequently unconnected with the specific conditions of pre-1848 France.

Many of these radicals were influenced by the early nineteenth-century socialist Claude-Henri de St. Simon, who inspired them to think that they were participants in a movement for social and economic change that dwarfed the feeble decisions of individual politicians. St. Simon predicted that the path to a just society would emerge from a long-lasting struggle between antagonistic groups over control of the tools of production. Those who had the upper hand in these battles were responsible for the unequal relationships that defined the period. To an extent, St. Simon would have agreed with Robert Owen about the importance of addressing this conflict through progressive initiatives. He advocated deliberate social planning and the amelioration of poverty through the abolition of unearned wealth. However, unlike Owen, he did not assume that this task could be entrusted to benefi-cent entrepreneurs and progressive associations. Rather, he argued that it should be carried out by an administrative elite with the techni-cal skills and expertise required to address the needs of every social stratum.

In sharp contrast to St. Simon's confidence in organizational solu-tions, Pierre-Joseph Proudhon, a seminal figure in the history of anar-chism, rejected his predecessor's readiness to entrust the fate of the common man to anyone at the top of the social hierarchy. Proudhon maintained that the transformation of social relationships could only be achieved if it moved from the bottom upward. To this end, he advo-cated a host of institutional innovations, including the establishment of communal banks and the formation of producers' cooperatives to increase workers' control over the products of their labor. In every case, he deemed a return to centralized government unacceptable.

Another influential thinker, the philosopher Étienne Cabet, did not consider himself a revolutionary and abhorred the use of violence. But he maintained that social equality would only be achieved by eliminat-ing the institution of private property. As one of the first persons to use the term "communism," Cabet envisioned a new form of political organization in which property would be held in common and every human action, from how people lived to how they dressed, would be shaped by the strict application of egalitarian values. To ensure compli-ance with these standards, Cabet also contended that overt expressions of individuality should be restrained. Uniquely among his peers, he succeeded in attracting tens of thousands of followers to his cause by tapping into the grievances of artisans and skilled laborers who were threatened by industrial growth.[5]

Unlike both Proudhon and Cabet, the ultraleftist Louis Auguste Blanqui espoused a doctrine of outright violence. The conflict between the rich and the poor, the ruling class and the proletariat, Blanqui pro-claimed in a famous courtroom defense in 1832, would not be resolved by the wealthy "dropping some crumbs from a splendid table." The achievement of a just society presupposed the eradication of the entire ruling elite. Thus, he urged his followers to wage a revolutionary war "until not a single enemy of the happiness of the people and of freedom is left standing."[6] This endorsement of violence would not have been new to anyone who had experienced the Revolution's descent into terror. What gave his approach lasting significance for future generations of radicals, including the founder of Bolshevism, Vladimir Ilyich Lenin, was its emphasis on the necessity of having a disciplined, conspiratorial core of revolutionaries to lead the people. In Blanqui's view, the working masses would not act on their own. Only an elite group would understand their true interests. For this reason, Blanqui emphasized that the coming revolution could not be democratic. It would require a dictatorship until socialism was fully realized.

The Militant Convictions of Itinerant Radicals

Owen, Lovett, St. Simon, Proudhon, Cabet, Blanqui—all of these figures would play major roles in shaping the views of future communists. Yet, many of the most prominent founders of the movement, such as Marx and Engels, operated under considerably less favorable conditions. Most came from cities like Berlin, Cologne, Vienna, and Warsaw, where even the advocates of modest reform had difficulty expressing their views. Parliamentary institutions were weak or simply nonexistent in Central Europe. Legislatures composed of nobles and property holders existed under the constitutional monarchies of southern Germany, but there were no equivalents to these representative institutions in the two powers that counted the most for the region's future, Prussia and Austria. In contrast to Britain and France, political parties did not exist at all. To find even the faintest glimmer of autonomous political organizations, one had to turn to rarified associations, such as the liberal student fraternities, or *Burschenschaften*, of Thuringia and Bavaria.

Additionally, the opponents of absolutism in Central Europe lacked many of the necessary opportunities to make their views known. As in other parts of Europe, newspapers provided limited forums for political debate, but they were heavily censored and easily shut down. Drinking clubs functioned as venues for discontent, but they were frequented by police spies. Members of secret societies and labor agitators were routinely jailed or sent into exile. Nonetheless, even if these impediments had not existed, the would-be revolutionaries struggled with the frustration that their messages did not resonate with local populations. Although incidents of social unrest occurred, Germany did not have a revolutionary tradition like France, at least until 1848. Journeymen, craftsmen, and common laborers staged intermittent protests and strikes against poor working conditions, low wages, and high rents. In 1844, a revolt of weavers in Silesia cascaded into violent demonstrations throughout the German states and Austria. Still, these disturbances did not last. Workers chose to keep their mouths shut and their heads down.

These conditions had a formative impact on the character of midcentury socialism. They meant that the driving ideas behind the movement were formulated primarily by people on the move, either as exiles or as émigrés, who were more stridently committed to the revolutionary cause than their British and French counterparts. A majority were educated and accustomed to middle-class lifestyles that allowed them to read books and meditate on great philosophical questions. Others were less privileged. They included tradespeople, artisans, and clerks who chafed against the remnants of feudalism. These itinerant radicals were also united by factors that transcended their socioeconomic status. The Germans were joined by Poles, Hungarians, and Italians who were determined to assert their national identities. There was also a high representation of persons typically excluded from political life—Jews, ethnic minorities, and women.

For these reasons, the experience of emigration hardened the radicals' convictions. When they arrived in cities like Paris in the mid-1840s, they were not only interested in learning from their hosts. They were also determined to inject their own, more militant perspectives into their debates. This process of reciprocal enculturation was a notable shift. Whereas the flow of ideas had generally moved from West to East in the seventeenth and eighteenth centuries, this historical current was partly reversed. The émigrés introduced French writers, artists, and budding activists to the thought of Russian revolutionaries, like the anarchist Mikhail Bakunin, and literary giants, like the Polish poet Adam Mickiewicz. They also exposed them to ideas with roots in German idealism. In contrast to the libertarian traditions of the French

Enlightenment that exalted individual volition, the German activists thought in terms of large-scale movements and the inevitability of human progress. Furthermore, they were confident about their ability to link the certainty of revolution with concrete political action.

When continental Europe ceased to be a hospitable setting, many German émigrés moved to London where their exposure to the working population's growing assertiveness encouraged them to fashion a less elitist, more democratically minded tradition of open meetings and public debate. Labor agitators rented meeting halls and called for the formation of trade unions. Socialists founded a German Workers' Educational Association, offering lectures to workers on history and political economy, and organized consciousness-raising social events. They also formed a protoparty, the Fraternal Democrats, to bring radicals of different nationalities together. Complementing their international orientation, they used periodicals, newspapers, and propaganda pamphlets to foster communications among clandestine cells and activists in cities as far afield as Geneva, Berlin, and Brussels.

Marx and Engels were direct products of this milieu. Constantly on the move in Europe, they were acutely conscious that one could not succeed at revolutionary activity without a cohesive movement. Accordingly, when the two men were forced to leave Paris for Brussels in 1845, they and other émigrés founded the Communist Correspondence Committee with the goal of coordinating the activities of radical groups across Europe. Their collaborators included the Chartists and a London-based secret society known as the League of the Just. The League's working-class members reinforced Marx and Engels's conviction that the urban proletariat was the emerging motor force of history. They were also converted to the idea that the moment was nearing when this class would overthrow its oppressors and replace a system based on the ownership of private property with a classless, communist society. In June 1847, at Marx and Engels's instigation, the association renamed itself the Communist League and embraced the radically democratic and egalitarian themes that would eventually make Marxism popular throughout the world.

Although Marx was not present at the Communist League's inaugural congress on June 2–9, 1847, the delegates voted to replace the old association's motto, "All men are brothers," with his slogan, "Proletarians of all Countries, Unite!" At the League's next congress in November, the delegates adopted a program that defined their aims as "the overthrow of the bourgeoisie, the rule of the proletariat, the abolition of the old bourgeois society which rests on the antagonism of classes, and the foundation of a new society without classes and without private property." Perhaps most appealing to those who joined the League's ranks and to subsequent generations of Marxists, the program idealistically endorsed a governing structure that was significantly less hierarchical and elitist than other conspiratorial organizations of the time. In a bottom-up fashion, grassroots communes were to elect the bodies above them. Although the League's Central Committee would conduct the organization's business, all legislative powers would be reserved to an annual congress of deputies from each of the circles.[7]

Simultaneously, Marx and Engels positioned themselves to define the League's other order of business, the formulation of a declaration of principles. With the backing of the League's most radical members, Engels arranged for Marx to compose a comprehensive statement of purpose—a "Communist Manifesto," as Engels called it—about the crisis of capitalism and the impending revolution. Engels provided some thoughts on the topics in a formulaic catechism, "Principles of Communism," in which he addressed the impact of the Industrial Revolution on the proletariat and the shortcomings of rival socialist groups.[8] But the final document was exclusively Marx's work. When he delivered the *Manifesto of the Communist Party* to the League on or around February 1, 1848, he clearly aimed to produce more than a declaration of the organization's intentions. He viewed the *Manifesto* as an invitation to all clear-thinking individuals to put themselves on the right side of history.

THE MANIFESTO OF THE COMMUNISTS

Against this background, one can appreciate why Marx did not feel compelled to devote himself to a detailed description of the communist party. While the League was attending to this mundane matter, he focused on justifying the call to revolution. Importantly, he did not write the *Manifesto* for the working class. Even if a worker could read, he or she did not have the time or wherewithal to act as Marx desired. Rather, Marx's audience was composed of other educated rebels who, like himself, needed good reasons for choosing his cause over many others. This was no small matter. In the process of making his case, he laid the groundwork for debates about the organ's functions that would continue for generations.

The first thing one notices about the *Manifesto* is how quickly Marx gets down to explaining why, after centuries of waiting, the oppressed masses will finally be freed from their shackles. His answer: history itself had ordained this moment. The record of humanity, Marx explains, is a living record of the struggles between antagonistic classes—free men and slaves, patricians and plebeians, lords and serfs, and guild masters and journeymen. These conflicts are driven by the craving of the class that controls the means of production to acquire new sources of wealth. It satisfies this desire by exploiting the labor of those who do not have these resources. Yet, Marx argues, the ruling class's productive powers are nearing a point at which the ability of the few to satisfy the needs of the many is exhausted. This development will result in a revolutionary upheaval that no amount of human will can resist. The proletariat will revolt against its masters and a new epoch in the class struggle will begin.

In this context, Marx presents his reader with an attractive reason for believing that he or she has been called to align with his cause. He glorifies the class to which most of his audience belongs. In its position as the driving force behind the Industrial Revolution, Marx declares, the bourgeoisie "has accomplished wonders far surpassing Egyptian pyramids, Roman aqueducts, and Gothic cathedrals; it has conducted expeditions that put in the shade all former Exoduses of nations and crusades." Indeed, Marx contends, no earlier generation had even a presentiment of what "nature's subjugation to man, machinery, applications of chemistry to industry and agriculture, steam-navigation, railways, electric telegraphs, clearing of whole continents for cultivation, canalization of rivers, whole populations conjured out of the ground" could bring about.[9]

Yet, Marx emphasizes to his potential converts, this is also a leap onto the right side of history. No matter how much one appreciates the bourgeoisie's contributions, this class is destined to become its own gravedigger. The bourgeoisie cannot survive, Marx maintains, unless it identifies additional sources of profit. Hence, it constantly develops new forms of production and seeks new markets in distant lands. But, Marx adds, this unrestrained pursuit of profit will blind the bourgeoisie to the perverse economic and social implications of its actions. In an absurd contrast with less developed societies, it will foster an epidemic of overproduction—or, as the *Manifesto*'s author colorfully puts it, of "too much civilization, too much means of subsistence, too much industry, too much commerce." As a result, capitalism will be convulsed with crises that undermine everything its creators have accomplished. In addition, Marx informs his readers that the bourgeoisie's unavoidably self-destructive activity is nowhere more dangerously manifested than in how it treats the class whose labor has accounted for its successes. In crowded factories, workers are organized like soldiers in an army. In these unforgiving conditions, they are not only transformed into the servants of the bourgeois class and the bourgeois state; they are enslaved by the machines they operate. Due to the ruling class's arrogant overconfidence, it fails to see that it is doomed by its avarice: "The more openly this despotism proclaims gain to be its end and aim, the more hateful and the more embittering it is."[10]

Anticipating his readers' skepticism, Marx adopts the pose of the realist. The working class's transformation into a revolutionary force, he observes, will not be instantaneous. This shift, too, will be governed by the laws of history. At first, disgruntled workers will act impulsively against their oppressors. They will smash their machines and burn down their places of work. However, as their numbers grow and they are brought together in the same halls of labor, these workers will acquire a more mature understanding of what they share in common. Their first step will be to form trade unions to lobby their employers for higher wages, better working conditions, and shorter days. But soon they will cross the line between reform and revolution. For the first time in history, the great majority, constituted as the proletariat, will rise up against its oppressors and eliminate every form of class exploitation.

At this point, Marx finally makes his case to his readers about joining the communist movement. Notably, he appeals directly to their self-interest. The logic of human progress guarantees that when the class struggle nears the decisive hour, a small section of the ruling class will be called to "cut itself adrift" and join the revolutionary class. In particular, this applies to "a portion of the bourgeois ideologists," presumably including Marx himself, "who have raised themselves to the level of comprehending theoretically the historical movement as a whole." Importantly, as I have indicated at the beginning of this chapter, Marx assumes that these communists do not represent any special interests. In speaking only for the proletariat, they are presented with a priceless gift—the chance to exemplify moral virtue. Their lives will not be easy, he emphasizes, because they will be falsely accused of opposing fundamental rights and values. But, Marx assures his reader, they will have justice on their side.[11]

What Marx does not say about this moral opportunity is also noteworthy. He is conspicuously restrained in addressing the communists' use of violence in carrying out his prescriptions. He borrows from Engels's "Principles of Communism" in noting that it will be necessary to make "despotic inroads on the rights of property and on the conditions of bourgeois production." Then, he matter-of-factly presents a list of unavoidably violent measures—the abolition of "property in land," the confiscation of the property of all "emigrants and rebels," and the "centralization of credit in the hands of the state"—as if they were nothing more than items on a laundry list.[12]

Perhaps Marx did not wish to tarnish an otherwise romantic conception of revolutionary change. In any case, he is much more deliberate in contending that only those who are willing to become communists have a legitimate chance of supplanting Europe's ruling bourgeois parties. The first victims of his disdain are the middle-class parties that came out of the French revolution of July 1830 and the English reform movement. These parties, he contends, foolishly imagine that they can help the proletariat by collaborating with the bourgeoisie and "singing lampoons of their new master and whispering in his ears sinister prophecies of coming catastrophe." In reality, they are just as venal as the old ruling class. "Despite their high falutin' phrases, they stop to pick up the golden apples dropped from the tree of industry and to barter truth, love, and honor for traffic in wool, beetroot-sugar and potato spirits."[13]

Other socialist groups are no better. In an attempt to conceal their opposition to the class struggle, those whom Marx labels the "German, or 'True,' Socialists" dress up the emancipatory ideals of the French Revolution with a "robe of speculative cobwebs, embroidered with flowers of rhetoric, steeped in the dew of sickly sentiment." They are no different from bourgeois reformers who seek to avert revolution by merely redressing the social grievances of the proletariat. Only a few early socialists, like St. Simon and Owen, receive praise from the *Manifesto*'s author. At a time when the proletarian movement was still in its infancy, Marx affirms, these theorists at least recognized the necessity of questioning the bourgeoisie's actions.[14]

For these reasons, it should be clear why Marx did not feel the need to outline the particular features of a communist party. He did not need to. There could be a manifesto of a "communist party" simply by virtue of the fact that the revolutionaries whom he idealized were devoted to realizing its destiny. And, the number of these followers was sure to grow when they recognized that they would have history and moral virtue on their side. In this spirit, Marx concludes the *Manifesto* with an affirmation of the communists' desire to work constructively with every progressive group. In France, he notes, they are already allied with other socialist forces against the bourgeoisie. In Switzerland, they support the liberals, and in Poland, the agrarian revolutionaries. In Germany, which Marx regards as having the best chance for revolution, they fight alongside the bourgeoisie "whenever it acts in a revolutionary way." Naturally, Marx emphasizes, there are limits to which these cooperative efforts can be taken. The communists must never lose sight of their basic principles. The main thing is that they ready the proletariat to begin its struggle against its masters.[15]

REVOLUTION RISING?

The problem with any prediction is that it might eventually be proved false. Yet, revolutionaries do not typically live in the world of "eventually." Looking forward, they are convinced that their day of victory is nearing. Naturally, their convictions are reinforced on occasions when society is thrown into turmoil. In times of concord, however, their position is more difficult. For the most committed among them, the challenge is to find ways of persuading their followers that their sacrifices will continue to be worthwhile.

Only three weeks after Marx turned in the *Manifesto*, stunning events in Paris gave him and Engels reason to think that their predictions were on the verge of being confirmed. On February 23, 1848, mass protests erupted against the decision by France's prime minister, François Guizot, to prohibit a banquet at which middle-class citizens planned to discuss electoral reforms and the expansion of the franchise. The Orléanist king, Louis-Philippe, desperately tried to calm the crowds by forcing Guizot's resignation and then abdicated the throne. On February 26, the National Assembly proclaimed the Second French Republic and declared its support for universal suffrage and social justice. But for those who expected that France's government would at last live up to the ideals of the Revolution, these measures ended in disappointment. It did not help the new government's credibility that its offices were filled by many of the same politicians who had ruled in the past, and France slid into a new era of polarization. Four months after the National Assembly's declaration, a confrontation between ordinary laborers and the government over relief for the unemployed led to a full-scale insurrection. Tens of thousands of ordinary Parisians erected barricades throughout the city and fought against National Guard soldiers. Only after thousands of people were killed was the revolt suppressed.

For European revolutionaries of all hues and variations, the fall of the Orléanist regime and its violent aftermath were bigger than France. This event was a catalyst for a perfect storm of protest and upheaval that engulfed the entire continent. Over the ensuing months, the constituent elements of the old European order were assaulted by uprisings that were united more by their timing, thanks to newspapers and other means of communication, than by a common cause. Grassroots insurrections broke out in Belgium, Galicia, and Wallachia over economic and social conditions. In Sardinia, Piedmont, the German states, and the Netherlands, liberal reformers staged demonstrations in favor of written constitutions, parliamentary governance, and the right to vote. In other locations, the protests were amplified by an impassioned rejection of the diplomatic system that had governed Europe since Napoléon's defeat in

1815. In Ireland and Hungary, revolutionaries and liberals from all social strata demanded national independence from their imperial overlords. German and Italian radicals battled for national unification.

Marx and Engels were fully aware of the significant differences among these protests. Thus, it is noteworthy that, far from acting according to any dogmatic blueprint, they turned their attention from France to their German homeland where they thought they had the greatest chance of influencing events. In late March 1848, they issued a declaration, "Demands of the Communist Party in Germany," that spelled out the terms under which millions of Germans could be liberated from their exploiters. However, aside from a few concrete references to socialist themes, such as the creation of a state bank and the nationalization of the means of transportation, this was not the stuff of revolutionary provocation. In fact, their demands would have been met with approval in many bourgeois households: Germany should at once be declared a single and indivisible republic, every citizen should be entitled to vote, and all remaining feudal institutions and obligations should be abolished.[16]

Still, Marx and Engels were far from willing to sacrifice their long-term goals for short-term gains. Through a newspaper, the *Neue Rheinische Zeitung*, which Marx started in Cologne, they showed their intention to have it both ways. The publication was filled with invective against established institutions. Its editorials dared the Prussian king to go to war with Russia to liberate the Polish people. Its reporters entertained their readers with biting criticism of budding parties and associations whose leaders were, in their view, insincere or uncommitted to overthrowing the status quo. When the German states' first freely elected parliament met in Frankfurt in May 1848, Engels ridiculed its deputies for their inability to agree about anything but their rules of procedure; they knew, he observed wryly, "that when two or three Germans get together they must have a set of rules, otherwise chair legs will be used to decide matters."[17] Yet, again testifying to its founders' adaptability, the paper's acerbic style was only part of the story. Although all five of its editors were members of the Communist League, they conspicuously distanced themselves from advocating solely for working-class interests. The daily proclaimed itself an "organ of democracy." It embraced the view that Germany's transition into a modern state would be completed under the leadership of a vibrant entrepreneurial class and with full democratic representation.

As 1848 came to a close, however, Marx and Engels found it increasingly difficult to maintain a balance between their perspectives. For revolutionaries across Europe, the following year was a time of disappointment and disillusionment. In particular, the events in France did not become a beacon for revolution but instead a harbinger of reaction and restoration. In December 1848, left-leaning radicals were appalled when the country's newly enfranchised citizens chose to elect Napoléon Bonaparte's nephew, Louis-Napoléon, as its first president. Two years later, a popular referendum in support of his policies would give him the pretext to stage a coup d'état against the republic and later declare himself Napoléon III. Everywhere one looked, there was reason for despondency. Workers' uprisings were crushed in Berlin and Vienna. The Frankfurt Assembly imploded under the weight of factional differences. Across central and eastern Europe, Austrian, Prussian, and Russian armies successfully restored absolutist governments and defeated movements for national independence.

In this context, when Marx and Engels returned to London in 1849, they faced a simple question with no obvious answer: How could one keep hopes for a revolution alive if those who were to be liberated were either unable or unwilling to stand up to their oppressors? One response, which enjoyed significant support within the Communist League, was to argue that these were merely temporary setbacks. According to this view, it was incumbent upon all communists to prepare for a new wave of popular unrest. The other, less happy response was that these defeats were exactly what they seemed. Because the working masses were not yet ready to accept their historical responsibility, the prudent approach was to avoid precipitous action, keep one's options open, and find ways to hold the revolutionary movement together.

In a period of less than a year, Marx and Engels swung from one extreme to the other. This was not a sign of weakness. It was a sign of the times. First, they chose intransigence. In March 1850, they advised the League's Central Committee that there was no point in seeking to reach an accommodation with the representatives of bourgeois democracy. The defenders of the latter would tolerate no serious challenge to their class supremacy. Therefore, the working people's sole chance of survival was to use both public and conspiratorial means to create a "party of the proletariat" that would not be seduced "for a single moment by the hypocritical phrases of the democratic petty bourgeoisie."[18] By September, however, Marx and Engels had seen enough of their hopes result in failure that they reversed their stand. In an invective-filled diatribe, Marx attacked his Central Committee allies for seeking to move too quickly. They wrongly assumed, Marx maintained, that revolution was a matter of *will* and that if one did not act *immediately*, one might as well "go back to bed." The conditions were not yet ripe for revolution, he insisted, and the working class needed to be told as much: "You have 15, 20, 50 years of civil war to go through in order to alter the situation and to train yourselves for the exercise of political power."[19] This assessment of the future course of history implied that they should seek to form a different kind of association with a more pragmatic approach to its mission.

The Advent of Organization

I have recounted the preceding shifts in Marx and Engels's thinking to show that it was unclear at this time what the global phenomenon later known as "Marxism" was. The two revolutionaries had produced thousands of pages of analysis about the crises of their times, but they could not have known what was ahead of them. The fact that they did not, and perhaps could not, pin themselves down to a single strategy had a decisive, long-lasting impact on the communist movement. For them and for coming generations of revolutionaries, it meant that their conception of the communist party was built around two, potentially contradictory agendas. One was based upon militant confrontation; the other emphasized organizational adaptation.

As the prospect of imminent proletarian revolution diminished in the 1850s and 1860s and was replaced by the rise of trade unions in Europe, Marx and Engels had growing reasons to think about their party in organizational terms. Benefiting from both the precedent of Chartism and the right to form labor associations, British reformers made steady progress in mobilizing skilled trades and engineers. Their goals were not at all revolutionary or, at this stage, even socialist, let alone communist. Instead, they formed consumers' cooperatives and set up mutual benefits funds for industrial disputes. As their membership grew to the hundreds of thousands, these unions matured into powerful political forces. In contrast to their British cousins, French workers did not enjoy the legal right to combination, but in Napoléon III's empire they gained the right to vote. Accordingly, when the emperor encountered opposition to his policies from middle-class politicians in the 1860s, he turned to the working class as a potential source of support. Even in Prussia, where workers had neither the right to form unions nor the right to vote, one could detect germs of labor activity. After 1858, under the regency of a seemingly moderate monarch, Wilhelm I, liberal politicians created hundreds of workers' educational societies that they hoped would reduce the ordinary laborer's appetite for class conflict. The facilitators of these societies had no intention of extending a political role to the working class. But once the idea of popular association was accepted, it was impossible to prevent the issue from being raised again. In 1863, a socialist agitator and member of the Communist League, Ferdinand Lassalle, took this step by forming a new organization, the General German Workers' Association, which aimed to win universal suffrage by peaceful means.

Several years passed before it would become clear that Lassalle's creation represented a serious challenge to Marx and Engels's conception of the proper agenda for the proletariat. For the time being, signs of independent labor activity appeared to put the two revolutionaries in the position of asserting direct control over a burgeoning international movement. On February 28, 1864, labor activists from a variety of countries—England, France, Prussia, Italy, and the United States—met in London to found the International Workingmen's Association (IWA), later to be known as the First International. Initially, Marx and Engels's influence was minimal. The idea of forming a common body was a British and French initiative to bring organizers from one country into contact with those from others. Its participants were wildly diverse, and it was not even socialist. Among the 2,000 or so people in attendance, there were Blanquists, Proudhonists, Chartists, Owenites, anarchists, nationalists, and radical republicans, all looking for a home apart from the forces of old-regime Europe. But the fact that the members of the organization's newly elected General Council invited Marx to deliver the inaugural address at their first session in October and draft the association's governing statutes had a substantial impact on what the First International was to become.

In the inaugural address, Marx laid claim to the position that the working class's immediate priority was to exert political power. Reading the speech today, one is struck by the absence of both the revolutionary proclamations of his *Manifesto* and its confident prophecies. Instead, Marx's message to the International reads like a panegyric to the industrial proletariat of a single country: Great Britain. Although he begins with the observation that the gap between the enormous wealth of the British bourgeoisie and the misery of the working class had shown few signs of narrowing, Marx uses the successes of the country's unions (e.g., forcing Parliament to pass legislation on a ten-hour day; undertaking novel experiments with workers' cooperatives) as evidence that organized labor can effectively act in its interests. Workers in France, Germany, and Italy are already learning from Britain's example, Marx notes. Now, they must join hands across national boundaries to serve the mutual good.[20]

Correspondingly, Marx's draft of the IWA's general rules provides a provocative glimpse into his increasingly concrete conception of the desirable functions of an international working-class organization. The interests and activities of each of the association's member bodies, he observes, will necessarily be influenced by local conditions and laws. Hence, it is only just that each should have the right to make its own rules and control its appointments. Because participation in the association is based upon a fraternity of ideals, anyone meeting this qualification can presumably enter or leave its ranks at will.

Nevertheless, Marx's assumptions also force him to grapple with a dilemma that typifies voluntary associations. To the extent that the IWA lacks a strong central authority, he points out, it will be at risk of degenerating into a debating club. How will the body function effectively, Marx asks rhetorically, if the General Council has to manage the demands of a plethora of disparate organizations in each country? Would it not be a good idea for the Council to prompt its delegates to use their "utmost efforts" to unify these disconnected bodies into national organizations? Marx also raises the thornier issue of internal disputes. Here, too, he believes that the leadership should have a hand in resolving such conflicts. However, aside from noting that the actions of its members should be "simultaneous and uniform," he does not have anything to add apart from the need to improve communications.[21]

The immediate response of both Marx and Engels to these problems was to build temporary coalitions within the IWA. They met with varying degrees of success. For example, they won the ready support of some sections of the organization in making the case against Louis Auguste Blanqui and other proponents of revolutionary conspiracy. British trade union leaders were understandably apprehensive about the appeal of the Blanquists' renunciation of any form of compromise with the bourgeoisie. Marx and Engels faced a more daunting challenge with marshaling opposition to Proudhon's followers. These militants viewed any type of collective or state ownership of property as a violation of human dignity. They enjoyed the support of a majority of the French delegates to the International. Had they been able to build a vigorous coalition, they would have presented a lasting challenge to the unity of the IWA. Nonetheless, they struggled to find a coherent strategy because of their philosophical disposition to downplay the work of formal organizations, including even trade unions.

Marx and Engels's most formidable opponents were to be found among radical anarchists, whose ranks swelled as those of the Proudhonists declined. The uncontested leader of the movement was the Russian agitator, Mikhail Bakunin. Bakunin's views may now seem purely quixotic, but anarchism enjoyed a sizeable following in many parts of Europe, especially in Spain and the newly created Kingdom of Italy. Additionally, like many Eastern European radicals, such as the founder of Russian socialism, Alexander Herzen, and the nihilist Sergei Nechayev, both of whom I shall consider in chapter 3, Bakunin's views were shaped by the experience of futile opposition to the tsarist autocracy. In many ways, he was cut from the same intellectual cloth as Marx and Engels. He was committed to the class struggle and convinced that the ruling class would be overthrown through an act of mass violence. He, too, believed that the revolution's goal should be to replace the state with direct rule by the people. The difference between Bakunin and his German contemporaries, which led to some of the fiercest battles of the IWA's short history, was about how to achieve this objective. Whereas Marx and Engels were cautiously prepared to advance the interests of the working class by engaging with bourgeois politicians and envisioned a transitional role for the state in the passage to communism, Bakunin opposed all forms of compromise. For him, revolution was an act of volition exerted by a community of true believers. Only when these revolutionaries had demonstrated their purity of purpose could they act in solidarity with the people.

In their efforts to retain control over these varied approaches to labor activism, Marx and Engels were presented with a challenge that appeared to provide Bakunin and other radicals in the voluntarist tradition, like Blanqui, with absolute proof that the masses were already primed to make history on their own. On March 28, 1871, a radical experiment in self-rule, the Paris Commune, seemed to discredit the two communists' judgment about the likelihood of an extended period of bourgeois rule. When the Commune failed, however, Marx not only rebuffed his critics but did so in a way that gave subsequent generations of radicals reason to focus on the second, revolutionary side of his conception of the communist party.

The Paris Commune was a desperate experiment in popular government. It grew out of Napoléon III's humiliating defeat in the Franco-Prussian War of 1870–1871 and the failure of a new conservative republican regime, under the leadership of Adolphe Thiers, to persuade the Parisian population that it would faithfully represent their interests. After a brutal siege by the Prussian army, the city appeared to relive the experiences of 1789, 1830, and 1848 when it was once again engulfed by spontaneous demonstrations and street protests. When Thiers made the fateful decision to move the National Assembly, its administrative apparatus, and the regular army to Versailles, he unwittingly gave Paris's aggrieved residents the chance to fill a political vacuum with their own ideas and institutions. This drama not only stirred the hopes of the anarchists. In two acts, it provided the substance for decades of international debate among left-wing radicals about contending forms of revolutionary governance.

The first act will never live up to its mythic reputation. The Paris Commune came into being as a result of direct elections under the supervision of sympathizers in the city's independent popular militia, the National Guard. Blanqui's supporters were the big winners, garnering over one-quarter of the vote and successfully having their hero, who was once again in prison, elected as honorary president of the Commune's governing council under the banner of a red flag. Yet, the body's social base was more diverse than these revolutionaries were willing to acknowledge, ranging from radical journalists and intellectuals to National Guard members, shopkeepers, artisans, ordinary workers, and feminists. As a result, the Commune's agenda was diffuse and few of its decrees were carried out. Had the Commune's leaders had more time, it is possible that they could have combined demands for workers' cooperatives, the categorical separation of church and state, and women's rights into a coherent revolutionary program. However, on May 21, Thiers launched a full assault on the city and the visionaries were quickly driven to fight for their lives.

The second act provided the emotional substance that instilled coming generations with the passion of self-sacrifice. From its first days, the battle to save the Commune was a hopeless enterprise. In the week of the heaviest fighting from May 21 to May 28, 10,000 people lost their lives, most of them Parisians. The carnage that came after the Commune's surrender solidified its lasting, antiauthoritarian mystique. Thiers's forces arrested tens of thousands of the city's residents, some of them combatants but many others innocent citizens, and subjected them to summary trials before military tribunals. Upwards of 30,000 people were executed, and thousands more were sent to prison or deported to island labor camps.[22]

Marx and Engels were bystanders in these events. But in one of his most creative acts, Marx transformed the Commune into a simultaneously poetic and apocalyptic narrative that seemed to support every position the communists had ever advocated. In an address to the General Council of the IWA on May 30, just two days after the Commune's defeat, Marx portrayed the Parisian revolt as a testimony to, and elaboration upon, the theses of the *Manifesto*. Under the title "The Civil War in France," he consolidated the Commune's various participants under a single heading: the proletariat. He informed his audience that, for the first time, Paris had been ruled by a working-class government, one that was born of the struggle between the expropriating class (the "Party of Order," as it was commonly known) and the producing class (the "Party of Movement"). On some future date, the overthrow of the former would result in the complete emancipation of labor. For the time being, as the embodiment of the "healthy elements of French society," the Commune deserved recognition as France's true national government. Moreover, it was the champion of the liberation of the working class throughout the world.[23]

Had one been present during the Commune's brief existence, and few of the members of the League's General Council were, one could easily have disputed the accuracy of Marx's account. Privately, Marx might have agreed because he regarded the Commune's leaders as insufficiently disciplined. Yet who among his allies would have wanted to dissociate themselves from a story that so clearly served their purposes? In his depiction, the Communards had signaled their determination to establish a totally new form of human governance. The people of Paris had proved that they were prepared to govern themselves. Rather than bowing any longer before the norms of state domination, they had insisted that the Commune be "a working body, not a parliamentary body, executive and legislative at the same time." The ruling class's reaction had been so brutal, Marx explained, because it feared that the proletariat would expropriate its property. Its representatives' fears were well founded. Although the workers of Paris had no ready-made, utopian formulas for taking this next step, the Commune proved that history was finally moving in their favor. For this reason, Marx emphasized, the Commune would be "forever celebrated as the glorious harbinger of a new society."[24] To an extent he could never have anticipated, Marx was right. For more than a half century after these events, communists of every hue, from Lenin to Rosa Luxemburg, Joseph Stalin, and Mao Zedong, found a way to use their personal interpretations of the Commune's significance to justify their policies.

However, Marx was wrong about the present. Based in chaos and arbitrary rule, the Paris Commune was not a harbinger of an ideal social order, let alone a communist one. Still, his failed prediction perfectly illuminates the choice faced by Europe's revolutionaries. On the one hand, they could place their faith in the outbreak of future uprisings, but the prospects of such events happening soon were dim. The French, German, Austrian, and Russian governments responded with renewed repression to the possibility that the collapse of central authority in Paris was not a one-time event. On the other hand, the revolutionaries could act on the assumption that the working masses had temporarily accommodated themselves to rule by their oppressors. By the end of the century, this second interpretation was the overwhelming choice of a majority of Europe's leftist movements. The most significant manifestation of this orientation was the formation of Europe's first mass party, the Social Democratic Workers' Party of Germany (SDAP). Notably, as support for the SDAP grew, its members described their organization as "Marxist."

Paradoxically, this new party eventually did more to hinder Marx's revolutionary goals than to advance them. This eventuality was not evident immediately. When Wilhelm Liebknecht and August Bebel met with other socialist activists in the Thuringian town of Eisenach on August 8, 1869, to found the SDAP, Marx and Engels did not regard the new organization as a competitor with the transcendent phenomenon they called the communist party. They had no love for the term "social democracy" because it lacked a sense of militancy; Marx rationalized using the term as a dispensable expedient should the movement fail. Nonetheless, they regarded Liebknecht and Bebel as trustworthy exponents of the class struggle who were advancing the proletariat's cause in the most realistic way possible. Thus, they backed the party's admission to the IWA.

The idea of an organized socialist party with a clear sense of purpose made good sense at this historical juncture. In 1867, Prussia's minister-president Otto von Bismarck embraced the principle of popular representation by incorporating universal male suffrage into the constitution of the North German Confederation. Bismarck's motives were not magnanimous. In his campaign to unify the German nation under Prussian control, he gambled—correctly, it would turn out—that the democratic process would harness the nationalist sentiments of the average German on the street. Like many other conservatives, he also assumed—in this case, incorrectly—that these new citizens would cast their votes for a government that provided them with jobs and social peace.

In this light, the "Eisenacher" party was compatible with Marx and Engels's pragmatic approach to the politics of the time. In a period when, in their view, opportunities for revolutionary action were limited, workers could still improve their well-being by expressing their demands through the ballot box and taking part in local and state assemblies. By the same token, if the party failed to take advantage of this opportunity, it would risk isolating itself from its natural base. The key criterion for this engagement, as Marx and Engels saw it, was for the party leadership to ensure that the working class's participation did not cause it to lose sight of its fundamentally antagonistic relationship with the bourgeoisie and its duty to overthrow the capitalist system.

The difficulty of maintaining this balancing act was concretely expressed in the popularity of Lassalle's ideas within the SDAP. Lassalle was killed in a duel in 1864 but not before introducing an alternative conception of the class struggle that proved to have enormous staying power. Lassalle had insisted that he was as much a revolutionary as Marx and Engels, but unlike his mentors, he had a more positive view about the role of the state in achieving progressive goals. Whereas Marx and Engels viewed the expansion of state power as a temporary measure that would eventually wither away, Lassalle regarded it as a permanent feature of society that was required to serve the needs of all of its members. In an influential speech in 1862, "The Working Man's Program," just prior to the formation of the General German Workers' Association, he had argued that the state was only a negative force when it served the interests of private-property holders. When it was in the hands of the working class, in contrast, it would become a moral agency, capable of bestowing true freedom upon every member of society. This "soaring flight of the human spirit," as Lassalle called it, would not be fully realized overnight. Yet precisely because the state was not going to disappear, workers' interests were best served by using their voting power to humanize its practices.[25]

There was no automatic confluence of interests between the "Eisenachers" and Lassalle's followers, and the personal animosity between its leaders was an unremitting source of tension. However, in the 1870s, following Bismarck's extension of universal male suffrage to all of Germany, the two groups of necessity combined their forces into a unified front against the imperial regime. In May 1875, they met in Gotha to create the Socialist Workers' Party of Germany (SAPD). The strength of this organization was its much larger size than its predecessor. As an agglomeration of different political forces, however, its founding program was a hodgepodge of potentially conflicting goals. The signatories committed themselves simultaneously to state socialism, the emancipation of the working class, institutional reform, and the right to free association.

Marx and Engels went along with a majority of these objectives and eventually made their peace with the formation of the new party. But they had significant reservations about how these goals were tied together. In particular, Marx was alarmed by the Lassallean imprint on the program's central profession to use "every lawful means to bring about a free state and a socialistic society."[26] In his marginal notes on the document, subsequently published by Engels under the title "Critique of the Gotha Program," he expressed deep concern that this supposedly free state would be nothing more than the existing Prussian-dominated German state. The working class's aspiration, Marx indicated, could not be to free the government machine to do what it wanted but rather to subordinate the state to society's wishes. One would know that this transition had taken place, he added, in an oft-cited passage, when the bourgeois dictatorship had been replaced by a new form of governance, *"the revolutionary dictatorship of the proletariat."* Otherwise, there would be nothing to prevent the old regime from continuing to impose its ideas and institutions.[27]

Despite the term's global reach over the coming decades, Marx never clarified what he meant by this cryptic reference to a "revolutionary dictatorship"; he referred to the concept only a handful of times in all of his writings. Nevertheless, two developments shortly transformed the SAPD into a political entity that he and Engels could not have foreseen. The first event was Bismarck's decision to destroy the socialists after concluding that they would never provide him with the support he desired. For twelve years, from 1878, when Bismarck successfully pushed antisocialist legislation through the Reichstag, until 1890, when the parliament refused to renew the laws, the SAPD ceased to be an effective public force. Although the party was never officially declared illegal and its members could run for office as independents, they were prohibited from holding or attending meetings; socialist publications and fund-raising were banned; and the police were given enhanced authority to suppress public dissent. Out of the spotlight, however, the SAPD succeeded in spreading its message and recruiting new members. Organizers ran party activities through secret cells and used trade unions as communications conduits. When these activities proved too dangerous, they shifted their operations to other countries. The party newspaper, *Der Sozialdemokrat*, was published in Zurich and then smuggled back into Germany through underground networks.

These conditions changed the SAPD's agenda, increasing the power of its left wing. There was no longer any point to engaging in arcane debates about whether the needs of the working class could be met by enlisting the state's support. This particular German state would have nothing to do with a socialist party. As a result, Bismarck's repression left an indelible mark on the kind of organization the SAPD was to become. As an underground association, the party's leaders could demand the unflinching loyalty and discipline of their members because the party's survival depended on these qualities. Hence, the SAPD acquired an avowedly militant cast.

The second development in the SAPD's evolution was its transformation into a democratic, mass organization. Far from weakening the party as Bismarck desired, the antisocialist laws had the unanticipated consequence of generating sympathy for its cause among German voters and enhancing its reputation as the authentic representative of the working class. Bismarck attempted to counter these sentiments by introducing a comprehensive system of health and disability insurance. Yet most workers viewed these measures for what they were, proof that the SAPD could force the regime to change its policies. As a result, the idea of a vibrant socialist party became a permanent fixture in German politics. When the Reichstag refused to renew the antisocialist laws in 1890, the socialists were in a stronger position than ever before to campaign for political office. Under a new name, the SPD won nearly 1.5 million votes and, signaling its ascent from illegality, filled 35 out of 397 seats in the Reichstag.[28]

Overnight, the SPD became the largest and most powerful socialist party in Europe. Yet the SPD's continued electoral success also presented its leaders with problems that would have been inconceivable during its years of illegality. The more they concentrated on winning seats in parliament and reaching out to broader segments of the electorate, the more their contradictory foundations were exposed. For example, the leaders of Germany's rapidly growing trade unions were naturally inclined to judge the party in terms of its efficacy in exacting concessions from employers on wages and improved work conditions. Conversely, the SPD's true believers abhorred these calculations, fearing that the party would compromise its Marxist soul.

On the surface, the case for orthodoxy seemed to win out. In 1891, the SPD adopted a new program in Erfurt affirming its Marxist credentials. Under the stewardship of the Czech-German socialist and popularizer of Marx's work, Karl Kautsky, the party underscored its founding fathers' basic line on history's ineluctable march toward socialism. Capitalism was the source of the proletariat's emiseration; the class struggle was intensifying; and true justice would be achieved only with the abolition of class rule. Thus, the concluding message at Erfurt was consistent with its founders' views—there could be no lasting accommodation with the bourgeoisie.

Just below the surface, however, a reformist wing was making the case for treating participation in bourgeois institutions not as a means to a higher end but as an end in itself. In an influential book, *Evolutionary Socialism*, Eduard Bernstein, a friend of both Engels and Kautsky, took issue with the core of Marx's claims about the inherent instability of capitalism. Living in England, Bernstein was impressed by the fact that British industrialists had not experienced the recurrent crises predicted by his predecessor. Instead, the bourgeoisie had survived—indeed, flourished—by using its wealth to buy the loyalty of the lower classes. Additionally, contrary to Marx and Engels's predictions, working-class living standards were improving, not declining. Accordingly, Bernstein concluded that the SPD's best strategy was to secure a position within the capitalist system as the permanent advocate of working-class interests. Over time, as he saw it, class boundaries would be overcome and a just distribution of resources would emerge.

For many SPD members, and especially those schooled in the harsh lessons of the antisocialist laws, Bernstein's prescriptions were sheer heresy. Down the road, this view would congeal into a serious fault line within the party. Still, as the social democratic movement grew, many of the party's rank-and-file members were attracted to a concept of political action that was not based upon an imminent confrontation, let alone a violent conflict with established instititions. From their leaders' perspective, one could still subscribe to the doctrine of the class struggle while pushing the revolutionary horizon further out.

One can appreciate the significance of the SPD's emergence as a formidable model of party organization by considering the plight of its socialist counterparts in the countries that first had parties, Great Britain and France. In the former, when a socialist movement finally took hold, it had few of the characteristics of what would soon be called a Marxist party. Not only had England played host to Marx when he produced his most influential work, but as the first European state to experience the full effect of the Industrial Revolution, it had also provided him with the historical template for his arguments about the inherent instability of capitalist production. To be sure, Marx was right about one thing. The English working class did not need outside help to assert its interests. The presence of well-organized, skill-based trade unions in the 1850s and their expansion to include unskilled trades in the ensuing years demonstrated that workers were capable of lobbying on their own behalf for social and economic reforms. The more success these organizations encountered, however, the less compelling was the case for radical change among their members.

Unlike in Germany, which lacked the long-established tradition of parliamentary representation, British workers could pursue their interests within the existing political system. Thanks to new suffrage reforms, they shared a sense of common citizenship with the ruling classes and, especially in England, nearly universal agreement about the legitimacy of the country's ruling institutions—Parliament, the crown, and the empire. These attitudes did not prevent them from asserting their will. Far from deferring to the wishes of their employers, their leaders used strikes and other forms of industrial action to press for higher wages and express their grievances. Their sense of collective power was enhanced when both Tories and Liberals, the Whigs' successors, recognized that they could no longer calmly discount the workingman's vote. By the elections of 1885, the Liberal Party was disposed to seek common cause with the larger trade unions on many issues, even agreeing not to campaign against independent labor candidates for Parliament.

Against the backdrop of this success story of trade unionism, Marxist and quasi-Marxist political groupings engaged in self-inflicted torments as they struggled to find points of traction between their ideas and the goals of the labor movement. For example, one association, the Social Democratic Federation, was noteworthy for its almost inexplicable rejection of trade unionism. Under the leadership of the dogmatic Marxist, Henry Mayers Hyndman, the Federation espoused the view that meaningful social change was only possible after the collapse of capitalism. Until this point, Hyndman argued, accommodation was not only pointless, it would impede the proletariat's recognition of its revolutionary destiny. A different but equally ineffective position was taken by the Socialist League, a breakaway faction of the Federation. The League's identity was shaped by William Morris, a utopian thinker and former Liberal, who shared many of the moralistic predispositions of Marx's precursors. As a fervent believer in a revolutionary path to socialism, Morris went further even than Hyndman in opposing any form of parliamentary democracy. Inadvertently, he set the stage for allowing the League's anarchist wing to take over the association by the end of the decade.

Notwithstanding their importance in the evolution of Marxism in Britain, both the Federation and the League were never more than small sects, composed of little more than a thousand members. The closest any organization came to the formation of a self-sustaining socialist party was the Independent Labour Party (ILP). Shaped by Keir Hardie, a Scottish miner, dynamic labor organizer, and member of Parliament, the ILP was created in 1893 as a response to the Liberals' efforts to co-opt the working-class vote. In its early years, it was a mélange of the discontented radical Marxists, Christian socialists, Scottish nationalists, and a heterogeneous intellectual club, the Fabians. Unlike its predecessors, the ILP's overriding goal was to bring the panoply of left-wing groups under a common roof. However, it accomplished the opposite. Its members' identification with different trade unions and divisions over collectivist approaches to controlling the economy had the unintended consequence of making a truly independent path to socialist unity impossible.

In this light, it was logical that if a viable party could not be imposed from on high to lead the working class, it would have to come "out of the bowels" of the labor movement itself.[29] In 1899, representatives of the omnibus Trades Union Congress (TUC) voted to create the Labour Representation Committee, which then changed its name to the Labour Party in 1906. On the surface, the new party appeared to be a unified body. All of its predecessors were involved in its formation, well represented on its executive board, and among its candidates for public office. But true to form, they proved to be their own worst enemies. The Socialist Federation and the ILP lost no time in coming to blows; in less than two years, the former had seceded from the organization.

The beneficiaries of these developments were the trade unions. For both good and bad, as far as the socialist movement was concerned, they became one of the most influential political forces in England on the eve of World War I. For the Labour Party, the good was that the TUC brought millions of skilled and unskilled workers from every sector of society to the polls. Either in concert with the Liberals or on their own initiative, Labour politicians capitalized on this success by passing progressive legislation on education, national insurance, and eventually women's suffrage. The undesirable consequence for Labour was that the TUC was an inconsistent supporter of the party's priorities. Its diverse and frequently antagonistic members—clothiers, miners, and yard workers—were all inclined to regard the party as their private agent. From a democratic perspective, this was a healthy arrangement because Labour was forced to be a more representative organ than its Conservative and Liberal rivals. However, the party's complex base was also the source of negative consequences. Even when Labour tried to profile itself as an independent working-class party before World War I, its leaders could not commit themselves to an exclusively socialist, let alone Marxist, program.

Labour's weaknesses in comparison with the German SPD may have disappointed many Marxists, but it was nowhere near the dismal, confusing lot of the socialists in France. At first blush, one would have thought that they were in an advantageous position. Thanks to the abiding spirit of the Revolution, leftist politicians were more comfortable in expressing their militant views in France than elsewhere. Moreover, there was much to complain about because French democracy failed to provide both elites and ordinary citizens with the stability for which they yearned. Only a few years after the carnage of the Paris Commune, moderate parliamentarians pushed for the promulgation of a new constitution that bestowed upon France's Third Republic the image of a popular government. Yet, the divisions that had permeated French society since the Revolution could not be wished away. In particular, liberal politicians were ineffective in countering the antidemocratic sentiments of a constantly shifting alliance of business owners, the Church, the army, and landowners.

Despite the fact that these divisions were ripe for exploitation, French socialists proved incapable of offering workable alternatives. In numerous cases, they were their own worst enemies. The country's first socialist party, the Federation of the Socialist Workers of France, was formed in 1879. Colloquially known as the Possibilists because of the temperate leadership style of its leader, Paul Brousse, the party was ambivalent about Marxism. On the other side of the political spectrum, a leftist faction led by Jules Guesde broke away from the Possibilists in 1880 to form the French Workers' Party. Guesde considered himself a true Marxist. In contrast to those socialists who had reconciled themselves to capitalism's relative stability, he was a rigid determinist who believed that a violent revolution was imminent and defined his party's priorities accordingly.

Compounding these difficulties, the socialist parties and their respective factions had to compete for the heart of the French worker with "antiparty" movements. Unlike in Britain and Germany, anarchism continued to be a powerful force. The leaders of the sizeable anarcho-syndicalist General Confederation of Labor were instinctively distrustful of any form of state rule and forbade its members from engaging in partisan politics. Preaching the language of "direct action," they encouraged workers to force concessions from employers through boycotts and sabotage. The ultimate expression of their attitudes was the revolutionary concept of the "general strike," the moment at which the working class would supposedly break the back of the capitalist system by laying down its tools, taking command of the factories, and reorganizing production according to direct citizen participation and union control. In the monarchists' view, the legacies of 1789, 1830, 1848, and 1871 testified to this possibility. Some anarchists went even further, calling for "propaganda by the deed," bombings and assassinations, to inspire the population to violent action.

The great misfortune of France's first truly viable, mass socialist party, the French Section of the Workers' International (SFIO), which was founded in 1905, was to inherit these deep conflicts. The party's subsequent difficulties were not due to a lack of inspiration. Its popular leader, Jean Jaurès, infused the SFIO's programs with the manifold symbols of the French Revolution—its moralistic fervor, rebellious distaste for political authority, and transcendent vision of republican democracy. Yet the hopes that Jaurès raised quickly turned into disappointment. For some observers, Jaurès was too open to compromise; for others, he was too willing to collaborate with the government. In the eyes of ordinary French citizens, he failed because he could not control the dynamic forces that the party unleashed. The SFIO was unable to rein in waves upon waves of strikes and protests that swept across the country from 1905 to 1914. This did not prevent a majority of Jaurès's compatriots from mourning his passing when he was assassinated by a French nationalist on July 31, 1914, only three days after the outbreak of World War I. It did mean that the issue of a unified socialist party in France was primed for contentious debate when the conflagration came to an end.

THE INTERNATIONAL AND THE NATIONAL PARTIES

Looking backward from this catastrophe, one is struck by how much the revolutionary landscape of Europe had changed in the sixty-six years since the publication of the *Communist Manifesto*. In this relatively short period, the abstract idea of a communist party had converged with the rise of electorally driven socialist and social democratic parties to take concrete form. In the 1840s, established parties had been based upon cultures of limited representation. Their members simultaneously looked down on the man on the street and feared the revolutionaries who could lure him or her into action. By the new century, however, strains of Marxist thinking, from its progenitors' advocacy of social and economic transformation to their confident predictions about the progressive course of history, could be found in the programs of diverse left-wing parties everywhere.

Nonetheless, the appearance of success brings one back to the potential contradiction in the transition from a period primarily characterized by the exchange of revolutionary ideas to one that is increasingly defined in terms of organizational effectiveness. In Marx and Engels's best of all possible worlds, as we have seen, it was unimportant to define the communist party in terms of a neat organizational structure. Marx in particular envisioned a party that would come together fluidly thanks to a shared vision. Its members would pledge their allegiance to truly revolutionary principles because their understanding of history proved to them that no other action was defensible. In return for their sacrifices, history would repay them by allowing them to assist in the birth of a new type of society.

The problem with this perspective is that history is rarely so obliging. As the outcome of the revolutions of 1848 demonstrated, the workers of Germany, Britain, France, and other European countries did not have enough grievances in common to constitute a unified proletariat. Some staged factory protests and strikes, but they were not prepared to undertake the risks of revolutionary confrontation. Others engaged in acts of rebellion, but they were motivated less by economic conditions than by republican values and demands for national independence. Contrary to Marx and Engels's predictions, a majority of workers were unwilling to commit themselves permanently to a victory that was still far down the road. Furthermore, as working and living conditions improved and the effectiveness of trade unions grew, they became convinced that their needs could be met within the established order.

In these respects, the formation of the IWA in 1864 was a sensible attempt to give credence to both Marx and Engels's ideas and those of many other leftist thinkers. It provided a common roof under which orthodox Marxists, Lassalleans, Proudhonists, radical anarchists, and

British trade unionists could coalesce. For a brief time, this international experiment benefited from both a surge in labor protest and the fact that it was the only significant membership option for the European Left. But the organization's dissolution after twelve years of creeping obsolescence testified to the difficulties of holding a movement together if the ideas that undergirded it became more diffuse. Little concrete progress could be made among people who were separated by fundamental differences. In the end, the IWA expired under the weight of two events. One, the failure of the Paris Commune, undermined its members' confidence that the benefits would outweigh the risk of putting one's life on the line. The other, Bakunin's expulsion from the body at Marx's instigation in 1872, caused a lasting rift between socialists and anarchists across the continent, especially in southern Europe.

In contrast, the so-called Second International, which was founded in Paris in 1889, had the attributes of a modern political organization. Whereas its predecessor was open to most self-professed representatives of the toiling masses, membership in the new International was restricted solely to the *national* socialist parties, including the SPD, the French socialists, and the British Labour Party, as well as to their affiliated labor organizations. The anarchists were prohibited. On these narrow foundations, the Second International's leaders painted a picture of socialist solidarity that was certain to please the orthodox revolutionary. Under the weighty influence of the German Social Democrats, they portrayed the organization as the voice of the proletariat of all countries. Its national parties used its meetings to expound the tenets of the ideology they now identified as Marxism: the primacy of the class struggle as the motor force of history; state control of the means of production; and opposition to the enemies of the international working class, including nationalism, great-power chauvinism, and imperialism.

Thanks to the SFIO's influence, the Second International also provided the vehicle for the propagation of the romantic iconography that communist regimes would adopt throughout the twentieth century. Through an exhaustive combination of red banners, slogans, songs, manifestos, and parades, agitators—or "comrades" as they now called themselves—gave birth to a mass political culture that Marx and

Engels could only have dreamed about in the 1840s. This exuberant spirit was embodied in the adoption of the "Internationale" as the official anthem of the proletariat. In glorification of the "damned of the Earth" (*damné de la terre*) and the "prisoners of hunger" (*forçats de la faim*), the voices of communists around the world exalted the world-wide cause of human liberation.

Maintaining the purity of these ideas, however, was clearly a more problematic enterprise than ever before. As a result of the Second International's desire to attract representative parties and unions from every nation, the organization adopted a highly decentralized structure. Unlike its disjointed predecessor, it did not form a central governing organ until 1900. This body, the International Socialist Bureau (ISB), was subordinated to the interests of the national party organizations that created it. It could make high-minded proclamations, but its representatives' hands were tied when the national parties failed to act on them.

This contradiction was epitomized in the ISB's relationship with the German SPD. No party espoused the International's principles with greater exuberance than the Social Democrats. But in practice, the electoral calculations of the SPD's leaders continued to fuel its transformation from the party of Marx into the party of Eduard Bernstein. The larger its mass base grew, the more they attempted to capitalize on the opportunity to work within the existing political order. Instead of confronting the state, they sought concessions on issues ranging from social security and education to taxation and foreign trade.

In 1914, a global tragedy fully exposed the disjunction between the International's revolutionary principles and the SPD's political calculations. As war clouds descended upon Europe in the early 1910s, the ISB initially reiterated Marx's proposition that the workers of each country should rally around their class identity and combat the predatory designs of the bourgeoisie. At the Basel Congress in 1912, the organization's representatives declared that no worker should be asked to take up arms against another, and they obligated their members to campaign for an immediate cessation of hostilities should war break out. It was thus with shock and horror that many socialists received the news that the SPD's parliamentary faction had voted on August 4, 1914—with a single abstention by the left-wing socialist Karl Liebknecht—to support war credits. The ISB immediately condemned the decision. But in the following weeks, the International's French, Belgian, and British members demonstrated that they had a different view, declaring themselves at war with their German partners. At this juncture, it became clear that the international character of the working-class movement was a mirage. The major socialist parties in Europe felt more beholden to the defense of their nation than to any abstract conception of class solidarity.

This turn of events was devastating for those believers who still held out hope that the European proletariat would coalesce into a single movement. Yet for the socialist parties' most radical members, it also marked a beginning. From one country to another, they had struggled to make their voices heard in their respective national parties. Now, their leaders' betrayal of the International's founding principles gave them reason to take responsibility for returning their movement to its original values. In considering their choices, these revolutionaries were understandably inclined to look for examples of parties that were pursuing more radical paths. One of these, the Russian Social Democratic Labor Party (RSDLP), had emerged in a setting that orthodox Marxists considered not yet ripe for a socialist revolution; even the RSDLP's leaders agreed with this judgment. Nevertheless, given that European socialist parties were making little progress on their own, it was at least conceivable that an alternative model of party organization could offer lessons about reinvigorating the ideals that Marx outlined in the *Communist Manifesto*.

CHAPTER 3

A Revolutionary Party Emerges

In March 1902, Vladimir Ilyich Lenin provided part of the answer to the question that had become obscured since the publication of the *Communist Manifesto*: What is the communist party? In his enormously influential tract, *What Is to Be Done?*, the father of the Bolshevik Revolution presented his supporters with a compelling picture of how they might achieve their objectives. To bring revolutionary consciousness to a slumbering proletariat, they would need an elite organization. This body's operations would be centralized and directed by disciplined professionals just like them, who were devoted to building a just society. Schooled in what Lenin colorfully called the "art of combat" and ideologically sophisticated, these Marxist heroes would be poised to do battle with anyone who dared to stand in the way of the liberation of the masses.[1]

Lenin's provocative ideas made sense to many readers. At this juncture, he was seeking to enlist the support of Russia's small and divided population of revolutionaries. In particular, the modestly sized Russian Social Democratic Labor Party (RSDLP), to which he belonged, was attempting to find its footing in conditions that were less suited for Marxist precepts than the party that inspired it, the Social Democratic Party of Germany (SPD). In Germany and elsewhere in Europe, the idea of confronting the unjust relationship between rulers and ruled was already gaining traction in major urban centers. In contrast, Russia's small working-class population was much less prepared to confront its oppressors, let alone attack the autocracy's institutions. Thus, many of Lenin's readers would have been attracted to the idea that a disciplined group of communist conspirators with a clear sense of its mission could push the exploited class into acting on its best interests.

In this light, scholars frequently treat *What Is to Be Done?* as a blue-print for what the communist party was to become within a decade after its leaders' ascent to power—uniform in its programs, tightly organized, and dictatorial. Notably, this desire to characterize the party in readily understandable terms was first evinced by Soviet theorists in the years after the Bolshevik Revolution and categorized as the doctrine of "Marxism-Leninism." Yet, these features were not what Lenin had in mind in 1902. Unlike his European counterparts who were already building organizations with the capacity to mobilize vast numbers of their countries' citizens and shape their governments' policies, Lenin and his fellow radicals were grappling with the challenge of applying their ideas to the overthrow of the established order. In this respect, the Lenin of *What Is to Be Done?* was not as far removed as one might think from the Marx of the *Communist Manifesto.* Like Marx, Lenin was convinced that a proletarian revolution was in the offing, even in his less-developed setting. As an agitator who had Marx's intellectual foundations to stand upon, he believed that he was called to identify the best strategies to use in the coming upheaval, even if his ideas were at variance with his predecessor's predictions.

An equally important reason for not interpreting Lenin's work out of context is that the conditions in which the RSDLP, or more precisely his Bolshevik faction, was acting were not yet conducive to success. Between 1905 and 1917, Russia experienced three major social and political conflagrations. But in all of them, the Bolsheviks were only one of many different insurrectionary groups. In the crowning event, the October Revolution of 1917, they would not have come to power—or, quite possibly, had the capability to distinguish themselves from their rivals—had not all major forms of political authority collapsed around them.

Against this background, it is important to appreciate that when Lenin and other Bolshevik leaders spoke of their party in the early 1900s, they still viewed it primarily in revolutionary terms and only secondarily appreciated the benefits of greater organization. As revolutionaries, they viewed their mission in terms of working together to ensure that the proletariat followed through on its historically appointed task. Thus, there was considerably more room for debate among them about the party's purposes than is commonly assumed. The organizational structures would eventually come. But this would be a slow process, reflecting an abiding tension between the idea of the party's function in the Revolution and the organs that were required for effective governance thereafter.

THE ROOTS OF REVOLUTION

The approach that Lenin and his contemporaries took to revolution was directly shaped by decades of frustration at their predecessors' failure to chip away at Russia's autocratic culture. Unlike in Great Britain, for example, where the state allowed its citizens the space for independent self-expression and eventually the emergence of mass organizations, there was very little room for political protest in Russia. On those rare occasions when overt challenges arose, the autocracy responded immediately with repression. In December 1825, the tsar and his supporters crushed a revolt by army officers who demanded a constitution and the end to serfdom. Likewise, in 1830, the Russian army quelled a violent uprising in Russian Poland, abolishing its constitution and imposing new restrictions on the territory's autonomy. For related reasons, Russian dissidents lacked the opportunities for self-expression available to their French counterparts. Although the tsars had long welcomed representatives of the French Enlightenment into their court, the horrific consequences of the Revolution of 1789 made them determined to prevent any would-be critics from acquiring the means to make their views known.

Accordingly, when the window for political change finally opened in Russia, it was because the tsar and his court wanted it to happen. After the country's humiliating defeat in the Crimean War in 1856, a new tsar, Alexander II, introduced sweeping reforms to unify the diverse segments of Russian society and increase popular participation in public life. Acting on an already existing consensus among his advisers, he approved the Emancipation Act of February 19, 1861, which abolished the tragic institution of serfdom. In 1864, he permitted the establishment of local assemblies in which elected delegates from the landed nobility and, to a lesser extent, townspeople and rural residents could deliberate over matters like road building, schools, and medical care. In these and other Great Reforms, Alexander II intended to lay the foundations for the modernization of Russia's backward economy and to recoup the autocracy's diminished authority. But he inadvertently spurred oppositional forces into action. The benefits of the end to serfdom were quickly perceived to be outweighed by its negative effects. Although former serfs were granted the right to own the commodity they coveted the most—land—they soon found themselves laden with new burdens. They were required to make redemption payments to the state at high rates of interest and to remain on their land holdings for years before they could move elsewhere. Similarly, Alexander II's failure to grant the local assemblies significant power alienated their educated participants.

In the 1860s and 1870s, these and other disappointments congealed into a broad and distinctively Russian movement known as populism. Unlike many middle-class intellectuals in countries like Britain and France, the populists shared a romantic belief in the innate goodness of the common man. They were deeply influenced by the thinking of the founder of Russian socialism, Alexander Herzen, a friend of Marx and Engels and a well-known figure in the circles of the First International. Herzen argued that Russia's privileged upper classes had a moral obligation to improve the lives of the peasantry. He was personally tormented by the executions of the so-called Decembrist rebels of 1825, which he saw as unequivocal proof that the autocracy could not be trusted to meet this challenge. As an alternative, he looked to the well-heeled children of the nobility to assume the responsibility that had been neglected by their parents. In his view, they were obliged not only to educate the masses but also to learn from them. In particular, Herzen and his populist followers were enamored with a peculiarly Russian form of land tenure, the village commune, which they regarded as a potential foundation for a just society. For many, the commune bore a resemblance to the early socialist vision of a classless society because property was held in common and distributed to individual households on the basis of need. They had little concern for how this ideal was to be applied to Russia in its entirety. Its primary attraction was that it served their egalitarian impulses. Indeed,

late in life, even Marx was intrigued by the possibility that this institution could provide a "starting point" for the transition into
socialism.[2]

Unlike these early populists, the political activists who came after
them were radicalized by the unfulfilled expectations of Alexander
II's reforms. Their disillusionment convinced them that meaningful
change was only possible if they were willing to invest their lives fully
in bringing it about. In fact, many of them concluded that the regime's inherently repressive nature could only be overcome by meeting force with force. These radicals found a hero in the writer Nikolai
Chernyshevsky, whose novel, *What Is to Be Done?* (1863), inspired
them to think about political action as a moral imperative in which
they would play a leading role. In this novel, written in a prison cell in
St. Petersburg's Peter and Paul Fortress, Chernyshevsky gave life to
the argument that Russia could only be changed by a revolutionary
elite that was committed to transforming the country from an un-
civilized backwater into a modern state. He portrayed his protago-
nists as "new people" who thought for themselves, cast aside their
parents' superstitions and outmoded beliefs, and treated each other as
equals.

In a climate of distrust and suspicion, educated young men and
women immediately identified with Chernyshevsky's heroes. As potentially "new people," they saw themselves as liberators endowed with
both the prophetic insight and the temperament to free the masses
from their physical and psychological chains. In 1874, in an extraordinary demonstration of youthful exuberance, more than 2,000 populists, most of them students, traveled to villages throughout European
Russia with this objective in mind. Dressed as peasants and professing
enthusiasm for the customs of the countryside, they extolled the virtues of socialism and rebellion against the autocracy. This "going to the
people" movement, as it became known, was a fiasco. Far from attempting to learn from the peasants, as Herzen had urged, the populists lectured them about putatively enlightened ways of thinking and urged
them to abandon the sentimental attachments of traditional society.
More often than not, village leaders received their visitors with suspicion, if not outright hostility.

Although this foray into mass mobilization was a failure, populism's shift from an amorphous idea to a palpable social movement led by the children of petty nobles, professionals, and priests confused and frightened Alexander II and his court. The tsar reacted to these affronts to his magnanimity with more repression, jailing activists and staging public trials to reinforce his authority. As these measures escalated, populist leaders faced a difficult choice. Should they continue to campaign for justice in full view, trusting that they would eventually awaken the sympathies of those they were trying to help? Or should they learn from defeat, organize their forces secretly, and launch the revolution on their own terms?

In the late 1860s and early 1870s, two left-wing populists, Peter Tkachev and Sergei Nechayev, took the lead in advocating the latter conspiratorial approach. In many ways like Louis Auguste Blanqui in France, Tkachev and Nechayev were convinced that the movement's weakness lay in a misguided faith in the masses' understanding of their true needs. In their view, the peasantry had the collective power to better its condition, but no progress would be made until this inert segment of Russian society was told what it had to do. For both radicals, this meant that the populists needed to learn to lead.

Tkachev concentrated on the organizational challenge of fomenting revolution. More of a theorist than his peers and better acquainted with Western radical traditions, including Marx and Engels's available writings, Tkachev was among the first activists to take on the task of showing why Russia was suited to have a revolution of its own. In a contentious exchange with Engels, he argued that his country's weak bourgeoisie and negligible proletariat made it "altogether exceptional." Accordingly, Russia's radicals required a special revolutionary program that would, in Tkachev's succinct characterization, differ as much from that of a country like Germany as German conditions differed from those in Russia. In this light, he observed, Russia was fortunate in having an educated class of men and women who understood that revolutionary action could no longer be postponed. To live up to their calling, he added, they needed "centralization, severe discipline, speed, decision, and unity in action." Only in this way could they surmount the doubts and divisions that had previously kept other radicals from achieving their goals.[3]

For his part, Nechayev was the quintessential conspiratorial revolutionary, someone noted for his ruthless opposition to compromise. His "Revolutionary Catechism," which may have been coauthored by the anarchist Mikhail Bakunin, was published in 1869 and took the principle of self-sacrifice further than anyone before him. Nechayev described the true revolutionary as a "doomed man." This man would have no personal interests, no emotional attachments, not even a name. He would be totally consumed by his cause and, therefore, prepared "to perish himself and to destroy with his own hands everything that hinders the revolution's realization."[4] Nechayev struggled over how his sacrificial hero should be reconciled with his contemporaries' desire to build a broader movement. Should this individual act on his own or should he link arms with his like-minded peers? Nechayev's solution was that his model revolutionary would seek the guidance of comrades who shared his convictions. Together, they would agree upon a common plan. But after this point, the "doomed man" would rely solely on his instincts. "In the fulfillment of a series of destructive actions," Nechayev wrote, "each must act himself and seek the counsel and help of comrades only when it is essential for success."[5]

I have singled out these currents of radical thought because of their centrality to Russia's first revolutionary associations and thereby to Lenin's thinking down the road. One clandestine group, Land and Liberty, which was formed in 1876, took the first steps in coordinating the activities of secret cells in Russia and abroad. Land and Liberty retained the early populists' fascination with the inchoate wisdom of the masses and their faith in the revolutionary potential of the countryside. Yet on one issue in particular—the use of violence—its members were deeply divided. Although they agreed that nothing short of the forcible overthrow of the regime was necessary, they differed on when such measures should be taken. One faction, led by Georgy Plekhanov, widely recognized as the father of Russian Marxism, and the Jewish anarchist and later Menshevik, Pavel Axelrod, maintained that the movement should primarily use violent means to defend itself against the regime's efforts to suppress its activities. The other, larger faction treated violence as a good in itself. Its supporters contended that the only way to gain the advantage over their adversaries was to attack them head-on.

Land and Liberty's split over this issue in 1879 resulted in the formation of two new associations with quite different objectives. One, a short-lived group of moderates known as Black Repartition and briefly led by Plekhanov, was committed to the redistribution of property. The other, the People's Will, was an avowedly terrorist organization. In a mere two years, it left an indelible mark on Russian history. People's Will was almost entirely at the mercy of the ambitions of its radical members. Formally, they echoed standard populist themes. They paid lip service to the familiar rhetoric about the nobility of the people; they promised to hand over land and factories to the masses; to guarantee freedom of conscience, speech, and association; and to create a society in which the need for state domination would eventually disappear. But in practice, they advanced these lofty goals almost entirely through destructive means.

This contradiction could not have been more starkly illustrated than in their most dramatic act. For over a year, a handful of adherents focused on a single goal—to kill the tsar. They achieved their objective on March 1, 1881, when a bomb thrown by one of their members mortally wounded Alexander II. Yet instead of precipitating waves of mass protest as they anticipated, the assassination left the populist movement as a whole with a devastating legacy. At the time of his death, the tsar had been seriously contemplating new political reforms. The accession of his son, Alexander III, to the throne, however, led to political retrenchment and a horrific backlash. Scores of the movement's members and sympathizers were executed, including Alexander Ulyanov, the brother of Lenin. Many more were sent to penal colonies in Siberia. Just as consequential, the Russian public reacted to the assassination with revulsion.

SOCIAL DEMOCRACY COMES TO RUSSIA

A basic law of politics is that times of despair for some people can be turned into times of opportunity for others. The key to understanding the advent of a Russian version of a Marxist party is that it grew out of the disorganized, divided, and futile tradition that had begun with populism. Technically, this was not supposed to happen. Marx and

Engels were writing about countries in the industrialized West that, in their estimation, had already moved into the later stages of capitalism and were on the verge of a revolutionary upheaval by the proletariat. In comparison, according to this interpretation, Russia had barely passed beyond the bounds of early modern feudalism.

Nevertheless, for the many left-wing activists who were looking for alternative models of political engagement, the social democratic movement provided some answers to their country's plight. For one thing, the conditions in the Russian empire were more favorable for radicalism than is sometimes appreciated. Although Russia was less developed than its Western neighbors, some sectors of its economy were undergoing significant growth by the 1880s and 1890s, thanks to selective government investments and trade tariffs, the influx of foreign capital, and a massive increase in the size of the population. Simultaneously, there was a sizeable gap at the end of the nineteenth century between this wealth and the welfare of the average laborer. Although there were only about 2 million workers in the empire out of a total population of around 128 million that was primarily composed of peasants, their openness to radicalization was substantial.[6] Heavily concentrated in major cities like St. Petersburg and Moscow, and non-Russian regions like Poland and the Baltics, their daily existence was akin to the dark circumstances that Engels encountered in Manchester—abject living conditions and poor employment prospects. Also like in Britain in the 1840s, these desperate conditions were exacerbated by a mass migration of peasants from the countryside.

Thanks to these conditions, radical socialists could offer their audiences something that the proponents of populism could not—a robust and apparently all-encompassing social theory that was relevant to the construction of an industrialized society. Whereas populist leaders based their appeals on the basic goodness of the common man and woman, Marxism, or "scientific socialism" as its proponents called it, seemed to provide a systematic way of connecting the certainty of Marx and Engels's predictions with the effects of Russia's industrialization. Despite the fact that many of these laborers were recent arrivals from the countryside, socialist agitators could creatively take advantage of the family resemblance between oppressed urban workers in the West and the Russian peasantry to deem the latter their "proletariat." Even leftists who were skeptical about the universal applicability of Marxist theory could readily see the advantages of an organized social democratic movement over a fanatical group like People's Will. The terrorists had tarnished the reputation of Russian socialism by reducing the idea of revolution to acts of will. In contrast, the social democrats were attractive because of their determination to link theory with practice. In the eyes of their supporters, they understood what was required to facilitate Russia's transition, first to capitalism and later to socialism.

Finally, Russia's socialists benefited from the fact that Western social democratic parties were already proving that they could put their beliefs into action. They were enthralled by the success of the German SPD. In particular, they admired the SPD's organizational discipline and its members' fierce commitment to their beliefs during years of oppression and conspiratorial action. Although the Russian socialists, too, were relegated to underground activity, they were not in a position to emulate the German example. The first quasi-Marxist associations in the empire were isolated, poorly organized, and lacking in direction. These included the South Russian Federation of Workers and two Polish groups, one called Proletariat and the other a Jewish labor association, later to be known as the Bund. Only in 1883 did Plekhanov, Axelrod, and three other prominent socialists found the Emancipation of Labor group that would evolve into Russia's first social democratic party.

At first glance, Emancipation of Labor's goals appeared to be anything but revolutionary. The group's initial objective was to spread the gospel of Marxism by distributing pamphlets and books to potential supporters. Nonetheless, as Plekhanov demonstrated by publishing the first Russian translation of the *Communist Manifesto*, its members were in a propitious position to advocate for their cause. With few rivals, they became the first guardians of Marxist orthodoxy in Russia. They could determine what constituted legitimate interpretations of Marx and Engels's works, which texts were worth publishing, and which should be rejected. In short, they stood to win the battle of ideas before a fully formed party came into being.

No figure was more important than Plekhanov, a former populist, for establishing the baseline against which the coming debates about social democratic leadership were to be waged. In an essay written in exile in Geneva in 1885, "Our Differences," he made the case for a Russian version of Marxism seem fresh and exciting. According to Plekhanov, the populists had mistakenly assumed that the march to socialism and communism could be driven by the peasantry. In fact, he argued, in tune with Marx before him, the best rural society had to offer was some type of "petit-bourgeois" ownership of land. In contrast, Plekhanov emphasized that it would not be necessary to lower one's aspirations if one acted on the as yet untapped yearnings of the proletariat. In this case, one could count on the working class to be resolutely opposed to capitalism.

At the time, anyone reading Plekhanov's essay would have recognized the complexity of this position. If the revolution was to be made by Russian workers and not by the peasantry, then capitalist production relations would need to develop more fully before the apocalyptic battle between the proletariat and its oppressors could take place. Plekhanov accepted this principle but also provided some good news for those who were anxiously awaiting the revolution—the proletariat's day of reckoning with its enemies was not as distant as it seemed. In response to his critics, among whom he included everyone from Bakunin and Tkachev to Russian "Jacobins," Blanqui, and People's Will, Plekhanov emphasized that Marx and Engels's conception of an international class struggle was as applicable to Russia as to any other country. Thanks to the fact that capitalism was already in crisis in the West, its presence in Russia would "fade before it has time to blossom completely."[7]

Drawing upon this argument, Plekhanov's major contribution was to translate a Russian idea of Marxism into the advocacy of a Russian social democratic party. This party's function, as he described it, would not be like that of the German Social Democrats since there was little chance of meaningful elections in Russia. Its task would be to bring "consciousness" to the working class by taking the "scattered efforts of the workers in individual factories and workshops" and giving them a class character. One could not know exactly when the time for action would arise. But, he underscored, the party would do well to learn from the populists' mistakes. Good will was no substitute for good organization. Accordingly, a Russian social democratic party would be charged with uniting its members into a "single, formidable, disciplined force."[8]

Naturally, other Russian Marxists had different ideas about how and to what end such an organization should be used to mobilize the proletariat. One group, known in socialist circles as the "Economists," sought to shift the locus of debate back to the economic foundations of Marxist theory. The Economists did not dispute the value of having a leading party, but in their view, it was sufficient to concentrate their immediate steps on improving the lives of workers and providing fair pay and decent working conditions. Furthermore, although the Economists believed that an eventual revolution against capitalism was necessary, they differed with Plekhanov on the necessity of violence. They contended that if progress could be made on these material goals, the need for a forceful confrontation with capitalism's defenders would diminish. On the same issue, another socialist group, known as the "Legal Marxists," was even more disposed to accommodate itself to the emerging order. In their view, socialists should welcome the advent of capitalism. Had not Marx himself characterized the bourgeoisie as a revolutionary class? According to Peter Struve, the group's best-known adherent, the lesson from the growth of democratic institutions in the West was that wherever the bourgeoisie was found, its representatives would support both economic reforms and political freedom. Accordingly, the Legal Marxists joined many Western reform socialists, including Eduard Bernstein, in contending that a gradual transition to socialism was preferable to fruitless upheaval.

For the time being, the prospects for Russian socialism were so poor that none of these voices prevailed. But their consensus that the revolutionary focus should be shifted decisively toward the working class resulted in one major development. On March 13–15, 1898, nine representatives of three social democratic groups—the Bund; a Ukrainian socialist newspaper, *Rabochee Delo*; and the radical League of Struggle for the Emancipation of the Working Class from St. Petersburg—met in secret in Minsk to found the RSDLP. The outcome of this meeting, the First Congress of the organization that would evolve into one of the dominant political parties of modern times—the Communist Party of the Soviet Union (CPSU)—was initially negligible. In a manifesto written by Struve, each of the participants at this tiny gathering found some cause to endorse. The problem for the attendees, as well as for other sympathetic socialists living in exile, was that the program offered no coherent plan of action on which they could all agree. Most of the congress's delegates were arrested by the tsarist police shortly after the meeting concluded. Still, several socialists who could not be present stepped in to prepare the new party for its next congress. One was the twenty-eight-year-old Lenin, who had been banished to Siberia for his involvement in one of many strikes in St. Petersburg at the end of the century.

LENIN ASCENDANT

Lenin's early association with the RSDLP gives his eventual command over the party an air of inevitability. In retrospect, it is tempting to imagine a straight line running from his authorship of *What Is to Be Done?* in 1901–1902 to the formation of the party's Bolshevik faction in 1903, the October Revolution in 1917, and from there to the militarization of the organization during the Russian Civil War (1918–1920). Yet this characterization, later transmogrified into the rigid doctrine of Marxism-Leninism, is totally misleading. Certain features of the party's structure would remain constant over these years due to Lenin's larger-than-life personality and his efforts to seal his control over the organization. Nonetheless, his conception of the party, like Marx's, should be viewed as an evolving project. It was subject to both the contending visions of other revolutionaries and his own ambivalence about the revolution's direction.

Like Plekhanov, Lenin was intent upon resolving the divisions within the social democratic movement. He was convinced that the RSDLP would only survive by closing its ranks to any involvement with the reformist currents, such as those embodied by the Economists, Legal Marxists, and other putatively revisionist streams. Furthermore, as the new century began, he and Plekhanov were not alone among the Social Democrats in facing an additional obstacle—the emergence of non-Marxist revolutionary parties. In particular, the many diverse sentiments that typified early populism were on the rise. In 1902, the formation of an explicitly populist party, the Socialist Revolutionaries (SRs), presented the RSDLP with a formidable rival. Unlike their predecessors, the SRs were well organized. They quickly attracted a large following with a simple formula. In opposition to the Marxists, they professed a willingness to lead both the peasantry and the working class directly into socialism.

In response to these pretensions, Lenin took the lead in founding a party journal to make the case for social democratic orthodoxy. It was no coincidence that the first issue of the publication *Iskra* appeared in 1901 in the same month as the Decembrist uprising seventy-six years earlier. Under the masthead "A spark will kindle a flame," *Iskra*'s editors offered a dynamic interpretation of Russia's prospects. Lenin adorned its front page with an editorial underscoring Plekhanov's views about the primacy of fundamental political change. He maintained that it was time to organize the proletariat and overthrow the autocracy. As they watched their readership grow, the journal's publishers initiated an aggressive campaign for a second RSDLP congress to address the outstanding issues involving the party's identity.

The fact that Lenin began writing *What Is to Be Done?* in anticipation of this meeting is a reason for both the historical importance of the document and the challenge of interpreting his message correctly. It is important because the congress provided him with his first chance to make a statement about how the work of the RSDLP should be understood by its members. At the same time, the pamphlet is challenging because Lenin's views were still developing. In contrast to the document's reputation, Lenin's goal was not to leave a blueprint for the organization. This would have been too much to expect when even the party's survival was uncertain. Furthermore, he recognized that too much was in flux to make definitive statements about what the party should do. Rather, we must read *What Is to Be Done?* as a contribution to the continuing debate, begun by radicals like Herzen, Tkachev, and Plekhanov, over how to promote revolutionary change when political power was exclusively reserved to an untouchable monarch and the vast majority of the population misidentified the sources of its discontent.

The title of Lenin's book is no accident. Like many young idealists of his generation, Lenin came from a well-off, educated family and was infatuated with the image of Chernyshevsky's "new people" who devoted themselves to communing with the masses. Thus, in considering his version of *What Is to Be Done?*, one must keep in mind that Lenin was appealing to a readership that was drawn to the idea of bringing truth—in this case, Marxism—to the unwashed people below them. This is a decisive moment, Lenin advises his reader in the tract, because Russia's Social Democrats are faced with the decision about the kind of party they will build. The correct decision, he declares, will allow the party to "overturn Russia." The wrong choice will lead it into despair.[9]

What is to be done to avoid the mistakes of Russia's early revolutionaries? Lenin provides us with two answers. One is about how the party's members should organize themselves, the other is about how they should act. Both of these answers must be interpreted with care. I opened this chapter with the all-too-familiar first response. To be successful, the RSDLP must be composed of individuals who commit themselves to full-time revolutionary activity. A conspiratorial party, Lenin underscores, must be "solid." It must be built around talented leaders who are, as he puts it, "schooled by long experience" and "working in perfect harmony." In short, they must be primed for battle.

From a comparative perspective, Lenin's emphases are significant. Despite their Marxist roots, the prominent Western European socialist parties had been reluctant to characterize their obligations in such elitist terms. Even the German SPD, which had been driven underground during the first years of its existence and insisted on its members' adherence to party discipline, was far more inclusive and democratic. Nonetheless, Lenin's depiction of the communists' role was not new to Russian radicalism, despite the reverence with which it was later regarded. Based upon the differences among the radical movements in the nineteenth century, all of the Russian Social Democrats agreed that some form of centralized leadership was essential to keep their cadres' attention focused on the tasks at hand. Much more than any of its Western counterparts, the party's survival was dependent upon secrecy.

Lenin's second response was about how the party should act. In a famous passage, which bears the distinctive imprint of Plekhanov's thinking, Lenin directly addresses the major ambiguity about the role of a Marxist party in fomenting revolution. "We have said," Lenin states, "that there could not have been Social-Democratic consciousness among the workers. It would have to be brought to them from without. The history of all countries shows that the working class, exclusively by its own effort, is able to develop only trade union consciousness, i.e., the conviction that it is necessary to combine in unions, fight the employers, and strive to compel the government to pass necessary labor legislation."[10] There is a problem, however, with focusing only on this section of *What Is to Be Done?* because Lenin makes other, equally provocative observations about the meaning of revolutionary activity. In turn, these remarks lead to additional ambiguities about his understanding of the party's function. Despite the book's title, Lenin actually concentrates on what is *not* to be done. On almost every page, he brings his ire to bear on a panoply of socialist groups, including the Economists, Legal Marxists, and Bernsteinian revisionists, whom he blames for engaging in a *"slavish cringing before spontaneity."*[11] The mistake of all of these groups, he asserts, is that they have convinced themselves that the workers will of their own volition rise up against their oppressors. As a consequence, while waiting for this spontaneous upsurge to occur, they seek only to improve the class's economic standing.

What makes Lenin's analysis potentially misleading is that he uses the word "spontaneous" in different ways. At times, the problem seems to be the workers' lack of spontaneity. This deficiency obliges the party's members to bring them consciousness from outside. Yet Lenin qualifies the point, noting that "there is spontaneity and spontaneity." In his view, the strikes of the 1890s in St. Petersburg and other cities indicate that the working class was capable of acting on its own. This is evidence, Lenin advises, of "consciousness in an *embryonic* form." To ensure their well-being, the workers wisely sought to extract concessions from their employers, including their right to form autonomous associations. These actions demonstrate, Lenin contends, that it is not the party's function to create consciousness out of nothingness. This stance would be inconsistent with Marxism's emphasis on the economic foundations of the class struggle. Instead, the party's role is to stir up what is already there, to enable the workers to see that there is an irreconcilable antagonism between their interests and those who exploit them. This idea, he stresses, is social democratic consciousness.[12]

Lest this point seem like a novel contribution, let us recall that in the *Communist Manifesto* Marx invoked the idea of proletarian consciousness in his cryptic admonition that the task of the communists is to "point out and bring to the front the common interests of the entire proletariat."[13] Marx assumed that a *party* of communists would recognize this responsibility and therefore act on it. In this respect, Lenin is simply reiterating a point that was already recognized by others. However, he introduces a qualification that is specific to his Russian context. Instead of merely affirming the elites' contributions, he questions their abilities. Whatever limitations the masses may have had in confronting their oppressors over the preceding half century, Lenin asserts, the radical intelligentsia's failings were much greater. The social democrats of his age, he continues, are still lacking in their *own* consciousness. All around them, people are expressing discontent—workers, students, and peasants. Only one group has lagged behind: the revolutionaries themselves. Why, Lenin asks? Because they have failed to establish "a constant and continuous organization capable of *leading* the whole movement."[14]

I have deliberately placed this part of Lenin's analysis in its historical context because it helps to distinguish his position from the fractures that would soon divide the Russian Social Democrats at their Second Congress in July–August 1903.[15] When the delegates assembled in Brussels and London, they were for the most part not divided over the arguments in *What Is to Be Done?*, including the primacy of the working class and the importance of party unity. To the contrary, *Iskra*'s editors used the pamphlet to frame the congress's agenda and assembled party-like *Iskra* committees in cities throughout Russia to propagate Lenin's views. After acrimonious and abstruse interfactional debates over a draft program, Lenin, Plekhanov, and their respective allies agreed on a document that affirmed the party's role in elevating the consciousness of the working class. More emphatically than Marx and Engels, they underscored the necessity of using force to counter the assaults of the capitalist class. When the few recognizable Economists at the congress complained that this type of organization would end up dominating the proletariat, they were derided by the other delegates. Similarly, the representatives from the Bund were swiftly outvoted when they insisted on preserving an autonomous status within the party.

The more serious division arose over a seemingly trivial exchange between Lenin and his partner in the St. Petersburg League, Julius Martov, over the definition of Article I of the party's draft constitution. Lenin argued that membership should be limited to those who were actively involved in one of the party's organizations (i.e., professional revolutionaries). Martov offered different language, suggesting that membership could be slightly expanded to include those who operated under the supervision of a party organ. This was a fine distinction indeed. But when it was combined with Lenin's desire to have the whole party behind him, the disagreement became insurmountable. As far as Lenin was concerned, anyone acting outside the party's organs was less than a full-time revolutionary and therefore could not be relied upon to submit to its dictates.

As a result, when the congress voted in favor of Martov's language, Lenin responded with indignation. In a flurry of Byzantine maneuvers, he temporarily increased his supporters' representation in the party's three governing bodies: the Party Council, the Central Committee, and *Iskra*. And he met with some luck. Thanks to the defection of the Bund delegates and the expulsion of the Economists, he had the votes to win this particular skirmish. Suddenly in the majority, he and his supporters adopted the name by which they would subsequently be known: "Bolsheviks" ("Majoritarians"). They dubbed their opponents "Mensheviks" ("Minoritarians") who, for inexplicable reasons, adopted this far less advantageous name as their own. Not one to miss an opportunity to rub salt in an adversary's wounds, Lenin blamed the entire split on his former allies. In a polemic entitled "One Step Forward, Two Steps Backward," he declared that the party had been divided all along into a revolutionary wing and an opportunist wing. Now it was time for the true supporters of social democracy to close ranks against the "self-satisfied exaltation of the retrograde-circle spirit" and the "tinsel and fuss of intellectualist anarchism."[16]

Lenin's new opponents, now joined by Plekhanov who was appalled by his collaborator's behavior, fought back. They accused Lenin of putting his own views ahead of the cause of party unity. They also criticized the assumptions of *What Is to Be Done?* Lenin's tactics, they contended, were a direct consequence of a narrow conception of party leadership. The dynamic, leftist revolutionary, Leon Trotsky, who was also attending the congress, castigated Lenin's tactics, sarcastically comparing him to the infamous despot of the French Revolution, Maximilien Robespierre. The danger in "Comrade Lenin's" thinking, he declared, was that he confused organizational questions with immediate political tasks and thereby put the party's wishes ahead of the historical mission of the proletariat. In this way, Trotsky contended in an oft-cited observation, Lenin's party organization would "substitute" itself for the party; the Central Committee would substitute itself for the party organization; and finally, the dictator—Trotsky presumably meant Lenin—would substitute himself for the Central Committee.[17]

No doubt, Lenin's critics were motivated as much as he was by personal ambition. Despite their attacks, they had agreed to participate in the congress, knowing that it would be organized largely according to Lenin's principles. It would have been hard to imagine anyone, and certainly not the equally opportunistic Trotsky, who would have been uninterested in asserting his will over the meeting. Yet this confrontation was a turning point. Although it did not resolve every ambiguity, it created a more conspicuous line of demarcation between opposing conceptions of the party.

THE REVOLUTIONARY IDEA IN PRACTICE

Looking back at the period between the Second Congress and the outbreak of World War I, one is struck by the extent to which Lenin balanced his desire for control against his recognition of the need for flexibility. At first glance, it might seem as though a person who had advocated a centralized version of party organization would have been unabashedly dogmatic. However, in a context in which loyalties to one faction over another were constantly shifting, Lenin cultivated the profile of a sage figure who could see the big picture from on high. In his view, the revolutionary party required both strong leadership and the agility to grasp the historical moment.

Lenin's emphasis on the first factor was manifested in full form through his organizational maneuvering in April 1905. Disregarding the party's statutes, he took the liberty of convening a Bolshevik-dominated Third Congress of the RSDLP in London. At the beginning of the meeting, he was constrained by the determination of a majority of the delegates to maintain a semblance of party cohesion. Nonetheless, his management of the congress's proceedings was a tour de force. In thrall to their leader, the participants obligingly voted to replace Martov's definition of party membership in their statutes with Lenin's more restrictive version. They also agreed to abolish the Party Council and to elect a Central Committee.

At the same time, Lenin's conception of the party's agenda was born out of a creative interpretation of the first revolutionary upheaval of twentieth-century Europe. In 1905, the tsarist autocracy was suffering from a massive loss of credibility as a result of its defeats in a war with Japan. With the government's resources drained and segments of its armed forces dispersed in the Far East, its opponents were emboldened to risk organizing demonstrations against the regime. The cities were engulfed by strikes, and peasants engaged in bloody confrontations with landlords. After a dramatic mutiny of sailors in the Black Sea fleet in June, Tsar Nicolas II chose the course of conciliation. He promised guarantees on civil liberty and agreed to form a quasi-representative parliament in which legislative power would be shared between a purportedly democratically elected lower house, or State Duma, and an upper house dominated by the nobility. Nonetheless, amid the crumbling social order, he could not prevent further protest. In St. Petersburg, demonstrations precipitated the emergence of self-governing strike committees, or "soviets," which claimed to speak directly for the workers. These bodies quickly spread to Moscow and other cities.

These developments could have been a serious setback for Lenin. Like most Social Democrats, his commitment to Marxism's progressive conception of history did not allow him, at least not at this point, to argue that working-class unrest in Russia could supersede Marx and Engels's assumptions about the shift of the international class struggle from West to East. Like many Bolsheviks, he also distrusted the spontaneous character of this unrest. Initially, he and his associates viewed the St. Petersburg Soviet, in which Trotsky had conspicuously inserted himself as a participant, with the ambivalent feelings of a neglected parent. By the time the Bolsheviks finally endorsed the committees, specifically urging the leaders of the Moscow Soviet to call for a general strike, the government had reasserted its authority, crushing the labor councils across Russia and splitting the revolutionary movement by promising political reforms.

As a result, the Social Democrats once again broke ranks over how to interpret these events. To many socialists, the Mensheviks' response seemed the most sensible. Plekhanov, Martov, and Axelrod retreated to Marxist orthodoxy. The year's upheavals, they contended, were the growth pains of a movement that would be long in gestation. Initially, the proletariat would have to put up with an extended period of bourgeois rule. During these years, the Social Democrats' primary responsibility was to work with the bourgeoisie to mitigate the extreme expressions of tsarist rule.

Lenin agreed that the party would have to adapt to these less than desirable conditions. But in a step that would redound to his advantage twelve years later, he stressed that his quarrel with the Menshevik leaders was not so much over the need to wait for the proletariat to mature as the meaning of the word "proletariat." Even in his earliest writings, Lenin had fudged on the term. For him, the concept of the working class was a big tent. It included not only industrial workers but anyone who worked with his or her hands, including segments of the peasantry. In a country where most of the population lived on the land, this approach made sense. Moreover, in 1905, the countryside was filled with revolutionary fervor. Immediately after the Third Congress, Lenin capitalized on this circumstance by arguing that these signs of class consciousness would eventually lead to the establishment of a "revolutionary-democratic dictatorship of the proletariat and the peasantry." This union would be a *democratic* dictatorship, he explained, in an indication that he did not foresee a quick transition to socialism, because it would have the support of a bourgeois class that had finally been forced to listen to the will of the people. This combination of forces was the best way to ensure the decisive victory over tsarism.[18]

In making this point, I do not mean to suggest that Lenin's Bolsheviks or, for that matter, the Mensheviks, perceived themselves to be natural allies of the peasantry. This was the ideological territory of the Socialist Revolutionaries. Moreover, the Social Democrats' long-standing distrust of the traditions of the peasantry was unabated. They viewed the peasants' demands for land as secondary to the construction of a workers' state. Rather, I mean to call attention to the extent to which the Marxist image of a struggle between the powerful minority and the impoverished majority could be translated to class relations in Russia.

In April 1906, the land issue provided the occasion for an arcane but revealing debate between the two social democratic factions. At the RSDLP's Fourth Congress, the Mensheviks' victory seemed likely since they had a slight majority of delegates. Their preferred solution was to take the land away from its owners and give it to local governments who would decide how it would be utilized. Lenin's solution was simpler and precedent-setting, as would become apparent during the October Revolution eleven years later. The land would be nationalized under a revolutionary government that would, in turn, delegate its administration to peasant committees. Of the two, the Mensheviks' position would have been less confrontational, but Lenin's approach appealed to many peasants because he was offering the shorter path to getting what they wanted.

On other questions, however, Lenin showed that he was willing to alienate the left-wing members of his faction when it served his understanding of the party's interests. In April 1906, after Nicholas II followed through on his promise to create a limited legislative assembly, the formation of the Duma put the entire RSDLP in an uncomfortable position. Up to this point, the Social Democrats had consistently opposed participation in bourgeois elections, arguing that their involvement would help to legitimize the autocracy and strengthen the hands of the oppressors of the proletariat. In contrast, the tsar's decision to move forward was less of a problem for the Mensheviks. Their acceptance of a conventional Marxist conception of history allowed them to rationalize political engagement during a long period of bourgeois rule. In their view, parliamentary participation was necessary to ensure that proletarian interests were defended. In fact, many Mensheviks concluded that participation was essential given the emergence of rival parties on the Right that would seek to confuse the working masses to garner their support. In October 1905, middle-class critics of the autocracy had come together to form a party of their own, the Constitutional Democrats, or Kadets. One of their prime targets was the recruitment of working-class voters. One year later, a breakaway faction from the Socialist Revolutionaries, the Trudoviks, came into being with the goal of representing both workers and peasants.

Compared with the Mensheviks, the Bolsheviks' position was much more complicated. In the competition for control of the RSDLP, they had consistently portrayed their Menshevik rivals as undisciplined and ready to compromise with the bourgeoisie on fundamental questions. This hyperbole had its purposes. For many members, especially those risking their lives in underground agitation, their faction's appeal lay precisely in its rejection of compromise. Accordingly, when the Mensheviks voted at the RSDLP's Fourth Congress to take part in the Duma elections, the Bolsheviks called for a boycott. But not Lenin. Only a few days after siding with his associates, he shifted to the Menshevik position, contending that the RSDLP's presence in the assembly would provide its deputies with an opportunity to expose the body as a sham. Predictably, many Bolsheviks were shaken by their leader's about-face from the faction's established position.

Lenin's critics need not have worried. In the vote on April 27, 1906, only Menshevik candidates were elected to the State Duma, and Nicholas II dissolved the assembly ten weeks after its opening. Less than one year later, when the tsar again decided to permit elections to a new Duma, Lenin swung back to a position that was in tune with his faction's uncompromising attitudes. At the RSDLP's Fifth Congress in May 1907, he condemned the Mensheviks for supposedly using the Second Duma to cozy up to the moderate parties. If there were to be any collaboration with non-Marxist parties, Lenin stressed, this could take place only with honest representatives of the people. Among these ranks, he included the SRs and the Trudoviks. For the time being, the tsarist government did the Social Democrats the favor of postponing a new row between the factions by dissolving the Duma again and imposing greater limitations on future assemblies.

From this point forward, there was little chance of patching up the divisions among the Social Democrats on the issue of intraparty cooperation. Nevertheless, the gyrations in Lenin's position understandably raised questions about his priorities. Would it be better for the Bolsheviks to seek a minimal accommodation with the Mensheviks in the hope of acquiring broader influence over the social democratic movement? Or should one bide one's time while awaiting the coming unrest by refusing to compromise the faction's radical identity? As I shall show in later chapters, variations on the functions of a revolutionary party would be raised repeatedly during the era of global communism.

In this case, Lenin turned against the left-wing Social Democrats first. Misrepresenting his critics' actions, he accused them of committing multiple offenses and falsifying Marxist theory. By 1909, he had successfully rid the faction of most of his adversaries. On the right, the Mensheviks proved to be an easier target. We can appreciate the depths to which the two factions' relations had fallen by the fact that both sides had lost interest in the debates that originally divided them. Their primary battles in the remaining years before World War I were over the oldest issues of politics: money and power. Unquestionably, the Bolsheviks showed the greater zeal. With Lenin's tacit approval, Bolshevik gangs staged "expropriations," robbing banks, post offices, and trains to compensate for their lack of dues-paying members. Through intimidation, blackmail, and deceit, their agents diverted funds to their coffers that would otherwise have gone to the RSDLP as a whole.

In January 1912, the Bolsheviks took the steps that sealed the division of the RSDLP. In a sparsely attended conference in Prague, from which they excluded nearly everyone to the right of their faction, Lenin and his supporters effectively formed their own party. They elected a new Central Committee, established a central bureau to coordinate underground work in Russia, and declared their refusal to deal with any social democratic representatives in the State Duma who had not been approved by their executive. Hoping that these measures could be rolled back, Menshevik leaders, including Plekhanov, appealed for the intervention of the socialist Second International. In a meeting in Brussels on July 16–17, 1914, at which the two factions were present, the International's governing body pressed the Bolsheviks to take part in yet another congress on the subject of party unification. Lenin and the Bolsheviks refused to oblige.

A week and a half later, the outbreak of the Great War raised the prospect that cooperation between the factions could be revived in the face of a shared danger. On this occasion, the Bolsheviks and the Mensheviks jointly affirmed the primacy of the international proletarian struggle. Unlike their socialist brethren in the West who responded affirmatively to the call for national defense, this was at least Marxist consistency. But of course, the terms of their agreement were open to interpretation. How one intended to speak for the interests of the proletariat was a different matter entirely.

HARDENING THE LINES

Russia's engagement in World War I was a godsend for both of the social democratic factions. Indeed, given their relatively small numbers and marginal political status, it is conceivable that they, and especially the Bolsheviks, would have withered into obscurity had this European calamity not occurred. Instead, Nicholas II and his advisers created the desperate conditions that provided untold numbers of Russians, imperial minorities, and marginal groups with an incentive to consider their revolutionary options. Over the three years of Russia's involvement in the conflict, the empire suffered millions of casualties. More than 2 million soldiers died on the battlefield, and over 1.5 million civilians were killed as a result of the fighting and related causes. The empire lost substantial portions of its wealthiest and most populous western territories, including Poland. Vast numbers of people were permanently displaced by the fighting and fled eastward in search of new homes and employment. Those who remained behind suffered under staggering inflation and the collapse of internal markets.

Initially, these circumstances had a salutary effect on relations among the Social Democrats who were able to escape the tsarist police or were living in exile in the West. Unlike the Kadets and other moderate parties who supported the war effort, many of the Bolsheviks and Mensheviks were like the Western and Central European socialists of the 1840s. They had lived abroad for years and were generally unburdened by direct association with the politicians in the Russian capital. Under the flag of Swiss neutrality, their leaders did what their peers were less capable of doing on their home soil. They congregated in meeting halls in Geneva, Bern, and Zurich to echo their opposition to the war and engage in complex theoretical debates about strategy. This was an imperialist conflict, they maintained, that was wholly at odds with the interests of the toiling masses of all countries. If one wanted to serve Russia's real interests, they told anyone who would listen, one only had to subscribe to the international message of Marxism.

But what were Russia's real interests and how should one pursue them? On these questions and in no small part due to Lenin's influence, the divisions between the Bolsheviks and Mensheviks became sharper. Of the two, the Mensheviks appeared best positioned to garner support for their views about ending the conflict. They were in the majority in the émigré community and, like many European socialists who had slowly come to see their mistake in supporting the war, they espoused a negotiated peace. It would do the working class no good, Plekhanov and others stressed, if it were to inherit a country that was carved up and humiliated by its enemies. A settlement that allowed Russia to regain its lost territories and diverted Germany's attention to the western front would provide for peace with honor. More importantly, it would be certain to accelerate the end to tsarist rule. The advantage of this position was that the Mensheviks did not have to ask their supporters to make the unpleasant choice between the party's revolutionary goals and fidelity to their homeland. They could have both.

For Lenin, in contrast, this position was apostasy. Once again, he shocked even his closest associates, proclaiming that it would be better for Russia to lose the war than for its representatives to soil themselves by making deals with the imperialists. Compromise was unacceptable.

The only defensible strategy, Lenin insisted at an antiwar conference in Zimmerwald, Switzerland, in 1915, was for the party to forego the focus on a just peace and confront the imperial regime head-on.

Lenin was slow to win converts to this stand. For our purposes, however, his first achievement was in defining the Bolsheviks' views on the functions of a communist party. He moved them into the position to claim possession of the strand within Marxism that emphasized the primacy of revolution over tactical collaboration with the bourgeoisie. In 1916, he published a slim volume, *Imperialism: The Highest Stage of Capitalism*, which made the emphatic case that only the Bolsheviks were on the right side of history. Lenin's premise in *Imperialism* was that the evolution of capitalism presented Russia's socialists with both a historical opportunity and a special responsibility. The inherent contradictions in capitalism's productive forces had led to the formation of powerful industrial and financial monopolies that were increasingly in search of overseas markets. Far from alleviating these contradictions, Lenin insisted, the pursuit of profit in the precapitalist world was fostering even more extreme forms of exploitation. Under these circumstances, radical parties such as his own were in a position to hasten the revolt against capitalism. Even in Russia, which had not yet undergone the full transition to capitalism, Lenin concluded, imperialism's victims could be induced to rise up against their oppressors.

Lenin's corollary to this argument, which he directed against various socialists, especially the Marxist theorist Karl Kautsky, was that the Social Democrats had simultaneously acquired an obligation. The bourgeoisie, he maintained, had prevented a revolution in the West by using its riches to pacify the working class. Now that the struggle for profits had entered an acute phase in the war, the leaders of industry in countries like Germany and Britain could no longer afford this strategy. As a result, their relations with their own laboring classes were increasingly susceptible to disturbances in any part of the world. For this reason, Lenin argued, Russian socialists were obliged to make capitalism's plight worse. Correspondingly, he accused those socialists who sought to ease these burdens, and especially those who would agree to a sordid peace with the imperialist powers, of violating this historical responsibility.[19]

Neither Lenin nor his many critics could have foreseen the advent of the tumultuous events that would press them into deciding whether the split within their party would become permanent. In January 1917, Lenin confessed to a socialist youth group in Zurich that "we old timers," as he put it, would not live to see the decisive battles of the revolution.[20] Only a month later, in late February, massive street demonstrations and the outbreak of a general strike led to the complete collapse of authority in Petrograd (St. Petersburg's official name during the war) and the reappearance of the rudimentary form of grassroots governance, the revolutionary soviet, which had last been seen in 1905. One week later, on March 2, the State Duma formed a Provisional Government and Nicholas II abdicated. The leaders of the new government announced that they would take the tsar's place until free, democratic elections could be held for a Constituent Assembly that would form a government and draft a constitution.

As embroiled in these developments as any other political group, the Social Democrats found themselves in a situation where their divisions over the war merged with the question of with whom they wished to ally themselves. Suddenly, Petrograd had two governments, one the Provisional Government and the other the Soviet of Workers' and Soldiers' Deputies, as the local organ became known. The Mensheviks tried to have it both ways. On the one hand, they linked arms with an array of political groups and parties—Kadets, liberals, monarchists, Trudoviks, and SRs—in supporting the Provisional Government. This was not a bad gamble. The new government presented itself as both a Western-style democratic regime and a defender of the crowds of Petrograd. It guaranteed basic rights and abolished class and hereditary distinctions while simultaneously declaring a blanket amnesty for political prisoners, replacing regular police organs with local militias, and assuring soldiers who had participated in the uprising that they would not be sent back to the front. On the other hand, the Mensheviks joined the SRs in seeking to take advantage of the chaotic conditions in the Petrograd Soviet. The faction's left wing had already been active within workers' groups in the city and, hence, they comfortably joined the SRs in forming an executive committee to represent the Soviet in negotiations with the Provisional Government.

Lenin's response was predictably defiant. Declaring that the Mensheviks could not legitimately avoid choosing between the two organs of government, he upped the ante in the interfactional battle over who was entitled to represent the working class. In back-to-back addresses, later known as the "April Theses," he stupefied his listeners, Mensheviks and Bolsheviks alike, with the intensity of his convictions. One could have anticipated his first thesis. He condemned all plans to end the war that were not based upon a complete break with capitalism and the proletariat's acquisition of political power. Lenin's second thesis represented a profound departure from the conventional wisdom about the applicability of Marxism to Russia. He flatly rejected the proposition, which he had previously expressed on multiple occasions, that Russia would enter a period of extended bourgeois domination. In his characterization, the existence of two types of government standing side by side indicated that the first phase of the revolution was already passing. The Provisional Government, Lenin noted sarcastically, had transformed Russia into "the freest of all of the belligerent countries in the world" by taking advantage of the masses' naïve trust in its intentions. Henceforth, it would be necessary—after only one month of supposedly bourgeois rule!—to reject all cooperation with this regime and, Lenin added, with its petit-bourgeois supporters among the Mensheviks and the SRs. The only acceptable step at this stage was for the Bolsheviks to throw their full support to the only truly revolutionary government, the Soviet of Workers' and Soldiers' Deputies.

We can easily appreciate the confusion and skepticism with which many of Lenin's supporters received this message, not least because he had been abroad and presumably could not fully understand the conditions they were facing. Suddenly, Lenin was telling them that Russia's long-anticipated bourgeois revolution was already coming to a close. All of the predictable doubts arose. Had there been enough time for a robust form of capitalism to develop in the cities? Had the transformation of the agrarian economy even begun? Predictably, Lenin intended to show that he was one step beyond these familiar debates. In his eyes, the question was no longer how the proletariat could be led to rise up. Rather, it was how the party should prepare the proletariat for taking power.

This is a key point in the development of Lenin's thinking. For the first time since the publication of *What Is to Be Done?* in 1902, we find him returning to a more concrete conception of revolutionary leadership. Many of Lenin's remarks in the "April Theses" are reminiscent of the didactic tenor of that document. Some workers will be slow to embrace socialism fully, he advises in his declaration, because they have been misled. They may suffer from an "unreasoning trust" in the capitalist government's claims about the war. For this reason, Lenin contends, the party's representatives must explain their error to them and, he adds, do so "with particular thoroughness, persistence, and patience." Similarly, because the masses have little experience with politics, they cannot be expected to recognize that the Mensheviks and other socialist members of the Soviet are actually willing collaborators with the Provisional Government. Again, the Bolsheviks' duty is to help the workers understand the betrayal of these purportedly socialist parties.[21]

In an equally significant move, Lenin takes his demands one step further by broaching the issue of nomenclature. In the ninth of the ten "April Theses," he informs his supporters that the RSDLP's name must be changed. Three days later, when the two addresses appeared in the party newspaper *Pravda*, those readers who had not already intuited Lenin's aspirations could learn something interesting from a footnote to the article. This organ would be called the "Communist Party." What could be more sensible, Lenin inquired rhetorically, than to adopt this title when social democratic politicians "*throughout* the world have betrayed socialism and deserted to the bourgeoisie"?[22]

Lenin's appropriation of the *Communist Manifesto*'s title marks a striking break in his relations with the Mensheviks. To get a full picture of his intentions, however, it is crucial to recognize that he seems to have been primarily concerned about the behavior of his own branch of the RSDLP. On the day of Lenin's return to Petrograd, the Bolshevik leadership had concluded a party conference at which it adopted a platform that was almost completely at odds with his demands. Two senior Bolsheviks, Joseph Vissarionovich Dzhugashvili ("Stalin") and Lev Kamenev successfully persuaded their colleagues to support a variety of moderate policies, including a more flexible position on the war, cooperation with the Provisional Government, and acceptance of the possibility of unification with the Mensheviks. Making this situation more noteworthy still, it was not at all clear that Lenin could overcome these views. The editorial board of *Pravda* promptly disavowed his arguments, and thirteen of the fifteen members of the party committee in Petrograd voted to reject his theses. Kamenev took the lead in denouncing "Comrade Lenin" for what he insisted was a demand for an immediate socialist revolution. In addition, he accused Lenin of seeking to form a *new* party. Such an organ, he declared, would transform the RSDLP into "a group of communist propagandists."[23]

Kamenev was stretching the truth. Lenin's references to the party's tutelary role show that he believed the masses were not ready for the leap into socialism. Furthermore, he was not advocating the formation of a new party, only a name change. But, as in politics everywhere, nomenclature matters. In returning to Marx and Engels's conception of a single communist movement, Lenin was seeking to persuade his audience that the entire party could be unified if only its members would accept his unifying vision. In a draft platform for the RSDLP's upcoming party conference, Lenin explained that his proposed name change was simply a chance to reaffirm the principles of the *Communist Manifesto*. The words "social democratic," he noted, had not only been used to fool the people and lead them in the wrong direction. They were also unscientific. True communists aspired to achieve much more than the social ownership of the means of production. "Our party looks further ahead," he emphasized. "Socialism must inevitably evolve gradually into communism." For similar reasons, he insisted that the words "social democracy" conveyed the wrong idea about the character of the revolutionary state. True Marxists understood that their goal was not a parliamentary republic. Their goal was to create "a state like the Paris Commune of 1871 and the Soviets of Workers' Deputies of 1905 and 1917."[24]

Thanks to his prestige within the faction and his political skills, Lenin converted many of his critics, Stalin among them, into allies. By the conclusion of the RSDLP conference at the end of April, a majority of the meeting's delegates voted in favor of nearly every resolution that he introduced. They agreed to a prohibition on participation in the Provisional Government, the nationalization of bourgeois landholdings, and the necessity of establishing Bolshevik control of Russia's soviets. Lenin was unable to secure the body's support for a motion to withdraw from the Second International, though this step too would be taken in due time.

Lenin's success in moving the Social Democrats in a more militant direction helped to spur an unprecedented period of growth for the Bolsheviks. Before the February Revolution of 1917, the faction had no more than 23,000 members, and these were scattered around Russia and abroad. By the end of April, this number had risen threefold to nearly 80,000, and by August, it approached 200,000. Initially, the Bolsheviks' representation in the soviets was smaller than that of the Mensheviks or the SRs. What they lacked in quantity, they made up for in an active presence in the central cities of Petrograd and Moscow and among sailors in the Baltic fleet. In these locations, they were much better organized than the larger parties, and because they were in the opposition on most issues, they were not as divided as their rivals. The more unbearable the war became for the Russian population, the more the Bolsheviks' clout in the soviets grew.

The State in the Revolution

Given the spirit of the "April Theses" and Lenin's proposal to rename the party, one might think that he would have been eager to clarify what he meant by "communist party" as his Bolsheviks took increasingly aggressive steps to confront the Provisional Government. In fact, he had the opportunity to do so in his greatest theoretical work, *State and Revolution*, which he completed in September 1917. Writing in Finland, where he had fled after an abortive revolt by soldiers and workers led the Provisional Government to institute repressive measures against its opponents, Lenin looked down the post-revolutionary road and asked himself what one could learn from Marxism about coming to power and "leading the whole people to socialism."[25] Yet, in a sign that he still regarded the communist party as a group of like-minded comrades, and not as a clearly definable organization, he made only a few passing references to the subject. Instead, he reserved the primary responsibility for building socialism to the state.

The crux of Lenin's argument in *State and Revolution* is that the overthrow of the bourgeoisie is not a sufficient condition for rising above capitalist exploitation. It is only the beginning of a process by which one form of state power, a capitalist dictatorship, is exchanged for another, a "dictatorship of the proletariat." The abolition of the bourgeois state, Lenin explains, does not mean that its former defenders will simply go away. They will fight to protect their class position. Hence, this transition will inevitably take the form of "a period of an unprecedentedly violent class struggle in unprecedentedly acute forms."[26]

Predictably, Lenin uses this point to make a sweeping indictment of every moderate form of Marxism. One of the greatest delusions of these "sham socialists," Lenin contends, is their conviction that they can simply replace the class struggle with the dream of class harmony. This attitude merely extends the political life of the bourgeoisie. The only way to ensure the transition to a higher stage of socialism is to "crush" and "smash" all manifestations of bourgeois power. This, Lenin suggests, was the hard lesson the proletariat had to learn during the Paris Commune. How else can exploitation be overcome if the class that is the source of all social contradictions is not destroyed?[27]

For the prospective members of a communist party, there is much that is advantageous in assigning these violent functions to the state. As long as the state sullies itself with the nasty business of exercising power, the party can take the higher road of discerning the course of history and inspiring society to follow its vision. In this case, as *one* of those communists, Lenin offers his readers wonderful news. After defending the necessary actions of the proletarian state, he paints a picture of life after the attainment of socialism that is richer and more detailed than any description of this phase of development in Marx and Engels's works. The creation of a workers' democracy in the place of these vestiges of bourgeois rule, Lenin maintains, will enable the majority to govern itself directly. As the state's functions shift away from fighting the capitalist class, officials will gradually turn their attention to serving the needs of society. This transition, he notes, would have occurred in the Paris Commune if only it had survived. In fact, Lenin lightheartedly compares this new system of governance to the presumably efficient, nonexploitive operations of the postal service. "We shall have a splendidly equipped mechanism," he writes, "freed from the 'parasite,' a mechanism which can very well be set going by the united workers themselves, who will hire technicians, foremen, and accountants, and pay them *all*, as indeed *all* 'state' officials in general, workmen's wages."[28]

On this basis, Lenin offers his supporters the ultimate payoff. The unifying objective of all communists, he argues, is to create the conditions under which state power of any kind will no longer be necessary. Logically, when the exploitation of one class by another no longer takes place, the state will wither away. Under "complete communism," as Lenin calls it, even democracy will no longer be necessary. The long-standing justification for the domination of one human being over another will vanish and, with it, all of the current conventions of political activity.

How will this postpolitical era be feasible? Here, Lenin provides a cryptic but provocative response: "habit." With the final victory over the last vestiges of capitalism and bourgeois institutions, he suggests, people will acquire the habit of acting in ways that serve the common good. Lenin admits that there will still be abuses. "We are not utopians," he states. But, he adds, undoubtedly seeking to win over skeptics, these errors will be confined to the mistakes of single persons and not social classes. Even this eventuality is not a cause for worry. Civilized people will step in to resolve these problems, just as they would intervene "to put a stop to a scuffle or to prevent a woman from being insulted."[29]

The withering of the state, the end to political domination, the conclusion of the class struggle—how could the downtrodden worker living in this turbulent time not find something appealing in these ideas? However, Lenin's reticence about the communist party's functions is likely to leave the close reader of *State and Revolution* with uncertainty. Presumably, there will be communists, like himself, in this higher form of society, although Lenin is not clear about this issue. More importantly, will the party wither away just like the state? Because Lenin does not regard the party as a conventional organization but only an expression of the will of the working class, one is left to wonder whether even this unique association will be necessary when habit takes the place of revolution.

THE BOLSHEVIK OPPORTUNITY

As I shall show in chapter 8, the Soviet Union's future leaders would come close to answering this question only once—under the populist leadership of Nikita Khrushchev. Nevertheless, they would leave no doubt about their conviction that a fully formed Bolshevik party was present to witness the revolutionary events of October 1917 and to prod the proletariat forward along its predestined path. Up to the breakup of the USSR in 1991, every Soviet schoolchild could recite the fable of the events that transpired just less than two months after Lenin offered his theoretical glimpse into the future. On October 25, 1917, sailors on the cruiser *Aurora* fired the opening salvos that called the soldiers of the Petrograd garrison to overthrow the Provisional Government. Arm in arm with militant factory workers, they marched on the ruling seat at the Winter Palace, the tsar's occasional residence. There, they engaged in pitched battles until the building's last defenders had fallen. Emboldened by their success, the Petrograd Soviet proclaimed a new government. Over the ensuing days, weeks, and months, the Russian empire's cities, towns, and villages were set afire with revolts. Soon all power came to rest firmly in the hands of the people. Crucially, none of these achievements would have been possible without Lenin's resolute direction and the backing of a disciplined core of Bolshevik cadres.

All founding myths are based upon exaggerations, half-truths, and fabrications. In their use of these devices, the official chroniclers of the October Revolution have had few masters. The heroic depiction of the Bolsheviks' actions endowed their successor, the CPSU, with an aura of legitimacy that would last for decades. The reality was much different—the *Aurora* fired only one shell, and it was a blank. Few of the garrison's soldiers took part in the day's fighting, and many were noncommittal. The fighting at the Winter Palace was sporadic at best, and there was little bloodshed. When a detachment of Bolshevik Red Guards finally broke into the building, they found that its protectors had fled, leaving behind a huddle of frightened servants to fend for themselves. As a French commentator observed, "the government was overthrown before it could say 'ouch.'"[30] Many of Petrograd's 2.3 million residents had already fled the city. Of those who remained behind, few were even aware of what had happened.

Under these conditions, the Bolsheviks became the beneficiaries of circumstances they could never have created and were unsure how to handle. Due to the continuing losses from the war, the collapse of the economy, and the radicalization of the soviets, the Provisional Government was in free fall when Lenin was hiding in Finland. Continuing defeats at the hands of German troops and mass desertions crippled the army, the soviets' power and their leaders' will to defy the government were escalating, and the countryside was pockmarked with peasant revolts. Adding to the disorder, Russia's new leaders displayed an uncanny talent for bringing misfortune upon themselves. The mass demonstrations in July led to the collapse of one governing coalition and the creation of an ill-fated government under the moderate Socialist Revolutionary Alexander Kerensky. In the belief that he was personally called to save Russia, the new prime minister alienated key actors across the political spectrum.

If we put ourselves into the shoes of the onlooking Bolsheviks, we can imagine their sense of raw anticipation at these events. For years, they had struggled to be heard. Suddenly, the mistakes and misfortunes of their adversaries raised the prospect that they could maneuver their way into power. Much less evident, however, was how and when they should make their move. Lenin demanded that they take immediate action. In mid-September, while still in hiding, he urged the handful of people who constituted the Bolshevik leadership to use the political confusion to foment an armed insurrection in Petrograd and Moscow. However, despite their mutual excitement, his fellow revolutionaries did not share his sense of urgency and, at Stalin's suggestion, called for more discussion. Only after his return to Petrograd in early October was Lenin able to defend his case. Because the Provisional Government had set the date for the elections to the Constituent Assembly for mid-November, he insisted that the revolutionary moment would be lost if the Bolsheviks failed to act immediately. Kamenev and Grigory

Zinoviev, a close associate of Lenin in Zurich, opposed him, arguing that the Bolsheviks had become sufficiently popular to influence the Assembly. Yet the tipping point for those who wanted to support Lenin in principle was provided by his longtime antagonist, Trotsky, who had recently joined the Bolsheviks. In his position as chairman of the Petrograd Soviet and its military arm, the Military Revolutionary Committee, he affirmed that a successful uprising was possible.

I am highlighting the contingent nature of these events because they provide insight into two distinct issues: how the Bolsheviks thought they could act when they found political power suddenly dropped into their laps, and how they reacted when they discovered that the October Revolution was not yet theirs to control. On the one hand, Lenin was quick to issue decrees. The most prominent, the Decree on Peace, expressed his government's intent to enter into peace negotiations without preconditions with the belligerent European states. The Decree on Land ordered the confiscation without compensation of the properties of large landowners, the state, and the churches and their transfer to village communities for their distribution to the peasantry. Then, in early December, Lenin invited the Congress of Soviets to form a Council of People's Commissars, or Sovnarkom, to administer the different branches of government (e.g., Interior, Foreign Affairs, Nationalities, etc.). It was no accident that these new organs were not called ministries. Unlike the latter, which were readily associated with bourgeois rule, the commissariats were meant to be direct extensions of the revolutionary spirit of the proletariat and its representatives in the soviets. More importantly, they allowed the Bolsheviks to establish control over these autonomous bodies and their grassroots followers.

On the other hand, Lenin and the Bolsheviks encountered violent resistance at every turn. Representatives of the old regime, constitutional democrats, officials, trade unions, and other revolutionary parties rejected their authority. Within seven months, these tensions and countrywide opposition to the Bolsheviks' policies spiraled into a bloody civil war that lasted until fall 1920 in European Russia. Compounding their difficulties, Lenin and his associates found that the support they expected from the masses of workers and peasants was either slow in coming or, in the case of the latter, easily transformed into hostility.

It is crucial to appreciate this disjunction between the Bolsheviks' hopes and their determination to hold on to power because it was, and would remain, a formative experience. For everyone involved, it confirmed that force and violence would become integral parts of the new regime's identity. Ironically, at a historical juncture that later generations of communists would regard as the October Revolution's finest hour, the Bolsheviks were fighting for their survival. Yet this was also an opportunity for grand mythology. In Lenin's depiction, this battle was not an indication of weakness. To the contrary, it justified everything he had argued about the necessity of dictatorship in *State and Revolution*. The state would not disappear simply because the proletariat had come to power. It would be needed for as long as elements of the former exploiting class were still around.

Accordingly, in January 1918, Lenin informed the delegates of the Congress of Soviets that their battle was only beginning. They should not expect socialism to be delivered on a silver platter. Not a single issue pertaining to the class struggle, he stressed, could be settled without a confrontation with the representatives of the old order.[31] Lenin was equally intent on cementing the government's grip on the population as a whole. After the coup, he systematically weeded out manifestations of dissent. He ordered the expulsion of Menshevik and Socialist Revolutionary officials who were still to be found on the membership lists of the local soviets. He also showed no compunction in drawing upon the coercive resources of the government's new security organ, the Cheka, to drive his adversaries into submission. These measures were merely a preface to the body's ascent into an omnipresent instrument of persecution and state terror during the civil war.

Given Russia's worsening conditions, it is difficult to separate the Bolsheviks' revolutionary motivations from their efforts to establish order. In spring 1918, spreading food shortages in the cities and industrial areas forced the new regime to face up to the long-standing contradictions in its message to the peasantry. After a few months of conciliatory signals, the Sovnarkom sent Red Army detachments to the villages to requisition purported grain surpluses. It justified its use of force not merely in terms of economic necessity but as an instance of class warfare against putatively bourgeois-capitalist, upper-class peasants, or kulaks. These measures devastated the economy. One decade later, as we shall see in chapter 5, Joseph Stalin would repeat this campaign in dramatic and unspeakably tragic proportions. For the time being, the assault on the countryside marked the first stage of a period of "War Communism," when the government extended its reach into every sector of the economy.

At this juncture, not surprisingly given the circumstances, we find Lenin making his most explicit demands for the use of state violence. In a secret telegram in August 1918, he ordered officials to destroy the kulaks. All of their grain should be confiscated, Lenin declared, and the wealthiest among them should be hanged without hesitation. These measures should be carried out in such a fashion, he emphasized, that for hundreds of kilometers around, people would "see, tremble, know and shout: they are strangling and will strangle to death the bloodsucker *kulaks*."[32]

The "Comradely Family"

At this point, it is essential to appreciate the difference between how the Bolsheviks understood the exercise of state power and how they viewed their party. The function of the Sovnarkom was straightforward. In line with *State and Revolution*, it was a tool for exercising dictatorship. In contrast, the identity of the party was much more fluid during these years. Just as they had done before the October Revolution, Lenin and his colleagues continued to view the party as Marx and Engels had seen it. It was an association of enlightened individuals operating beyond the bounds of conventional political activity. As communists, they were charged with discerning the course of history and inspiring others to follow their lead.

The ambiguity was how this association of like-minded revolutionaries could operate effectively without the clearly defined organizational rules that were taken for granted in established political institutions. This was no mean question. Despite the fact that party leaders demanded that their rank-and-file members exercise discipline and obedience to

Central Committee dictates, the upper echelons of the Bolshevik hierarchy initially retained the debating-club features that had typified the party during its years of illegality and exile. No one seriously questioned Lenin's status as a first among equals. Nevertheless, his associates still firmly believed that revolutionary decision making was a collective enterprise. They were comfortable disagreeing with Lenin on nearly every issue and expected that their views would be taken seriously. Kamenev, Zinoviev, Trotsky, and many others regularly questioned their leader's judgment. To be sure, there was no change in Lenin's domineering personality. He frequently expressed his consternation at his colleagues' supposed impertinence. Whether he wanted to or not, however, he put up with expression of these differences; at times, he publicly made a point of insisting that his critics be allowed to retain leading positions in the organization.

This culture of intraparty debate could not have been borne out in any more conspicuous way than in the circumstances leading up to the humiliating Treaty of Brest-Litovsk that the young regime reached with Germany on March 3, 1918. From the beginning, Lenin's approach was purely pragmatic. With vast numbers of desertions from Russia's armies and the likelihood of civil war looming on the horizon, he stressed that his government had no realistic alternative to laying down its arms. Russia needed a breathing space, he argued, to stabilize its economy and to build a broader base of support for socialism. Yet in a continuing demonstration of the limits of his power, Lenin was unable to find unanimous support for his position. The party's so-called Left Communist faction maintained that the survival of the Revolution was precisely the reason to keep fighting, either through direct military action or underground guerrilla operations. In the view of the faction's leader, Nikolai Bukharin, whose writings had played a major role in shaping Lenin's analysis of the consequences of imperialism, the Russian proletariat had a special responsibility. Until its brethren in Germany and other advanced capitalist states were ready to launch the ultimate assault on the bourgeoisie, its function was to keep the fire of revolution alight.

Only after threatening to resign did Lenin get his way. Even then, when the issue came to a vote, the motion was carried only because four of the Central Committee's members, including Trotsky, who had negotiated the treaty, agreed to abstain. At the Bolsheviks' Extraordinary Seventh Congress, which took place only a few days later on March 6–8, 1918, Lenin could not contain his displeasure with those who had disagreed with him. Singling out Bukharin by name, he sarcastically observed that the readiness of the party's members to assemble under one roof was evidence that the majority was "90 percent" in agreement with him. Still, he added, the party was a "comradely family." In such company, there was no reason for its members to hide their opinions. Now that the party had made up its collective mind, however, it was necessary to grit one's teeth and rally behind its decision.[33]

Amid these tensions, Lenin must have been pleased with one development that came out of the party congress. After months of discussion, he finally secured his colleagues' agreement to change the party's name. It would henceforth be the Russian Communist Party (Bolsheviks) (RCP[B]), in recognition of its roots. Under this banner, there could no longer be any doubt about which socialists were the authentic heirs to the tradition of Russian Marxism.

What did this claim mean in practice? On this matter, Lenin and others provided hints that the party needed to clarify its relationship with state institutions, especially the Sovnarkom. For purely practical purposes, if the party were to be more than a simple source of inspiration for the masses, it needed to have clearer lines of command and be open to professional expertise in making its decisions. At the RCP(B)'s Eighth Congress in March 1919, the Central Committee created two organs to streamline its activities. One, a seven-member political bureau, or Politburo, was designed to handle urgent policy questions that needed to be resolved before a full Central Committee session could be convened; such a body had been set up in 1917, but never met. The other, an organizational bureau, or Orgburo, was charged with managing personnel. These bodies were to work with the Central Committee's administrative office, the Secretariat, in coordinating their decisions and making appointments.

There was nothing unusual about these developments. Yet in the context of the Bolsheviks' sudden ascent to power, they provided those who emphasized the party's revolutionary identity with cause for concern. The more regimented and predictable the party's activities became, the more likely it was that future leaders would raise questions about the kind of organization they needed to undertake the construction of socialism. In particular, these questions would be about the necessity of the dynamic qualities—the idealism, spontaneity, and comradely collegiality—that many Bolsheviks regarded as typical of their early years.

For Russia's new leaders, this uncertainty underscored how important it was that they not find themselves alone in the world. Fortunately, from their perspective, Marxism affirmed that their experience was only a part of an unpredictable but infinitely more powerful, historical movement: the worldwide proletarian revolution. Lenin and his fellow radicals believed that they stood at the beginning of a universal conflagration that would eventually surpass their achievements. In fact, given the unexpected train of developments that had led the Bolsheviks to victory before their more advanced European counterparts, they were convinced that their survival depended upon an imminent cascade of revolutionary upheavals in the capitalist countries that were meant to have them first.

Earlier, when Lenin addressed the state of the class struggle in Germany in his political report at the RCP(B)'s Seventh Congress on March 7, 1918, his concern was palpable. "If the German revolution does not come," he insisted, "we are doomed."[34] In chapter 4, we shall see that his hopes were tested in January 1919, when the Communist Party of Germany suffered a devastating defeat. Only two months later, however, on March 21, Lenin rebounded when a fledgling Hungarian Soviet Republic was established in Hungary. The advent of this workers' government, he affirmed in his concluding address at his party's Eighth Congress, showed that a European revolution was finally taking off. The fact that this event had come to pass, Lenin added, in a "more cultured country" than his own, made it even more promising, proving that the proletariat was not merely driven by "the peculiar conditions prevailing in Russia."[35] The major uncertainty, or so it seemed at the moment Lenin was speaking, was how the Bolsheviks should proceed until the entire European proletariat threw off its chains. The success of Hungary's small working-class population could only be a beginning. One had to assume that its heroic example would soon be emulated by the working masses of neighboring countries. This would prove to be a big assumption indeed.

CHAPTER 4

Internationalizing the Party Idea

On March 2, 1919, Lenin and the Bolsheviks' romantic dreams of a fraternity of equally militant communist parties seemed to be fulfilled. Fifty-two representatives of an assortment of left-wing parties, labor associations, and émigré groups gathered in the cramped quarters of the old Court of Justice in the Kremlin to found the Third Communist International, or "Comintern." Lenin began the meeting with a solemn tribute to the founders of the Communist Party of Germany (KPD), Rosa Luxemburg and Karl Liebknecht, who had been killed two months earlier by a right-wing paramilitary group linked to Germany's social democratic regime. Their deaths, he proclaimed, showed that civil war was already a fact in Europe. It would soon spread to other countries, even to Great Britain.[1] Trotsky appeared in military garb, pronouncing the congress to be proof that "the mole of history did not excavate poorly beneath the Kremlin walls."[2] At a moment when the "worst pyromaniacs in history" were picking through the debris and smoking ruins of war, he declared, it was time to unify the efforts of all genuine revolutionary parties and to "generalize" the experience of the proletariat throughout the world.[3] At the congress's concluding session on March 6, Lenin announced that victory on a world scale was assured. The Bolsheviks would no longer be the only party to lead a workers' state: "The founding of an international Soviet republic is on the way."[4]

Never before would Lenin's words have made so much sense to those revolutionaries outside Russia who were wondering where their countries stood alongside the Bolshevik Revolution in the Marxist scheme of history. From Germany to France, Britain, and the remains of Austria-Hungary, the same conditions existed that had propelled the Bolsheviks into power. In Austria-Hungary alone, roughly 3.5 million soldiers and 3.7 million civilians perished; there was a deficit of over 15 million births.[5] The survivors of this bloodletting incurred massive material losses and were left with deep psychological traumas. Yet in the eyes of the left-wing socialists and self-declared communists who suffered along with them, this was a time of opportunity. The gutting of the imperial institutions and traditional ways of thinking that fueled the tragedy of war simultaneously raised the intoxicating prospect that the unfulfilled dreams of a proletarian revolution were finally realizable. Overnight, the outbreak of labor strikes, mass protests, and violent uprisings throughout Europe gave them reason to believe that Marx and Engels's prophecies were coming to pass.

How striking it is, then, that only a year after the Comintern's founding, not a single one of a plethora of the new communist parties was close to exercising state power. Most had either been driven underground or were so weakened by political repression, internal divisions, and poor election results that it was unclear whether they would ever have a significant influence on their societies, let alone stir their populations into overthrowing their governments. In an indication of the extent of their failure and the significance of the Bolsheviks' success in holding on to power, they were suddenly forced to look for leadership to revolutionaries whom they had long expected to follow their example.

This historical reversal set the stage for the transformation of the Comintern into an all-powerful organization with a global reach. When the Comintern held its Second Congress between July 19 and August 7, 1920, in Petrograd and Moscow, its Russian hosts treated their European members as well as revolutionaries from states like China and the United States as secondary players who had much to learn from their example. Lining them up like so many privates in a proletarian army, Lenin and the chair of the Comintern's Executive Committee, Grigory Zinoviev, demanded that they adhere to an *international* model of party leadership that mimicked the Bolsheviks' idealized, if historically inaccurate, image of the movement that had brought them to power. In effect, this was to be an empire of both ideas and organizations. Among twenty-one conditions for affiliation, each of the communist parties was expected to be organized "in the most centralized way possible and governed by iron discipline"; it would undertake a "complete and absolute rupture with reformism"; it would purge its ranks of petit-bourgeois elements "that worm their way into it"; and finally, it would change its name to the "Communist Party" to set itself apart from the social democratic and socialist parties that had betrayed the working class.[6]

Not every Comintern party accepted this international organizational imperative immediately. The head of the KPD, Paul Levi, initially balked over the inclusion of an ultraleftist party of German communists. The left wing of the French Section of the Workers' International, led by Ludovic-Oscar Frossard and Marcel Cachin, butted heads with Zinoviev over whether they should be required to expel their party's moderate socialists. But in a sign that the Soviets were not alone in thinking that the Comintern's members should adhere to a uniform structure and set of goals, other European delegates, such as the virulently dogmatic Hungarian communist leader Béla Kun, rushed to defend the organization's stipulations. After the Soviets indicated that there was no room for opposition, the congress's participants resoundingly adopted the twenty-one conditions on August 6, 1920. At the end of these battles, there was little left of the notion that European communists were entitled to come up with their own ideas about party leadership. Ironically, at a time when the Bolsheviks were still trying to work out the correct balance between their revolutionary ideals and the need to form a stable government, they were demanding that their counterparts accept rigid rules that were, in many cases, unsuited to their specific conditions.

What happened to make the European communists fall into line so quickly and definitively? In this chapter, I shall argue that the same factors that made the Bolshevik Revolution possible in Russia—above all, the catastrophe of World War I—had the opposite effect in Europe. In different ways, as I shall show in the key cases of Germany, Hungary, Great Britain, and France, communist leaders sought to present their ideas about the path to socialism as uniquely suited to move Europe forward. But for equally different reasons, each ended up accepting the Comintern's directives. The KPD advocated a mass-based conception of revolutionary action that contrasted sharply with Lenin's advocacy of a conspiratorial vanguard. However, the credibility of this idea was undermined by failed uprisings against the social democratic governments of the Weimar Republic. Hungary's communist leaders attempted to transform their society according to a radically voluntarist conception of party rule during the short-lived Hungarian Soviet Republic. However, their extremist approach perished when their country was overrun by foreign troops and its population turned against them. Well before the British Communist Party was even formed, the party's founders were overshadowed by the postwar popularity of the reform-minded Labour Party. Due to factional infighting, only Moscow's intervention was enough to keep them from self-destruction. Finally, France's communists seemed to have the greatest chance of establishing an independent identity. Nonetheless, this prospect failed to materialize when the pro-Comintern forces within the party's ranks consolidated their power.

In a strange twist of fate, only in distant Mongolia did a putatively revolutionary party succeed in coming to power. But this party, the Mongolian People's Party (MPP), ascended in a different kind of war, and at the time it was neither communist nor a member of the Comintern. Interestingly, its success was a harbinger of an imposed type of party rule that would become prevalent in Eastern Europe after World War II. For the moment, however, both it and the Comintern parties shared one thing in common. They were dominated by the only party in the world with the credibility to claim that its idea of leadership should be the model for the entire communist movement.

THE QUEST FOR A GERMAN ALTERNATIVE

If any group of European communists should have been predestined to represent the alternative to the Bolsheviks' understanding of party rule, it was the founders of the KPD. Nowhere on the continent did the devastation wreaked by world war seem more propitious for fulfilling the dream of Marxist revolution. Well before the war's end, cities across the country were engulfed in strikes as over a half million factory workers took their protests against the war into the streets. Among the most vocal demonstrators were the revolutionary shop stewards from the metal industries who, following the example of Soviet Russia, set up self-governing councils to contest the regime's monopoly on political power. By fall 1918, Germany's population faced a nationwide crisis of central authority. In early November, sailors in the northern naval base in Kiel revolted against the Naval High Command's decision to send them on a suicide mission to maintain the illusion that Germany could still win the war. After establishing an autonomous governing council, the mutineers called for military garrisons in other coastal cities to follow suit. Simultaneously, Kurt Eisner, a socialist politician in the southern German state of Bavaria, rallied disaffected soldiers to force the abdication of King Ludwig III. Taking the revolt one step further, on November 7, Eisner proclaimed Bavaria to be Germany's first Soviet Republic. Within two days, this turmoil culminated in a decisive event: the German emperor Wilhelm II abdicated his throne.

The left-wing socialists who took part in these confrontations with the imperial regime were filled with a profound sense of vindication. Militants like Karl Liebknecht, the sole Reichstag deputy to have refused to vote for war credits in August 1914, were exhilarated by the prospect that Germany was at last experiencing its revolutionary moment. From their standpoint, this event confirmed that they had been right all along to oppose the transformation of the Social Democratic Party (SPD) into a reformist organization. In their self-portrayal, they alone had recognized the faulty assumptions behind Eduard Bernstein's claims about the abatement of the class struggle. These mistakes, they contended, had led the party to focus exclusively on electoral politics and the extraction of marginal concessions on wages and working conditions from employers. In the process, both the party and its trade union partners had allowed themselves to be taken over by petty bureaucrats who had no appreciation for the actual needs of the proletariat, and hence no interest in pursuing real justice.

These leftists also treated the war's outcome as a validation of their position. The primary target, for many, was the ideological godfather of German Social Democracy, Karl Kautsky, whom they accused of failing to follow through on Marx's teachings. In the radicals' view, Kautsky had begun with the correct premise. In accord with the principles of the Erfurt Program of 1891, of which he was the primary author, Kautsky had correctly emphasized that there could be no long-term accommodation with the capitalist class. Yet, they maintained, his actions showed that he could not be counted upon to defend this basic principle. Instead of leading the proletariat toward a confrontation with the ruling classes, he and his sympathizers had bent over backward to appease the Social Democrats' reformist wing. This stance proved that they had lost sight of the goal of overthrowing the capitalist system.

Notably, the SPD's left wing did not confine its attacks on the reformists' support for the war to the conflict alone. For them, this disastrous decision was merely the bitter culmination of a record of repeated betrayals of the interests of the working class. In their estimation, this shameful behavior was starkly illustrated by the party leadership's decision to show its solidarity by suspending hostilities with Germany's bourgeois parties for the duration of the war. This treachery was made even worse, the radicals contended, by the high price the SPD's leaders paid to secure a seat at the government's table. They abused the norm of party discipline by forbidding their members from publicly disagreeing with these policies.

The left-wing Social Democrats had a powerful spokesperson in Rosa Luxemburg, whose views on the party's responsibilities contrasted sharply with Bernstein's revisionism, Kautsky's reformist Marxism, and Lenin's elitism. Born in Russian Poland, educated in Switzerland, a Jew, and a woman in a dissident culture dominated by men, Luxemburg was the living embodiment of the international character of the communist movement. In her life as an activist and innovative contributor to Marxist theory, she was the equal of Lenin in rallying supporters to her side. Like the Bolshevik leader, Luxemburg had been active in the underground, had suffered arrest and imprisonment, and as a cofounder of the Polish and Lithuanian Social Democratic Party, had proven her skill as a political organizer. The most significant aspect of Luxemburg's appeal to the SPD's militants was her identification with an anti-elitist conception of the party's role that borrowed on the democratic traditions of early socialism. Most likely, had Luxemburg lived to attend the Comintern's Second Congress in 1920, Lenin's followers would have found her to be a formidable opponent of the twenty-one conditions.

Luxemburg's most influential work, *The Mass Strike, the Political Party, and the Trade Unions* (1906), provides a particularly instructive contrast with the conspiratorial orientation of Lenin's vanguard party in *What Is to Be Done?* Notably, Luxemburg was provoked to write the book by the central event in the Bolsheviks' early history: St. Petersburg's Bloody Sunday massacre of January 22, 1905. Like her peers throughout the Russian empire, she was appalled by the tsar's callous brutality toward his people. At the same time, she was enthralled by the spontaneous character of the popular uprising and its escalation into an assault on the foundations of the autocracy. After years of waiting for the revolution to occur, she and scores of other insurrectionists were convinced that they were seeing their dreams come to fruition. This period was, as Luxemburg later described it, "the happiest of my life."[7]

When reading *The Mass Strike, the Political Party, and the Trade Unions* today, one is immediately struck by its similarity in tone and content to Marx's idea of revolutionary change in the *Communist Manifesto*. Just like her forebear, Luxemburg does not focus on the communist party, even though she too includes the word "party" in her title. Instead of talking about an organization, she directs her reader's attention to the people who will actually make the charge against capitalism and asserts that their assault on the established order is inevitable. She calls this revolution "the mass strike." This strike, Luxemburg maintains, is not a specific form of industrial action. Nor is it a single, cataclysmic event. Rather, the mass strike is the culmination of multiple, historically contingent actions by proletarian groups in years past. In the case of the St. Petersburg uprising, she tells the reader, the foundations for these actions were laid by multiple events over the preceding decades: strikes by weavers and spinners in 1896, violent protests by socialist agitators in 1897, and the refusal of tram operators and sailors to negotiate with government officials in Odessa in 1904. In the absence of these precedents, Luxemburg explains, the Revolution of 1905 might not have occurred, or certainly would not have taken the form that it did.

These points give us insight into Luxemburg's well-known disagreements with her contemporary, Lenin, over the communists' revolutionary role. In *The Mass Strike*, she maintains that the key to understanding the working-class struggle lies in the appreciation of the role of indeterminacy. Human will cannot dictate the coalescence of disparate events into full-scale revolution, she emphasizes. The overthrow of the oppressor class is "not artificially 'made,' not 'decided' at random, not 'propagated.'" Rather, she points out, it "is an historical phenomenon which, at a given moment, results from social conditions with historical inevitability."[8]

As I have suggested in chapter 3, one must be cautious in characterizing Lenin's views on this topic. The author of *What Is to Be Done?* would have agreed with the assumptions behind this position. He, too, was convinced that the proletariat required specific social and economic circumstances to take control of the class struggle. A revolution could not be made on volition alone. But there is a markedly different accent to Luxemburg's interpretation that, in my view, accounts for both her acrimonious exchanges with Lenin and her distinctive message to the German Social Democrats. Whereas Lenin argues that a cohort of revolutionary professionals is needed to push the working class "from without," Luxemburg's understanding of the party's purposes is more nuanced. A disciplined party, she agrees, is necessary to inspire the masses and guide them toward their goals. It will provide "cues" for the fight; offer tactical advice; and contribute to "a feeling of security, self-confidence, and a desire for struggle."[9] Nevertheless, she stresses, in an emphatic contrast with Lenin, the party is worthless without the masses. As she concisely puts it, "the organization does not supply the troops for the struggle, but the struggle, in an ever-growing degree, supplies the recruits for the organization."[10]

On this basis, one can understand why *The Mass Strike* would have special meaning for the German communists who were waiting for their day of glory to arrive. The Russian Revolution of 1905, she argues in the book, confirms Marx and Engels's characterization of revolutionary change as a complex and unpredictable process in which the confrontation between antagonistic classes assumes different forms in different times. The broad stage of the mass strike would not have been set without the two great upheavals in the centuries before it: the "reckless radicalism" of the French Revolution and then, as she describes the event, Germany's "smothered" revolution of 1848. For this reason, she advises, Germany's clear-thinking Social Democrats can take comfort in the recognition that the conflagration in St. Petersburg is not as remote to their country's fate as it might seem. To assume otherwise, she asserts, would be typical of the "bureaucrats of the German labor movement [who] rummage in their office drawers for information as to their strength and maturity." Conversely, committed revolutionaries understand that they are part of an international proletarian movement. These events are integral to their own experience. They are "*a chapter of their own social and political history.*"[11]

In making these points, Luxemburg emphasizes that one cannot be sure when Germany's revolution will occur. The contradictions of capitalist development, she points out, do not "proceed in a beautiful straight line but in a lightning-like zigzag." Nonetheless, Luxemburg assumes that this truth will be reassuring to those Social Democrats who fear that the reputation of Germany's workers is being overtaken by Russia's smaller, less sophisticated proletariat. Even if her country's workers should follow a slower course than their neighbors, she assures the reader, they are guaranteed an honored place in history. Marxism teaches that countries in the most advanced stages of development will be the first to *complete* the revolution from capitalism into socialism. According to this line of reasoning, Luxemburg argues that because the bourgeoisie has been in power in Germany for much longer than in Russia, it will be the first to experience the full furor of the oppressed masses. Logically, the German working class will then be first in line to implement the full extent of the dictatorship of the proletariat. The only uncertainty, Luxemburg adds, is whether her party's leaders will have enough insight to take full advantage of these events. If not, the workers will leave them behind.[12]

In light of her convictions, Luxemburg was outraged when the SPD's leaders failed to live up to her expectations in 1914. Following her imprisonment in 1916 for organizing protests against the war, she composed a blistering attack on the party in a lengthy essay, *The Crisis in the German Social Democracy*. Writing under the pseudonym "Junius" (after the founding consul of the Roman Republic), Luxemburg condemned the SPD's centrist politicians for pronouncing a death sentence on the socialist Second International. In her stinging assessment, there was no longer any point in seeking to reconcile the warring constituencies of the German Left since Europe's largest party had sacrificed the class struggle to the twin evils of militarism and imperialism. If only the Social Democrats had used their party's "moral prestige" to rally the socialists of other nations, she lamented, "peace sentiments would have spread like wildfire and the popular demand for peace in all countries would have hastened the end of the slaughter."[13]

To the extent that Luxemburg found any grounds for hope about the future of European socialism, it was not in the prospect of an early peace. Rather, as she explained, it would be found in tragedy. The "blood and smoke of the battlefields" would disprove the falsehoods on which the war was based.[14] From a political standpoint, this analysis proved to be startlingly correct. The longer the war lasted, the more it exacerbated the multiple fissures within the SPD. The outcome of these tensions testified to the aptness of Luxemburg's convictions about the indeterminate character of history. Despite their best efforts, neither she nor any of the radical Social Democrats could foresee, let alone control, the zigzagging course of events that led to the creation of Germany's first communist party.

One year earlier, in 1915, the veiled hand of history had appeared to call the Left to action. Luxemburg, Liebknecht, and other militants fired the first shots in the internal battle within the SPD by organizing a dissenting faction, the "International Group," in opposition to the party's continued support for the war effort. Originally, the activists did not intend for their small group to have the features of an organized party. After all, such an association would have been antithetical to Luxemburg's idea of charging the masses with the leadership of the revolution. By 1916, however, the group could not avoid assuming some of the features of this role. Under a new name, "Spartacus League"—in honor of the leader of the heroic, though unsuccessful, slave revolt against Rome—its adherents were holding regular meetings, distributing leaflets, and inciting protests against the war.

In spring 1917, the radicals' fortunes took another turn when they were confronted with a formidable rival. On April 6–9, pacifist politicians from the SPD's left-center wing walked out on their party to form a new association, the Independent Social Democratic Party (USPD). Initially, the USPD's founders had not wanted to take this step. They preferred to change SPD policy from the inside. But their hands were forced when the SPD's executive body expelled their Reichstag deputies for sponsoring an antiwar conference. At their First Congress in Gotha, the same city where the "Lassalleans" and the "Eisenachers" brought the socialist movement together in 1875, the Independents won immediate support from the war's opponents and attracted members from an array of political camps. In a demonstration that all ideological gyrations were possible, even Kautsky and Bernstein joined the protest to demonstrate their love for peace!

This shift to the left forced the Spartacists to commit to a single course of action. One of their options, as they saw it, was to increase their numbers by joining the USPD. However, this step would have meant associating themselves with people who were unprepared to commit themselves fully to the necessity of revolution. Their alternate option was to take the purist path and resist affiliation. But this step would have had an even more adverse consequence. It would have marginalized their voice on the major issue—the war—on which they shared the most in common with the protesters in the streets. For the time being, the Spartacists attempted to have it both ways. They joined the Independents but insisted that they be allowed to assert their own views within the party's ranks.

In fall 1918, the unpredictable march of events again confounded the Spartacists' plans. In the wake of the sailors' revolt in Kiel in October 1918 and the renewed outbreak of nationwide strikes and demonstrations, the Independents recalculated their options. In view of Germany's imminent defeat in the war and the likelihood of a new form of government coming into being, the SPD's leaders faced what they presumed was an easy choice between two images of the German future. In one case, social peace would be reestablished under a strong central authority; in the other, it would be obliterated through revolutionary violence. Incredibly, this perception took vivid form on a single day. On November 9, the kaiser abdicated and Germany was proclaimed a republic not once but twice: at noon as the "German Republic" by the cochair of the SPD's parliamentary group, Philipp Scheidemann, and in the afternoon as the "Free Socialist Republic" by Liebknecht. Even before these developments, it had become clear to most politicians that the weight of public opinion was leaning in the first direction. Thus, three of the USPD's leaders switched sides and agreed to take part in a provisional government, the six-member Council of People's Deputies, under the leadership of the SPD's chairman Friedrich Ebert. They were followed by other Independents, who in turn were joined by representatives of the most powerful workers' and soldiers' councils. In line with these developments, the new government promptly agreed to an armistice with the Entente powers and made plans to hold elections for a national constituent assembly on January 19, 1919.

Regardless of their leaders' desires, the SPD's success created conditions that forced the Spartacists to commit themselves unequivocally to revolutionary action. Under the magical spell of the Bolsheviks' ascent to power only a year earlier, the supporters of this position remained confident that a German revolution was coming. The militant council leaders, such as the shop stewards, were fiercely distrustful of the moderate politicians. They demanded immediate support for their cause. They were joined by legions of demobilized soldiers who felt betrayed by the former government and were desperate to identify political forces that would help them make new lives for themselves. Paradoxically, the greatest pressure on the Spartacists was unintentionally generated by Ebert. Mistakenly interpreting these expressions of discontent for something they were not—signs of an imminent social explosion on the scale of Russia's October Revolution—Germany's provisional leader went on the offensive to protect the republic against its enemies. In so doing, he reinforced the Spartacists' convictions that their faction was firmly on the correct side of history.

Ebert's decision to go to war with his adversaries was triggered by the occupation of the imperial palace by several hundred disgruntled sailors on December 23, 1918. Far from espousing a radical political program, let alone throwing in their lot with the radical Left, the sailors merely demanded that the government pay their back wages and provide them with jobs. But on the following day, Ebert made the fateful decision to call in regular troops to storm the palace. Although the number of casualties was not high, the use of force against the veterans marked the point at which an essentially peaceful standoff over competing visions of the ideal German future was transformed into a violent confrontation.[15]

These events marked a fundamental transition from Luxemburg's idea of a revolutionary party to a party that pursued this goal through more organized means. On the one hand, "Ebert's Bloody Christmas," as Liebknecht called the assault, confirmed what Marxists had maintained about the bourgeoisie since the nineteenth century. No matter what its representatives called themselves, the ruling class would never voluntarily relinquish power. On the other hand, Spartacist leaders, including Liebknecht, found in these developments the rationale to convince their followers that the formation of a separate party had become necessary for the movement's survival. Initially, Luxemburg had reservations about the decision, fearing that its elitist implications would rob the party of Marxist authenticity. Nonetheless, she allowed herself to be persuaded that the risks of political organization were preferable to the threat of oblivion. At the party's founding congress in Berlin on December 31, she emphasized that the organization should never lose sight of its responsibility to the working masses. It should represent "true Marxism" as opposed to the "ersatz Marxism" of the SPD.[16] On January 1, 1919, the new party was officially proclaimed the KPD.

In what proved to be an enduring feature in the story of German communism, the congress demonstrated that one could not just wish away the divisions within the party elite. On the question of what steps the KPD should take first to assert its interests, Luxemburg again took the minority position, arguing for restraint. The working class, she insisted, was not yet primed for revolution. On this ground, she shocked many of her listeners by suggesting that its representatives participate in the upcoming parliamentary elections. As surprising as Luxemburg's accommodating gesture may have been, it was consistent with her past emphasis on the importance of proletarian maturity. Once again, however, she was outvoted in the KPD's Executive Council, which demanded instead a frontal assault on the Ebert government. Capitalizing on a failed attempt by the regime to replace Berlin's radical USPD police chief, Liebknecht called on January 6 for a general strike and formed a revolutionary council, which he claimed to be the sole, legitimate government of the German people. Even he must have been surprised by the success of this appeal. On the following day, over a half million workers filled the streets, shutting down the city.

Yet, these numbers were misleading. This massive demonstration of popular opposition against the regime's policies was not an endorsement of the tiny KPD. Communists constituted only a small percentage of the protestors. Most of the strikers were unaffiliated council members, soldiers, and ordinary laborers who simply seized the moment to express their distress. What mattered most for the KPD, however, was that the government's reaction to the crisis justified the party's call for greater militancy. Perceiving the KPD's actions to be a putsch attempt, Ebert again responded with force, allowing troops from the paramilitary *Freikorps* to hunt down the communists. The ensuing confrontations between the two branches of the German socialist movement were replete with violence, but no development was comparable in its long-term significance than two particular deaths in mid-January. On January 15, just four days before voters went to the polls to elect the National Assembly of the Weimar Republic, Luxemburg and Liebknecht were kidnapped and murdered by the *Freikorps* troops. With these blows, the two revolutionaries were elevated into the hallowed temple of martyrdom and became permanent reminders to their followers of the SPD's perfidy. Thus, every subsequent battle between the Ebert regime and the communists over the following spring, including the killing of more than a thousand protesters in Berlin in March and the brutal suppression of a newly established and equally violent Bavarian Soviet Republic in May, was a further confirmation that the SPD and the KPD could never be reconciled.

In view of Luxemburg's opposition to the Spartacist uprising, it is understandable that the KPD's more circumspect leaders subsequently wondered whether their party had made a fundamental error. Would not the party's interests have been better served by participating in the national elections? As they saw it, this was not a question of renouncing the recourse to violent means to achieve the communists' long-term goals. Luxemburg had never hesitated to defend the use of violence as long as the circumstances justified it. In her eyes, the issue was whether the KPD's ability to take advantage of popular discontent would not have been greater if it had allowed itself more time to develop an effective organization and a broader social base.

The sobering consequences of the KPD's premature call for revolution and the revulsion of much of the German Left at its violent tactics led to the party's transformation into an organization that was, for a time, significantly different from what the militant communists desired. For ten months after the January uprising, the KPD's members were forced to conduct their business in hiding. When they resurfaced in the late fall under the direction of Paul Levi, one of Rosa Luxemburg's collaborators, they denuded the KPD of much of its outwardly confrontational character and embraced cooperation. In Levi's view, the greatest danger facing the party was represented by the all-or-nothing thinking that would lead to its permanent isolation from German society, and especially the Left. The remedy to this disorder, as Levi saw it, was to compete openly for the loyalties of the people. This strategy entailed both taking part in elections and engaging aggressively in trade union agitation, a realm that had previously been monopolized by moderate socialists. Levi had his way, and the KPD flourished as a result of the social democratic government's growing trials. Under his direction, the party took on many of the attributes of an electorally oriented mass party and could claim over 375,000 members. In June 1920, it won four seats in the first elections to the Weimar Reichstag. In December, the KPD merged with the left wing of the USPD to become the junior partner in the second largest parliamentary party.

At first blush, one might anticipate that this transformation in the KPD's public posture would have put it at odds with the Comintern's stringent demands of its member parties. However, Lenin and his co-leaders were not at all repelled by the idea that fraternal parties should seek to subvert the bourgeoisie by working within its institutions. At minimum, this strategy provided Moscow with an opportunity to foment internal discord among its Western foes. Given this focus, it would be fanciful to think that the communists could have recaptured Luxemburg's dream of a workers' party that received its primary impetus from below. The KPD had already branded itself with the damning reputation of elitism, having presumed that it could dictate to the masses when it was time for them to act.

Still, as we shall see, the memory of the past hung over the KPD like a heavy weight. It could not escape its tortured history with the party that held the reins of power. No matter how great their attunement to Levi's pragmatic instincts, many of the KPD's most prominent personalities were incapable of shaking their hatred for the Social Democrats. As a consequence, they remained open to the possibility that their party's focus would change once again. For the time being, this was not a serious concern. As long as Levi's strategies served Moscow's interests, most of the KPD's militant members were content to live with their party exactly as he desired.

THE HUNGARIAN COMMUNISTS COME TO POWER

In Hungary, too, the tragic consequences of World War I led to the formation of a communist party, but this time in a country where such an organization might have easily been relegated to insignificance. With little fanfare, a group of communist exiles and former prisoners of war (POWs), most of whom had recently returned from Moscow, met with the left-wing faction of the Social Democratic Party of Hungary (SDP) on November 24, 1918, to create the unified Hungarian Communist Party (HCP). Oddly, this party had already been founded on Russian soil a few weeks earlier. This second founding was an emphatic statement. Under the direction of the Moscow-trained propagandist Béla Kun, the communists' union with their SDP allies was meant to prepare them for the daunting task of fomenting revolution under the desperate conditions created by the fall of the Austro-Hungarian dual monarchy.

In many respects, the HCP was born of the same miserable circumstances that would lead only a few weeks later to the founding of the KPD in Germany. As in Germany, Hungary's human losses were staggering. Of the 3.2 million ethnic Hungarians who fought on the side of the Austro-Hungarian monarchy, as many as 531,000 were killed, 500,000 were seriously injured, and 833,000 were imprisoned.[17] When the survivors returned to their homeland after the signing of the ceasefire with the Entente powers in November 1918, they converged on its few cities in search of work and food. Thanks to the agitation of radical socialists and syndicalists, wildcat strikes and protests shut down entire sectors of the economy.

Yet in other respects, conditions in Hungary were uniquely debilitating. More than in Germany, the war's outcome exacerbated a spectrum of already existing social and class tensions. Prewar Hungary was distinguished by socioeconomic cleavages and cultural antagonisms that made it more like Russia than its Central or Western European neighbors. At the turn of the century, two-thirds of the population was engaged in agricultural production, where a handful of conservative noble families owned most of the tillable land.[18] Some peasants were locked into a state of semiservitude that was actually expanding at the same time that the remaining features of serfdom were waning in Russia. As a result, when these simple farmers returned home after fighting for the monarchy, they were driven by a sense of entitlement to the commodity that had previously been denied to them—land. When they did not receive what they wanted, their embitterment left them open to recruitment by extremist parties on both the Left and the Right. In addition, the war's outcome sharpened the divide between town and countryside and created fertile ground for demagoguery and the advocacy of simplistic solutions to Hungary's plight. While the nobility and its sympathizers in the state bureaucracy and the army were swayed by the appeal of hypernationalism and xenophobia, middle-class intellectuals and a growing segment of the urban working class were moved by the promise of social and economic radicalism.

Finally, the appeal of extremism was fueled by Hungary's enormous territorial losses after the war. The victors allowed the Romanian government to annex sizeable portions of the country's territory and merged Hungarian lands with neighboring regions to craft entirely new states, including the Republic of Czechoslovakia and the Kingdom of Serbs, Croats, and Slovenes (Yugoslavia). By the signing of the Treaty of Trianon in 1920, Hungary had lost more than two-thirds of its prewar territory and three-fifths of its population, including over 3 million ethnic Hungarians. In the process, the country was deprived of a substantial portion of its industrial capacity.[19]

These tumultuous conditions put Hungary's moderate postwar rulers in an impossible position. Formed in October 1918, under a democratically minded aristocrat, Mihály Károlyi, the fledgling National Council of the Hungarian People's Republic hastened to express its good intentions. It declared an immediate end to military hostilities and promised major economic reforms, including a sweeping overhaul of the electoral system, administrative reorganization, and the redistribution of land. Nonetheless, the coalition of middle-of-the-road parties that constituted the new government was not the equal of Friedrich Ebert's socialist government in Berlin. With the exception of the Hungarian SDP, which had a clear program and sophisticated organizational structure, the coalition's members showed that they were more adept at engaging in abstract disputes than building effective institutions. They issued hundreds of decrees but were unable to implement them.

The inability of Károlyi and other moderate politicians to master Hungary's divisions was a boon to the communists, and especially Kun. A small-time, leftist journalist, Kun had found his calling in Russian POW camps, where he came into contact with left-leaning radicals from across Europe who shared his exuberance over the Bolshevik victory and confidence that capitalism was in its last days. In a manner that would become common practice in the Comintern, Kun's captors took note of his sympathies and sent him to Petrograd to work in the propaganda division of their party's International Department. In this position, he established a reputation for his zealous convictions and was included in the formation of Hungary's first communist organization, the Hungarian Group of the Russian Communist Party (Bolsheviks).

Without these experiences, Kun would probably have fallen into oblivion. With them, he was able to tap into the militant idealism of countless other converts to Bolshevism. It was no matter that these returnees were unequipped to provide the remedies that had eluded Károlyi's government. Kun's primary objective in forming the unified HCP was to sustain their followers' faith in the immediacy of the revolution and their readiness to use any means to force it through.

Kun's fledgling HCP was much smaller and less disciplined than the social democratic members of the National Council, but it had one major advantage over its rivals. As long as the SDP was associated in the public mind with the government's ineptitude, Kun and his comrades could portray the HCP as the only left-wing party that was seriously committed to redressing the population's grievances. In taking advantage of this discontent, Kun benefited from a critical blunder by the Károlyi regime. Fearing Kun's growing popularity in the streets, it ordered his arrest and imprisonment. Kun might have remained in confinement were it not for the resignation of Károlyi and his ministers in March 1919 after the French head of the Entente commission in Budapest demanded that the government relinquish more of its territory. Now sanctified by these events, Kun was released from prison, and the improbable became reality. Claiming that it was time for the SDP to prove its revolutionary credentials, he muscled through the formation of a unified party of Communists and Social Democrats on March 21, 1919, to govern the country. Under a new name, the Socialist Party of Hungary, the former opponents joined in proclaiming the world's second revolutionary socialist state, the Hungarian Soviet Republic, or "Commune" as its founders called it. In tune with the iron law of the class struggle, the Social Democrats pledged to combat "the bandits of counter-revolution and the brigands of plunder" and to create a new social order by nationalizing major industrial corporations, confiscating landed property, and instituting the dictatorship of the proletariat.[20]

From this unlikely beginning to the new party's uncelebrated end, the communist leaders of the Socialist Party of Hungary gave voice to the triumphant bravado that is commonly found among people with little experience in real-world politics. They justified the unification of the Left and the founding of the new Hungarian Soviet Republic by appealing to Marxist clichés. According to Kun, the two currents of international socialism had merged with no other purpose than to serve the proletariat. "We have achieved what we have achieved," Kun boasted, "namely that we have become practical models for the proletariat of Central Europe."[21] His deputy commissar for education, the renowned philosopher György Lukács, went into greater detail. It was undeniable, Lukács conceded, that the Russian proletariat had taken the first step toward socialism. Yet this achievement had degenerated into an ongoing, fratricidal civil war. In contrast, the unification of the Hungarian Left proved that the representatives of the advanced working class could set aside their differences. In this way, Lukács concluded, the Socialist Party of Hungary showed that the bourgeois concept of the political party was no longer needed. The proletariat had moved beyond it. *"The parties have ceased to exist,"* he affirmed, *"now there is a unified proletariat."*[22] Later, he proclaimed that even the communist party would eventually pass away.[23]

Looking back on the Hungarian Soviet Republic's short 133 days of existence, one could easily fault the moderate Social Democrats for assuming that they could conduct business as usual with revolutionaries whom many of them despised. Yet, in the face of the communists' control over the protests in the capital and the even more disturbing growth of nationalist parties on the Right, they had few choices. For a brief period, they countered Kun's scarcely concealed efforts to dominate the regime. But they were no match for his demagoguery and his skill in exploiting their internal divisions. By early summer, the communists exercised full control over the government and were implementing policies that eroded, rather than enhanced, its faint claims to legitimacy. Some of these measures verged on the bizarre. Lukács set up an audaciously named National Council for the Products of the Mind, which focused on cultural reeducation. He ordered the closing of bookstores and their replacement with "flying bookstands" to distribute communist literature in public places. He paid handpicked writers to write sympathetic tributes to the regime and opened proletarian theaters to raise the consciousness of the working class. Other policies had disastrous consequences. The Soviet Republic followed through on a promise to confiscate the property of large landholders. But instead of turning over this land to the peasantry, as long promised, it created lasting enemies in the countryside by declaring its intention to form large-scale collective farms.

Above all, this period should be remembered for the communists' unabashed endorsement of violence. The more the Social Democrats took issue with these policies, the more ferociously Kun and his coleaders fought back. To an extent that even Lenin questioned, they showed no mercy in dealing with anyone who dared to challenge their policies. In a party communiqué, the regime declared its intention to "drown the bourgeois counterrevolution in blood."[24] It dispatched teams of armed thugs, known as "Lenin's boys," to terrorize its critics. It conducted show trials and executed hundreds of purported counterrevolutionaries. One of the high-ranking officials involved in these measures, Mátyás Rákosi, the commander of the Soviet Republic's domestic militia, would later play a central role in post–World War II Hungary's transformation into a Soviet satellite.

The most acute analysis of Hungary's descent into anarchy came from outside the country. Looking on from Germany, Paul Levi denounced Kun and other HCP extremists for following a misconceived path. Their fatal error, Levi maintained, was to conflate two different historical stages, the fall of the bourgeoisie and the victory of the proletariat. In Levi's view, one could legitimately argue that the bourgeoisie, as he colorfully put it, had "kicked the bucket." However, Levi emphasized, it was much too early to speak about victory. In this case, the experience of Germany's communists was instructive. At the cost of considerable pain, they had learned that the dictatorship of the proletariat would not come into being merely because the party wanted it. Rather, Levi advised, the proletariat could only establish its supremacy if it fully understood its interests. To reach this level of self-understanding, it would need to acquire "the intellectual maturity, the determination, and the insight to recognize that salvation lies in its dictatorship alone." This point had not yet been reached.[25]

When the Hungarian Soviet Republic finally dissolved on August 1, it was significant that the regime was brought down by nationalist misadventures, not the wishes of the proletariat. Rhetorically, Kun sought to define the Socialist Party's strategy in dealing with the hostile powers surrounding his country in much the same way as Lenin. He counted upon the proletariat's victory elsewhere in Europe. Pronouncing himself "secure in the knowledge and conviction that the world revolution is here, is coming," he declared that detachments of the proletariat from other countries, "whose historical calling is to make their own revolution, just as we had to make ours," would soon come to Hungary's defense.[26]

But in practice, Kun defiantly muddied the waters of Marxist orthodoxy by moving in a direction that both the Bolsheviks and the German communists had resisted. He increasingly treated the party as an agent of national rather than class interests. Shortly after the establishment of the Soviet Republic, Kun sought to take advantage of popular outrage over the loss of Hungarian territory by invading the newly created state of Czechoslovakia. For a brief period, the offensive paid off. By early June, Hungarian troops had taken control of most of Slovakia and set up a new socialist state, the Slovak Soviet Republic. At the end of the month, however, the army was forced to retreat. A month later, Kun attempted to exploit his population's nationalist sentiments one final time, declaring war on Romania. When Romanian units easily routed their attackers and marched toward Budapest, there was nothing to hold the Soviet Republic together. Few Hungarians were willing to shed any more blood or tears to defend this tortured experiment.

As in the case of Lenin's support for an unconditional peace settlement with the Central Powers a year earlier, it would be difficult to make the argument that Kun's use of the party's leading role as a tool for defending Hungarian territory had much to do with the organization's Marxist foundations. However, it says a lot about the elasticity of the language of Marxism that Kun used it to account for the demise of what he thought to be the first step toward the inevitable leap into socialism. After announcing his resignation, Kun explained that the failure of the Soviet Republic confirmed the unpredictable course of the class struggle. The proletariat, he explained, as if it were an expression of history and not a concrete class, had "left *itself* in the lurch" by not defending the Soviet Republic. This was not its fault, Kun allowed. Its fate simply testified to the sad circumstance that it was not yet possible "to convert capitalism, that dirty, ugly capitalism, into anything but the dirty, ugly system we have in this country."[27] In fact, confirming that the prospects for Hungarian socialism had evaporated, the Soviet Republic was followed by an "ugly" period. It was replaced by an ultranationalist, right-wing government led by a former admiral in the Austro-Hungarian Navy, Miklós Horthy, which promptly unleashed a reign of "white terror" against officials from both the Károlyi and Kun governments, communists and socialists, intellectuals, ethnic minorities, and Jews. The communists did not forget these events. When they returned to power twenty-five years later under the rule of Kun's deputy, Rákosi, they responded in kind to every hint of opposition to their policies.

THE PLIGHT OF THE BRITISH COMMUNISTS

In contrast to the leaders of the communist parties in Germany and Hungary, the left-wing socialists who founded the British Communist Party (BCP) in 1920 barely had the opportunity to establish an independent identity. At the end of the war, they faced the daunting challenge of organizing themselves in an environment in which the case for radicalism was undercut by national victory. Britain, too, had incurred enormous losses in the conflict. Among the 2.5 million casualties overall, three-quarters of a million British citizens perished.[28] The population suffered the privations of any sustained military confrontation, including significant economic dislocations, painful inflation, and widespread food shortages. Nonetheless, while these losses created the space for leftist politicians to prove themselves, the absence of recrimination and the bitterness of defeat meant that Britain's would-be communists were at a loss to compete with the message of the moderate socialists.

The Labour Party benefited the most from the war's favorable outcome. After years of being a minor player in British politics, its leaders were encouraged by the fact that the attitude of the British electorate toward the Left had changed over the course of the conflict. In 1914, the average man or woman on the street had anticipated a limited engagement in Europe that would be heavy in heroism and short in duration. Well before the end of the fighting, however, the same population was demoralized by the conflict's immense cost. In this atmosphere, citizens distanced themselves from the Liberal and Conservative Parties that had drawn the country into the conflict. Adding to the possibilities for Labour, these parties had been forced to adopt state-centered economic policies, including price controls and direct involvement in private industry, which they had previously decried as socialist. Hence, the more the average voter grew accustomed to greater state involvement in the economy, the less threatening the prospect of a left-wing government appeared.

Under these propitious circumstances, Labour's leaders took a step that would not only redound to their good fortune for years but also significantly weaken the prospects of the party's radical left wing. They publicly committed themselves to socialism. Labour's first constitution of 1918 endorsed measures for a "national minimum" in social services, full employment, higher taxes, and democracy in the workplace. In fact, the party came just short of endorsing the nationalization of industry. Although the constitution did not use this incendiary term, the infamous Clause IV of the document, which was written by the Fabian Society's Sidney and Beatrice Webb, advocated the "common ownership of the means of production, distribution, and exchange" and called for "the best attainable system of popular administration and control of each industry or service."[29]

Had Britain's radical Left only been faced with Labour's successes, the challenge of making even a small mark on postwar politics would have been significant. But its even greater problem was that it was fractured into a multiplicity of small parties, factions, militant groups, and labor associations. Logically, the far Left's best choice of action was to bring these competing bodies under a common roof. To this end, a growing number of its representatives called for the most ambitious option—the formation of a unified communist party. In weighing the merits of this step, however, the leaders of each constituency were compelled to ask themselves the classic question about any form of cooperation: Would alignment increase their respective chances of meeting their objectives, or was it better to go their separate ways in the interest of preserving fundamental principles?

As the largest of Britain's three best-known radical socialist parties, the 5,000-member British Socialist Party (BSP) was the most likely candidate to have its interests met through unification. Formed in 1911 by disenchanted members of the Social Democratic Federation and the Independent Labour Party, the BSP began as a loose collection of breakaway factions and labor agitators who were bound together by the simple conviction that the working class should be led by a genuinely Marxist party. As a result of two developments, these elements slowly congealed into a more substantial entity. The first was the departure of a handful of the nationalist politicians from the party leadership in 1916, including Henry Mayers Hyndman. Their absence gave the BSP the opportunity to define itself as a radical alternative to Labour by adopting an explicitly antiwar platform. The second was the Bolshevik Revolution. Given the absence of the domestic turmoil in Germany and Hungary, it would have been fanciful to imagine that the radical Left would be animated by the same call to emulate the Russian example that propelled its continental counterparts into action. Instead, the BSP's leaders treated the Bolshevik victory as a call to moral responsibility. Despite their modest size, they vowed to keep the idea of an eventual revolution alive until the British working class was ready to act on its true interests.

In attempting to live up to this responsibility, the BSP's leaders defined their party as the natural unifier of the Left. In their view, the interests of the proletariat, both in Britain and abroad, would only be served if all elements of sectarianism were removed from the movement. Thus, in much the same manner as Paul Levi, they argued that left-wing parties of all types should not be allowed to reduce themselves to narrowly focused interest associations or, worse still, to obscure cults. To create a just world, it was essential to work within it. In the final decades of the nineteenth century, even Marx and Engels had grudgingly acquiesced to the participation of socialist parties in elections. But the BSP showed just how flexible it was willing to be by taking this way of thinking one step further. In 1916, it allowed its members to stand as Labour Party candidates in the general elections. From the beginning, the relationship between the two socialist parties was fraught with tension, which became increasingly pronounced as a result of Labour's continued defense of the war and open hostility to the Bolsheviks. Nonetheless, the BSP's openness to this level of collaboration showed that even an avowedly Marxist party could find pragmatic grounds for moderation.

Britain's second largest Marxist party, the militant Socialist Labour Party (SLP), initially seemed a much less likely supporter of unification. Based in the grim industrial centers of Glasgow and Edinburgh and boasting less than one hundred members, the SLP was heavily influenced by the American Marxist Daniel De Leon, who advocated direct industrial action and the organization of workers in workshops and factories. For this reason, the SLP's leaders primarily viewed their party as a vehicle for raising the level of consciousness of the proletariat. Although they insisted on strict party discipline to maintain a consistent message, they were opposed to all forms of centralized leadership.

Thus, in 1918, the party ran candidates in the general elections who unabashedly espoused turning over the means of production to the working class and replacing Parliament with a Congress of People's Councils. Just the same, the supporters of unification found a grain of hope in the SLP's willingness to participate in elections, even though its objective was to subvert the existing order. This suggested that there was a chance its leaders would consider the possibility of working with the BSP.

Such a meeting of minds was practically inconceivable for the even smaller Workers' Socialist Federation (WSF). As an organization, the WSF can barely be distinguished from the personality of its founder, Sylvia Pankhurst. Pankhurst had grown up in a left-wing household as one of the daughters of the leader of the British suffragette movement, Emmeline Pankhurst. But she was more radical than both her mother, with whom she publicly broke ties over the latter's support for the war, and the suffragettes, who were uncomfortable with political agitation among working-class women. Initially, Pankhurst established her reputation as a grassroots organizer, setting up a network of service centers in London's East End to provide indigent women with access to health clinics and nurseries. The creation of the WSF encouraged her to go far beyond these measures. In a seven-point program, the Federation advocated policies—the dismantling of the armed forces, the abolition of the capitalist system, and the creation of a national assembly of workers' councils—that would have made even alignment with the SLP difficult.

In this light, one can see why the founding of the Comintern would have been attractive in different ways to each of the above parties. When the Executive Committee of the Communist International (ECCI) demanded that they unify their forces into a single communist party and set up a Unity Committee to realize this objective, the leaders of each organization naturally looked to the ECCI to champion their respective strategies. This was no small matter. It showed that in the absence of the definitive social and economic conditions to justify one approach over another, the determination of which party was best suited to speak for the interests of the working class was left up to Moscow.

The resolution of this uncertainty came down to the Comintern's deliberations over the BSP's affiliation with the Labour Party. Not surprisingly, as the leader of the smallest party with the most to lose, Pankhurst hastened to lobby the Bolsheviks' founder for support. At first, she appeared to win this battle for influence when Lenin expressed concern that Labour might swallow up its smaller partner. However, he soon changed his mind. After several members of the SLP left their party to join the BSP, the prospect of a stable party with the power to unite the Left became a realistic possibility. In response, Pankhurst took a remarkable step. She formed her own communist party, the "Communist Party (British Section of the Third International)." It turned out that she had good reason for fearing that the course of events was moving against her. When her rivals asked Lenin to take a position on their decision, he notified them on July 8, 1920, that he saw no problem with their "adhesion" to the Labour Party, provided that it allowed for "free and independent communist activity."[30]

I am recounting these interparty skirmishes to illustrate how the Comintern was more than an instrument of domination. It also became an agency for addressing the extraordinarily complex divisions within the radical Left. Pankhurst's opposition was only the first hurdle along this path. When the Unity Convention finally took place on July 31–August 1, 1920, the BSP controlled more than half of the delegates. But when they voted to found the BCP, the new party nearly foundered on its first decision. On the question of affiliation with the Labour Party, its Executive Council was opposed by an array of guild socialists, shop steward committees, Welsh socialists, and other independent groups with radically different views about what kind of party should represent their interests. Hence, the resolution for affiliation barely passed with only a margin of 100 votes to 85.

This less-than-heartening beginning to the BCP is instructive. It showed that this slim victory would not have been achieved without Lenin's intervention. Just prior to the convention, Lenin published a fiery polemic, *"Left-Wing" Communism: An Infantile Disorder*, in which he railed against those communists who, in his view, had allowed dogmatic thinking to cloud their good judgment. The matter of cooperation with bourgeois parties, Lenin stressed, had nothing to do with forgiving the "social traitors" who had sold their souls to capitalism. Referring to Labour's first cabinet member, Arthur Henderson, he wryly advised the communists to support such politicians "in the same way as the rope supports a hanged man!"[31] The main thing, Lenin underscored, was to do whatever was realistically possible to advance the cause of the proletariat. In this way, the working class's true representatives would be on hand to take power when the appointed day of revolution arrived.

Lenin's case was helped by an unanticipated development that had nothing to do with his maneuvering. After the Unity Convention, the BCP matter-of-factly asked the Labour Party's National Executive Committee to allow communist candidates to retain their membership in their own party. A positive response seemed to be a foregone conclusion. To the communists' surprise, the committee summarily rejected the application. With good reason, it argued that Labour could not have people speaking on its behalf who were fundamentally opposed to its constitutional principles. This decision would eventually marginalize the communists even further, but it had a temporarily salutary effect. It removed the divisive issue of Labour affiliation from the table. On January 29, 1921, representatives of the BCP, Pankhurst's party, and sundry other groups gathered in Leeds for a second Unity Convention. This time, they made a show of patching up their differences and established a truly unified organization. In a revealing choice of words that captured these unusual developments, Arthur MacManus, the BCP's first chairperson, aptly summed up the news: "The Communist Parties are dead. Long live the Communist Party."[32] At the same time, the prospect that these communists would ever be strong enough to assert their independence from Moscow died as well.

THE UNIFICATION OF THE FRENCH LEFT

If one could count the unification of the socialist Left as a sufficient criterion to establish an independent identity, the French communists would be worthy of commendation. Unlike their counterparts in Germany, Hungary, and Great Britain, France's left-wing socialists actually achieved this goal. On December 25–30, 1920, 285 delegates of the French Section of the Workers' International (SFIO) assembled in Tours to address the questions of whether and under what circumstances their party should join the Comintern. The congress provided the setting for one of the most remarkable debates in the history of French socialism. On the concluding day of the meeting, these self-appointed representatives of the working class arrived at their decision in a truly democratic fashion. They voted on it. By a margin of 3,208 to 1,022 votes, with each delegate receiving a number of ballots in proportion to the party members they represented, the congress accepted the twenty-one conditions of Comintern membership and founded a new party, the French Section of the Communist International (SFIC).

Outside France, socialists, communists, and other left-wing radicals must have been amazed that one of the most divisive issues in the international workers' movement could be resolved with such apparent ease by voting "oui" or "non." The French penchant for replacing individual self-expression with centralized control had seemingly won the day. In addition, the Comintern's new members treated their good fortune in a way that undoubtedly pleased the organization's leaders in Moscow. In October 1921, the radical faction within the SFIC dutifully renamed itself the French Communist Party (PCF). In what would turn out to be an abiding predilection, its representatives made a point of looking to Russia's example, and not to some homegrown version of communist identity, in choosing their priorities.

Nevertheless, appearances were deceiving. The SFIO's choice for the Comintern and its governing principles was as much about the socialists' weaknesses as their strengths. On the one hand, the spirit of the times seemed to provide ample grounds for confidence. France's left-wing socialists benefited from a resurgence of the radical cast of working-class protest that had prevailed in the years before World War I. In 1914, many Frenchmen had gone to the trenches with as much, if not more, ardor as combatants elsewhere, determined to recapture the glory the country had lost to Germany in 1871. By 1917, however, the combined impact of France's enormous losses on the battlefield—10 percent of the working population was killed—and the misery of the populace made it seem as though the violent class conflict of the 1880s had returned with greater force than ever. Workers seized control of armaments factories, miners left their fields, soldiers were on the brink of mutiny, and entire municipalities were taken over by demonstrators. To be sure, similar unrest could be found elsewhere in Europe, especially in Germany and Hungary. However, in the eyes of the French worker, there was a crucial difference. France had been the victim of aggression, not its instigator. Hence, those persons who had lost the most during the war felt that their government had not compensated them for their sacrifices.

Additionally, the SFIO's militant Left appeared to be ideally positioned to take advantage of the working class's disillusionment with their government's wartime policies. The moderate socialists' willingness to participate with the establishment parties in the *union sacrée*, or "sacred union," had damaged their reputation by forcing them to defend military engagement. Compounding this difficulty, they had underestimated popular enthusiasm for the Bolsheviks among workers and intellectuals and, in 1918, had even gone along with the coalition's support of the White forces in the Russian civil war. Under these circumstances, a vocal minority of SFIO members argued that the leadership had lost touch with its base. It campaigned to end the party's collaboration with the government and engineered a broad shift to the Left at the party's national congress in October 1918. Ludovic-Oscar Frossard, a Marxist pacifist and master tactician, was elected general secretary, and Marcel Cachin, a self-described "common man," was chosen to be the editor of the party's powerful newspaper, *L'Humanité*. Under their influence, the reorientation of the party's profile quickly paid off, and its membership climbed beyond its prewar levels.

On the other hand, the SFIO proved to be no more capable of managing its internal divisions than in the past. At the center of the political spectrum, the party's recognized spokesperson, Léon Blum, an acolyte of Jean Jaurès, openly expressed doubts about whether the French proletariat had anything to learn from its Russian peers and warned his colleagues about the dangers of neglecting France's democratic traditions. In his view, it was a fatal mistake for the party to accept "a compulsory discipline that proceeds from the top down" or to allow itself to become "some kind of vast secret society."[33] In contrast, on the far Left, enthusiasts of the Bolsheviks, such as the unionist Fernand Loriot, demanded that the party prove itself worthy of its vanguard role and take immediate steps to spur the masses to action.

A related problem for the SFIO was that it lacked direct means of communication with the working class. Despite the party's revolutionary rhetoric and its leaders' confidence that the march of events was on their side, even its most radical members had few ties with the working masses. With only a few exceptions, such as Frossard, who came from an artisan family, most had bourgeois backgrounds and were more comfortable arguing about Marxist theory than dealing with the plight of the average worker. Ideally, the latter function should have been fulfilled by the General Confederation of Labour (CGT). Like the party, it too profited from a sizeable influx of new members toward the end of the war. However, the CGT was much weaker than its British and German equivalents. Its reputation for political moderation and its willingness to negotiate with employers made it suspect in the minds of militant trade unionists. Furthermore, the dispositions of the Confederation's radical fringe were as deeply influenced by France's strong syndicalist traditions as they were by Marxism. Given the CGT's federal structure, these factors prevented its executive council from acting without the explicit support of the major unions. In fact, even the description of the CGT as a national organization must be qualified. Most of France's workforce was not unionized at all. Hence, workers were subject to easy manipulation by other associations and political parties.

In 1919, these weaknesses were exposed when both the SFIO's and the CGT's momentum during the previous year stalled. In France's first postwar election in November, a coalition of conservatives, middle-of-the-road liberals, and Catholic politicians, known as the National Bloc, took advantage of the popular desire for stability by portraying the vote as a referendum on the applicability of Bolshevism to French conditions. They were swept into office, winning over half the popular vote and more than two-thirds of the seats in the National Assembly. In response, a divided SFIO effectively deprived itself of the chance to influence the new government by ruling out any form of cooperation with nonsocialist parties. Compounding these setbacks, a renewed wave of great strikes raised further doubts about the Left's effectiveness. On May 1, 1919, the CGT made a bid to bolster its bargaining power by calling for national work stoppages. Over the ensuing months, nearly three-quarters of a million workers walked out on their jobs. Nevertheless, the Confederation lost control of the protests when they splintered into hundreds of contending groups and employers used the divisions to buy off their workers with minor concessions. One year later, the CGT again asserted its authority over the labor movement and a staggering 1.3 million workers went on strike. With railway workers in the lead, the organizers expected that these protests would spread throughout French society. Yet, the government successfully shut the campaign down. It arrested the CGT's leaders and stood by employers when they dismissed more than 20,000 of the union's members from their jobs. With tepid public support, the Confederation was forced to call off further strike action.

These defeats shed light on why the socialists' debates over Comintern membership were about something more substantial than formal affiliation or mere nomenclature. They were about defining the SFIO's identity from a position of weakness. In the end, it was not the heavy hand of history that led the party to move in one direction rather than another, but instead the influence of specific personalities. In mid-June 1919, Frossard and Cachin traveled to Moscow to take part in the Comintern's Second Congress. Upon their arrival, they voiced all of the socialists' ambivalent feelings about membership in the organization. Yet, they quickly found that their hosts were not interested in compromise. In contrast to their handling of the other European parties, which had virtually no bargaining power, Lenin and Zinoviev subjected their guests to an unnerving combination of criticism and cajoling. They agreed that Frossard and Cachin's task was not easy, but stressed that there were no halfway positions on the road to communism. One was either fully committed to proletarian unity or not at all. It cannot have hurt that everywhere the two French socialist radicals were taken, they were impressed with the Bolsheviks' dedication to building a new society. Upon their return to France, they had made up their minds to support the Comintern's wishes at the upcoming party congress.

From its opening session on December 25, 1920, onward, the Tours Congress was a raucous affair as rival factions battled over their party's destiny. It was clear to the delegates that the SFIO needed to reach an unequivocal decision about its commitments. But they also recognized that the choice for the Comintern would result in a split within the party. Cachin took the lead in making the case for membership regardless of its internal consequences. The Bolsheviks, he argued, had the interests of the international proletariat at heart and were eager to learn from every party's experiences. In fact, the spirit and traditions of the French Revolution were among their greatest inspirations. Accordingly, it made good sense that Russia's "great nation" should now become the revolutionary example from which other parties could learn. He and Frossard, he emphasized, had seen extraordinary accomplishments during their travels around Russia. It was true, Cachin conceded, that the Bolsheviks had made these achievements by imposing a dictatorship on their people and violently suppressing their enemies. Nonetheless, he stressed, such measures were unavoidable in an "epoch of barbarism." For the same reason, it was time for the SFIO to recognize that a specific type of political party was needed to wage battle with its opponents. This party would be "thoroughly organized, totally centralized, and vigorously led."[34]

In response to Cachin's defense of the Bolshevik model, Blum tried to convince the congress delegates that the democratic values of French socialism would be impaired by Comintern membership. The organization's twenty-one conditions, Blum maintained, were evidence that Moscow was seeking to impose a conception of communist rule upon other parties that had little to do with the founding ideals of Marxism. In impassioned terms, he warned of the potentially undesirable consequences of Lenin's approach to political power. Lenin's idea of the party, he contended, was nothing less than Blanquism in its most extreme form. It would stifle freedom of thought, eviscerate democratic procedures, and permanently divide socialists and communists. Moreover, it would allow a committee of unknown personages in a distant city to decide the fate of the French party.[35]

Blum ended his address with a famous admission, indicating his recognition that the vote at the congress would go against him. In view of the SFIO's impending split, he announced that he intended to stay behind with those who were needed to "guard the old house."[36] In this way, his response to the party's weaknesses was to take what one could of its good features and let the bad drift away. Why were a majority of the SFIO's members prepared to break with his conception of socialist principles and make their home under the aegis of a party that would be dominated by the Comintern? No doubt, many were caught up in the thrill of the moment. The defeat by the National Bloc in 1919 had not yet convinced them that the prospects of revolution had diminished. Quite the contrary, the government's heavy-handed treatment of the labor movement reinforced their conviction that a mass rebellion against bourgeois rule was all the more likely, even if the event itself was not at the moment around the corner.

Nonetheless, even after the congress delegates voted overwhelmingly in favor of the Comintern, the case that Frossard and Cachin made for membership was hardly as self-evident as they made it seem. To achieve their desired outcome and avoid alienating party members who were still ambivalent about the decision, they refused to let themselves be pinned down on the meaning of adherence to the Comintern's conditions. They simply declared that the body's expectations would be interpreted according to French circumstances. In fact, both Frossard and Cachin hoped that the Comintern Executive Committee would respectfully observe the party's special interests. Nevertheless, after the SFIC finally adopted the full name of the French Communist Party (PCF) in 1921, it quickly became clear that the proper definition of these interests would be determined in Moscow, not Paris.

A PARTY OF A DIFFERENT KIND

In contrast to the sinuous paths that European socialists followed to Comintern membership, it says a lot about the international organization that it found its greatest source of unadulterated support among the assorted groups of revolutionary fighters and insurgent forces of the less developed, nonindustrialized world. One-quarter of the voting and nonvoting delegates at the Comintern's Founding Congress in 1919 were from the distant territories of the old Russian empire as well as the states and regions on the periphery of the young Soviet Republic. These revolutionary groups were also heavily represented at the Comintern's Second Congress. Although few of them represented communist parties and even fewer could claim to speak in any meaningful way for proletarian interests, their weakness in comparison with the advanced socialist parties in Europe had a noteworthy consequence. It made them even more receptive to the idea that the Bolshevik Revolution was their best hope for the future. Whether they came from Japan, China, Persia, or India, they found a host of ways to translate the Bolsheviks' victory into terms that made sense in their struggles against traditional despotism and colonial rule.

For the Comintern's leaders, and especially those in Moscow, this outpouring of enthusiasm from the East could only be regarded positively. In their interactions with these followers, they encountered little of the ideological baggage that they associated with the European communists. There were few debates over the historical significance of the Bolsheviks' ascent to power or contending views about the desirable form of communist leadership. These groups were simply happy to have found a common home. In addition to enhancing the Comintern's prestige, these relationships were also strategically significant for Soviet Russia. In 1920, the Bolsheviks were still fighting a civil war on several fronts. Furthermore, they were acutely aware that surrounding powers, like China, Japan, and Great Britain, would at some point test their will and ability to defend their achievements. In these respects, the Marxist idea of a global proletarian revolution could be readily translated into a broader imperative to serve the Kremlin's passing needs.

For these reasons, the Comintern Executive Committee was intent upon supporting its new allies, both financially and militarily. Notably, it pursued this objective in a much more flexible and less ideologically demanding manner than in the case of the European communists. In September 1920, less than two months after the Second World Congress, the Comintern convened the Congress of the Toilers of the East in Baku. In this forum, its representatives instructed the 1,891 delegates, most of whom could hardly be classified as communists, that they were equal partners moving along the path to a worldwide revolution. Conveniently putting aside his own catastrophic failure and lack of connection with their world, Béla Kun shared with them the words they wanted to hear. He informed his listeners that they would play a central role in overthrowing the forces of feudalism and foreign imperialism. No one should tell them, Kun stressed, that they were any less equipped to accomplish this task than their Western peers. While the latter were charged with leading the proletariat to power, the peoples of the East, as he portrayed them, were obliged to lead the poorest peasantry. There was no longer any excuse for waiting; this would only prolong the misery of their oppressed populations. "The ability to rule," Kun underscored, "like the ability to use a weapon, demands that you make a start and get some practice in: he who never handles a rifle will never learn to shoot."[37]

Kun's rallying cry was nowhere more appropriate than in the case of the relatively unknown MPP. In March 1921, it accomplished a feat that no other Soviet-backed party would accomplish for a quarter century. It presided over the founding of a "People's Government," soon to be called the Mongolian People's Revolutionary Government. This development was significant for two reasons. The first is that the MPP could scarcely be called a communist party. Although the founders were inspired by the Bolshevik victory in a general way as a triumph of the masses over the forces of repression, they had little more than a hazy acquaintance with the issues and controversies that animated the Russian and European debates over Marxism and socialism. The tiny group of nobles, court officials, common laborers, and even a Buddhist lama who came together in a clandestine meeting in the Outer Mongolian capital, Urga, on June 15, 1920, had a simple goal in common. They were dedicated to liberating their nomadic country from Chinese occupation. Otherwise, they shared only an inchoate understanding of the meaning of revolutionary change, and even this was based on an uneasy blend of traditional and semimodern values. In the party's loyalty oath, the element with the closest resemblance to Marxism obliged its members to "let people live free from suffering, neither oppressing nor being oppressed." Another clause, however, did the opposite. In a quite unrevolutionary way, it obliged party cadres to defend a theocratic monarchy, to "purge cruel enemies who are hostile to the faith and the nation, to restore lost authority, loyally to protect and encourage state and church, to protect our nationality."[38]

The second noteworthy feature of the MPP's success is that, in the beginning, it was almost entirely self-initiated. Although these rebels had fleeting contacts with Soviet agents in the Far East and traveling Comintern officials, the Bolsheviks were preoccupied with the Civil War and reluctant to take any steps that might add a conflict with

China to their burdens. As a result, the fledgling MPP found itself in the unusual position of initiating contacts with Moscow. Not long after the party's founding, its leaders dispatched a secret delegation to Irkutsk to seek financial and military assistance. While awaiting a response from the Bolshevik authorities, two of the party's future leaders, Damdinii Sükhbaatar and Khorloogiin Choibalsan, took advantage of the opportunity to receive military training from their hosts and learn more about their revolutionary goals. Yet, the Mongols' entreaties had little effect. Thus, it could not be more revealing about Moscow's ambiguous goals outside Europe that it took a military threat to convince the Kremlin to look eastward. In February 1921, a White Army general, Baron Roman von Ungern-Sternberg, and a motley army of White Russians, Cossacks, Tatars, and Japanese soldiers drove the Chinese forces out of Urga and set up a government with the expressed aim of defending Mongolia against the communist threat. This development instantaneously raised the MPP's stature in the Bolsheviks' eyes. With Moscow's backing, the Mongolian party convened its First Congress in the Russian city of Khyakta on March 1–3, 1921, and promptly founded the provisional People's Government. Using this body's appeal for protection as a pretext for intervention, the Red Army marched into Mongolian territory and crushed Ungern-Sternberg's forces in August.

If ideological considerations played a role in these military measures, the Kremlin did not express them. True to the accommodating spirit of Kun's remarks at the Congress of the Peoples of the East, Moscow demonstrated that it had little interest in forcing the new government to adopt the organizational model that it demanded of the European parties. Accordingly, even with Comintern agents taking part in the MPP congress, the party's official program was a hodgepodge. It dutifully paid tribute to the valor of the international proletariat, made obscure references to an imminent transition from feudalism to capitalism, and advised its members to act on a variety of issues, including the management of religious affairs in accordance with the "spirit of our times, the experience of the peoples of the world, and in conformity with the character of future changes in world events."[39] Indeed, even after the MPP solidified its control by establishing the People's Revolutionary Government and christening itself the Mongolian People's

Revolutionary Party (MPRP), Moscow gave it a free hand in defining its priorities.

In a telling contrast with Europe's communist parties, the Mongolian party would have preferred even greater integration within the Comintern. When a delegation of its leaders visited Moscow in November 1921, it was granted the opportunity to meet with Lenin and ask the Bolshevik leader whether the MPRP would soon have the privilege of calling itself a communist party. Lenin's answer was unequivocal. "I should not recommend it," he advised, "because one party cannot be 'transformed' into another." In Lenin's estimation, the essential task of a communist party was to be a party of the proletariat. The Mongols were clearly not ready for this step. "The revolutionaries," he solemnly advised, "will have to put in a good deal of work in developing state, economic and cultural activities before the herdsman elements become a proletarian mass, which may eventually help to 'transform' the People's Revolutionary Party into a Communist Party." For the time being, Lenin concluded, "a mere change of signboards is harmful and dangerous."[40]

At this juncture, no judgment about a party's identity could have been more revealing. Moscow did not love the Mongolian communists for the militant ideas they could bring to the global revolution. It simply wanted an obedient organization that would loyally serve Soviet Russia's national security interests. It was no coincidence that when the MPRP was finally admitted to the Comintern in 1924, the Executive Committee was in no hurry to impose the twenty-one conditions of membership. In accord with Lenin's earlier judgment, the international organization's new member was not even asked to change its name. Demonstrating the MPRP's function was to serve a cause other than its own, when Sükhbaatar's successor as head of state, the chair of the Central Committee Soliin Danzan, expressed reservations over a Soviet-Mongolian friendship treaty at the party's Third Congress, he was summarily executed.

In retrospect, both these experiences and those of the MPRP's European counterparts allow for a provocative point about the Bolsheviks. In both regions, Moscow's determination to use the Comintern as an instrument to underscore the primacy of the Soviet experience meant that their leaders had less and less control over their parties' identities.

In the latter case, their early claims to a distinctive route to socialism led the Bolsheviks to induce them to adhere to a unified model of communist rule; in the former case, this model was denied to them despite their wish to be full participants in a historically divined movement. Certainly, the Bolsheviks showed that they knew a lot about telling other parties what do to. But it is significant that they were much slower to reach agreement in the early 1920s about the meaning of communist leadership within their own country. Although it was not fully apparent, they were about to engage in a decade of acrimonious disputes that would eventually prove profoundly more destructive than those that beset their allies.

1. Karl Marx and Friedrich Engels spread the word about the looming specter of communism in their newspaper, the *Neue Rheinische Zeitung*.

2. Imprisoned revolutionaries in Trier, Germany, plot their next move.

3. Citizens in the National Guard prepare to defend the Paris Commune against the imminent assault of the regular French Army in May 1871.

4. Standing between portraits of Ferdinand Lassalle (*left*) and Karl Marx (*right*), Rosa Luxemburg agitates for a proletarian revolution at a rally in Stuttgart, Germany, in 1907.

5. Vladimir Ilyich Lenin storms across Red Square in 1918.

6. Bitter confrontations at the Congress of the French Section of the Workers' International, in Tours in December 1920, lead to the founding of the French Communist Party.

7. Ernst Thälmann, the uncompromising German communist, fires up a crowd on Berlin's Schloßplatz on May Day, 1931.

8. Mao Zedong poses with political commissar Zhou Enlai (*left*) and Red Army commander Zhu Deh (*right*) during the formative Long March to Yan'an.

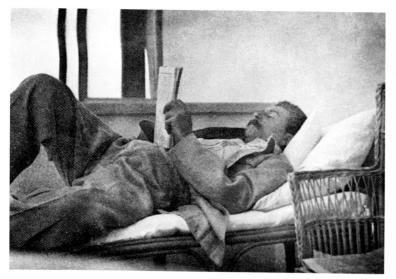

9. Frequently isolated from his advisors, Joseph Stalin was free to make decisions at his whim.

10. Communist demonstrators in Barcelona hold high the banner of revolution during the Spanish Civil War.

11. Josip Broz Tito (*far right*) is joined by members of his cabinet and his fellow guerrilla fighters in the mountains of Yugoslavia during World War II.

ЛЕНИН
СТАЛИН

12. Communist party leaders contemplate the future as Joseph Stalin's remains are added to Lenin's mausoleum on March 9, 1953. From left to right: Gheorghe Gheorghiu-Dej (Romania); Bolesław Bierut (Poland); Pak Den-Ai (North Korea); Walter Ulbricht (East Germany); Dolores Ibárruri (Spain); Otto Grotewohl (East Germany); Valko Chervenkov (Bulgaria); Mátyás Rákosi (Hungary); Socialist Party leader Pietro Nenni and Palmiro Togliatti (Italy); Jacques Duclos (France); Klement Gottwald (Czechoslovakia); Nikolai Bulganin, Vyacheslav Molotov, Kliment Voroshilov, Georgy Malenkov, Nikita Khrushchev, Lavrenty Beria, and Maksim Saburov (Soviet Union); Zhou Enlai (China); Mikhail Pervukhin, Lazar Kaganovich, Nikolai Shvernik, and Anastas Mikoyan (Soviet Union).

13. Hungarian Stalinist Mátyás Rákosi (*left*) barely contains his disdain while his reform-minded premier, Imre Nagy, speaks during a parliamentary session in 1954.

14. Nikita Khrushchev's report to the Communist Party of the Soviet Union's Twentieth Congress will culminate in his denunciation of Stalin in the "Secret Speech" on February 25, 1956.

15. Fidel Castro flaunts his guerrilla *machismo* in Cuba's Sierra Maestra Mountains in 1959.

16. Thousands of exultant Red Guards wave their copies of Mao Zedong's "Little Red Book" on Beijing's Tiananmen Square in 1966.

17. Two directions in 1968: East Germany's party leader Walter Ulbricht (*left*) is determined to preserve the status quo, while his Czechoslovak counterpart, Alexander Dubček (*middle*), seeks to give socialism a "human face."

18. Władysław Gomułka, one of the few remaining representatives of the communist old guard, celebrates his sixtieth birthday with Polish miners.

19. The Soviet Union's Leonid Brezhnev (*left*) and Bulgaria's Todor Zhivkov, both symbols of the pragmatic spirit of "developed socialism," are greeted by cheering crowds in Sofia, Bulgaria.

20. Epitomizing the corruption of communist ideals in the 1980s, Romanian dictator Nicolae Ceauşescu concentrates on carving a barbecued pig.

21. General Secretary Mikhail Gorbachev demonstrates his commitment to regaining the trust of the Soviet people in a visit to Armenia after a devastating earthquake in 1988.

22. Solidarity leader Lech Wałęsa (*middle*) arrives at the negotiations between prodemocracy forces and the government in early 1989 that will lead to the unraveling of communist party rule in Poland.

23. China's Paramount Leader, Deng Xiaoping (*left*), with Communist Party General Secretary Zhao Ziyang, whose reforms will precipitate antigovernment demonstrations in Beijing in spring 1989.

24. President Xi Jinping headlines the celebrations of the 150th anniversary of Sun Yat-sen's birth, drawing from China's precommunist past to legitimize party rule.

25. As Cubans mourn the passing of Fidel Castro in November 2016, they must wonder what will come next.

CHAPTER 5

Creating the Leninist Party

In August 1924, the Bolsheviks finally gave a name to their conception of the communist party: Leninism. Joseph Stalin, a cobbler's son, onetime bandit, political commissar, and newly designated general secretary of the Russian Communist Party (Bolsheviks), deserves much of the credit for promoting the concept. Certainly, he rushed to make it his own. In early April of that year, less than three months after Lenin passed away on January 21, Stalin delivered a series of lectures on the topic at the Sverdlov Communist University. These statements subsequently became the definitive text of the new doctrine under the title *Foundations of Leninism*. In contrast to his predecessor's tendency to modify the language of party leadership according to changing conditions, Stalin's message was a model of precision. The Leninist party, he instructed his listeners, had exactly six characteristics: it was the "vanguard of the working class"; an "organized detachment of the working class"; the "highest form of class organization of the proletariat"; the "instrument of the dictatorship of the proletariat"; the "embodiment of its unity of will"; and the enemy of all forms of opportunism. By definition, wherever one found these elements, one had a Leninist party.[1]

The timing of Stalin's lectures was no coincidence. With the passing of the party's founder, he and the other senior Bolsheviks needed to tell their citizens what came next. As they showed by placing Lenin's embalmed corpse in a temporary structure next to the Kremlin wall, later to be replaced by a full-blown mausoleum, and broadcasting his immortality ("Lenin lived, Lenin lives, Lenin will live!"), their objective was to give a tangible form to the idea that both the substance and the spirit of the October Revolution would be carried forward. Hence, the naming of their party's functions was essential. The right formula would justify its decisions, put the stamp of authority on its policies, unify its rank-and-file members, and galvanize mass support.

If only a change in nomenclature could be a recipe for success! But life is more complicated than this. Stalin was wrestling with the same problem that we have encountered in the case of the less powerful European communist parties. He and the other Bolsheviks had to figure out how to define their party's responsibilities in a time when its mission was no longer shaped by the guns of military conflict. Even before the end of the Russian Civil War, the leaders of the new Bolshevik regime were faced with daily decisions over which type of party they preferred to emphasize—a revolutionary party or a ruling party. There was no easy answer to this dilemma. On the one hand, the first type of party was best suited to maintain their early ideals and emphasize their continued commitment to the class struggle against what they regarded as a transitional, capitalist order. But after seven years of fighting, this was a potentially costly strategy. No matter how intensely its leaders wanted to change the world, the fragile regime could not afford to ignore its population's hopes to return to some semblance of social and economic normalcy. On the other hand, the development of a ruling party had the advantage of stabilizing expectations and promoting greater identification with the regime's policies. But here, too, there was a potential drawback. A party that focused primarily on meeting immediate demands would quickly lose the momentum required for following through on the revolutionary transformation of society. For many, this risk was particularly great if the revolution failed to spread to other countries and there was no force to maintain its original ideals.

Lenin's successors would have undoubtedly been delighted to act on each of these conceptions of leadership with equal fervor. Yet, as I shall suggest in this chapter, the powerful personalities who were involved in making this choice were not easily persuaded that a neat balance could be found between these poles. For much of the 1920s, a group of so-called Right Bolsheviks led by Nikolai Bukharin and Joseph Stalin, and largely supported by Lenin before his death, had the upper hand in this battle. They pressed for a party with the capacity to lead Soviet Russia out of the turmoil of war and international strife. The other group, composed of left-wing Bolsheviks including Leon Trotsky, Lev Kamenev, and Grigory Zinoviev, favored a militant party that was attentive to the social and economic roots of the revolution and determined to drive the country toward the eventual realization of socialism. By the late 1920s, the Left opposition was soundly defeated. But this was a pyrrhic victory for the advocates of sobriety, especially Bukharin. Once one set of rivals was eliminated, a suddenly uncompromising Stalin turned on his former allies and transformed the party into a rigid organization that was expected to carry out an orchestrated revolution from above.

Under other circumstances, Stalin's revolution should have been a milestone for those figures who called themselves communists. As the party's general secretary, Stalin drew upon the principle of party dictatorship to lead the Soviet Union into a period of unprecedented growth, establishing the USSR as a modern industrial state and a global power. In November 1936, he made the ultimate pronouncement, declaring at the Extraordinary Eighth Congress of Soviets that his country had "achieved the first phase of Communism. Socialism."[2] The Congress sanctified this statement, as well as its leader, in a new constitution that proclaimed the USSR a socialist state. Nonetheless, as I shall demonstrate, the dictatorial structure of the same party organization that formally allowed Stalin to take credit for these feats also put him in the position to destroy it. In the second half of the 1930s, his determination to eliminate anyone who dared to question his frequently disastrous policies led him to declare war on the party. His primary target was the founders of the party. By his death in 1953, the party apparatus was not only reduced to a secondary status under a centralized state; more importantly, the more fluid understanding of its mission that had existed in Lenin's time was dead.

THE UNCERTAINTY OF VICTORY

The Bolsheviks initially had no plans to govern. This fact is hardly surprising. Before their ascent to power, their focus was on tearing down institutions. In their view, the path toward socialism could be cut simply by eliminating the bodies that stood in their way. The first institution to go was the Provisional Government. However, they quickly realized that their survival depended on their ability to replace old institutions with new ones. In the face of this challenge, it was easy for them to maintain, as they continually insisted, that this function would be fulfilled by their party. Yet, the principle of party rule could not feed returning war veterans, house refugees, restart damaged industries, and restore domestic trade. Lenin admitted as much in an exchange with Trotsky. "You know," he said immediately after the Bolsheviks shut down a newly elected constituent assembly in January 1918, "from persecution and a life underground, to come back so suddenly into power.... *Es schwindelt* ('It makes your head reel')."[3] In the confused conditions of the late 1910s, Soviet Russia required practical solutions to complex problems.

In this context, one is struck by how little convincing Lenin and the other Bolsheviks required to look primarily to their newly formed state organs to address these challenges. They made the Council of People's Commissars, or Sovnarkom, the central instrument of governance. Although this body had all of the trappings of a revolutionary government, such as its division into "commissariats" rather than "ministries," its officials were quickly consumed by the business of restoring order to their society. In this spirit, Lenin brought his considerable charisma and single-mindedness to the task of leadership and rallied the commissars to attend to their assignments.

The Bolsheviks did not stop here. At a time when the Civil War was spreading and they were aggressively taking control of the "commanding heights" of the economy, they could easily have rejected any form of accommodation with representatives of the "class enemy." But as Lenin admitted, serious revolutionaries could not afford the luxury of pretending that they could solve all of their country's problems on their own. If the Bolsheviks' dreams were to survive during a period when Russia was "a fortress besieged by world capital," the regime required the skills and talents of everyone who was not resolutely opposed to their goals. This meant, in Lenin's assessment, that the party was obliged to combat the "pseudo-radical but actually ignorant and conceited opinion that the working people are capable of overcoming capitalism and the bourgeois social system without learning from bourgeois specialists." As distasteful as this step was, one needed to "make use of their services" and "work side by side with them."[4]

No concession could have been more painful than the decision to form a majority of the commissariats by grafting them onto the pre-existing ministries. In the first year after the October Revolution, 80 percent of the officials in eight of the fourteen commissariats were holdovers from the tsarist and provisional governments. During the Civil War, the thorniest issue involved the Sovnarkom's inclusion of former military officers and experts. In the first three months of 1918 alone, and with Lenin's blessing, the People's Commissariat for War and Naval Affairs incorporated over a third of the commanders from the old general staff and comparable numbers of specialists into the Red Army.[5] As both creator and commander of the revolutionary army, even Trotsky showed that he had the capacity for occasional bouts of flexibility by supporting the policy. This stand made him a convenient target for his Politburo adversaries, such as Stalin, as well as the so-called Military Opposition, which accused him of compromising the Bolsheviks' militant ideals.

In view of these difficult choices, one might be tempted to see the pragmatic focus on the Sovnarkom as a sign of a fundamental ideological shift—the ascendency of state power over the party's authority. But this conclusion would cloud a major question: What was the communist party at this juncture? In many ways, it was no more than the sum of the loose collection of Bolsheviks who filled its senior ranks. To an extent that resembled Marx's assumptions seventy years earlier, these revolutionaries' first inclination was not to think of their party as an organization governed by hard-and-fast rules. In their eyes, *they* were the party. As the makers of the Revolution, they naturally believed that they were charged by history to exercise the role of the vanguard. For this reason, they regarded the Sovnarkom as one of many official organs that reflected their collective will.

In this circumstance, Lenin's position was complicated. Although he insisted on his right to dictate party priorities, he seems to have recognized that the regime could not afford a rift among the Bolsheviks. Thus, he allowed fellow communists in the Sovnarkom, such as

Felix Dzerzhinsky (the commissar for internal affairs), Stalin (the commissar for nationalities), and especially Trotsky (the war commissar and chair of the Defense Council), considerable room to maneuver within their respective spheres of responsibility. For a short period, this precarious balancing act appears to have functioned effectively. Although the Sovnarkom's meetings were the site of rancorous debates, bitter adversaries were nonetheless able to reach crucial decisions. On some occasions, Lenin, too, was forced to bargain to get what he wanted.

Yet, the Bolsheviks had an additional building project. No matter how important they perceived themselves to be as individuals, the party could not exercise its appointed role without a structure to oversee the Sovnarkom. The party was so far from living up to Stalin's formulaic conception of a "Leninist" institution that its central command was essentially run by two persons during its first year of operations. One was Lenin himself, who did not even hold a formal party title. Although Lenin sought to keep abreast of the organization's activities, he was also chair of the Sovnarkom and the de facto head of several other bodies. The other, more important figure was Yakov Sverdlov, the secretary of the Central Committee, who ran the party apparatus. With the help of only a few assistants, Sverdlov supervised all personnel appointments, arranged the Committee's meetings, and took responsibility for the flow of information among its offices. Trotsky aptly described both Sverdlov's skill and the organization's potential weakness: "all the threads of practical connections were gathered in his hands."[6] After Sverdlov's death on March 16, 1919, Lenin succinctly captured the gravity of the event: "He's gone. He's gone. He's gone."[7]

The task of mastering this concatenation of diverse posts and stubborn personalities could not have been easy. Because channels of communication across the party were still being formed, key personalities in one part of the country had no idea about the actions of their peers elsewhere. In addition, Sverdlov's authority was routinely tested by other communists. In the non-Russian territories of the former empire, such as the Baltics, Byelorussia, and Ukraine, native elites set up separate communist parties of their own to assert their regional and ethnic interests. Local agitators and factory cells frequently resisted his efforts to rein in their activities. Compounding these difficulties, Sverdlov himself had divided loyalties. As head of the Central Executive Committee of the Congress of Soviets, the state agency that theoretically paralleled the Central Committee, he was not bound to either organ in making his decisions.

Against this backdrop, it is a telling sign of the Bolsheviks' reluctance to pin themselves down that it took them until their Eighth Congress in March 1919, which began two days after Sverdlov's death, to reach a consensus about the party's central organs. At this point, they formed three functionally distinct bodies under the command of the Central Committee. The first was a new, five-member Politburo that was charged with addressing major questions and making decisions that could not wait until the next Central Committee meeting. The second, a large Organizational Bureau (Orgburo), was tasked with making senior appointments and delegating personnel assignments. The third body, initially assumed to be the least important, was the party Secretariat. Its assignment was to run the Central Committee departments and make lower-level appointments.[8]

It would take some time before these organs were strong enough to manage the different spheres of party activity. Additionally, the leading Bolsheviks were still stubbornly committed to their respective conceptions of the regime's priorities. However, the party's gradual stabilization as a ruling institution did not result in it becoming a more representative organization. Stalin would make vividly clear that the person in charge of the party apparatus was best positioned to define what it meant for a Leninist organization to exercise its leading role. Nonetheless, before this point would be clear for everyone to see, it was necessary to begin with the battle over ideas.

THE IDEA OF THE RIGHT TO RULE

On a day-to-day basis, the party's new offices and clearer lines of command strengthened its operations. But for a majority of the most prominent Bolsheviks, the party's identity was still only minimally defined in terms of its organizational attributes. This circumstance meant that its responsibilities in representing the proletariat remained open to dispute. One view was that the party had won its leading role simply by virtue of the fact that it was in power. In July 1919, Lenin underscored this qualification. "Yes," he told a congress of educators, "it is a dictatorship of one party." "This is what we stand for, and we shall not shift from that position because it is the party that has won ... the position of vanguard."[9] A different view was that the party was a direct expression of the popular insurrection that had precipitated the Revolution, most notably the people's soviets. Logically, if one chose the first interpretation, the regime could decide the party's policies of its own accord. However, if one emphasized the second interpretation, the party organization was obliged to take account of the demands of the grassroots forces that had made the Revolution possible.

The tension between these positions was borne out by the protests of left-wing Bolsheviks. Many regarded the party's consolidation as a sign of the leadership's creeping alienation from its rank-and-file members and its working-class constituencies. Worse still, some saw it as the harbinger of a corrosive drift toward overcentralization and dictatorship. One group, the Workers' Opposition, which was led by the commissar for labor, Alexander Shliapnikov, contended that the rights of factory workers had been eroded by the party's excessive recruitment of non-communist specialists, and demanded that it correct this abuse of power by providing greater autonomy to trade unions. Another opposition group, the Democratic Centralists, demanded that local party organs be allowed to choose their own representatives on the basis of open debate, rather than commands from on high.

The expression of these contrary views did not occur in a vacuum. As the chaos of the Civil War receded, the Left Bolsheviks found a receptive audience among broad segments of the Russian population and non-Russian nationalities who had yet to be persuaded that the Bolsheviks were interested in addressing their needs. Between 7 and 8 million people perished over the course of the conflict, more than half of them civilians.[10] In this context, as the regime took more concrete form, the survivors understandably pressed their new government to reverse the draconian measures that had been undertaken during the conflict. To provide resources for the war effort, the Bolsheviks had eliminated all semblance of the rule of law, allowing for the arbitrary arrest of anyone deemed to be the enemy. They had nationalized major industries and plundered farms and villages to address food shortages in the cities. By 1921, the Volga and Ural Mountain regions were caught in the grip of the worst famine in a century, a tragedy that alone claimed over 5 million lives.

Amid frequent uprisings in the countryside, work stoppages in major industries, and other forms of mass protest, the Left Bolsheviks could easily make the case that the regime had dangerously lost touch with its citizens. Nowhere were their arguments more vividly demonstrated than in an explosion of antigovernment demonstrations in Petrograd. Beginning on February 23, 1921, just two weeks before the opening of the party's Tenth Congress on March 8, labor protests gave the Bolsheviks reason to fear that the Revolution was starting all over again. Workers shut down factories and demanded that the regime provide them with both food and the freedom to govern themselves. When word of these demonstrations spread to the nearby Kronstadt naval garrison, the crew of the battleship *Petropavlovsk* took what was, for the Bolsheviks, an unthinkable step. The mutineers cobbled together a far-reaching list of demands that included the right to free assembly, new elections to the soviets, and the abolition of the political sections of the military. But their act of defiance was not to last. On March 21, when the insurgents formed a Provisional Revolutionary Committee to represent their views, Trotsky ordered the Red Army to crush the rebellion. After two weeks of bloody combat, the garrison surrendered.

The Bolshevik leadership lost no time in blaming this upheaval on provocateurs and the machinations of agents of foreign imperialism. However, Lenin and the rest of the party's inner circle clearly knew the truth. They had, as yet, failed to convince the working class that the party was acting on their behalf. Furthermore, they must have been aware of the perversity of their resort to brute force. In Kronstadt in particular, where the party had almost no representation, they had turned their weapons on the same sailors who rallied around their cause in 1917. The rebels were not trying to overturn the Revolution. They were appealing to its original principles. As a result, the regime was forced to decide which steps it would take to restore its authority.

At the Tenth Congress, which had been deliberately postponed until the day of the Kronstadt attack, Lenin provided an unequivocal response to this challenge. He committed himself to the proposition that the party should first make sure that its own house was in order before dealing with the discontent outside its walls. In keeping with his wishes, the congress adopted two resolutions on party unity. The first resolution explicitly banned all forms of "factionalism" within the party's ranks and ordered the dissolution of any groups with independent platforms. In a particularly controversial section, which Lenin asked to be temporarily withheld from publication, the resolution authorized the Central Committee to expel violators from their positions and, in cases it deemed extreme, to remove them from the party. In any organization, the threat of exclusion is disquieting. But, as we have seen, membership in the Bolshevik party was not like belonging to a book club or a debating team. Given the party faithful's intense devotion, expulsion could be psychologically devastating. The second resolution was more specific. It condemned the Workers' Opposition and, to a lesser extent, the Democratic Centralists for purportedly propagating anarchist and syndicalist deviations.

Strictly speaking, the ideas behind the congress's measures were not new. None of the Bolshevik leaders seriously contested the sanctity of party unity. However, Lenin's identification of the party's shortcomings as a contributing factor to the country's ills was as close as he would ever come to describing what a properly functioning communist party should look like once it held power. To this end, he informed the congress that the Bolsheviks were entering new territory. In the past, he maintained, the party could readily identify the class enemy. Yet, the events in Petrograd and Kronstadt demonstrated that its foes had developed more devious ways of waging their attacks. Rather than exposing themselves to full view, as they had done during the Civil War, they were disguising "themselves as communists and even as the most left-wing communists, solely for the purpose of weakening and destroying the bulwark of the proletarian revolution in Russia." Due to this new form of battle, Lenin stressed, the party needed to take forceful steps to regulate the boundaries of disagreement among its members. If it failed to do this, he explained, its enemies would work their way into factional groupings, exploit their cleavages, and then use these footholds to advance their counterrevolutionary objectives.[11]

Looking ahead to the 1930s, we know that Stalin would take advantage of Lenin's call for vigilance to justify a reign of terror against his party and the broader Soviet population. However, it would be hard to prove that Lenin intended to go as far as Stalin. In my view, his primary goal was to provide the regime with a much-needed opportunity to step back from its internal quarrels. Two months after the Tenth Congress, on August 28, 1921, Lenin candidly stated in an article in *Pravda* that the proletariat needed a "respite" to recuperate from the strains it had incurred on the road to political and military victory. Its next challenge, he suggested, would be on the economic front. It was called to build large-scale industry and "electrify" a country that had only recently broken through the bonds of feudalism and was still held back by a peasant-based economy. In the face of these weighty challenges, the party needed to reconcile itself to the fact that progress toward socialism would be slower than expected. Citing the positive outcome of the Brest-Litovsk treaty that had generated so much conflict in the party, Lenin advised the regime to approach its task "dispassionately, cautiously, and prudently."[12]

Lenin's call for sobriety made sense, especially in view of the fact that the expected proletarian revolution in Europe had stalled. However, I believe it is equally important to underscore what he did not say. He did not assert that the party's commitment to revolution had changed. To the contrary, to ensure that the proletariat's forward march proceeded without interruption, he insisted that its vanguard wage battle against anyone who would hinder its advance. This imperative meant constantly being watchful for the intrigues of an enemy that, in Lenin's estimation, was "still far stronger than we are."[13] Accordingly, when Lenin and other leaders, such as Bukharin, turned to the business of governance, they pursued two potentially contradictory strategies simultaneously. On the one hand, they committed themselves squarely to an economic recovery program, the New Economic Policy (NEP). On the other hand, they counterbalanced this strategy with a campaign to create a national party organization that could effectively defend their founding ideals.

A Sober Policy, an Ascendant Party Organization

The thinking behind the NEP could not have been more straightforward. Its proponents' goal was to initiate a retreat from the most extreme economic policies of War Communism. Up to the Tenth Party Congress, the Bolsheviks had been wedded to the principle that growth should begin in the cities and human and material resources should be concentrated on heavy industry. Accordingly, the regime accorded little more than secondary significance to the development of the countryside. It treated peasant farmers as no more than providers of foodstuffs and raw materials, and otherwise left them to fend for themselves in desperate conditions. However, as the Bolsheviks discovered to their horror in catastrophes like the Volga famine, one could not ignore the realities of a peasant-based economy. If one deprived the peasantry of the incentive to produce surplus goods, it would simply produce for personal consumption. And if the state took away these goods, it would starve. Furthermore, the regime's extractive policies confirmed the peasantry's long-held conviction that the Bolsheviks would never have their interests at heart.

Accordingly, one of the regime's first steps in implementing the NEP was to address the imbalance between town and countryside by revising tax policies, allowing peasants to sell goods on semiopen markets, and reducing the mandatory delivery of grain and livestock to the cities. In the same way, while the regime jealously guarded its monopoly of the "commanding heights" of large industries, the railways, banks, and foreign trade, it returned small enterprises and shops to private hands. It also encouraged entrepreneurs and merchants to produce and sell goods for their personal enrichment. Under these more relaxed policies, production in numerous sectors of the economy gradually returned to prewar levels, markets expanded, and the currency was stabilized.

These policies did not sit well with those Bolsheviks who expected the party to emphasize its revolutionary side. From its upper echelons down to its lower-level cadres, many members were repulsed by the idea that their leaders, including Lenin himself, would accept even a temporary accommodation with an apparently bourgeois economic system. They had grave reservations about the appeal to the peasantry's pecuniary motivations. In their view, only the better-off peasants, the so-called kulaks, would benefit from the NEP, while poorer peasants would be left to struggle as they had in the past. Moreover, they were convinced that the NEP would undermine socialism's egalitarian values. Many saw their fears confirmed in the emergence of a class of capitalist profiteers, or NEPmen, who reaped enormous profits by selling scarce goods in open markets.

As we shall see, these concerns would soon provide the fuel for fierce battles within the Politburo about the regime's priorities. Notwithstanding these conflicts, the critics were wrong in arguing that the NEP's architects had lost sight of the party's importance. To the contrary, figures like Bukharin were determined to ensure that the communist party would play the leading role in meeting the demand for economic growth. To this end, they turned their attention to the task of building the robust organization that Stalin would soon glorify as the cornerstone of Leninism.

It may have surprised some party members that the momentum of this campaign would swing toward the Central Committee Secretariat. This body was easily the least scintillating of the leadership organs because of its occupation with the nitty-gritty aspects of party management. Nonetheless, as the demands on party officials escalated, the need grew to exercise these competences more efficiently. With only eight full and candidate members in 1921, the Politburo was too small to attend to this business. It was overwhelmed by the immense responsibility that the Bolsheviks' desire for centralized control imposed upon it. Likewise, the ongoing battles within the forty-member Central Committee made it a cumbersome forum for dealing with minutiae.[14] As a result, the Secretariat as well as the Orgburo became the administrative crossroads at which multiple dimensions of the party's expansion were addressed. These functions ranged from the entire appointment process and the extension of control over local party organizations to the collection of records, the distribution of propaganda, and the preparation of meetings.

Once again, the senior Bolsheviks' tentativeness showed through. They took until 1922 to create a formal position within the Secretariat, the general secretaryship, to coordinate the body's functions and organize its bourgeoning staff. It was probably for this reason that Lenin himself chose Stalin, a man who had a reputation for being a skilled manager and a voice of moderation, to assume the post. Under Stalin's leadership, the Secretariat quickly emerged from the shadows. As the sole figure to have a position in all four of the party's decision-making bodies—the Politburo, Central Committee, Orgburo, and Secretariat—Stalin was well placed to make sweeping appointments and to take control of party business at every level of its administrative apparatus. In one of his first victories, he successfully asserted the Secretariat's power over the Central Control Commission, taking advantage of the latter body's responsibility to discipline purportedly wayward members who were judged guilty of corruption and the abuse of power.

In 1923, complementing the increased attention to the Secretariat, the Politburo established a class of administrative officials, the *nomenklatura*, which would eventually extend the party's reach into every sphere of Soviet society. Under this system, the Central Committee empowered party committees to review the performance of its representatives and to make appointments or recommend dismissals at every level of the hierarchy. Initially, the leadership focused on party personnel, but it soon expanded this review process to include the entire Sovnarkom apparatus. Predictably, state officials rebelled against what they regarded as the party's unwarranted intrusion in their affairs. But once put into effect, the idea of the party's entitlement to scrutinize the performance of state organizations went a long way toward settling unresolved questions about its authority. One issue involved the Central Committee's right to make appointments in a top-down fashion rather than having to wait for local agencies to act (it could); another was about the need to counterbalance the reliance upon technical expertise with ideological oversight (it was necessary).

Not every battle was quickly or definitively resolved. Party officials encountered their most intense opposition in seeking to exercise control over the armed forces and the security organs. Military commanders objected to the idea that party organs, and particularly local party officials, would question their expertise. The security organs were even more defiant. Given the monopoly on the domestic use of force held by the People's Commissariat for Internal Affairs (NKVD), it was natural that party officials would want to subject its activities to direct supervision. Yet, this issue was never fully resolved. Due to a consensus within the leadership that even party representatives should be subject to external review, the ministry maintained a significant and, it would later turn out under Stalin's control, ultimately horrific degree of autonomy.

As the party's apparatus of control was extended, the *nomenklatura* system proved to be much more than a set of rules. To have one's name associated with a post that was deemed of central importance to the party, of which there were 5,562 positions in 1923 (out of roughly 380,000 party members), was quite like what Lenin had to offer his followers in the first decades of the century.[15] This was the satisfaction of belonging to an elite club. Under the party's aegis, one held a privileged role in the construction of a new society. Stalin increasingly used this idea to co-opt Sovnarkom officials by offering them privileged positions in the party. Accordingly, his personal power over the state apparatus, and especially the security police, grew.

Finally, the regime took deliberate steps to affirm the party's Marxist credentials by changing its membership qualifications. To offset the appointment of skilled professionals under the NEP, as well as the frequent purges of unqualified or supposedly disloyal members, it undertook a mammoth recruitment campaign to increase the representation of workers and peasants in the party's ranks. Coming just after Lenin's death, this drive, the Lenin Enrollment, represented a notable return to the mythology of the proletarian roots of the Revolution. Stalin dedicated his *Foundations of Leninism* to the campaign and declared that the hundreds of thousands of names that were added to the party's rolls were evidence of the "intangible moral threads which connect the party with the non-party masses."[16] As general secretary, he had reason to be pleased. During this drive alone, the party more than doubled its size and many of its new members became his clients and devotees.[17]

As in many instances of Bolshevik mythology, not all aspects of the Lenin Enrollment were quite what they seemed. To meet its enrollment targets, the party was forced to lower its standards and accept recruits with little formal education. Many of its new cadres had no exposure to Marxist ideology. Moreover, this was hardly the proletariat Marx and Engels had envisioned. Although some of the recruits could claim to have begun their working lives in factories and shipyards, most were already holding positions in the state bureaucracy. In comparison, the party's efforts to recruit new members from the countryside were conspicuously unsuccessful.

Yet, as always, the appearance of success was more important than the facts on the ground. If anyone questioned the Bolsheviks' commitment to their founding principles, they could argue that these measures were proof that they were committed to incorporating all social strata into their ranks. Ideally, these efforts should have been enough to bring the party elite together. Nonetheless, it was far from self-evident how this meeting of minds among the party's most prominent members was to occur.

THE LEADERSHIP DIVIDES

From a rational standpoint, it was in the Bolsheviks' collective interest that the myriad personalities who comprised their inner circle would subordinate their particular passions and commitments to the cause of party unity. Nonetheless, as I have emphasized in the cases of other communist parties, a willingness to compromise is not a common characteristic of revolutionaries. Despite the leadership's attentiveness to its rank-and-file membership, this focus had little effect on the arena of decision making where change was required the most. Until the last years of the 1920s, the key posts in the Politburo and the Central Committee, as well as the commissariats, were held by the same individuals who had joined the movement in the months and years before October 1917. In contrast to the majority of the party's new members, who were young and primarily focused on the demands of building a new political and social order, these "old Bolsheviks" could justify their continuing grip on the reins of power by harkening back to conspiratorial activities against the tsarist autocracy and struggles in exile. Their claims to be authentic representatives of the Revolution made each of them determined to ensure that their views were taken into account. It also meant that their desire to work together on a common cause was constantly tested.

On May 25, 1922, a single event confirmed the fragility of this party consensus. Lenin suffered, but did not succumb to, the first of several strokes that would eventually claim his life. Had he died immediately, it is conceivable that the event would have thrown the regime into turmoil because of the tensions within its upper echelon. With the loss of his larger-than-life presence, there would have been little to hold his colleagues' fragile egos and combative instincts in check. Instead, over a period of one and a half years during which he intermittently penned articles and interjected his voice into internal debates, Lenin provided them with an interlude for staking out their respective positions and preparing for battle.

The immediate cause for discord was the NEP. In 1923, two years after Lenin gave his blessing to the policy, the NEP was threatened by an unanticipated consequence of its success. The regime's decision to allow peasants to share in the profits of their labor was a boon to agricultural production. Yet rather than promoting a healthy balance of trade between town and countryside, as its planners had envisioned, it generated a price crisis, which Trotsky colorfully likened to the diverging blades of a scissors. Contrary to expectations, the recovery of the industrial sectors of the economy proved to be much slower than in agriculture. As a result, peasant farmers were put in the invidious position of having to sell their grain surpluses while the prices for manufactured goods soared. Finding themselves unable to purchase consumer products to improve their lives and too poor to live off their sales, many peasants retreated into subsistence farming and hoarded their grain.

The regime temporarily resolved this crisis within a year by cutting the staffs of inefficient industries and regulating prices. Nonetheless, this setback provided the NEP's critics with ammunition for spreading doubts about the policy's consistency with Bolshevik principles. On October 26, 1923, forty-six party notables signed a letter to the Politburo that excoriated the leadership for supporting the NEP. The critics pointed to the "scissors crisis" as proof that the policy was leading the Soviet Union toward catastrophe. They also attributed the failure to the party's degeneration into an apparatus of specialists and functionaries. These bureaucrats, they argued, were defacing party traditions by deliberately walling themselves off from the masses.

The outbreak of renewed incidents of industrial unrest at this time, including wildcat strikes in Moscow and Petrograd, added to the Politburo's troubles. Although the NEP's supporters initially dismissed the protests as evidence of factionalist tendencies, Zinoviev and Stalin worked out a compromise. In a resolution passed at a joint meeting of the Politburo and the Central Control Commission, the two sides agreed to continue the NEP while also acknowledging that the regime could have done a better job explaining to its rank and file why the policy was not a capitulation to capitalism. The recognition of these mistakes, the resolution affirmed, had nothing to do with calling into question the party's competence. It merely demonstrated that its leaders needed to be more open to the views of all of its members. The sole constraint upon the NEP was that there could be no toleration of factional groups that threatened the dictatorship of the proletariat.[18]

Before the Tenth Party Congress, this statement would have been little more than a recapitulation of the standard argument about the principle of democratic centralism: party members were entitled to express their personal views in formulating policy, but once a decision was made, they were obliged to support it. Nonetheless, in the wake of the promulgation of the "ban on factions," the persisting debate over the NEP's revolutionary credentials suggested that one could interpret the idea of party discipline in a much more restrictive way. Regardless of Lenin's original intentions, once the party's leaders decided that there was such an entity as a faction and that its existence contradicted the norm of party leadership, they could argue that they were no longer bound to consider this group's views. Indeed, one could even maintain that it was a violation of the principle of party unity to do so.

Trotsky took the lead in calling attention to the destructive impact of this way of thinking on the original idea of intraparty behavior. In an open letter to the party that appeared in *Pravda* on December 8 and 10, 1923, he demanded that the Politburo adopt a "new course" to return the organization to its revolutionary foundations. To this end, he summoned the classic defense of the party member's right to voice his or her opinions in a community of equals. Beginning with an attack on the mushrooming size of Stalin's Central Committee staff, he berated his colleagues for using the need of centralized administration as an excuse for stifling individual initiative.[19] This practice, Trotsky underscored, had sapped the party's spirit. Conversely, the way to overcome the problem was to return to the idea that each member could contribute to the collective good. "A party is a party," Trotsky emphasized. "We can make stringent demands upon those who want to enter and stay in it, but once they are members, they participate most actively by that fact, in all the work of the party." The party member was not only owed this privilege. This freedom, Trotsky added, was essential to overcome the country's domestic and international trials, including the failures of the NEP and the "retardation" of the world revolution.[20]

Trotsky sought to curry support for his views by offering an all-too-familiar but no less alluring picture of the benefits of his conception of party membership. To advance the revolution, he stated, one required a special type of person. "A Bolshevik is not only a disciplined man," he explained. "He is a man who in each case and on each question forges a firm opinion of his own and defends it completely and independently." Naturally, Trotsky emphasized that this individual would abhor any step that could lead to the erosion of party unity. To keep the revolutionary spirit alive, it was essential to raise questions about a majority view "a second, a third, and a tenth time, if need be" to keep the party vibrant and alive.

This was not the first time Trotsky had accused his comrades of being insufficiently open to criticism. But, given the potentially incendiary character of these remarks, he might have chosen to keep any further attacks within the confines of the Politburo. This was not to be. Trotsky publicly insisted that the first step in his "new course" should be to purge the party's upper ranks of "mummified bureaucrats" who "brandished the thunderbolts of penalties" against their critics. Adding fuel to the fire, he recommended that these representatives of the "old guard" should be systematically replaced by younger communists. They would have fresh perspectives to keep the revolutionary flame alight.[21]

Trotsky's attack was a remarkable display of confidence coming from an individual who was increasingly on the margins of the Politburo. But the Politburo refused to be cowed. In a five-part article that appeared in *Pravda* between December 28, 1923, and January 4, 1924, and was undoubtedly authored by Bukharin, the paper's editorial board maintained that Trotsky was in fact guilty of the sin of factionalism. His aim, the article asserted, was to devise a "full-blown, platform-shaped political statement" to take advantage of the naïveté and lack of experience of its younger members. Thus, to ensure a truly democratic spirit within the party, it was self-evident that the most advanced members of the organization should take charge of its activities. At the current moment, there could be no doubt about who was best suited to lead. "The old Bolshevik guard," the article advised, "is the most precious capital of our party, and that is why this old guard must lead the young generation."[22]

Pravda's statement was a sign that open debate about the party's purposes was still possible. One communist (Trotsky) was appealing to traditional party values in making the case for a younger leadership. The other (Bukharin) was making the case for the old Bolshevik leadership by defending new policies. Despite the actors' choice of audiences, their debate made sense in terms of the contending, but equally understandable, justifications of party rule in the early 1920s. Still, there is little solace to be found in being true to history. It would not take long before both positions were replaced by an entirely new approach to the party.

Stalin Arrives

This altercation and many other clashes within the Politburo were held in check as long as Lenin was alive. His passing in 1924 changed everything. The loss of the cohesive force that held the contending egos and passions in check unleashed a struggle that could not be contained by the invocation of abstract principles. Each of Lenin's successors faced the possibility that a gain for a comrade in battle could result in a loss of both personal prestige and the power to influence the country's course.

The first act in this drama was all about Trotsky. Recognizing that he was losing his battle but unwilling to concede defeat, he initially sought to allay his colleagues' apprehensions by assuring them of his intention to abide by the collective will. At the Thirteenth Party Congress in May 1924, he insisted, in an oft-quoted speech, that he would not oppose the party's decisions because "the party in the last analysis is always right." He added: "We can only be right with and through the party for history has not created other ways for the realization of what is right."[23]

Trotsky must have had an ideal conception of the party in mind, since he soon showed that he had no intention of jettisoning his understanding of the Revolution. In November, he indicated that he was unwilling to wait for his rivals to come to their senses. Under the pretext of writing a new history of the October Revolution, he advised his readers in an essay on "The Lessons of October" that the regime's greatest error had been to assume that its work was done once it was in power. The opposite was true. The lesson that Trotsky derived from the events of October 1917 was that the party should constantly strive to prove its worth to the proletariat. Otherwise, it would be no better than the former ruling class. Lest his colleagues have any doubt that his message was directed at them, Trotsky turned to the example of Germany's failed revolution. He likened the Communist Party of Germany's (KPD) weaknesses to the behavior of those Bolsheviks—an unmistakable reference to Zinoviev, Kamenev, and Stalin—who had either doubted Lenin's call for action in 1917 or opposed it outright. Compounding the impact of the barb, Trotsky added that one could expect to see further manifestations of this "irresolute, skeptical, conciliationist, capitulatory, in short, Menshevik" behavior in the future.[24]

These attacks provided the context within which the normally left-leaning Zinoviev and Kamenev and the centrist Stalin shed their ideological differences and came together to oppose a common foe. They excoriated Trotsky for distorting party history and accused him of formulating a new doctrine—Trotskyism. In Kamenev's depiction, Trotsky was guilty of nothing less than aspiring to "improve" Leninism. Even if he did not intend to divide the party, Kamenev continued, his criticisms would allow petit-bourgeois elements to impede its work and undermine its authority.[25] In like fashion, Stalin condemned Trotsky for casting doubt on the party's monolithic character.[26] Against this powerful alliance of convenience, Trotsky was helpless. On December 17, 1924, his detractors condemned him for threatening to "de-Bolshevize" the party and forced him to relinquish his remaining post in the

Sovnarkom. The penalty could have been worse. As events were to show a decade later, even the hint that someone was seeking to advance an alternative to the official doctrine of Leninism—a definition that Stalin happened to have devised—would have fatal consequences. Although Trotsky retained his influential seat on the Politburo, his political defeat marked a critical juncture. In the shadow of the ban on factions, it demonstrated that not even the most distinguished Bolsheviks were immune to punishment.

The second act in the Bolshevik crisis of the 1920s proved to be a confirmation of Lenin's reasoning at the Tenth Party Congress. A divided party could not live up to its mission. The effect of Trotsky's defeat was almost predictable. Without a mutual foe to bind them together, there was less to prevent Zinoviev and Kamenev, on the one hand, and Stalin and his ally, Bukharin, on the other, from voicing their long-standing differences and going to battle. As ever, the rivals paid tribute to the principle that party unity was a fundamental good, but each side was determined to ensure that it would be in the position to decide the preferred form of this united stand.

By 1925, Stalin was a formidable adversary. Drawing upon the Secretariat's powers of appointment and the resources of the Central Control Commission, he had successfully built an enormous, clientelist network. Tens of thousands of party members were able to rise to higher positions thanks to his beneficence, and they remained comfortably dependent upon his patronage. Stalin also demonstrated his skill in whittling away at his rivals' positions. In particular, he went after Zinoviev, removing one of the latter's key supporters in his stronghold in Leningrad (Petrograd's name after Lenin's death) and inserting himself into the routine business of the Comintern of which Zinoviev was president. Yet Zinoviev struck back. He mobilized the Leningrad party apparatus against its distant general secretary by appealing to the city's traditional disdain for the quality of leadership in Moscow. After all, Leningrad was the sacred home of the Revolution.

This infighting soon evolved into a storm of political hyperbole in which no form of accommodation was possible. The Left Bolsheviks sought control of the ideological heights. They maintained that their adversaries had abandoned Marxism and showed themselves to be incapable of understanding events in terms of class analysis. The party's support for the NEP was proof that it was no longer in sync with the needs of the working class or the international proletariat. Far from being a Leninist organization, they stressed, like Trotsky before them, that it was degenerating into a purely bureaucratic institution. In response, the Politburo majority countered that its opponents were defaming the achievements of the Revolution. In its portrayal, the leftists' criticisms of the NEP showed that they had no confidence in the power of the proletariat and were no longer prepared to abide by Leninist norms of discipline. Bukharin accused his rivals of dallying with the dangerous "idea of *two parties*."[27]

By the party's Fourteenth Congress on December 18–31, 1925, these battles over both power and policy converged in a form that neither side professed to desire: the inclusion of both majority and minority reports to the Central Committee. It also led to the erosion of the Left's power. The minority platform, which called attention to the deficiencies of the NEP and made the case for greater state investment in the socialized sectors of the economy, was easily outvoted by the majority. Then, Stalin hastened to cripple his opponents. With the assistance of his deputy, Vyacheslav Molotov, he took a mere three weeks to wrest control of the Leningrad party organization from Zinoviev. Showing that Trotsky's demotion was only a prelude of things to come, he arranged for Kamenev to lose his posts in the Sovnarkom and the Moscow Soviet. By fall 1927, the Left's defeat was a foregone conclusion.

REVOLUTION FROM ABOVE

Stalin's victory amounted to much more than his successful consolidation of power. It allowed him to make the case for a radical approach to the party's role that broke with those of his rivals. Whereas Trotsky was prepared to subject the party's decisions to criticism in every way in order to maintain the purity of its revolutionary credentials, and Bukharin advocated an accommodating style of leadership in order to prevent the revolution from spinning out of control, Stalin combined elements of both positions into an entirely new approach. Balancing Trotsky's convictions about an ongoing revolutionary struggle against the purported enemies of socialism with Bukharin's focus on the dangers of instability, Stalin embraced the idea of using the party to impose a revolution strictly from above.

One can detect the early signs of Stalin's novel synthesis in a concept that he first articulated in 1924: "socialism in one country." He began with the premise that Russia could no longer afford to wait for a successful proletarian uprising in the West. To survive the continuing threats from its enemies at home and abroad, he emphasized that it was necessary for the party to push ahead in laying the foundations of socialism on its own soil. This was a simple argument that Stalin liberally borrowed from his peers, including Bukharin. But it was based on an intriguing blend of both the old and the new. The old was the recognition of the exceptional character of the Russian Revolution. Like Lenin before him, Stalin was merely restating the implications of this fact. By virtue of coming first in the Marxist progression of history, the Bolsheviks had incurred a holy obligation to keep the spark of revolution alive. The "*final* victory of socialism," Stalin emphasized, would still require the combined triumphs of multiple communist parties. Yet, there was a new element in his argument that was not present in Lenin's thinking. In his depiction, the "vast Soviet country," as he put it, was already "by its very existence, revolutionizing the whole world." Indeed, Stalin emphasized, the Bolshevik experience had become the "precondition" for this revolution, one from which the more industrialized world had much to learn.[28]

This was a bold statement. Still, as we have seen in chapter 4, it had a basis in fact. The Western communists had failed to sell themselves to their dubious populations. The last European uprising of note took place in 1923, when hundreds of thousands of factory workers and miners shut down the industrial Ruhr Valley region. In response, the Comintern issued an urgent call for a national insurrection. Yet, when the KPD rushed into action, its luck was no better than it had been in 1919 and 1921. It failed to muster the support it needed from the masses on the street to sustain the rebellion.

In fact, the Bolsheviks were already acting on the idea that their country's revolution would remain unique for some time. In a signal that they were settling in for the long haul, the Congress of Soviets formally adopted the Constitution of the Union of Soviet Socialist Republics (USSR), on January 13, 1924, creating a new federal state composed of Russia, Byelorussia, Transcaucasia, and Ukraine. The birth of this new entity, the Soviet Union, was denoted by all of the conventions of a fully functioning state—the power to conclude treaties, to establish a uniform monetary system, and to approve budgets.

The deeper and more far-reaching implications of the doctrine of socialism in one country were forced into the open by the march of events. Between 1926 and 1928, a confluence of domestic and international developments precipitated a final split within the party leadership. In winter 1927, the fragile consensus over the NEP collapsed when a grain procurement crisis erupted over a shortage of deliveries to the cities. The regime swiftly introduced emergency measures to coerce peasants to increase their grain transfers. Of greater consequence, however, was Stalin's decision to use this crisis to turn against his ally, Bukharin. After an impromptu inspection tour of Siberia in which he threatened local officials with reprisals if they failed to intensify their pressure on the peasantry, Stalin declared that the country had entered a more arduous phase of the class struggle. It was necessary to combat the criminal actions of the wealthy peasants, the kulaks, who were bent upon restoring capitalism in the countryside.

For many in the party elite, Stalin's call for renewed militancy seemed to be justified by a number of other developments, some real, others imagined. In 1928, the Joint State Political Directorate, or security police, claimed to discover a counterrevolutionary plot by anticommunist engineers in the Shakhty mines of the Donets Basin. Stalin quickly pronounced the alleged conspiracy to be proof of an insufficiently vigilant party. Simultaneously, the leadership was wrestling with growing fears of encirclement by hostile capitalist powers. In 1926, Poland's government fell to a military coup led by an anti-Russian general, Józef Piłsudski; in 1927, China's Nationalist leader, Chiang Kai-shek, massacred tens of thousands of communists in Shanghai. By the summer, this sense of national vulnerability culminated in a war scare, when officials convinced themselves that Great Britain was planning a military offensive against the USSR. In a speech before party activists in April 1928, Stalin announced that the precarious equilibrium between "the two worlds, the two antipodes, the world of the soviets and the world of capitalism" was on the verge of exploding.[29]

In this tense atmosphere, the Bolshevik leadership came to a breach. When the party notables debated the NEP's future, they showed that it was possible to espouse radically different, and even opposed, conceptions of socialism in one country. Stalin was on one side. Underscoring the supposed lessons of the grain crisis, he argued that the government should strike back against the kulaks and speculators who had brought hunger to the people. Rather than continuing to make concessions to the peasantry, the party of the working class needed to renew its militant focus, build collective and state farms, and give priority to industrial production.[30] Taking the opposite side, Bukharin pleaded for caution lest the peasants turn their backs on the cities. The sensible approach, he argued, was to rescind the emergency measures and acknowledge that the conversion of the economic and social structures into socialism would be long in duration.[31]

Behind the scenes, the power of conviction had already given way to the struggle for survival. On the day before the plenum ended, Bukharin arranged for a clandestine meeting with Kamenev at which he proposed, incredibly in light of past animosities, that they work with Zinoviev to remove Stalin from the Politburo. If they failed to unite their forces, Bukharin emphasized, Stalin would surely return the country to War Communism and disaster.[32] This meeting was illuminating because it demonstrated that the comradely bonds of Bolshevik culture were still strong enough that bitter adversaries could trust each other to forge an alliance against a formidable opponent. The meeting was also the last occasion for two prominent participants in the October Revolution to act without significant constraints. In the unusual fraternity in which the most senior party members lived, the Politburo briefly reinstated Kamenev's and Zinoviev's party membership and Bukharin brought his opposition to the regime's impending shift of direction into the open. Although he did not address Stalin by name—he used Trotsky's name instead—Bukharin accused his foe of ignoring the complex balance between agricultural and industrial production and claimed that his policies would lead to a "super-centralization" of the economy.[33] This warning failed. On February 9–10, 1929, the Politburo invented a new threat to party unity, the "Bukharin faction"; on November 17, the majority removed Bukharin from his post.

Unlike Bukharin, Stalin had no reservations about calling his opponent by name. His defense of the Politburo's decision went beyond listing his adversary's sins to justifying a confrontational posture that would color the party's identity for the next quarter of a century. He accused Bukharin of misrepresenting the Revolution. His adversary had made the fundamental error, Stalin declared in April 1929, of assuming that capitalism, whether it be found in the cities or the countryside, could grow peacefully into socialism. The harsh reality, Stalin insisted, was that the closer one came to realizing socialism, the more the exploiting classes would fight back. This desperate fight for survival was what the wrecking activities of the bourgeois intellectuals in the Shakhty affair were all about; this was why the kulaks were capable of committing any crime to protect their property. What, Stalin inquired, should the party do to subdue these dying classes? Here, Stalin invoked the fiery images of class war. A truly revolutionary party was called to inspire the working class and the exploited masses to "increase their fighting capacity and develop their mobilized preparedness for the fight against capitalist elements in town and countryside, for the fight against the resisting class enemies."[34]

This strident rhetoric was reminiscent of the party's militant culture under War Communism. Nevertheless, it was not a simple return to the recent past. Whereas War Communism was fueled by a combination of desperation and missionary passion, Stalin and a growing number of Politburo members were inspired by the belief that socialism could be constructed from above. The initial expression of this idea had been presented during the unveiling of the USSR's First Five-Year Plan in May 1927. The plan's goals were incomplete and fuzzy on details, but demonstrably aggressive and grandiose. Its architects promised to spur industrial growth by introducing new technologies and machinery and by concentrating resources on heavy industrial sectors, such as coal mining and steel production. Not surprisingly, they began by promptly demolishing the defining institutions of the NEP, shutting down private trade and small-scale manufacturing, and reining in independent entrepreneurs. Yet the plan went beyond a straightforward focus on accelerating the transition to socialism. As the regime showed by undertaking enormous construction projects, such as the building of the steel-fabricating behemoth, the city of Magnitogorsk, and the Chelyabinsk tractor factory, Stalin and his colleagues were intent upon making a vivid point to their adversaries, both at home and abroad. If the Soviet Union's citizens showed the will and dedication, a centrally planned, socialist economy was a credible alternative to any system the bourgeoisie had to offer.

To serve this purpose, Stalin took advantage of the hundreds of thousands of new party members to whom the Secretariat had given its stamp of approval in the 1920s. In his first revolutionary act, he made them his army and declared war on the peasantry. In November 1929, the regime followed through on his ambition to reorganize the economy of the countryside and supply grain and other edible goods to the cities by forcing the kulaks to give up their private landholdings and enter large-scale state and collective farms. Given the absence of significant party representation in rural areas, party officials, Komsomol (party youth league) members, and shock workers descended upon these regions like the Russian populists in the 1860s and 1870s, intending to convince peasants that it was in their interest to pool their land and machinery into large farms. Everywhere they met fierce opposition. Well-off and poor peasants alike fought to retain their property and preserve the structures of communal governance. Far from being as easily managed as their zealous instigators had assumed, these confrontations between town and countryside were so destructive to the landed economy that even Stalin was persuaded in 1930, albeit for a brief period, to relax the campaign.

Nonetheless, collectivization, like the industrialization drive, was about something more fundamental than bringing a new economic program to the peasantry. The deployment of cadres to the countryside was about the education of a revolutionary vanguard in its duties. In the person of the kulak, Stalin and his confederates found a symbol of the prerevolutionary order that could be painted in as reprehensible a fashion as Marx and Engels had done with the urban capitalist. Conveniently, this black-and-white portrayal had a way of proving itself. When peasants resisted the efforts to expropriate their land, the regime described their actions as proof that the class struggle between an oppressive minority and the oppressed majority was as real as ever. True to his ideological ambitions and his desire for personal gain, Stalin argued that the conflict was actually getting worse. Thus, it was not only important to deprive individual kulaks of their property; it was essential, as Stalin chillingly told his followers, to "liquidate the kulaks as a class."[35]

This manufactured version of the class struggle provided the occasion for the emergence of a phenomenon not seen since Lenin's passing. This was the idea that one person, Stalin, and the party were inseparable. On December 21, 1929, Stalin's colleagues organized a nationwide celebration of his fiftieth birthday. They lauded him as Lenin's rightful successor and the guarantor of their party's sacred course. Although Lenin had consistently resisted such encomia, his successor was happy to oblige. In a bizarre tribute, he intimated that the party was his mother. All of his accomplishments, Stalin stressed, were due to the "party which bore me and reared me in its own likeness." He would continue to sacrifice everything, he promised, for the cause of world communism, "all my strength, all my ability, and if need be, all my blood, drop by drop."[36] This was not the first time these words had been uttered. Since 1924, Stalin had made sure that such high praise was a routine feature in Lenin's hagiography. In this case, the telling difference was that Stalin was still alive.

"The Complete Victory of Leninism"

If one were to take Stalin's public pronouncements at face value, the launching of the revolution from above should have been an occasion for satisfaction for the party faithful. Their organization had evolved from an assortment of independently minded individuals working their way toward the creation of a coherent organization in the early 1920s to a point at the turn of the 1930s at which the contests over its priorities had seemingly been resolved. In fact, on January 28, 1934, four years and a month after the first of many birthday celebrations, Stalin informed the delegates to the Seventeenth Party Congress, the so-called Congress of Victors, that their dreams had come true. Under the "flag of the complete victory of Leninism," their policy of accelerated industrialization had triumphed. Collectivization had succeeded. A majority of the counterrevolutionary groups had been smashed. "Everyone sees," Stalin boasted, "that the line of the party has triumphed." Who, he inquired, could doubt that it was possible to build socialism in one country?[37] The Congress of Soviets' declaration of the achievement of socialism in 1936 formally put this question to rest.

Provocatively, most of the "victors" who were (very temporarily) allowed to enjoy the privilege of basking in Stalin's proclamation of glory were old Bolsheviks. Over 80 percent of the delegates to the Congress had become members of the party before 1921. Many of them had been active before 1917 and could remember the factional debates within the Russian Social Democratic Labor Party. Moreover, in a seeming testimony to comradely collegiality, Stalin invited his senior rivals, including Zinoviev, Kamenev, and Bukharin, to pay tribute to their generation's accomplishments. After showing sufficient contrition for their sins, they joined the general secretary in affirming the USSR's advance toward socialism.

However, to claim at this juncture that the party was victorious was sheer braggadocio. Although the regime could take satisfaction in the belching smokestacks of new factories and a creeping improvement in agricultural production, the Soviet Union was only beginning to sort out the myriad problems that it had created for itself. In the cities, the abandonment of the NEP meant that the entire system for providing goods and services had to be rebuilt. Following the elimination of private trade and production, urban dwellers faced renewed conditions of scarcity, shortages of basic commodities, food rationing, and depreciating wages. A mass influx of peasants in the wake of collectivization made the situation worse. In a mere four years, the cities' populations grew by 38 percent. In a manner that would haunt Soviet policymakers until their country's dissolution more than a half century later, the regime's obsession with centralization and gigantic industrial projects gave birth to an economy that was suffused with inefficiencies, shortages, and failed promises.

These trials paled in comparison with the destruction of ordinary life in the countryside. After Stalin reintroduced collectivization in full force, wide swaths of the USSR were devastated by famine. In Ukraine, the largest grain-producing territory in the USSR, this tragedy unfolded in two stages. In the first, the worst excesses of the original collectivization drive were exceeded. Officials imposed impossible procurement quotas on farmers and implemented draconian punishments for underperformance. Just as before, peasants fought back. But this time, Stalin's response was different. He moved from war to annihilation. The horrific consequences of this second stage were not the result of excessive zeal or miscalculation. Ignoring explicit warnings from his deputies that further action would lead to famine, Stalin declared the peasantry guilty of anti-Soviet crimes and "wrecking" and stripped the countryside of the most elementary means of subsistence. With no way to escape the resulting catastrophe, peasants were reduced to eating bark and rotting carcasses; thousands of villages disappeared. From 1932 to 1933, up to 4.5 million people died from starvation and disease, more than 15 percent of Ukraine's population.[38]

There is a final reason why the old Bolsheviks should have tempered their enthusiasm. Stalin had already begun to redefine the party's role in a way that significantly modified the original Marxist understanding of revolution. In a passionate speech before a meeting of industrial managers in 1931, he announced that the party's responsibility was not limited to overthrowing the bourgeoisie. It was obliged to overcome centuries of Russian backwardness. This was not the first time, Stalin argued, that the Russian people had suffered at the hands of stronger powers. Long before the proletariat's subjugation to capitalist exploitation, its predecessors had been beaten by legions of enemies—Mongol khans, Turkish beys, and Japanese barons. As a result, in Stalin's reasoning, the party had a duty to the working class of the world to ensure that the "socialist fatherland," as he called it, would no longer be dragged down by its weaknesses. "We are fifty or a hundred years behind the advanced countries," Stalin advised. "We must make good this distance in ten years," or, he added, "we shall go under."[39]

It seems not to have bothered Stalin that previous generations of communists had consistently maintained that the proletariat had no fatherland. Yet, it mattered a great deal for his understanding of the kind of party that was required to serve this purpose. One could assume from

Stalin's words that its members would be filled with passion and show "Bolshevik tempo" in acting on their assignments. However, Stalin's endorsement of this catch-up mentality had direct implications for the longstanding debate over the party's revolutionary identity. To close the gap between the Soviet Union's low level of development and the capitalist world, one could no longer assume that virtuous intentions would be the key to transforming the economy. Alongside the scientists and engineers who were already contributing to this effort, Stalin emphasized, it was essential that the party's cadres become masters of science and technical expertise.[40] In other words, their primary task was to serve the same catch-up functions of the state.

Stalin's admonitions were borne out in a marked shift away from the egalitarian precepts that had guided the party's preceding recruitment drives. This correction went quickly. In 1932–1933, the Central Committee launched an extensive internal purge. Its goal was to remove not only careerists and political undesirables from its membership but also many of the uneducated and unskilled cadres who had been welcomed as members during the first euphoric years of industrialization. With growing frequency, party leaders emphasized the importance of recruiting members with the expertise to get things done. Good communists, it was clear, should be as intimately acquainted with the production process as they were with their party's ideals. Finally, in 1936, in his report to the Extraordinary Eighth Congress of Soviets on the new Soviet Constitution, Stalin endorsed this pragmatic mind-set by inventing a new social stratum, the "working intelligentsia," which now joined the working and peasant classes in building a classless society.[41]

When future Soviet Union leaders, such as Nikita Khrushchev and Leonid Brezhnev, looked back at this early period of Stalin's rule, they took pains to distinguish between their predecessor's achievements and what came later, the Great Terror. For example, when Khrushchev used his famous "Secret Speech" at the Twentieth Party Congress in February 1956 to expose Stalin's crimes, he emphasized that great things had been accomplished under Stalin's leadership. Above all, Khrushchev emphasized that one should never forget that the full potential of socialism had been realized. Beyond calling attention to the regime's marquee achievements such as the construction of new cities and vast increases in industrial production, he and subsequent leaders credited Stalin with proving that socialism could improve the lives of ordinary citizens. By the end of the 1930s, most of the Soviet population could read and write; schools and technical institutes could be found in the most distant reaches of the USSR; and women were guaranteed equal educational opportunities. Socialism not only eliminated unemployment. It meant that the regime addressed issues directly affecting workers' lives.

Privately, Stalin's successors may have recognized the risk in viewing the party's primary task in terms of building a modern society. To the extent that its members were judged according to this standard, one could legitimately inquire how their work was any different from that of the state officials who did not happen to belong to this fraternity. It would take decades before the full implications of this transition would play themselves out. But for the moment, the shift raised a question that would haunt the Soviet Union until Stalin's death. If the party somehow failed to realize its appointed tasks, who was to be held responsible?

STALIN ATTACKS THE PARTY

In retrospect, the period associated with Stalin's Great Terror was all about blame. Between 1934 and 1938, every stratum of Soviet society was swept up in a whirlwind of mutual recrimination and character assassination. People who worked in the realm of ideas, members of the "working intelligentsia" whom Stalin had just canonized, engineers, technicians, and journalists suddenly found themselves singled out as wreckers, saboteurs, and counterrevolutionaries. They were joined in these dubious categories by foreign communists living in exile in the USSR and non-Russian nationalities, such as Ukrainians, Georgians, and Armenians. As the ferocity of these campaigns spread, they inevitably reached into the lives of ordinary citizens who were far removed from positions of authority and fell into no discernible classification. In 1937–1938, according to Soviet-era archives, the NKVD arrested a staggering 1.5 million people for an assortment of purported crimes and convicted 85 percent of them. More than half of those arrested were shot. Over the same period, the number of people residing in labor camps or housed in prisons doubled, from 1 million to 2 million.[42] Few Soviet citizens went through this period without in some way being scarred by these events.

Yet Stalin's focus on eliminating any person or group who threatened to interfere with his quest for total domination was at the center of the Great Terror. For this reason, it is no accident that Stalin and his collaborators devoted their energy to attacking the last remnants of meaningful dissent—the old Bolsheviks. Stalin justified his actions by appealing to his own theory. If it was true, he reasoned, that the class struggle became more intense as one moved closer to socialism, it was logical to think that the most dangerous enemies would be found in the ranks of the party. In support of this position, Stalin reached back to the ban on factions to create a new offense against the Revolution. Because these enemies represented threats to the Soviet Union's existence, one should no longer judge their behavior according to the standard of party unity. Rather, their actions should be classified as crimes against the state.

In acting on this reasoning, Stalin and his confederates methodically went about building a lattice of culpability from one opponent to the next. When M. N. Ryutin, a former district party secretary from Moscow, was arrested in fall 1932 for organizing a petition to remove Stalin from office, the security police promptly rounded up everyone with even the slightest ties to him. Merely for having copies of the document, Zinoviev and Kamenev were once again expelled from the party. In December 1934, the justification was provided for a wider attack on Stalin's rivals when Sergei Kirov, the popular chief of the Leningrad party organization, was assassinated. Designating Kirov's murder a political crime, Stalin directed the NKVD to expose the activities of a purported "Leningrad center." Laying the foundations for the coming Great Terror and the construction of a vast archipelago of internment and labor camps, thousands of people were arrested, many of them party members. Simultaneously, Stalin raised the political stakes by arresting Zinoviev and Kamenev for allegedly associating with the persons behind the crime. To the extent that this move was a test of the extent of Stalin's control, it was a mixed success. In a tortuous example of Bolshevik reasoning, Zinoviev confessed that he might have unintentionally bolstered the hopes of antiparty elements. Yet, he denied any personal involvement in the crime. Kamenev refused to admit to anything. For the time being, Stalin had to be content with the sentencing of the two figures to lengthy prison terms.

Two years later, Stalin moved decisively against his adversaries. In an indication that he had finally consolidated his grip on the party leadership, he orchestrated three public show trials between 1936 and 1938 that confirmed that the time of the old Bolsheviks was over. The first trial, in August 1936, focused on Zinoviev and Kamenev; the second, in January 1937, concentrated on industrial managers and diplomats who were accused of being Trotskyists; the centerpiece of the third trial, in March 1938, was Bukharin. Without exception, the charges against the defendants were preposterous. These long-serving party members were accused of engineering Kirov's assassination, organizing criminal cells, and spying for British, French, and German intelligence agencies. Not surprisingly, they were also charged with plotting to kill both Lenin and Stalin himself. Incredibly, most of the accused obligingly confessed to their crimes, impassively reading carefully crafted scripts before hundreds of spectators, many of them foreign journalists, in Moscow's House of Unions. In tandem with these proceedings, the regime conducted a secret trial of senior military officers in June 1937. Following their convictions for espionage, their executions were announced to the press.

While these trials were under way, Stalin's deputies devoted the same deliberate attention to waging war on party members at all levels of the *nomenklatura*. In the case of Central Committee members, they drew on quasi-legal procedures in assessing evidence against their accused comrades; they followed ostensibly strict rules of protocol in issuing arrest orders; and they pretended to deliberate carefully over the sentences they meted out to the guilty. This care for detail was no accident. The trials' organizers used their decisions to fabricate a public record of specific crimes that they could then use to justify further prosecutions. When guilt was successfully ascribed to someone at the top of the party hierarchy, everyone below them became a potential target for investigation.

At the time, there was no way to know how many of the party's members were swept into this maelstrom. Only in 1956 was it revealed that the human losses were worse than anyone imagined. At the party's Twentieth Congress, Khrushchev cited graphic statistics about the fate of the delegates at the Seventeenth Party Congress, the Congress of Victors. Of the 149 full and candidate members who were elected to the Central Committee in 1934, 98 were arrested and shot for being enemies of the people. Of the 1,966 delegates to the congress, Khrushchev added, 1,108 were subsequently arrested for counterrevolutionary crimes.[43]

In describing the Great Terror in this way, I am consciously emphasizing its specificity. The party's most prominent members did not commit suicide in the 1930s. In effect, they were murdered. When Stalin and figures like his secret police chief, Nikolai Yezhov, issued the orders in their one-sided war against an unarmed enemy, their directions were not carried out by abstract entities. They were carried out by human beings who were fully aware of the consequences of their decisions. Many believed that their party was under threat from within. In their denunciations of rivals, others were motivated by the prospect of personal gain. In countless cases, the Great Terror was driven by the fear that if one member did not go along with pressures to denounce another, he or she would be denounced instead.

For Stalin, the destruction of the party elite was a deeply personal affair. In Bukharin's case in particular, Stalin let his longtime comrade in arms and friend swing in the air of uncertainty. At one moment, he assured Bukharin that he would protect him against allegations of being a member of a so-called Zinoviev-Kamenev-Trotsky bloc; at another, he ordered that Bukharin's case be turned over to the NKVD. Until Bukharin's execution, he allowed his rival to believe—falsely—that he could somehow negotiate the terms of a confession that would save his reputation and the good name of his family. As in many of the prominent cases before him, Bukharin's sense of discipline shone through. He emphasized that he did not want to put his own needs ahead of those of the movement. "I know all too well," he wrote, "that *great* plans, *great* ideas, and *great* interests take precedence over everything."[44] To the misfortune of the party and the country he led, Stalin was no longer focused on the great ideas of 1917.

In a confirmation that the Great Terror was instituted and sustained by individuals extending down to the lower reaches of the Soviet Union's communist party hierarchy and was not an inevitable outgrowth of Leninism, Stalin and his small circle showed that they were equally capable of reining in the instruments of violence that made the purges possible. In fall 1938, as the threat of an expansionist Germany hovered ominously over the USSR, the Politburo pointedly criticized the NKVD for "excesses" in carrying out arrests; it faulted the organs for disregarding proper judicial procedures; and it ordered the state procurator to exercise greater supervision of police operations. In an especially telling measure, it removed Yezhov from his post, replacing him with another Stalin confidant, Lavrenty Beria, who pretended to be less directly connected with the purges. By spring 1939, the leadership tentatively broached the possibility of reexamining some NKVD convictions.

To be sure, none of the Soviet regime's powers was abridged in getting to this point. And there would be no rehabilitations. As if to make this point, the NKVD executed Yezhov on the appropriately far-fetched charge that its former chief had conspired to assassinate Stalin. Nonetheless, the reversal of the mayhem of the preceding years demonstrated an important point about the ability of those with a monopoly on power to control their destiny. It showed that what Stalin's government did with one hand, it could take back with the other.

In this light, one cannot help wondering how the Soviet Union would have been differently shaped if another Bolshevik leader had become Lenin's eventual successor. A Bukharin, for example, might not have been a saint. But based upon his advocacy of the NEP, it seems unlikely that he would have turned his country's path to socialism into a bloodbath. Still, Stalin's success in controlling the party was not a political version of the apostolic succession. He wrested his position from others' hands through a combination of political skill and a ruthless determination to gain power at any cost. In this respect, the odds were stacked heavily against Stalin's opponents by a political system that provided no means for constraining a man who had willfully abandoned all scruples.

WHAT REMAINED?

By the end of the 1930s, the Soviet communist party as it had existed under Lenin's tutelage was dead. A majority of the old Bolsheviks who had given the party its spark in its founding years were gone. With their passing, the collective memories of exhaustive debates over priorities, strategies, and long-term goals had perished as well. Soviet politics was no longer about the contest over ideas; it was about state power. This development was heavy with irony since the same Congress of Soviets that proclaimed the USSR to be a socialist state in 1936 had also, for the first time, recognized the party as the leading force in all public and state organizations.[45] But this was also a tragedy. The party that Lenin had led was already being replaced by a new generation of less reflective but more disciplined cadres. These *apparatchiki* owed their positions to Stalin and took their patron's pronouncements as gospel truth. The times of fighting to achieve socialism were over. The time for shaping the new socialist order had begun.

Still, responsibility for the party's demise was as specific as it was in the case of individuals. Stalin's coup de grâce was to destroy the party idea with the same determination that he exhibited in killing its leaders. He accomplished this goal by making the concept irrelevant. In his official report to the party's Eighteenth Congress on March 10, 1939, he once again showed some theoretical imagination by endorsing the party's replacement by the state as the leading force in Soviet society. Certain ideological gyrations were necessary to accomplish this task. According to Stalin, Marx had only been speaking in general terms when he predicted that the state would wither away after the attainment of socialism. He assumed that socialism would already be victorious in the advanced industrial world. Yet far from this development having come to pass, Stalin once again reminded his listeners that only the Soviet Union had experienced such glory. Accordingly, it was useful to rethink Lenin's intentions. If the father of the Revolution had lived longer, Stalin suggested, he would undoubtedly have written a second volume of *State and Revolution* in which he would have given the state greater prominence to accord with "the experience gained during the existence of Soviet power in our country." As if this speculative exercise were not enough, Stalin dared to take his argument one step further. In a profound break with his Marxist predecessors, he declared that the state would not only play a major role under socialism. It would exist for as long as the USSR's encirclement by capitalist powers continued, even under communism.[46] Two years later, to clear up any possible ambiguity about what this argument meant for him personally, Stalin symbolically allowed his disciples to appoint him chairman of the Sovnarkom.

Stalin's complementary contribution to the demise of the party idea was to divest the institution of its lived history. In late 1938, the Central Committee cast its imprimatur on a text, *The History of the All-Union Communist Party of the Soviet Union (Bolsheviks): Short Course*, which it described as the party's definitive statement about its history. From the beginning, however, the *Short Course* was Stalin's personal project. While party experts composed the book, he pored over every draft, revising chapters and excising paragraphs. The work that emerged was meant to stifle every manifestation of critical thinking about the party's past. In the characterization of the *Short Course*, the party's history was defined not by reflective individuals but by stock figures who battled over socialist destiny. One side was noble, the other purely malicious. According to this simple dichotomy, Lenin and his faithful disciple Stalin were models of dedication, clear-sightedness, and Bolshevik discipline who wanted nothing more than to fight for the good of the Soviet citizen. In contrast, their opponents, Trotsky, Zinoviev, and Bukharin, were renegades and revisionists whose only goal was to split the party.[47] Lest anyone doubt Stalin's desires, the Comintern made the *Short Course* the standard work by which communists in every part of the world would judge their progress. By the time of Stalin's death, 42,816,000 copies of the book (exactly!) had been printed in 67 different languages.[48]

What remained after Stalin's demolition of the idea that his former comrades had any role to play in building the Soviet state? The answer is simple: Stalin. On December 19, 1939, in preparation for the celebrations of the general secretary's sixtieth birthday, the Central Committee hailed its leader's greatness by proclaiming that the party and the Soviet people were "united as never before under the banner of

Lenin and Stalin and ready to continue the struggle for the complete victory of communism." The encomium was just right. As a larger-than-life personality who, in the body's words, was "surrounded by the warm love of workers of the Soviet Union and around the world," Stalin had achieved the mythic stature to allow him, like the Bolsheviks' founder, to control the meaning of the October Revolution.[49] The Soviet Union had moved on from building socialism in one country to embracing socialism in one heroic person.

In this respect, it is revealing that after Germany launched its invasion of the USSR on June 22, 1941, Stalin responded to the attack by once again daring to reformulate the Marxist conception of history. He inserted the Revolution into the context of Russia's centuries-old battle against foreign invaders. In an address to Red Army soldiers on November 7, 1941, the twenty-fourth anniversary of the Bolshevik takeover (according to the Gregorian calendar), he called the soldiers to be inspired not only by Lenin ("our lodestar") but also by the "manly images of our great ancestors." Among these heroic defenders of the "Glorious Motherland," he included Alexander Nevsky, the thirteenth-century prince of Novgorod, Dmitri Donskoy, the fourteenth-century grand prince of Moscow, and Alexander Suvorov, the eighteenth-century generalissimo of the Russian empire.[50] As the war progressed, Stalin never quite resolved the tension between the invocation of these traditions and the idea that the Revolution was based upon a fundamentally different way of looking at history. Yet, his desire for a usable past to conduct the war effort trumped such minor concerns. In late 1942, at the middle of the battle of Stalingrad, the regime pointedly subordinated the powers of political commissars to military commanders. In 1943, the army adopted titles and traditions from imperial times. A new Soviet anthem was composed to replace the "Internationale." Stalin himself assumed the title of Marshal, adorning himself with the tabs and epaulets that his party had once banned.

The fact that Stalin was most comfortable fighting a war of *national* defense, a Great Patriotic War, would remain a central part of Soviet foreign policy. The end of World War II and the emergence of questions about the political status of the newly liberated states of Eastern

Europe provided him with an opportunity to determine how the USSR's interests could be served in a part of the world that had not yet had its appointed revolution. Rhetorically, he paid tribute to the virtues of proletarian internationalism. Yet in practice, as we shall see in chapter 7, he filled the new governments of these countries with compliant communists and sycophants who could be counted upon to follow his command.

More importantly, the end of the war invited Stalin to make a decision about which principle of leadership would govern the Soviet Union in the years to come, one based on the party or another based on the state. He made the unmistakable choice for the latter. Out of the ruins of total war, he instructed his deputies to fashion a system of state administration that was exclusively focused on rebuilding the country. In March 1946, the Sovnarkom was replaced with a council of ministers that was entrusted with the task of managing the economy. In comparison with its predecessor, whose culture was infused with the militant traditions and symbolism of early Bolshevism, the council was a modern organization. It had a streamlined chain of command, a clear division of roles and responsibilities, and set routines. In due course, it was populated by a younger cohort of technocrats and specialists who were equipped to handle complex decisions in profoundly less turbulent times.[51]

To the unending aggravation of its administrators, the council of ministers was never able to insulate itself from the all-too-frequent interventions by the Soviet leader and his confederates. But the body's supremacy over the party in Stalin's eyes was never in doubt. Despite his constant references to the party's valiant role during the war and his religious invocations of its leading role, Stalin was disinclined to assign a significant status to an organization that had been the source of internal dissent and opposition to his policies throughout the early years of Bolshevik rule. Until his death in 1953, he showed little interest in the workings of the Politburo and the Central Committee. In fact, he only once saw the need to call a meeting of the full party that had last met during the Eighteenth Congress of 1939. When the organization's representatives came together for the Nineteenth Congress in October 1952, only five months before Stalin's passing, their most notable achievement was to adopt the name it would hold until its own demise in 1991: Communist Party of the Soviet Union. One wonders whether this was an afterthought. Given the fact that there was little substance to the idea of communist rule at this point, this change in nomenclature, like Stalin's creation of "Leninism" in 1924, was certain to raise more questions than answers for the Soviet leaders who came afterward.

CHAPTER 6

A Different Type of Party

In March 1927, a thirty-three-year-old communist agitator, Mao Ze-dong, presented the Central Committee of the Chinese Communist Party (CCP) with a stirring call for revolutionary action. Mao's appeal, the "Report on an Investigation of the Peasant Movement in Hunan," was the culmination of several trips to his home province in 1925 and 1926 to study rebellious peasants' associations. In nearly apocalyptic terms, he described the peasants' drive to speak for themselves as evidence of an imminent tidal wave in human history. In a very short time, Mao declared, "several hundred million peasants will rise like a mighty storm, like a hurricane, a force so swift and violent that no power, however great, will be able to hold it back. They will smash all the trammels that bind them and rush forward along the road to liberation."[1]

Reading the Hunan Report today, one is immediately struck by the resemblance between Mao's pronouncement and the prophetic tenor of the *Communist Manifesto*. In the same spirit with which Marx predicted the rise of a "self-conscious, independent movement of the immense majority" that would overthrow "the conditions for the existence of class antagonisms," Mao's mighty storm is to arrive with existential finality.[2] This impending upsurge, in his words, will "sweep all the imperialists, warlords, corrupt officials, local tyrants and evil gentry into their graves." It will be "a revolution without parallel in history."

Nevertheless, when one examines the Hunan Report more closely, there is also a revealing difference between the way Mao and his fore-runner, Marx, assess the issue of the leadership of this upheaval. Marx was so confident about the communist party's qualifications to lead the proletariat that he barely addressed the organization's characteristics in the *Manifesto*. In contrast, Mao is practically disdainful of the CCP. In the Report, he chides the party's representatives for their timidity in acting on the imperative that has been laid before them. "A revolution is not a dinner party," he lectures, "or writing an essay, or painting a picture, or doing embroidery. . . . A revolution is an act of insurrection, an act of violence by which one class overthrows another." The poorest peasants understand the necessity of using terror to achieve their goals and, he adds, they have "never been wrong on the general direction of the revolution." If the party does not join ranks with them immediately and "march at their head," he warns, it will be left with two damning options, either to trail behind them or to stand in their way and oppose them. Then, in a taunting tone, Mao challenges his comrades to make the right decision: "Events will force you to make the choice quickly."[3]

Mao's bluntly disparaging assessment of the revolutionary organization that is meant to lead the masses to victory is striking. However, as we shall see in this chapter, he was by no means alone in seeking leaders who would possess the courage to fight for the interests of the Chinese people. Well before Mao presided over the establishment of the People's Republic of China (PRC) on October 1, 1949, China had gone through a different kind of revolution, one that officially began with an uprising of railway workers and a military coup in the city of Wuchang on October 10, 1911, and culminated in the founding of the Republic of China on January 1, 1912. At this juncture, Mao was only a single voice among an entire generation of discontented intellectuals, liberal reformers, and radicals who were enthralled by the prospect that their nation would be rescued from the disastrous legacy of the preceding Qing dynasty—political breakdown, social upheaval, and foreign exploitation. Accordingly, when the republic's leaders proved to be unequal to this task and China descended into a renewed period of turmoil, the conclusion that Mao drew from this failure represented only one of many contending perspectives about what should come next. Indeed, in the aftermath of the Republican Revolution, Mao's thinking was still evolving. Nonetheless, by the time he wrote the Hunan Report, he was already laying the foundation for an innovative conception of revolutionary action that would inspire his future followers. His view, which transcended the reliance on conventional political organizations that we have encountered among communist parties in the Soviet Union and across Europe, was to be based on the power of human will and centered in the countryside.

Decades later, Mao would have the opportunity to act on this vision in the PRC. Tragically, many of his decisions would have horrific consequences for millions of people. Yet, there was nothing preordained about this outcome. Although Mao would present the communist victory in 1949 as the inevitable result of the class struggle and the death battle with imperialism, his success in establishing his perspective as the predominant conception of political action was not the result of a logical progression from one stage of history to the next. Like Russia's revolutionaries in the nineteenth and early twentieth centuries, he benefited from the misperceptions and missteps of others, friends and foes alike. In fact, had certain events not occurred, it is conceivable that the ideas embedded within the Hunan Report would never have taken concrete form. To understand both the evolution of Mao's thinking and his circuitous path to power, we must turn to the circumstances more than a century before his travels to Hunan, which convinced legions of Chinese radicals like himself that the creation of a fundamentally different type of political order was necessary and achievable.

SETTING THE STAGE FOR THE REPUBLICAN REVOLUTION

The collapse of any state is a traumatic experience. But the devastating fall of China's last dynasty, the Qing, in 1911 was the product of more than a century of traumas. At the height of their rule, the dynasty's Manchu emperors had lorded over an empire that easily matched its European counterparts in size, military might, and imperial grandeur. Under successive rulers, China experienced long periods of growth and material prosperity as well as times of political and social stability that had too often eluded earlier dynasties. Despite being foreigners, an identity they guarded by walling off their affairs from the surrounding society, the Manchus displayed a keen sense for securing the cooperation of their subjects. In their relations with the majority Han Chinese, they tapped into Confucian traditions to portray the emperor as the "Son of Heaven" who was devoted to the people's welfare. Additionally, the Qing court was adept at co-opting native elites.

It gave them a stake in the imperial order by fostering a privileged class of palace, metropolitan, and provincial officials to administer its affairs. In return, these officials buttressed the court's authority by administering communal works projects, collecting taxes, and guaranteeing public safety.

By the turn of the nineteenth century, however, this complex edifice had begun to break apart. China's long era of prosperity had generated a demographic explosion that undermined social stability. With a population of over 400 million and inadequate food supplies and arable land, officials at all levels of the Qing administrative hierarchy were suddenly overwhelmed by the law of scarcity. In order to make up for shortages in its treasury, the central government pressed regional authorities to raise taxes and transfer resources from the countryside to the cities. Magistrates and village officials were thrust into the impossible position of having to meet these demands while simultaneously contending with the needs of local populations. Their efforts to resolve these problems by currying the favor of diverse power holders, landowners, tax collectors, and militia leaders led to rampant corruption.

Importantly, the victims of these circumstances were predominantly among the lowest levels of society. Millions of poor peasants and itinerant laborers faced the daily threat of starvation. In the past, such conditions had frequently led to spontaneous protests and violent uprisings in the countryside. Yet as these strains grew, the Qing court was presented with a new phenomenon, the mass millenarian movement. The first great upheaval, the White Lotus Rebellion of 1796, began as an isolated tax revolt but swiftly expanded into a full-scale assault on the imperial order that spread throughout central China. By the time of its eclipse a decade later, the rebellion had taken the lives of thousands of people. Showing that Mao Zedong was not out of touch with Chinese reality, many more devastating mass uprisings were still to come.

The fury of these rebellions was matched by equally debilitating challenges to the Qing emperors' credibility from abroad. Like Russia's tsars in earlier centuries, the Manchus had cautiously sought to strengthen their empire by selectively opening their borders to Western visitors, merchants, and missionaries. However, despite their efforts to control these contacts, they were quickly overpowered by the demands of colonial powers for full access to their ports and internal markets. Beginning with humiliating defeats in the Opium Wars of the mid-nineteenth century and Great Britain's imposition of a punitive peace, the court was forced to agree to a succession of ignominious treaties with other European states, such as Russia and Japan, that undermined its subjects' faith in its ability to defend China's interests.

Setting the stage for the revolutions to come, the ensuing turmoil in China was far worse than any of the conflagrations experienced by the European autocracies of the nineteenth century. In the 1850s and 1860s, the imperial system was shaken by a torrent of civil wars. Foremost among these cataclysms was the Taiping Rebellion, possibly the largest and most devastating civil war of all time, which lasted an extraordinary thirteen years from 1851 to 1864 and, by conservative estimates, took the lives of 20 million people. Notably, the Taiping revolutionaries were better organized than earlier movements and had a clearly articulated social agenda that gained them support wherever they went. In a foreshadowing of themes that Mao and other Chinese radicals would appropriate in the coming century, they aimed to purify society, put an end to political and moral corruption, and institute an enlightened social order based on regulated markets and the equitable distribution of land.

Once again like Russia's tsars, the Qing rulers sought to reassert their power through so-called self-strengthening policies. They sent emissaries to Europe and the United States to purchase machinery and military hardware and brought Western technicians to China to train manufacturers. They wooed regional authorities by looking beyond the imperial army for security. In what would later prove to be fateful steps for the empire's internal stability, they allowed provincial governors, nearly half of whom were Han Chinese, to form independent armies and tolerated the creation of gentry-led private militias to defend villages from roving bands of rebels and bandits.

Far from satisfying their subjects, however, the Manchus' measures emboldened native elites to press for more extensive reforms. In the wake of China's defeat in the Sino-Japanese War of 1894–1895 and the outbreak of the antiforeigner Boxer Rebellion of 1899, the Qing court responded to these demands with a series of "new policies." It replaced

the 500-year-old examination system with Western educational practices, routinized tax collection, and condemned traditional practices
such as the foot-binding of women. None of these reforms had greater
political magnitude, however, than the court's agreement to adopt a
written constitution and to permit elections to local, provincial, and
national assemblies. Although the first assemblies were predictably
weak and reflected the views of only a minuscule segment of the population, they and the convening of a National Assembly in Beijing in
1910 had a profound impact on the expectations of China's educated
strata. They presented them with both a taste of self-government and
powerful grounds for indignation when the Qing rulers showed that
they had no intention of living up to their promises.

THE RISE AND DEMISE OF REPUBLICAN GOVERNANCE

The generation of radical activists and intellectuals who would soon
participate in their nation's twin revolutions was born of these circumstances. Given the suffocating conditions of Manchu rule, it is not
surprising that many of them discovered their calling outside China.
Japan, in particular, was an incubator for independent thinking and
rebellion. By 1905, more than 8,000 Chinese students were attending
Japanese schools and universities, ironically thanks to the Qing regime's
self-strengthening policies. In addition to acquiring the skills their
country needed in engineering and science, they were exposed to the
alluring writings of Enlightenment thinkers and a plethora of beliefs and
perspectives that were unknown in their homeland—not only republicanism, but also anarchism, liberalism, socialism, and especially nationalism.
Inspired by these ideas, they took advantage of the Meiji government's
tolerance of their activities to compose manifestos, publish inflammatory newspapers, and organize study groups and revolutionary cells.

No figure better represented the passions of these young radicals than
Zou Rong, a Sichuanese student who was infatuated with the French
and American Revolutions. Zou's short but influential popular tract,
The Revolutionary Army (1903), which he wrote at the age of eighteen,
excoriated the Qing rulers for allowing China to be subjected to the
whims of outside powers. Invoking popular racialist ideas and

nationalist fervor, Zou implored his readers—the "Han race"—to "wipe out the five million barbarian Manchus, wash away the shame of two hundred sixty years of cruelty and oppression, and make China clean once again."[4] Once this purifying act was completed, he assured his fellow rebels, it would be possible to build a Chinese republic in which every individual, male and female, would enjoy the rights of life, liberty, and self-fulfillment. Should any future government violate these rights, Zou wrote, invoking Western revolutionary themes, the people would be justified in overthrowing it to "satisfy their hopes for peace and happiness."[5]

The primary figure to whom Zou and his contemporaries looked for guidance was the republican revolutionary Sun Yat-sen. Living in exile for nearly sixteen years due to his conspiratorial activities, Sun did more to publicize the idea of popular rule than any other person. He also had the organizational aptitude to make this objective seem realizable. On August 20, 1905, he and other revolutionaries met in Tokyo to found a secret association, the Tongmenghui ("Revolutionary Alliance"), to lead the republican movement. Although a majority of the Tongmenghui's members were from South China, this rudimentary party had many of the features of a mass organization. It could credibly claim to speak for all of China because its members also included ethnic minorities, Christian Chinese, exiles, and members of secret societies. Sun himself came from the Hakka minority.

One source of the Tongmenghui's broad appeal was Sun's propagation of a specific doctrine, the Three People's Principles, as a roadmap to a future republic. The first principle, "nationalism," was the most straightforward. In his eyes, the primary purpose of the republican movement was to restore the empire's lost glory. To this end, the Tongmenghui was organized around the goal of extricating China from the grip of outsiders. Sun's second principle, "people's democracy," was more elusive. Notwithstanding the term's appeal to Sun's Western supporters, neither he nor most of the Tongmenghui's members were prepared to endorse a full-blown democratic system. Writing in 1905, only a few years after Lenin formulated his conception of a vanguard party in *What Is to Be Done?*, he too endorsed the establishment of a tutelary democracy in which the masses would be led by educated elites with the "foresight to progress and apply the most suitable law and norm to our crowd to stand among other countries in the world."[6] Sun's final principle, "people's livelihood," was the most ambiguous. At this point, he seems to have wanted only a tax on land speculation to protect the peasantry. Still, by touching upon one of the most sensitive issues of his time, the unequal distribution of property, he planted the germ of an idea of socialism that future radicals could act upon.

Furthermore, many of Sun's youthful admirers found his conception of revolution particularly persuasive because of its hard-edged military core. In much the same way that Lenin's conception of the revolutionary party appeared well suited to the Russian environment, Sun gave his most radical supporters confidence that his ideals could be brought to fruition in China's conditions. At his direction, in 1907, the Tongmenghui publicly committed itself to a three-stage plan for the period after the Revolution that was predicated as much on the use of force as were the ideas of European Marxists. Due to the "chaos and disturbance" of the time, Sun's first stage was to be a period of military dictatorship. During this phase, which the Tongmenghui confidently predicted would last a mere three years, the Manchus and their Chinese collaborators who resisted the revolution would be "killed without mercy." In the second stage, following the "pacification" of the nation, a provisional constitution would allow the Chinese people to elect their own representatives. But, the plan made clear, this transition would take place under military supervision. "Political tutelage" was necessary because the people still "needed time to acquaint themselves with the idea of liberty and equality." Only after this orderly process was completed could the Tongmenghui invest full governmental power in their hands.[7]

If ideas alone could make a revolution, the founding of the Chinese Republic on January 1, 1912, would have allowed Sun and his supporters to apply this particular blend of inclusionary and authoritarian principles immediately. Nevertheless, in the same way the Bolsheviks would discover in Russia six years later, these revolutionaries did not so much win power as found it placed in their laps. The difference for the republican revolutionaries is that they were unable to retain power once they had it. The Republican Revolution was largely the product of the Qing court's ineptitude and failure to appreciate the adverse consequences of its policies. Peasants and small landowners protested against inordinate tax burdens, business leaders withdrew their support because of the regime's favoritism toward foreign investors, secret societies fomented local rebellions to protect their trade in drugs and contraband, and urban radicals organized strikes by textile workers and dockworkers. Most important, the increasingly powerful Han army commanders and provincial governors chafed at the Manchus' heavy-handed tactics. As a result, when a wave of rebellions spread throughout China, they could no longer defend the regime against those who were determined to overthrow it.

The fact that these crises, and not so much republican dreams, led to the toppling of the dynasty was decisive. It meant that the new republic was built upon an unsteady foundation and that every misstep was likely to discredit it. Still, the extent of the regime's weaknesses was not apparent at first. When Sun was named the country's provisional president, he voluntarily turned over the position to the powerful head of the regional Beiyang army, Yuan Shikai, in a gesture of conciliation. In exchange, Yuan agreed to call elections to the first National Assembly. In the ensuing months, members of the gentry, former Qing officials, businesspersons, and constitutionally minded democrats formed over a dozen political parties to voice their interests. These included Sun's new Nationalist Party, the Guomindang (GMD), which won a plurality of the seats in both the upper and lower houses of parliament in early 1913. Nonetheless, the prospects for republican governance were only as strong as the goodwill of those who were in the position to lead it. Maintaining that the Nationalists could not be trusted, Yuan Shikai ordered his troops to attack the armies of military governors sympathetic to the party. He arrested parliamentary deputies and provincial representatives who opposed him. In fall 1913, he completed this assault by forcing the remaining parties to elect him president and ordered the GMD's dissolution. In late 1915, he exchanged power for parody by inducing his rubber-stamp parliament to "elect" him emperor.

It is impossible to know whether a truly republican politician such as Sun could have built the necessary consensus among China's elites to defend the country's experiment with popular government. Yet the possibility of holding China together dissolved when Yuan turned a majority of his supporters against him. In rapid succession, the governors of multiple provinces declared their independence from Beijing. When their seats of power fractured into scores of quarreling warlord satrapies, some huge and others small, some bellicose and others enlightened, it was reasonable to argue, as Mao did, that if China were ever reunified, it would require a very different form of rule.

Toward a Chinese Communist Party

Up to this point, I have emphasized the failure of the Republican Revolution and China's descent into dictatorship and warlord rule because these events provided the context in which a conception of revolution based upon Marxist and Leninist thinking could gain political traction. The founding fathers of the People's Republic of China were not ambivalent about their goals. They were convinced that conventional republican institutions, including the diverse parties that participated in them, had proven to be unequal to the task of unifying China and eradicating the belief systems and traditions that had led their nation into misery.

The conditions for the communists' emergence were generated by a powerful wave of urban protest in the mid-1910s known as the New Culture Movement. Whereas their predecessors had aspired to change China with the introduction of Western-style representative bodies, the intellectuals, writers, and educators who inspired this movement conceived of their challenge in much broader terms. Echoing Sun Yat-sen's concerns about the immaturity of the Chinese "crowd," but generally avoiding the endorsement of specific institutions, they sought to provide their followers with a salve to the republic's failures by emphasizing the need for even greater social change. In their view, this transformation could only be realized if one swept away the superstitions, bigotry, unquestioning obedience to authority, and militarism of China's past. Notably, they directed their criticisms at every segment of society, including their fellow educated elites.

The ideas behind the New Culture Movement gained nationwide attention in the pages of an array of newspapers and other publications, including the iconoclastic magazine, *New Youth*. Founded in 1915 by

Chen Duxiu, the soon-to-be-named dean of the humanities at Peking University, the magazine was a magnet for legions of young Chinese men and women, including a Hunanese peasant named Mao Zedong. In rebellion against their parents' wisdom, they initially looked to inspirational figures like Zou Rong and Sun Yat-sen for enlightenment, even though the latter was skeptical of the movement's Westernizing focus. In the same spirit as the youthful members of the Russian intelligentsia who went "down to the people" in the second half of the nineteenth century, *New Youth* inspired its readers with a sense of common purpose and direction. Chen encapsulated *New Youth*'s message when he urged them to "bury the old youth whose narrow-mindedness led to conservatism and corruption." He dared them to "Be Different!"[8]

Idealistic students found the chance to act on this command in the classrooms and courtyards of Peking University, ironically a product of the Qing reforms that were meant to reinvigorate the dynasty. Under the inspired leadership of a German-educated philosopher and former minister of education, Cai Yuanpei, the university became a seedbed for radicalization. As chancellor, Cai encouraged students to abide by high moral standards and reject the corrupting temptations of their high social stations. As a fierce defender of academic freedom, Cai recruited some of the most dynamic thinkers of the age to the university to give lectures and to join its faculty. They, in turn, convinced their listeners that China was on the verge of a profound cultural transformation.

One of these stars, Hu Shih, had studied under John Dewey at Columbia University and was captivated by the notion that cultural change should begin with education. Upon returning to Beijing, he used the pages of *New Youth* to support the popular "vernacular movement" in Chinese literature. Hu's campaign won an extraordinary victory when, in 1920, the Ministry of National Education adopted the vernacular as the official written language of elementary school education. Additionally, because the majority of Chinese could not read, Hu and other intellectuals pushed simultaneously for the adoption of a spoken national language based on the Mandarin dialect. This campaign had potentially revolutionary implications. It meant that ordinary people could be unified behind a common cause.

Lu Xun, the essayist and novelist, was among the regular visitors to Peking University. Like Hu Shih, Lu Xun campaigned for the Chinese people's liberation from their stifling conventions and implored them to think for themselves. But his vision was angrier. His breakthrough to national attention came in 1918 with the publication of his vernacular essay, "My Views on Chastity," in *New Youth*. In the essay, he directed his furor at the hypocrisies of traditional Confucian scholars who, he argued, were responsible for defending a culture in which men could behave as they pleased while women were degraded. More than a defense of equality between the sexes, the essay was a call to action. "We must tear off every mask," Lu Xun declared. "We must do away with all the stupidity and tyranny in the world which injures others as well as ourselves."[9]

This climate of intellectual ferment provides an essential clue to understanding the initial appeal of Marxism in China. The radicals who first called themselves Marxists were not equipped to engage in rigorous class analysis or to offer sophisticated explanations for their choice of one path to socialism over another. Far from it; few had any but the most rudimentary exposure to the doctrine they claimed to support and little interest in the laws of economic determinism. Until 1918, even the word "Marxism" was practically unknown in China. The first Chinese version of the *Communist Manifesto* had not appeared until 1908, and it was poorly translated and misleading. Marxist theories were filtered through translations of broader studies on European radicalism. Serious analysis of core texts only became possible when a Fujianese journalist, Chen Puxian, returned from Japan in 1919 to publish full translations and detailed commentaries on Marx and Engels's works. As a result, Marxism's few adherents subscribed to a hodgepodge of beliefs that they deemed best equipped to respond to their nation's tribulations—anti-imperialism, humanism, guild socialism, and anarchism.

On one count, however, these early communists could be distinguished from other expositors of the ideas behind the New Culture Movement: they were unequivocally committed to violent revolution. The first major defense of a Marxist position was taken by Peking University's chief librarian, Li Dazhao, in the waning months of World

War I. In October 1918, Li published a sensational essay in *New Youth*, "The Victory of Bolshevism," which went far beyond Hu Shih's and Lu Xun's hopes that enlightened education alone would be sufficient to loosen the hold of traditional beliefs and practices. Inspired by the success of the Bolshevik Revolution, an event that had received scant attention among educated circles, Li predicted that China, too, would soon be swept up in the "crashing waves of revolution." The Bolshevik victory, he argued, was not an isolated national event. It signaled the birth of an international mass movement in which the winds would roar, the clouds would surge, and the mountains and valleys would echo with the sounds of rebellion. "In the face of this global, mass movement," he wrote, "historical remnants—such as emperors, noblemen, warlords, bureaucrats, militarism, capitalism—and all other things that obstruct the advance of this new movement will be crushed by the thunderous force."[10]

Given the similarity in style, one can reasonably assume that Mao Zedong, who worked as Li's library assistant, had this apocalyptic narrative in mind when he crafted the Hunan Report nine years later. To the good fortune of the handful of active communists at this moment, the timing of the publication of "The Victory of Bolshevism" could not have been more propitious. On May 4, 1919, China was swept into a renewed period of violent protest. Thousands of students assembled on Tiananmen Square to denounce a new blow to the nation's sovereignty. Word had just reached Beijing that the Western delegations to the Versailles Peace Conference had reneged on promises to compensate China for its contribution to the war effort by returning German concessions in Shandong. Instead, they extended these rights to neutral and, in Chinese eyes, culturally inferior Japan. Within days, the Beijing protests spiraled into a nationwide outpouring of patriotic indignation that transcended all social and class boundaries.

Significantly, the May Fourth Movement was only the most public expression of an embittered desire among these rebels for an alternative to conventional republican ideas. Although Yuan Shikai had died in 1916, the sitting government in Beijing was a desperately poor example of a constitutional regime. Operating in the shadow of regional warlords, the political factions and cliques that claimed to be representative parties engaged in unending battles over commercial, financial, and military interests. Personal loyalties and political corruption trumped institutional obligations. The most telling indication of the regime's weakness was its inability to contain the May Fourth demonstrations. When the government instructed its representatives at Versailles to refuse to sign the peace accord, its opponents blamed the debacle on their supposed lack of honor. Correspondingly, by confirming the protestors' skepticism about the applicability of republican ideas and institutions to Chinese conditions, the government's weakness fueled the attraction of radical approaches to national salvation and social transformation. In this favorable climate, interest in Marx and other European revolutionaries exploded. Chinese translations of Marx's classic works, such as the "Critique of the Gotha Program" and "The Civil War in France," appeared overnight. They were followed by Lenin's *State and Revolution* and a host of works by Trotsky, Luxemburg, and Bukharin. As in Japan, students set up study groups and political societies to distill what they could from these texts and fantasize about their future.

These events led to Chen Duxiu's conversion to Marxism. For years, Chen had held out hope that his nation's cultural transformation could be accomplished through democratic means. But the power of the protests led him, along with a growing number of like-minded intellectuals, to look to the October Revolution for inspiration and guidance. Unlike Li Dazhao, who was transfixed by the prospect of a spontaneous, mass uprising but ambivalent about the use of violent means, Chen was impressed with what he took to be the superior organizational features of a Leninist party. In his view, which was consonant with Sun Yat-sen's skepticism about Western democracy, the Chinese people did not yet have the capacity for active citizenship in a republic. They were, as Chen crassly put it, "a partly scattered, partly stupid people possessed of narrow-minded individualism with no public spirit who are often thieves and traitors and for a long time have been unable to be patriotic." Lenin's conception of a vanguard party represented exactly the approach to bring them around.[11]

Interestingly, Chen concentrated on the type of organization needed after the communist victory and not, as in Lenin's case, on the challenge of coming to power. He may have been influenced by the fact that he could already observe the outlines of such a party in Russia. As the center of gravity of the May Fourth Movement shifted southward and Chen moved to Shanghai to engage in conspiratorial activities, he found the answer to this challenge. In spring 1920, a two-person Comintern delegation, led by the secretary of the Department of Far Eastern Affairs, Grigory Voitinsky, arrived in China to explore the possibility of forming a compliant Chinese communist party. The visit, which preceded the convening of the Congress of the Toilers of the East in Baku, was meant to extend the Comintern's reach into the colonial world. With Voitinsky's guidance, Chen assembled the rough components of a party organization, including a provisional Central Committee, a youth league, and a monthly magazine to complement the thoroughly radicalized *New Youth*. Finally, on July 23, 1921, thirteen self-proclaimed communists and two Comintern advisers met in the back room of a girls' school in Shanghai's French Concession to found the CCP.

This First Congress did not have an auspicious beginning. Neither Chen nor Li Dazhao could attend the meeting because of concerns for their safety. Still, Chen was elected the party's general secretary in absentia. The delegates, including the young labor agitator Mao Zedong, could claim to represent a grand total of fifty-three members nationwide. Their program was a combination of boilerplate and ambiguity. On the one hand, the party's functions were defined in strictly orthodox Marxist terms. It was to be the "revolutionary arm of the proletariat." Its goal was to "overthrow the capitalist class." And it would be based on the dictatorship of the proletariat. On the other hand, the program had nothing to say about the organization's membership requirements or its authority over its members.[12] After several days of deliberation, the delegates were still unable to reach agreement on strategy. Some insisted that the party concentrate on clandestine agitation among factory workers. Other delegates argued that the CCP should be open to the public and that its members should seek to influence the government by participating in parliamentary elections. As a result, the new party offered outsiders, both communists and noncommunists alike, few clues about how Marxism would be applied to conditions quite unlike those confronted by revolutionaries in Europe or Russia.

The Communist Party's First Phase

As an organization that came into being quickly and from virtually nowhere, there was a certain pathos to the fledgling CCP's existence. According to a participant in the Congress, three facts were recognized by all: "party members are very few; it is necessary to increase party membership; and the methods of organizing workers and making propaganda have to be improved."[13] Unlike Russia's Social Democrats whose thinking had been shaped by two decades of rancorous debates over tactics and doctrines, China's communists had no historical memory of Marxism to draw upon. At this juncture, they were conspicuously more militant than the Bolsheviks, who were just entering the period of the New Economic Policy. But at best, their party was a project. They had only a vague sense of how to work with the diverse motivations—labor activism, cultural transformation, anti-imperialism, and patriotism—that had brought them together. In this light, it is no wonder that other revolutionaries, including Sun Yat-sen, barely acknowledged the CCP's founding.

Intriguingly, it took only five years for this tiny organization to become a major force in Chinese politics. Some of the party's successes can be attributed to its leaders' canny recruitment strategies and their cadres' growing comfort with labor organization. But more importantly, the party's rapid growth was due to two highly unusual political opportunities that the communists could not, and probably would not, have created of their own volition. The first grew out of the Soviet leadership's decision that it could most effectively increase its influence in China by supporting both the CCP and Sun's resurgent GMD. The second was the formation of a united front between the CCP and the GMD in which the latter remarkably agreed to accept a division of labor between the two parties. While the Nationalists focused their attention on the unification of China, they allowed the communists, as well as sympathetic left-wing GMD members, to take the lead in the task of spurring social revolution.

For the GMD, the first development must have seemed like a stroke of good fortune. Amid the wild optimism of the May Fourth Movement, Sun Yat-sen had returned to political life to re-found the party.

It was no accident that he chose October 10, 1919, as the official date for this event and appended the words "of China" to the party's name. In choosing the month and day of the Wuchang uprising in 1911, he underscored the GMD's responsibility to rebuild the nation. Not surprisingly, Sun put the Three People's Principles at the center of this project. He then set the tenor for the organization by requiring the party's members to swear an oath of loyalty to him. "To obey me," Sun advised, echoing the all-too-familiar role of the dominant leader in Chinese history, "is to submit to the revolution that I advocate." "And if one obeys my revolution," he added, invoking Christ-like imagery, "naturally one should [also] obey me."[14]

Just the same, appearances were deceiving. Sun had the ideas, but the GMD still needed to transform itself from a largely overseas organization into a party with a mass following at home. Additionally, although Sun assumed, in the tradition of the Tongmenghui, that he could accomplish his goals by forming a national army, the military arm of the party was sorely deficient in financial and material resources. In fact, only a year and a half after setting up a purportedly representative government in Guangzhou, Sun and the GMD were expelled from China for plotting against the northern warlords. Sun was only able to return in 1923.

In this circumstance, a Western observer might have anticipated that the Soviets' desire to accentuate the Comintern's impact would have forced them to choose between two mutually exclusive options. On the one hand, alignment with Sun and the GMD would give the Nationalists the best chance of building a functioning national government. On the other hand, the Comintern's insistence on adherence to the Bolshevik model of revolution seemed to require a focus on the CCP. Yet, Moscow adopted a third option. In early 1923, a Comintern agent, Mikhail Borodin, persuaded the two parties to form a united front. Under the terms of the agreement, the GMD gained by co-opting a potential rival into its government. For their part, thanks to the Kremlin's intervention, the communists were given the option to join the GMD as individuals while retaining their membership in the CCP.

This was an unstable marriage of convenience, but it proved to be an additional confirmation of the Comintern's value for the communists.

Initially, Sun was reluctant to allow an outside power to meddle in his party's affairs. Despite his growing sympathy for socialist views on land reform and the role of a strong state, he regarded the CCP with distrust. For their part, Chen Duxiu and his fellow communists were even more anxious about the implications of their association with the GMD. As the leaders of a small party—in 1923, the CCP had only 432 members—they risked being swallowed by their partners.[15] At minimum, they were wary of the GMD's appeal to social forces on the Right. In their view, the party's close ties to the bourgeoisie and well-off landowners threatened to dilute the CCP's Marxist views. Nonetheless, in a demonstration that Moscow's wishes could not be ignored as well as his appreciation for the power of the national ideal, Chen was among the first to join the Nationalists.

Initially, the GMD seemed to get the better part of the deal. In return for Sun's acceptance of the united front, Moscow provided his government with the financial and technical support it needed to recruit soldiers and equip a modern army. Additionally, Soviet advisers played a key role in transforming the GMD into an organization that could easily have qualified as a Leninist party had it shared communist values. At the GMD's First National Congress in January 1924, Sun proclaimed that China was in such disarray that it would have to accept a Nationalist government before it made the transition to a republican one. This situation, he argued, made it necessary to build the state "through the party." Accordingly, the delegates, including their communist members, formally endorsed the Soviet-style principle of party supervision at every level of the government's operations. They assigned the GMD the leading role in implementing the Three People's Principles, and in the spirit of democratic centralism, bound its members to strict party discipline. They also obliged those who belonged to affiliated organizations, such as trade unions or provincial assemblies, to adhere to party priorities. Finally, the congress adopted a Comintern-style set of Three Great Principles: collaboration with the Soviet Union, the CCP, and the working class and the peasantry.[16]

Yet, far from being relegated to a second-class position, it was the self-identified Leninist party that benefited the most from this arrangement. This "bloc within" strategy, as the Comintern termed the CCP's role in the alliance, allowed the communists to step out of the GMD's shadow. Joint affiliation meant that communist agitators could identify potential recruits by emphasizing issues—labor activism, the formation of peasant unions—that set the CCP apart from the Nationalists. The party could also forge alliances with sympathetic, leftist members of the GMD. In May 1924, the CCP leadership adopted a resolution to accomplish precisely this objective by publicizing the differences between the GMD's right and left wings and expressly including the latter in its class-based, anti-imperialist struggle.[17] In 1925, the communists gained an unusually favorable platform for expressing their views when Mao Zedong was appointed director of the GMD's propaganda bureau.

Simultaneously, the alliance with the Nationalists forced the CCP's leaders to address their party's weaknesses. Until its Third National Congress in June 1923, the CCP resembled the early Bolsheviks. It was little more than a collection of intellectuals and regional activists, each of whom had his own ideas about the party's priorities and felt no greater obligation than to himself. Under the Comintern's direction, the party adopted a unified chain of command, functionally specific departments, and explicit procedures and regulations. At Chen's urging, the Central Bureau committed itself to collective decision making to unify its policies. These changes easily meshed with a Leninist focus on conspiratorial action. The Central Executive Committee created cells in factories, schools, and other workplaces to expose its members to concrete social needs and spread propaganda. It also formed bloc organizations to integrate these activities and reinforce cadre loyalties.[18]

Nowhere were the benefits of the "bloc within" strategy more clearly spelled out than in the inclusion of CCP members in the Whampoa Military Academy. The Academy's purpose was to build a professional officer corps. It was funded by the Soviet Union and supplied with Soviet advisers to instruct cadets in the ways of modern warfare. Under its first commander, Chiang Kai-shek, the Academy offered a curriculum that emphasized patriotic duties and obedience to centralized authority. Since the communists were no less immersed in the militarized and nationalistic culture of the time, they easily adapted to these norms.

Furthermore, the CCP had the incredibly good fortune of being able to use the school as a platform for promoting Marxism. Notably, the new deputy head of the Political Department, Zhou Enlai, was an experienced party activist who had converted to communism while in a work-study program in Europe. Although Zhou, too, was committed to national unification, he was typical among the communists for having a subversive understanding of the term "unity" based upon the overthrow of existing class relations. Under his direction, the CCP established two central organs within the Academy, one to expose students to Marxist theory and the other to coordinate clandestine operations. Under the slogan "A good communist is a good member of the Guomindang nucleus," the CCP added to its influence by placing party workers in nearly every political department of the National Revolutionary Army (NRA).[19]

The second major benefit of the "bloc within" strategy was the GMD leadership's acceptance of the division of labor within the united front. After Sun Yat-sen's death in 1925, Chiang Kai-shek emerged as the principal proponent of his party's military ambitions. Under his command and with the encouragement of the Soviets, Chiang enlisted the support of southern military governors and, in July 1926, launched the Northern Expedition that Sun had hoped to undertake three years earlier. As the Nationalist armies marched northward, Chiang and his generals were immediately presented with a choice. During their advance, they could focus on winning the support of the urban working class and disaffected peasants, a stratum that was central to Sun's concept of "people's livelihood." Or, since this emphasis risked alienating the industrial interests and large landowners whose financial support and political connections were integral to their campaign, they could turn over the work of cultivating the grassroots to others. They chose the apparently less risky path and allowed the CCP to pursue the latter task.

It was far from apparent at the time, but the CCP's approach to this question hinted at a possible shift in its conception of revolutionary politics. During the late Qing and early republican periods, the promotion of major change was primarily understood to begin at the top of the social hierarchy. Chiang espoused this position as well. Educated elites concentrated on attacking traditional institutions and seeking to replace them with representative bodies whose enlightened policies would eventually trickle down to the masses. In contrast, there was an alternative route to revolutionary change. This approach would begin at the bottom of the social order and rise upward. The party would still play a leading role in this process, but its success would depend on its cadres' skill in turning mass discontent into action.

Nonetheless, the mixed record of the CCP's effort to spur labor unrest in the cities suggested that such a reorientation of party strategy would have been problematic. With scant resources at their disposal, communist agitators formed clubs and schools to educate workers and laid the foundations for trade unions by organizing factory committees. Yet, their ability to sustain these undertakings was constrained by both the difficulty of managing these associations and the hostility of employers and local officials. Although communists played active roles in a spate of labor disturbances throughout this period, including a massive sea workers' strike in Hong Kong in 1922 and a railway workers' strike along the Beijing-Hankow Railroad in 1923, these instances of industrial action were largely one-off events.

At least theoretically, one could make the case that militant protest was more likely to be found amid China's overwhelmingly peasant population. By the early 1920s, the breakdown of the traditional governance structures in the countryside that had begun at the turn of the nineteenth century was complete. During the warlord era, regional officials and the gentry abandoned all pretense of looking after the welfare of peasant communities. Facing the erosion of their means of subsistence, recurrent natural disasters, and the attacks of marauding bandits, peasants were driven by rage and the threat of starvation into spontaneous acts of rebellion.

Chen Duxiu and other communist leaders were clearly aware of these incendiary conditions, but they were hesitant to modify the tenets of orthodox Marxism to accommodate them. This is not to say that the CCP ignored the countryside. One agrarian activist, Peng Pai, the secretary of the GMD's Peasant Department, set up a political training institute and established large-scale peasant associations in Guangdong Province in 1922. Still, these bodies were not the revolutionary organs that Mao glorified in the Hunan Report. Rather than addressing the explosive issue of land distribution, they concentrated on everyday complaints over rents, wages, and food prices.

Just as with other traumas from China's past, such as the punitive settlements after the Opium War and the war with Japan, a single event was sufficient to transform both the CCP's understanding of its priorities and its prospects for acquiring equal standing with the GMD. On May 30, 1925, British soldiers in Shanghai fired on a peaceful demonstration of students who were protesting the killing of a striking worker in a Japanese textile factory. When several students died, even larger protests broke out in Guangzhou. Within two days, an eruption of antiforeigner unrest swept across multiple regions. Students flooded into Beijing's Tiananmen Square to demand redress for the killings, and southern China was crippled by strikes.

This outcry catalyzed the CCP. Emboldened by the possibility of directing a nationwide uprising, the party's leaders hastened to link one form of mass fervor, patriotism, with another, the call for class rebellion. Lending credibility to this charge, the party achieved its first great success in Shanghai in 1925 when the Consolidated Workers' Union led hundreds of thousands of factory workers into the streets to protest the collusion of Chinese capitalists and foreign imperialists.

The May 30 upheavals were especially significant for forcing the CCP's leaders to confront a defining question: What kind of party did they wish to have? In October 1925, the Central Executive Committee provided part of the answer. Breaking with the practice of recruiting the majority of the party's members from the upper reaches of society, it loosened its requirements to facilitate the admission of the workers and peasants it claimed to represent. The Committee justified the decision by maintaining that it was a "mistaken view" to insist that candidates for membership be familiar with the intricacies of Marxism or already have extensive revolutionary experience. These matters could be learned. Instead, the Committee emphasized, recruits should exhibit "class consciousness and loyalty to the revolution." Accordingly, the party should exercise flexibility in selecting its cadres.[20] This decision paid off in a massive increase in the party's size. Whereas the CCP had a mere 994 members in 1925, its ranks swelled to 10,000 one year later. By April 1927, it could claim over 57,000 members.[21]

This strategy also provided the CCP with an incentive to publicly redefine its relationship with the GMD. At the October meeting, the Central Executive Committee essentially changed the conditions of the united front by adopting a two-track policy toward its partners. One of these tracks, it specified, was to bring sympathetic members of the GMD's left wing "close to the majority of the masses." The other was to "oppose the rightists" and "expose [their] slogans and strategies."[22] One year later, the Comintern affirmed this two-pronged approach by underscoring the CCP's responsibility to prevent the rightists from turning the GMD into an exclusively bourgeois party.

THE WRITER FROM HUNAN

These gyrations in the CCP's conception of its functions provide a valuable opportunity to speculate about Mao's motivations in writing the Hunan Report. In some ways, Mao's examination of the conditions in his home province in 1927 coincided neatly with the CCP's growing appreciation of the need to incorporate ordinary Chinese workers and peasants into its ranks. In this respect, Mao's Report was a strategic document designed to amplify the party's appeal. At the same time, however, it was truly distinctive in breaking with the conventional understanding of the party's leading role and focusing on the sources of revolution from below.

Born in 1893 into a well-off peasant family in the vicinity of Changsha, Hunan, Mao experienced many of the tumultuous political and intellectual mood swings of the educated strata of his generation. He was initially impressed by the desperate struggles of officials in the late nineteenth century to reform the monarchy but converted to Sun Yat-sen's vision of a republican China as the Qing dynasty evaporated. Like many early communists, he was then swept up in the moral righteousness and indignation of the New Culture and May Fourth Movements. Yet instead of embracing his peers' faith in Western institutions and liberal-democratic values, he sought a home in the writings of anarchists like Mikhail Bakunin and Peter Kropotkin. Mao was especially taken by their conviction that educated people should find their way to truth by laboring alongside the common man. After meeting Chen

Duxiu and Li Dazhao at Peking University, he began to call himself a communist. But his conception of Marxism, which he acquired from only a few secondary accounts, was already tinged with the voluntaristic, antiorganizational sentiments that would shape his policies until his death. Revolution, as the young Mao understood it, was not a matter of waiting for the dialectics of historical progress to present a sure opportunity. It was an act of heroic will, driven by the determination to replace corrupt institutions and reactionary traditions with healthy forms of human interaction and the observance of high moral standards.

In 1921, Mao was already building a reputation as a political commentator and ran an activist bookstore and newspaper in Changsha. Unlike many leftists, however, he was not merely a man of ideas acting above the fray. Mao was an agitator. Through the All-Hunan Federation of Labor Organizations, which sought to speak for an array of workers' groups, such as carpenters, miners, masons, and railway employees, Mao rallied the union's members to stage work stoppages and factory protests. Most of his efforts did not get very far; some were ruthlessly suppressed. Still, they were early indications of Mao's talent for mobilizing believers to serve higher ideals.

In my view, this context is crucial for understanding the stark differences between the Hunan Report and the formulaic, Comintern-style statements of a majority of the CCP's leaders. Every line of the Report is the work of an activist who is fervently seeking to engage his party in the plight of the lower classes. Naturally, there is much that is hyperbolic about Mao's prediction that hundreds of millions of peasants would rise "like a mighty storm" to engulf the nation. Although the movement to form peasant associations had spread throughout large portions of southern China by the mid-1920s, political infighting within the GMD and repression by local authorities had sapped much of its energy by the time Mao returned to Hunan. Hence, on strictly empirical grounds, there was little to support his claims. But, as I have suggested earlier, it was not sheer historical fantasy to imagine a mass uprising that would, in Mao's words, "sweep all of the imperialists, warlords, corrupt officials, local tyrants, and evil gentry into their graves." The White Lotus, Taiping, and Boxer Rebellions were evidence of the overpowering fury of the lower classes. All of these upheavals, and especially the last, which occurred while he was young, were products of the breakdown of central authority in the empire. In fact, in the mid-1920s, a unified China was far from being restored. Adding to the force of Mao's claims, the long duration of these incidents of unrest lent credibility to the proposition that one did not need to wait for social unrest to occur. In the right circumstances, the assault upon central authority could be consciously carried out according to a coherent body of ideas. Why, then, the Report provokes its readers to ask, should one be surprised that China's peasantry was primed to turn the world upside down?

Finally, Mao's appeal is a foreshadowing of a coming divide within the CCP over the party's identity as both a revolutionary idea and a revolutionary organization. As I have indicated at the opening of this chapter, the Report is not directed at the peasantry at all. Mao's target is his fellow party members. Instead of responding to the peasants' courage and heroism with concrete action, these privileged elites, as Mao portrays them, have essentially become bureaucrats. They have joined the GMD, the legal trade unions, and other establishment bodies in fostering an antirevolutionary culture of officialdom. "All without exception have their executive committee members," Mao emphasizes, "it is indeed a world of committee men."

Mao's fascination with voluntarist approaches to political change during his days at Peking University shows through in this diagnosis. Naturally, he underscores that it is not the party's function to take the place of the masses in overthrowing their oppressors. "It is wrong for anybody else to do it for them," he insists. However, he places the burden of responsibility on the party's will to act. Given the imminence of the revolution, the party must reconnect with its mass base. It is time to step forward, Mao explains, to "draw the bow" and to "indicate the motion."[23]

The Party's Turning Point

The few CCP members who took the Hunan Report seriously at this time may have wondered whether significant numbers of communists would come around to Mao's more nuanced understanding of the party's leading role. If so, the CCP leadership provided a negative answer. When the party's leaders raised Mao's themes, but not the Hunan Report itself, at its Fifth National Congress in late April 1924, they emphasized that their organization was to be regarded as "not only a mass party but a Bolshevik Party."[24] To retain this identity, they stipulated that the party should concentrate on further centralizing its operations. Most revealing with respect to Mao's analysis, they reaffirmed the central role of the proletariat in the revolution. Although the leadership paid lip service to addressing the sources of inequality in the countryside, the punitive measures it recommended were to be imposed only on the wealthiest landholders.

This disjunction between Mao's understanding of the party's purposes and the thinking of the organization's leaders leads one to wonder what form their movement would have taken if they had retained the upper hand. What if the author of the Hunan Report had never succeeded in making his views known, let alone been in the position to impose his idea of revolution on an entire nation? Fortunately for Mao, a tragedy provided him with the unexpected opportunity to make his case. On April 12, 1927, Chiang Kai-shek declared war on the CCP, launching an assault on the communist-led General Labor Union in Shanghai. With the support of local militias and criminal gangs, NRA troops swept through the city, arresting labor leaders, beating agitators, and shooting protestors. Chiang's campaign quickly escalated into a full-scale attack on communists and union organizers in other cities and culminated in the slaughter of thousands of members of peasant associations.

Far from provoking this bloodshed, the leaders of the General Labor Union had actually prepared the way for Chiang's troops to enter Shanghai by organizing a citywide strike of 800,000 workers and setting up a new municipal government. But their influence over these forces was enough to convince Chiang that the communists had become too powerful to justify further collaboration. Over the following summer and fall 1927, the CCP's attempts to counter the Nationalists' attacks all ended in failure. In August, communist organizers fomented an uprising in Nanchang, hoping to convince GMD leftists to join their side. However, the faction's leaders refused to break ranks with their party. Likewise, when Moscow urged the CCP to instigate revolts against local authorities during the autumn harvest season, the party suffered more ignominious defeats. Finally, in December, an attempt to set up a communal government in Guangzhou, purportedly along the lines of the Paris Commune of 1871, was crushed by local warlords and NRA troops.

These events marked the beginning of the Chinese Civil War and an epoch in which Chiang Kai-shek and the GMD dominated national politics. In 1928, the Nationalist government proclaimed victory in the Northern Expedition. Once the NRA had taken control of the rich Yangtze River valley and Shanghai, its troops marched northward to capture Beijing. Chiang made Nanjing the nation's new capital and swiftly set up a quasi-dictatorial government. Although the militarized regional governors' support for the regime was more tenuous than the GMD's leaders let on, the appearance of success gave the party's leaders credibility. Everywhere Chiang's forces went, the GMD acquired new members and thousands of Chinese of all social classes leaped onto the bandwagon of national unity.

In contrast, the CCP entered a period of desolation. In only a year, the party lost nearly 20,000 members; many were killed in the fighting but even more defected in the wake of the party's defeats. This adversity was compounded by the loss of prominent personalities. Some died for their beliefs; Li Dazhao was executed in Beijing. Others fell victim to internal battles within the CCP. Chen Duxiu was made a scapegoat for the party's failures and ostracized. Dismayed by the proletariat's failure to rise up against their new enemies and reduced to fighting an underground battle with Chiang's armies, the CCP's remaining leadership in Shanghai initially turned to an idealized version of Leninism. According to this conception, the party would continue to rely upon the centralized decision making and discipline required of any clandestine organization. In recognition of the movement's dispersion and perilous state, however, they pledged to respect the decisions of party branches in other cities and rural locations.

Yet, the efficacy of this shift was undermined by infighting. Arguing that China was the weak link in a chain of imperialist power, a new general secretary, Li Lisan, ordered the party's fledgling Red Army to stage attacks on the cities and promote large-scale urban insurrection. These efforts failed miserably. But instead of leading to a reassessment of the party's position, they opened the way for even greater rigidity. Li was replaced by an equally dogmatic group of young communists who had drifted back to China after studying at Moscow's Sun Yat-sen University. These "returned Bolsheviks," as they became known, expanded the party's dictatorial role and instituted Stalinist-style witch hunts to cleanse its ranks of supposedly counterrevolutionary elements.

Despite these developments, an assortment of communists who fled to the south after the Shanghai massacre were spurred to think about their party in a different way. In the barren mountains and border regions of Jiangxi and Hunan Provinces, they organized small armies and established rural base areas to defend themselves against Chiang Kai-shek's troops. In the course of struggling for survival, they wrestled with a difficult question. Was the CCP primarily a political organization acting in the name of the dictatorship of the proletariat? Or had it become a military organization responsible for mobilizing the people to fight their enemies?

Mao was forced to confront this issue earlier than many of his comrades. In October 1927, he and a tiny contingent of Red Army soldiers were driven into the Jinggang Mountains by advancing NRA troops. Mao arrived in his new home with the stubborn convictions of a young communist determined to bring justice to a needy population. He immersed himself in the violent business of taking from the rich and giving to the poor. In a testimony to his lack of political experience, he ordered the indiscriminate confiscation of the landholdings of the few property owners who could be remotely categorized as wealthy, with the result that the local economy was fractured. More importantly, Mao directed his attention toward building what he needed most—a viable army. Far away from the scrutiny of the CCP center, he sought to bring together the motley collection of vagabonds, NRA deserters, mercenaries, and poor peasants who had chosen to follow him.

A different commander might have been overwhelmed by this challenge. After all, Mao's soldiers had nothing in common with the disciplined cadets with whom he had previously interacted at the Whampoa Military Academy. In an essay in November 1928, "The Struggle in the

Chingkang [Jinggang] Mountains," Mao conceded that his troops lacked the skills and training of the NRA and its warlord allies. But, he argued, they made up for their shortcomings by embodying the power of will in action. In his assessment, they showed in unending marches under sweltering heat and seemingly hopeless guerrilla battles with superior, conventional armies that they were endowed with nobility. Indeed, in Mao's mythological depiction, these simple soldiers embraced a "democratic" culture. Their disposition to cooperation gave them the confidence to fight with high moral purpose. Supposedly, officers did not beat their underlings. Food was shared equally. According to Mao's flight from reality, the army supposedly treated even enemy prisoners with respect and solicitude.[25]

Mao's characterization of the army as a virtuous agent is especially illuminating because of the contrast it represents with his treatment of the party. His essay on his Jinggang Mountains experience treats the CCP with much of the same condescension that he evinced in the Hunan Report. According to Mao, the party was always welcomed by village communities because it professed strong values and virtuous behavior. Its problem, however, was that it turned out to be full of opportunists. In his description, many comrades lacked the will to fight; those who found the will resorted to acts of "blind insurrection" that inevitably led to disaster. Furthermore, party branches were weighed down by the malady of localism. Instead of orienting themselves around the good of the entire movement, their representatives merely cared about the narrow interests of their clans and villages. One could hardly build a militant Marxist party on these foundations, he insisted.[26]

On a personal basis, Mao matched this juxtaposition of the image of the noble soldier and the imperfect party organization with a greater inclination than ever to assert his views against the prevailing policy of the central party leadership. In a letter to a fellow Red commander, Lin Biao, written on January 5, 1930, shortly after leading his beleaguered troops out of the highlands into the borderlands of Jiangxi and Fujian, Mao sounded a lot like Trotsky in his interpretation of the concept of party discipline. He maintained that one should only feel required to follow the instructions of higher authorities when they were based upon an informed understanding of local conditions. Contending that the

Central Executive had grossly underestimated the peasantry's readiness for revolution, he accused his distant comrades of promoting a culture of pessimism. Although they had appropriately emphasized the centrality of the class struggle in the cities, he stressed, they failed to appreciate the opportunities that existed in rural China.

In addition, Mao contended that this shortsightedness had led the party center to make major errors in military strategy. It was foolhardy, he lectured, to focus solely on the "objective" capabilities of the Red Army. Objectively, its numbers were small. But despite this weakness, the army was "subjectively" strong. Thanks to a deep familiarity with their setting, its guerrilla soldiers could take advantage of the manifold expressions of the class struggle in Chinese society—labor strikes, peasant uprisings, NRA soldiers' mutinies, and student protests—to incite the masses to action. Once again, Mao turned to hyperbole to make his case. "All China is littered with dry faggots which will soon be aflame," he proclaimed. "The saying, 'A single spark can start a prairie fire,' is an apt description of how the current situation will develop."[27]

THE LONG MARCH MYTHOLOGY

In the coming decades, Mao's depiction of the revolutionary challenge in the countryside would shape the official definition of the CCP's leading role in much the same way as Stalin's very different *Foundations of Leninism* did for the Soviet Union. Still, one must be careful not to exaggerate Mao's initial ability to promote this "prairie fire." For one thing, despite his highly developed sense of self-worth, he was not yet a dominant figure within the party. Moreover, his unique interpretation of the application of Leninism to Chinese conditions was still evolving. After arriving in the city of Ruijin, he immediately set about transforming a military base into a full-fledged socialist experiment, the Jiangxi Soviet. Demonstrating that he was not totally dismissive of the need for political organization, Mao and his supporters built a functioning government with a local administrative apparatus, courts, schools, and even a postal system. In contrast to his impulsive behavior in the mountains, Mao showed that he had learned something about the delicate balance of a functioning economy. He encouraged cadres to experiment with different models of land reform and to practice bottom-up work styles that took into account the perspectives of the local populace. He also won support by attacking traditional practices, such as arranged marriages. Still, this was not the only face that Mao brought to his new constituency. He had no inhibitions about using violent means. Under the pretext of responding to Chiang Kai-shek's "communist extermination campaigns," he joined other communist leaders in conducting brutal purges of purported enemy agents within the party and the army.

Mao's control over the Jiangxi Soviet was far from uncontested. He was opposed by local communists who found his agrarian policies too extreme. From their positions in Shanghai, Li Lisan's supporters attacked him for shirking party orthodoxy about the proletariat's leading role. When the "returned Bolsheviks" took over, they presented Mao with a new obstacle by moving the party headquarters to Jiangxi. To cement their authority, they relieved Mao of his position as commissar of the Red Army and appointed him to a titular post as head of the Soviet government.

It is provocative to think about what would have happened to the CCP if, at this point, Mao had been permanently relegated to the sidelines. Would his nuanced understanding of party leadership have been replaced by a formulaic conception of Stalinist dictatorship? Looking two to three decades down the road, would a different leader have undertaken the devastating experiment in forced economic development of the Great Leap Forward or allowed the war against established institutions of the Great Proletarian Cultural Revolution? As I have argued in my examination of Stalin's policies in chapter 5, different leaders can make a difference. Still, this does not necessarily mean that their policies will be any less violent or erratic.

Once again, contingent events intervened to give Mao the opportunity to assert himself. In fall 1934, the leaders of the Jiangxi government concluded that they were no longer capable of defending the Soviet from the unremitting attacks of the Nationalist armies. In mid-October, two army corps began a strategic retreat. With no clear idea about where they were going and leaving thousands of wounded soldiers and family members behind, two columns of roughly 86,000 soldiers, party officials, and government personnel broke through the NRA blockade and began the arduous journey known as the Long March. Over a period of twelve months, under the command of Lin Biao and Peng Dehuai, they climbed mountains, crossed arid grasslands and bogs, and ferried rivers while conducting guerrilla warfare against NRA forces. By the time the Red Army commanders decided on their destination, the remote Yan'an Soviet in northern Shaanxi Province, an unforgiving combination of battle casualties, starvation, disease, and desertions had cut their numbers to fewer than 6,000 people.

At first blush, one might think that these desperate survivors had little to offer their movement. The Long March was not a victory march. It was all about defeat. In Mao's hands, however, the struggle to surmount their misfortunes became the stuff of grand mythology. Along the way, the CCP held a party conference in the city of Zunyi at which Mao scored a major victory over the "returned Bolsheviks." He was appointed a full member of the five-member Standing Committee and assigned a key role in military planning. Thus, upon his arrival in Yan'an in late 1935, Mao was quick to take advantage of his increased power in the party by laying claim to the idea that both he and his Red soldiers had accomplished a world-historical feat. The Long March, he pronounced in an essay in December, was "a manifesto, a propaganda force, a seeding-machine." It was a manifesto, he stressed, because it showed the world that "the Red Army is an army of heroes, while the imperialists and running dogs are impotent." It was a propaganda force because it announced to "some 200 million people in eleven provinces that the road of the Red Army is their only road to liberation." And it was a "seeding-machine" because it sowed "many seeds which will sprout, leaf, blossom, and bear fruit, and will yield a harvest in the future."[28]

Mao's description of the Long March was grossly exaggerated. When the Red soldiers and party members entered villages, this "array of heroes" was greeted with manifest mistrust. In the eyes of ordinary peasants who had rarely traveled far from home, these urban bearers of the good news about Marxism were a threat to their precarious existence. The soldiers' arrival meant that the village would be caught up in battles with the NRA that had no relevance to the daily struggle of life on the land. Moreover, like the Russian peasantry a half century earlier who had been repelled by the populist "going to the people" movement of the 1860s and 1870s, they were easily alienated by the communists' pretensions to educate them and offer foreign remedies for their troubles.

Correspondingly, the communist cadres among these soldiers often had no more than a vague idea of what they were supposed to do. At best, they had only a superficial understanding of Marxism. Giving little thought to the ramifications of their actions, they summarily expropriated landlord property. They labeled local officials as "bad elements," regardless of their standing in the community. Worse still, despite the orders of commanders, including Mao, to show respect to the villagers who greeted them, Red Army soldiers were often driven by hunger and despair to steal their hosts' food and property.

Where the Long March did have a positive impact was in affording the leadership the opportunity to depict the Marxist cause as far superior to the dictates of a distant GMD government. In addition to offering local populations the promise of social justice, the communists presented themselves as the legitimate representatives of the Chinese nation. In this task, they were helped immeasurably by a critical mistake by Chiang Kai-shek in the face of the looming threat of yet another war with Japan. Four years earlier, China's age-old enemy had annexed Manchuria and was already staging intermittent attacks on cities as far south as Shanghai. As the possibility of all-out war escalated, Chiang gave priority to the destruction of the Red Army over repelling Japan's advancing troops. This error was a blessing for the communists. As they moved from one region to the next, officers and party officials could draw upon the broadly interpreted Marxist dichotomy between the wrongdoers and the wronged, the few and the many, to enlist the support of ordinary Chinese who were looking for an easily intelligible way of understanding their plight. In the CCP's characterization, one campaign was against a historical foe, imperialism, this time represented by perfidious Japan. The other was against the class enemy, including NRA forces, rich landlords, and their allied warlords, who had supposedly confirmed their indifference to the cause of national unity. This was not the first time that Chinese radicals had conjured these images. Elements of each argument could be found in the patriotic appeals of the May Fourth Movement.

In response to Comintern pressure, Mao took the high road in 1935, calling for a united front with the GMD to fight Japan. The threat to China, he told his presumably dubious comrades, required the CCP to exercise the same flexibility as the guerrilla armies that had enabled it to survive. At a moment of national peril, he asserted, there was no room for dogmatic behavior. The narrow-minded "closed-doorism" advocated by communists who were obsessed with the "Holy Writ" of Marxism would result in certain defeat. They needed to accept the fact that revolution "always follows a tortuous road, and never a straight one." Then, too, Mao added, true communists were open to viewing the class struggle in a more flexible way than they had in the past. Thus, an authentic united front should be composed of all patriotic forces, including even rich peasants, moderate trade unions, and the progressive bourgeoisie. According to Mao, this broader view of revolution would provide the basis for the creation of an eventual "people's republic."[29]

Mao's residency in the Yan'an Soviet provided him and other communists living in guerrilla bases with the opportunity to develop new ideas about what it meant to serve the people. By virtue of their isolation from the outside world, Red cadres and soldiers had to learn what it meant to live among simple villagers. Accordingly, their leaders instructed them to adopt the same flexible attitudes and readiness for adaptation that they practiced in their battles with the NRA and the Japanese. Under these conditions, and with the same quixotic spirit as the European utopian socialists, like Claude-Henri de St. Simon and Étienne Cabet, they dreamed that they were forming a new type of human community. In Yan'an in particular, soldiers and party members lived together in caves, grew their own food, and engaged in earnest discussions about Marxist texts and current affairs. No one was more adept at cultivating this heroic mystique than Mao. As the de facto leader of the Soviet, he made a point of conspicuously practicing the doctrine of self-sacrifice. In his cave home, he affected the coarse habits and mannerisms of the simple peasant; he even tended his own vegetable garden. Of course, the line between appearance and reality in these measures was obscure. Still, this vision of a culture of sublime asceticism was magnetic. By the end of the 1930s, tens of thousands of youthful idealists had rushed to Yan'an and other soviets to join the party and fight for their nation.

In this light, the CCP's dual commitment to communist revolution and national unification was an incalculable advantage when Japan launched a full-scale invasion of China in July 1937. Up to this point, it was possible for skeptics of Mao's appeals for a renewed united front to argue that the Nationalists and their bourgeois supporters could never be trusted. But at the urging of the Soviet Union, the war compelled the two adversaries to join forces to fight a common enemy. At this juncture, however, in contrast with the mid-1920s, the CCP could count itself as an equal. By 1940, the party had 800,000 members and 500,000 troops under its command, as well as the expressed support of the Soviet Union.[30] Hence, the preservation of its distinctive identity was not dependent on good fortune. The CCP could defend itself on its own terms. Naturally, Mao assumed that he should play the pivotal role in defining the party's mission.

Toward a "Sinified" Marxism

By the second half of the 1930s, Mao had clearly acquired the power to dictate the CCP's policies. But control of the party organization was far from being his preeminent goal. He was determined to command the realm of ideas. In his secluded residence in Yan'an, which he rarely left for nearly a decade, he set out to make his mark as a Marxist theorist by familiarizing himself with the writings of Marx, Lenin, Stalin, and others from the pantheon of communist history. Some of Mao's works during this period, such as a treatise on dialectical materialism, will not go down as classics in the annals of Marxism. However, he made a lasting contribution by articulating what he called a "Sinified" path to communism. Practical as always, Mao focused on China's specific conditions. There was no such thing, he declared at the CCP's Sixth Plenum in 1938, as "abstract Marxism." "What we call concrete Marxism is Marxism that has taken on a national forum, that is, Marxism applied to the concrete struggle in the concrete conditions prevailing in China." The CCP's function, Mao explained almost sentimentally, was to discern the policies most appropriate to his nation's needs and then to express them in a "new and vital Chinese style and manner, pleasing to the eye and to the ear of the Chinese common people."[31]

One year later, in December 1939, Mao spelled out the defining characteristics of this Sinified approach in a chapter in a party textbook, *The Chinese Revolution and the Chinese Communist Party.*[32] In his clearest statement to date about China's uniqueness, he maintained that the Chinese revolution would not be a proletarian revolution like that which had taken place in Russia. His country first needed to undergo the capitalist stage of development. Yet, showing just how far Marxism's dichotomous structure could be stretched, he maintained that two interrelated struggles would serve to accelerate China's special path beyond capitalism and into socialism. The first was the struggle against imperialism that had begun in the nineteenth century. The war with Japan alone, Mao contended, could not account for the rapid coalescence of very different social classes into the united front. Their sense of shared purpose was the product of China's long battle against colonial exploitation, beginning with the Opium Wars and leading to the Taiping Rebellion, the Republican Revolution of 1911, the May Fourth Movement, and the Northern Expedition.

Mao's second struggle, which reflected the idea of Chinese exceptionalism, was against the feudal landlord class. Unlike in Europe and America, Mao explained, the abolition of this class would not simply lead to the ascendancy of the bourgeoisie. Thanks to the advances of the "world proletarian-socialist revolution" (i.e., the Comintern), he informed his readers, China would experience a revolution of a new type, a "new democratic revolution," which would unite its supporters around the destruction of imperialism and its reactionary allies. In this way, it seemed, a Sinified approach would be consistent with Marxist principles. It would just have a broader reach. The new democratic revolution would lead to a "joint dictatorship of several revolutionary classes under the leadership of the proletariat."[33]

These were stirring words. Naturally, they begged the question of how the CCP, as the vanguard of the proletariat and presumed leader of this coalition, would hold such a collection of diverse interests together. Mao's answer, enshrined as "Mao Zedong Thought" in a new party constitution in 1945, was to advance an innovative approach to the education of party members based upon the concept of "rectification." In the early 1940s, the CCP had faced a dilemma that was all too familiar to its Soviet mentors. As the party expanded, it encountered the enormous challenge of having to educate hundreds of thousands of new members about party priorities and the lessons of two decades of seeking to put them into practice. Many knew nothing about Marxism and Leninism; more had joined solely out of nationalist fervor; others were simply opportunists.

One way of dealing with these problems was to offer cadres in base camps rudimentary classes on party history and acquaint them with the unique challenges presented by the war with Japan. Naturally, true to the CCP's revolutionary roots, Mao and his associates had an even more comprehensive conception of political education that went far beyond the inculcation of facts. Beginning in 1942, the party required tens of thousands of cadres to engage in public acts of "self-criticism." In the presence of their peers, members were forced to bare their breasts about their personal failings. These sins ranged from arrogance and elitism to corruption and self-centeredness. When cadres were judged to have exhibited sincere contrition and a readiness to improve their thoughts and actions, they were absolved of their sins and welcomed back to the fold. Those who failed these tests were expelled.

What made Mao's approach stand out is that he did not intend for rectification to end here. In a seminal lecture, "Rectify the Party's Style of Work," which he gave at the inauguration of the Central Committee's party school in Yan'an in December 1942, Mao emphasized that good communists had to *earn* the right to lead the people by educating themselves. With the same forceful language he had used in criticizing the haughty and uninformed behavior of party members in earlier years, Mao observed that there was something "not quite right, not quite proper" in many comrades' behavior. One impediment to correct thinking was the "malady of subjectivism" that led them to assume that they could make effective policy on their own volition without having to engage directly in practical work. Another was the more damaging offense of "sectarianism" when members put their own interests ahead of the whole. This malady not only promoted factionalism within the CCP, it prevented the party at a time of national urgency

from reaching out to diverse segments of Chinese society who were prepared to fight alongside it. Finally, some cadres were guilty of "stereo-
typed party writing"—a "vehicle for filth," as Mao called it—which
led them to treat Leninism as a lifeless dogma rather than a scientific
guide to action. This was a manifestation of the broader malady of
"dogmatism" that prevented the party from exercising the flexibility to
hold the national struggle together.[34]

From today's vantage point, these seem like arcane failings. Yet at
a time of war and social struggle, Mao had good reason for wanting to
counter the assumption that party cadres should have a ready-made
formula for success. As he saw it, the lesson of the Long March and the
guerrilla battles for survival was that the party needed to "free the minds"
of any comrades who assumed that their judgment was better than
others'.[35] In fact, many of the CCP's fresh recruits found Mao's demands that they confront their failings exhilarating. Seeing themselves
in their new roles as the revolutionary elect, it made sense that the CCP
should have higher expectations of them than a bourgeois party like
the GMD.

Above all, Mao's radical understanding of correct thinking meant
that these cadres' understanding of the party's functions should be based
upon a correct relationship with the masses. In an essay written in
June 1943, "Some Questions concerning Methods of Leadership," Mao
expressed this perspective in a formulation called the "mass line." In what
may be the most frequently cited paragraph in all of Mao's works, he
instructed his followers to "take the ideas of the masses (scattered and
unsystematic ideas) and concentrate them (through study turn them
into concentrated and systematic ideas), then go to the masses and propagate and explain these ideas until the masses embrace them as their
own, hold fast to them and translate them into action, and test the cor-
rectness of these ideas in such action. Then once again concentrate ideas
from the masses and once again take them to the masses so that the
ideas are persevered in and carried through. And so on, over and over
again in an endless spiral, with the ideas becoming more correct, more
vital and richer each time."[36]

Not every feature of this Sinified version of Marxism is novel. The
top-down element of the Leninist concept of revolutionary agitation

suffuses the paragraph. The masses still require guidance from above. They need someone to explain their true interests and show them how they should act. Mao's ideological innovation, however, is that his cadres and the masses must constantly work together to identify the truth. In the same spirit that was embodied in the Hunan Report's break with the intellectuals who had first inspired him to action, both communists and noncommunists, Mao's message to the party's members was that they should begin with the nascent ideas of those below them if they wanted to call themselves Marxist.

It made sense that Mao would arrive at such a conception of the party's role. In contrast to Lenin and Stalin, who had mainly focused on revolution from on high, he knew something about the masses by virtue of having lived among them. Still, it would take two years before the war with Japan was over and an additional four years before a renewed civil war concluded with the CCP's defeat of the GMD. When that day arrived in 1949 and the communists' supremacy was no longer threatened by total war, China's leaders—and especially Mao himself!— would need to discern what it meant to apply a doctrine of Mao Zedong Thought to a country that was finally under their control.

CHAPTER 7

Monolithic Socialism

On May 15, 1943, the Presidium of the Executive Committee of the Communist International (ECCI) made a shocking announcement. The Comintern, the organization that had inspired and coordinated the actions of a majority of the world's communist parties for a quarter of a century, would be dissolved. Since 1919, the statement affirmed, the Comintern had played a historic role. Everywhere, it had saved working-class parties from collapse by defending "the teachings of Marxism from vulgarization and distortion by opportunistic elements in the working-class movement." It had guided these parties in mobilizing the proletariat to defend the "chief bulwark against fascism," the USSR. Nonetheless, the authors of the statement maintained, the Comintern had "been outgrown by the growth of this movement and by the complications of its problems in separate countries." For this reason, the reliance upon "any sort of international center" had become, in the Presidium's word, a "drag" upon these parties' further development.[1]

This was unsettling news for communists around the world. For twenty-four years, the organization had been the primary communications vehicle, aside from one-on-one meetings, through which Moscow had conveyed its commands. Still, it is unlikely that the seasoned leaders of these parties would have regarded this event as a signal that they could finally move beyond the "drag" on their development and freely adapt their policies as needed. They had too much experience with the difference between Moscow's words and its actions to take Andrei Zhdanov's pronouncement literally. Thus, when the Soviet Union established a new "international center" four years later in September 1947, its closest allies would not have been surprised or, in most cases, even disappointed. This body, the Communist Information Bureau, or Cominform, had a much narrower focus. Aside from the

Russian Communist Party (Bolsheviks) (RCP[B]), it was composed of only European parties, seven from the East and two from the West. Furthermore, it was primarily a tool for legitimation and propaganda. In Eastern Europe in particular, its function was to enable its members to justify their control over recalcitrant populations and to ensure that Moscow's pronouncements about the correct road to socialism were affirmed.

It would be tempting to characterize these developments as a simple story of Soviet domination. In such a depiction, one could emphasize the deliberate manner in which the Kremlin combined its military and economic might with its virtual monopoly on the rigid doctrine of Marxism-Leninism in order to impose its desires.[2] These factors are unquestionably important. Still, for two reasons, I believe that it is misleading to interpret this long period in communist history in such a narrow fashion. First, the records of the Comintern and the Cominform are interesting precisely because the Soviet Union's leaders were constantly trying to sort out what they wanted from the two organizations' members. From the 1920s onward, the twin pressures of a rapidly changing international environment and the Soviet transition from Bolshevism to Stalinism compelled Moscow to revise its expectations of its fraternal parties at least five different times. In the initial phase, the Soviets behaved like any power that suddenly finds itself in charge of an international movement. They struggled to balance their demands with their recognition of their allies' differing expectations. Then, in the late 1920s, they chose certainty over ambiguity, demanding that the Comintern's members adhere to a single political line based upon confrontation and class struggle. After Adolf Hitler's rise to power in 1933, the Kremlin's tactics changed again, leading it to support considerably more flexible "popular front" alliances with progressive parties, including those allied with the bourgeoisie. Then, for a brief period after 1939, Moscow threw the Comintern's members into confusion by demanding their accommodation to an unthinkable non-aggression pact with Nazi Germany. Finally, Germany's invasion of the USSR in June 1941 and the defeat of the Axis powers four years later led to the return of a uniform conception of the European parties' purposes under the narrow aegis of the Cominform.

Second, and even more central to my argument, the leaders of these parties were not always prepared to define their identities exclusively in terms of Moscow's wishes. Like politicians anywhere, they had their own ideas about how they should discern their roles in their respective settings. Although they felt ideologically bound to the Soviet Union and, thanks to the Comintern's directives and material support, were prepared to make significant sacrifices on its behalf, this did not mean that they were indifferent to their specific situations. The issue, as I shall show, was whether they were in the position to act on them. In some cases, they could. Much like the Chinese Communist Party (CCP), the parties that came into being through insurgent warfare against foreign occupation forces and domestic collaborators, such as those in Italy, France, and Yugoslavia, had greater freedom of maneuver. Independently of Moscow's dictates, they were able to convince diverse segments of their populations that the Marxist class struggle and the cause of national liberation were two, intertwined expressions of the same cause.

In contrast, as I shall demonstrate, those parties that came into being as a result of their leaders' long years in Moscow and their postwar dependence on the support of the Red Army's troops were at a monumental disadvantage. Importantly, their association with the Soviet Union meant that they were deprived of the national narrative; indeed, they were regarded by their populations as agents of an enemy power. Since most of the Eastern European parties fell into this category, it is no wonder that they welcomed the black-and-white simplicity of the Cominform. There was a cost to this conformity, however. Their acceptance of a Stalinist, state-centered model of leadership meant that they, like their Soviet overseers, were prepared to sacrifice the motivating idea of communist party rule. Given the fact that they had few alternative sources of legitimation than state power, most paid this price, even at the cost of ignoring their national identities.

Between Revolution and Accommodation

The early stages of Moscow's policy toward the Comintern's member parties in the 1920s were as open to dissension and controversy as the RCP(B)'s decision to adopt the New Economic Policy (NEP). None of the Bolsheviks questioned the importance of using these parties to pave the way toward a worldwide revolution. The whole point of the Second Congress's twenty-one conditions of membership was to create the disciplined organizations that could be efficiently steered into supporting this cause. But as with the NEP, Soviet leaders were divided over strategy. On one side of the continuum, leftists, such as Trotsky and the Comintern's president, Grigory Zinoviev, espoused a militant conception of the party's role, arguing that a spirit of combat and confrontation was necessary to keep the spark of revolution alive; on the other side, rightists, such as Nikolai Bukharin and Stalin, were cautiously open to allowing individual parties to adopt accommodating postures when the conditions for upheaval were not yet ripe. Yet, as Zinoviev found when he tried to steer the Comintern through the ebb and swell of European affairs in the early 1920s, the task of identifying which approaches were most appropriate in a given context was not easy.

In Weimar Germany, the conditions for a revolutionary upheaval appeared suddenly propitious in 1923. The republic's Social Democratic coalition government was reeling under the weight of multiple crises. In January, France and Belgium used Berlin's failure to make timely reparations payments as a pretext to occupy Germany's industrial Ruhr Valley. The economy was wracked by hyperinflation, and strikes were spreading throughout the country. Hence, when Zinoviev ordered the Communist Party of Germany's (KPD) cochair, Heinrich Brandler, to prepare for a nationwide insurrection, Brandler and the party's other leaders were once again forced to ask the question that they had debated in 1919 and 1921. Was the depth of their party's national support at this moment sufficient to guarantee that the working class would respond to the call to overthrow its oppressors? Brandler was unconvinced that the KPD was strong enough to take this risk. But under pressure from Moscow, he made the case for joining Saxony's left-Social Democratic governing coalition, arguing that this alliance would allow the communists to launch a general strike. Yet, even this venture proved to be too much, too soon. When the central government sent troops to Dresden to put pressure on the coalition, the Social Democrats refused to support the strike and the KPD had to call it off.

Worse than this loss of face, however, were the catastrophic results of the KPD's attempt to take power in the northern city of Hamburg. For two days, local communists, including the dockworker and war veteran Ernst Thälmann, engaged in street battles with municipal police and right-wing militias. But Zinoviev's predictions were proven wrong again. The rebels failed to gain the support they anticipated. Instead of coming to the aid of those who claimed to speak for the interests of the proletariat, the city's trade unions and other leftist groups watched from the sidelines as the Reichswehr and the militias crushed the revolt.

These uprisings had a poignant dimension. Never one to admit that he was on the wrong side of history, Zinoviev cynically attributed the KPD's defeat to Brandler and arranged for his expulsion from the party leadership. Yet, the debacle was hardly the German communist's fault. If he had not been forced to bow to Zinoviev's dictates from afar and instead pursued a more cautious strategy, he might have been able to hold the Saxon coalition together. In this light, it was a provocative sign of the growing political uncertainty in Europe that Zinoviev soon made an about-face. In reaction to the rise of Benito Mussolini's fascist government in Rome, he instructed the ECCI to adopt a more flexible strategy toward the more heterodox Italian Communist Party (PCI).

At first glance, Zinoviev's decision might seem surprising since the PCI resembled the KPD in many ways. Like its counterpart, it was born out of the same incendiary combination of high expectations and deep disappointment of the times. In October 1919, the left wing of the Italian Socialist Party (PSI) seemed poised to lead the Italian proletariat into revolution when 30,000 automobile workers in the Piedmontese city of Turin took control of their factories and set up self-governing workers' councils. In the ensuing months, these protests swelled to include hundreds of thousands of workers in industries in other cities. Yet even though these revolts took place in regions where the concentration of Italy's working class was the greatest, they could not be sustained. The major employers refused to be cowed by the workers' demands and labor leaders were divided over the goals of the protests.

As in Germany, this defeat set the stage for the classic socialist debate between the PSI's reformist and radical factions. Was the lesson of these failed uprisings that the party should return to a conventional focus on labor agitation, or should it instead gamble on overthrowing the entire political system? At the PSI's national congress in Livorno in January 1921, this dispute led to a bitter conflict over whether the party should adhere to a Comintern directive to expel its right-wing members. When a majority of the delegates, many of whom were no less radical than the Comintern's supporters, refused to accede to this condition, the party's left wing broke away to form the PCI.

Notwithstanding the PCI's similarities to the KPD, there was a major difference between the two parties. At this point, only Italy was beset by a rising fascist movement. Hence, for purely tactical reasons, Zinoviev concluded that the PCI offered the Comintern a realistic opportunity to exert its influence in Europe. His reasoning was shaped by a bitter conflict over the party's identity between its two most prominent personalities, Antonio Gramsci and Amadeo Bordiga. Gramsci, a labor activist and prolific political theorist, advocated a democratically minded approach to mobilizing the working class that would combine the views of the revolutionary elite with the perspectives of different social and economic segments of the population. In contrast, Bordiga was a purist. He maintained that the proletariat's interests could only be expressed by its vanguard and opposed any form of collaboration outside of the communist fold.

Bordiga was well positioned to win this battle because he had the majority of the newly established PCI leadership on his side. Yet, Zinoviev and the ECCI reasoned that Gramsci had a better sense for how communists might respond to the growing rifts in Italian society by building a broad working-class following. Hence, they threw their support to Gramsci's conception of the party. When King Victor Emmanuel III invited the fascist leader Benito Mussolini to form a government in 1922, Gramsci repaid the Kremlin's trust by pursuing a strategy during the parliamentary elections that simultaneously appealed for the support of Comintern sympathizers within the PSI and cut across traditional class, regional, and ideological boundaries. From a strictly electoral standpoint, the outcome of the general election of 1924 was not a monumental achievement for the PCI; the party won a modest 3.7 percent of the national vote and only 19 of the 535 seats in the

Chamber of Deputies.[3] Still, Gramsci's flexibility gave the Comintern a legitimate voice in the parliament of a major industrial power.

Based upon these events, it is telling that when Zinoviev took the opportunity to make a definitive statement about the Comintern's expectations of its members, he chose ambiguity over clarity. In a dense and frequently contradictory address at the organization's Fifth World Congress in July 1924, Zinoviev showed that he had learned something from the failure of the German revolution by advising the delegates that the timetable for capitalism's collapse was no longer certain. Despite the inevitability of proletarian revolution, he conceded, the class's day of destiny had been obscured by the bourgeoisie's new policy of "concealment." Under the guise of promoting democracy and peace, Zinoviev explained, capitalism's acolytes were building alliances among a diverse and unpredictable array of political forces, ranging from social democrats to reactionary parties. In Mussolini, the capitalists had found a new ally, fascism, which gave them even greater latitude in pursuing their goals.[4]

What were the implications of this period of concealment for the communist movement? Zinoviev preferred two approaches. On the one hand, he introduced his listeners to a new concept: "Bolshevization." Given the fact that the bourgeoisie was still intent upon unleashing a new era of reactionary policies and imperialist wars, he stressed, every communist party was required to intensify its commitment to Leninist essentials: tight centralization and the elimination of every manifestation of factionalism. Each party should be "fused in one mold." Naturally, he added, this focus entailed the adoption of every aspect of "Russian Bolshevism" that bore international significance.[5]

On the other hand, Zinoviev underscored the wisdom of the ECCI's support for the flexible strategy that had worked for the PCI. Singling out Bordiga for criticism, he noted that communist parties did not always need to act in the same way. Since the Comintern's goal was to become, as he put it, "not in words, but in deeds, a real world-wide, invincible communist party," it was wise to combine its members' best ideas into a truly collective undertaking. In this case, he drew a distinction between united fronts "from above" and united fronts "from below." The former, as they had been practiced in the years after World War I, were unacceptable. The Comintern's commitment to revolution precluded participation in parliamentary coalitions with bourgeois parties, including reformist socialist parties. Yet, he added, this constraint did not mean that communists should limit themselves to interacting only with fellow believers. Many of the most fruitful opportunities were to be found by working from below. Indeed, one could judge communist parties by their skill in agitating among the masses, organizing factory cells, and infiltrating trade unions. In these circumstances, cooperation with progressive workers of all political allegiances, including members of social democratic parties, was not only legitimate, it was necessary to free them from the corrupting influence of bourgeois democracy. Provocatively, Zinoviev hinted that this logic could even be extended to discussions between communists and social democratic officials about policies that served the purpose of mass mobilization, but only if Comintern parties retained their absolute independence.[6]

A majority of the members of the Soviet Politburo must have agreed with Zinoviev's sentiment. Only ten months later, the ECCI stressed that it was willing to soften even the concept of Bolshevization. At its Fifth Plenum in May 1925, the body announced that the world crisis of capitalism was no longer intensifying. In fact, it had slowed down. In this situation, a strict adherence to Bolshevik principles was still required of all parties. However, the ECCI stressed that there was no single formula that could be applied universally to address the plight of the proletariat. Hence, it was essential that each party carefully consider what was required for its specific circumstances. The ECCI even modified its language about the universal applicability of the Russian model. Bolshevization did not mean that the Russian experience should be applied mechanically. Rather, its guiding approach should be to apply "the general principles of Leninism."[7]

The "Third Period" and the End to Soviet Ambiguity

How antiquated—and dangerous—Zinoviev's words must have seemed only three years later! Even he agreed. In 1928, in an abrupt departure from its previous policies, the ECCI redefined its expectations of its members. When the Comintern's delegates met for their Sixth

World Congress on August 29, they were informed that capitalism had entered a new era, the so-called Third Period. Unlike its assessment of earlier stages of the conflict between the bourgeoisie and the proletariat, the first marked by the severe defeats of the Western European communists and the second by capitalist stabilization, the ECCI described this phase as one of extreme instability. In view of the growing threat of imperialist wars and intensified class conflict, the Comintern's members could no longer proceed as before. Henceforth, national identities were irrelevant to the victory of socialism. There could be no illusion of collaboration with noncommunist parties, especially social democratic parties. Instead, they were to use all of the weapons at their disposal—mass strikes, agitation among the rural poor and the peasantry, and assistance to the anticolonial struggle—to defend the cause of the world proletariat.[8]

This period, or "the turn" as it became known, is worth examining particularly closely because of the relative ease with which a majority of the Comintern's members redefined their missions to comply with the Comintern's about-face. It is not difficult to account for the shift in Soviet policy. In line with the internal battles within the Soviet Politburo, the decisive factor was who was in charge. Two years earlier, in 1926, Bukharin had achieved a major coup by toppling Zinoviev from his post as Comintern president. As a reward, the ECCI promptly granted to him and, of course, Stalin the authority to "decide all urgent questions themselves."[9] In 1928, when Bukharin was seeking to assert his authority, Stalin found the idea of the Third Period to be ideal fodder for his campaigns against his rivals. This was the circumstance in which, as we have seen in chapter 5, he justified renewed militancy in the struggle between the "the two worlds, the two antipodes" of socialism and capitalism.[10] In a direct parallel to the case for going to war with the Soviet countryside, he underscored the urgency of rallying behind the USSR as it prepared war with the class enemy.

The more difficult issue is *why* Stalin and his colleagues were able to secure the cooperation of their fraternal parties. Context played a huge role. As I have shown in chapter 5, Stalin twisted and turned the events that led to the war scare of the late 1920s—Józef Piłsudski's seizure of power in Poland, the war scare, the massacre of the Chinese

communists in Shanghai by the Comintern's Guomindang allies—
into a confirmation that the irreconcilable contradictions between the
"two worlds" and "two antipodes" had come to a head. An even more
compelling justification of Stalin's position was provided by events in
Europe and America that suddenly seemed to confirm Marx's and Lenin's prophecies about the self-destructive nature of capitalism and imperialism. At the end of the 1920s, the supposedly imminent threat to the
USSR's security was transformed into an opportunity for new thinking.
This time, the Comintern would take the offensive. The Wall Street
Crash of fall 1929 and the onset of the Great Depression provided Stalin and his Politburo with seemingly indisputable evidence that the
conditions for proletarian revolution had dramatically improved. The
collapse of international trade, bank failures, monetary chaos, and
the explosion in the numbers of the unemployed—all of these developments seemed to confirm that the working class and its true representatives, the communists, would come together as never before.

Nevertheless, I believe that these events alone are not sufficient to
explain the Comintern members' acceptance of the Third Period. As I
have demonstrated in the case of the CCP, the world's communist parties were hardly identical. Hence, it is important to appreciate that
when they were called to abide by the Comintern's dictates, they did so
for different reasons. In the case of the KPD in particular, the party's
leaders would have probably had a belligerent understanding of their
mission regardless of the Soviet Union's wishes. In contrast, less powerful parties, such as the Communist Party of the United States (CPUSA),
bowed to Moscow's wishes because they had no other options. However,
in the case of at least one party, the PCI, compliance came more slowly
and with greater ambiguity.

At the end of the 1920s, the German communists needed no convincing about the legitimacy of "the turn." They had come to the conclusion
well before the Sixth World Congress that meaningful cooperation
with the bourgeoisie was impossible. Wherever they looked in their
short history, they found betrayal—by the Social Democrats who had
fought against them, the leaders of reformist trade unions who rejected
the inevitability of the revolution, insufficiently class-conscious workers
who had repeatedly let them down, and their own "rightist" comrades

who had called for restraint. Conversely, they remained transfixed by the achievements of their Soviet counterparts. If one took Stalin at his word, and most of the KPD's members did, the USSR was on the verge of even more exemplary feats.

The pervasiveness of this sentiment within the KPD's ranks was facilitated by the outcome of internal struggles in the party's highest echelons. Even earlier than in the Soviet Union, the KPD leadership was nearly homogeneous. Only two of the sixteen major figures in the 1923–1924 Politburo remained in place in 1929; eleven had been expelled from the party for purported acts of infidelity. Over the same period, more than half of the organization's major functionaries had been either forced out or left of their own accord. In replacing these figures, the KPD followed Stalin's example. It recruited thousands of true believers who had no experience with or patience for the doctrinal quarrels of the past. Only one-tenth of the party's 360,000 members in 1920 were still around in 1927.[11]

No figure had a greater influence on the KPD's identity than Ernst Thälmann, who became the party's leader in September 1925 and ruled it with an iron fist until his arrest in March 1933. From the time of his involvement in the ill-fated Hamburg uprising, Thälmann had impressed the Soviets with both his unflinching loyalty and his contempt for social democracy. Accordingly, the ECCI used him as a vehicle to announce one of the most significant ideological formulations of the Third Period, the doctrine of "social fascism." The doctrine held that all Social Democratic parties, their affiliated trade unions, and other allied organizations were not simply rivals. They were enemies, presenting themselves in a disguised form of fascism that was meant to confuse the working class. Thälmann committed the KPD to exposing these forces as the greatest threat to German democracy.[12]

Had the KPD remained a fringe party with a marginal following, its extreme stands would have had little consequence. However, in contrast to the party's repeated failures in the early 1920s, the deepening crisis of Weimar democracy and the rapid rise of National Socialism were electoral boons. In the national elections of 1928, the KPD won an astonishing 10.6 percent of the popular vote and became the fourth strongest party in the Reichstag. Although the Social Democrats retained the support of organized labor, the KPD's success in tapping into the bitterness of unskilled and unemployed workers gave it a powerful voice in German politics.

The significance of the KPD's intransigent radicalism for the tortured history of the Weimar Republic has long been a subject of debate. For the party's adversaries, it was proof of its leaders' inability to see that National Socialism was a much greater threat to Germany than the shortcomings of the republic. For generations of historians, it has been the subject of counterfactual speculation. Could Hitler's rise to power in January 1933 have been averted if the KPD had moderated its stands and allied itself with the Social Democratic Party (SPD)? Whatever response one gives to this question, one cannot deny the perversity of the communists' position. In the early 1930s, the KPD cheered alongside the National Socialists at the Social Democrats' struggles and ultimate failure to maintain viable governing coalitions. They even cooperated with the Nazis in organizing one strike. Only a party as blinded by its militancy and as infatuated with its foreign mentors as the KPD could have assumed that its enemies on the extreme Right were less threatening than its competitors on the Left. Indeed, it took Hitler's installment as chancellor on January 30, 1933, for Thälmann to concede that a change of course was necessary. In desperation, he appealed to the SPD for help with a general strike. This was too little, too late. Two months later the KPD was outlawed, and Thälmann was arrested, imprisoned, and later executed.

Unlike the KPD, the CPUSA was typical of a majority of the world's communist parties in having a weak hand in its dealings with the Soviet Union. However, its subservient behavior during the Third Period was not simply due to pressure from Moscow. It was the fear of irrelevance. The party's weaknesses were caused by the unique American conditions—the absence of a feudal aristocracy, broad mobility across class divisions—that made it difficult for any party to persuade the working class of the need for radical economic change. Furthermore, the American Left was suffused with multiple, cross-cutting divisions over priorities that exceeded those of most European parties. In their competition to win popular support, Jewish émigrés from Europe squared off against US-born activists, Europeans from one region against those from another, orthodox Marxists against anarcho-syndicalists, and proponents of reform against revolutionaries.

As a result, when the moderate wing of the American Socialist Party sought to increase its electoral appeal credibility by expelling its most radical members in 1919, it was telling that the radicals did not link arms in opposition to their former party. They stubbornly held on to their differences and formed not one but two distinct communist parties. Two years later, the Comintern ordered the two parties to merge into a unified organization. But even this measure could not hide the tensions that coursed through the party's ranks. The centrists, led by the CPUSA's founder, Charles Ruthenberg, and its later national secretary, Jay Lovestone, insisted that only united-front tactics with other progressive parties and associations would be effective in a country that presented such poor soil for revolution; the radicals, led by the labor activist James Cannon, opposed any accommodation and demanded that the party's members increase their agitation among factory workers and within trade unions.

However, on one issue the two factions were not at odds. The Kremlin's frequently heavy-handed interference in the CPUSA's affairs grated against their respective efforts to make headway with American voters. When Lovestone became head of the party, he took a bold step. In May 1929, he led a party delegation to Moscow where he challenged the ECCI's authority by publicly contesting the Third Period's premise that his party should ready itself for a proletarian upheaval. This act of defiance marked a precipitous moment in the CPUSA's relationship with Moscow. Fresh from his victory over Bukharin, Stalin demonstrated his intention to eliminate even the faintest memories of dissension within the organization's ranks. "Who do you think you are?" he demanded of Lovestone and his other guests. "Trotsky defied me. Where is he? Zinoviev defied me. Where is he? And you? Who are you? Yes, you will go back to America. But when you get there, nobody will know you except your wives."[13]

Stalin was right about the extent of his reach. The CPUSA Politburo promptly expelled Lovestone. Yet it was not simply the party's subordination to Moscow that drove it deeper into the Soviet fold, to the point in fact at which many of its best-known members engaged in fawning defenses of Stalin's purges. At least until Hitler's rise in the 1930s, the party had few claims to distinction aside from its association with Moscow and the international movement.

The same could not be said for the Italian communists. In stark contrast to the KPD's uncompromising posture and the CPUSA's impotence, the underground PCI's path toward the acceptance of the Comintern's dictates was much more circuitous. Gramsci, who had replaced Bordiga as the head of the party in 1924, was arrested and imprisoned. Yet, his absence did not mean that his conception of the interplay between the PCI's vanguard role and the enlightenment of the masses was forgotten. Although Gramsci's successor, Palmiro Togliatti, had more of the canny instincts of the Leninist strategist than his collaborator and a greater appreciation for organizational discipline, he waged the same battle with the party's orthodox wing over the party's strategy and the prospects for revolution.

In Togliatti's view, Italy could go one of two ways. One possibility was that the working class would live up to its historical mission by overthrowing Mussolini's fascist dictatorship and moving "at once to the establishment of a dictatorship of the proletariat." The other possibility was that Italy would need a broad "people's revolution" before it could move on to form a socialist government.[14] Togliatti agreed with his opponents about the desirability of the former scenario. But, in his judgment, the Italian workers' passivity in the face of Mussolini's rise was a sign that they were not yet ready to live up to their destiny. Thus, like Gramsci before him, Togliatti maintained that the revolution was best served when the PCI actively sought the assistance of noncommunist forces in uniting the proletariat.

Togliatti's position was not only heretical for those communists who brooked no diversion from the Comintern line, it came at a particularly inauspicious moment. In late 1928, the Presidium of the ECCI sent an "open letter" to the KPD that was clearly meant to apply to all of the Comintern parties. Thälmann's policies, the Presidium emphasized, necessitated disciplinary action against any party member who advocated so-called transitional theories about the road to socialism or conciliatory strategies toward the bourgeoisie. Yet, amazingly, Togliatti was unmoved by this implicit threat. He immediately denounced the use of such "organizational measures," as he called them, to resolve internal party disputes.[15]

One can only speculate about Togliatti's motives. He may have simply reasoned that the PCI could not ignore its specific circumstances when it was battling for its life. Still, given the ECCI's demands of the KPD, Togliatti's display of independence was an invitation for internal opposition. In early 1929, a group of younger communists declared that he was unfit to lead the party. With a zeal that matched Bordiga's earlier clashes with Gramsci, the radicals accused Togliatti of blurring the differences between the bourgeoisie and the working class and forsaking the revolution. They demanded a renewed commitment to overthrowing the existing system. They were joined by Comintern officials who pressed for Togliatti's transfer from the party leadership. But Togliatti surmounted these attacks. Apparently, Stalin recognized that there was no comparable figure in the PCI with the national credibility to replace his errant comrade. Still, Togliatti did his part to avert a serious conflict. In 1929, he showed that he had not forgotten his Leninist formation when he denounced loyal supporters for purported deviations that he had previously endorsed.

"Popular Fronts" in the Service of the Soviet Union

In retrospect, it is easy to see why Hitler's rise to power in 1933 would have undercut the logic behind the Third Period doctrine and paved the way for a renewed shift in Comintern policy. While Stalin and the ECCI were forbidding the organization's members from collaborating with noncommunist parties, the National Socialists proved to be a far more dangerous adversary. However, ideological convictions are never easily reversed. A revealing testimony to this maxim is how long it took Stalin and the heads of the European parties to recognize the need for a corrective. For example, many communists, like the leaders of the KPD, could not easily forget the wrongs done to them by the "class enemies" and "social fascists." Furthermore, Stalin had his own reasons for hesitation. A revised policy would have diluted the language of class warfare that undergirded his domestic collectivization and industrialization drives. Thus, as late as the Seventeenth Party Congress on

January 26, 1934, a full year after Hitler's ascent, Stalin refused to concede that a change of course was necessary. In his official report, he took issue with the notion that the National Socialists' success was the manifestation of something new; it was, he suggested, merely the outgrowth of the ongoing economic crisis of capitalism. His government was "far from being enthusiastic" about the new German regime, but, he emphasized, it would do what was required to avoid provoking a new war.[16]

Not all of the Comintern parties were in this comfortable position. In a way that was provocatively similar to the situation in which socialist parties found themselves at the outbreak of World War I, they faced a choice between adhering to a purely revolutionary conception of their mission and defending the nation. In early April 1933, Maurice Thorez and Klement Gottwald, the general secretaries of the French Communist Party (PCF) and the Communist Party of Czechoslovakia (CPC), respectively, chose the latter course, explicitly calling for an end to the Third Period policies. Undoubtedly motivated by their countries' proximity to Germany, they proposed that the Comintern immediately begin talks with the socialist Second International about joint action against the fascist threat. As the leaders of Europe's largest and still legal communist parties, both leaders recognized that they would lose the support of their voters if they did not reach out to other antifascist parties. Yet, Stalin and the ECCI rebuffed their initiative. True to their Leninist instincts, Thorez and Gottwald backed down.

For these reasons, it was fitting that when the Soviet leader and his allies finally moderated their stand, it was because the working class forced them to do so. On February 12, 1934, thousands of French communist and socialist trade union members joined in a general strike against the toppling of their country's centrist government by right-wing extremists. This spontaneous demonstration of solidarity between two normally antagonistic movements was not instigated from above in the PCF's typically mechanical fashion. Instead, it came from below. Thorez was instantly thrown into the quandary of having to decide whether to rein in the unions or accept the idea of repairing his party's fractured relationship with the French Section of the Workers' International (SFIO). He finally decided that there was no alternative to collaboration. When the SFIO expressed its desire to form a "united front" with the PCF, Thorez not only accepted the offer but proposed that it even be extended to a "common front of liberty and peace" with nonsocialist, middle-class parties. On October 12, Thorez's speech was published in *L'Humanité* under the headline for which the new policy of cooperation between communists and noncommunists would become universally known: "For a Broad Anti-fascist Popular Front."[17]

It cannot have been easy for Thorez to make this shift. This step went far beyond the organization's hesitant endorsement of united-front tactics in the early 1920s. It undoubtedly helped that a preeminent figure in the Comintern, the Bulgarian communist leader Georgy Dimitrov, was working behind the scenes to persuade Stalin that fascism had become a greater threat to peace in Europe than capitalism. Dimitrov enjoyed enormous prestige in Stalin's eyes for successfully defending himself against Nazi accusations that he had taken part in the burning of the Reichstag in 1933. There can be no doubt, however, about the galvanizing effect of Thorez's stand on the PCF. At a time when France was once again beset by a hardening of the lines between the Left and the Right, he succeeded in transforming the party from the marginal clique that it had become after the Congress of Tours in 1920 into a permanent force in twentieth-century French politics. Within two years, the PCF's membership grew nearly threefold. In the national elections in spring 1936, its participation in the Socialist-led Popular Front resulted in it receiving twice as many votes and six times as many seats in parliament as in 1932. Although the party leadership adhered to the orthodox Comintern line and refused to accept cabinet posts in the new government, its support for the ruling coalition allowed it to push aggressively for significant reforms in economic and labor policy.

Thorez's policies became the model for the Comintern's formal acceptance of the Popular Front policy in 1935. On August 2, at the Seventh World Congress, Dimitrov, the newly appointed Comintern president, formally endorsed the concept.[18] For two reasons, his address marked a fundamental turn in the Soviets' understanding about the role of communist parties. The first change was the shift in strategy. Although Dimitrov began the speech by emphasizing the insurmountable gulf between capitalism and socialism, he argued in unmistakable terms that the fascist danger necessitated cooperation among all parties that opposed it, including the Social Democrats and other socialists. It did the working class no good, Dimitrov stressed, if communists practiced "self-satisfied sectarianism" or "ranted about the leading role of the communists." The working class needed "real political parties," parties that could take the form of mass organizations and serve the people.

Accordingly, Dimitrov found no problem with the idea, for which Thorez and Gottwald had been rebuked two years earlier, of united action by the two Internationals. The organizations' collaboration would make it easier to repulse the fascist onslaught. In fact, Dimitrov was so supportive of the idea of cooperation with social democratic parties that he even held out the possibility of eventual reunification into a single party of the proletariat. Furthermore, albeit more cautiously, Dimitrov endorsed the formation of broader, antifascist coalitions that could include nonsocialist bourgeois parties. The key criterion was that careful steps be taken to distinguish the true opponents of fascism from its potential supporters.

On the surface, Dimitrov's approach—he dubbed it "revolutionary realism"—would have been welcome news for any communist who was seeking to apply the Marxist message to the specific conditions in which he or she was operating. But the second reason for the significance of Dimitrov's stand had even more far-reaching implications. Just between the lines, Dimitrov seemed to downplay the conventional assumption that the fight against fascism would have to be led by truly revolutionary parties. Fascism's ascent, he noted, was novel in one crucial respect. It was "not an *ordinary succession* of one government to another." Rather, it was a *"substitution* of one state form of class domination of the bourgeoisie, bourgeois democracy—by another form—open terrorist dictatorship."

At first glance, Dimitrov's shift in focus from party to state domination may seem slight. However, his characterization was not only, or even primarily, an expression of class interest. It was a form of national self-assertion. Thus, when talking about the rise of right-wing movements, he emphasized their national dimensions. Mussolini marched on Rome, Piłsudski moved into Warsaw, and Hitler descended upon Berlin. In Dimitrov's description, the fascists not only sought the support of bourgeois economic interests, they rummaged through the entire history of every nation to "pose as the heirs and continuers of all that was exalted and heroic in its past." In Germany in particular, he asserted, fascism had become an enemy of humanity on multiple fronts. It was the "spearhead of international counterrevolution," the "chief instigator of imperialist war," and, in his view as head of a Soviet-led organization, the "initiator of a crusade against the Soviet Union."

In these respects, the Popular Front policy signified a major shift in the Comintern's identity from being an international organization of the proletariat to an organization in the service of the nation. The logic behind collaboration between communists and their former socialist and nonsocialist adversaries was that these agreements were necessary to combat a common foe. But now, the foe had changed. For the moment, the struggle between classes was subordinated to the struggle between different types of states. Dimitrov confirmed the shift in a provocative and previously unthinkable suggestion. Communist parties should go beyond tolerating bourgeois governments. They should actively participate in them. There was, in his estimation, no longer any reason to wait for the "victory of the revolution."[19]

THE INTERESTS OF THE SOVIET UNION

Dimitrov's observations were far from being rhetorical flourishes to a controversial policy. In the second half of the 1930s, Stalin demonstrated his determination to internationalize what he was already undertaking at home. Paralleling his campaigns to transform the Soviet Union into a mighty industrial power, he candidly defined the cause of the revolution in terms of the promotion of his country's national interests. In every respect, this shift changed the way that communists were expected to think about their parties' functions.

The unmistakable indication that the struggle between states and not the class struggle had become the driving element in Stalin's thinking was provided by the Soviet Union's engagement in the Spanish Civil War. Even before the war began on July 17, 1936, when an attempted military coup by right-wing military officers against the Second Spanish Republic fractured the country between defenders of the

Republic and nationalist rebels, Stalin had grown concerned about the prospect of yet another fascist takeover in Europe. In early 1936, he had instructed the Spanish Communist Party (PCE) to take part in the formation of a pro-Republican Popular Front government. Thus, after the war began, Moscow secretly sent planes, weapons, and food to off-set the insurgents' superior military forces. Additionally, in a gesture of proletarian solidarity, the Comintern lived up to its internationalist credentials by sponsoring International Brigades of volunteer soldiers to take part in the fighting. Under the banners of revolutionary heroes and events, more than 40,000 earnest young communists and social-ists from over fifty countries as diverse as the United States, Germany, Hungary, and Belgium travelled to Spain. There, they joined Abraham Lincoln, Thälmann, Rákosi, and Paris Commune brigades to defend the Republic against the fascist menace. For these idealists, this oppor-tunity to take their beliefs into battle was a confirmation that the in-vincible hand of history was finally turning their way.[20]

Moscow's engagement was good news for the PCE. Although the party's general secretary, José Díaz Ramos, had been an early propo-nent of collaboration among leftist parties, the PCE was dwarfed by the powerful Spanish Socialist Workers' Party. Furthermore, the Republican coalition included members of the Trotskyist Workers' Party of Marx-ist Unification (POUM) and was associated with radical groups like the anarcho-syndicalist National Confederation of Labor. In Barcelona in particular, anarchists had achieved enormous success in stirring rev-olutionary ferment. With a passionate intensity that seemed to its par-ticipants to fulfill the dreams of the Paris Commune, they proclaimed an end to centralized government, set up workers' collectives, confiscated property, and formed independent militias. Nevertheless, it soon turned out that the communists had a noteworthy advantage. When it became clear that the Soviet Union would be the only major power to come to the aid of the Republic, the PCE's popularity soared. Most im-portantly, its participation in the government allowed it to tap into the national narrative. The party's claims that it was serving the good of the Republic and not just the class struggle allayed many Spaniards' fears about its revolutionary identity. One year before the military coup, the PCE had fewer than 13,000 members; in Barcelona, Spain's working-class hub, it could count a mere 1,171. Yet, two years later in 1937, it had 249,000 members.[21] With this growth in membership, the PCE acquired the features of a mass party. Its ranks were filled not only with industrial workers but with significant numbers of agricultural laborers, peasant proprietors, and middle-class professionals. For the first time, it could credibly claim to represent broad swaths of Spanish society.

Still, the PCE's successes did not make it a moderate party. They merely strengthened its leaders' resolve to ensure that the Republic moved in a direction that served both its objectives and those of its Soviet sponsors. While Moscow pursued its interests by deploying military advisers and People's Commissariat for Internal Affairs (NKVD) agents to serve as political commissars in the International Brigades and liquidate purported "enemies of the people" in rival leftist parties, the PCE concentrated on maximizing its role in the government. Arguing that the Left's primary goal should be to serve the Popular Front, the communists portrayed themselves as defenders of the people against extremism. In particular, they set their sights on the anarchists and other radical groups. Confirming that its democratic professions were questionable, the PCE defiantly resorted to force to get its way. In early May 1937, the party and its affiliated Unified Socialist Party of Catalonia goaded the Republican government into supporting an assault on the anarchists and the POUM in Barcelona. After a week of bloody fighting in which its opponents were eventually defeated, the PCE laid claim to being the preeminent leftist party in Spain.

This was a pyrrhic victory. At first, the PCE seemed to have its day of glory. The ECCI dispatched Palmiro Togliatti to Spain with instructions to work with the party to lay the foundations for a revolutionary democracy. Togliatti immediately recognized, however, that the Popular Front was dissolving. As Nationalist troops marched toward the government's remaining strongholds in Madrid, Valencia, and Barcelona, the last semblance of cooperation among the coalition partners broke down. Worse still, the communists were torn by internal divisions. Under these circumstances, Stalin decided that there was no point in continuing to support either the Popular Front or the PCE. The USSR's disengagement from the conflict in late 1937 may not have caused the Republic's demise. However, by failing to come to the aid of a fraternal party, Stalin showed that he was prepared to make crucial decisions in a way that was scarcely different from the strategic calculations of other European leaders.

No decision more graphically confirmed this change than Stalin's attempt two years later to extricate the USSR from the looming threat of war with Nazi Germany. When the Soviet and German foreign ministers, Vyacheslav Molotov and Joachim von Ribbentrop, met in Moscow on August 23, 1939, to sign a nonaggression pact, the Soviets' change of course put the Comintern's members in an impossible position. After years of being told that the main threat to socialism was fascism, they were suddenly asked to accommodate themselves to a guarantee of nonbelligerence with the enemy. They could either do the unthinkable, which was to stand up to the Soviet Union and risk expulsion from the international fraternity, or they could accept their ally's about-face with all of the ideological shortcomings it entailed and accept the lifeless rhetoric of proletarian solidarity.

In a telling demonstration of the true believer's capacity for rationalization and the communists' subordination to Moscow, most of these parties' leaders prostrated themselves at the altar of fidelity. After all, who would dare to deny what had been confirmed once and for all by Stalin's supremely self-interested action! Devotion to the idea of revolution had been replaced by loyalty to a single state. The affirmation of this principle did not mean that every party acceded to Soviet expectations without protest. In the few countries where communists had not been driven underground, some leaders initially attempted to preserve the basic idea of the Popular Front. In every case where Moscow could not get what it wanted one way, it secured its interests by other means. With few exceptions, these parties' attempts to assert their independence were futile.

For example, the British Communist Party's (BCP) general secretary, Harry Pollitt, put up a heroic but fruitless defense of the proposition that the safeguarding of his country's national security interests was compatible with a policy of friendship with the USSR. When Pollitt supported Britain's entry into the war with Germany after Hitler's invasion of western Poland on September 1, 1939, however, other less independently minded members of the BCP leadership followed the Kremlin's instructions and removed him from his position. The German-Soviet Nonaggression Pact was the cause of even greater turmoil within the PCF, which had experienced a surge in membership after the formation of the Popular Front government. When the USSR acted on a secret protocol in the pact and sent the Red Army into eastern Poland, 27 percent of the PCF's deputies in the National Assembly left their parliamentary group and set up an alternative parliamentary faction. Yet, Maurice Thorez showed, at considerable cost to his party's reputation, that despite its previous efforts, the PCF intended to remain a different kind of party. He denounced his country's leaders when France entered the war. As a result, the French government ordered the PCF's dissolution and forced its members into hiding.

The fate of the CPUSA would have been equally disconcerting for the true believer who assumed that a Leninist party could be equally committed to the nation. Like its European counterparts, the CPUSA enjoyed an upsurge in popularity in the mid-1930s thanks to both the growing power of trade unions in the United States and its leaders' early warnings about Hitler's bellicose intentions and the rise of fascism in Spain. As a consequence, the pact was an instant source of internal disruption within a party that had never wanted to foreswear its American identity. While the party's head, Earl Browder, stretched credulity by characterizing the agreement as a "wonderful contribution to peace" and "a serious blow for German fascism,"[22] other communists demanded continued opposition to Hitler. This position did not survive the partition of Poland between Nazi Germany and the USSR. The ECCI ordered Browder to advise his comrades that the times of the Popular Front were over. Operating under these constraints, the CPUSA was forced to reconcile itself to the less popular appeal for US neutrality and, as a result, soon found itself back on the margins of American society.

Against this background, one can imagine that the Comintern's members were relieved when Stalin once again ordered a change of course after Germany's invasion of the Soviet Union on June 22, 1941. Instantaneously, the crusade against fascism returned as the Comintern's battle call. The logic of the Popular Front was back as well. All alliances with freedom-loving peoples were justified in the name of defeating fascism. But the Comintern's members also had to accommodate themselves to a new ideological gyration when Stalin took the position that had earlier been articulated by Dimitrov. The hallowed goal of revolution would be postponed. In a forceful radio address in which he spoke to the Soviet people as the commander of the "national patriotic war," Stalin did not mention the word "revolution" once. Instead, he invoked Lenin's name to justify a new type of commitment. The chief virtues of the new Soviet man and woman, he declared, should be "courage, valor, fearlessness in struggle, [and the] readiness to fight together with the people." But this was not the Lenin of *What Is to Be Done?* or even Stalin's earlier dogmatic depiction of his predecessor's thinking. This was the language of national self-defense. Listening from abroad, foreign communists must have noticed that Stalin only mentioned the revolutionary institution that they shared in common—the party—a single time. He merely referred to the organization's "self-sacrificing support to the Red Army and the Red Navy."[23] Indeed, in light of the Soviet leader's focus on national rather than party interests, they might have wondered whether it mattered that they represented communist parties at all. Looking down the road, the answer depended on Stalin's conception of the organization's utility as well as the views of the individual communists who were expected to carry out his wishes.

From International Revolutionaries to National Apparatchiki

The Comintern had been preparing since its founding to resolve the tension between its international and national focuses. Beginning in the 1920s, the ECCI had brought thousands of idealistic students from every continent to the Soviet Union with the expressed intent to educate them in the theory and practice of communist leadership and prepare them for future roles in the international movement. In special schools, such as Moscow's International Lenin School and the Communist University of the Toilers of the East, these visitors were exposed to the foundational works of Marxism and Leninism, instructed in the glories of the October Revolution, and taken to factories and farms in order to engage in lively discussions with "hero workers." In the early years, these prospective leaders were caught up in the swirling ideological debates and controversies over the Revolution's short- and long-term goals, its tempo, and its costs. Following Stalin's ascent, however, everything about this experience changed. In the same way that Stalin and his supporters systematically replaced their country's independently minded old Bolshevik cadres with a new generation of loyal apparatchiki, Comintern officials concentrated on forging their own army of tightly focused cadres who would dutifully replicate the Stalinist model of communist rule.

Accordingly, when Stalin subordinated the proletarian revolution to the cause of national security, the development of organizations to effect this goal became a priority. For example, during the early 1940s, Comintern training programs were specifically designed to prepare young communists from the states with which the Soviet Union was at war for the day when they would return to their homelands and set up new governments. In the Comintern school in the Bashkir city of Ufa, students were divided according to the respective countries of origins, received lectures on carefully crafted versions of their national history, and learned to rebut fascist propaganda. Within these closed confines, they engaged in acts of obligatory self-criticism that resembled the practices of China's communists in Yan'an, and they learned to appreciate the self-control and "right attitudes" of the mature communist. Above all, they were taught to stick unquestioningly to the Soviet line. In the words of a young German communist, Wolfgang Leonhard, who later participated in the administration of the Soviet Occupation Zone in Germany, "everyone was trained to be able to react immediately in a politically correct manner to every question in Soviet politics. We were thus all in the position, in the absence of directives, to be able to adopt the corrective and to propagate it in our own initiatives."[24]

In the case of those believers who could not come to the Soviet Union, the Comintern brought the Soviet Union to them. It makes sense that the most prominent vehicle for conveying the good news about communism was Stalin's introductory *Short Course* on the history of the RCP(B). In 1938 and 1939 alone, nearly 700,000 copies of the text appeared in translation. If a Chinese, Mongolian, Albanian, or Cuban communist wanted an authoritative statement on any major event in the RCP(B)'s history—the Bolshevik-Menshevik struggle, the NEP, collectivization, and the "liquidation of the remnants of the Bukharin-Trotsky gang of spies, wreckers, and traitors to the country"— one could read the *Short Course* in sixty-two different languages.[25] By this point, the text's circulation far exceeded that of the *Communist Manifesto* or any of Lenin's works.[26] In addition, one could learn about Moscow's priorities. This testimony to the power of mass propaganda had virtually nothing to say about the Comintern or the specific experiences of its members. This made sense. If one assumed that an official recounting of the Bolshevik record, complete with methodical simplifications and distortions, was all one needed for a reliable catechism, it was logical that other parties' revolutionary experiences had little significance next to the Soviet model.

The flip side to the fabrication of this generation of communist devotees was the elimination of anyone deemed a threat to the Soviet Union and Stalin's supremacy. In the same calculated manner with which he eliminated competitors like Zinoviev, Kamenev, and Bukharin, Stalin set about cleansing the Comintern's ranks of potential dissenters. In Dimitrov's presence in 1937, he uttered this chilling warning: "All of you there in the Comintern are working in the hands of the enemy."[27] Of course, the definition of a threat was highly elastic. Under Stalin's tutelage, accusations of "Trotskyism," sabotage, and deviationist behavior became clichés. The Soviet leader was especially obsessed with ridding the international movement of the foreign communists who were living reminders that he had not been alone at the creation. Left unchecked, such individuals had legitimate claims to representing the font of diverse ideas that inspired the Revolution. For this reason, Stalin devoted special attention to the long-lionized communists who were, for his purposes, conveniently congregated in the Comintern's residence in Moscow, the Hotel Lux. In many cases, the arcane ideological debates that had been integral features of the organization's evolution in the 1920s came back to haunt them. Many were tortured because of their inability to keep up with the twists and turns in their leader's policies.

Notably, Béla Kun was among the victims. As the leader of the short-lived Hungarian Soviet Republic of 1919, he had the singular misfortune of presiding over the only other example of a successful communist revolution. No stranger to the art of survival in periods of internal intrigue, Kun had shown little compunction in denouncing fellow communists. Thus, in a stroke of poetic justice in June 1937, he fell victim to his own methods when a fellow party member accused him of sabotaging the Hungarian "Commune" and, worse still, insulting Stalin. Like senior communists who had begged for his mercy, Kun appealed to his benefactor, Stalin, for exoneration. Never one to let sentiment get in the way of absolute power, the Soviet leader denied the request; Kun was forced to confess to imaginary crimes and later put to death.

Stalin also directed his attention toward those Comintern parties that he deemed guilty of exhibiting nationalist tendencies. Among the most tragic cases was the small Communist Party of Poland (KPP). As an underground party that had struggled for its life since Piłsudski's coup, the KPP represented no tangible threat to the Soviet Union. Most Poles regarded it with deep suspicion because of its ties with Moscow and the fact that it was mainly composed of national minorities and marginalized groups, including Germans, Ukrainians, Byelorussians, and Jews. Hence, in its struggle for survival, the KPP was directly beholden to the Comintern. Nevertheless, despite the KPP's hardships, Stalin barely concealed his animus toward the party. Regarding it with the distrust of centuries of ingrained Russian hostility to the Polish people, he directed the Comintern to take measures against the KPP that far exceeded its importance. Between August 1937 and November 1938, the NKVD arrested every member of the KPP's Politburo and Secretariat, as well as most of the Central Committee. Nearly all of these figures died by execution or perished in prison. Taking these measures even further, Stalin ordered the Comintern to dissolve the party. This was no mere administrative measure. The ECCI set up a special department to eliminate all vestiges of the organization. In the end, 143,810 Poles living in the Soviet Union, communists and noncommunists alike, were convicted of espionage or conspiratorial activity and more than 111,000 were executed.[28]

A TALE OF TWO EUROPES

Stalin's campaign to rid the Comintern of perceived adversaries and stock it with his devotees provides a helpful lens for interpreting the event with which I began this chapter: the organization's demise in 1943. Although communists throughout the world were stunned to learn about the death of the body that symbolized the unity of the proletarian cause, Stalin's reasoning was simple—he no longer needed it. After years of bending and twisting scores of communist parties to serve his bidding, he could count on all of them—at least, so he thought—to fall into line without having to wait for directions from a putatively representative international body. In fact, by definition, the Comintern was incompatible with Stalin's national focus. As long as it existed, the organization was a reminder to everyone, and especially the USSR's wary, wartime allies in Europe and the United States, of the Soviet Union's revolutionary roots.

Less than two months after the announcement of the Comintern's dissolution, Stalin confirmed his thinking in a letter to a correspondent from the British news agency Reuters. Invigorated by the Red Army's victory in the bloody, five-month battle over Stalingrad and expressing himself in a manner that was simultaneously totally insincere and highly revealing, Stalin indicated that he was already mulling over the Soviet Union's postwar aims. The insincere side to his remarks was meant to allay fears in the West. The decision to dissolve the Comintern, he asserted, had exposed "the lie of the Hitlerites to the effect that 'Moscow' allegedly intends to intervene in the life of other nations and to Bolshevize them" and that "the communist parties in various countries are allegedly acting not in the interest of their people but on orders from outside." To the contrary, Stalin intoned, his government only wanted what was best for Europe. Correspondingly, the revealing side to his comments was that he did not restrict his observations to the role of communist parties. Once the "fascist beast" was destroyed, Stalin advised, his government's aim was to clear the way for patriots in all countries to join "the future organization of a companionship based upon their equality."[29] Naturally, Stalin was being disingenuous; he had every intention of using his agents, including loyal communist parties, to meddle in other countries' affairs. Still, his appeal to the concept of a "companionship" of patriots confirmed that he was contemplating a new strategy.

In 1945, many Western European politicians were receptive to this message. In confronting the monumental task of lifting their societies out of the rubble, rebuilding industries, and finding jobs and housing for millions of refugees and returning soldiers, they were disposed to support state-centric plans for economic recovery and to give left-wing governments the power to realize them. In this climate, native communists had both the antifascist credentials to counter lingering doubts about their national loyalties and the fiery rhetoric to excite voters into thinking that they could provide solutions for their problems. As a consequence, party enrollments exploded in the mid-1940s. Tens of thousands of Swedes, Greeks, Belgians, and Danes rushed to align themselves with the purportedly progressive cause. Just as leading intellectuals had exulted over the glories of the October Revolution nearly three decades earlier, they were joined by scientists, philosophers, artists, and writers who were armed with romantic ideas about emulating the Soviet Union's creation of new socialist men and women.

Three parties in particular—the PCF and the PCI in the West and the CPC in Central Europe—had the credentials to represent both working-class and patriotic interests. The first, the PCF, emerged from the war as a potent political force because communists had constituted the majority of the fighters in the Resistance. For this reason, the party was a natural purveyor of the gospel of antifascism. In the public mind, it was no longer the "foreign party" of the 1920s and 1930s. In the words of its followers, it was the *parti des 75,000 fusillés* ("party of the 75,000 who were shot"). The payoff in terms of national popularity was instantaneous. The PCF grew from 300,000 members at the end of 1944 to more than a half million members in June 1945; by December, it had three-quarters of a million members.[30]

Adding to the PCF's patriotic credentials, its leaders successfully neutralized pressures from within the party ranks to return to its radical roots. During the war, the communists had already made the strategic decision to cooperate with the varied groups that comprised Charles de Gaulle's French Committee of National Liberation. As a result, the

PCF leadership had an indisputable claim to take part in a united-front government. Upon his return from exile in Moscow, Maurice Thorez expressed the point succinctly: "The recovery of France cannot be the task of a single party" but of "a whole nation." This responsibility could only be shouldered by a "government of broad national and democratic unity."[31]

The results of the PCF's self-transformation were stunning. In October 1945, Thorez aggressively campaigned to change public perceptions of the party. In the elections to France's interim Constituent National Assembly, the party's leaders combined their advocacy of trade union agitation, worker participation in factory management, and the nationalization of major industries with appeals for cooperation with bourgeois parties. The PCF won the largest share of the national vote and, with surprising ease, formed a coalition government with both its age-old socialist adversaries in the socialist SFIO and the Christian-democratic Popular Republican Movement. In the elections to the second Constituent Assembly in June 1946, the party did nearly as well, coming in a close second to the Christian-democratic Popular Republican Movement. Thorez was made vice prime minister in the new government. Finally, following closely on the popular approval of a new constitution that bore the communists' heavy imprint on such issues as the right to work and the right to strike, the PCF was the leading vote-getter in the November elections to the First National Assembly. Were it not for the SFIO's refusal to participate in a coalition with the PCF alone, the communists could have played a decisive role in shaping the policies of the Fourth French Republic and Thorez might have been its first prime minister.

The Italian communists were in an even more propitious position. Thanks to the PCI's decades-long opposition to Mussolini and its survival in the underground, the party's patriotic credentials were impeccable. Unlike in France, where the PCF had to compete with the reputation of the stronger French Committee of National Liberation, the PCI was the preeminent party in the Italian resistance movement. Moreover, it received widespread recognition for its subsequent restraint during the last year of the war. Amid the disruption wrought by Mussolini's rule and the accentuation of regional and class divisions in Italian society, the PCI could have ordered its partisan militias to seize power in the urban centers of the liberated north. Yet, Togliatti wrenched the country from the brink of civil war by parting ways with the most radical partisan militias and announcing that the PCI, too, would be willing to enter a democratic coalition government in the spirit of national reconciliation.

Togliatti's declaration, the "Salerno turn," was approved by Stalin. Still, it was a gutsy call that was consistent with Togliatti's past advocacy of Popular Front policies. Despite stiff resistance within the communist movement, Togliatti portrayed the PCI as both a vigorous defender of working-class interests and a democratic mass party. Like the PCF, membership in the PCI soared, rising from 400,000 in July 1944 to 1.7 million members in December 1945.[32] In the first general election in 1946, the party came in third in the national vote and won 104 of the 556 seats in the new Constituent Assembly. In 1948, the party joined the Socialists in a Popular Democratic Front. Although the coalition was beaten by the Christian Democracy (DC) party, the PCI nevertheless won nearly one-third of the popular vote and, in the process, established itself as a permanent presence in Italian politics. Testifying to the close association between the party's identity and the magnetic personality of its leader, Togliatti won successive terms as vice prime minister and justice minister in two governments. He was a member of the parliament's Chamber of Deputies from 1948 until his death in 1964.

Finally, the CPC, too, enjoyed a legitimate claim to electoral viability. Alone among the states in its region, Czechoslovakia had been a functioning democracy in the interwar period. During these years, the CPC had comported itself well enough, professing working-class values and its desire to work within the democratic order, that it received more than 10 percent of the popular vote in the parliamentary elections of 1929 and 1935. Unlike its French and Italian counterparts, the CPC was no different than the country's other parties in playing only a small role in the resistance to German occupation. During the war, most of its leaders, including its general secretary, Klement Gottwald, were in Moscow. But when these communists returned from exile, they benefited from two factors. Interestingly, one of them, which had worked to the detriment of every other communist party in the region, was their close relationship with Moscow. This disposition was reinforced by a long tradition of pan-Slavism. In the eyes of many of Czechoslovakia's citizens, the Soviet Union alone had stood by their country when its British and French allies gave in to Hitler's threats. Following his resumption of the presidency in 1945, Edvard Beneš made the cultivation of a special relationship with Stalin a personal priority. The Soviet leader reciprocated this attention by withdrawing the Red Army's occupation forces not long after Germany's surrender. The second factor, which benefited all of Czechoslovakia's leftist parties, was the banning of the major right-wing parties that had collaborated with Nazi Germany.

In this auspicious climate, the CPC presented itself as a party for all seasons. It championed workers' control over the instruments of production and state ownership of major industries; it joined the nationalist charge to expel the Sudeten Germans from Bohemia; and it won the favor of peasants by rewarding them with dispossessed properties. From the beginning, Gottwald confidently predicted that the CPC had the popular support to win office. He was exactly right. In the country's first postwar elections in 1946, the CPC won 31.2 percent of the vote (38.1 percent, if one included its Slovak branch), the most by any European communist party in a democratic election. Notwithstanding many citizens' misgivings about the communists' intentions, Beneš promptly invited Gottwald to be prime minister and the CPC was awarded nine cabinet posts in a left-leaning National Front government.[33] For a brief period, it seemed possible that Czechoslovakia would have the first communist-led democratic government in Europe.

In contrast to Czechoslovakia, Stalin's message of patriotic "companionship" was much less favorably received in other parts of Eastern Europe. Most of the communist parties were burdened by their association with Moscow. In the view of local populations, they shared the blame for the violence and recrimination following their countries' "liberation" by the Red Army. When Comintern-trained communists, such as Mátyás Rákosi (Hungary), Bolesław Bierut (Poland), Valko Chervenkov (Bulgaria), Ana Pauker (Romania), and Walter Ulbricht (Germany), returned to their homelands with the good word about the Soviet Union, working-class rule, and socialist grandeur, these "little Stalins" were dismissed as renegades. As a consequence, their understanding of their parties' functions was hardened. When they could not win power through popular approbation, they used the parties instead as instruments of domination.

Poland presented a particularly difficult challenge. It was practically preordained that a people who had witnessed the rebirth of their nation in 1918, later dismemberment under the terms of the Molotov-Ribbentrop Pact, and an invidious postwar settlement would regard the presence of foreign troops on its soil as yet another instance of national humiliation. In fact, Poland already had a legitimate constitutional government in London. Based on a broad coalition of socialist, peasant, and Catholic-nationalist parties, this regime-in-exile was recognized by all of the Allied powers, including the Soviet Union (until 1943). Furthermore, it had its own army, the Home Army, whose more than 400,000 soldiers fought courageously against the German occupation.

In this circumstance, the Soviets would seem to have been at a disadvantage. Due to Stalin's decision to liquidate the KPP in 1938, Moscow's sole source of local support was a weak underground party, the Polish Workers' Party (PPR), which Soviet agents had founded in 1942. Nonetheless, the Kremlin did have one monumental advantage. Stalin benefited from the goodwill of his British and American allies. After founding an alternate coalition government in 1944, the Lublin-based Polish Committee of National Liberation, he secured the Allies' agreement to recognize this regime, and not the one in London, as Poland's legitimate government in exchange for his promise to include representatives from every party and to hold early elections. Once the new government was in place, however, it did not take Stalin long to undermine it. He stacked the coalition in favor of Soviet interests and installed sympathizers in the state ministries. In January 1947, when Stalin decided that he could afford the risk of holding parliamentary elections, the PPR formed a coalition with a supposedly "democratic bloc" of parties and used vote-rigging and police intimidation to capture 80 percent of the seats in the legislature and remove its rivals from office.

Six months later, the Hungarian Communist Party (HCP) attained virtually the same outcome, though it followed a different path. When the Red Army marched into Hungary in 1944, its troops committed atrocities that reminded many Hungarians of the bloodshed during

Béla Kun's revolutionary dictatorship in 1919. Still, the communists who returned to their country were confident that they would be welcomed as liberators. Led by Kun's former deputy, Mátyás Rákosi, they tried to appeal to different segments of the population. They promised to meet some groups' demands for social and economic change, such as the implementation of land reforms, but simultaneously invoked the quite unrevolutionary language of national self-determination, democracy, and multiparty rule. Assuming that victory was certain, the party welcomed the opportunity to compete in the country's first democratic elections of November 1945. In what would turn out to be the last reasonably free opportunity for Hungarians to express their preferences until 1990, the HCP was soundly beaten. The middle-class Independent Smallholders Party received 57 percent of the vote, while the HCP came in third, just below its old nemesis, the Social Democratic Party.

Rákosi had not returned to Hungary to give away power. In fact, even if the HCP had received the most votes, it is unlikely that either he or Stalin would have tolerated the coalition government that emerged from the election. The communists furiously moved to repair the damage. With the Red Army to back them up, they deprived the Smallholders of their share of cabinet posts and arranged to have László Rajk, a home communist who had been imprisoned in Germany, appointed minister of internal affairs. One of Rajk's first acts was to create a secret police force that fomented defamation campaigns against members of anticommunist parties and used rumors, threats, and arrests—"salami tactics," as Rákosi later called them—to whittle down their numbers. Finally, Rákosi called for new elections. Testifying to the population's continuing hostility to the communists, the HCP won a mere 22 percent of the national vote. But this was enough to allow it and a few associated front parties to take control of the government.

In two other countries, Bulgaria and Romania, the willingness of the USSR's Western allies to recognize Soviet control made the prospect of noncommunist governments extremely unlikely. Hence, the returning communists viewed their mission primarily in terms of taking power. For historical and cultural reasons, Bulgaria was notably receptive. The country's population was already disposed to accept what it regarded as its liberation by fellow Slavs. Furthermore, the Bulgarian

Communist Party (BCP) had been one of the best organized parties in the Comintern. Led by the second most famous communist official in the world, Georgy Dimitrov, the party had prepared for its home return well before the war's end. As the leader of a Fatherland Front with other anti-Hitler groups, it staged a successful coup against the country's fascist dictatorship. True to plan, when Bulgaria held its first elections in November 1945, the Front, which was the only political organization on the ballot, won an overwhelming victory. A year later, when elections were held to the Grand National Assembly, the BCP won a majority of the votes. Dimitrov became the new government's prime minister.

The Romanian Workers' Party (RWP) did not enjoy the BCP's advantages. Due to a century of poor relations with Russia, which included two periods of tsarist military occupation, the country's population viewed the arrival of the Red Army as a prelude to domination from the East. Unlike the Bulgarian communists, the RWP was not in the position to counter this perception. When the communists returned to Bucharest in summer 1944, the party had no more than 1,000 members. Accordingly, with Moscow's encouragement, the leadership presented itself as a fervent defender of Romanian and non-Slav interests, a force for conciliation, and an advocate of moderate social and economic change. To enhance the RWP's credibility, the Kremlin also took a step that would inadvertently complicate its relations with Bucharest down the road. It replaced the party's Muscovite leadership with so-called prison communists who had fought in the underground during the war. Their most notable figure was the new general secretary, Gheorghiu Gheorghe-Dej, a radical labor activist who had spent eleven years in Romanian jails and labor camps.

Nevertheless, rather than waiting for the RWP to gradually win over the Romanian population, the Soviets imposed the regime from above. In March 1945, they induced King Michael I to form a national-front government under the premiership of Petru Groza, a compliant leader of a small nationalist party. In November 1946, they backed fraudulent parliamentary elections that led to a predictably resounding victory for the communist-dominated Bloc of Democratic Parties. Groza was again chosen to be prime minister, but only as a figurehead. After taking over the key Interior, Justice, and Communications Ministries, the RWP quickly asserted its total control.

Predictably, the KPD faced the most complex circumstances of any of these parties. When the Moscow-trained communists returned to Berlin in the tracks of the Red Army and equipped with Stalin's orders, they encountered deep-seated hostility. For hardened believers and especially the party's general secretary, Ulbricht, who had been a deputy in the Reichstag during the Weimar Republic, an associate of Ernst Thälmann, and a Comintern functionary, it was inconceivable that their compatriots would not eventually be won over to the vision of a socialist Germany. In their view, the KPD was an antifascist "people's party" and a "party of peace." When the Soviet Occupation Authority legalized the party along with a host of others—a Christian democratic party, a liberal democratic party, and a social democratic party—he presented the measure as a bold step toward the realization of true democracy. Hence, as one of Moscow's emissaries, he made a show of appointing members of these and other bourgeois parties as mayors and local administrators. However, there could never be any doubt about Ulbricht's determination to select people for these positions who would serve his and the Soviet Union's purposes. As he told Wolfgang Leonhard about the selection of public officials: "It's quite clear—it's got to look democratic, but we must have everything in our control."[34] Finally, he confirmed that his primary objective was to set up a functioning state, not to make a revolution, by expelling those home communists from the party who were intent upon asserting its radical identity.

Despite Ulbricht's optimism, the KPD's efforts to improve its standing with the German population failed to take hold. Worse still, the popularity of the revitalized Social Democratic Party of Germany (SPD) grew rapidly, despite the fact that the party entered the postwar period with roughly the same numbers as the KPD. In response to this trend and undoubtedly acting in accord with Stalin's wishes, Ulbricht took a step that resonated with the party's past. Effectively reversing the decision of the left Social Democrats to leave their party in 1919, he called for the unification of the KPD and SPD. The announcement immediately divided the Social Democrats. Many were in favor of cooperation but feared Ulbricht's intentions. Accordingly, in March 1946, the party's members in Berlin's western sectors voted resoundingly against unification. Despite the misgivings of even some of the KPD's members, Ulbricht forced the merger through.

Even after the formation of the new Socialist Unity Party (SED), the communists could not count on strong support within the entire Soviet Zone of Occupation. In fall 1946, when the SED put up candidates in regional elections in the first and, it would turn out, last free elections in eastern Germany until 1990, the results were profoundly dispiriting. Although the party easily won control of the Soviet zone in Berlin, it struggled against the "bourgeois" parties in other cities with large working-class populations. When separate elections were held in all four occupation zones in Berlin, the communists came in a humiliating third place. The Social Democrats received nearly half of the popular vote, while the Christian Democratic Union won more than 20 percent.[35] These disappointments were only the beginning of a desperate search for legitimacy that would plague the SED over the next four decades.

A Unitary State System

It would be fanciful to think that any of the Eastern European communist parties that came to power with the support of the Red Army would have remained in office without Moscow's continuing presence. Whatever they promised, the communists who returned to their homelands had no intention of compromising the visions of socialist grandeur that they had nurtured while abroad. As good Stalinists, they lived through their convictions. As a result, when these true believers encountered opposition, they did not consider it an indication that they needed to change their views. To the contrary, it was evidence of a fundamental Stalinist precept: the class struggle would intensify with the nearing of socialism. If there was any room for doubt about this proposition, it was overcome by the swift deterioration of relations between the USSR and the Western democracies.

In this circumstance, the Soviets left nothing to chance. On September 22, 1947, they and representatives of eight other European communist parties gathered in the Polish resort town, Szklarska Poręba, to found the Cominform. In a stirring statement, Andrei Zhdanov, the party's expert on ideological and cultural affairs, conjured the darkening cloud of East-West relations to outline the organization's mission. According to Zhdanov, two huge superpower blocs stood face to face. One was led by the USSR, "the leading force and spirit in the military defeat of Germany and Japan." This alliance had "withstood the worst trials of the war" and "the life-and-death conflict with its most powerful foe." The other bloc was led by the United States. It had cynically adopted the expansionist plans of the "Hitlerites" and was intent upon sabotaging the peace, fostering economic expansionism, and preparing for a third world war. Under these conditions, Zhdanov asserted, the sole hope for mankind was for peoples of good faith to unite their efforts to "fight for a democratic peace, for the liquidation of the remnants of fascism" and to affirm the "principle of equality of rights and respect for their sovereignty." These goals could only be realized by following the leading example of the Soviet Union, which had consistently demonstrated the "will and desire for cooperation" with its adversaries.[36]

In one respect, the dichotomous structure of Zhdanov's analysis harkens back to the rigid, us-versus-them message of the Comintern's Second World Congress, albeit with fewer global aspirations. But there is a key difference. Reflecting the evolution of Soviet priorities under Stalin, the Cominform was designed to coordinate policies against the threats of great powers, not great ideologies. To this end, Zhdanov's primary focus in his address was on the entities that were most useful as bulwarks against the Western threat—states. In his description, these "people's republics," subsequently known as People's Democracies, would not be full-blown copies of the Soviet Union. They still needed time to rise to the USSR's extraordinary achievements! But, Zhdanov argued, they could certainly prepare themselves to begin the transition to socialism.[37]

Just as in the Soviet Union, the victim of the ascendancy of this state-centered way of thinking was the idea of party rule. Notably, Zhdanov devoted only a single section of his speech to the issue of party leadership. In this case, he focused solely on the Western European communist parties that, he hinted, were not yet fully committed to the cause. The Comintern, Zhdanov stressed, had ensured these parties' existence by uniting the international working class. But after its work was finished, their leaders had retreated into their national shells and become isolated from the progressive movement. This condition, he contended, was "incorrect, harmful, and essentially unnatural." For this reason, they should return to the international fold and devote their energies to "enlisting all anti-fascist, freedom-loving elements into the struggle against the new American expansionist plan for subjugating Europe."[38]

The fact that Zhdanov did not demand more of these parties is an instructive indication of how much had changed since the days of the Comintern. Representatives of both the PCF and the PCI were present in Szklarska Poręba. Yet, Zhdanov was accommodating. Rather than insisting that they fall into line with the rigid model of Stalinist discipline that was expected of the People's Democracies, he merely criticized them for being excessively fond of parliamentary politics. This was no accident. In both cases, the Soviet Union had more to gain from authentically democratic parties. Their success at the voting booth was a potential opportunity to shape public thinking in the West. In light of this comradely largesse, it was unfortunate that 1947 and 1948 turned out to be difficult years for both the PCF and the PCI. In fact, for the PCF, they were terrible. In May 1947, the PCF's five cabinet ministers were thrown out of the Socialist-led coalition government because of the party's pro-Soviet stands and its doctrinaire approach to socialism. In April 1948, the less intractable PCI went into the general elections with surging optimism. Yet despite making significant gains in parliamentary seats, the PCI lost its bid for power to the Christian Democrats. Although the communists remained a formidable presence in Italian politics for decades to come, they would never again enter a national government.

The Soviets had a more immediate cause for concern, however, in the case of a different Cominform member within their sphere of influence: Yugoslavia. Under the charismatic leadership of Josip Broz Tito, the Yugoslav Communist Party (YCP) had come to power without the aid of Soviet troops. In the process of conducting an insurrectionary war against their country's German occupiers, Croatian fascists, and Serbian nationalists in the hills and mountains of Bosnia and southern Serbia, his Partisan guerrilla fighters acquired a sense of mission that bore a greater resemblance to the revolutionary culture of Mao Zedong's rebel army than to the imposed parties of the People's Democracies. Many were idealistic university students and veterans of the Spanish Civil War. Like the Chinese communists, they too were keen to act on a conception of the class struggle that was intertwined with the cause of national liberation. In their country in particular, this blend of revolutionary and patriotic goals seemed naturally suited to addressing the tensions that the war had exacerbated among the myriad ethnic and religious groups—Slovenes, Croats, Serbs, Montenegrins, and Bosnian and Albanian Muslims—that constituted the Yugoslav state. In their official mythology, the YCP's role would extend beyond divesting the old ruling classes of their power. By reinforcing their shared national identity, it would provide a mechanism to prevent these groups from tearing the country apart.

When Tito and the Partisans emerged from the mountains, they were free to decide for themselves how to pursue these objectives. In an ironic contrast with the other People's Democracies, they chose to implement Stalinism immediately. In only the first year after forming a government in Belgrade, the YCP showed what it meant to be the victor. With the zeal of underground freedom fighters who finally had the chance to realize their dreams, Yugoslav communists threw themselves into establishing total power and engaging in full-scale socialist construction. They conducted ruthless extermination campaigns against purported collaborators and repressed potential rivals, such as the Slovenian People's Party and the Catholic Church. Simultaneously, the YCP instituted a crash program of industrialization and laid the groundwork for collectivization by transferring farmland acquired by peasants during the war to new state farms. In these campaigns, the party exalted Tito's leadership.

The Kremlin might have found these Stalinist measures to be merely premature were it not for one aspect of their implementation. Tito used them to demonstrate his party's independence. Although he proclaimed his undying loyalty to Moscow, it was not the Soviet Union that he had in mind. It was its revolutionary ideal. In May 1945, he infuriated his allies when, in an attack on the West, he chose terms that could have been as easily applied to them as to the capitalist world. The Yugoslav communists, he declared, did not wish to be treated as "small change" or to become an object of exchange in "a policy of spheres of interests."[39] In an indication of Yugoslavia's strategic importance, Stalin initially showed uncharacteristic patience in putting up with these acts of defiance. However, his restraint was not to last. In February 1948, he summoned Tito to Moscow for a pledge of allegiance. When Tito refused to come, Stalin's response was unequivocal. He devoted the Cominform's Second Conference on June 21, a meeting the YCP refused to attend, to putting Tito in his place. On Stalin's behalf, Zhdanov delivered a stinging attack on Belgrade, accusing Tito and the YCP of being everything they were not. In a flawless enunciation of Stalinist newspeak, he declared that the Yugoslavs had become followers of the "Narodnik-Kulak" line, deniers of the class struggle, anti-Marxists, and enemies of Leninism.[40] On June 28, the assembled parties, including even the French and Italian delegates, made a remarkable decision. They expelled their wayward ally from the Cominform. As if to prove that his former mentor had been right all along, Tito hunted down Stalin's purported supporters in Yugoslavia and declared his intention to create an independent path to socialism.

THE RISE OF THE STATE, THE FALL OF THE PARTY

Yugoslavia's ouster from the Cominform clarified everything Zhdanov had declared at the organization's founding. Dutiful states and not freewheeling parties were needed at a time when the class struggle had taken the form of a life-or-death confrontation between the defenders of peace and democracy and the capitalist powers that were preparing for a new war. Conveniently for Moscow, its Eastern European allies did not need to be forced to view the world in this way. Even before Tito's excommunication, most were instituting policies that showed that, whether they were called People's Democracies or not, they would not tolerate any deviation from their policies. This inclination was almost universally characteristic of those communists who received their formation in Moscow. Nearly everywhere, they used their party organizations to engage in acts of self-Stalinization. These measures culminated in the formation of a belt of Soviet-style dictatorships with demonstrably similar profiles. The Bulgarian government forced its king to abdicate and expelled dissident members from the Fatherland Front. Romania's communists forced through a merger of their party with the opposition Social Democrats, leading to the creation of the Romanian Workers' Party. The Hungarian communists renamed their party the Hungarian Workers' Party, a notably unrevolutionary relative of its militant ancestor in 1919. In Poland, the communists absorbed the Polish Socialist Party into a Polish United Workers' Party.

The consolidation of these dictatorships was matched by the introduction of equally uniform economic policies. Regardless of their countries' level of development, state planners acted as though there was only a single formula for building socialism, one based upon the accelerated production of steel, chemicals, coal, and electric power. To meet these governments' unrealistically high production quotas, hundreds of thousands of agricultural laborers were moved into the cities. Industries not yet fully nationalized were taken over by the state. Although their tempos differed, all but one of the People's Democracies followed Stalin's example of assaulting the countryside. Under the pretext of providing food and clothing to the cities, officials used "anti-kulak" campaigns to justify the conversion of small farms into massive collectives. Only in Poland, where full-scale collectivization would have led to a national uprising, did private farming continue.

Two states, Czechoslovakia and the soon-to-be formed German Democratic Republic (GDR), took different paths, although they ended up with similar results. At the beginning of 1948, Czechoslovakia was still a functioning democracy, but just barely. Thanks to the CPC's domination of key ministries, the communists could have simply forced their will on their opponents. They controlled the armed forces and the security services, monopolized the media, and presided over a plethora of paramilitary groups. Instead, Gottwald took an indirect route, provoking a cabinet crisis over claims that the CPC was abusing its police powers. He may have thought this approach would create the impression that the CPC was simply defending its honor. One way or the other, he achieved his goal. When the cabinet split apart, President Beneš had no choice but to ask Gottwald to form a new government.

But the time for communist pretense was over. The CPC swiftly staged a coup against the regime, attacked its members, and held sham elections in May 1948 in which citizens could only vote for a communist-dominated National Front. After the formation of a new parliament, it declared Czechoslovakia a People's Democracy.

The GDR was genetically different from its eastern neighbors. Its founding on October 7, 1949, was the result of Great Power competition, not national self-assertion. It was not invited to join the Cominform and could not even be called a People's Democracy. Since 1945, Stalin himself had been reluctant to commit to the formation of a separate East German state, fearing the loss of Soviet authority over Germany as a whole. But he grudgingly concluded that any influence on the West was contingent upon the Eastern zone's stability. Hence, he consented to the GDR's creation. With control over their own state, Walter Ulbricht and the other Moscow-trained communists pursued the same policies as in the other People's Democracies. Under the pretext of fostering an antifascist alliance, they founded a Democratic Bloc (later, National Front) of obedient parties and mass organizations. They installed communist officials in every major state position. They nationalized large industries, imposed exorbitant work quotas on factories, and laid the groundwork for agricultural collectivization. Finally, they cracked down on their critics. Aside from targeting Social Democrats and Christian Democrats, they purged their own ranks of anyone suspected of putting the cause of national reunification ahead of the construction of a separate East German state.

THE PARTIES DEVOUR THEIR FOUNDERS

If there was any doubt at this point that the focus of the Eastern European states' leaders was on aggrandizing power, and not on abiding by Marxism's lofty internationalist principles, it would have been laid to rest by the deliberate manner in which they mimicked Stalin's infamous achievement—the Terror. Even more quickly than their Soviet exemplars and in an even more focused manner, communists in each country turned on their fellow party members. They accused old friends and comrades in battle of the all-too-familiar crimes of Trotskyism, Bukharinism, and Zionism. They also added a new offense, Titoism.

Tens of thousands of rank-and-file party officials and regular members were purged; many thousands were arrested, tortured, and sent to labor camps. In textbook fashion, each regime followed Soviet precedent by conducting public show trials at which the accused were forced to admit their guilt before being led to their execution.

The first major communist to be arrested was the Romanian justice minister, Lucrețiu Pătrășcanu, who in April 1948 was charged with being a Titoist-American agent. Pătrășcanu's execution was followed by the show trial of Hungary's foreign minister and former interior minister Rajk, who was accused of plotting with Tito to assassinate Mátyás Rákosi. In a trial of eleven senior party members, the president of the Bulgarian Council of Ministers, Traicho Kostov, was condemned for anti-Soviet activities. The most publicized trial of all was the prosecution of Rudolf Slánský, the general secretary of the CCP (Gottwald was the party chairman). In November 1952, he and thirteen other prominent figures were sentenced to death. The head of the Polish Workers' Party, Władysław Gomułka, was fortunate to escape execution. Thanks to his high public profile he was merely sentenced to house arrest following his expulsion from the party.

It was no accident that a majority of the accused in these cases were home communists, especially those with Jewish backgrounds. For Muscovite communists like Rákosi, Chervenkov, Gottwald, and Bierut, their rivals shared with Stalin's old Bolsheviks the one quality that they lacked—revolutionary authenticity. Rajk had fought heroically in the Spanish Civil War and was a leader in the Hungarian underground. Kostov had been active in the Bulgarian resistance. Slánský had parachuted into Slovakia to lead the uprising against the Germans. Although Gomułka had spent time in Moscow, he had returned to Poland during the war to participate in the refounding of the communist party. In only a handful of cases were the home communists the victors in these power struggles. Not surprisingly, they involved leaders who were not totally dependent on Soviet support. Romania's Gheorghiu-Dej purged his three major rivals, all Muscovites, from the Politburo. In Albania, where the communist party had come to power on the basis of an independent guerrilla struggle, the country's leader Enver Hoxha used Stalin's break with Tito to justify the execution of his principal rival, Interior Minister Koçi Xoxe.

There was, however, one major difference between these purges and Stalin's Terror. The Soviet leader did not have an equivalent "Stalin" to lord over him. He was free to do what he wanted with his allies. Hence, he was frequently active behind the scenes, even when the victims were loyal to his command. For example, he personally ordered Kostov's execution after a dispute over trade policy. In Slánský's case, he initially ruled that the Czechoslovak leader's crimes were insufficient to justify harsh punishment, but after a period of reflection changed his mind and ordered Gottwald to carry out Slánský's execution.

Nevertheless, it says a lot about the motivations of the leaders of the People's Democracies that most would have likely carried out these purges without Stalin's bidding. To be sure, the Soviet leader provided the tools for these campaigns. NKVD agents were actively engaged in the purges of the parties' upper echelons. Its agents were conduits for the Kremlin's directions and seasoned educators in the arts of interrogation and forced confessions. Still, we cannot account for the furious dimensions of the Eastern European purges unless we take into account the willing engagement of the figures who were behind the arrests, trials, and executions. Just as in the Soviet Union, guilt was specific. Their actions were the product of internecine struggles within each of these regimes over who was entitled to rule. Some of these battles grew out of disputes over social and economic priorities. More often than not, however, their intensity derived from personal ambition and a lust for power. Also like the Soviet Union, the perpetrators were invariably those individuals who had the support of strong patronage networks and the police and security organs. They knew what was required to manipulate popular perceptions to their advantage.

In the end, the most important victim of this violence was the old European conception of the communist party. Thanks to Stalin's example in pioneering the perversion of the party's purposes, these self-serving measures shattered the mythology that the global communist movement was woven together by a tapestry of noble hopes and beliefs. In the process, the party was stripped of its honor. In September 1949, when Hungary's new interior minister, János Kádár, asked his predecessor, Rajk, to sign a full confession, he conceded that no one actually believed he was guilty. The act of confession was simply something one did for the good of the cause. "The party has chosen you for the role of traitor," Kádár explained, "and you must sacrifice yourself for the party." He added: "This is terrible, but after all, you are an old militant and cannot refuse to help the party."[41] In the ultimate act of cynicism, Kádár promised Rajk that his life would be spared if he cooperated. When Rajk complied, he was executed anyway. However, history would wreak its revenge. Two years later, Kádár was caught up in the same whirlwind of violence. At Rákosi's command, he was arrested and tortured. However, Kádár somehow managed to escape Rajk's fate. His good fortune, as I shall show in chapter 8, would allow him to play a formidable role in his party's history.

As long as Stalin was alive, it was enough for survivors like Rákosi to know that the Soviet Union would come to their aid if their hold on power was threatened. Due to their supreme confidence in their abilities, they probably did not give much thought to what would happen if the great leader were not around to back up this guarantee. One thing was certain. Thanks to their actions, they could no longer look to the institution, the party, whose mystique had once legitimated the communists' right to rule.

CHAPTER 8

Rediscovering the Leninist Idea

On March 6, 1953, *Pravda* and *Izvestia* solemnly announced the news that would arguably become the most important event in international communism since the October Revolution: "The heart of Lenin's comrade-in-arms and the inspired continuer of Lenin's cause, the wise leader and teacher of the Communist Party and the Soviet people—Joseph Vissarionovich STALIN—has stopped beating." Had Stalin himself scripted the announcement, much as he had done for momentous and trivial matters alike in the past, he would have been pleased with these words. This was not any man who had succumbed to the condition of his mortality. Together with Lenin, "Comrade Stalin" had, in the newspapers' announcement, forged the mighty party of communists, formed the world's first socialist state, led his country to victory over fascism, and armed the party and the entire people with a clear program for building communism.[1]

In this situation, the powerful figures in the Communist Party of the Soviet Union (CPSU) Presidium, as the Politburo was called after 1952, were presented with two immediate challenges. One was to decide who among them should step into the great leader's shoes. Not surprisingly, Stalin had conspicuously failed to appoint a successor. This step would have been unthinkable to him. In his self-serving fantasies, even in the unlikely event that one could find an individual with sufficient gifts, that person would have begun plotting against him immediately. The other challenge for Stalin's successors was even more daunting. At the height of his power, Stalin's persona had been the glue that held the Soviet Union together, as well as nearly the entire communist movement. Thus, as these figures rushed to identify the best courses of action, they asked themselves where they should look to find a force that was powerful enough to take Stalin's place. The easy answer to both questions was the one that had prevailed in principle since Lenin was in power: the communist party.

True to ritual, *Pravda* and *Izvestia* came right to the point. The workers, collective farmers, intelligentsia, and working peoples of all countries, the newspapers proclaimed, should come together "in a great fraternal family under the tested leadership of the communist party, created and reared by Lenin and STALIN." In turn, the party would reciprocate their devotion by maintaining a "steel-like and monolithic unity." The Presidium's members were quick to echo these sentiments. They let it be known that they, too, would carry on their predecessor's example of holding the banner of party leadership high. In charting the course of socialism in the post-Stalin era, they intoned, this common bond would lead them forward.

If only the principle of party rule were so resilient! As we have seen in chapter 5, one of Stalin's most prominent accomplishments was to destroy the institution that brought him to power. Whether through calculated design or sheer impetuosity, Stalin demonstrated that there was no middle ground between the pursuit of absolute power and the preservation of the party's founding ideals. He went after the party precisely because the institution provided an umbrella under which other communists, and especially his old Bolshevik comrades, could articulate rival conceptions of Marxism and Leninism and build the internal coalitions needed to implement them. Without the party to protect them, there was nowhere these individuals could go. They could either hew to Stalin's interpretation of the Soviet Union's priorities or face expulsion from the party's ranks, or worse.

Against this background, we can understand why *Pravda*'s and *Izvestia*'s romantic conceptions of a "great fraternal family" would have represented an intuitively compelling alternative to what Stalin's successors had experienced over the preceding decades. A party-centered approach, or "collective leadership" as the concept became known, would be predictable in a way that Stalin's dictatorship had never been. If it worked, it would be more collegial and provide room for more responsible decisions. From a strictly self-interested standpoint, collective leadership was also a form of self-protection. It would ensure that one could come to work in the morning without having to fear that a misstep in one's interactions with a new great leader would result in a trip to the Gulag at the end of the day.

Yet, for all of Stalin's successors, the idea of party leadership had a powerful rival: the seductive appeal of personalistic rule. In a system in which trust in institutions had broken down and been replaced with fealty to a single person, it must have been difficult for them to believe that their political system could survive if it were not in some way fortified by the power of personality. Indeed, their ingrained Leninist sense of superiority undoubtedly led them to assume that they were individually called to take on some aspect of this mission.

I shall argue in this chapter that in the first ten years after Stalin's death, the temptation to address the Soviet Union's challenges through personalistic rather than institutional means represented the single greatest impediment to the restoration of the party's authority. Under the populist leadership of the CPSU's first secretary, Nikita Khrushchev, as I shall show, the party's centrality to the USSR's future was rhetorically returned to the forefront of the regime's proclamations. Yet it was all too frequently trumped in deed by the "great man" principle. The same dictatorial proclivity was present throughout the communist world, especially in the People's Democracies of Eastern Europe. In the wake of their mentor's passing, "little Stalins," like Walter Ulbricht in East Germany, Bolesław Bierut in Poland, and Mátyás Rákosi in Hungary, were acutely aware of their vulnerability. Accordingly, although they paid tribute to the concept of collective leadership, they simultaneously subverted it.

This is not to say that the investment of significant power in certain individuals always had negative consequences. Paradoxically, as I shall show, Khrushchev's supreme position gave him the power to bring about one of the most far-reaching political shifts in communist history. At the CPSU's Twentieth Congress in 1956, he delivered an earth-shattering attack on Stalin's role in the Terror. In the process, as I shall also suggest, Khrushchev provided his listeners with a tantalizing picture of a revitalized form of Leninism as it had supposedly existed in Lenin's time. This development culminated in his announcement at the CPSU's Twenty-Second Congress in 1961 that the party would lead the Soviet people into the "orbit" of communism. In contrast, in other socialist countries, personal despotism resulted in heartache, disillusionment, and violence. The stubborn refusal of the leaders of the People's Democracies to contemplate a responsive form of leadership to deal with their citizens' hardships led to outright conflict, both with their populations and within their respective parties. In one case, Hungary, the failure to appreciate the necessity of a change of course resulted in the total collapse of the regime's authority and military intervention by the Warsaw Pact.

STALIN'S COMRADES

To understand the mentality of Stalin's successors in 1953, it is essential to begin with a simple fact. They were all Stalinists. After all, they had become members of Stalin's inner circle by hewing faithfully to their leader's commands. Furthermore, unlike many other members of the communist aristocracy, each had been shrewd enough to survive the Terror. The three personalities, or "troika," who delivered the eulogies at Stalin's funeral—Georgy Malenkov, the senior secretary of the Central Committee; Lavrenty Beria, the minister of the interior and grand inquisitor of the People's Commissariat for Internal Affairs (NKVD) since 1938; and Vyacheslav Molotov, soon to be reappointed foreign minister—were willing participants in their leader's manipulation of higher communist ideals and beneficiaries of his patrimony. As Stalinists, they had consciously used the concept of proletarian dictatorship to justify the violent proclivities of the "teacher and leader, the great genius of mankind" (Malenkov);[2] they had preached a doctrine of class warfare that made it impossible for any Soviet citizen to envisage a time without secret police repression; and, they were complicit in their mentor's darkest deeds. As head of the NKVD, Beria was conspicuously involved in Stalin's crimes. But Malenkov, Molotov, and the others in Stalin's circle were knowing participants as well. They had denounced their friends and former comrades in battle and looked the other way as they were shipped off to NKVD camps. They had also joined Stalin in signing death warrants.

The open question in March 1953 was whether they wanted to *remain* Stalinists. In this matter, the case for a substantive, as opposed to a merely abstract, concept of collective rule was compelling. In his final years, Stalin had given everyone around him specific reasons for concern about their livelihoods and lives. Molotov, his longtime confidante, had fallen out of favor. He was removed from his position as foreign minister in 1949, and watched helplessly as his wife was deported to a Siberian labor camp. In 1951, Stalin sent an ominous signal to Beria, whom he apparently felt had acquired too much power, by ordering the arrest of officials from his home region of Georgia. In January 1953, Stalin's hand seemed to come dangerously close to the entire Presidium when he claimed to have discovered a plot by physicians in the Kremlin to assassinate him. In this sense, his successors were "all in the same boat."[3]

Only these figures' motivations were unclear. Were they interested in reviving an old institution because they hoped to initiate policies and reinvigorate high ideals? Or were they merely taking these steps to aggrandize personal power? Politicians everywhere know that the pursuit of power and the advocacy of policy are frequent bed partners. Still, there were early signs that some of the Soviet Union's new leaders were more adept than others at pursuing both objectives.

The leadership's first step was to fashion a power structure that would give its members control over their destiny. In late 1952, Stalin had replaced the Politburo and the Orgburo with a new body, the Presidium, which had a grand total of thirty-six members. No doubt, his goal was to dilute the organization's authority all the more. Although the older organs had rarely met, it did not escape the attention of these senior members that the new appointees were predominantly younger cadres whom Stalin could have used at will to replace them. Literally within hours of his death, they retook what they were apparently on the verge of losing by removing twenty-two of the new members. They also moved quickly to divide the Presidium's corresponding state ministries among themselves. Malenkov was made chairman of the Council of Ministers, or premier, and three others, including Beria, were appointed as his deputies.

The elite group's next step was to end the fusion of state and party offices that had facilitated Stalin's grip on power. On March 14, Malenkov apparently voluntarily gave up his position as senior party secretary and the Presidium turned over the Secretariat's daily affairs to Nikita Khrushchev. The choice of Khrushchev proved to be momentous, though its full significance was not evident at the time. In accord with his technocratic focus on the state ministries, Stalin had reduced the Secretariat's functions to being little more than a mouthpiece for ideological policy. Furthermore, Khrushchev, an uneducated peasant's son and dutiful apparatchik, did not appear to be a threat. He had successfully built a reputation as an advocate of his coleaders' collective interests by instituting measures to place the state security organs under the Secretariat's direct supervision.

The Presidium's final move could not have been bolder. On June 26, a loose coalition composed of Malenkov, Khrushchev, and Marshal of the Soviet Union Georgy Zhukov trapped Beria in the Kremlin and arrested him. Following nearly two months during which Beria's fate was unknown to the outside world, the Soviet press announced that the man who had presided over millions of deportations and killings was guilty of conspiring with British intelligence agents to defame the party and overthrow the government. On December 23, Beria was executed.

The plotters' immediate goal was self-preservation. Khrushchev made the point succinctly: "While this bastard is around, none of us can feel safe."[4] Yet at least one of the Presidium's members appears to have been thinking about something more substantial than saving his own skin. In the July 1953 Central Committee sessions in which Beria's fate was discussed, Malenkov showed that he was willing to risk the animosity of his colleagues by asking what had happened to the party during Stalin's tenure. Why was it the case, he inquired at the opening session on July 2, that Central Committee plenums had rarely taken place over the preceding decades, that the Politburo had ceased to function, and that there had been only two party congresses since 1934? These "abnormalities," in his estimation, could not be reduced to Beria's perfidy. Rather, Malenkov argued, everyone in the leadership was guilty of losing sight of the primacy of party leadership. Only the restoration of collective rule could ensure that these transgressions were not repeated.[5]

By taking the risk of lifting the veil from the issue of responsibility, Malenkov invited his colleagues to speculate about the deeper sources of these dysfunctions. In particular, he addressed Stalin's dictatorial behavior. At the concluding session of the plenum on June 7, he laid the major share of the blame on the "cult of personality," as he called it, which surrounded the party's leader. This deformation, Malenkov maintained, had led to the destruction of collective decision making in the Politburo, the neglect of criticism and self-criticism at the regime's highest levels, and countless flawed policies. Citing an 1877 letter from no less an authority figure than Karl Marx on the dangers of elevating the individual over the collective, Malenkov hinted that the Presidium had already waited too long to correct these offenses. The only way to prevent the personality cult from recurring was to restore the party to its leading role.[6]

Shortly thereafter, in a further indication that he was determined to address substantive matters, Malenkov confronted the great shibboleths of Soviet domestic and foreign policymaking. In a speech before the Supreme Soviet in August 1953, he announced a program of balanced economic growth, soon to be known throughout the Soviet bloc as the "New Course," which broke away from his predecessor's infatuation with heavy industry and centralized planning. Arguing that the Soviet people had a *right* to expect better living standards, Malenkov declared that the ministries under his command would henceforth increase the supply of food and high-quality consumer goods. To accomplish this task, they would reallocate to light industrial production budgetary resources normally restricted to heavy industry and the military. He also directed government agencies to stimulate agricultural production by reducing delivery quotas on private plots and promoting trade among collective farms.

In the same address, Malenkov was no less daring in calling for a searching reassessment of Soviet foreign policy. In particular, he challenged the Stalinist dogma that the conflict between socialism and capitalism precluded cooperation with the West. The idea was not totally new. For propaganda purposes, the Kremlin had previously mouthed the rhetoric of "peaceful coexistence" between the superpowers. However, Malenkov showed that he meant what he said. He explicitly parted ways with those members of the ruling circle, such as Molotov, who religiously intoned Stalin's observations about the intensification of the class struggle and demanded vigilance in the face of imperialist intrigues. The threat of nuclear obliteration, Malenkov contended, had permanently altered the nature of the conflict between the superpowers. Although he did not go so far as to say that the contradictions between socialism and capitalism had disappeared—he was, after all, a Marxist—he emphasized that the nuclear powers were obliged to seek peaceful means of resolving their differences.[7]

There is a certain poignancy to the fact that Malenkov espoused these positions. By the end of the 1950s, they would become standard features of Soviet domestic and foreign policy. But he would not have the honor of acting on them. Within two years, Khrushchev, and not Malenkov or any of Stalin's other successors, would become the prime mover in the Soviet leadership. Initially, the senior party secretary appears to have been cautious about playing his hand. Aside from joining his colleagues in an emotional denunciation of Beria at the June 1953 Central Committee meetings—"Beria's views of the party," in his opinion, were "no different than the views of Hitler"—Khrushchev presented himself as a voice of reason, someone who was intent upon restoring the party's lost luster.[8] Looking back, however, we can detect hints of what was to come. In mid-April 1953, after Khrushchev had taken control of the Secretariat, *Pravda*, the Central Committee's public voice, published an article under the title "The Collective Principle of Party Leadership," which suggested that a shift in the locus of decision-making authority was under way. As head of the Secretariat, Khrushchev must have been behind the article's endorsement of restoring party organizations to their central place in policymaking.[9] He also had different reasons than Malenkov for invoking the party's leading position. Like Stalin before him, he would have known that control of a revitalized Central Committee was the first step toward absolute power.

On September 3, Khrushchev showed that he had both policymaking and the satisfaction of his personal ambitions in mind when he convened a special Central Committee session on the advancement of his greatest passion: agriculture. Normally, such an initiative would have come from the state planning ministries, but that was Malenkov's territory. In his address to the Central Committee's members, Khrushchev outdid his rival's promises—he pronounced one of Malenkov's policies "strange"—by pledging to raise the living standards of collective farmers, to reduce their taxes, and to provide them with greater incentives to bring their surpluses to market. There was nothing antisocialist about appealing to people's self-interest, Khrushchev lectured, as if Malenkov would never have considered this point. The "great Lenin" had taught that the road to communism would take many years. Thus, one had to provide Soviet citizens with palpable reasons for maintaining their faith in the journey.[10]

At the meeting, Khrushchev also offered an early indication of the emotionally charged, populist style that would run throughout his years in power. He presented himself as the tribune of the people, battling against the elitist attitudes of communist functionaries. Too many district party officials, Khrushchev advised an assembly of collective farmers, had a "lordly and bureaucratic" attitude toward village life. They thought they could simply show up at a village and issue instructions without leaving their car. This behavior violated a basic rule of party behavior. Their role was to motivate their fellow citizens, not dominate them. They should immerse themselves in the lives of the working masses, explain the party's policies, and guide them in the pursuit of mutually beneficial goals.

Khrushchev's remedy for this dysfunction was suggestively reminiscent of the mass mobilization strategies of the early 1930s, when Soviet citizens were spurred to transform their country into a modern nation. It even had a tinge of the Russian "going to the people" movements of the 1860s and 1870s. Whereas Stalin had called for the construction of massive industrial cities in his country's hinterland, Khrushchev exhorted the party's young members to move to the countryside, where they could learn the ways of those who worked on the land. "Now that a Soviet intelligentsia has grown up among us," Khrushchev queried, "why should we not issue a call from the party and summon the best people from the cities—say, for example, 50,000 communists—to strengthen rural work?" There would be no problem finding ample numbers of cadres to volunteer for this assignment, he pointed out, because they would immediately see the advantage of living where they worked.[11]

Khrushchev's ability to put these claims into practice was fortified by the Presidium's decision to promote him to the newly created post of first secretary in September 1953. Like so many of his undertakings, Khrushchev's sheer force of will seems to have pushed him forward. In the summer of 1954, he threw himself into a campaign to open millions of acres of virgin land in western Siberia and Kazakhstan to cultivation. The initiative proved to be enormously popular. The CPSU's youth organization, the Komsomol, mobilized hundreds of thousands of volunteers to travel to these regions where they tilled the soil, planted maize and sunflowers, and received their first exposure to the hardships of Soviet agriculture. Many of these young enthusiasts settled in these areas permanently and, together with legions of seasonal workers and soldiers, built huge state farms. The "Virgin Lands" program suffered a major blow during its first year when drought conditions destroyed these crops. Nevertheless, later successful harvests made Khrushchev look like a miracle worker.

These ventures alone would probably not have sufficed to challenge Malenkov's position in the leadership. But after allowing his colleagues to underestimate him, Khrushchev skillfully built a coalition against his rival. With the support of Nikolai Bulganin, the defense minister, and Zhukov, he took the premier to task for supposedly breaking with time-tested priorities. Every good party worker knew, Khrushchev advised, that the large industrial sectors like steel, mining, and chemicals were the bulwarks of sustained growth. With equal fervor, Khrushchev asserted that Malenkov had deviated from the orthodox "Marxist-Leninist-Stalinist" line about the inevitable conflict with capitalism. Capitalism, he underscored, would meet certain defeat in such a conflict, whereas communism would emerge victorious. To think otherwise was tantamount to rejecting the doctrine of the class struggle.[12]

Khrushchev won this battle decisively. In early February 1955, the Presidium announced that Malenkov had been replaced by Bulganin as premier. What may have surprised those around Khrushchev was the vitriol he directed toward Malenkov. To listen to the first secretary, one would have thought that his longtime associate's demotion had saved the Soviet Union from certain catastrophe. Malenkov, it seemed, had been second only to Beria in the damage he inflicted in less than two years in command. He was responsible for every major failure in economic and foreign policy since Stalin's death. To be sure, the Presidium had accused Beria of a greater crime—treason. But in Khrushchev's self-serving assessment, Malenkov's policies had been no less damaging. He was guilty of everything from spinelessness to "anti-party behavior."[13]

This was an astonishing choice of words. The critics of Lenin's New Economic Policy had been accused of antiparty behavior at the Tenth Congress in 1921. More ominously, Stalin had used the term to serve more sinister purposes, denouncing opponents like Bukharin for their supposed crimes against the faith. In this way, Khrushchev's action was a foreshadowing of the blustery, confrontational use of power that would turn most of his closest associates against him a decade later. The difference is that this was not Stalinism. Only a few years earlier, the charges against Malenkov would have been enough to send him to prison, or worse. Yet apparently recognizing that a majority of the Presidium's members were unwilling to invest him with uncontrolled power, Khrushchev chose to hold back. He refrained from calling for any further action against his rival. For his part, Malenkov dutifully engaged in an act of self-criticism. In return, he was allowed to remain in the Presidium and hold a position, albeit a diminished one, in the Council of Ministers.

The Persistence of Stalinism in Eastern Europe

To outside observers in 1953, a break with Stalinism must have seemed even more necessary in Eastern Europe than in the Soviet Union. A majority of the People's Democracies, as well as the German Democratic Republic (GDR), literally owed their existence to the USSR. Yet precisely this relationship made their leaders' claims to authority problematic. Thus, rather than embracing meaningful change, these "little Stalins" relied upon two means to retain power: dogged opposition to any political rivals, especially reformists, and, when necessary, the recourse to brute force.

Stalin's death instantly exposed the fragility of these regimes. In early May 1953, tobacco workers went on strike in Bulgaria's second-largest city, Plovdiv, in opposition to draconian work quotas. One month later, the Czechoslovak government declared martial law in Plzeň when thousands of workers protested a planned currency reform that would have destroyed their savings. The prospect of further instability was most vividly confirmed by successive crises in the GDR, Poland, and Hungary. In all three countries, their Stalinist leaders—Walter Ulbricht, Bolesław Bierut, and Mátyás Rákosi, respectively—were threatened by both popular discontent and discord within their party's ranks. But in these cases as well, they drew upon their internal supporters and Moscow's determination to satisfy its security interests to retain power.

The extent of this crisis of legitimacy was demonstrated by the nearly total breakdown of political authority in the GDR in 1953. As a result of Ulbricht's decision to accelerate the transition to socialism, East Germany was beset by widespread food shortages, the collapse of the transportation system, and labor unrest. On June 16, three months after Stalin's death, construction workers in East Berlin walked off their jobs in protest against the regime's refusal to rescind its high production quotas. On the following day, June 17, the city exploded. As strikes and demonstrations spread throughout the GDR, only the intervention of Soviet troops and the deaths of hundreds of citizens were enough to keep the East German government in power.

Looking back at these events, one might wonder whether this convulsion would have been prevented if Ulbricht's ambitions had been checked. One of the most intriguing dimensions of the crisis is that key figures in the Socialist Unity Party's (SED) highest echelons recognized the need to move beyond the policies of the Stalin era. Several weeks before Malenkov announced the New Course, a majority of the members of the Politburo of the SED, led by the minister for state security, Wilhelm Zaisser, reached a consensus about the desirability of a more conciliatory approach to the population. They endorsed the return of confiscated property to its original owners, a halt to further collectivization, and the redirection of investment priorities toward private consumption. At the Central Committee's meeting on May 13–14, they successfully secured Ulbricht's agreement to modest reforms, but with the fatal concession that they increase the controversial work norms.

Nevertheless, in the wake of the workers' revolt, Ulbricht's opponents seemed to win the opportunity to turn against him. All but two members of the Politburo were in favor of removing the SED chief from office. At a session on July 8, Zaisser accused the first secretary of having "spoiled" the party's reputation and declared that he could not be trusted to implement serious economic reform. Zaisser proposed replacing Ulbricht with Rudolf Herrnstadt, a less dogmatic candidate member of the Politburo and the editor of the party's official newspaper, *Neues Deutschland*. Another member, Fred Oelßner, went further, arguing that the party did not even need a first secretary. What really mattered was that they engage in "collective decision-making."[14]

In assessing these attacks, one needs to be careful to avoid assuming that Ulbricht's adversaries would have abandoned the institutional mechanisms that had allowed their leader to aggrandize power. After all, they were led by the head of the security police. Had the Politburo majority had its way, it would presumably have gone no further than to adopt a path like that of its Soviet allies. However, there was a fundamental difference between the two regimes' circumstances. Unlike Malenkov and his comrades, Ulbricht's opponents needed to secure the support of an omnipotent external power. Yet, despite the fact that nearly the entire CPSU Presidium regarded Ulbricht's intransigence as calamitous, their gamble failed. For the Kremlin, Ulbricht was at least a known entity; his intransigence worked, even if it worked badly. Accordingly, Malenkov and his associates reluctantly threw their support behind the SED chief.

Predictably, the equally hard-line leaders of the Polish United Workers' Party (PUWP) had strong misgivings about the Soviet leadership transition. Notably, they waited a full year following Stalin's death before finally holding a party congress. With Malenkov's star on the rise, Bierut and his coleaders initially made a show of embracing the New Course. They mouthed the CPSU's rhetoric about collective decision making and obligingly amended their statutes to separate the leadership of the party apparatus from the state ministries. Bierut held on to his position as secretary general of the PUWP but ceded the premiership to a fellow Presidium member, Józef Cyrankiewicz. In tune with Malenkov's policies, they paid lip service to increasing the supply of consumer goods and housing and providing the peasantry with relief from high delivery quotas and taxes. Despite this posturing, however, the regime soon made it clear that it intended to stick with its policies. Far from making the lot of the peasantry any easier, Bierut announced that the pace of collectivization would be stepped up. He also introduced repressive measures against Poland's sole independent institution, the Catholic Church, jailing hundreds of priests and placing Poland's primate, Stefan Cardinal Wyszyński, under house arrest.

Unlike Ulbricht, Bierut benefited from strong internal support within the PUWP's inner circle. The party's older members were aware that they had made little progress in portraying themselves as loyal sons of the nation; a sizeable percentage of the Polish population regarded them as agents of a hated neighbor. Many also shared with Bierut a specific reason for avoiding hasty action. This was the shadowy presence of the home communist and former party leader, Władysław Gomułka, who had managed to escape execution and was living out his years of banishment under house arrest. Gomułka was no closet reformer. But he was the one communist notable who appeared to be a credible representative of the national road to socialism.

The dilemma for Bierut and his supporters was that developments in Moscow made it equally as risky to do nothing. Their vulnerability was exposed in fall 1954, when Radio Free Europe broadcast sensational interviews with a high-ranking defector from the Polish secret police, Jožef Światło. In gruesome detail, Światło recounted stories of sadistic interrogations and the arrest of thousands of innocent persons. These revelations should not have surprised anyone in the upper party elite, not least those members with firsthand knowledge of the suffering of former comrades. But until the broadcasts, the PUWP leadership had consistently told its rank-and-file cadres that Poland's purges had been less severe than elsewhere in the bloc—as if one could somehow quantify the burden of terror. Just as demoralizing for ordinary PUWP members were Światło's depictions of a culture of self-serving, cynical behavior that suffused the party's highest echelons. He named Bierut as one of the major offenders.

Had the PUWP's first secretary or coleaders chosen to address Światło's charges in a serious fashion, they might have ameliorated the feelings of betrayal that subsequently spread throughout the party's lower ranks. Yet true to form, they chose prevarication over objectivity, blaming the abuses entirely on the secret police. After making a show of abolishing the Ministry of Public Security, they merely turned over its functions to the Ministry of the Interior and the Council of Ministers. Just as was seen in East Germany, they underestimated the level of discontent in the party's lower echelons. When the Politburo met with officials from the Central Committee staff in early December 1954, its members were shocked to be subjected to blistering criticism from their subordinates for failing to appreciate their lack of credibility. In the ensuing months, rank-and-file party members called for authentic dialogue between the regime and the population. Discussion groups about the goals of Polish communism sprang up in party cells. Importantly, the primary topic of debate was not about abandoning socialism. It was about what was required to restore the reputation of an institution that had consistently boasted about its adherence to high moral standards.

In contrast to these pressures on the PUWP leadership, a single development in the immediate aftermath of Stalin's death gave party members in another country, Hungary, reason to hope that a reformed version of communist rule was possible. On July 4, 1953, the moderate former minister of agriculture, Imre Nagy, resurfaced from political isolation and was appointed to replace the Stalinist party chief, Mátyás Rákosi, as premier. Given the enmity between the two communists, this was a shocking development. But it was not the opportunity to heal the wounds of the purges of the 1940s and 1950s that it seemed to be. Rákosi still controlled a heavy majority within the Politburo of the renamed Hungarian Working People's Party (HWPP) and would not of his own accord have agreed to give up the position, especially to Nagy. Rather, the decision was made in Moscow where Rákosi was intensely disliked because of his political inflexibility. Malenkov decried his "bossiness" and flagrant abuse of party norms. Citing Rákosi's failure to reconsider his policies, Khrushchev held him personally responsible for alienating the working class and impoverishing the peasantry.[15]

Perhaps the tensions between the HWPP's general secretary and his new premier would have been attenuated had Nagy sought to work his way slowly back into power. However, true to the form he had displayed in his previous positions and emboldened by his support in the Kremlin, he rushed to introduce sweeping reforms. He directed the state ministries to take immediate steps to reduce the pace of industrialization and collectivization and directed new resources toward improving the quality of daily life. He committed the government to observing basic standards of socialist legality, ordering the closing of the country's network of internment camps. Just as prominently, Nagy outdid Malenkov's reforms by suggesting that he would open up the political realm. He proposed that the Politburo create a Patriotic People's Front—a more autonomous version of the rubber-stamp People's Front—to provide nonparty members and independent social groups a role in the formulation of state policies.[16]

Not surprisingly, Nagy's maneuvers hardened Rákosi and his supporters' opposition to any form of change, regardless of the reformist currents emanating from Moscow. Nagy fought back, defending his more flexible conception of leadership and taking his opponents to task for perpetuating the us-versus-them mentality that had led to the regime's immobilization. Instead of taking diverse views into account, they had chosen "stupidity," as he indelicately put it, as their strategy for addressing the complex demands of a modern socialist economy.[17]

Nagy was clearly a more sophisticated figure than Rákosi. But, of course, talent alone is never sufficient for political survival. He lacked the instinctive sense for political calculation that the general secretary had nurtured since the days of the Hungarian Revolution of 1919. In his two years as premier, Nagy did little to build a power base, preferring instead, much like Malenkov, to advance his policies by championing good ideas and practices. As a result, Rákosi easily used Khrushchev's victory over the Soviet premier to move against his counterpart. Describing Khrushchev's triumph as a vindication of his opposition to the New Course and benefiting from Moscow's fears of making a bad situation worse, he rallied his supporters to remove Nagy from office and expel him from the party.

The Yugoslav Exception

In all of the above cases, I have emphasized the role of distinct leaders because they show how the absence of a consensus about the overarching idea of communist party rule made the invocation of collective leadership an empty promise. In the case of the Yugoslav Communist Party (YCP), a single charismatic figure, Marshal Tito, played the same role. However, by virtue of Yugoslavia's ostracism from the Soviet bloc, his policies did not fit into the formulaic Soviet conception of Leninist leadership. Well before Stalin's death, Tito signaled that if he was not allowed to be a Stalinist, he was determined to develop policies that would rival Stalin's in their grandeur. To this end, he sought to reinvent the party idea. Under Tito's direction, the delegates at the YCP's Sixth Congress in November 1952 changed the party's name to the more inclusive-sounding League of Communists of Yugoslavia (LCY). The new nomenclature was not mere window dressing. In formulating the party's new statutes, Tito and his coleaders took pains to set themselves apart from the Soviet model of leadership by promising a clear division of labor between the LCY, which would assume responsibility for "political and ideological work in educating the masses," and the state, which would directly manage economic and social policy.[18]

If one knew nothing about the Communist Party's fate under Stalin and the People's Democracies, one might conclude that the LCY had been relegated to a diminutive role. To the contrary, as we have seen, the party idea had basically been put to rest by Moscow and the People's Democracies. In contrast, the LCY statute's focus on the institution's educational identity was quite different. It was a way to bring back the concept of political tutelage that was at the heart of early Marxism and Leninism. In fact, in the Yugoslav context, it was something more. The use of the word "League" expressed Tito's conviction that his country could only be held together if each of its national groups perceived itself to be equally a part of the building of a Yugoslav nation-state. Accordingly, the statutes provided for the transformation of the country's regional communist parties into eight additional Leagues of Communists to represent each of Yugoslavia's six republics and two autonomous regions.

These changes made sense in light of Tito and his fellow communists' experiences as partisan guerrilla fighters. In their struggles in the mountains and countryside, they had not had to worry about organizing state bodies. Just like Mao Zedong and the Chinese communists in Yan'an, they had cultivated a mythology that was distinctively populist and antielitist. In this spirit, Tito depicted the LCY as the defender of the people's interests against the encroachments of the bureaucratic state. Emphasizing the party's proletarian foundations, his regime introduced a prominent ideological innovation, "workers' self-management," which theoretically gave factory workers a greater say in production decisions.

The seriousness with which Tito and his associates took these issues had an ironic consequence. Once they announced the transition from a revolutionary to a ruling party, they were vulnerable to being attacked for not living up to these high principles. In late fall 1953, Milovan Djilas, the LCY's propaganda chief, launched a direct assault on the party leadership in nearly a score of articles in its official newspaper, *Borba*. In unusually candid terms, Djilas accused his longtime comrades in battle of using the party organization to elevate themselves over the people. "No one in the party," he declared, "not even a single class, can be the exclusive expression of the objective imperatives of contemporary society." Every attempt to restrict freedom of thought would diminish the honor of those who perpetrated it. Djilas even intimated that if his colleagues failed to mend their ways, they would risk the return of crimes on the scale of the Spanish Inquisition, Hitler's concentration camps, and Stalin's labor camps.[19]

Coming from a party insider, these accusations were incredible. Tito did not wait long before responding. In January 1954, Djilas was removed from his posts and expelled from the party. Still, these attacks testified to the incendiary potential of returning to open discussions about the appropriate functions of the party. Simultaneously, they raised the opposite question for Moscow. How might a frank discussion with their estranged adversaries serve Soviet interests?

Fresh from his victory over Malenkov, Khrushchev decided to address his country's problematic relationship with Belgrade by making the restoration of diplomatic relations his first big foreign policy initiative to complement the Virgin Lands campaign. On March 26, 1955, he and Bulganin journeyed to Yugoslavia to meet with Tito. There, he advised his host that his government "sincerely regretted" the breach between the two countries. By the end of the visit when Bulganin and Tito signed a joint declaration, Khrushchev showed that he was considering an even bigger step, the enunciation of a new way of conceptualizing the idea of communist international relations. The Belgrade Declaration effectively confirmed a position that the Yugoslavs had taken since their country's expulsion from the Cominform. The signatories expressed their "respect for sovereignty, independence, territorial integrity, and for equality between the states in their mutual relations." They also pledged "mutual respect and noninterference in internal affairs for any reason," and agreed that "differences of concrete forms of developing socialism are exclusively a matter for the peoples of the different countries."[20]

This statement was a turning point. It led many European communists, both in the East and in the West, to conclude that Moscow was ready to step away from the lockstep, international principle of party uniformity that had begun under the Comintern in the 1920s and been stripped of all subtlety and nuance under Stalin. One year later, the Soviet leadership seemed to confirm this interpretation by formally dissolving the Cominform. Even this event was overshadowed, however, by an extraordinary party congress in Moscow.

THE FIRST SECRETARY SPEAKS!

In the days leading up to the CPSU's Twentieth Congress in February 1956, very few of Khrushchev's associates knew that their first secretary had made up his mind to make a definitive break with the Stalin era. Over the preceding year, the Presidium had issued a review of the fate of hundreds of thousands of unjustly convicted persons, among them fellow party members, who had been sent to the vast reaches of the Soviet Union's Gulag archipelago. By the time the body's carefully circumscribed report reached Khrushchev's pen, however, the first secretary had concluded that only an open denunciation of the crimes committed under Stalin's rule would suffice.

The consequences of his decision were explosive. Let us imagine that we are sitting among the 1,436 privileged representatives of the CPSU elite—all foreign communists were excluded—who are told with no forewarning in the late hours of February 25, 1956, that the father of Soviet socialism is guilty of monstrous acts of inhumanity. We sit in stunned silence as Khrushchev accuses Stalin of waging war on the party. In grim detail, he describes the fates of the delegates to the "Congress of Victors" of 1934. For the first time, we hear that Stalin presided over the branding of 70 percent of the Central Committee's members and candidates elected at the congress as "enemies of the people." We are horrified to learn that a majority of the nearly 2,000 delegates were subsequently arrested for supposedly counterrevolutionary offenses. Khrushchev drives these perfidies home with concrete examples, such as the case of former commissar for agriculture and Politburo candidate member Robert Eikhe, who pleaded with Stalin to address "the provocation, slander, and violation of the elementary basis of revolutionary legality." A faithful communist to the end, Eikhe was nonetheless executed for crimes he did not commit.[21]

In an equally devastating manner, Khrushchev eviscerates Stalin's reputation as the military genius who led the Soviet Union to victory in World War II. To the contrary, Khrushchev declares, Stalin was at least partly responsible for some of the country's worst defeats. His arrogance left the USSR totally unprepared for war with Germany. During the purges, he destroyed the upper echelons of the officer corps. Stalin was even informed of Germany's imminent invasion, but he did nothing. In fact, when he recognized the extent of his errors, Stalin's response was to go into hiding. Only a Politburo delegation could induce him to take action against the invaders.

Notwithstanding these broadsides, Khrushchev is careful to prevent his revelations from cascading into a blanket indictment of the socialist system. Thus, he praises Stalin for playing a "positive role" in suppressing party members who sought to derail the inevitable march toward socialism. What would have happened, Khrushchev inquires, if the Trotskyite-Zinovievite bloc and the Bukharinists had gained the upper hand in 1928–1929 and imposed its anti-Leninist theses on the party? The answer is self-evident: "We would not now have a powerful heavy industry; we would not have the kolkhozes [collective farms]; we would find ourselves disarmed and weak in a capitalist encirclement." Indeed, in his desire to protect the reputation of this formative period in Soviet history, Khrushchev practically describes the early years of Stalin's battles as a time of civility. Party leaders, it seems, merely *explained* their opponents' faults to their rank-and-file members who, in turn, conscientiously sought to apply Leninist principles in correcting them.

Without a doubt, one of Khrushchev's motives was to protect himself and other members of the ruling elite. They were all implicated in

Stalin's crimes. Whether through acts of commission or omission, each had blood on his hands. Hence, by focusing the congress's attention on Stalin's personal culpability, Khrushchev was providing his colleagues with a means of self-exculpation. "Where were the members of the Politburo?" Khrushchev asks rhetorically. Like most Soviet citizens, he explains, they were under the spell of Stalin's charisma. Over time, they became aware of the extent of Stalin's wrongdoing, but they were impotent. As evidence, Khrushchev recounts a private conversation with Bulganin. "It has happened sometimes," Bulganin told him, "that a man goes to Stalin on his invitation as a friend. And, when he sits with Stalin, he does not know where he will be sent next—home or to jail."[22]

It is not surprising that Khrushchev has nothing to say about the extent to which the party's centralized structure allowed a single individual, Stalin, to abuse his power. Nonetheless, in an often neglected part of the "Secret Speech," he presents a return to a dynamic version of Leninism as an antidote to this dysfunction. He resurrects the Bolshevik founder's mythology of the virtuous cadre. Insofar as he and the party elite were prevented from doing the right thing under Stalin's grip, Khrushchev tells his listeners, they can now be entrusted with this responsibility because they are good communists. They have the good fortune that the Soviet Union was founded upon ideals, or as Khrushchev called them, "our holy Leninist principles." These ideals will enable them to surmount its tragedies.[23]

Khrushchev's device for conveying this message in the speech is to use the ultimate symbol of the October Revolution, Lenin, as a model of communist leadership. This Lenin is not the Lenin of historical fact. This is the imagined Lenin who will restore the party's good name. Khrushchev's Lenin has three related personality traits. He is modest, he is collegial, and he makes decisions on the basis of facts.

Khrushchev sets up the first image as a contrast with Stalin's cult of personality. The modest Lenin, Khrushchev explains, did not think of himself as a "genius" as Stalin did. He was aware of his human limitations. "Lenin always stressed," Khrushchev emphasizes, "that modesty is an absolutely integral part of a real Bolshevik. Lenin showed respect for others." Whereas Stalin was "rude" and "suspicious," Lenin focused on convincing and educating. He was recognized for his "patient work with people, stubborn and painstaking education of them, the ability to induce people to follow him without using compulsion, but rather through the influence on them of the whole collective." To clarify this point, Khrushchev shocks his listeners by quoting from Lenin's so-called testament, a December 1922 document in which he recommended removing Stalin from office.[24] At this point, Khrushchev may envision himself as a more qualified successor. Stalin should be replaced, Lenin wrote, by "a man who, above all, would differ from Stalin in exhibiting greater tolerance, greater loyalty, greater kindness, and a more considerate attitude toward comrades."[25]

In conjuring this image of Lenin's supposedly collegial style, Khrushchev is not making the case for a less than revolutionary conception of leadership. Rather, his question is about when and under what circumstances revolutionaries should use violent means to achieve their goals. In this light, Khrushchev's portrayal of Lenin's decisions is a testimony to the allure of historical fiction. When the Socialist Revolutionaries defied the Bolsheviks in 1918, he informs his audience, this Lenin explicitly endorsed the use of force. However, he only advocated extreme measures against "actual class enemies" of the Revolution. In contrast, Khrushchev notes, Lenin did not call for violence against "those who blunder, who err, and whom it was possible to lead through ideological influence and even retain in the leadership." Supposedly, this mythical Lenin ordered Felix Dzerzhinsky, the head of the Cheka, to desist from any further use of mass terror after the defeat of the Bolsheviks in January 1920.

Had Khrushchev wanted to be a better, or a more candid, historian, he could have qualified this interpretation by bringing up two defining events of March 1921: Lenin's support for the massacre of the Kronstadt sailors and the "ban on factions." Yet his aim in the speech is not to tell the whole story. It is to provide his listeners with an ideal standard. Hence, he assigns to his Lenin a familiar second attribute. The father of the revolution epitomized collegiality. Unlike Stalin who built a personality cult, Khrushchev stresses, "there was no matter so important that Lenin himself decided it without asking the advice and approval of the majority of the Central Committee members or the members of the Central Committee's Politburo."[26]

Finally, Khrushchev's Lenin demanded that the party's decisions be well-informed and grounded in facts. This maxim might appear self-evident. Yet, the first secretary asserts, Stalin was not interested in these mundane matters. He assumed that he alone knew what was best. "How could it be admitted that he, Stalin, had not been right!" Khrushchev jeers. "He is after all a 'genius,' and a genius cannot help but be right!" Of course, everyone makes mistakes. But, Khrushchev added, Stalin always thought he was right, even when his policies were disastrous. Predictably, Khrushchev's Lenin had the opposite trait. He knew what needed to be done because, unlike Stalin, he addressed concrete conditions. The party could never do what was right for the Soviet people unless its cadres worked among them, listened to them, and learned about their daily trials.[27]

CRISIS IN THE SOVIET BLOC

Had Khrushchev chosen to be less explicit in his assault, the implementation of his "holy Leninist principles" would have been challenging enough for the Stalinist leaders of other countries who had been inclined to be more boastful than modest, more distrustful than collegial, and more dogmatic than discerning. For this reason, every word that he uttered was subject to anxious scrutiny by his fraternal counterparts. Was the Soviet first secretary truly leaving it up to them, they wondered, to decide how to approach their past? In theory, Khrushchev had affirmed the point during his 1955 trip to Yugoslavia. Also, at the CPSU's Twentieth Congress's opening session on February 14, 1956, he had taken it one provocative step further. After matter-of-factly claiming ownership of Malenkov's arguments about the threat of nuclear holocaust and the noninevitability of war between bourgeois and proletarian states, he declared that the international working-class movement had become so strong and the victory of communism so certain that the forms of the transition to socialism would become "more and more varied." Achieving these objectives, Khrushchev explained, did not even necessitate violence. The Bolsheviks' tragedy was that they had not had this option in 1917. But the world had changed thanks to the Revolution. Indeed, Khrushchev added, it might even be possible to "go over to socialism" by parliamentary means.[28]

In view of the tortured history of the relationship between Moscow and Warsaw, it is fitting that Khrushchev's assurances would be tested in the country where animosity to the USSR was the greatest. On March 12, 1956, the Polish leader, Bolesław Bierut, died under mysterious circumstances after taking part in the Twentieth Congress. When Khrushchev journeyed to Warsaw for the funeral, he arranged for the PUWP to invite him to speak at a Central Committee meeting. There, he affirmed the narrowest version of his allies' prerogatives, lecturing them about how they should interpret Stalin's rule. The speech, known among Polish communists as the "Second Secret Speech," was in one part a blistering attack on Stalin's behavior and in another a reaffirmation of his predecessor's accomplishments. What stood out to Khrushchev's audience, however, was his imperious manner. He had little to say about the implications of his position for Poland. In fact, he barely referred to the country, noting without a hint of self-irony, that he had "a lot of Polish friends" and adding that Stalin had once joked about him being Polish.[29] One not-so-hopeful indication of Khrushchev's intentions occurred on the following day. To the consternation of those PUWP members who expected a new political wind from Moscow, he vetoed the party's preferred candidate for first secretary, Gomułka, and pushed through the appointment of a lower-profile Stalinist, Edward Ochab.

Most likely, Khrushchev was drawn to Ochab because of his vociferous opposition to Gomułka. Interestingly, the new first secretary responded to his opportunity by raising expectations that far-reaching changes were in the offing. He proclaimed an amnesty for thousands of political prisoners. He advised officials to exercise restraint in their interactions with students, intellectuals, and factory workers who questioned the government's policies. Ochab's greatest contribution to changing the popular mood was his handling of a national crisis. On June 28, 1956, riots broke out in Poznań over working conditions and other economic hardships. On the next day, the Polish defense minister, Marshal Konstantin Rokossovsky, who like many other generals was a Soviet citizen, used military and police forces to impose a bloody end to the demonstrations. Yet rather than declaring that the protests had been engineered by imperialist agents and antisocialist provocateurs, Ochab adroitly used a Central Committee plenum on July 18 to do a remarkable thing: he told the truth. The riots were not instigated by Poland's enemies, he admitted. The party had failed the working class, and it was up to its leaders to put things right.[30]

In a testimony to the limitations of the idea of party unity, Ochab's stand immediately divided the PUWP leadership. One group, the so-called Natolinites (named after a palace near Warsaw), was constituted of former underground fighters and warned Ochab against making concessions. This was not the time, they contended, to let down one's guard against the class enemy. In opposition, a less cohesive group, the Puławska faction (named after a meeting place on a Warsaw street), challenged the hardliners with an array of demands, ranging from modest economic reforms to the reversal of collectivization and the expansion of political freedoms. Looming above both factions was the prospect of Gomułka's return to politics.

To understand this period, one should appreciate just how close the Soviet Union came to intervening militarily in the conflict. Certainly, no one in the PUWP leadership was arguing for anything as drastic as the end to single-party rule or withdrawal from the Warsaw Pact. Nevertheless, by early fall, Khrushchev and his colleagues had an added reason for concern. Not only did both of the PUWP factions support Gomułka's reinstatement, but the former first secretary made it clear that he would only return under specific conditions. Declaring that "everything that has so far been done [is] wrong," he demanded that Poland be allowed to craft its own path to socialism.[31]

Fearing that the Polish government had lost touch with the situation, Khrushchev returned to Warsaw on October 19, the day Gomułka was to be renamed head of the party. The moment Khrushchev descended from the plane, he berated both Ochab and Gomułka for taking their country down a slippery path and insisted that they call off the Central Committee session set to begin that day. "We have decided to intervene brutally in your affairs," Gomułka later recalled Khrushchev saying, "and we will not allow you to realize your plans."[32] Yet he soon reversed himself. As he informed the CPSU Presidium, the risk of war with the Polish nation was too great. "Finding a reason for an armed conflict [with Poland] now would be very easy," he explained, "but finding a way to put an end to such a conflict later on would be very hard."[33]

Once again, the absence of any institutional checks on the pursuit of power allowed a single individual, in this case Gomułka, to present himself as a solution to a country's trials. With the same populist flourish as Khrushchev, he blamed the party's inner circle for fostering the conditions that fueled the upheaval in Poznań. The proletariat, Gomułka advised the Central Committee, should not be held accountable for the riots. The workers had taught the party a "painful lesson." They had "shouted in a powerful voice: Enough! This cannot go on any longer! Turn back from the false road." Like the Soviet Union, Gomułka noted, the PUWP was now called to be responsive to the people. Even more than in the past, the essence of its leading function was to guide, *not* govern. The latter task, Gomułka indicated, should be left to the state ministries; they were equipped to decide which policies would or would not work. In particular, he insisted that collectivization should be rolled back.[34]

In a second speech a few days after his appointment, Gomułka affirmed Poland's bond with the USSR. Standing in front of the towering Palace of Culture, Stalin's unpopular "gift" to the Polish people, he informed a rally of 300,000 people that he intended to abide by the strict parameters of his country's agreements with the Soviet Union. In line with Khrushchev's proclamations about different paths to socialism, his government would strive to address the specific needs of the Polish people. At the same time, Gomułka indicated that the class struggle was very much alive. As long as NATO continued to "foment chauvinism and revisionism against our borders," his regime would "with even greater decisiveness" combat all of the reactionaries' attempts to weaken "the alliance between our fraternal nations."[35]

Gomułka's reassurances allow us to appreciate Khrushchev's good fortune in refraining from using the Soviet army to reverse the course of events in Poland. Notwithstanding any policy differences between the two leaders, the Polish first secretary showed in his first years in office that he had won the domestic credibility to maintain a fine balance between addressing his country's needs and exhibiting fidelity to Moscow. In contrast, Khrushchev was not so fortunate in his relations with the Hungarian government. On October 23, 1956, the day before Gomułka's Palace of Culture speech, a chain of events in Budapest threatened to undermine both of the precepts that Gomułka had defended: party rule and the leading role of the Soviet Union.

Just as tensions were ebbing in Warsaw, spontaneous demonstrations broke out in the Hungarian capital in support of the Polish reforms. The immediate cause of these protests was an apparently minor offense: students at the city's Technological University had compiled a list of sixteen demands of the government. Their demands were quixotic, ranging from the specific—the removal of an enormous statue of Stalin near Heroes' Square and the restoration of Imre Nagy as prime minister—to the fantastic, including the withdrawal of Soviet troops from Hungarian soil. But when Rákosi's successor, Ernő Gerő, summarily denounced the students as enemies of socialism who were bent upon "creating disorder, nationalist well-poisoning, and provocation," he precipitated unrest throughout the city as workers, military veterans, and passers-by gave vent to long-felt grievances.[36] In a symbolically charged act, one group removed Stalin's statue from its concrete pedestal and dragged portions of it throughout nearby streets. In response, the regime made a bad situation worse. The security police opened fire on unarmed demonstrators. On the following day, October 24, the Kremlin ordered Soviet troops stationed on the outskirts of the city to restore order.

The revolutionary upheaval that burst forth from these clashes was a tragedy within a tragedy. The most visible impact of the battles was its human toll. Between October 24 and November 4, 1956, when the Soviet army moved again into Budapest, more than 3,000 insurgents and Soviet soldiers were killed, tens of thousands of Hungarians were arrested, and 200,000 others fled to the West. An equally compelling aspect of the tragedy is that the extent of these losses might have been reduced had Khrushchev and his coleaders fully appreciated the Hungarian regime's crisis of legitimacy.

Eight months earlier, Khrushchev's denunciation of Stalin had thrown the HWPP on the defensive. Rákosi reacted in the cynical fashion at which he excelled. He paid his obeisance to the goal of eradicating the "cult of personality" within the party. In addition, he promised to provide forums within official institutions to facilitate the free exchange of dissenting views. The most notable of these were the so-called Petőfi circles in the state writers' association, which were named after the nineteenth-century poet and national hero, Sándor Petőfi. But behind the scenes, with the party standing behind him, Rákosi had already launched a plan to arrest hundreds of current and former party members, writers, intellectuals, and army officers. The centerpiece of these actions was to be the trial of Imre Nagy and members of a purported "Imre Nagy anti-Party plot."

When the Soviet Union's leaders recognized that Rákosi's measures would make a bad situation worse, it would have been a masterstroke had they immediately named Nagy as his successor. Like Gomułka, Nagy enjoyed widespread support within the party apparatus and among the Hungarian populace. In fact, some members of the CPSU Presidium favored Nagy. "Had Imre Nagy remained in the party," Anastas Mikoyan wrote optimistically, "he would have had to obey party discipline and carry out the will of the party."[37] Still, even if the Presidium's members had not chosen Nagy, they could have turned to someone with a modicum of popular support, such as János Kádár, a victim of Rákosi's show trials and purported centrist. Instead, they erred by endorsing Rákosi's closest ally, Gerő, as party chief. Confirming their lack of insight, a secret CPSU Central Committee directive informed Gerő that he should "eliminate all factors responsible for the collapse of party conduct in Hungary, restore discipline among Central Committee members and the party's rank and file, and launch a fierce struggle on the ideological front."[38]

Under ordinary circumstances, the Hungarian regime's willingness to march in lockstep with this directive would have merely demoralized the party's members. But at this juncture, Gerő was presented with a burden that his Polish counterparts had not had to shoulder. He was operating in the uncertain context created by the PUWP's change of leadership. If Gerő had disassociated himself immediately from the policies of his predecessor, he might have won credibility with his opponents. Yet his hesitation to engage in anything but atmospheric changes (e.g., he removed Rákosi's name from public buildings) led to the erosion of his position within the Presidium. When Gerő went on vacation in early October, his coleaders made a pointed decision. They arranged for the disinterment and reburial of Rákosi's most famous victim, László Rajk, in a place of honor. On October 13, after weeks of negotiations, Gerő grudgingly consented to Nagy's readmission to the party—his harsh treatment was blamed on Rákosi—in return for his promise to show Leninist discipline.

These conciliatory gestures were scant consolation for a rapidly growing number of party members who regarded them as too few and too late. Correspondingly, the party's internal turmoil emboldened university students and the news media to stand up to the regime. Instead of serving as compliant tools of the government, the Petőfi circles became hotbeds of opposition. Simultaneously, discontent spread to the provincial towns and villages of rural Hungary.

In this light, Moscow's initial use of force was paradoxically a sign of both military strength and political ineffectiveness. The Soviet government immediately gave its blessing to the HWPP's desperate attempt to restore order by reappointing Nagy to his second stint as prime minister; Gerő was replaced as first secretary by Kádár. But with Soviet tanks confronting insurrectionists throwing Molotov cocktails in the streets of Budapest, the situation could not have been more different from the circumstances surrounding Gomułka's return to power five days earlier. The Polish communist leader whom Khrushchev met at the Warsaw airport on October 19 had the backing of his party and could summon an entire population to Poland's defense. In contrast, the return of Nagy, who lacked Gomułka's populist appeal, took place in the context of open rebellion.

There is considerable pathos in Nagy's efforts to restore order amid the chaotic conditions in his country. After all, he inherited a situation in which the psychological supports for breaking with Stalinist rule—a unified party apparatus, popular quiescence, and Soviet military restraint—had vanished. Far from being the instigator of a "counterrevolutionary armed uprising," for which he was later tried and executed in Budapest in July 1958, Nagy's primary failing was that he could not keep pace with events. Once the spell of the regime's control over society was broken, he was unable to contain his compatriots' demands. In the end, he gave the protestors what they wanted. He endorsed demands for the immediate withdrawal of Soviet troops, the dissolution of the security police, and the legalization of hundreds of autonomous workers' councils. Most important for our purposes, he responded to vast defections from a paralyzed HWPP by confirming what had already become fact. He declared the end to single-party rule and promised to form a multiparty government.[39]

There was nothing inevitable about the Soviet decision on October 31 to crush the Hungarian Revolution. The transcripts of the CPSU Presidium sessions between October 21 and 31 present an image of a group torn between fear over the risks of using force and the recognition of the absence of alternatives. Khrushchev initially expressed support for Nagy, calling him courageous and acknowledging that conditions had changed since the days when the Soviet Union used the Comintern to impose its will. "If we wanted to operate by command today," he insisted, "we would inevitably create crisis."[40] When the crisis in Budapest failed to let up, however, Khrushchev informed his colleagues that Moscow will defend socialism in the bloc by any means necessary: "We have no other choice."[41]

WITHIN THE COMMUNIST REALM

The Hungarian Revolution was a terrible shock to Khrushchev, a "nail in my head," as he later told his son.[42] The use of troops against a fraternal ally was a sign of weakness, not strength. Despite Khrushchev's wishes to move beyond the Stalinist model of managing the bloc, the crisis showed that a decade of enforced discipline could not easily be replaced with an idealized notion of Leninist enthusiasm. The point of the attack on Stalinism, as Khrushchev saw it, was to identify other means of supporting socialism. But the events in Poland and Hungary raised questions in the minds of communist leaders throughout the world about where the denunciation of Stalin would lead.

There was no black-and-white answer to this question. In China, as we shall see in chapter 9, Mao and his coleaders were shocked when word spread about the contents of the "Secret Speech," not least because their representatives to the party congress, along with those of the other communist parties, were excluded from the CPSU's closed session. It was not Khrushchev's attack on Stalin that bothered Mao the most. The Chinese Communist Party (CCP) had decades of mixed experiences with Stalin's erratic and self-serving policies. Thus, in a session of the CCP Secretariat on March 17, 1956, the chairman expressed support for Khrushchev's decision to "take the lid off" the superstitious belief in Stalin's infallibility. Yet, Mao also noted that his counterpart had committed a "blunder" in moving so quickly.[43] In his view, which he subsequently found confirmed in the events in Poland and Hungary, Khrushchev had been no more interested than Stalin in the consequences of his actions for the rest of the communist world. In the former case, Mao bluntly let the Kremlin know that the CCP would consider siding with its Polish comrades in the event of military intervention. In the case of Hungary, he conceded that the use of force was unavoidable. Nonetheless, both crises underscored for Mao the inherent instability of an international system that was primarily based on the decisions of a single power.

The lot of a neighboring communist party, the Korean Workers' Party (KWP), was considerably more complicated. Since the end of the Korean War, the KWP had been riven with conflicts over both the regime's international loyalties and contending economic priorities. One group, led by party chairman Kim Il-sung, a former guerrilla fighter, advocated an unabashedly nationalist agenda based upon Stalinist-style heavy industrial production and forced collectivization. In Kim's eyes, this approach would give his country the leeway to reduce its dependency on all foreign powers, especially the Soviet Union and China. Another, the so-called consumer-goods group, used the uncertainty of the post-Stalin transition to push for a scaling back of accelerated growth to emphasize light industry and the satisfaction of popular needs.

The conflict came to a head when the advocates of slower growth took advantage of Khrushchev's attack on Stalin to accuse Kim of the same sins. In a letter to the Central Committee, on October 5, 1956, the ambassador to the USSR, Li Sangjo, took Kim to task for fostering a personality cult that harkened back to "the epoch of feudalism and Japanese occupation." In this atmosphere, Li argued, party members would rather "go to their knees before the authority of an individual leader" than to engage in healthy Leninist criticism. Unfortunately for him and his allies, Li's diagnosis was correct. In a move that would lay the foundation for the elimination of all opposition currents within the party, Kim marshaled his forces to expel Li and his critics from the Central Committee.[44]

In Europe, the Hungarian debacle also raised questions among the Western communist parties, especially the powerful Italian Communist Party (PCI), about the health of the international working-class movement. Like Mao, the PCI's general secretary, Palmiro Togliatti, stepped into line to support the Soviet invasion. In view of the party's dependence on Moscow, he reluctantly concluded that the movement would collapse if its member parties simply chose to do as they pleased. But the PCI suffered enormously from the decision. Its sustained success as Italy's premier leftist party, regularly winning 30 percent of the vote in national elections, had derived from the traditionally fierce loyalty of its members. Yet the crushing of the Hungarian uprising, combined with Khrushchev's shocking revelations about Stalin, demoralized the party's moderate, younger followers. In combination with defections that had already begun during the preceding year, the PCI lost over 400,000 members between 1955 and 1957.[45]

Not surprisingly, these developments complicated Togliatti's postwar balancing act between fidelity to Moscow and PCI's record of responsiveness to the wishes of the Italian electorate. In the wake of Khrushchev's speech, he showed that he had the ideological agility to justify both priorities. In an interview with the left-wing literary magazine *Nuovi Argumenti* in July 1956, he not only defended Khrushchev's attack on Stalin, but in sharp contrast to Mao's misgivings, he complained that his Soviet counterpart had not gone far enough. Khrushchev's emphasis on the role of a single person to account for the Terror, Togliatti asserted, was "outside the criterion of judgment intrinsic in Marxism." The shortcoming of the "Secret Speech" was that it failed to ask why "Soviet society could reach and did reach certain forms alien to the democratic way and to the legality which it had set for itself, even to the point of degeneration." The primary cause of this pathology, Togliatti stressed, sounding a bit like Trotsky, was the bureaucratization of the centralized structures, and above all the party, which had been required for the attainment of socialism.[46]

Building on Khrushchev's acknowledgment of the possibility of different paths to socialism, Togliatti defended his position by maintaining that the communist world was appropriately becoming "polycentric." When this process was completed, he maintained, no single state would be able to claim that it should be the guide for any other.[47] It is hard to see how Togliatti's support for the use of Soviet troops against a fraternal ally was consistent with this assertion. Most likely, he reasoned that a direct confrontation with Khrushchev was not worth having, especially if it might undermine the principle of proletarian solidarity. However, simply by enunciating the principle of polycentrism, which harkened back to the pre-Comintern idea of diverse working-class parties, he planted a seed for dissension within every communist party.

The Return to Personality

If the position of CPSU first secretary had been occupied by a more cautious person than Khrushchev, such as Malenkov, the argument for measured steps to build socialism might have seemed self-evident. At first, Khrushchev was weakened by these crises. Internally, members of the Presidium were no less concerned than their Italian and Asian comrades about the implications of Khrushchev's assault on the memory of Stalinism. For some, the "Secret Speech" was rankling both for what he said and his motivations in saying it. By appropriating the issue, he prevented them from taking a different approach to the darkest passages in the party's history. They perceived the crisis in Eastern Europe as a vindication of their views.

Khrushchev's initial response to his critics was to temporize. At a December 1956 party plenum, he appeared to give in to pressures to downgrade some ambitious economic growth targets. He even made positive references to Stalin's record as a Marxist revolutionary. Nonetheless, his self-restraint was short-lived. In February 1957, he once again went around his colleagues to announce the reorganization of the administration of Soviet industry. Under this plan, he abolished key economic ministries in the republics and replaced them with territorial departments to run their respective industries. Ideally, these measures were to result in greater efficiencies in the production and distribution of goods. However, Khrushchev had a much more ambitious goal in mind than economic reform. He declared that the government would revise its investment priorities to enable the Soviet Union to outpace the United States in the per capita production of meat and dairy products in three years. In his estimation, these bold steps, along with massive new investments in housing construction and education, would mark the first step toward realizing the USSR's historical destiny.

Khrushchev's pronouncements set events in motion that resulted in his acquisition of unquestioned power. Because these measures would have substantially reduced the power of Presidium members whose support was in the state ministries, they led a majority of the body's full members, headed by Malenkov, Molotov, and Deputy Premier Lazar Kaganovich, to stage a coup against their leader. Although they mustered an 8–4 vote to remove Khrushchev, the first secretary was not cowed by this turn of events. In a demonstration of his appointment power in the Secretariat, he convened an emergency session of the Central Committee to rally to his defense. Thanks to the support of the many persons whose careers he had promoted over the preceding four years, Khrushchev was reaffirmed as the party's leader and the perpetrators of the coup were removed from their positions.

The coup attempt is revealing because it exposed the unresolved elements in the break with Stalinism. In a manner that evoked memories of his predecessor's organizational maneuvering in the 1920s, Khrushchev survived by using the party organization to elevate himself above his opponents. With justification, his opponents had accused him of violating the same precepts that he had held up as noble features of Leninism. On a new note, they threatened to eliminate the post of first secretary "with the goal of preventing the appearance of a [Khrushchevian] personality cult."[48] Nevertheless, Khrushchev showed that he had the monopoly on interpreting the meaning of de-Stalinization. The plotters were not defenders of collective leadership, he insisted, but representatives of a new "anti-party group." This was an amazing choice of terms given the fact that Stalin had used it two decades earlier to destroy his adversaries. Even Khrushchev could not escape his past! Still, in this case, power came before principle. Andrei Gromyko, his future foreign minister, spoke for a majority of Central Committee members when he lauded the party chief's "huge contributions ... to the country and the party." In Gromyko's estimation, Khrushchev had remained the CPSU's faithful servant, while the coup plotters sought to prevent a new generation of communists from replacing them. These members of the old guard had put themselves, in Gromyko's words, "in a position of some sort of priests." But, he added, there was now "no need at all for these priests."[49]

Gromyko may have failed to appreciate the contradictory implications of paying homage to Khrushchev while simultaneously invoking the party's authority. The essential question about Khrushchev's victory could have been applied to Stalin at any stage of his rule. Should a single "priest" in the form of Nikita Khrushchev be allowed to elevate himself completely above the party? Thanks to his skill in promoting his clients to the Presidium, including future leaders Leonid Brezhnev and Alexei Kosygin, the answer was that he could. Khrushchev solidified his grip on power in late October 1956 by dismissing Marshal Georgy Zhukov, the one figure with equal gravitas in the Presidium, from his post as defense minister. Finally, in March 1958, he completed the sweep by pushing Bulganin aside and appointing himself premier.

In focusing on Khrushchev's maneuvers, one must be careful not to dismiss his profound idealism. He undoubtedly believed that he needed this power to do what was necessary to move his country forward. In the late 1950s, his hand was strengthened by a series of successes that seemed to confirm, to him at least, that he had been called to this mission. His signature program, the Virgin Lands campaign, had provided a record harvest in 1956. After a shortfall in 1957, the 1958 harvest was even more successful. Significant gains were also made in some sectors of factory production. In October 1957, the Soviet Union's launch of the world's first space satellite, Sputnik, confirmed to millions of his fellow citizens that the USSR's scientists could compete, both scientifically and militarily, with any of their Western adversaries. To amplify this message, Khrushchev became the grand master of asserting his country's international interests. In 1959, he fulfilled his dream of visiting the United States, regaling his hosts with the combination of conviviality and bombast that he considered fitting for the leader of a superpower.

These achievements provide us with insight into the frenetic pace with which Khrushchev appealed to the power of the human will to ensure the successful leap into communism. By all accounts, this populist approach appears to have won over significant segments of the populace. In the short span between the CPSU's Twenty-First Congress in January 1959, which he convened one year early, and the Twenty-Second Congress in October 1961, Khrushchev announced more changes in the lexicon of socialist construction than in the two and a half decades since the "Congress of Victors" of 1934. This was "Bolshevik tempo" in modernized form!

One marvels at Khrushchev's self-confidence at the Twenty-First Congress. On January 27, 1959, he announced what had never been more than a distant promise in the forty-two years since the October Revolution. Thanks to the Soviet Union's domestic accomplishments and international stature, he declared that the country was entering "a new period of historical development in which socialism grows into communism." The first secretary cautioned his listeners that this goal would not occur instantaneously. There could be "no calendar date marking the entry into communism" because the Soviet working class still needed to create the absolute abundance of goods to satisfy the needs of every citizen. Also, it would take more time for people to develop the "inner need" to live up to their abilities. Yet, Khrushchev declared, two developments ensured that this stage was attainable. First, the scales of world production were on the verge of tipping in favor of socialism over capitalism. Second, the era of capitalist encirclement had ceased to exist.[50]

In addition, Khrushchev used the congress's pulpit to present himself as the authoritative interpreter of Lenin's vision. In contrast to Stalin's emphasis on the dictatorial aspects of the Bolshevik founder's thinking in his *Foundations of Leninism*, Khrushchev turned to the more attractive images of the future in *State and Revolution*. Like Lenin, he stressed that the eventual withering of the Soviet state did not mean that all state organs would disappear when communism was achieved. In his description, this process was not like "the turning of leaves in autumn, when the branches are left bare as the leaves fall." Rather, the state's functions would undergo qualitative change. In accord with Lenin's predictions, its operations would acquire a predominately administrative character. Ordinary people would take charge of public organizations, such as health services, people's courts, and popular militias. In these happy times, the use of force would decline. Khrushchev could envision only two exceptions to this rule—the armed forces and the security police. Even the improvement in the Soviet Union's international position did not mean that its enemies had gone away. "How then," he exclaimed, "can we abolish agencies which have the duty of securing the socialist state!"[51]

Most important, Khrushchev clarified what Lenin had left ambiguous: the party's role as it moved toward communism. Alongside his judgment that most of the state's functions would wither away, he emphasized that "the role of the party must grow, and not decline." The Soviet people regarded this Leninist institution as "their tested leader and teacher, and in its farsighted guidance, they see fresh victories for communism." Accordingly, Khrushchev stressed that the party's responsibilities would continue to evolve in tandem with the USSR's achievements. As a "party of the whole people," it would engage its members in every level of the production process, in each republic, district, factory and farm to remind them of the nobility of their cause.[52] As Khrushchev characterized this responsibility, possibly borrowing from an image that Lenin had penned in 1922, the party was like an advance contingent of mountain climbers "boldly and courageously storming new, seemingly inaccessible heights and blazing the path for those who follow behind."[53]

At the Twenty-Second Congress in October 1961, Khrushchev took this triumphant image even further, unveiling a new CPSU program that officially recognized the Soviet Union's transition to a higher phase of historical development. Khrushchev likened this achievement to a three-stage rocket. The party's first program (1903), as Khrushchev interpreted it, had been promulgated to wrench Russia out of the grip of early capitalism. The second stage (1917) lifted the country onto the path of socialism. This final program would carry the Soviet people into the "orbit of communism." "This is a remarkable rocket, comrades," he proclaimed, with equally remarkable confidence. "It is the greatest energy of all—the energy of the builders of communism."[54]

What should be the task of these builders? Khrushchev's response was as utopian as anything in Lenin's writings. The "party of the whole people" should create a "state of the whole people." Socialism had required a dictatorship of the proletariat to protect it from its enemies, but the elimination of class distinctions and the achievement of social equality meant that coercion should no longer be construed as the state's primary means of implementing policy. Since the interests of the individual and the interests of society were on the verge of becoming indistinguishable, its representatives would logically turn their attention to the construction of public institutions—trade unions, workers' councils, youth organizations, and cooperatives—in which citizens would naturally devote their loyalties to the good of all. In short, the state would preside over its own obsolescence.[55]

To this end, Khrushchev advised the congress's delegates that the CPSU's goal should be to create a "new man" out of the rising generation of young communists who had been born into the advanced stages of socialism. Initially, they might need to be pushed into appreciating the benefits of a just and socialist society. But, he added, the party would ensure that they were educated properly. There cannot be any "moral cripples," he clarified about this final stage. "If young fruit trees have been damaged to any extent," he added, "how much trouble must be taken to nurse them back to health, and even this cannot always be accomplished."[56] Undoubtedly, this was welcome news for Khrushchev's appointees who feared that their positions within the party would recede along with the state. "Always," he rhapsodized, "when the sun shines brightly or when the sky is overcast, in days of victory or in days of grave trial, the party is with the people, the people are with the party."[57]

Skeptical listeners—and there must have been many—would have wondered what new development had transpired to guarantee this merging of the interests of rulers and ruled. Would the principle of party leadership not continue to serve as a justification for the dictatorship over the ordinary citizen as had been the case since the Bolsheviks' ascent to power? In anticipation of this question, Khrushchev reinvoked his populist credo. Just as state officials had been subject to scrutiny on the basis of their performance, he emphasized, party members, too, should be judged according to meritocratic standards. It was no secret that some comrades had "lost the capacity to work creatively and lost the sense of the new." For this reason, Khrushchev noted, it would not only be a disservice to the Soviet citizen to retain these people. It would affirm the same cult of the individual that had permitted the party's perversion under Stalin. Therefore, he concluded, the only way to justify the party's leading role was to replace self-centered members with new leaders, both young and old, who showed their commitment to the good of all.

Khrushchev's Defeat

It cannot be more significant that when Khrushchev's colleagues successfully removed him from office on October 14, 1964, exactly three years after the Twenty-Second Congress, they drew upon the principle of collective leadership to justify their decision. Without mentioning Khrushchev by name, a statement on the front page of *Pravda* on October 17 condemned as "alien to the party" all practices based upon "hare-brained scheming; half-baked conclusions; and hasty decisions and actions divorced from reality; bragging and bluster; and attraction to rule by fiat."[58] This was the kind of behavior that Khrushchev himself had deemed antithetical to Lenin's example. In his idealized portrayal of the father of the October Revolution, the good communist was modest in demeanor, eager to work with others, and studiously attentive to real conditions. Thus, the suggestion by *Pravda*'s editors that their first secretary was lacking in all of these qualities was a rare opportunity to tell the truth.

Pravda's diagnosis captured the disjunction between what Khrushchev said he wanted and what he was actually doing. Since Stalin's death, he had constantly emphasized his determination to return the party to its leading position. He may have believed what he said. Yet despite this assertion, Khrushchev's method for leading his country into the higher stage of development that Marx and Lenin had barely dared to describe was not to entrust the party with this responsibility. Rather, it was to use the organization's resources to put himself, his ambitions, and his ideas over everyone else.

The instigators of the coup, which included both Brezhnev and Kosygin, did not come together overnight. Given the risks of moving at the wrong time or misjudging the intentions of their fellow conspirators, the ouster of a sitting party chief took time. In this respect, the success of the coup, unlike the earlier attempt in 1957, is an indicator of how bad things had become in their leader's final years in power. In fact, it is difficult to say which of an array of different factors mattered most in steering the coalition against Khrushchev. I shall suggest only a few possibilities.

One of Khrushchev's most pronounced vulnerabilities was in the area that propelled his way into power, agriculture. In late summer 1963, he paid the price for identifying himself personally with this economic sector when the Volga Valley and Kazakhstan were hit with a drought that led to a crisis in the supply of food. Ordinarily, the government would have dealt with the calamity by drawing upon the stockpiles of past harvests. But these reserves had already been depleted due to Khrushchev's various experiments—"hare-brained scheming"—with accelerating the pace toward communism. Consequently, the government could only prevent the outbreak of famine by using its scarce trade reserves to purchase food from abroad.

Khrushchev's remarks at the Twenty-Second Congress about replacing ineffective party members also made his removal easier. Suddenly, the Central Committee functionaries who had come to his aid in 1957 faced the prospect of losing their jobs. In 1962, Khrushchev made matters worse by announcing a plan to divide the entire provincial and district party apparatus into separate agricultural and industrial sectors. He argued that he had no intention of diminishing the party's leading role. In fact, he increasingly filled his speeches with Leninist language about "trust in cadres" and "cadres decide everything." But in creating two independent party organizations at every level of the economy, Khrushchev inevitably alienated the scores of regional party secretaries upon whom his power base was grounded.

Khrushchev was also implicated in disastrous developments in Soviet foreign policy. None was more damaging than his decision in 1962 to challenge American strategic superiority by secretly sending missiles loaded with nuclear warheads to Cuba. For thirteen days, from October 16 to 28, the first secretary's "hasty decisions and actions" led the world to the brink of nuclear war. Despite this show of force and bravado, the US government refused to be intimidated. In the end, Moscow suffered a humiliating defeat when it was forced to withdraw the missiles.

This debacle was matched by the total breakdown in the USSR's relations with China. As we shall see in chapter 9, Khrushchev's efforts to devise an effective formula for maintaining the Soviet Union's tutelary role over the diverse states and parties that constituted the socialist bloc could not withstand the criticisms of leaders, like Mao Zedong, who were sure they knew better how to serve their own people. By 1962, the Soviet Union's claim to a monopoly of revolutionary truth was replaced by a conflict with the People's Republic of China over diametrically opposed conceptions of Marxism.

Nevertheless, even if Khrushchev had met with economic success or been more adept at managing his country's foreign affairs, his ego proved to be his worst enemy. The key to his ability to outflank Malenkov in 1955 and his survival of the coup attempt in 1957 had been the loyalties he gained in rebuilding the party apparatus. Without these connections, Khrushchev would never have been able to put his grandiose plans into motion. Yet by the early 1960s, his consolidation of power seems to have brought out his worst instincts. A common theme in the recollections of individuals who worked closely with him was the impact of his unbounded personality. Whereas Stalin frightened his subordinates into submission, Khrushchev belittled and humiliated those who were closest to him. In this way, he turned the whole Presidium against him.

In Khrushchev's final year in office, even his smallest affronts became grounds for removing him. In July 1964, he authorized his son-in-law, Alexei Adzhubei, to represent him in negotiations with the West German government. It was bad enough, in the Presidium's view, that Adzhubei had little experience in foreign affairs; incredibly, he told his hosts that the first secretary was prepared to discuss the removal of the Berlin Wall, which Moscow had supported to stem the East German refugee crisis in 1961. It was worse that Khrushchev showed that he had no compunction about putting familial connections over his country's interests.

Khrushchev's loss was the Soviet Union's gain. By showing his disregard for the high standards that he had espoused at the Twentieth Congress to describe the qualities of a good Leninist, he provided his colleagues with definitive proof that the factors that made the cult of personality possible should be eliminated. Accordingly, the formation of the new government, which was matter-of-factly announced in the press on October 16, 1964, was a seamless affair. The ruling coalition that succeeded Khrushchev, a troika composed of Brezhnev as general secretary, Alexei Kosygin as premier, and Anastas Mikoyan as chairman of the Presidium of the Supreme Soviet, did not require an internecine battle, let alone the death of a party leader. At this point, these coleaders' priority was to find a new formula to justify their claims to authority.

CHAPTER 9

The Charismatic Leader and the Party

On December 2, 1961, Fidel Castro, the prime minister and later president of the Republic of Cuba, gave a characteristically spirited, three-hour speech on the radio station of the People's University of Havana in which he announced a new political agenda. As Cuba moved into a higher stage of development, he declared, it required a strong, well-disciplined party. A party of the bourgeois type would not do. The latter could recruit millions of members, he explained, but as past experience had shown, this type of party would quickly be taken over by representatives of the old ruling class, "a bunch of politicians, a conglomerate of individuals," who were more interested in money than in justice. Cuba, he asserted, needed a revolutionary Marxist party. The members of this organization would be absolute believers. They would be chosen on the basis of rigorous standards. They would represent all segments of society. Lest there be any doubt about his own convictions, Castro for the first time proclaimed himself a "Marxist-Leninist," indeed, "one to the last day of my life."[1]

Looking in from the outside, one might have assumed that Castro was completely committed to his new party. Created only four months earlier, this organization, the Integrated Revolutionary Organizations (ORI), bore a marked resemblance to the putatively representative bloc parties of postwar Central and Eastern Europe. It was composed not only of members of Castro's rebel army, the 26th of July Movement, but also of Cuba's long-existing communist party, the Popular Socialist Party (PSP), and the so-called Revolutionary Directorate March 13, an underground student organization. In March 1962, the ORI was renamed the United Party of the Cuban Socialist Revolution. Three years later, the full-fledged Communist Party of Cuba (PCC) was founded on October 3, 1965, with Castro as its first secretary. At last,

Cuba seemed to be ruled by the same type of Leninist organization that could be found throughout the communist world.

If only Castro's promises had been true! However, despite his repeated assurances in the address—in which he referred to himself revealingly as "we"—that he did not aspire to be "a Caesar" and that he had every intention of abiding by the norm of collective leadership, he would become precisely such a figure. From a historical perspective, this was a highly significant development. Long before the PCC's creation, Cuba had already had an organized and far less personalistic communist party. The first Cuban Communist Party (CCP)[2] was founded in 1925 and renamed the PSP in 1944. It was a stereotypical Leninist organization, obligated in every way to follow the instructions of the Comintern. For this reason, ironically, the CCP would be easier to characterize than would later be the case with Castro's PCC. The CCP was not an insurrectionary party and its history was beset with missed opportunities. Up to the 1950s, its leaders could have articulated a realistic alternative to the consistent failure of the country's middle-of-the road parties. But due to strategic mistakes and policies that were at odds with most of the population's wishes, they were unable to sustain a galvanizing message.

In this way, Castro's personal domination of the party by the 1960s represented a clear break with the standard Soviet model of Leninist leadership. In contrast, it should be understood in terms of two factors. The first was Castro's agility as a guerrilla fighter in the 1950s and thereafter as Cuba's leader in tapping into nearly a century of popular frustration and anger at the failure of established organizations, and especially political parties, to meet the country's interests. For decades, Cuban politicians assured their citizens that they would foster responsible governance, social justice, and national self-determination. Instead, they all too frequently rewarded the population's patience with the opposite results—political instability and corruption, increased economic disparities, and compromised sovereignty.

The second factor was the successful propagation of a cult of "Fidel." For this achievement Castro owed much to his confederates and adulators. In the first years after the victory of the 26th of July Movement in 1959, they ruthlessly and efficiently eliminated his rivals and weeded out potential critics within the state and military apparatuses. Just as energetically, they presented the exploits and teachings of their leader in hagiographic terms. Castro's disciple and fellow guerrilla fighter, Che Guevara, captured this mystique by likening his *compañero*'s connection with the people to a dialogue between tuning forks. "Fidel and the masses," Guevara gushed, "begin to vibrate together in a dialogue of growing intensity until they reach a climax in an abrupt conclusion crowned by our cry of struggle and victory."[3]

This is not to say that Castro ruled Cuba exclusively according to revolutionary principles. Unlike Guevara, who had an expressly anti-institutional bias that frequently put him at odds with Fidel, Castro was more of a pragmatist than his mythology implied. During the 1960s, the PCC was only one of numerous organizations, including the armed forces and grassroots organs of mobilization, which he used to head off opposition and institute progressive social and economic policies. In fact, when his authority was threatened in the early 1970s as a result of a severe economic crisis of his own making, he granted the PCC a small measure of autonomy. Nonetheless, during his nearly five decades in power, Castro never gave up the charismatic style of leadership that set his rule apart from that of party leaders in many other parts of the communist world. Before turning to Castro's role or the existence of Cuba's two communist parties, I shall begin with the turbulent conditions in the late nineteenth century and twentieth century under which successive Cuban governments and political parties inadvertently made his socialist vision attractive and credible.

THE UNFULFILLED PROMISE OF REVOLUTION

Prerevolutionary Cuba had political parties since the 1830s, long before most Latin American states. Yet, rather than being inspirational agents of change, let alone becoming reliable defenders of democracy, these early associations were weak and ineffective. The country's dominant Spanish Party, composed of Spanish-born Cubans, or *peninsulares*, applied itself to strengthening the island's ties with Spain. Its competitor, the Cuban Party, was primarily composed of *criollos*, or native-born elites of European ancestry. It represented the interests of plantation owners and skilled professionals who resented, but were unable to shake, the *peninsulares'* domination of most political institutions.

This simple arrangement might have lasted longer had it not been for the development in the 1850s and 1860s of serious fissures in Cuba's relationship with Spain. In large part due to the colonial administration's heavy-handed policies, high taxation, and toleration of discriminatory behavior by the *peninsulares*, broad segments of the population coalesced to demand truly representative institutions that would speak for Cuban interests. When a reformist party unexpectedly won a majority in the Spanish parliament in 1858, members of the Cuban Party, sugar producers, and business owners rushed to take advantage of the opportunity to open the political arena. With the support of sympathetic Spanish politicians, they established interest groups, cultural societies, and newspapers to foster public debate about representative government, the abolition of the slave trade, and national economic independence. In a manner that resembled the energetic idealism of Russia's youthful populists, students and radical intellectuals argued over previously unexplored ideologies, including republicanism and anarchism.

At this juncture, arguably, both Spain and its allies in the Spanish Party missed a valuable opportunity. Had they taken steps to address their opponents' demands, they might have averted a political crisis. Instead, they chose the opposite course. In response to the emergence of a rebellious separatist movement among plantation owners in eastern Cuba, the same region where Fidel Castro would later conduct guerrilla operations, Madrid sent over 100,000 troops to the island in 1868. After nearly a decade of bloody fighting, indiscriminate executions, and mass deportations, Spain and its Cuban sympathizers crushed the insurrection. Rather than currying the favor of Cuban moderates by loosening control over the press and offering amnesty to the rebels, the Spanish court showed its disdain for democratic representation by refusing to extend universal suffrage to the island, even while bestowing this right on its own citizens. Simultaneously, it renewed military operations against a burgeoning Cuban independence movement.

The Cuban revolution that would eventually bring Castro to power was born out of these circumstances. During the period when politicians in the moderate parties debated the merits of home rule, revolutionaries in exile and in the underground were galvanized by a sharper, national passion that had grown out of the conflict—patriotism. No figure was more important in promoting the cause of independence than the renowned poet and essayist José Martí. Under Martí's leadership, the revolutionaries founded a new type of political party, the Cuban Revolutionary Party (PRC), in the United States in 1892. Its simple goal was to overthrow Spanish rule.

It is crucial to appreciate the influence of Martí's thought because it provides insight into both what motivated these early revolutionaries, as well as other insurrectionists throughout Latin America, and the abiding dissatisfaction and alienation of Cuban elites that would continue into the next century. In a widely read essay, "Our America," published on New Year's Day, 1891, in New York City, Martí painted a picture of a coming revolution that was every bit as gripping as Karl Marx's invocations of the specter of communism in the *Communist Manifesto*. This conflagration would be far more profound than a military battle, Martí prophesied. It would arrive as a "cloud bank of ideas" that "no armored prow" could cut through. Like the "mystical flag of the last judgment," it would achieve victory because it was driven by "weapons of the mind" that could stop a fleet of iron-clad ships. Accordingly, the chief responsibility of Cuba's revolutionaries was to move the masses in the right direction. To this end, Martí demanded that they become "real men" with the courage to overthrow the repressive institutions of colonial rule, fight for the oppressed, and found a new nation.[4]

Decades later, Castro would repeatedly summon the same masculine imagery to inspire his rebel fighters. But there is a significant difference between Martí's idea of revolutionary leadership at the end of the nineteenth century and Castro's later preferences. Whereas Castro brought charismatic dictatorship to the island in the years after his ascent to power, Martí was not enamored with socialism; he even criticized Karl Marx for promoting violence. Instead, Martí advocated direct democracy. The PRC's founding statutes, of which he was the primary author, stand out for their emphasis on decentralized governance. According to these guidelines, the revolutionary party's authority would derive from grassroots associations, or clubs, which would guide the decisions of local councils. The party would inspire the people, but it would be subservient to a national executive elected by these popular councils.[5]

Martí was killed in combat in 1895, only two months after the outbreak of the Cuban War of Independence, which would end with the defeat of Spain. Had he lived to see his country's liberation, however, Martí would have undoubtedly shared his fellow revolutionaries' bitter disappointment over the outcome of their struggle. When the United States intervened in the last months of the war, Cuban's established politicians proved to be ambivalent about standing up to their neighbor. Initially, two embryonic parties, the Republicans and the Nationalists, successfully forced Washington to grant the island full independence. After the proclamation of the Cuban Republic in March 1902, however, they and another major party, the Democratic Unionists, failed to condemn measures, such as the US Platt Amendment, which restricted the island's sovereignty. In an indication that party affiliation remained an ambiguous commitment, elected officials routinely took advantage of these conditions by exchanging political influence for personal financial gain in their dealings with American companies. Government jobs were bought and sold, and electoral fraud was rampant. When Washington repeatedly sent troops to quell popular unrest and sporadic revolts, the population's disdain for its representatives grew.

In this light, when Cuba finally attained a semblance of stability, it was because much of the population, like their Latin American neighbors, preferred populist demagoguery over democracy and foreign tutelage. In 1925, widespread discontent over the ineffectiveness of successive governments led to the election of a military officer, General Gerardo Machado, as president. To great acclaim, Machado presented himself as the no-nonsense leader Cuba needed. In a classically populist manner, he instituted long-needed public works projects, created jobs, and promoted foreign investment. But this "tropical Mussolini," as he was described by the radical student leader, Julio Antonio Mella, also exacted a stiff price for his beneficence.[6] In a manner that bore little resemblance to the democratic aspirations with which the revolution had begun, Machado systematically eliminated every semblance of political competition and Cuba's Congress became little more than a rubber stamp for his decisions.

FOUNDING THE FIRST COMMUNIST PARTY

Cuba's first communist party was born out of these conditions. In the early 1920s, a panoply of radical groups emerged to challenge the regime. Although their leaders' ideas and strategies were as yet unformed, they shared the conviction that Cuba's seemingly permanent state of democratic dysfunction could only be resolved through a concerted assault on its political system. War veterans assembled to demand higher pensions. Socialists formed the Havana Labor Federation to coordinate strikes of railway and dock workers; eventually, this organization grew into the larger Cuban National Labor Confederation (CNOC). Additionally, as happens in so many instances of prerevolutionary turmoil, students played a central role in fomenting discontent. At the University of Havana, young militants were inspired by the success of the Bolshevik and Mexican Revolutions and the activism of their peers throughout Latin America to form a national Federation of University Students. Over the next few years, these activities provided the sparks for even more radical associations. Prominent among them was the clandestine terrorist group, ABC, which briefly caught the attention of a young Fidel Castro.

The nine future Central Committee members who were present at the founding of the CCP in Havana on August 16, 1925, represented an amalgam of these different tendencies.[7] Some were workers, such as the house painter José Peña Vilaboa, who soon became the party's general secretary; others, like Julio Antonio Mella, were student and labor organizers; one, Blas Roca, was a shoemaker-turned-socialist theoretician. A member of the Mexican Communist Party was also present to represent the Comintern. Only a few of these founding fathers could claim to know much about Marxism. Unlike Cuba's anarchists who were exposed to the writings of their Spanish brethren, few had read the seminal works of their political forefathers.

What these early communists lacked in ideological formation and organization, they made up for in the appearance of authenticity. They not only looked like the revolutionary workers whom Marx had heralded in the *Communist Manifesto* seven decades earlier; they were also well positioned to act on their ideals. Whereas a majority of communists in other parts of the world were still wrestling with the vestiges of feudalism, Cuba's sugar industry and textile factories had already made the transition to capitalism. This circumstance eased their adaptation to the Comintern's understanding of the requisites of revolution. According to official policy, they represented issues that were more profound than opposition to a corrupt government; they were standing on the side of the working class in confrontation with global capitalist exploitation. More than simply opposing US domination, therefore, they were fighting with other communist parties against world imperialism. In these ways, the party's founders contended, the class struggle and the progressive logic of history placed them squarely on the road to a new type of revolution: Leninism.

The CCP's weaknesses initially played to its advantage. Given the party's small size and ineffectiveness, Machado's government focused on curtailing the activities of the larger, better-organized opponents. These dissenters included both radicals and burgeoning groups of moderate reformers and exiles who had grown alienated by the established parties' failures. The Wall Street Crash of 1929 and the collapse of the world economy provided exactly the conditions the CCP required to find its footing in the opposition to Machado. Expounding the rhetoric of anti-imperialism, the party's leaders spoke a language that was immediately intelligible to urban and agricultural workers. With the backing of these strata, they rapidly extended their control over the CNOC and its affiliated unions. When the Confederation showed its muscle by carrying out a crippling general strike in Havana in 1930, the CCP's popularity soared.

Yet, despite the recognition by the CCP's leaders that the party should adapt its Marxist message to Cuba's specific conditions, they were constrained by their commitment to the Comintern. In perfect tune with the body's "Third Period," the party leadership defiantly refused to pursue tactical alliances with other anti-Machado forces, dismissing their activities as futile protests that would strengthen the bourgeois order. Even when it became clear that Machado's government was losing the support of the population, the communists continued to define their primary function in terms of labor mobilization, not revolution. In August 1933, the CCP took a step that paralleled the nearly simultaneous opportunism of the German Communist Party during Hitler's rise to power. They and the CNOC struck an agreement with Machado to call off a planned strike by transportation workers. In return for Machado's promise of legalization, they ordered the workers to return to their jobs. This appeal to proletarian discipline turned out to be a gross misreading of circumstances. To the CCP's detriment, the protestors refused to heed its orders and took to the streets.

The "August mistake," as the CCP's decision became known, was a major blow to the party's prestige, providing its critics on the Left with fodder to accuse its leaders of selling out the organization's principles. Yet, the CCP's leaders were not ones to learn the lessons of history. After Machado was forced out of office by the army and the US government, they tarnished their reputation anew by their dismissive reaction to his successors. In September 1933, an uprising of noncommissioned army officers, the so-called Sergeants' Revolt, precipitated the formation of a military-backed government under a progressive president, Ramón Grau San Martin. This development should have been the dream of every Cuban leftist. For one hundred days, Grau led his working-class, student, and agrarian supporters down a path that promised to resolve the injustices of colonialism and political cronyism. Under the slogan "Cuba for Cubans," the regime abrogated the conditions of the Platt Amendment, established an eight-hour working day, and granted expanded rights to women and small farmers. Yet, instead of welcoming these measures, the CCP rebuffed Grau's overtures to collaborate and denounced him as a "social fascist." Accordingly, the party leadership looked on with indifference when the army replaced Grau with a more compliant president five months later.

Even if the CCP's leaders had agreed to cooperate with Grau, they would not have been much help to a government that was resolutely opposed by moderate segments of Cuba's ruling class. Nevertheless, Grau's brief experiment with leftist rule set up the communists for an even greater test to their reputation in their dealings with the figure behind the Sergeants' Revolt, Fulgencio Batista. In their first interactions with the man behind the scenes in the new Cuban government, the two sides were implacably at odds. When the CCP joined other revolutionary groups in organizing a nationwide strike in 1935, Batista responded with a brutal display of military force, imprisoning and torturing many of the party's members. However, when Batista slowly moved away from these repressive policies in the ensuing years and broached the possibility of legalizing the CCP, the communists shocked many observers by choosing the benefits of working within the system over fruitless sacrifice. After previously likening Batista to Mussolini and Hitler, they suddenly discovered his virtues. Blas Roca, the CCP general secretary, clumsily observed that the colonel had "begun to cease to be the center of reaction." Batista returned the favor, declaring that the party had become "the promoter of democratic formulae."[8]

To the CCP's benefit, its openness to working with Batista coincided directly with the Comintern's enunciation of the Popular Front policy. As in Europe and in the United States, the party's leaders indicated their readiness to put their public pronouncements about the "class enemy" and the inevitability of the revolution on hold in the interest of preventing the rise of even more reactionary forces. Although this policy involved tortuous rationalization in view of their recent experiences, the party's fortunes improved when Batista began to drift politically leftward. Taking advantage of improved economic conditions and the restoration of political stability, he used the armed forces to implement popular social programs, build schools, bring medicine and better health care to remote rural areas, and educate farmers in new planting techniques.

The communists' response to these policies was resoundingly positive. Recognizing the possibility of finding a permanent place in the halls of power, they openly pursued an alliance with Batista. They changed the name of the CNOC in 1939 and agreed to transform its successor, the Cuban Workers' Confederation, into an essentially state-governed trade union confederation. Three years later, at a time when the Soviet Union was allied with the Western powers in the campaign against European fascism, the party committed itself to a no-strike policy for the duration of World War II. In return, an increasingly popular Batista invited his former enemies to join a host of moderate parties, including former Machado supporters, in promulgating a model democratic constitution. Thanks to the communists' inclusion in the process, the document gave the government wide leeway to intervene in the economy and provide for social security. After the CCP threw its support behind Batista in the national elections of 1940, the president kept his promise to legalize the party and named two of its deputies as ministers in his cabinet. Four years later, the communists affirmed their acceptance of the status quo by adopting a less provocative name, the PSP.

It is easy to understand why cooperation with Batista made sense to many communists who had suffered repression during the party's years in the underground. An antagonistic relationship with the regime would have returned the PSP to the political margins. Cooperation gave the party the chance to improve its national standing. In its leaders' eyes, the gamble paid off. By 1940, the PSP had the largest paid membership of any communist party in Latin America and was the Comintern's crowning example of a successful revolutionary movement. However, not everyone in the PSP agreed. For its left-wing members, the price of accommodation was to compromise the party's revolutionary values.

This tension within the communists' ranks would resurface on a regular basis throughout the years of Castro's rule. For the time being, the PSP's good fortune did not last. In 1944, a rejuvenated Grau returned from political isolation to defeat Batista's handpicked candidate for the presidency. One of Grau's first steps was to oust the communists from their controlling position in the trade union confederation and their presence in various government offices. His successor, Carlos Prío Socarrás, was even more determined to weaken the PSP; he imposed new restrictions on the party's public activities, closed its newspaper, and curtailed its radio broadcasts. In these hard times, the PSP's leadership might have at least consoled itself with the knowledge that it had won a legitimate place in Cuban politics. But this achievement was an illusion. In March 1952, Batista used the pretext of rampant corruption in Prío's government and the collapse of public order to stage a second military coup. He immediately canceled the upcoming elections. A year later, in November 1953, he outlawed the PSP.

An Insurrectionist Party

In the eyes of many Cuban radicals in the 1950s, the suppression of the PSP and other leftist organizations was part of an old story. Once again, their country's democratic institutions had proven too weak to restrain the worst instincts of their leaders. When given the chance to prove themselves worthy of revolutionaries like Martí, even leftist parties had proven ill-equipped to present serious alternatives. Under these circumstances, Batista's coup gave rise to a renewed wave of popular discontent and violence. The University of Havana again became a center for organized opposition; leftist students and professors disseminated political tracts and engaged in street battles with the police. Underground terrorist groups, such as the Insurrectionary Revolutionary Union (UIR), a peculiar amalgam of *gangsterismo* and crude anarchism, assassinated public officials. Workers and peasants rebelled against employers and local governments. The difference this time, however, was that the failure of Cuban democracy gave rise to the populist movement led by Fidel Castro. This movement not only overthrew a dictator but, in the following decade, provided the republic with a government that ensured political stability through the acceptance of the charismatic authority of a single person.

From the beginning, Castro's insurrectionist following, the 26th of July Movement, was imbued with the belligerent idealism of its cofounder. The son of an affluent landowner, Castro had the privilege of attending the University of Havana where he focused his energy on radical politics. Like many of his peers, he was deeply frustrated with the failure of establishment parties to live up to the promises of the 1940 constitution and despaired over the poor prospects for democracy throughout Latin America. He took part in an unsuccessful attempt to overthrow the Trujillo dictatorship in the Dominican Republic, participated in student riots in Colombia, and briefly associated himself with the terrorist UIR. Yet, unlike many of his radicalized peers, Castro had an acute sense for changing course when it suited his self-interest. Thus, after graduation, he became active in the moderate Ortodoxo Party, a breakaway faction from Grau's party, and campaigned on its list for the scheduled congressional elections.

It is impossible to know what kind of politician Castro would have become if Batista's coup had not taken place and he had instead won a seat in Congress. There is no ambiguity, however, about the coup's impact on his thinking. It turned him completely against the prevailing political order and its middle-of-the-road parties. On July 26, 1953, Castro led a group of fewer than one hundred poorly trained rebel soldiers in an attack on the Moncada military barracks in the eastern city of Santiago de Cuba. Batista's army easily repulsed the assault. The regime summarily executed many of the combatants and sentenced to lengthy prison terms a handful who happened, like Castro, to come from the upper classes.

In most cases, the Moncada debacle would have meant the end of a revolutionary's career. For Castro, it was only the beginning. Despite, or even because of, the fact that he spent the next two years behind bars, the sheer audacity of his assault and his subsequent defiant defense of his actions won him national visibility. It also gave him the opportunity to outline a message about his intentions that serves as the first major example of the simplicity—or, in other respects, complexity—of the phenomenon known as Castroism.

Conveniently, the initial expression of Castro's thinking is available in a prison essay of May 1954, *History Will Absolve Me*, in which he self-servingly embellished his courtroom defense in the Moncada trial. On one level, the essay is much more than an attempt to justify a particular, violent act. *History Will Absolve Me* is a defense of a moral imperative reaching back to the revolutionary tumult of the late nineteenth and early twentieth centuries. Castro begins by painting a romantic picture. "Once upon a time," he begins, there was a republic with vibrant democratic institutions that guaranteed its citizens the right to elect their representatives. However, these institutions were destroyed by tyrants and capitalist exploiters who did not share the people's love of liberty. One day, the citizenry awakened to find that the ghosts of earlier years had seized it "by its hands, its feet, and its neck." "Poor country!" Castro declares. In this account, it does not seem to have mattered to Castro that such an ideal Cuba had never existed. His deliberately provocative message is that there is a moral obligation to make it exist. Thus, Castro recalls telling the members of the court that their actions will be judged by posterity. The people, he explains, crave justice and abhor "the hairsplitting of jurisprudence." They also hate all forms of favoritism and inequality. Thus, he stresses, simple logic dictates that they will rebel against any decisions that transform the "maiden of justice" into a "prostitute wielding a dagger."[9]

In contrast, Castro's judgments in other sections of the essay are surprisingly measured. Indeed, for a person who led an armed attack on his government, they are practically unrevolutionary. Had his rebel army come to power, Castro says, it would have promulgated five laws to restore power to the people. It would have returned to the progressive principles of the 1940 Constitution. It would have given property to tenant farmers and squatters, although it would also have compensated landowners for their losses. It would have granted workers in large industries the right to share in the profits of their enterprises. It would have given the same right to sugar planters and tenant farmers. Finally, the movement would have confiscated property that had been illegally acquired by the regime and the agents of foreign powers.[10]

In comparison with other revolutionaries in similar positions, Castro's cautious approach is by no means exceptional. As we have seen, both Lenin and Mao exhibited moments of moderation, either to deal with difficult economic and social circumstances or to gain the allegiance of potential antagonists. What distinguishes Castro's approach from his Marxist counterparts at this point is how little he has to say in *History Will Absolve Me* about revolutionary organization. Instead, Castro focuses clearly and unabashedly on the subject of the essay's title—himself. In this self-portrayal, the person whom history will absolve is merely a "humble citizen" acting in the spirit of the great apostle, Martí. In this capacity, he is carrying out the will of the "Master," as he calls him, and other revolutionary heroes, "in my heart and in my mind, the noble ideas of all those who have defended the people's freedom everywhere!" As a participant in this holy succession, Castro advises, he holds no bitterness toward those who claim to judge him. He does not even seek vengeance against the murderers of his *compañeros*. His obligation is merely to speak the truth so that, one day, the Cuban people will enjoy justice. Thus, Castro happily assumes the martyr's pose, noting that imprisonment will be "harder for me than it has ever been." This does not matter. History itself will absolve him of his faults.[11]

In many respects, Castro's self-congratulatory words are remarkable. Even at the height of their personality cults, Joseph Stalin and Mao Zedong rarely used their public statements to put themselves at the center of history; they preferred that their sycophants do that for them. Now history itself was finally putting one man, and *not* a ruling class, at the head of its forward march. In 1954, this claim was a particularly noteworthy demonstration of Castro's hubris because he was not yet a prominent personality in Cuban politics. At this point, Batista had more immediate worries in dealing with subversive student associations, rebellious textile workers, constitutional challenges from the Ortodoxos, and factionalism within the military. In fact, the president showed that he was so unconcerned that Castro represented a serious threat that he pardoned the rebel leader less than two years into a twenty-six-year prison sentence.

At first, Batista's judgment appeared to be well-founded since Castro's subsequent attempt to foster a revolt resulted in disaster. In early December 1956, Castro and an expeditionary force of eighty-one rebels set sail from Mexico with the aim of joining urban members of the 26th of July Movement in an uprising in Santiago de Cuba. Led by the underground agitator Frank País, the insurrectionists successfully organized factory protests and sabotage actions for several days. But Castro's boat was delayed and the revolt was easily suppressed. Once again, however, Castro managed to turn defeat to his advantage. Much like Mao Zedong in the aftermath of the Shanghai massacre, he took the remnants of his army into the Sierra Maestra Mountains where they engaged the regime's military forces in a different type of warfare as guerrilla fighters. They initially suffered more defeats than victories against the better-trained national army. But just like in China, the heroic reputation that they acquired in these battles was as important, if not more so, as the facts on the ground.

From isolated locations, Castro and his fellow fighters, including his brother Raúl and an Argentine doctor-turned-military strategist, Ernesto "Che" Guevara, both of whom described themselves as communists, purveyed his message that revolution was an act of will in service of the people. According to this depiction, the 26th of July Movement was not merely waging a military campaign against a corrupt government. Its primary goal was to rescue the soul of the Cuban nation. Styling themselves as the only legitimate representatives of the people, they espoused the noble virtues of honor, patriotism, and self-sacrifice in a war in which the odds were stacked against them. Like Martí before them, they characterized their mission as a struggle of "real men" and they grew beards, flaunted pistols, and smoked cigars to emphasize their masculinity. Thanks to Guevara's influence, they also propagated the idea that this guerrilla struggle was more than a specifically Cuban event. It was, Guevara consistently argued, an example that could be followed by revolutionaries throughout the hemisphere.

A major factor behind the success of this mythology was Castro's intuitive sense for shaping public opinion according to his self-image. In a widely read interview with the *New York Times* leftist war correspondent Herbert Matthews in February 1957, Castro allowed himself to be portrayed as the guarantor of his movement's noble intentions. Like his *compañeros*, it seemed, he was simply fighting for a democratic Cuba and an end to dictatorship. He had no hatred, he stressed, for the soldiers fighting against his army; they were simply following the orders of their commanders. Nor did he harbor any animosity toward the United States; he merely wanted the Americans to stop supplying Batista with arms. In return for Castro's generous self-assessment, Matthews, who had once glorified the communist participants in the Spanish Civil War, described his subject in beatific terms. Castro was an educated "man of ideals," he wrote, "and of remarkable qualities of leadership." He was a commander who was worshipped by his troops and a source of inspiration for every young Cuban. As if this praise were not sufficient, Matthews added that it was hard to imagine that Castro could be defeated. He was "almost invulnerable."[12]

This mythology would live on long after Castro's ascent to power. Nevertheless, as I have shown in the cases of other communist movements, ideas alone cannot make a revolution. Their impact is to infuse a movement with meaning and to shape its future direction. Fortunately for Castro, his guerrilla army, and the participants in the 26th of July

Movement in the urban underground, Batista's policies fostered the tumultuous conditions in which political power was there for the taking. As the president tightened his grip on the public arena, the establishment parties did what they had done countless times in the past. They splintered into warring factions. Simultaneously, business owners deplored the high cost of operating in a climate suffused with graft and corruption. Even at a time when the national economy was stronger than in any other Latin American country, middle-class Cubans grew demoralized because they compared their standard of living to that of their neighbors in the United States. Most significant, Batista's commanding position within the armed forces was eroding. His nepotism and disregard for meritocratic standards in making promotions fueled disgruntlement and conspiratorial activities.

Over the same period, Castro's standing among the Cuban Left grew. As the country lurched toward Batista's last days, fewer groups could offer viable alternatives to his populist appeals. The PSP continued to be burdened by its reputation for opportunism and its record of support for nonrevolutionary governments. In 1953, its general secretary, Blas Roca, had denounced Castro's assault on the Moncada barracks for its "putschist methods" and depicted the rebels' heroism as "false and sterile."[13] The PSP had also opposed the 26th of July Movement's failed insurrection in 1956. Another threat to Castro's authority was defused in 1957 when the terrorist student organization, the Revolutionary Directorate, fell into disarray after a failed coup attempt to storm the presidential palace and assassinate Batista.

The remaining leftist challenge to Castro's mystique was presented by Frank País, whose record as an underground fighter would have given him a formidable claim to lead a new government after Batista's fall. As head of the National Directorate of the 26th of July Movement, País ran a tight, Leninist-style organization that successfully coordinated insurrectionary activity under conditions that were more dangerous than those in the mountains. His operations inflicted more damage on Batista's forces than Castro's smaller army. País also had a different personal profile. Whereas Castro's conception of political engagement was rooted in the image of the rebel soldier, País was an articulate advocate of civilian leadership. Once more, however, fortune was on Castro's side. País was assassinated in July 1957. One year later, the idea of an urban-centered revolution died when the National Directorate's call for a general strike received almost no support.

Accordingly, as members of one of the few revolutionary groups left standing, Castro and his guerrilla fighters were ideally positioned to take advantage of Cuba's political crisis. On January 1, 1959, a perfect storm of developments that had been accumulating over the preceding year—a precipitous downturn in the economy, the suspension of US arms shipments, and widespread revulsion against attempts to rig the upcoming presidential election—coalesced to force Batista to leave office. As he marched toward Havana, Castro must have been surprised, just like Lenin's Bolsheviks on the eve of the October Revolution, at the suddenness of the regime's collapse. Although his soldiers had begun to score victories in open battle with the national army since 1958, his plans for a takeover were still vague. This did not matter. True to his talent for sensing a political opportunity, Castro stepped into the vacuum. In a carefully choreographed performance, he and his troops entered Havana on January 8, 1959, where they were met by throngs of cheering citizens.

An Idea in Search of an Organization

From the moment Castro stepped into office, he faced the same question encountered by other successful revolutionaries, such as Lenin and Mao. How should one make the transition from a diffuse movement that had been primarily focused on taking power to a government with the capacity to rule? The 26th of July Movement was hardly suited for this task. With only a few hundred members, it was a stretch to call it a movement at all. Of these, only a handful were acquainted with the concrete challenges of meeting the expectations of an economically and socially heterogeneous population. Castro's solution to this dilemma, which ultimately shaped the character of the second PCC when it was founded in 1965, was twofold. On one level, he and his close circle took advantage of the momentum generated by Batista's capitulation to throw themselves completely into the task of revolutionizing society. On the other, more practical level, they took deliberate steps to create an organization with the capacity to sustain this agenda. In both cases, Castro—or, rather, the burgeoning phenomenon known as "Fidel"— was the glue that held these objectives together.

Another leader in Castro's shoes might have waited to measure the depth of his support before introducing substantial policy changes. However, the new prime minister left no room for doubt in the minds of his citizens that the revolution was not yet finished. To the contrary, in Castro's eyes, it needed to keep moving forward until his under-standing of the unfulfilled ideas of the republic's founders, above all those of Martí, were finally realized. Castro asserted that this goal would only be attained under his command. Supposedly, his success as a guerrilla fighter demonstrated that he was made of a different stuff than the politicians who had come before him. Like Martí, he knew what it meant to be a man of the people. Despite his opponents' charges, Castro insisted that he espoused no doctrine or ideology. And, he emphasized, he was certainly not a communist. Rather, in line with Herbert Matthews's portrayal two years earlier, he claimed that he sim-ply meant to offer a message of revolutionary humanism. "Government of the people without dictatorship and oligarchy," he explained during a visit to New York City on April 24, 1959, "with bread and without terror—this is humanism."[14]

In support of this view, Castro went to great lengths to emphasize that this new government of the people represented the happy conclusion to a long history of second-class status. For too long, he emphasized, the Cuban people had been treated as though they were incapable of governing themselves. Their enemies believed that "we were going to be victims of disunity, of unpreparedness, of the incapacity to organize ourselves."[15] Now, the Revolution's task was to prove its doubters wrong. To this end, the regime organized huge rallies and demonstrations around this vision of self-actualization. It dispatched newly minted activists to spread the good word to towns and rural communities across the country. Making an art form of political symbolism, it opened the beaches to all citizens, preached racial equality, drastically reduced rents, promised to improve working conditions for women, and established heavily subsidized "people's stores." These measures were accompanied by public campaigns to improve health care, promote mass literacy, and ensure a more egalitarian distribution of wealth. Additionally, the regime pointedly imposed stringent controls on the conduct of public officials to eliminate the corruption that had tarnished the country's governments for decades.

Of course, Castro was far from being the reincarnation of Martí. The revolutionary he revered was neither a socialist nor an advocate of centralized government. Furthermore, the point of the Republican revolution had changed since the turn of the century. To establish this position, Castro and his coleaders demonstrated that there was more to socialist humanism than letting people live as they wanted. Castro, Guevara, and other rebels made colorful figures when they showed up at international events wearing battle fatigues and berets. But they were not only showing off. Just like former guerrilla fighters everywhere, they were deadly earnest about their goals. In a popular handbook on guerrilla warfare, Guevara explained that one of the primary lessons of the rebel experience was that "it is not necessary to wait until all conditions for making revolution exist; the insurrection can create them."[16]

During the so-called Year of the Revolution, 1959, the regime seemed to adhere to precisely this voluntarist philosophy. It introduced the first of two agrarian reform laws, imposing significant limits on land ownership and distributing unused agricultural property to peasants. It launched the expropriation of the holdings of supposedly counter-revolutionary farmers. Finally, in 1960, it set its sights on the socialist transformation of the entire economy. With Guevara acting as the director of both the government's Department of Industries and the National Bank, the regime committed itself to accelerated industrialization and the nationalization of foreign property.

Over the same period, Cuba's new leaders showed that they were not willing to wait for the entire population to come to their side. They summarily executed more than 600 of Batista's former officials, most of whom were in the police, and imprisoned thousands of dissenters and members of moderate parties. In a manner that was eerily similar to its predecessors, the government cracked down on independent journalists, civic groups, and student associations. Professing the need for intensified public security, it consolidated its control over trade unions and abolished the sacrosanct right to strike. Additionally, in the context of intermittent battles with remnants of Batista's army and aggrieved peasants, it enlisted hundreds of thousands of volunteers into popular militias and created so-called Committees for the Defense of the Revolution (CDR) to police local communities.

There is no reason to think that Castro and his coleaders would have acted differently in less turbulent circumstances. But one development, Cuba's rapidly deteriorating relationship with the United States, presented a rationale to justify an atmosphere of revolutionary militancy for decades thereafter. In the years of opposition to Batista, Castro's criticisms of Washington had been muted. Once in office, however, he took advantage of the long-standing resentment against Cuba's northern neighbor to boost popular support for his policies. His government's nationalization of American-owned properties and the fact that he turned increasingly to the Soviet Union as a source of trade and economic aid were sufficient for US policymakers to gamble on overthrowing the Cuban regime. On April 16, 1961, a contingent of 1,000 American-trained Cuban exile soldiers landed on the coast of the Bay of Pigs with the aim of fomenting a popular rebellion. The invaders were easily routed by Cuban troops. Of greater, lasting significance, the attack gave Castro the evidence he needed to maintain the spirit of continuous struggle that underlay his path to power. A vigilant and permanently mobilized citizenry, he contended, was necessary to repulse future incursions upon Cuban soil. In October 1962, the crisis in US-Soviet relations surrounding Nikita Khrushchev's decision to install nuclear missiles on the island made this posture even more credible.

At the same time that Castro and his fellow leaders were urging their population to support these policies, they were turning toward the considerably more mundane task of building an organization that would keep them in power. To this end, Castro took the surprising, but entirely logical, step of seeking the assistance of the old communists. The PSP's conventional Leninist structure provided the disciplined organization that Castro lacked. In addition, unlike the 26th of July Movement, the PSP had full-time, experienced cadres who were strategically distributed in cities and towns across the country. Thus, in July 1961, Castro set the tone for a seeming accommodation with his old rivals by incorporating them into a new body, the ORI. He named Aníbal Escalante, an orthodox Marxist, the organization's secretary and gave his blessing to the appointment of thousands of PSP members to official positions. Complementing this turn, he even rewrote history. In an incredible statement to the Italian Communist Party's official organ, *L'Unità*, he credited the PSP for being the only Cuban party that had, in his words, "consistently called for a radical change of social structures and relations." It was true, he admitted, that the communists had originally distrusted him and his fellow rebels. But, he added with feigned humility, this attitude was entirely understandable: "We of the Sierra who were conducting the guerrilla war were still full of petty bourgeois prejudices and defects."[17]

No doubt, Castro had the same careful calculations in mind in December 1961 when he precipitously declared himself a Leninist. However, he soon showed his real intentions. In March 1962, in a revealing demonstration of his political skill, he accused Escalante of espousing sectarian views and expelled him from the leadership. Castro justified his decision in a speech that said a great deal about his unconventional understanding of the role of the communist party. Escalante's offense, it seemed, had been to create a "nucleus" within the party that would allow him and the "old militants" to control every decision made by government ministries. The situation was so bad, Castro suggested, that "if a cat gave birth to four kittens," it was necessary to refer the matter to the ORI leadership to make a decision about what one should do. This was not Marxism-Leninism, he contended, but merely an attempt to create a culture of favoritism and "political fawners." A real Leninist party had only one goal: "To orient." The party was to orient the government, but not govern on all levels. And, Castro noted, a real Leninist would avoid all sectarian tendencies by acting only according to the principle of collective leadership. Naturally, he judged himself to be the exemplar of this trait. Arguing that "history is written by the masses," he described this style of decision making as if it were an act of purification: "I believe that when the best opinions, the opinions of the most competent men, the most capable men are discussed collectively, that they are cleansed of their vices, of their errors, of their weaknesses, of their faults."[18]

Castro coupled these observations with a different kind of cleansing. Immediately after removing Escalante, the prime minister's supporters in the ORI purged thousands of the old communists from its rolls, removing over half of the members from Havana Province alone. In February 1963, Castro matter-of-factly announced that a new omnibus organization, the United Party of the Cuban Socialist Revolution, would replace the ORI. Finally, on October 3, 1965, he presided over the formation of the virtually identical PCC.

WHAT KIND OF PARTY?

The open question was what kind of party this new communist party should be. On the one hand, it was clear to Castro and his inner circle that the party could not be like the PSP. Even if that organization's members now pledged their allegiance to the PCC, the old communists' conventional understanding of Leninism was anathema to the Sierra Maestra rebels. On the other hand, most of the leadership agreed that there was a limit to the uncertainty the population would tolerate. In 1964, for example, the regime had been forced to retreat from Guevara's policy of accelerated industrialization because of severe dislocations in the economy and a sharp decline in sugar production. Thus, the key issue before the PCC's leaders was what balance they should strike between the party's revolutionary objectives and their desire to control the population.

Provocatively, the idea of the Cuban Revolution had gradually emerged as a point of contention between Castro and Guevara in the period after the ORI's founding. It would be too much to assert that there was an irresolvable conflict between the two personalities; Guevara incessantly professed his devotion to "Fidel." Nonetheless, while Castro was settling down to the business of governance, Guevara had different ideas. He continued to champion views, such as the need to combat socialist bureaucratization and to extend the Cuban model of armed struggle to other shores, which showed that he was not content to let the revolution slow down. In a fascinating letter to the Uruguayan weekly *Marcha*, published on March 12, 1965, only seven months before the PCC's founding, he asserted that the goal of the revolution should not be reduced to the mundane demands of changing social and economic conditions. It should be to create "the human being of the twenty-first century."[19]

Guevara was full of inventive ideas about how this transformation could be accomplished—intensified exposure to Marxist writings, artistic experimentation, and the assignment of a new status to manual labor. But he was vague about whether a political organization should be entrusted with this task. He noted elusively that he aspired for the PCC to become a "mass party." But, he added, the party's elevation would only be possible "when the masses have reached the level of the vanguard, that is, when they are educated for communism."[20]

In a turn of events that seems too convenient to have been coincidental, Guevara did not have the opportunity to clarify how this intriguing concept of a vanguard of the masses might be related to the PCC. In a radio address on October 4, following the party's founding, Castro announced that his longtime comrade in arms had resigned from his official posts and left Cuba to carry on the armed struggle in "new battlefields." This destination would turn out to be the Republic of the Congo.[21] Also to the point, on October 24, Castro used an address to the PCC's first Central Committee to convey an image of the party that was far more conventional than anything Guevara would have liked. He praised the new body as a major step toward the establishment of a "single line" in the government's decisions, especially in matters of ideology and economic planning. Too often in the history of the Cuban Republic, Castro lectured, "the dissolvent and centripetal forces of our society" had outmatched "the agglutinating and centrifugal forces." The people had wasted their energies in pointless internal quarrels. Henceforth, adherence to the party line would unite them firmly behind a revolution that had been long in the making. Moreover, Castro added that this party would emphasize the primacy of rules and institutions over the whims of the individual. The early days of the Revolution, he observed, without a hint of self-irony, had been marked by the deeds of heroic personalities. Now, it was time to make room for a more predictable system of rule.[22]

Castro's praise for the PCC sounded good, but one could have easily predicted that he would not allow a mere organization to take primary responsibility for a ruling idea that he and a handful of associates had monopolized since 1959. To the contrary, the PCC was an expression of "Fidel's" wishes, not the reverse. In fact, the first congress of the new party would not be held until 1975. Its ten-member Politburo was dominated by members of the 26th of July Movement. Of these, six were officers in the Cuban Revolutionary Armed Forces (FAR). Two old communists, Blas Roca and Carlos Rafael Rodríguez, were appointed to the party Secretariat. But, to prevent these individuals from taking advantage of their positions, both this organ and the Politburo were controlled by Castro and his brother, Raúl. Finally, although one-third of the members of the Central Committee were former members of the PSP, the body was dominated by the FAR; sixty-three of the organ's one hundred members came from the military.[23]

The presence of so many military officers in the PCC was not a sign of the militarization of the party. Rather, it reflected Castro's desire to supplement one crucial component of the regime's power with another. In this respect, the PCC had many of the functions of a Soviet-style party. It quickly assumed the leading role over the country's mass organizations, such as the Federation of University Students, the Federation of Women, the General Workers' Association, and the CDR, passing down commands from on high, educating members in Marxist-Leninist doctrine, and organizing public demonstrations in support of the regime's policies. Notably, the PCC's reach was also extended into the FAR. In contrast to the first half of the decade when the OIR's influence was negligible, party cells became more active in the army's ranks. For the first time, in a notable indication that the FAR was not invulnerable, criticism of the conduct of low-level officers was permitted.

The link between the formation of the PCC and the regime's increasingly risk-averse policies did not mean that Cuba's revolutionary impulse had died with Guevara's departure. The idea was very much alive where it mattered most: in Castro's head. There were simply limits to the extent to which he and his supporters could recapture the popular exuberance of the years immediately before and after their victory. Indeed, Castro encountered a storm of reality in a disastrous attempt to produce a record 10-million-ton sugar cane harvest. Beginning in November 1969, his government sought to summon the will of the masses once again by sending hundreds of thousands of workers, students, housewives, and soldiers to the fields to cut cane. In practice, there was little about this campaign that resembled Guevara's romantic revolutionary ideals, let alone a Maoist, consciousness-raising exercise. It was about hard, grinding work. But for a combination of reasons ranging from the lack of machinery to the inexperience of the volunteer laborers, the harvest fell far short of its primary advocate's goals.

Notwithstanding the campaign's outcome, Castro's handling of the crop failure provides revealing insight into his calculations at the beginning of the Revolution's second decade. On July 26, 1970, the seventeenth anniversary of the attack on the Moncada barracks, he gave a solemn speech in which he outlined the mistakes that had been made and their adverse impact on numerous sectors of the economy. The address was a characteristic tour de force. In one breath, Castro pinned the blame for the fiasco on himself and the party, and then, in another, declared that no one was to blame. He offered his and his coleaders' resignation, but then observed that they would be hypocrites to step down. The most notable feature of the speech was the way Castro turned the need for a more sober economic strategy into an all-important demonstration of revolutionary purity. The Cuban people, he declared, were not cowards. It was a sign of the "depth of their moral spirit" that they had the courage to admit their mistakes. Likewise, he and his colleagues were not afraid to say that they had no "magic solutions" to their country's woes. Rather, this situation, too, was a chance to celebrate the heroic deeds of the people. If he and the rebels who had finally brought Cuba its revolution had "an atom of value," Castro stressed, it was because of their service "to an idea, a cause, linked to the people."[24]

Interestingly, Castro's defeat led him to take the major step that he had resisted since the founding of the PCC in 1965. To restore his authority, he turned to the party to play a leading role in realizing this idea. This was no mean change of course. With the exception of the Politburo, the PCC's major organs, including the Central Committee and the Secretariat, had rarely met. The party had relatively few members, and its cadres had lost touch with their constituencies. In fact, the PCC had not held a single party congress in its history. At this point, thanks to Castro's backing, the PCC slowly acquired the features of a conventional organization. Its various departments began to meet on a regular basis. Party membership nearly quadrupled, from a mere 55,000 in 1969 to more than 200,000 members six years later.

Correspondingly, the representation of PCC officials in the leadership rose markedly. In 1965, the party had only provided 10 percent of the Central Committee's members, but within a decade, it accounted for nearly 29 percent. In a demonstration of party unity, Castro conspicuously reinstated old communists to both this body and the Politburo. For these reasons, when the PCC's members finally assembled for their First Congress in 1975 and endorsed a new constitution and a program of moderate economic growth, it seemed as though the party was finally coming into its own. According to Article 5 of the constitution, the PCC was "the vanguard of the working class" and "the highest leading force in society."[25]

Of course, Castro had not given up the idea that *he* remained the preeminent force in Cuban society. Still, the fact that he turned to the PCC in a time of crisis demonstrated that an idea of leadership based primarily on the instincts of a single individual is not always sufficient to guarantee the attainment of a government's goals. As in the Soviet Union and China in the 1970s, as I shall show in chapter 11, the affirmation of the party's leading role had the advantage of providing an atmosphere of constancy and predictability in complex conditions. Nonetheless, this particular party's days of glory were not to last. Within a few years after the PCC's elevation, Castro regained the confidence he had exhibited in the early period after the 26th of July Movement's ascendance and looked for new means of asserting his authority through a return to revolutionary action.

CHAPTER 10

The Revolution Returns

On June 30, 1949, three months before the founding of the People's Republic of China (PRC), Mao Zedong published an essay, "On the People's Democratic Dictatorship," in which he had this to say about the Chinese Communist Party (CCP). "Like a man," he began, "a political party has its childhood, youth, manhood and old age. The communist party of China is no longer a child or a lad in his teens, but has become an adult." "When a man reaches old age he will die," Mao continued, and "the same is true of a party. When classes disappear, all instruments of class struggle—parties and the state machinery—will lose their function, cease to be necessary, therefore gradually wither away and end their historical mission; and human society will move to a higher stage."[1]

Mao's reference to the CCP's adulthood is what one would expect from the leader of a movement on the verge of victory. The party's members had every reason to be proud of their achievement. But henceforth, they had to prove themselves worthy. The Chinese people would not wait around for their new rulers to get their bearings. Thus, in a manner that bore a striking resemblance to Lenin's admonitions after the October Revolution, Mao informed his readers that there was "still much work to do," and their struggle for power was only the first step in a new long march. The remnants of the enemy had yet to be wiped out. The tasks of rebuilding the economy, combating crippling inflation, and restoring public order were immense. For the time being, these responsibilities meant that the party should put aside what it did best—fomenting revolution—and concentrate on state-building. In the Soviet Union's infancy, the Bolsheviks had been up to this task. Now, the CCP could demonstrate its prowess as well.[2]

Yet, in one respect, Mao's description of the party's fate was new. In nearly every case I have considered in this book, the creators of Leninist orthodoxy seem to have taken it for granted that the communist party would survive, in one form or another, the attainment of communism. In the canonical works of Marx, Engels, and Lenin, only the state withers away. In Mao's essay, however, one finds him confronting what others have failed to consider—the party's mortality. In line with Mao's analogy, there is no reason to think that the party's demise should be any less inevitable than the passing of those who have brought the revolution to completion. Indeed, Mao suggested that the ultimate indication of the party's success will be its obsolescence. It will not be overthrown. Rather, it will be part of a historical process in which all institutions, "classes, state power, and political parties, will die out very naturally." At this point, he concluded, humanity will enter "a realm of harmony."[3]

In another respect, however, the difference between Mao's view of the party's destiny and a major strand of Marxist thought is not as great as it appears at first glance. At the heart of his thinking, Mao shared with predecessors like Marx, Rosa Luxemburg, and Leon Trotsky the instinctive distrust of all political organizations, the party included. Such human constructs threatened to sap the revolutionary moment's potential. Later, and even more than these iconic figures, Mao extended his animosity beyond the state to the party. But his target was the organizational party, not the idea of the revolutionary group that he had cultivated in Yan'an. Far from abandoning this conviction, he aggressively returned to it again and again after the PRC's founding.

There are two reasons for viewing Mao's intentions in this way. First, this perspective helps us to see why attempts by scholars to equate Maoism with other extreme forms of Leninism, and especially its Stalinist variant, are misleading or simply wrong. To be sure, Mao and Stalin were scarcely inhibited in using the pretext of communist party rule to serve their megalomania. Their desire for absolute power and their certainty that no other person was capable of acting with the clarity of vision and sense of historical purpose led them to inflict unimaginable suffering on their fellow human beings. Still, there is an essential difference between Mao's and Stalin's understanding of the party's functions. Stalin viewed the organizational party as a hothouse of independent thinking and an impediment to his particular brand of socialism. Hence, he subordinated the idea of party rule to an all-powerful state. In contrast, Mao was driven by the conviction that the organizational party should be reinfused with its original ideals.

Second, Mao's disdain for formal organizations meant that there was a contradiction built into the construction of socialism that Stalin and his Eastern European allies would have abhorred. To the consternation of many of his lifelong comrades in battle, Mao viewed the prospect of socialist stabilization with deep suspicion. In a conversation with the sympathetic Cambodian communist leader Pol Pot in 1975, he noted that socialism's struggle with its enemies would last more than 10,000 years; indeed, it would exist even under communism.[4] As we shall see, Mao's refusal to compromise this conception of revolutionary history had devastating consequences. In two distinct periods, his undercutting of the CCP's authority in the Great Leap Forward in the late 1950s and his assault on the institution during the Great Proletarian Cultural Revolution a decade later, he weakened the primary force that kept the revolution from turning in on itself and tearing the country apart. Notably, Pol Pot was infatuated with this revolutionary vision. From 1975 to 1979, he and his fellow insurrectionists in the communist Khmer Rouge subjected Cambodia to genocidal policies in the name of cultural and social "purification" that resulted in the deaths of a quarter of the country's population.

However, the era of Maoist rule shared one feature in common with Stalinism. Like the Soviet Great Terror, the turmoil that engulfed China might not have reached such unfathomable proportions under a different and possibly less powerful ruler. In making this point, I do not mean to suggest that another leader would have objected to the use of violence to achieve his goals. After all, just like Stalin's opponents in the 1920s, the key figures in the CCP were committed revolutionaries. Nonetheless, as I shall demonstrate in this chapter, some of Mao's deputies had different ideas about what was, and was not, required for the successful construction of socialism. In fact, years later, in the late 1970s and 1980s, their conceptions of single-party rule would lead China down a path that was much less turbulent than the years of Maoist supremacy.

Boundless Exuberance

To understand the Chinese communists' conception of their party's priorities after the founding of the PRC on October 1, 1949, one must appreciate the comparatively favorable circumstances in which they came to power. Only a few years earlier, the communists' prospects had seemed far from propitious. When the war with Japan ended in August 1945, Chiang Kai-shek's National Revolutionary Army (NRA) had nearly four times as many troops as the newly named People's Liberation Army (PLA) and enjoyed a vast superiority in weaponry. It controlled most of China's territory and nearly all of its major cities. Furthermore, Chiang was officially the country's president. He had both the United States and the Soviet Union at his side, each seeking to expand its sphere of influence. Nonetheless, through a combination of shrewd diplomacy, guerrilla warfare, and patriotic appeals, the PLA and the CCP soon turned these adverse conditions to their favor. Thus, when Mao stood atop Tiananmen Square's Gate of Heavenly Peace and proclaimed the new republic, he and his compatriots accomplished a feat that had eluded their predecessors. For the first time since the fall of the Qing dynasty, China was ruled by a single government. With this victory serving as proof of the communists' claims to represent a national agenda, they could direct their energies exclusively toward putting their social and economic values into practice.

Initially, the PRC's new leaders were cautious. After two decades of civil war and eight years of Japanese occupation, none would have believed that China was ready for an immediate transition into socialism. Their young regime was faced with the challenge of resolving the myriad problems that had made its rise to power possible. Thanks to the Guomindang's (GMD) intransigence and flailing leadership in its final years, the communists inherited a fractured economy. China lacked even a unified monetary system. There was no coordination of state, regional, and local budgets. Entire industries had been shut down, and there existed few reliable sources of transportation. Cities were threatened with food shortages and disease.

Compounding these problems, China's new rulers were in a similar position to the Bolsheviks in 1917 and 1918. They were not yet equipped to exercise the power they had won. Despite their prowess on the battlefield, they had few of the skills required for administering a demanding national government. The police forces and court system were in disarray and public order had broken down. The state's bureaucracies were suffused with graft and corruption. Many GMD officials with the experience and know-how to attend to the routine matters of governance had fled to Taiwan along with their president. Before coming to power, even Mao conceded the complexity of the situation. In contrast to his characterization of the party's adulthood in "On the People's Democratic Dictatorship," he also summoned the image of an earlier life stage. "We are like a girl," he told a Soviet emissary, "who, when marrying, knowing that she will have to bear children but not knowing how it will be, she still knows that it will be inevitable and [so] she marries."[5] This turned out to be an apt metaphor. Although the CCP was technically a robust twenty-eight years old, Mao and his comrades recognized that they had to face their limitations and build strong institutions.

Given the support they had earned among the peasantry and their appreciation of the danger of inflicting new blows on the agrarian economy, the communists appreciated the acute need for pragmatism in the countryside. In the final years of the war and immediately thereafter, the PLA had been the image of socialist beneficence, rewarding poor peasants with plots of land and livestock. But to restabilize the economy, the regime soon placed strict limits on the confiscation of property. Former landlords were allowed to keep small plots of land for personal use. Well-off peasants were able to continue employing tenant farmers. The case for moderation was even more compelling in the cities where the GMD had enjoyed the bulk of its support. For an all-too-brief period, middle-class urban residents and GMD officials were surprised to find that their fears of recrimination by the victors were unfounded. The communists presented themselves as liberating patriots. To compensate for their lack of experience, they, like the Bolsheviks before them, retained tens of thousands of civil servants. Although they hastened to take control over prices and wages, they tolerated wholesale and retail trade in private hands. Under the party's purview, the number of privately owned industries actually increased.

These strategies paid off. With greater incentives to attend to the cultivation of property, both large and small farmers rewarded the government with modest increases in productivity. As the unification of the country under a centralized authority took hold, the regime slowly reined in inflation, restored commerce, and boosted urban industry. In addition, the communists won public favor by skillfully characterizing their goals as principled alternatives to the moral bankruptcy of GMD rule. In a manner that harkened back to the idealistic fervor of the New Culture Movement of the late 1910s, they railed against the ills of old China—opium addiction, prostitution, and gambling. They introduced divorce laws and banned concubinage and polygamy. Across the country, cadres staged mass literacy campaigns, built schools, and formed neighborhood committees to educate citizens in basic health matters and sanitation.

Of course, Mao and his coleaders did not come to bring social peace alone. Once China's recovery was set in motion, they had less cause for restraint, especially against the party's purported opponents. In a conversation with one of Stalin's emissaries in early 1949, Mao had hinted at darker times to come by likening his country to a dirty house filled with "firewood, trash, dust, fleas, and lice." This home, he emphasized, needed to be purged of its enemies before it could be fully reopened.[6] In 1951, the regime began the housecleaning. Under the evocative "Campaign for the Elimination of Counterrevolutionaries" and the "Three-Anti Campaign," authorities claimed to uncover covert GMD agents, American spies, and imperialist collaborators everywhere, all of whom were supposedly bent upon fomenting a new civil war. Likewise, cadres whipped up popular hysteria with mass meetings and rallies, and conducted "tiger hunts" and public trials of the same officials the regime had previously retained. By the end of 1952, the government had executed upwards of 700,000 people for alleged crimes against the state; thousands more fell victim to the petty grudges of neighbors or died at their own hands.[7]

Moreover, the regime's dependence on the Soviet Union for material goods and expertise was unmistakable. In a manner resembling the noblesse oblige of his tsarist predecessors, Stalin came to the aid of his junior partners. In the name of proletarian solidarity, his government sent over 10,000 engineers, scientists, and other advisers to take part in the reconstruction effort; simultaneously, it welcomed eight times as many Chinese students to universities in the USSR. By the end of the 1950s, Moscow had provided the PRC with millions of dollars in financial assistance, long-term loans, industrial equipment, and military supplies, almost all of which was directed to modernizing sectors of the economy.

Despite Stalin's aggravating slights over the years, which had included support for a friendship treaty with Chiang Kai-shek in 1945, Mao held firm to his conviction that the leadership of the Soviet communist party was "China's best teacher and we must learn from it."[8] In an affirmation of this principle, following the country's stabilization, the CCP fashioned its First Five-Year Plan around the core element of the Stalinist economy: the priority of heavy-industrial development. In the words of Beijing's mayor, Peng Zhen, "Chairman Mao wants a big modern city; he expects the sky there to be filled with smokestacks."[9] From an ideological perspective, it helped that the Soviets had already gone through the tortuous debates about reconciling Marxist theory with their desire to accelerate the leap from precapitalist forms of economic organization to full-scale socialist construction. Thanks to its massive population, China already had a virtually unlimited supply of workers to emulate the Soviet model of labor-intensive growth. At a pace that outstripped Moscow's expectations, the regime acted according to the same storming mentality that had typified High Stalinism. It emphasized the production of steel, chemicals, and electric power; nationalized remaining private businesses; built massive industrial cities in the country's interior regions; and beyond its Marxist goals, mobilized millions of workers in the name of restoring the glory their nation had lost over the past century.

In the countryside, in contrast, the communists pursued policies that were more akin to the Bolsheviks' New Economic Policy than the mass collectivization drive that came later. Although the First Five-Year Plan referred to eventual collectivization, the policy's implementation was slower and generally less violent than in the Soviet Union. Recognizing the CCP's long-standing dependence on the peasantry, state planners formed mutual-aid teams in which small groups of households would do nothing more radical than work together, tilling the land and harvesting crops. After the adoption of the First Five-Year Plan, the regime's tactics became more ambitious. It formed larger production units, or Agricultural Producers' Cooperatives (APCs), in which peasants pooled their resources and were paid for their services. In theory, the APCs were meant to lay the ground for eventual collectivization. Still, these measures were nothing like the extremes of Stalinism. Property owners retained title to their holdings and were formally allowed to withdraw from the cooperatives.

THE IDEA OF THE PARTY IN DISPUTE

This period of restraint was not to last. When the Politburo's members began to consider the next step in China's development, they were forced to wrestle with a matter that was considerably more consequential than a change in economic policy. This was the party's leading role. In principle, no one questioned the CCP's importance in pursuing the twin goals of revolution and modernization. Nonetheless, there were significant differences between Mao and his closest colleagues about what this meant.

The APCs provided the occasion for the first major dispute. Initially, the peasantry had welcomed the new units as an opportunity to achieve financial security and improve their standard of living. But in 1955, their enthusiasm dissipated. Following two disappointing harvests, the government forced them to increase the delivery of grain to the cities. Poor peasants in particular found their livelihoods threatened by the meager returns of their private plots. As discontent grew, a majority of the Politburo's members concluded that one could only defuse the crisis by rescinding the state's demands and slowing the creation of new APCs. However, Mao undermined the consensus. On July 31, 1955, he went around the leadership to inform a gathering of provincial and municipal party secretaries in Beijing that the state should undertake even more aggressive steps. The misguided assumption of the First Five-Year Plan, he underscored, had been to prioritize industrial growth. This approach had allowed for the persistence of vast disparities in wealth among the peasantry. Now it was incumbent upon the CCP to redress this injustice by imposing its will on the countryside. The Soviet Union had done this after Stalin's death. China could, too.

In a testament to his authority, Mao achieved what he wanted. A suddenly compliant Politburo revised the government's agricultural production targets radically upward. Under the banner of the "Socialist High Tide"—later dubbed the "Little Leap Forward" by Mao's critics—it committed to doubling the number of APCs by the end of 1956. In fact, this goal was not only met; Mao's expectations were soon surpassed. Thanks to the frenzied efforts of local cadres and their promises of bountiful rewards to come, 95 percent of agricultural households were transformed into APCs. By the end of the decade, almost all of these cooperatives had become functioning collective farms.

For our purposes, the revealing aspect of the agrarian policy is what it said about Mao's view of the communist party. His understanding of the party's functions remained essentially unchanged from those of the fiery young revolutionary who had written the Hunan Report in 1927 and the report from the Jinggang Mountains one year later. The party was called to act on the inevitable flow of historical events. In a July 1955 speech, published as "On the Cooperative Transformation of Agriculture," Mao justified the acceleration of the cooperative movement by once again conjuring up the imagery of stormy seas and crashing waves to show that history was on the side of the oppressed masses who wanted to change the world. "The high tide of social transformation in the countryside," he proclaimed, would soon sweep through the whole country. This was "a vast socialist revolutionary movement" with more than 500 million members. It could not be defeated.

The problem, Mao argued with the same self-assuredness that he had evinced in the 1920s, was not with the masses. It was with the party. As an organization, the CCP had lost sight of its founding purposes. "Some comrades," Mao told his audience, in an unmistakable reference to his Politburo associates, "are tottering along like a woman with bound feet." They were "complaining all the time, 'You are going too fast, much too fast.'" But, Mao stressed, their diagnosis was completely wrong. The party was lagging behind those it was meant to lead. The mass movement was "running ahead, while the leadership cannot keep pace with it."[10]

In pushing the party to overcome its fear of "dragons ahead and tigers behind," Mao also presented his listeners with a familiar argument about how true communists should act. The way to inspire the masses, he maintained, was for cadres to engage in productive activity. One could never learn how to do a good job, he emphasized, by listening to instructors in a training class. A true communist was called to plunge into the battle, work alongside the people, and lead them into socialism. In so doing, each of the party's members would learn from those below them what it meant to act with courage and conviction.[11]

In theory, Mao's summoning of the holy spirit of the mass line was a reasonable approach to maximize the CCP's impact. In practice, the Socialist High Tide was a disaster. Far from stimulating the economy, it destabilized the countryside. Entire villages were threatened with starvation. Just as in the Soviet Union under collectivization, farmers hid their grain and others fought back, demanding that they be allowed to leave the APCs. Making matters worse, major industries were simultaneously beset with shortages of raw materials. For the first time since the PRC's founding Mao found himself vulnerable to charges that he was "going too fast, much too fast." At the time of the Socialist High Tide's enunciation, party veterans, such as Zhou Enlai, the new premier, and Liu Shaoqi, the chairman of the Standing Committee of the National People's Congress and author of the Civil War tract *How to Be a Good Communist*, had expressed misgivings about the policy's risks. This turmoil not only confirmed their fears, it raised questions about the wisdom of allowing their leader, and not the Politburo, to dictate party priorities.

This circumstance alone would have presented Mao with a major challenge. But his position was made even more precarious by the fact that these troubles coincided with Nikita Khrushchev's exposure of Stalin's crimes at the CPSU's Twentieth Party Congress in February 1956. As I have suggested in chapter 8, Mao's long association with Stalin and his reliance upon his personality cult meant that he was as vulnerable to the Soviet leader's attacks as his Eastern European counterparts. Accordingly, he hastened to inform his colleagues that he would take Khrushchev's revelations seriously. In an illuminating essay, "On the Ten Major Relationships," Mao admitted what had long been assumed about his party's relationship with the Soviet dictator. Stalin's treatment of China's communists, he pointed out, had not always been correct. He had mistakenly enjoined them not to press forward in their battles with the GMD and Japan. "He took us half seriously," Mao asserted, "half skeptically." After giving ground on these points, however, Mao showed that he was not willing to concede anything more to his colleagues than absolutely necessary. He ridiculed certain unnamed party members, both in the Soviet Union and in China, "who once extolled Stalin to the skies [but] have now in one swoop consigned him to purgatory." Quoting a Central Committee statement, Mao contended that "only 30 percent of Stalin's decisions were bad, whereas 70 percent were good." Ironically, precisely these terms would be used two decades later to characterize Mao's rule. But at this moment, the lesson for the CCP was that it should emulate Stalin's actions when they made sense for China and avoid them when they did not. By implication, the same standard could be applied to Mao himself.[12]

To demonstrate his readiness to abide by this standard, Mao raised no objection at the party's Eighth Congress in September 1956, when his colleagues revised the PRC's constitution, adopted only two years earlier, to restrain him from acting unilaterally. Invoking the norm of collective leadership, they strengthened the party Secretariat by eliminating the provision that made Mao its chairman. They also created a new position, that of CCP general secretary, which reported directly to the Politburo. Deng Xiaoping assumed this title, taking charge of the Central Committee apparatus. Finally, they removed the constitution's extraordinary reference to the primacy of Mao Zedong Thought.

These changes were far from a fatal blow to Mao's authority. He retained his key positions as both chairman of the PRC and Central Military Commission. Nonetheless, the dents in Mao's reputation provided an opening for serious discussion about the possibility that China could be led in a meaningful way by a vibrant party, and not a charismatic hero. Liu Shaoqi took the lead at the Eighth Congress, arguing that the CCP was fit to usher the country into a higher stage of historical development. Since the enunciation of the First Five-Year Plan, he emphasized, the party had made significant progress in preparing the population for the transition into socialism. It had eliminated feudal class structures, reformed former exploiters, and secured the proletariat's position as the leading class. Thus, it was time to look ahead. "We are now confronted with new conditions and new tasks," Liu told the congress, "and we must solve many problems which are more complicated than those of the past, and with which we are unfamiliar." Above all, in Liu's estimation, the party's members needed to accept that socialism would not be achieved overnight. Concretely, this recognition meant that the party would have to pursue its goals on a "step-by-step basis."[13]

In making this case, Liu could not have avoided brushing against at least some of the adverse effects of Mao's rule. The mistakes of the preceding few years, Liu declared in a clear reference to the Socialist High Tide, had been due to the rashness and impetuosity of "trying to do things by coercion and command." These mistakes could have been avoided if those in charge had made an "earnest effort to analyze correctly the actual conditions of things and to sum up the experience of the masses." In the absence of these correctives, party functionaries had grown conceited and complacent. Rather than formulating policy on the basis of investigation and listening to experts, they reached decisions solely on the basis of impressions. For the CCP to become more effective, Liu stressed, it had to learn from cadres who understood local conditions and ask whether its policies were sensible. Finally, given its aspiration to improve the lives of the Chinese people, the party needed to be open to new ideas and approaches.[14]

Naturally, Mao could not be faulted for slighting the *idea* of seeking truth from below. This was a central feature of Maoist rule. For Liu and other senior leaders, the problem was that he was inconsistent. Could one not deduce, therefore, that he bore a degree of responsibility for the regime's misguided policies? Liu was not quite willing to take this bold leap. Thus, he approached the dilemma of correcting a leader who, unlike Stalin, was still very much present in the flesh, by proceeding with caution. On the one hand, he fawned over the Great Helmsman's achievements. Since the Zunyi Conference in 1935, Liu affirmed, Mao had repeatedly demonstrated his genius for integrating the truth of Leninism with China's unique conditions. His brilliant instincts had guaranteed that the party had *never* made a mistake in its general line.

On the other hand, Liu used these encomia to justify the new face of party rule. In his portrayal, Mao was steadfastly committed to inner-party democracy and collective leadership. According to this logic, the CCP would only thrive, Liu pointed out, if the personalistic approach to revolution that had served the organization well in wartime were now replaced with a principled emphasis on party rule. This shift, Liu suggested, would be exemplified by greater consultation with the organization's ranks and a serious consideration of all views.[15]

It says something about the businesslike spirit within the CCP's upper echelons at this moment that even those individuals who were less critical of Mao embraced the theme of political stabilization. Nevertheless, it is equally telling that few, if any, of the Politburo's members dared to choose between the party and their leader. One day after Liu's address, Mao's protégé Deng Xiaoping conveyed the hope that this situation would never arise. Where Liu had set the stage for enhancing the CCP's position, the general secretary characterized the party as an institution that was built to last. Seven years after the PRC's founding, Deng argued, the CCP had established its leading role in "the work of the state." Party units had spread to every town, county, and district. Their representatives were active in every government office and economic enterprise. They were tirelessly engaged in educating the masses about the fundamentals of Marxism and Leninism.

This did not mean, Deng stressed, that the party was above criticism. He made a point of noting that cadres had not always lived up to their responsibilities. Many had fallen prey to the maladies of bureaucratic thinking. Notably, Deng formulated his response to these problems in a textbook description of democratic centralism. On the one hand, he underscored the need to guard against excessive centralization. In some matters, he contended, the organization's effectiveness would be increased by encouraging its lower-level functionaries to take the initiative. They were best positioned to know how to act because of their proximity to the masses. On the other hand, Deng emphasized that it was equally important to guard against excessive decentralization or, as he expressed it, the danger that cadres would "turn their particular department into a little world of their own." In these cases, he observed, the party's leaders should listen patiently to the views of their lower ranks. However, once they reached a decision, their representatives should carry it out without question.

In expressing this perspective, Deng must have provoked a question in the minds of everyone in the congress hall. How could one square the need for a stable set of understandings about party operations with the unremitting inclination of a particular individual—that is, Mao Zedong—to intrude upon its decisions? Deng showed that he was less inclined than Liu to address the contradiction. Notwithstanding an obligatory bow to collective leadership, he carefully observed that Marxism had never denied the importance of "outstanding individuals." The decisive issue, it seemed, was how this person acted. A true leader would maintain close contact with the masses, follow the party's rules, and obey its commands. Indeed, Deng added, when these conditions were met, it was reasonable to show one's love for the party by expressing one's love for the leader! Without a hint of irony, Deng noted that Mao had shown that he deserved this recognition by prohibiting the celebration of officials' birthdays. If one took Deng at his word, there was evidently no reason to believe that the chairman would fail to exhibit this beneficent disposition.[16]

FLOWERS BLOOMING, SCHOOLS CONTENDING

Based upon the other cases of personalist despotism that we have encountered in this book, one could easily conclude that Deng's attempt to reconcile the need for stable party rule with Mao's countervailing desire to assert his interests at will was destined to be a futile exercise. Still, Deng's address provides us with insight into the issue that would confound him and other party figures over the coming two decades. No matter what governing principles they endorsed, Mao's distinctively anti-institutional approach to leadership was deeply engrained in the political culture of the CCP.

On May 2, 1956, Mao surprised his colleagues by assuming a conciliatory pose. He invoked the words of a classical Chinese poem to "let a hundred flowers blossom" and a "hundred schools of thought contend." The speech was never published, although it was broadcast on radio. But Mao's thinking was subsequently clarified in an article on May 26 by the head of the CCP Propaganda Department, Lu Dingyi. In words that Mao must have approved and may have written, Lu expressed enthusiasm for the open spirit emanating from the Kremlin by encouraging writers and artists ("the hundred flowers") and the scientific and technical elite ("the hundred schools") to express themselves freely.

Initially, there was nothing to indicate that the government would actually live up to these words. Lu emphasized that the class struggle was still very much alive, especially in cultural and intellectual domains. Correspondingly, educated Chinese were understandably hesitant to test the government's toleration of independent thought. Nonetheless, following the Hungarian Uprising in October 1956, Mao took a shocking step. Instead of ordering an immediate crackdown on potential sources of opposition, he invited the elite to engage in precisely the active scrutiny of official policy that less-educated party and state functionaries feared the most.

Once again, Mao circumvented his senior colleagues to make his views known. In an initially unpublished speech to the Supreme State Conference on February 27, 1957, "On the Correct Handling of Contradictions among the People," he used a familiar Leninist formulation to announce the shift in policy. All socialist societies, Mao argued, were bisected by two types of contradictions. One, the antagonistic contradiction between the people and its enemies, could only be resolved through a resolute battle to the death of the latter. The other type, nonantagonistic contradictions among the people, could be addressed through patient discussion and persuasion according to the principle of democratic centralism.

This was hardly the first time Mao had suggested that Chinese society was divided into different groups. The new dimension was the extent to which he blurred the line between these opposing groups in favor of nonantagonistic contradictions. The first thing one notices in the address is that Mao does not refer to the class struggle at all. In fact, the putatively newly enlightened chairman seems to view this way of understanding society as less useful than in the past. Antagonistic contradictions, he explains, such as those between the working class and the national bourgeoisie, "[may], if handled properly, be transformed into non-antagonistic ones." This is good news for the exploiting class.

Whereas it was previously threatened with extinction, now it is presented with a chance for revelation. As Mao points out obligingly, "as long as one is not an enemy, one belongs to the people."[17]

In addition, Mao's way of justifying this argument is a revealing indication of his growing expectations of the Chinese Revolution. Instead of simply observing that the PRC has ascended to a higher stage of development, as Liu Shaoqi had done, he intimates that the party's handling of class conflict is already superior to that of the Soviet Union. To make the point, Mao singles out Stalin. Despite his many achievements, Mao advises his listeners, Stalin spent too much time looking for contradictions between the enemy and the people and, hence, "made a mess of it." As a result, the Soviet leader's policies had made it impossible for the USSR's citizens to contribute fully to their country. Under this system, Mao explains, "one could only say positive things, not negative things; only glorify, not criticize." Whoever had anything critical to say, he adds, "was suspected of being an enemy and risked landing in jail or having his head chopped off."[18] In contrast, Mao paints a positive picture of the CCP. In the PRC's first years, he stresses, there was no alternative to eliminating the hundreds of thousands of counterrevolutionaries who threatened the young republic; the Chinese people demanded their execution. But, Mao boasts, this number had quickly dropped. Indeed, over the preceding year, the government had killed almost no one, "only a very small number of odd ones."[19]

At this point in the address, Mao could have simply let his party comrades bask in this purported record of moderation. But he takes the argument one step further. Rather than limiting himself to the proposition that the contradictions in China have essentially been reduced to the nonantagonistic variety, he opens the room for political engagement to virtually every segment of society that is willing to contribute responsibly. There are many types of blooming flowers, Mao argues. The primary task is to distinguish between "fragrant flowers" and "poisonous weeds." On this basis, one should identify those citizens best suited to lead the people and weed out those who are holding it back.

In this matter, significantly, Mao makes an inflammatory point. Notwithstanding his praise of the CCP's record, it turns out that many of the party's leaders have been providing the soil on which many of the "weeds" are growing. Nine out of ten party members, he declares, oppose or only partially support political change. They insist on defending dogmatic approaches to socialism and refuse to accept criticism, punishing anyone who finds fault with their policies. Even within the party's senior ranks, from the district committees up to the Central Committee, leading figures endorsed "bureaucratism" and "departmentalism." As a result, Mao concludes, these personalities are not only incapable of solving pressing problems, they are contributing to the growth of new weeds "in Marxist garb."[20]

Most likely, Mao's criticism of the CCP's shortcomings would not have been news to those who knew him. Yet, instead of limiting himself, as he had done in the past, to inviting peasants and workers to investigate the party's behavior, he invites previously suspect groups, such as intellectuals and students, to take part in the process. In a remarkable segment of the speech in which Mao addresses recent incidences of student unrest, he suggests that mass protest against the party's decisions can be useful for correcting misguided policies. Provided that those who create "disturbances" are doing so for the right reasons, he declares, "Let them go ahead." "If they do not want to stop," he adds provocatively, "let them go on until they feel they have made enough disturbances."[21]

One can speculate about Mao's reasons for making these observations. Undoubtedly, he was trying to assert his authority over his critics. He may have also interpreted the collapse of communist rule in Hungary as a lesson about the dangers of Stalinist rule. Yet, it quickly became clear that his gamble had backfired. For two months, Mao got the "disturbances" he thought he wanted, but rather than increasing the party's credibility, they weakened it. Ever attentive to the slightest shift in official policy, educated Chinese readers found his clarification of the purposes of the "Hundred Flowers" campaign to be an invitation to voice dissatisfaction. With a fervor that recalled the protests of the New Culture and May Fourth Movements in the 1910s, they demanded that the government permit the free expression of opinion. Journalists documented instances of corruption in the party's ranks. On the campus of Peking University, students erected a "democracy wall" on which they posted placards venting their grievances. These protests snowballed into attacks on the entire socialist system, leading the regime to fear the collapse of social order.

Mao later sought to salvage his reputation by insisting that he had meant all along to trick counterrevolutionary elements into exposing themselves. It was, as he put it, like luring snakes out of their holes.[22] However, it is difficult to take this explanation at face value. It seems implausible that he would have undertaken such a risky venture if he did not wish to explore citizens' belief in the party. Assuming this latter interpretation is correct, his experiment was entirely consistent with his anti-institutional conception of political action.

Nonetheless, the damage was done. In June 1957, the Politburo swiftly reversed course. In contrast to the unconventional strategy of the Hundred Flowers campaign, it embraced entirely conventional means of coercion to restore public order. In the same unforgiving manner in which Hungary's new government and its Soviet occupiers were simultaneously suppressing their opponents, although without the context of foreign invasion, the regime arrested prominent participants in the protests and shut down independent newspapers and forums. Party leaders took particular care to identify and expel reform-minded critics within their own ranks. Overall, more than 500,000 people, ranging from writers and artists to scientists and engineers, were denounced for rightist tendencies. In the process of mobilizing millions of citizens to carry out this campaign, party activists reinforced a parallel strain within Maoist thought that denigrated all forms of intellectual activity.

Mao gave his imprimatur to this about-face in a subtly revised version of "On the Correct Handling of Contradictions among the People" on June 19, 1957. He pointedly removed the ambiguities and nuanced distinctions of the original speech. Gone was the suggestion that the enemies of socialism could become its friends. He underscored the class struggle and warned his colleagues about the resurgence of counterrevolution. Whereas the word "revisionism" had not appeared in the original speech, Mao not only invoked the term in the new version but used it as a counterpoint to his original condemnation of dogmatism. To safeguard his personal standing, he also noticeably softened his criticisms of Stalin's cult and accused Khrushchev of going too far. Although he retained the imagery of the "hundred flowers," it was clear that independent thought could only blossom with his explicit permission.

A GREAT LEAP FORWARD

Mao's failure did not cow him into political retreat. To the contrary, it emboldened him to look elsewhere to recommit the party to a particular conception of its leading role. He found this opportunity in what would become the disastrous politicization of the Chinese economy. At the Second Session of the CCP's Eighth Congress in May 1958, he demonstrated his power by entrusting his critic, Liu Shaoqi, with heralding and thereby sharing responsibility for the success of a new policy of economic development, the Great Leap Forward. The essence of the Great Leap Forward, as Liu described it in the Central Committee report, was that the CCP would undertake a qualitatively different approach to the construction of socialism than its Soviet allies. Whereas the Stalinist regime had emphasized urban growth strategies, the Chinese government would, in line with Mao's earlier emphasis on pursuing industrial and agricultural development simultaneously, take advantage of its huge population to advance labor-intensive growth strategies in all sectors of the economy.[23]

Mao's timing was no accident. In the aftermath of the Hundred Flowers debacle, he had to convince his comrades that he was fit to lead the party. In this respect, his choice of Liu to give the address was a conscious act of co-optation. Happy or not, Liu returned the favor by repeatedly praising the chairman's wisdom. Additionally, the Great Leap Forward coincided with indications of escalating tensions between Beijing and Moscow. When Nikita Khrushchev declared at the Moscow conference of communist parties in November 1956 that the USSR would outstrip the industrial production of the United States in fifteen years, Mao promptly asserted that the PRC would surpass Great Britain over the same period. China, it seemed, might not be the equal of the Soviet Union, but it was steadily on the rise.

Yet, for Mao, the Great Leap Forward was more than a platform on which to demonstrate China's economic prowess. Before announcing the new policy, he gave a flurry of speeches in Hangzhou, Nanning, and Chengdu outlining a conception of historical development that went far beyond the straightforward categories of classical Marxism. In Mao's portrayal, revolutionary activity was not a finite event. It was an enduring feature of human existence. In only a few years, he indicated, China had gone through multiple revolutions: the seizure of power in 1949, land reform, collectivization, and the antirightist campaign. A technological revolution was already under way.[24] This was by no means the end of the story. Revolutions would continue on an "uninterrupted" basis, one after the other. In fact, in a draft memorandum to the CCP apparatus Mao subsequently emphasized that they would never cease. Even after the class struggle had come to a conclusion and communism was achieved, people would continue to struggle over ideology, politics, and techniques. It was sheer foolishness to think otherwise.[25]

Additionally, in line with this argument, Mao clarified his understanding of the proper responsibilities of the party cadre. According to this characterization, the function of the archetypical party member at the current stage of China's development, the technological revolution, was to be both "red" and "expert." In their interactions with the masses, Mao explained, "red" cadres should not only address political matters; it was equally important to respond to the needs of ordinary people. By the same token, it was not enough for the "expert" cadre to know about business matters and technology; one needed a firm ideological footing to make the right decisions.[26]

Had Mao stopped here, these expectations would have remained largely in accord with those of Khrushchev and his Eastern European allies; they, too, were seeking to combine their demands that communists have the expertise to function in a complex economy with the expectation that they be stout defenders of the party line. However, the chairman's understanding of what it meant to unify "red" and "expert" was far more ambitious. In Mao's view, the cadre's proper purpose was no less revolutionary than it had been during the Long March. He was to go down to the masses on a regular basis and work alongside them to fulfill the party's goals. This obligation entailed using his experience and insights to assess current practices. He should experiment with new techniques and make recommendations about alternative approaches. It was his duty, if necessary, to eliminate ineffective or erroneous methods.[27]

Concretely, Mao gave life to this spirit of party engagement in a quasi-utopian People's Commune Movement, the central feature of the Great Leap Forward. At an enlarged Politburo conference in August 1958 in the coastal resort of Beidaihe, he announced that China would move toward agricultural self-sufficiency by amalgamating the APCs into massive administrative units that would go far beyond conventional collectivization. In these communes, or "sprouts of communism," as he called them, rural cadres would revolutionize the organization of society. People would eat together in large mess halls where food would be free. Official ranks and wages would be abolished. Everywhere, opportunities would abound for education, child care, and adult leisure. Mao even speculated about such minutiae as the number of airplanes in each province ("a couple hundred"). Of course, party members and their families would live in these communities as well. It was just, he declared, that they should share in the glory.[28]

Concurrently, the cadre's equally vital function in the APCs was to spur production, or in the words of a popular slogan, to produce "more, better, faster, and more economically." Under the CCP's supervision, agricultural workers were exhorted to experiment with new seeding techniques and methods of fertilization, and to use advanced machinery, such as "baby tractors," to increase crop yields. To capture new land for cultivation, they were enlisted to construct gargantuan dams and irrigation canals. To reduce demands on urban industries, they were told to pool their human and material resources and to engage in small, locally based industrial projects. Emblematic of the latter, peasants built hundreds of thousands of primitive backyard furnaces in their villages to forge their own tools and construction materials.

Why could China accomplish these incredible feats when they had eluded the Soviet Union? Mao's answer was characteristically voluntaristic. Unlike the homeland of the revolution, the CCP's cadres were filled with "the communist spirit" as a result of decades of struggle and self-sacrifice. "If human beings only lived to eat," he asked rhetorically, "isn't that like dogs eating shit?" "What meaning is there [to life] if

[you] don't help others a bit, or don't practice a bit of communism?"
The Soviets' mistake, according to Mao, was to assume that the only
way to convince people to do what one wanted was to induce them
with high material rewards or harsh punishments. The Chinese path,
Mao claimed, worked because its leaders understood that people needed
to treat each other as equals and become one in spirit.[29]

The speed with which communization was put into effect was staggering. Within a year, more than 700,000 APCs were consolidated
into approximately 23,000 communes comprising 99 percent of the
rural population. The last vestiges of private property vanished. Looking on from more comfortable conditions in Beijing, Mao and his
colleagues were like many European socialists in the first half of the
nineteenth century. From on high, they wanted to believe that their
experiment would take hold. Thanks to the initial enthusiasm of the
communes' inhabitants, as well as new irrigation projects and favorable weather conditions, the 1958 harvest improved in comparison with
the preceding year. At their root, however, the communes and a host of
equally quixotic experiments to boost agricultural productivity were
deeply flawed, leading to enormous imbalances. To meet exorbitant agricultural targets, rural cadres falsified production statistics. Crops
were neglected as a result of the dispersion of a sizeable portion of the
labor force to build roads and hydroelectric plants. Dramatic population growth in the cities led the government to augment the extraction
of grain from the countryside. Predictably, these hardships led the communes' residents to resent the regimentation of their lifestyles and livelihoods. It was one thing to support the abstract principle of sharing
one's time, talent, and treasure with fellow human beings, but quite
another to accept continuing sacrifices in a time of growing economic
uncertainty. Soon, the dream of harmony in the countryside was punc-
tuated with mutual recrimination and rampant violence.

By spring 1959, even Mao recognized these dysfunctions, just like
Stalin after the initial phase of collectivization. Under the influence of
more pragmatic Politburo members, like Zhou Enlai and Chen Yun, he
was persuaded to begin scaling back the government's unrealistic plan
targets and to allow limited forms of private production in the communes. Nevertheless, this period of moderation was shattered by an

event that threatened Mao's domination of the party. On July 14, 1959, in the midst of a month-long party conference in Lushan, the minister of defense, Peng Dehuai, sent Mao a letter attributing the perilous economic situation to "petty-bourgeois fanaticism," an insult in itself, given the chairman's responsibility for the crisis. The overreliance on mass movements and the attempt "to enter into communism at one step," Peng argued, had "done tremendous harm to the prestige of the party."[30] Notably, the minister was not a disinterested observer; he feared that the Great Leap Forward would weaken the PLA. In response, Mao seized upon Peng's letter as a pretext to force his colleagues to choose for or against him. Should his defense minister be allowed to split the party, Mao threatened chillingly, he would "go to the countryside to lead the peasants to overthrow the government." "If those of you in the Liberation Army won't follow me," he added, "then I will go and find a Red Army and organize another Liberation Army."[31]

This was incredible language. Perhaps to mollify his listeners, Mao feigned an act of contrition. Yes, he conceded, the Great Leap Forward had led to difficulties. Some mistakes, especially the backyard furnaces, were entirely his fault. In this case, he was telling the truth. Households had been stripped of everything from their cooking pots to their door hinges to provide scrap iron for the furnaces. In the end, the quality of steel produced by these methods was so poor that it could never be used. Nonetheless, Mao was unwilling to confuse contrition with an admission of personal defeat. Even Karl Marx, he emphasized, had made mistakes. The founder of the communist movement had initially doubted the Paris Commune, but after further reflection, he recognized that it was the first instance of a true, proletarian dictatorship. Mao admitted that he, too, had been impatient. Two Five-Year Plans would not be sufficient to make the transition to full communism. Still, that day was sure to come, even if it took twenty Five-Year Plans.[32]

INTERREGNUM

It says a great deal about the power of absolute leaders in Leninist systems that it took the unfathomable loss of millions of human lives caused by the Great Leap Forward to force a retreat from Mao's experiment with social engineering. The famine was primarily a rural phenomenon. The death estimates of Western scholars vary, from 30 million to an even more staggering 42 million people. Even Chinese officials estimate that 19.5 million people lost their lives.[33] Due to the government's favoritism toward urban workers, there were far fewer deaths in the cities. But here, too, enormous numbers of people suffered from impossibly high production quotas, and an increase in industrial accidents and criminality brought about by the influx of peasants from the countryside. Overall, China's economic collapse greatly exceeded the extent of the American Great Depression.

Mao refused to admit the catastrophic dimensions of the Great Leap Forward; he even extended the policy an additional year. Yet, after ensuring that Peng Dehuai was replaced as defense minister by another Long March loyalist, Lin Biao, Mao retreated to the isolation of his compound in Beijing, and on rare travels outside the city, hid behind the protective shield of his bodyguards and sycophants. He was oblivious to the horrors the population was experiencing. Concurrently, when senior party figures returned from inspection tours of the countryside with tales of the misery in the communes and popular uprisings broke out in the most calamity-stricken regions, the Politburo turned its attention to rescuing the country. Beginning in 1961, under the direction of Liu Shaoqi, Deng Xiaoping, and Chen Yun, the party's economic expert, Mao's associates unequivocally rejected the economic thinking behind the Great Leap Forward. The regime ordered an immediate reduction of compulsory deliveries from the communes and created new incentives for production by restoring the right to hold small, private plots and sell products in local markets. Correspondingly, it divested local cadres of their right to set production quotas and intervene in matters beyond their competence.

Expressing its desire to assume a hands-off attitude in matters beyond its competence, the regime reduced its emphasis on "redness" by elevating the role of scientific knowledge and expertise in decision making. It raised the level of respect accorded to scientists, engineers, and economists, regardless of their degree of political engagement, and encouraged the cultivation of "expert" values in secondary schools and universities. Naturally, the CCP's leaders had no intention of reawakening the uninhibited criticism of the Hundred Flowers campaign. Still, they relaxed controls over cultural activities and allowed intellectuals to engage in controversial topics, provided that they did not share their views publicly.

Liu Shaoqi and his allies did not regard the effort to project an alternative image of communist leadership as a mere stopgap measure. China's perilous circumstances gave them both the reason to assess the consequences of Mao's conception of an everlasting revolution and the opportunity to shift to a different course. In many ways, Liu and like-minded policymakers resembled Lenin's successors in the 1920s who faced the intractable contradiction between a continuation of War Communism and the necessity of stabilizing the economy and restoring the features of a functioning state. For a distinct historical moment, much like Nikolai Bukharin and, for a time, Stalin, China's moderates chose the latter option.

In fact, the CCP's new course only lasted a few years. But, moving forward, Liu and his allies were emboldened to address two fundamental questions about the CCP's leadership over the preceding years. What responsibility should the party take for the outcome of the Great Leap Forward? What was their supreme leader's role in this debacle? Liu left no doubt about his answer to the first question. In a report to a huge party meeting in January 1962, popularly known as the "Thousand Cadres Work Conference," he took issue with the attempt by Mao's supporters to attribute the Great Leap Forward's failures primarily to adverse weather conditions ("seventy percent") and only secondarily ("thirty percent") to human error. Citing a recent investigative tour of Hunan Province, he reported that peasants had told him that the reverse was the case. China's current predicament was due in large part to the mistakes and shortcomings of individuals, not to the party. Some communists, he observed frankly, had not only shown poor judgment, they were guilty of the greater sin of immodesty. In what must have been intolerable temerity in Mao's eyes, Liu even suggested that Peng Dehuai had been right to raise questions about this behavior. Not long thereafter, Liu called for the rehabilitation of party members who were purged after the defense minister's demotion.[34]

In responding to the second question, no one in the CCP's ruling circle dared to go as far as Khrushchev in attributing blame for the debacle to their leader's personality cult. After all, Mao Zedong, the phenomenon, was an integral component of the party's identity. Also, unlike Stalin, Mao was still breathing. Nevertheless, the Politburo again took steps to deemphasize the chairman's leading role. It informed officials that they no longer needed to adorn every achievement with a tribute to Mao. In support of this position, they were instructed to increase the population's awareness of other thinkers in the Marxist tradition. Accordingly, party propagandists actively disseminated Lenin's works and returned Liu's formulaic tract on party discipline, *How to Be a Good Communist*, to the shelf of required reading. In a major break with past practice, the regime also allowed the distribution of a variety of satirical essays and plays in which Mao was implicitly depicted as, if not flawed, at least a little bit imperfect. The most popular of these was *Hai Rui Dismissed from Office*, by Beijing's deputy mayor, Wu Han. This allegorical play recounted the story of an honorable Ming dynasty official who is unjustly punished by a tyrannical emperor. No one in the audience would have missed the allusion to the conflict between Peng and Mao.

In this context, the task of articulating a revised conception of communist leadership fell to Deng Xiaoping. In his capacity as CCP general secretary, Deng followed Liu's report at the Thousand Cadres Work Conference with a carefully crafted speech about the nature of party rule. The address is revealing because it was neither an overt criticism of Mao nor an endorsement of a return to the revolutionary intensity of the preceding years. Rather, Deng's objective was clearly to find a middle ground that would enable the CCP to become, in his words, what it had ceased to be over the preceding years, "a Marxist-Leninist party worthy of the name."[35]

On the one hand, Deng left no room for doubt about Mao's special place in the Chinese Revolution. The speech is replete with laudatory references to the chairman's teachings. The truth of Mao Zedong Thought, Deng affirmed, had been borne out by history itself. Its guidance and inspiration, and "not that of any other ideology," had led the masses to victory.[36] On the other hand, Deng sought to restore the party's good name by distancing it from the excesses of Maoism. A major shortcoming, in his view, was that the party's leaders had lost sight of the principle of democratic centralism. Some defenders of past policies, he noted, had promoted the idea that the organization's failings were due to excessive centralization. But the opposite was true. Decision-making power had been incorrectly passed down to middle-level cadres who were incapable of making responsible choices. As a result, senior officials had given their blessing to policies ("excessively high targets and absurd deadlines") that had no connection with reality. The key to restoring the population's confidence, therefore, was to establish clear lines of communication from above. Indeed, Deng declared, "when we corrected the mistakes, they said the *real* communist party was back."[37]

In addition to this oblique criticism of Mao's policies, Deng emphasized that the party's leaders had not always earned the trust of their fellow communists, especially those cadres who were capable of making informed decisions. As a consequence, instead of drawing upon Mao's wisdom of "seeking truth through facts," a concept Deng would use to describe his own policies two and a half decades later, they had attempted to solve problems in a simplistic fashion, for example, by encouraging mass movements to wrestle with complex decisions. "It is not good to have movements so frequently," Deng explained. The best way to build confidence was for the party to make good decisions on the basis of facts that are "accumulated bit by bit with great care."[38]

Finally, in a manner that resembled the pronouncements of Stalin's heirs in the 1950s, Deng underscored the primacy of the party over the individual. For the party to fulfill its functions, he stressed that none of its members, even those at the most senior levels, should regard themselves as superior to its rules. "Supervision," he advised, "should be exercised over the party's leaders at all times." One form of control was in the conventional top-down manner. Party committees and their secretaries should routinely scrutinize the decisions of their subordinates. Not surprisingly, the other form was collective leadership or, as Deng called it, "mutual supervision." Under this model, party members should meet on a regular basis and act just like responsible leaders everywhere. They would discuss matters that came before them, engage in acts of criticism and self-criticism, and eventually reach agreement.

Deng did not let on in the speech whether he had specific persons in mind who were guilty of transgressing the principle of collective rule. Still, his listeners would have recognized his primary target. They would also have detected a shift in the degree of respect he accorded his mentor. Although no individual receives greater praise than Mao in the address, Deng singled out Liu's contributions nearly half as many times. In fact, he intimated that the balance of power in the Politburo had changed. Rather than choosing Mao's words for the customary list of tributes at the end of the speech, he turned to the wisdom of the chairman's incipient rival: "Comrade Liu Shaoqi has challenged us to aim high, and let us do as he says."[39]

TOWARD THE CULTURAL REVOLUTION

Deng's address and the tenor of the Thousand Cadres Work Conference provide a compelling image of a China that might have been. To an extent that bore a striking resemblance to the hopeful perspectives of many communists in the Soviet Union in the 1920s, Liu, Deng, and others were convinced that their ideals could be realized through internal debates and the guidance of a party that pursued a gradual approach to building socialism. As in the Soviet Union, however, their dreams were not to be realized. Within a year, they were swept up in an internal party battle over both political power and revolutionary ideas that not only consumed them personally—Liu would die in prison, while Deng was sent to the provinces—but engulfed China in one of the most tumultuous disturbances of the twentieth century, the Great Proletarian Cultural Revolution.

At the center of the power struggle was the status of Mao himself. It was not accidental that the CCP moderates had been able to assert their views. Mao had made their work easy by removing himself from the quotidian business of party life. His attention during this period was largely reserved for the PLA. Yet, around his seventieth birthday in 1963, Mao became increasingly focused on his mortality and the question of who was to succeed him. In the party's upper echelons, Liu was regarded as his most likely heir. Deng confirmed this internal consensus in his Thousand Cadres speech. Mao, however, apparently had a different view. On personal grounds alone, he bridled at Liu's skill in using his growing prominence to assert his views. Mao was also obsessed with his legacy and feared that he would be remembered not as China's liberator and founder of the PRC, but primarily as the instigator of the Great Leap Forward. In fact, the way Khrushchev's successors castigated their former first secretary in 1964 for his "harebrained schemes" gave Mao reason to think that this was precisely what would happen to him.

This air of uncertainty led to the outbreak of an acrimonious, but also richly revealing, conflict between Mao and Liu over the CCP's proper functions. One year earlier, Mao had begun a new campaign, the Socialist Education Movement (SEM), to send investigative work teams into the countryside. The teams' specific charge was to combat corruption and malfeasance among local party organizations by reinstilling discipline and educating them about their responsibilities. As titular head of the campaign, Liu chose to push for internal rectification, forcing party officials to own up to their crimes and mistakes in public criticism sessions. Mao had no objection to Liu's treatment of wayward comrades. However, he became steadily dissatisfied with his deputy's limitation of the SEM to a purely internal party affair. In a flurry of essays and speeches, Mao took Liu to task for failing to see that the greater threat to the party's integrity was represented by revisionists and "capitalist-roaders" within its ranks. In his view, these hidden enemies could only be rooted out if the nonparty masses were incorporated into the campaign. In a display of self-confidence, Liu held his ground and refused to expand the SEM.

This dispute, which formed the ideological nucleus of the coming Cultural Revolution, was no mere battle over conflicting interpretations of the "mass line." Mao and Liu agreed about the party's leading role and the necessity of molding the revolution around the inchoate ideas of a noble population. But Mao soon demonstrated that his intention was not confined to establishing closer ties between the rulers and the ruled. Again, it was to save the idea of the revolutionary party idea from the party organization. On numerous occasions, he evinced contempt for the work teams by dismissing their efforts to revamp the party's image among the peasantry. In his description, local cadres were hopelessly unequipped to win the attention of the poor and lower-middle-class peasants. Instead of taking action, they showed that they would rather spend time reading documents and books. If the revolution were left in their hands, it would take one hundred years to complete. Mao reduced the explanation for their ineptitude to a single factor: "The more books one reads," he argued, "the more stupid one becomes, knowing almost nothing."[40]

In place of the cadres' feeble attempts to anticipate what was required of them, Mao advised that China needed a party that was prepared to get to work. Its representatives should organize mass rallies upon their arrival in the villages. They should listen to the people patiently and learn about the problems of each locale. In Mao's eyes, this approach required the party's members to shed the protective shell of the work teams and engage in struggle sessions over their duties. If some comrades were lazy, they should be made to return to work. If they were dishonest or corrupt, they should be forced to confess their crimes at once.

In this charge, one can find all of the elements for Mao's coming attack on the party in its form as a ruling organization—its overreliance on books, its rigidity, its distance from ordinary people, and its susceptibility to abuse. Nevertheless, Mao could not have instigated the Cultural Revolution of his own volition. To translate his sentiments into practice and to launch an assault on the party establishment, he needed two mutually reinforcing conditions: the active support of others in powerful positions and a population that was open to mobilization. He met the first condition with the help of Lin Biao. Like other Civil War veterans, Lin viewed Liu and Deng's efforts to use the CCP to stabilize the country as a threat to the PLA's status and revolutionary élan. With the help of sympathizers on high, he reinvigorated the role of the Military Affairs Committee in the party apparatus, cultivated closer ties with the security forces, and organized PLA committees in factories and schools. Lin's objective was not to denigrate the party's leading role. Far from it—he purged the PLA of military professionals, replacing them with party activists. Rather, like Mao, he was intent on demonstrating what a return to revolutionary values would look like. In the massive Lei Feng propaganda campaign, based upon a largely fictionalized account of a soldier killed in the Korean War, the PLA presented itself as the champion of moral and political rectitude and discipline. To demonstrate that it was truly a people's army, and not an elitist organization like segments of the CCP, Lin abolished the use of insignia that denoted differences between officers and enlisted persons.

Furthermore, Lin demonstrated his personal dedication to Mao by publishing and disseminating the phenomenally popular *Quotations from Chairman Mao*, and making it required reading for the PLA. The "Little Red Book," as the title became known, was a classic example of mythmaking in its most deliberate form. Actually, it was not a book at all, let alone a manual. It was simply a collection of aphorisms from Mao's speeches and writings that addressed themes as wide-ranging as the class struggle, war and peace, the people's war, and revolutionary heroism. Published in over 1 billion copies, the Little Red Book invited its readers to reflect upon, debate, and put Mao's words into action. It is doubtful that such a compilation of quotations could have provided meaningful guidance to anyone. But this was not the point. The Little Red Book's significance lay in the fact that one could hold it up, as enthusiasts did, as a symbol of Mao's transcendence of any established institution.

In conducting his assault, Mao also had the support of a diverse group of loyalists who had specific reasons for coming to his aid. One, Kang Sheng, a former head of the security police, had been at Mao's side in denouncing Khrushchev's revisionism. Another, Chen Boda, had been with Mao since Yan'an. As editor in chief of the party's theoretical journal, *Red Flag*, he was a fierce defender of Mao's conception of revolution. Zhou Enlai, the premier, was less of a hard-liner but aligned himself with the chairman out of self-interest. Of all of Mao's supporters, the most distinctive was arguably his wife, the actress Jiang Qing. Despite having little experience with politics, Jiang joined Kang Sheng in spearheading a cultural campaign to "purify" art, literature, and musical performance by expunging bourgeois influences. With the assistance of the propaganda department of the Shanghai party apparatus, she pointedly orchestrated an attack on Wu Han, accusing him of using *Hai Rui Dismissed from Office* to distort Mao's teachings about the role of the masses in history.

Complementing these demands for a return to the core values of Maoist ideology were the circumstances in which they came into being. The apocalyptic fury of the Cultural Revolution was driven by widespread discontent among China's citizenry. For reasons that were apparently poorly understood by those persons at the apex of power, the divisions within the party elite fostered conditions under which disparate and frequently antagonistic social groups coalesced in opposition to the regime's policies. The most vocal were the sons and daughters of former capitalists, landlords, and intellectuals who had long been used as scapegoats for the regime's mistakes. As ostensive "bad elements" and "rightists," they had been deprived of opportunities for advancement in the party and military due to the regime's preferential treatment of previously disadvantaged workers and peasants. They were joined by sizeable segments of the urban workforce, such as unskilled laborers, the employees of small enterprises, and temporary workers from the countryside, who were embittered by their low wages and poor job prospects. Overall, Mao's attacks on centralized political authority and bureaucratic practices resonated with many Chinese who believed that they were no longer the beneficiaries of the revolution.

The Cultural Revolution Begins

These circumstances put Mao in the position to receive both what he wanted and, paradoxically, more than he desired. Thanks to the intrigues of his confederates on high and the groundswell of popular support from below, he achieved a state of near deification by the end of the decade. With no one in a position to challenge him, there was little to prevent his obsession with the idea of permanent revolution against the class enemy from penetrating every niche in the apparatus of official policymaking. At the same time, in yet another episode of tragic dimensions, Mao's destruction of the organization, the party, which he considered the greatest impediment to the realization of his goals, deprived his government of the single most important institution for holding the country together. The unforeseen result of his success was the onset of a period of social turmoil that lasted for years and took the lives of between 750,000 and 1.5 million people.[41]

The tumult began with a power struggle. At Mao's request, the Politburo had authorized the formation of a new committee in early 1965 to deliberate over the enactment of a "Cultural Revolution" against the remaining vestiges of traditional thought and practice. The group, chaired by Peng Zhen, a member of the Politburo's Standing Committee and former mayor of Beijing, disappointed Mao by failing to endorse a radical agenda. In a pointed gesture, the body's members came to the defense of Wu Han's play, arguing that his depiction of Hai Rui should be judged by literary standards and not as a political provocation. Clearly, Peng and his allies meant for their statement to be a defense of the rationale behind Liu and Deng's moderate policies. Recognizing this threat, Jiang Qing and Lin Biao marshaled their forces to give Mao his first great victory in the conflict within the leadership. At a meeting in May 1966, Lin led the charge, attacking a nonexistent "antiparty clique" and demanding a purge of revisionist elements in the party. Peng was immediately demoted, and in the ensuing days scores of senior officials in the Central Committee's propaganda and ideology sections were removed from their posts. In short order, the Politburo majority obligingly replaced Peng's committee with a new body, the Central Cultural Revolution Group (CCRG), which was composed entirely of radicals, all of whom, like Chen Boda, its chair, Kang Sheng, and Jiang Qing were beholden exclusively to Mao.

Ominously, the May meeting concluded with a warning that party members who did not line up with the CCRG would suffer Peng's fate. Precisely this development came to pass. In a development that was probably coordinated from on high, Peking University erupted in demonstrations by formerly lower-class students over the disciplining of a radical professor for writing a big-character poster decrying the moderates' favorable treatment of Wu Han. Mao defended the poster, describing it as a "manifesto of the Beijing commune of the 1960s," a clear reference to the Paris Commune of 1871. When the protest spread to other universities and high schools, Liu fought back, dispatching CCP work teams to restore order. However, Mao refused to be upstaged, and ordered their withdrawal.

The fact that Liu sent young party cadres to the schools to contain the protests foreshadowed a nationwide confrontation between the forces of the "new" and the "old." The children of workers and peasants who had benefited most from the CCP's rise to power were pitted against the angry progeny of the former elites. Mao took advantage of these tensions to advocate renewed revolutionary fervor. On August 5, 1966, four days after the opening of a Central Committee plenum, Mao affirmed this stand in a big-character poster affixed to the door of the meeting hall. He called on the student groups to "bombard the head-quarters" and accused "some leading comrades," presumably including Liu, of empathizing with the reactionary policies of the bourgeoisie.

The party plenum proved to be a decisive moment for the articula-tion of the goals of the Cultural Revolution. True to Mao's wishes, the delegates endorsed a declaration of "Sixteen Points" on August 8, which proclaimed in no uncertain terms that the main target of the campaign was "those within the party who are in authority and taking the capi-talist road." According to the statement, some of the worst "bad" elements had wormed their way into the party; others were imprisoned by old thoughts and ways of acting. One could be certain that both would put up stiff resistance to anyone who sought to drive them from power. Ac-cordingly, its authors advised that the masses and those who were on their side, especially the students, should prepare for an impending battle with the enemy.[42]

The "Sixteen Points" declaration is particularly notable because it went beyond the conventional Leninist interpretation of the class struggle. The document only referred to the concept once, and only then in conjunction with Mao Zedong Thought. Rather than address-ing the transformation of class relations during the construction of so-cialism, the authors underscored Mao's loftier vision of transforming human consciousness. The Cultural Revolution's goal, they stressed, should be to create "new ideas, culture, customs, and habits of the proletariat to change the whole of society." To achieve this end, they endorsed the establishment of a multiplicity of grassroots Cultural Revolution groups, committees, and congresses. These supposedly demo-cratic associations were to be set up in every school, enterprise, urban government, and village, where members would criticize established practices and, correspondingly, be subjected to criticism of their own behavior by the masses.

Lest there be any doubt about the significance of this proclamation, the CCRG organized eight massive rallies to confirm Mao's preeminent position. Between August and November 1966, the PLA transported 13 million students from all over China to Beijing to venerate the chairman. In the first rally, on August 18, Mao appeared in military garb atop Tiananmen Gate to greet his youthful army. There he showed his solidarity with their movement by solemnly donning a red armband presented to him by one of the student participants from the so-called Red Guards. With Mao's blessing and Lin Biao's instruction on the same day that they should demonstrate their devotion to their leader by destroying the "four olds" (old customs, culture, habits, and ideas), these young rebels embraced the idea that they were elevating the revolution to an even higher stage than had been envisioned by their grandparents and parents. With the government's assistance, they descended upon cities, towns, and villages in search of "antiparty" elements, reactionaries, and saboteurs. At first, their actions were benign. They wrote posters and renamed streets after revolutionary heroes. But their restraint quickly degenerated into violent confrontations with all forms of authority. With unrestrained zeal, Red Guards crashed into homes and businesses in search of bourgeois property and reactionary literature. They subjected teachers, employers, party officials, and family members to public humiliation, forcing them to confess to preposterous acts of revolutionary infidelity. Many of these supposed enemies of the people were beaten to death; others were driven to suicide.

Toward a Different Revolutionary Order

I have emphasized the Cultural Revolution's degeneration into violence because it demonstrates how difficult it is for the leaders of authoritarian states to foresee—and then control—the consequences of their decisions. Although the CCP had initially been singled out as the primary hiding ground for capitalist roaders and other enemies, the institution's leading role had not been questioned. Moreover, although the moderates' policies had been criticized, their backers, including Liu and Deng, still occupied key positions and, it appeared, would safeguard the party. What these figures could not fully comprehend was the significance of Mao's promotion of a revolution from the ground up. There was no suggestion in the "Sixteen Points" that the uprising of the masses would take the form of student protest. But once Mao and the CCRG had given the rebels permission to attack power holders and institutions and they had gained traction among workers and other disaffected groups, one could not prevent them from focusing their attention on the party establishment. At every level, from the Central Committee apparatus down to factory cells, Mao's supporters subjected party officials to public excoriation and hounded them out of their positions. Once this movement had taken hold, the party's institutional authority could not be won back.

Nevertheless, Mao and his inner circle soon became aware of an unexpected consequence of these protests. In their efforts to build a self-generating revolutionary order, they were forced to recognize that there was a fundamental contradiction between continual revolts from below and the establishment of a new type of social order. In 1967, after the Red Guards splintered into warring factions, even Mao conceded that he had not foreseen the extent of the turmoil. But rather than address the source of the chaos, he initially acted as though one could simply strike a balance between tumult and stability.

When rival workers' associations emerged in Shanghai in fall 1966, Mao seemed to lean toward the primacy of revolution. One group, the Shanghai Workers' General Headquarters, which had the support of student Red Guards and unskilled workers and was backed by the CCRG, demanded the replacement of the provincial government with a dictatorship of the proletariat. The other, the Scarlet Red Guards, composed of older, skilled workers, made conventional demands for higher wages and inclusion in managerial decisions. When these associations came to blows in February 1967, Mao and the CCRG had to decide which of the two "proletariats" they would support. Initially, the radicals had the advantage and declared the formation of a Shanghai People's Commune. For nineteen days, the Commune's leaders maintained, in the same ebullient spirit as the Parisian Communards nearly a century before them, that they were substituting the CCP's organizational features with direct rule by the working class. Yet when the city was convulsed by demonstrations against the experiment, Mao intervened. Arguing that Shanghai's example threatened the country with anarchy, he ordered the Commune's dissolution and enlisted PLA troops to restore order.

Mao's engagement of the PLA in this case might lead one to assume that he had made a self-evident choice for political stability over rebellion. Nevertheless, his handling of an equally violent turn of events in Wuhan in July 1967 showed that he was not so easily judged. Just like in Shanghai, the city was paralyzed by battles among rival Red Guard organizations. Reasoning that there was no alternative to intervention, the commanding general of the region, Chen Zaidao, ordered his troops to take control of the city's industrial sectors and arrest the rebels. Instead of stabilizing conditions, however, these measures precipitated renewed violence. At this point, the CCRG called for the protection of the more radical of the two groups. With the support of Mao, Zhou, and Lin Biao, it dispatched air force and army units to Wuhan to disband the radicals' opponents. They rebuked Chen for his behavior and relieved him of his command.

I am highlighting the events in Shanghai and Wuhan because they provide insight into the extraordinarily complex situation that Mao and his close allies faced in the first years of the Cultural Revolution. They were aware of the limits to the turmoil their country could withstand. Yet even as their country was being thrown into a whirlwind of violence, they were intent upon preserving the anti-institutional thrust of the movement. Mao found the solution to this conundrum by turning away from the Red Guards to a stronger and seemingly more reliable source of power—the armed forces. In fall 1967, he called an official halt to the Cultural Revolution and ordered the PLA to restore order. This was no small development. Mao's decision effectively allowed the military to usurp what little remained of the ruling authority of the CCP.

With a decisiveness that matched its performance in the final years of the Civil War, the PLA systematically set about reestablishing stability by neutralizing the factional struggles that were ripping the country apart. Rather than simply attacking rebel groups, the army formed revolutionary committees in schools, factories, and municipal governments to co-opt Red Guards and other radical elements. These committees were invariably led by military officers, not party officials. Even in its own ranks, the PLA responded with force, attacking factionalism and disciplining soldiers who sympathized with the radicals.

Nevertheless, although references to the term "Cultural Revolution" waned, the PLA showed its determination to remain as "red" as it was "expert" by carrying on the spirit of the movement in practice. Beginning in 1968, it sent millions of young people, large numbers of them Red Guards, to locations throughout China where they were told to gain political enlightenment from the masses. Most were dispatched to the countryside. In untilled lands and never-ending rice fields, they engaged in crippling manual labor while simultaneously undergoing ideological reeducation in struggle sessions. Significantly, they were joined by their former targets, the millions of party cadres, officials, and intellectuals who were judged to be either insufficiently radical or, conversely, too radical for the public good. Simultaneously, the military undertook nationwide "cleansing" campaigns to expose class enemies and counterrevolutionaries.

One might reasonably ask whether, at this point, China was now ruled by the military. At the CCP's Ninth Congress in April 1969, the first such meeting since 1958, 35 percent of the members of the newly elected Central Committee came from the ranks of the military. Moreover, the congress affirmed a revision of the party constitution to designate Lin Biao as Mao's "close comrade-in-arms and successor."[43] But this description of the regime would be misleading. Instead, it is more appropriate to characterize the shift as a militarization of Chinese politics. In fact, multiple personalities, not all of them active in the armed forces, agreed about the necessity of using force to re-ensure the country's passage to socialism. Despite serious differences over political priorities, they shared the conviction that the ultimate source of ruling authority was, or should be, Mao Zedong. Their chairman was the sole link that bound them together and the only person who could protect them from each other.

At the Ninth Congress, Lin had the honor of delivering the political report that transformed Mao from an object of reverence into one of deification. The address, which was partly written by the journalists who had penned the initial attack on Wu Han, was more akin to an epic poem than to a speech. Its subject was the Cultural Revolution's life-and-death battle between the forces of good and evil, and its principal characters were Mao and Liu Shaoqi. On the one side, in Lin's depiction, stood Mao, the rightful successor of Marx, Engels, and Lenin, who had dedicated his life to leading the proletariat and peasantry to war against the bourgeoisie. On the other side stood Liu, recently exposed as a "Hidden Traitor and Scab as far back as the first revolutionary war." The Cultural Revolution represented the highest stage in the confrontation between these contradictory forces. Mao had wisely emboldened the masses to bombard the headquarters of reaction, whereas Liu had sought to confuse them by propagating the fallacy of the demise of the class struggle. Fortunately for the people, Mao had never flinched. Thanks to him, Lin resolutely pronounced, the Cultural Revolution was victorious and China was poised to realize the "grand ideal of communism."[44]

By themselves, these were only words. The PLA and the revolutionary committees systematically translated them into practice by integrating a mythic depiction of the chairman's life into the daily life of the citizen. Under the ensuing "Three Loyalties" and "Four Boundless Loves" campaigns, every segment of the population, from city managers and high school students to factory workers and itinerant peasants, was expected to proclaim their undying loyalty to Mao and love for his revolutionary line. When they woke up in the morning, went to work, and returned home, they were to face the chairman's picture and ask themselves the eternal question: What would Mao do? Through an endless procession of public rituals—parades, mass celebrations, collective recitations from the Little Red Book, and loyalty dances—millions of people voiced the belief that their lives were intertwined under a single, unifying force. Arguably, to a greater extent than ever before, China was unified under a single leader.

The Party Reappears

The fabrication of the cult of Mao Zedong once again testifies to the power of a small group of well-placed persons acting under few institutional constraints to transform an indisputable case of individual charisma into a nationwide reality. Still, Mao's indebtedness to his associates did not compromise his authority. To the contrary, his position was strengthened all the more. Given the fact that multiple factions were jockeying for influence, each depended upon his largesse to further its interests. This dependency put him in a prime position to promote not collective leadership but collective rivalry.

By 1970, there were unmistakable signs that Mao was tiring of the PLA's prominence. It was one thing to insist that political power should control the gun. But given the crucial role of the armed forces in reversing the extremes of the Cultural Revolution, it was another to assume that the military would never overstep its bounds. Thanks to the outbreak of deadly skirmishes with Soviet troops on the Ussuri River in 1969, the PLA was suddenly in the position to do so. Its soldiers' heroism in battle was an enormous boost to its popular prestige. Then, too, Mao's relationship with Lin Biao had become frayed. Mao had begun to perceive his defense minister's longtime promotion of his divinity as a self-serving strategy to enhance his own position. When Lin asserted himself in the Politburo and took issue with Mao on some questions, such as the chairman's unexpected decision to explore an opening of relations with the United States, Mao turned against both him and the military.

Given the rivalries within his inner circle, Mao could count upon the support of opposing leadership factions in making this move. Although the CCRG had been officially disbanded in 1969, its members' relationship with the military was fraught with tension. A different group, with which Zhou Enlai and Chen Yun were associated, viewed a return to full civilian control as essential to national recovery. With the latter's support, Mao returned to a familiar source of leadership: the party. In a matter-of-fact way in summer 1970, he brought the issue of CCP rule back into official discourse. The regime took the first steps toward revitalizing the institution that it had destroyed by setting up provincial party organs to replace the PLA's revolutionary committees. Members of the new organs were still expected to demonstrate their ideological credentials by devoting themselves to the study of Mao Zedong Thought and interacting with the masses, but they were freed of the burden of adhering to their predecessors' transformational goals. Slowly, the CCP apparatus acquired the professional demeanor to which Liu Shaoqi and Deng Xiaoping had aspired before the Cultural Revolution.

Naturally, there was a difference between rebuilding the party organization form and acknowledging its full authority. In an apparently opportunistic gesture of respect for the CCP, Mao rebuked Lin for calling him a genius: "Genius does not depend upon a person or a few people. It depends on a party, the party which is the vanguard of the proletariat."[45] But as Mao showed by turning against Lin, he was determined to prevent any challenge to his preeminent position, whether it came from a person or an organization. Beginning at a party conference in Lushan in September 1970, he attacked Lin for ostensibly seeking to split the party and build an independent power base. One year later, under murky circumstances, Lin was killed in a plane crash, supposedly trying to flee the country after an aborted coup attempt. The real circumstances of Lin's demise may never be known, but there is no mystery to Mao's response. He immediately ordered the removal of PLA officers from prominent party and state positions and their replacement with civilian authorities. At the same time, he allowed Zhou Enlai to undertake the rewriting of recent history to hold Lin responsible for the excesses of the preceding decade. Overnight, the new party line held that the late defense minister had been a leftist all along and the chief advocate of the Cultural Revolution.

However inaccurate these claims may have been, Zhou expertly turned them into the rationale for a period of social and political relaxation. In a manner that resembled the Soviet leadership's de-Stalinization measures, he arranged for the return of party veterans to their former jobs and the rehabilitation of cadres who had been unjustly accused of crimes. His most consequential step was the political rehabilitation of Deng Xiaoping in 1974. Upon his return to Beijing after years spent as a lowly machinist in Jiangxi, Deng was appointed first vice-premier and elevated to the Politburo. Accompanying these moves, Zhou revamped the government's economic priorities. To this end, he outlined a strategy of "Four Modernizations," focusing on industry, agriculture, science and technology, and national defense, that would, in his eyes, fulfill Mao's 1949 vision of making China a major world power by the end of the century. Within a decade, thanks to Deng's return, this goal would be realized!

Zhou's innovations would not have been possible without Mao's acquiescence. Yet, what the chairman gave with one hand, he took away with the other. In a confirmation of his determination to safeguard his revolutionary ideals, he gave his blessing to a renewed, but thematically different campaign against Lin Biao. This time, Mao designated Lin a rightist and likened his views, improbably, to those of Confucius. Mao may not have meant this act of historical revisionism to be interpreted as a criticism of Zhou. However, his suggestion that the greater threat to China's well-being now lay with the moderates presented the radicals in the Politburo, including Jiang Qing, with a final opportunity to assert their opposition to Zhou. They were particularly furious with the premier's decision to allow Deng Xiaoping's return. Their worries were justified. Due to Zhou's declining health, Deng had taken over the premier's functions. Calling for a renewal of the Cultural Revolution, Jiang and her allies lashed back. Denouncing putatively reactionary elements for sullying the party, they organized street demonstrations and factory protests to make their weight felt.

In allowing the radicals this leeway, Mao was undoubtedly searching for a desirable balance between the contending Politburo factions. Thus, he pointedly warned Jiang and three other members against becoming a "Gang of Four." Nonetheless, the popular response to Zhou's death on January 8, 1976, confirmed that the hostilities between the warring factions could not be contained. Only a few days after the premier's funeral, protests broke out in Nanjing and other cities against what the participants perceived to be the regime's tepid commemoration of Zhou's legacy. By early April, this discontent had spread to Beijing where millions of the city's residents visited Tiananmen Square to lay wreaths and paint posters in tribute to Zhou. Stricken by illness and with only six months to live, Mao showed that he had no intention of abandoning the ideals that had motivated him since his days as an agitator in Hunan in the 1920s. He joined the radicals in denouncing these acts as counterrevolutionary and ordered the arrest of tens of thousands of demonstrators.

Amid this crackdown, there was a conspicuous political demotion. Deng Xiaoping was again dismissed from his party and state posts. Yet, in a confirmation that there was still much to be resolved in a regime that was tied so completely to the whims of a single person, he was allowed to retain one significant honor, his membership in the CCP. In the words of an anonymous observer, perhaps Mao himself, the decision was made "so as to see how he will behave in the future."[46] Deng's retention was a significant sign for the party, even in its fallen state. The possibility that he might one day return to prominence showed that there was still a glimmer of life in the institution. Not long thereafter, this possibility became a reality. Mao died on September 9, 1976. Confirming the ebb and swell of the Politburo's internal politics, Jiang and the other members of the Gang of Four were arrested for ostensibly attempting a coup d'état. Deng reentered office ten months later and was soon named Mao's successor. One could only wonder what the return of a party reformer would mean for the restoration of the party's authority.

CHAPTER 11

The Party Comes Back

On November 3, 1967, Leonid Brezhnev was blessed with an opportunity that his predecessor, Nikita Khrushchev, would have relished. As general secretary of the Communist Party of the Soviet Union (CPSU), he headlined the celebrations of the fiftieth anniversary of the October Revolution. In what was, by his normally unimaginative standards, a colorful address to the members of the Central Committee and the USSR Supreme Soviet, Brezhnev gave the party central billing. The victory of the Revolution and the successful construction of socialism, he proclaimed, were the result of the "ideas of the communist party" and a "great triumph of the Leninist general line." There was "not a single major problem" over the past fifty years to which the party had failed to contribute its "wisdom, will, and inexhaustible energy." The battle against the class enemy had been won, the country's backward conditions overcome, and the basic elements of socialism established. Henceforth, the party was poised to act upon a new agenda that would lead to the attainment of communism.[1]

Looking on from his modest home in the countryside, Khrushchev must have taken satisfaction at one aspect of Brezhnev's peroration. As the person directly responsible for shattering Stalin's despotic mystique, he could bask in the restoration of the party's authority. In this sense, Khrushchev's successors owed him a considerable debt. However, Brezhnev did not come to praise his predecessor. He came to supplant him. Far from embracing Khrushchev's populist conception of the party's role, Brezhnev's focus was on the use of the party as an agent of stabilization. In this new, lower-intensity stage of the Soviet Union's evolution, which he called the "developed socialist society," Brezhnev specified that the party's functions were to be understood in organizational, not transformational, terms. Its leaders should intensify their efforts to "help every member of society to better determine his place, his role in the process of communist construction and the place where his talents and responsibilities will yield the best results." In this way, he emphasized, "the party sees to it that even the smallest streams of everyday activity merge harmoniously into a single mighty current."[2]

Scholars often describe the period associated with the general secretary's remarks, roughly between Khrushchev's ouster in 1964 and Brezhnev's death in 1982, as a time of inertia, decay, and disillusionment. In view of the accumulated problems that led to the worldwide crisis in communism of the 1980s and early 1990s, there is undeniable truth to this perspective. The CPSU and the overwhelming majority of its peers ultimately failed to convince both their members and their populations that the status quo was worth maintaining.[3] However, I believe that this perspective can be misleading. It obscures the fact that the early years of Brezhnev's "developed socialism" were a time of notable, if unspectacular, tranquility in at least one part of the communist world—the Soviet Union and its narrow band of Eastern European allies. With the exception of the eight months of far-reaching reforms during Czechoslovakia's so-called Prague Spring in 1968, which were crushed by a Warsaw Pact invasion, and the Polish government's frantic efforts to repair its fractured relations with its citizenry in the early and mid-1970s, these regimes' decisions were rarely dramatic. After the "little Stalins" of the preceding era were replaced, there were no bold proclamations about the future and no radical experiments in countries like Poland, Bulgaria, and the German Democratic Republic (GDR); at most, Hungary's government tinkered around the margins of economic reform. After years of jockeying uneasily between the norms of confrontation and accommodation, these regimes committed themselves to an ethos of sobriety, predictability, and, above all, normalcy. Under the terms of what I call the "Brezhnev consensus," their parties cultivated a tacit understanding with both their populations and their rank-and-file members that was based upon the promise of stable expectations and collective rewards. The party of developed socialism would no longer have an antagonistic relationship with society. Instead, its cadres would work diligently to meet the needs of their populations and provide them with regular improvements in their quality of life. In return, citizens would respect the party's authority and the norms of communist rule.

The communist regimes outside the Soviet sphere were in a different position. Without Moscow lording over every decision, they enjoyed the freedom to decide for themselves how they wanted to build socialism. In these circumstances, powerful personalities emerged to define each of these parties' paths. As we shall see, in some cases, such as Yugoslavia in the 1960s and 1970s and especially in China in the second half of the 1970s, they went significantly beyond the economic boundaries of the Soviet model. In others, however, such as Romania, Albania, and North Korea, leaders manipulated nationalist passions to establish new cults of personality antithetical to the Soviet idea of party rule.

Looking back at these diverse efforts to maintain order in the communist world, one might reasonably credit the Soviet regime and its "small bloc" allies with seriously attempting to preserve some of the international movement's original ideals. In an important way, "developed socialism" meant that their populations could expect to enjoy relatively decent lives. Nonetheless, I shall contend that the primacy of single-party rule made it increasingly difficult to sustain the basic elements of the Brezhnev consensus. Despite the best efforts of socialist planners to modernize their economies, these regimes could not keep up with their citizens' rising expectations. As conditions grew more uncertain, party members undercut their credibility by seeking to insulate themselves from these trials and using their positions to their exclusive benefit.

There was, however, one sign of hope for Western Marxists who still believed that the promise of communism's founding ideals was realizable. In the mid-1970s, the Eurocommunist parties of Italy, Spain, and France seemed poised to assume dominant roles in their respective governments. Yet in the end, they were unable to escape the constraints of an institutional culture that had originally been framed in revolutionary times and made much less sense in robust multiparty democracies.

HUNGARY COMES FIRST

The first instantiation of developed socialism did not come to the country at the center of the communist revolution. It came to Hungary. When one considers the circumstances in which Janos Kádár and the other leaders of the renamed Hungarian Socialist Workers' Party (HSWP) found themselves after the crushing of the 1956 Revolution, this development makes sense. Imre Nagy's successors were hated by a majority of Hungarians who viewed them as traitors to the nation. Furthermore, the HSWP had few followers. The party had been eviscerated by mass defections and postinvasion purges. Of the party's 871,497 members in August 1956, fewer than 40,000 remained in December.[4]

In seeking to devise a formula for establishing their authority, Kádár and his associates faced a conundrum. They were determined to guarantee that there would never again be room for questioning the party's leading role or the existence of socialism. It was also essential to reassure Moscow that Hungary's loyalty to the Warsaw Pact was guaranteed. Yet, they were also acutely aware that they needed to convey these messages in ways that would not totally alienate their citizenry.

In the years immediately following the uprising, the HSWP emphasized the first agenda. Although its actions never came close to the ferocity of Mátyás Rákosi's terror, the regime nevertheless concentrated on eliminating the remaining threats to its power. "If the counterrevolution sticks its nose out of its maggot hole," Kádár announced in February 1957, his government would "strike [it] right away."[5] Thus, the regime swiftly suppressed independent workers' councils and writers' associations, cracked down on independent media, and ordered the arrest and prosecution of purported enemies of socialism. By 1961, tens of thousands of people had been removed from their jobs, 13,000 had been sent to internment camps or imprisoned, and 341 had been executed.[6] The HSWP paid special attention to its own ranks. Although few of the party's new leaders could legitimately be described as Stalinists—Kádár himself had been arrested and tortured under Rákosi's rule—this did not prevent them from designating "revisionism" the greatest threat to Hungarian socialism. The regime imprisoned thousands of party members for allegedly harboring counterrevolutionary and "Titoist" sympathies. In a dramatic move in February 1958, Kádár ordered the trial of nine former members of the Hungarian government; four of them, including Imre Nagy, were subsequently hanged.

In light of these measures, one can readily appreciate the difficulty Kádár and his inner circle faced in restoring any semblance of normalcy. Still, they skillfully played two features of Hungary's postrevolutionary environment to their advantage. One might be called "the Soviet excuse." Given the more-than-hypothetical possibility that the Soviets would use military force again if they felt their interests were threatened, they conveyed the message that the HSWP had no choice but to adhere to Moscow's commands. In this respect, they intimated, the party and the population were bound together by a common constraint. The leaders' other advantage was that the party's depleted numbers allowed them to build the organization anew. To this end, they recruited tens of thousands of new members who welcomed the challenge of moving beyond the extremes of Rákosi's and Nagy's rules and were confident that they could win the hearts and minds of their alienated compatriots.

On these bases, Kádár skillfully crafted a message to both his citizens and his fellow party members that anticipated Brezhnev's theme of developed socialism. In the late 1950s, he signaled his desire to move forward along a path of social reconciliation. To reassure onlookers about his good intentions, he pushed through the de-Stalinization measures that Rákosi had refused to implement. The regime rehabilitated prominent figures who had been persecuted before 1956 and proclaimed a general amnesty for political prisoners. Correspondingly, the HSWP expelled Rákosi, Ernő Gerő, and numerous other Stalinists from its ranks. It also announced that aggressive socialization measures, such as the collectivization of agriculture, would be slowed down.

Kádár's most evocative gesture was his enunciation of a new way of understanding the break with the Stalinist past. Invoking a biblical theme, he reversed his predecessors' confrontational definition of the HSWP's functions: "Whereas the Rákosiites used to say that those who are not with us are against us," he wrote in the HSWP daily *Népszabadság* on January 21, 1962, "we say whoever is not against us is with us."[7] This phrase, which Kádár would repeat throughout his years in office, is revealing both for what he did and did not say. On the one hand, he did not say that the HSWP's leading role could be questioned. In fact, his choice of the distinguishing term "us" confirmed that there was still an essential gap between those who were in the party and those who were not. On the other hand, he clearly wanted to change the party's understanding of its mission. As he explained in a speech one month later, one could hardly "live on a war-footing" with fellow Hungarians who happened to have different points of view. An uncompromising stand was only necessary against the small minority who sought to overthrow socialism. Otherwise, Kádár indicated, the HSWP's duty was to show its citizens that it was worthy of their trust. It should "work as hard as if there were 20 parties in Hungary and we had to win votes by secret ballot every day."[8]

Simultaneously, Kádár signaled that the times of internal confrontation within the HSWP were over as well. After removing senior members who stood in the way of his policies, the general secretary pointedly promoted a culture of stability and predictability. From the early 1960s onward, turnover throughout the party's ranks plummeted, especially within its highest echelons. In addition, although no one would have questioned Kádár's desire to maintain his leading position in the party, he showed that he was made of different stuff than Khrushchev. He promoted an atmosphere of collective leadership, making a practice of visibly delegating power in major policy decisions. In the 1960s, the names of other senior figures were frequently conjoined with his own.

In 1962, the party's culture tsar, György Aczél, took the lead in advancing a policy, known as the "Three T's," that went even further than Kádár's simple we-versus-they dichotomy. He advised artists and intellectuals that the government would actively "support" (támogat) those whose work conformed to Marxist-Leninist standards; it would "tolerate" (tűr) the production of those who were not at odds with these principles; and it would "forbid" (tilt) behavior that was antithetical to socialism.[9] Simultaneously, under the direction of the Secretariat's head of economic affairs, Rezső Nyers, the regime introduced economic reforms focused on raising living standards ("goulash communism," as the policy was popularly known) and strengthening Hungary's competitive position in foreign markets. Under Nyers's direction, enterprises were given greater leeway in meeting production targets and, in some industries, market mechanisms were introduced to inform investment strategies. All along, Kádár emphasized that there would be no compromise on the party's role in setting economic priorities. Still, these reforms, which were subsequently known as the "New Economic Mechanism," testified to how far Hungary had come since 1956. They quickly established the country's reputation as the preeminent source of economic innovation in the Soviet bloc.

THE SOVIET UNION COMES NEXT

When Brezhnev and the CPSU's other leaders enunciated the principles behind the idea of developed socialism in the years after Khrushchev's ouster, they did so in a much less dramatic way than Kádár. Their approach was hardly surprising since they did not need to rebuild a functioning government or regain the trust of an embittered population. Instead, they aimed to make a statement about what the Soviet Union had already achieved. In their view, the tumult of Khrushchev's rule—the "ostentatious ballyhoo and boasting, paper shuffling and rashes of meetings, petty tutelage over economic bodies and incompetent interference in their activities, administration by fiat and command-giving"—had obscured an indisputable fact: the USSR was already a great power at the time of Stalin's death.[10] Under the party's tutelage, their government had successfully built socialism, played a decisive role in the defeat of Germany, and established the Soviet Union as the equal of major powers like the United States, Great Britain, and France.

It was no accident that Khrushchev's successors held these views. Most were born a decade later than Khrushchev. Their formative experiences were not rooted in the early stages of the Revolution but in their country's extraordinary growth in the 1930s. Thus, they understandably took pride in their contributions as party members to this period of social and economic transformation. Brezhnev, the CPSU's first secretary (soon to be called general secretary) had been a military commissar and regional party leader; Alexei Kosygin, the prime minister, was an industrial manager; Nikolai Podgorny, who replaced Anastas

Mikoyan as chairman of the Presidium of the Supreme Soviet, was a career party functionary. Having lived through the Terror, these cautious personalities had no romantic ideas about Stalin. They wanted to continue their country's steady progress toward fulfilling the promise of socialism.

As a result, the essence of the Brezhnev consensus, as it evolved over the second half of the 1960s and into the 1970s, was to present an image of constancy and competence. Unlike Hungary's leaders who had to overcome the animosity of a hostile population, Brezhnev and his associates concentrated on gaining the confidence of their fellow party members. The Politburo's appointment of three different individuals, a "troika," to hold Khrushchev's state and party posts was meant to signal that it would pay more than lip service to the principle of collective leadership. Although Brezhnev positioned himself to become the most powerful figure in this circle by taking advantage of the Secretariat's appointment powers, he was never more than a first among equals. As party chief, he weighed in on the introduction of new policies. For example, in 1966–1967 he engaged in an extended battle with Kosygin over the merits of the centralization of the planning process and the relative priorities of defense spending and consumer goods production. Also, in the interest of conveying the image of unity at the top of the party hierarchy, the CPSU's leaders were willing to grant the general secretary the accoutrements of senior status. For example, Brezhnev's public speeches were carefully crafted to ensure that he received an appropriately high amount of applause. But this was not the cult of personality that had infused Stalin's or even Khrushchev's rule. In setting priorities, a majority of the Politburo's members would have rebelled had he attempted to impose his views with no consideration of their interests.

Of equal consequence, the CPSU's leaders were intent upon affirming the prestige of party membership. Brezhnev informed the rank and file that there would be no doubt about their central role in building the "state of the whole people." To belong to the party was a high honor. Each of them, he averred, showed that it was possible for people with talent to "not only think as one but also act as one." Naturally, to belong to this special club they had to prove themselves worthy. The party would "hold each one responsible for the task entrusted to him and stringently penalize any violation of party or state discipline." But to those who were chosen to represent the highest of causes, these expectations were an integral part of the institution's appeal. Assuming that they lived up to this standard, each would enjoy the privilege of leading the fight for the "creation of a socialist society."[11]

In return for party members' dedication, the CPSU leadership offered predictability. It dismantled the division of regional party offices into separate industrial and agricultural units that had taken place under Khrushchev. The experiment had not only proven to be an administrative nightmare but also threatened the party's claim to be a unified actor, raising the possibility of creating two different classes of party membership that would undermine its cadres' careers. In a related gesture, the Politburo dissolved the so-called party-state control committees that Khrushchev had established to monitor the performance of party and government officials.

In his report to the CPSU's Twenty-Third Congress in March 1966, Brezhnev was quite frank about this focus on stability. He condemned his predecessor's "unwarranted shuffling and replacement of cadres."[12] Under a new rubric, "trust in cadres," the regime reduced turnover rates at nearly every level of the CPSU hierarchy. The leadership's commitment to job security was particularly evident in the Central Committee. Whereas Khrushchev had overseen the replacement of 50 percent of the body's members at the Twenty-Second Congress in 1961, that figure dropped to 27 percent in 1966. At the Twenty-Sixth Congress fifteen years later, only 22 percent of the members of Brezhnev's Central Committee were replaced. In fact, the lot of those at the party's highest levels was even better. Thanks to the largesse of Khrushchev's successors, not a single member of the CPSU Politburo or Secretariat failed to be reelected in 1981. The same patterns of extraordinary stability could be found throughout the *nomenklatura* and the halls of the state ministries.[13]

Complementing this focus on internal stability, the Brezhnev consensus was based upon the cultivation of a tacit understanding with Soviet citizens. In return for their acceptance of the proposition that the party was working on their behalf—another form of "trust in cadres"—the regime would address their concerns in a conscientious and responsible fashion.[14] Although this commitment was never as far-reaching as the comparable gestures in Hungary, the Soviet man and woman on the street experienced a noticeable improvement in their quality of life in the late 1960s. Coveted consumer goods, such as refrigerators and television sets, were more plentiful and citizens bene-fited from large-scale investments in apartment construction. As aver-age wages rose, workers were able to take advantage of better-stocked stores. The regime also showed a willingness to tolerate the country's "second economy" as a provider of scarce goods and commodities.

Yet, here too, Brezhnev and his colleagues did not need to approach the idea of developed socialism with the same degree of openness to new ways of thinking as their Hungarian counterparts. In their eyes, the fact that the USSR had already achieved a high level of develop-ment meant that their citizens should naturally appreciate the benefits of life under socialism. To this end, they conspicuously avoided Khru-shchev's penchant for making bold predictions about the communist future. Instead, they embraced a new socialist norm: the "Soviet way of life." No mere appeal to material self-interest, this strategy underscored the distinctive features of life under socialism—full employment, free health care, and high-quality education—and exalted Soviet military strength and national pride. The leadership's message was simple and straightforward. Although it might take decades for their country to catch up with the material prosperity of the capitalist world, Soviet citi-zens could take satisfaction in their ability to compete with its adver-saries in the construction of a just and morally superior society.

Conversely, the Brezhnev regime showed that it was prepared to punish anyone who called into question the foundations of these achieve-ments. Unlike in Hungary, where party officials felt the need to tolerate some forms of independent expression, it showed little hesitation in repressing writers and intellectuals who were deemed to have crossed the fine line between being "with us" and "against us." It is debatable whether the CPSU's authority was seriously threatened by these critics. Among the dissidents whom it targeted, relatively few could be called out-and-out opponents of communist rule. Most, like the writers Andrei Sinyavsky and Yuli Daniel, were products of the government's own de-Stalinization measures. Furthermore, aside from exceptional figures like Alexander Solzhenitsyn who enjoyed a worldwide reputation, few were well known outside their intellectual circles and their complaints were too diffuse to have a nationwide impact. Rather, the regime's measures reflected the psychology of a ruling elite that felt that its beneficence should be rewarded with unquestioned compliance with its policies.

Czechoslovakia Goes Too Far

To the contemporary observer, it might appear as though one can draw a straight line between the dramatic reforms of Czechoslovakia's Prague Spring in 1968 and the Kremlin's decision to use military force to topple its government. Yet, this conclusion would not only be incorrect, it would prevent us from appreciating the considerably more interesting challenges that Moscow's "small bloc" allies faced in the 1960s. Unlike in Hungary, where Kádár and his coleaders had been forced into reform, most of the other communist leaders, such as Antonín Novotný in Czechoslovakia, Walter Ulbricht in East Germany, and Władysław Gomułka in Poland, were still imbued with the combative mentality of Stalinism. It was by no means obvious to them how or to what extent they should modify their policies to accord with the changed attitudes in Moscow.

Czechoslovakia's communist regime epitomized this uncertainty. In the first half of the 1960s, Klement Gottwald's successor as president and first secretary of the Communist Party of Czechoslovakia (CPC), Novotný, took a consistently cynical approach to the Soviet calls for de-Stalinization. In the judgment of the country's future foreign minister, Jiří Hájek, his policies were replete with "absolute halfway measures."[15] On some occasions, Novotný had raised hopes that he would finally break with the past. In 1962, he dynamited the enormous Stalin monument that overlooked Prague and removed Gottwald's embalmed remains from their mausoleum. Yet, on the matters that counted most, Novotný did little. He refused to consider any but the most limited rehabilitation measures of the victims of the CPC's purges and attributed past injustices to the personal defects of his predecessors. Novotný's desultory handling of a deepening economic crisis was even more divisive. After a precipitous drop in national income, he formed a commission under the direction of a prominent economist and Central Committee member, Ota Šik, to explore ways of modernizing the economy. However, when the body recommended significant changes in economic planning and administration, he instructed his ministers to water down the subsequent measures to the point where they were barely distinguishable from existing policy.

Novotný's domination of the CPC might have continued had he not provoked an open conflict with party moderates in October 1967 over the proper function of Leninist leadership. Acting on a report by the head of the party's Ideological Commission, Jiří Hendrych, which warned against any further experimentation, Novotný demanded that the entire party fall into line. To the first secretary's surprise, his critics fought back. Alexander Dubček, the leader of the CPC's Slovak section, emerged as their natural spokesperson. Making the case for a regenerated style of party leadership, he maintained that the CPC's function was to lead the people, not to immerse itself in every aspect of governance. To this end, Dubček argued, the party only needed to take advantage of the broad experiences of its members, while allowing the state to implement its promises.[16]

These were appealing terms. What gave them substance was Brezhnev's decision to intervene in the conflict. At first, he sided with Novotný's defense of the status quo. But after he became aware of the depth of the CPC's divisions, he shifted to the side of the reformers, demanding that Novotný turn over to Dubček his most important post of first secretary. From the start, Dubček was determined to carve a new path for his country, but he had no intention of emulating Imre Nagy. Accordingly, on February 22, 1968, he took the opportunity provided by the twentieth anniversary of Czechoslovakia's imposed "February Revolution" of 1948 to assure his Soviet allies that he would defend the CPC's vanguard role. In his eyes, the pressing issue was simply "how to enforce the leading role of the party more effectively in the existing conditions of socialist construction."[17]

In my view, the terms according to which Dubček made this commitment could not have been more significant. They explain why Brezhnev and his associates allowed the regime to undertake one of the most innovative attempts in communist history to resolve the contradiction between the use of the party as a tool of domination and its employment as a tribune of the people. In April 1968, the CPC published an Action Program that provided a distinctively Czechoslovak answer to this dilemma. Reading it today, one is immediately struck by its authors' aspirations to think in big ways about an institution, the party, which in their view had yet to fulfill its promise. Echoing Dubček's remarks the preceding October, the Action Program informed its readers that the CPC's founders had never meant for it to become a "universal caretaker" to monitor the implementation of every directive and speak for every social group. This focus had repeatedly prevented state and societal institutions from meeting their responsibilities in the past. By trying to do too much, the party had lost credibility. To regain its authority, the CPC needed to return to its original mission of "arousing socialist initiative, showing the ways and real possibilities of communist perspectives, and winning over all workers."[18]

To this end, the Action Program's recommendations were notably concrete. For example, its authors recommended that the rubber-stamp National Front (the umbrella organization overseeing the trade unions, youth organizations, and the post-1948 bloc parties) be given greater autonomy to stimulate popular engagement in the day-to-day business of socialist governance. Rather than limiting the agency's functions to implementing the party's commands, the authors suggested that the National Front be used to ensure that the insights of workers, intellectuals, and other social groups would percolate their way up to the top policy-making bodies. In the process, the CPC's authority would not be undermined, it would be enhanced. Using the same reasoning, the Action Program advised the party to get out of the business of economic management. This task, it specified, was best left to the state ministries; only these organs were equipped to make responsible decisions. In cultural policy, too, the Action Program recommended that once the CPC had set the tone for the "the humanistic and democratic character of socialism," it should "step back and allow the forces of creativity free rein."[19]

Looking back years later with the knowledge that Moscow would use these statements to justify its invasion, the author of the political section of the Action Program, Zdeněk Mlynář, lamented the decision to include the National Front in the document. In Mlynář's view, the references to the noncommunist bloc parties were guaranteed to antagonize anyone who was suspicious of the regime's intentions.[20] However, I believe that such retrospective judgments are misleading. They prevent us from appreciating the most revealing aspect of the Action Program. Unlike Nagy in 1956, Dubček and his fellow reformers, including Mlynář, had not proclaimed an end to the principle of single-party rule. They were wrestling with the same difficulties that had bedeviled communists from the early Bolshevik debates onward. There was no hard and fast boundary between acceptable and unacceptable attempts to reform Leninism.

For this reason, the ultimate test of doctrinal purity was reduced to the mundane issue of maintaining political stability. In much the same way that Nagy had provided room for independent thinking twelve years earlier, the Action Program inspired diverse segments of Czechoslovak society to test the limits of official policy. Student groups, trade unions, and churches confidently explored new agendas. Newspaper publishers exposed political scandals and corruption. No development had a greater impact than the publication of the "Manifesto of 2,000 Words" on June 27. Authored by the writer Ludvík Vaculík, and cosigned by sixty writers, scientists, journalists, and even a few Central Committee members, the "Manifesto" was meant both to support Dubček and to embolden him to defend the party's new course. It praised the first secretary for his bold convictions but warned that the reforms were in danger of being reversed by the same antidemocratic forces that had suppressed them in the past.

Notably, the authors of the "Manifesto" made a point of not questioning the party's authority. Instead, they called upon their readers to speak up for the cause of humanizing socialism. In these respects, the "Manifesto" was arguably more cautious than the Action Program. It was distinctive, however, in one key respect. It was produced outside the party's purview. As a result, both it and similar expressions of social discontent fueled a debate within the CPSU Politburo about whether Dubček should be allowed to remain in office. One topic was theoretical: At what point did justifiable efforts to revitalize a communist party's leading role spill over into its extinction? Because the answer to this question was dependent on context, Brezhnev and his colleagues were put into the difficult position of any public official who is asked to describe an indefinable offense. At best one could say, "You know it when you see it." The other question was immediate and concrete. If the CPC's first secretary and his coleaders were no longer able to safeguard their exclusive right to set their country's priorities, could they still be counted upon to defend Soviet interests?

Despite heated disagreements among Soviet leaders and those of fraternal parties, like Ulbricht and Gomułka, Brezhnev initially stood up for Dubček, gambling on his ability to defuse the CPC's feuding factions. Nevertheless, by August he concluded that his Czechoslovak protégé was no longer up to the task. On August 20, Soviet and other Warsaw Pact troops moved into Czechoslovakia to put an end to the Prague Spring.

THE OPPONENTS OF REFORM

The Soviet Union's use of force against the Dubček regime provides a stimulating opportunity to distinguish between the old and the new. The old is that Moscow had already used its military might against a wayward ally, Hungary, in 1956. The rationalization for the decision in 1968, known as the "Brezhnev doctrine," was largely the same as that which the Kremlin had used twelve years earlier. The Czechoslovak government, the argument went, had forfeited its sovereignty by deviating from Leninist principles and transgressing the vital interests of the world proletariat.[21] Brezhnev made the point succinctly in November 1968. "When external and internal forces hostile to socialism try to turn the development of a given socialist country in the direction of restoration of the capitalist system," he maintained, "when a threat arises to the cause of socialism in that country ... this is no longer merely a problem for that country's people, but a common problem, the concern of all socialist countries."[22]

The new factor is that unlike Imre Nagy and his supporters, the Soviet Union's leaders and a majority of their Czechoslovak counterparts did not disagree about the importance of taking measured approaches to the construction of socialism. Brezhnev explained three years later at the CPSU's Twenty-Fourth Congress in March 1971 that Lenin himself had anticipated developed socialism in 1918. The sacrificial labors of the Soviet people had shown that "the material and technical base" for the transition to communism could be laid.[23] The difference between Czechoslovakia and other countries within the "small bloc"— such as East Germany and Poland, which I shall explore in this section— was that although these states' leaders faced similar challenges in the 1960s, they were considerably less open to new ideas than their peers in Prague.

By the 1970s, the GDR had become a model of what its leaders called "actually existing socialism." However, due to East Germany's location at the epicenter of the East-West conflict, their path to this consensus was unusually difficult. With the exception of unresolved issues involving Poland's boundary, none of the GDR's allies had to face questions about their territorial integrity. Even more daunting, none of them had to compete for their citizens' sympathies with a bourgeois-capitalist state, the Federal Republic of Germany, which boasted a significantly higher standard of living and extensive personal freedoms.

Given these circumstances, it is easy to appreciate why Ulbricht and his fellow leaders maintained the combative spirit that had defined the policies of the Socialist Unity Party (SED) in its early years. The Western powers' refusal to recognize the GDR's sovereignty, they argued in good Marxist terms, was proof that only unflinching vigilance against the "class enemy" would ensure the survival of socialism on German soil. Hence, they emphasized that one could not expect a letup in the class struggle until the GDR's right to exist was recognized.

Paradoxically, the SED's ability to make this case was facilitated by the ultimate act of weakness. On August 13, 1961, the regime began the construction of the Berlin Wall to halt the unremitting flight of East German citizens to West Berlin. One is hard-pressed to imagine a more dramatic illustration of a ruling party's failure. Ulbricht admitted as much: "No one can say that we enjoy having barbed wire."[24] Yet, for the first time, he and his colleagues had a literally captive audience. Given the population's inability to leave the country and the SED's determination to enforce its commands, ordinary East Germans had little choice but to accommodate themselves to their fate.

For these reasons, the Wall was a boon to Ulbricht's domination of the SED. More than anyone else in the party, he could take credit for the GDR's survival. Accordingly, he applied himself to the construction of socialism with the same ideological conviction and aversion to compromise that he had acquired during the turbulent times of the Weimar Republic. At first, some of his policies appeared to be innovative. Even before Kádár, he empowered a team of economists in 1962 to explore the possibility of reforming the GDR's planning system. Similarly, between 1963 and 1966, he opened the Wall just enough to allow thousands of West Berliners to visit relatives in East Berlin. But in every instance, Ulbricht was a source of disappointment. In the first case, he frustrated planning officials by sharply circumscribing the extent of economic reform. In the second, he deflated his population's hopes for expanded freedom of movement by making unrealizable demands of the West.

By the end of the decade, a growing number of Politburo members had come to the conclusion that their general secretary's "absolute half-way measures" (to quote Jiří Hájek's observation about Antonín Novotný) proved that he had lost touch with the GDR's actual conditions. As if to confirm this assessment, Ulbricht was increasingly prone to making the exaggerated proclamations that had characterized Khrushchev's tenure. He predicted that East Germany was on track to exceed West Germany's production of basic goods and commodities. This achievement and countless other successes, he declared, would lead to the birth of a new "socialist nation."

Most likely, the internal opposition to Ulbricht would have taken longer to coalesce had it not been for a major shift in Soviet foreign policy. In the late 1960s, Moscow went around the GDR to begin four-power negotiations over the status of Berlin and to initiate contacts with West Germany over improved bilateral relations. Quite rightly, Ulbricht viewed this change of course as a threat to his all-or-nothing conception of interactions with the capitalist world. Invoking his roots in the German communist movement, he suggested that he was the servant of a higher cause than the Kremlin's wishes. He informed his allies that the GDR was on the verge of making the "transition to communism."[25] While attending the CPSU's Twenty-Fourth Congress in

April 1971, he asserted rank over Brezhnev. Citing a fleeting acquaintance with Lenin, he claimed that even the "Russians" (a derogatory reference in itself) had "things to learn."[26]

Ulbricht's defiant behavior made it easy for the Soviet and East German Politburos to reach an agreement on forcing him out of office. The departure of this venerable communist on May 3, 1971, not only marked the removal of a personality who embodied the Stalinist temperament. Just as importantly, it signified the acceptance of the logic of developed socialism. Ulbricht's successor, Erich Honecker, underscored this point. In a lengthy address to the SED Central Committee on the day his predecessor's ouster was announced, he advised his listeners that the party would henceforth be guided by the slogan, "To learn from the Soviet Union is to learn to be victorious." The CPSU, Honecker affirmed, had established the "general line" for every proletarian party in the world. Accordingly, the CPSU's directives would have "general theoretical and political validity for the SED in living up to its responsibility to shape the developed socialist society in the GDR."[27]

The new general secretary and his coleaders lived up to this pledge. In words that could have easily been mistaken for Brezhnev's, they instructed their cadres that the SED's policies were grounded in collective leadership and stable routines. The all-around promise of socialism, they asserted, would not be realized in a day. Building a better society was a long-term process that required patience, sobriety, and the readiness to accept cautious approaches to complex problems. Thus, instead of mimicking Ulbricht's assurances of glorious times on the horizon, the SED presented itself as a servant of the public good. It appealed to the population in down-to-earth terms, stressing values that the average man or woman could readily comprehend. Because of its citizens' acute awareness of the higher living standards in West Germany, it particularly emphasized the advantages of socialism over capitalism, including the maintenance of law and order and the provision of fitting rewards for hard work.

In many ways, the Polish United Workers' Party (PUWP) would undertake a similar redefinition of its functions in the early 1970s. But to an even greater extent than the SED, its leaders had to contend with the will of an individual, Władysław Gomułka, who viewed himself as his nation's savior. In standing up to Khrushchev in 1956, Gomułka had won enormous goodwill from both the party elite and the Polish population. In the first years after this confrontation, it looked as though he would take advantage of this opportunity. He halted collectivization, promised to punish police officials for the abuse of power, and released thousands of political prisoners, including Poland's primate, Stefan Cardinal Wyszyński. He even experimented with multicandidate elections to the country's rubber-stamp parliament, the Sejm. Yet hopes that Gomułka would take these steps even further collapsed at the end of the 1950s. To an extent that was profoundly demoralizing to many of his supporters, he singled out the PUWP for attack. He likened putatively "revisionist" elements in the organization to "tuberculosis" and, in contrast to Khrushchev, declared that Stalinists were no worse than the flu. Confirming his step backward, he denounced his critics for diverging from the socialist cause.

Gomułka's refusal to consider anyone his equal made it impossible for the PUWP to establish an autonomous profile. Yet, in an attempt to guarantee his authority, Gomułka took a step that inadvertently destabilized Polish society and led to his downfall. Rather than promoting a consensual atmosphere within the Politburo, he sought to augment his stature by playing party factions against each other. One group, the so-called Partisans, was composed of former underground fighters who were wedded to Stalinist values. Passionately nationalistic and intolerant of political diversity, they faulted Gomułka for not doing enough to defend the country's sovereignty against Moscow. A second group, known as the "Technocrats," was composed of pragmatically minded functionaries, such as the popular Silesian party chief Edward Gierek, who pressed their colleagues to be more responsive to popular demands. A final group was composed of younger, midlevel cadres, engineers, and scientists who chafed at the underutilization of their skills and expertise.

Had Gomułka been able to maintain a balance of power among these factions, he might have solidified his position. However, by the mid-1960s, successive domestic crises forced him to take sides. Following the outbreak of the Arab-Israeli Six-Day War in June 1967, he supported a wave of anti-Semitic attacks by the Partisans. There was no love lost between Gomułka and the instigator of this campaign, Interior Minister Mieczysław Moczar. But because one of the purposes of the Partisans' offensive was to remove Jewish communists from senior leadership positions, Gomułka evidently calculated that he needed to curry the support of those who replaced them. The anti-Semitic campaign had barely reached its peak when Gomułka was confronted with an eruption of protest by students and professors at the University of Warsaw in support of Dubček's reforms in Prague. When the protestors demanded that the PUWP consider similar reforms, Gomułka ordered the police to use brute force against the demonstrators and purged the university's faculties.

An even more consequential crisis emerged over a precipitous economic downturn at the end of the decade. To counter a sharp decline in industrial production and growing food shortages, planning officials convinced Gomułka to freeze wages at the current levels, limit productivity bonuses, and even allow for layoffs. In less turbulent times, these measures would have led to a public outcry. But the regime made the situation worse in December 1970 by announcing substantial increases in the prices of consumer goods. Coming just days before Christmas, the news threw the country into chaos. Dockworkers in the northern port cities of Gdańsk, Szczecin, and Gdynia took to the streets. Party offices were set ablaze and protests spread to other urban centers. Confirming his recognition of his regime's failures, Gomułka ordered the army to crush the protests. Hundreds of demonstrators were killed and thousands injured.

Just like in East Germany only half a year earlier, Brezhnev and his coleaders did not need to be convinced that Gomułka was no longer fit to rule. On this occasion, conveniently, they did not have to risk the incendiary consequences of military intervention. On December 14, Gomułka's opponents forced their first secretary to resign and selected Gierek to replace him. No sooner had Gierek entered office than he announced his intention to restore the PUWP to its rightful place. After removing Gomułka's Partisan supporters, he followed Brezhnev's example by committing himself explicitly to collective decision making. To regain the support of the party's rank-and-file members, he charged them with the straightforward task of satisfying the population's material needs.

As Gierek soon discovered, however, the Polish population's deeply engrained distrust of its rulers meant that there was a problem with defining the PUWP's functions in service terms alone. When he hesitated to act on all of the workers' demands from the December protests, activists staged a coordinated strike in the Gdańsk shipyards. Gierek rushed to the city to appeal to the protestors for patience. "Help me, help me," he pleaded, "I am only a worker like you. . . . But now, and I tell you this in all solemnity as a Pole and as a communist, the fate of our nation and the cause of socialism are in the balance."[28] Most likely, many protestors did not care whether Gierek considered himself a good communist. But, for the moment, he made his appeal to national solidarity credible by revoking the planned wage freeze and price hikes. Nonetheless, as much as Gierek hoped that this strategy would result in the domestic stability enjoyed by his Soviet and East German counterparts, his solution was made on shaky ground. Whereas the leaders of the CPSU and the SED had removed rulers from office who refused to adapt to a new phase of socialist development, blood had been spilled in Poland's streets and dockyards. A disaffected population was even less convinced that the party was acting on its behalf.

Tito's Way

In Stalin's time, these developments would have had an immediate impact on communist regimes everywhere. The Soviet Union would have intervened forcefully to determine exactly what political stance it desired of its allies. With the declining reach of Moscow's sphere of influence, however, there was less to prevent other regimes, and especially those that came to power without the assistance of the Red Army, from choosing for themselves how they wanted to build socialism. Provocatively, in nearly every case, with the partial exception of the West European communists, these parties remained heavily under the sway of the individuals who led them.

In Yugoslavia, every aspect of the identity of the League of Communists (LCY) was imbued with Josip Broz Tito's persona. In the official hagiography, Tito was lionized for his leadership of the Partisan movement during World War II and his subsequent defense of his country's independence from Moscow in 1948. Most prominently, he was regarded as the cohesive force that held the multiethnic state of Yugoslavia together. Under his direction, the LCY demonstrated how a Leninist organization based upon a Marxist idea of proletarian unity could be creatively modified to respond to manifold societal problems. The party embraced the concept of *Jugoslovenstvo*, or "Yugoslavism," as a strategy for overcoming the persisting conflicts among Slovenes, Serbs, Croats, Bosnian Muslims, and other ethnic and religious groups. Indeed, Tito increasingly treated the issue of national unity as if it were no longer in question. "No one in Yugoslavia," he confidently declared, "any longer points out whether someone is a Serb, a Croat, or a member of any other nationality."[29]

Tito would have been fully aware that such an assertion was unfounded. Even a party as purportedly enlightened as the LCY could not easily overcome the memories of injustice, both real and imagined, that had been committed by one ethnic group against another. Still, Tito's centrality to the project of national reconciliation helps us to understand why both he and all of the members of his inner circle became increasingly preoccupied with a single question: Who could possibly step into Tito's shoes after his death? No one could have known that their septuagenarian leader would be with them until his passing at the age of eighty-seven in 1980. But the centrality of this concern indicated the depth of the party's dependence on his personality.

In this context, when Tito expelled his presumptive heir, Aleksandar Ranković, from the Yugoslav Communist Party leadership in 1966, the event precipitated open conflict among incipient factions within the regime. As secretary of the party's Organizational Department and chief of the security police, Ranković used the threat of recrimination to ensure that his commands were carried out. With his removal, party moderates were emboldened to call for greater political transparency. In the same spirit as Kádár's and Brezhnev's promotion of a closer relationship between rulers and ruled, they contended that Yugoslav citizens could not be expected to make lasting contributions to socialism, let alone be persuaded that they were part of a common cause, if the party treated them as children. Each citizen should take charge of his or her own thoughts and deeds. Of course, just as in Hungary and the Soviet Union, the reformers did not intend to question the party's authority. Hence, the secret police routinely targeted free-thinking intellectuals, like the editors of the revisionist Marxist journal *Praxis*, with harassment. Nonetheless, the moderates' encouragement of some forms of critical reflection spilled into other aspects of LCY policymaking. At the League's Eighth Congress in December 1964, Tito threw his support behind the former Partisan fighter and reform-minded economist Edvard Kardelj. With Ranković out of the way, Kardelj advanced an ambitious modernization strategy, the New Measures, which led Yugoslavia to have the most open economy in the socialist world by the end of the decade.

The greatest impact of the atmosphere surrounding Ranković's ouster was on the self-perception of party leaders in each of the republics. It exposed a latent conflict between their role as representatives of their home regions and their responsibilities to the Yugoslav federation. For the politicians of the northern, most-developed republics, Slovenia and Croatia, Ranković, a Serb, had symbolized the negative features of the consensus on which the federal state was based. In their eyes, Belgrade's proclamations about abiding by the principles of Leninist solidarity were contradicted by the fact that Serbs held a disproportionate number of the central government's senior economic and military appointments. In addition, the republics' representatives accused Belgrade of promoting policies that unduly benefited the country's less-developed southern regions. When they pressed Tito to address their grievances, he responded positively. In a decision that would have fateful long-term consequences for the Yugoslav state, he transferred many of the federal LCY's powers to its republican party organizations. For the first time, the latter were given direct control over the selection of cadres, from local cells up to their respective Central Committees. In 1968, the LCY amended the constitution to give each republic sovereignty over all matters not explicitly reserved to the federal government. In a novel interpretation of Leninism, Tito justified these changes by arguing that they represented a specifically Yugoslav refinement of the concept of "democratic centralism." They would, he claimed, strengthen the LCY's leading role.

I am calling attention to this shift because it illustrates the continuing problem—in this case an extreme one—of defining the criteria for party unity. Suddenly, in Yugoslavia's case, the possibility arose that *multiple* claimants to the principle of single-party rule would jeopardize the authority of a single-party state. Tito responded by forming a fifteen-member Executive Bureau of the Presidium composed of representatives from each of the party's republican and provincial organizations. In theory, this was a good idea. In practice, it deadlocked the government. The more that republican parties asserted their prerogatives, the harder it became for central party organs to make effective decisions. In addition, the devolution of decision-making authority exacerbated long-standing republican rivalries. In 1969, a decision by the federal government to divert World Bank funding for a Slovenian road-building project to poorer regions in the south precipitated a full-blown crisis. Croat leaders joined their neighbors in denouncing Belgrade for slighting their interests. In response, the Serbs and Macedonians accused the northern republics of promoting factionalism. A considerably more ominous consequence of these decentralization measures was that they exposed deeper forces of ethnic chauvinism. In the Croatian republic, perceptions of external exploitation gave rise to nationalist and populist sentiments. In turn, fears of Croat separatism and nationalism stirred similar feelings in the Serbian republic and among Serbs living in Croatia.

Tito's reaction to these developments testifies to his faith in the idea of a unified Yugoslav nation-state. In September 1970, at the age of seventy-eight, he put the question of his succession squarely on the table by proposing a collective presidency that would eventually replace him. Adopted a month later, the plan was a classic expression of the balancing act that typified his rule. With representatives from the republics, the new organ was charged with ameliorating tensions among state organizations in the same way the Executive Committee was meant to serve the party. However, in 1971, the flaw within this formula was manifested by the near collapse of central authority in Croatia. In response to Tito's encouragement of republican identities, the activist cultural organization Matica Hrvatska, among other groups, called for the recognition of a separate Croatian language. University students demanded the right to organize themselves independently.

Policymakers pressed the federal government for greater autonomy and control over foreign currency reserves.

In some respects, the Croatian Spring that grew out of these demands had the same intoxicating effect as the rush to reform socialism in Czechoslovakia three years earlier. The movement's advocates stemmed from the Croatian LCY's claim that it could revise the party's role without undermining it. In fact, many old communists who had fought alongside Tito stood behind this effort. From Tito's perspective, however, the experiment was tantamount to allowing a subordinate segment of the party to dictate the terms of Yugoslav unity. He had good reason for concern. Matica Hrvatska behaved more and more like a separate political party—indeed, an anticommunist party—demanding a greater say in political and economic policy. Tito was not alone in seeing these dangers. For reasons ranging from ideological conviction to political opportunism, a majority of the Croatian party's leaders concluded that their republic needed the father of the Yugoslav Revolution on its side. Accordingly, they joined the leaders of the other republics in August 1971 in formulating an Action Program quite unlike the document that inspired the Prague Spring. Their declaration condemned the disturbances as antisocialist and antinational. When the student federation of the University of Zagreb called for a republicwide strike, the Croatian leadership linked arms with Tito in denouncing the "rotten liberalism" and "counterrevolution" that had despoiled their republic and demanded the resignation of the LCY members who supported the Croatian Spring.

In retrospect, one wonders whether Tito's assertion of authority would have taken place as smoothly had he lost the support of the Croatian party. In any case, he let it be known that he was prepared to use military force, if necessary, to restore the federal party's supremacy. When the worst did not transpire, Tito demonstrably returned to familiar national and ideological territory. First, he emphasized that Croatia's problems were not limited to a single republic. This was a national crisis that required a Yugoslav solution. When the LCY leadership reassembled in January 1972, he sharply reduced the size of the Executive Bureau from fourteen to eight members, and removed its most conspicuous supporters of regional autonomy. With the same intent, he took parallel steps against uncompliant members of the Serbian party leadership at the end of the year.

Second, Tito emphatically returned to a Leninist vocabulary. Using words that could have easily come from the mouth of Brezhnev, Honecker, or Kádár, he asserted in a speech in the Croatian seaport of Rijeka on September 4, 1972, that Yugoslav socialism was open to all types of people. The sole requirement was the acceptance of the "class character" of the struggle against separatism. Those who insisted on taking the country backward needed to know that the proletarian vanguard—that is, the party center—would not hesitate to turn to older methods. "You know how they used to do these things in other countries," Tito emphasized in an unmistakable nod to his Stalinist roots: "Heads rolled; there was hard labor and all sorts of things. We do not want to do that but, by God, if anyone is persistent in hostile activity then we must put him into isolation somewhere. And you know what isolation means. There is no other way."[30] Still, Tito emphasized that his version of Leninist rule would withstand the test of time. He concluded his address by referring to certain unnamed Western "forecasts" that Yugoslavia would disintegrate after his death. "I consider that people abroad have no right to tell lies," he declared. "Our country is stable. We suffered together, we fought together, and we made enormous sacrifices."[31]

Deng Xiaoping's Way

A single decision in China at the end of the 1970s demonstrated that Tito's inner circle was not alone in allowing a commingling of personalistic leadership and the idea of communist party rule. In July 1977, Mao's immediate successor, Premier Hua Guofeng, persuaded the Politburo's Standing Committee that the Chinese Communist Party's (CCP) break with the Cultural Revolution required the reinstatement of his best-known surviving critic, Deng Xiaoping. Deng was not given a top party post, but he required little time to act on the differentiated conception of party leadership that he and Liu Shaoqi had advocated in the late 1950s and early 1960s. Although Deng would never rise above the level of vice chairman of the Central Committee, he would play the preeminent role in shaping China's trajectory until his death in 1997.

There is a certain pathos to the fact that one of the first steps Deng took to establish his authority was to turn the Standing Committee against Hua. Although Hua was originally chosen to be Zhou Enlai's successor because of his reputation for being the most desirable—or least undesirable—person to execute a gradual retreat from the extremes of the preceding decade, he played an important role in facilitating the break from Maoism. In 1977, Hua sought to placate the remaining leftist Politburo members with words of reassurance. For those who feared the diminution of the CCP's revolutionary heritage, he endorsed a "two whatevers" policy—support whatever "decisions" Mao made and whatever "instructions" he left behind. At the same time, Hua's policies bore a distinct resemblance to Brezhnev's efforts to stabilize expectations. He assured party members and potential recruits that the chaotic times of the Cultural Revolution were over. He praised the noble virtues of party life and promised to infuse the institution with new energy. Unlike Mao, who had rarely left China, he also traveled to other socialist countries to learn about alternative approaches to socialist management.

Notwithstanding Hua's contributions, Deng took the lead in formulating a new conception of Chinese politics that would result over the coming decades in the country's emergence as a major world power. In his capacity as Paramount Leader, as he became known, Deng engineered the CCP's transition from a party of revolution to a party of organization. In a path-breaking speech on December 13, 1978, just before the convening of the Third Plenary Session of the Eleventh Central Committee, he signaled the definitive break with the Cultural Revolution by endorsing Zhou Enlai's Four Modernizations as the party's new line. In living up to the obligations of "our new Long March," Deng stressed, the primary task for every communist was to emancipate his or her mind by "seeking truth from facts." For too long, cadres had sought comfort in the bad habits that served as survival tools under extremists like Lin Biao and the Gang of Four. Yet, Deng underscored, these days were over. China could only advance if the party recruited members who could look beyond tried-and-true methods and dedicate themselves to solving demanding social and economic problems.[32]

In this spirit, Deng took up the thorny issue of Mao's record. To seek truth from facts, he argued, one needed to confront the party's mistakes. Although some wrongs could never be rectified, others could. In the interest of party unity, he emphasized, comrades who had made mistakes should own up to their errors and take steps to correct them. In this case, Deng's Khrushchevian moment was to address the cult of Mao Zedong. Even Chairman Mao, he stated, was not infallible. "To demand that of any revolutionary leader," it seemed, "would be inconsistent with Marxism." Surely, Deng added cryptically, Mao had good reasons for initiating the Cultural Revolution. Nonetheless, the party had to confront this dark chapter in its history. Deng did not say how or when this step should be taken. In fact, he cautioned against undue haste. Yet even raising the issue of Mao's fallibility was a monumental leap.[33]

It is instructive that Deng's guarded critique evoked the same question about the fragility of the party's authority that we have encountered in Yugoslavia. Given the fact that China's entire domestic order was linked to the personality of a single individual, how could one make the transition to a meaningful and viable concept of party rule without simultaneously disrupting society as a whole? Even some of Deng's strongest supporters worried that the country was not ready for such an examination of its past. These concerns were justified. Not long after Deng's speech, Beijing's tacit acceptance of its residents' use of wall posters to give vent to their grievances exploded into a Democracy Wall movement when disaffected students and intellectuals throughout China tested the limits of the regime's tolerance of dissent. In numerous cities, they were emboldened to organize sit-ins, start underground newspapers, and demand expanded freedoms. In particular, they called for the rehabilitation of the protestors jailed after the April 1976 demonstrations over the insufficiently respectful handling of Zhou Enlai's funeral arrangements. Deng had never intended the pursuit of "truth through facts" to be taken this far, and he showed his displeasure by turning to the same remedy that had been used in the other socialist states: force. On March 29, he ordered the arrest of the movement's leaders. On the following day, he rebuked their sympathizers in the party for promoting anarchism. China would only progress, Deng insisted, if it adhered to four long-established principles: the primacy of the socialist road; the dictatorship of the proletariat; the leadership of the communist party; and the tenets of Marxism-Leninism and Mao Zedong Thought.[34]

What Deng and other victims of Mao's terror seemed to fear the most about the Democracy Wall movement was not the protestors' specific demands. Rather, as he and the CCP's inner circle would affirm by returning to the use of force against antigovernment demonstrations a decade and a half later in June 1989, it was a return to the disorder of the 1960s. Otherwise, Deng showed that he was determined to transform the CCP into an organization that was principally suited to managing a complex economy. Invoking Maoist language, but with a very different objective, Deng used the protests to challenge party members to prove that they were worthy of being the people's vanguard. At a Politburo meeting on August 18, 1980, he declared that China would not become a modern socialist state unless its cadres adopted new ways of thinking and acting. In his view, even those with the requisite skills to move forward were still being held back by the feudal mentality of an earlier generation. There was no longer room for the clannish practices of yesteryear when, as Deng put it, someone's promotion to a leadership position meant that "even his dogs and chickens" ascended with him. The "dignity of our state and national self-respect," he stressed, required that no one should be above the law.[35]

For a rising, increasingly more educated, and hopeful generation of Chinese communists, these were heady words. The admission that the CCP's representatives were imperfect did not call the party's infallibility into question. Rather, it provided room for these members to believe that they could join in realizing the organization's high ideals. Now that Deng had created this opportunity, they naturally expected that he and all public officials would live up to this standard as well.

Persisting Personality Cults

One cannot avoid making an important qualification to Deng's commitment to reestablishing the CCP's leading role. He was personally involved in every aspect of the undertaking. Given the extent to which China's political and social order was suffused with Mao's cult, it is hard to imagine how a break with the past would have been possible without a dominant figure to direct it. At the same time, in many other socialist states, the absence of a momentous event, like Mao's death, to force such a transition meant that it was even easier for dictatorial personalities to resist the subordination of their desires to a collective principle of leadership. The leaders of Romania, Albania, and North Korea found a convenient rationale for maintaining absolute power by presenting themselves as both torchbearers of the class struggle and defenders of national dignity.

Romania is a case in point. When Nicolae Ceauşescu, a home communist, succeeded Gheorghe Gheorghiu-Dej as general secretary of the renamed Romanian Communist Party (RCP) in March 1965, he faced a situation quite like that of Rákosi's and Novotný's successors in Hungary and Czechoslovakia. Under Gheorghiu-Dej, the party leadership had alienated its citizenry and much of its rank-and-file membership. Like its counterparts in other socialist states, the RCP unabashedly defended Stalinist economic and social policies that left it out of touch with the population's needs. Furthermore, thanks to Gheorghiu-Dej's success in opposing any form of collective leadership, the upper echelons of the RCP lacked a reform-minded cohort to offer an alternative course.

As a senior member of the leadership since the communist takeover in 1947, Ceauşescu was as ensconced in these policies as anyone. Hence, he initially surprised observers by seeming to distance himself from this legacy. As party chief, he assumed both the posture and tone of Brezhnev's regime. He courted the support of RCP members by assuring them of his respect for collective decision making and promising opportunities for professional advancement. To free up positions for new cadres, he forbade party officials from holding more than one position simultaneously. He also tentatively indicated his willingness to take a long, hard look at the party's sordid past. No measure played a greater role in establishing a positive image for Ceaușescu than his defense of Romania's independence. In a dramatic break with Moscow on August 21, 1968, he condemned the Warsaw Pact's invasion of Czechoslovakia for violating the sovereignty of a fraternal socialist state. For many Romanians, party members and nonmembers alike, the speech was a tour de force. It demonstrated that adherence to the doctrine of proletarian internationalism was fully compatible with Romanian nationalism. "One cannot be internationalist," Ceaușescu affirmed, "if one does not love one's own nation and if one does not struggle for the building of the new socialist and communist nation."[36]

Yet, this synthesis was also Ceaușescu's key to establishing that he, and not the RCP, would be the father of this nation. After his return from an extended tour of China, North Korea, and North Vietnam in summer 1971, all countries that exhibited independent policies against Moscow, he abandoned the conciliatory tone of the preceding decade. Invoking seventeen "theses" that were reminiscent of the battle themes of Stalinism, Ceaușescu ordered the RCP to intensify political education among party members, rein in disloyal writers and journalists, and promote socialist patriotism. This campaign, or "Mini–Cultural Revolution" as it became known, was a far cry from China's Cultural Revolution. Instead of replicating Mao's campaigns to elevate the idea of party rule by attacking the practice of party organizations, Ceaușescu's goal was simply to assert his control over all spheres of Romanian life.

To be sure, the RCP's general secretary was not the first communist leader to put his personal interests above the collective good. But at least by European standards, his cult was on par with Stalin's in both its extent and mythic pretensions. In official statements, the government portrayed Ceaușescu as the natural heir to a long line of Romanian heroes extending back to the ancient and equally mythologized Dacian people of the first century AD. His written works were celebrated as among the greatest contributions to Marxist theory. In newspaper articles, television documentaries, literary works, and poetry, he was acclaimed as a genius and secular deity. Not one to let such tributes go ignored, Ceaușescu likened his role to that of an orchestra conductor, or *Conducător*, who "blended" his call to leadership with the needs of the masses. "One might compare the role of personality and of the masses to an orchestra," he explained. "A good orchestra is nothing without a good conductor, just as the best conductor is nothing without a good orchestra, with each contributing to the performance as a whole."[37]

In one respect, Ceauşescu's quest differed from Stalin's. The Soviet leader distrusted close personal relationships, while Ceauşescu's proclivities were unabashedly familial. The more suspicious he became of collegial decision making, the more he sought security in his own clan. In particular, he elevated his wife to a status that rivaled that of Mao's spouse, Jiang Qing. At her husband's side, Elena Ceauşescu fostered her own personality cult. She was exalted simultaneously as the mother of the Romanian nation and as its daughter. Just as important politically, her husband charged her with making all cadre appointments in the Central Committee. By the 1980s, nearly thirty members of the Ceauşescu clan held top party and state positions. This was not socialism in one country. This was socialism in one family!

Like Ceauşescu, Albania's Enver Hoxha skillfully established his position by combining Marxist and nationalist appeals. When Hoxha became first secretary of the Party of Labor of Albania (PLA) in 1944, he assumed the pose of the quintessential Stalinist. He praised both Stalin and Tito, whose Partisan fighters had been instrumental in founding the PLA's predecessor, the Communist Party of Albania, in 1941, and for demonstrating how a developing country could make the leap out of backwardness. Following his heroes' example, the new regime swiftly expropriated the property of large landowners, nationalized the country's few industries, and jailed and executed former officials and internal critics. By the early 1950s, Hoxha had deservedly earned the reputation for heading one of the most brutal regimes in the communist world.

Hoxha soon showed that he did not view Albania's path to socialism as contingent upon Belgrade's or Moscow's desires. His break with Tito came first. Following Yugoslavia's expulsion from the Cominform in 1948 and Tito's innovations in party organization and economic management, Hoxha jumped on the bandwagon of condemning his neighbor for joining the forces of counterrevolution. Then, in an even more explicit declaration of independence in the mid-1950s, he turned his attention to Khrushchev, denouncing the "Secret Speech" as a manifestation of revisionism. When the extent of Sino-Soviet tensions came into full view at the turn of the decade, Hoxha alone among Eastern Europe's communist rulers joined Beijing in attacking the Soviet Union for great-power chauvinism. After Moscow severed diplomatic relations with Tirana in 1961, he glorified the People's Republic of China (PRC) and Mao as the standard-bearers of communism.

Yet there was a twist. In one respect, Albania's relationship with China from this point forward had the characteristics of a conventional alliance. After Hoxha severed diplomatic relations with the USSR, China became the major source of economic aid to Tirana. Still, Hoxha's interest in the PRC was also proof of the continuing power of ideas in the communist world. From his vantage point, the PLA's association with the Chinese communists was an opportunity to share in the assault on the Soviet model of developed socialism. In tribute to his partner, Hoxha launched his own Ideological and Cultural Revolution immediately after Mao's appeal to the Red Guards in 1966 to "bombard the headquarters." However, his objectives were only partly like Mao's. Like China's leader, he was contemptuous of traditional culture, including the institution of the family and all forms of religion. Yet, like Ceaușescu, Hoxha did not aim to foster a permanent revolution. Rather, he intended to use his position to establish his supremacy over both the party and the state. Thus, the Ideological and Cultural Revolution was all about taking control of society. In the name of eradicating Soviet "revisionism," Hoxha deployed compliant PLA cadres, youth organizations, and soldiers to purge party and state offices of supposed "bureaucrats" and "technocrats" and wage war on traditional culture. He abolished military ranks, launched literacy campaigns, and declared full equality for women. On a triumphant note, he proclaimed Albania the world's first atheist state.

Hoxha found the ideal justification for these policies in the Soviet invasion of Czechoslovakia. Writing in the party daily, *Zëri i Popullit*, in early 1969, he accused the "Khrushchev revisionists" of using their troops against another country to conceal their nefarious plans to establish "capitalist states of a new type" and military dictatorships throughout the world. In his estimation, the Soviet Union had long ago given up the ghost of Leninism. The "Brezhnev-Kosygin clique," Hoxha argued, wanted other socialist states to believe that the class struggle was over and that all exploiting classes had been liquidated. But, he emphasized, bourgeois influences would continue to contaminate socialism "even after the victory of communism." By implication, the only way to guarantee the survival of the communist ideal was to "achieve the full victory of socialist ideology in every individual country."[38] Presumably, Hoxha believed that Albania had already achieved this goal.

In itself, Hoxha's variant on the theme of "socialism in one country" was audacious. Speaking as the representative of a country that was scarcely known in other parts of the world, he aimed to establish himself as a preeminent Marxist thinker. It would take an even more distinctive turn in the early 1970s when Mao outlined a "Three Worlds Theory" that posited the existence of a second world of peaceful capitalist states between the superpowers and the nonaligned movement. Hoxha denounced the concept as a dangerous blurring of the lines between revolution and counterrevolution. Making relations between Albania and the PRC even worse, in February 1972, Mao committed the unpardonable sin, in Hoxha's eyes, of welcoming the symbol of American imperialism, US president Richard Nixon, to Beijing. Thus, after the defeat of the Gang of Four, the two states' partnership collapsed. In 1978, Hoxha accused China's leaders of seeking to make their country a superpower. Taking this denunciation one step further, he declared that Mao Zedong Thought had been anti-Marxist all along. Mao himself, it seemed, was no more than a Chinese Bukharin, who had used the CCP to build a personality cult that rivaled those of "Emperor Bokassa, the Shah of Iran, or the King of Nepal." Hoxha even denounced the Gang of Four as a "group of megalomaniacs, ambitious, outright babblers."[39]

In fairness to Beijing, Hoxha's assessment was "babble," too. Nonetheless, this was instructive babble. Hoxha's justification of Albania's divorce from the PRC should have exposed the poverty of his position. After all, if it was hard to realize the fruits of socialism in the Soviet Union and China, why should Albania be up to this charge? Yet, provocatively, Hoxha's stature was enhanced in some parts of the world. By the 1980s, he was practically alone among ruling communists, save for Kim Il-sung in North Korea, in defending the Stalinist themes of ideological struggle and class warfare. With faith in communism in decline everywhere, "Hoxhaism" became an ideological aphrodisiac for scores of minute splinter parties throughout Africa, Asia, and Europe. Its appeal lay not so much in Albania's growth strategies. Rather, for the Chilean Communist Party ("Proletarian Action"), the Communist Ghadar Party of India, the Voltaic Revolutionary Communist Party in Burkina Faso, and the Communist Party ("Reconstructed") in Portugal, among many others, Hoxha's amalgamation of diverse elements of Marxism was a way to focus on overthrowing the established order at a time when established socialist regimes were determined to stabilize it.

Against this background, it says something about the characteristics of North Korean socialism that the cult of Kim Il-sung was even more pervasive than those in Romania and Albania. In establishing his authority, Kim had an advantage that was unavailable to most of the communist world—a sustained military threat. After an agonizing three-year war that took the lives of nearly 5 million people and ended in a stalemate with South Korea and the United States, he could persuasively argue that North Korea's survival depended upon maintaining a state of battle readiness. By the early 1960s, Kim had achieved this goal, combining Stalinist strategies of accelerated economic development with high levels of armaments production. However, despite the fact that North Korea had a higher percentage of party members among its population than any other socialist state, this focus had little to do with advancing the leading role of his party, the Korean Workers' Party (KWP). Just like Stalin, Kim simultaneously purged the KWP's upper elite. By the party's Fourth Congress in September 1961, only twenty-eight out of eighty-five full members of the Central Committee were retained from the preceding congress five years earlier. Most of those removed were members of the Soviet and Chinese factions who did not share Kim's roots in the Manchurian guerrilla movement. Not one to let sentiment get in the way of personal ambition, Kim also turned on his former comrades in battle. In October 1966, under the banner of a so-called monolithic ideological system, he removed nine of the sixteen members of the party's highest body, the Political Committee. One-fifth of the Central Committee's members met the same fate.[40]

Confirming his determination to restrict the parameters of the North Korean Revolution to his vision alone, Kim undergirded his cult with a doctrine of national "self-reliance," or *Juche*. When he initially broached the concept in the mid-1950s, he claimed that *Juche* was merely a supplement to Marxism-Leninism. Yet the doctrine quickly evolved into a profound rationale for asserting North Korea's independence. In the early 1960s, when Moscow took issue with his government's military ambitions and threatened to withdraw economic aid, Kim publicly broke ranks and threw his support to Beijing. Later in the decade, when the Cultural Revolution presented an all-too-vivid image of socialist instability, he distanced himself from the PRC. By the 1970s, although Kim still sought military and economic assistance from both countries, he had abandoned any meaningful connection to the idea of proletarian internationalism.

Then again, Kim was convinced that he did not need to rely on the guidance of outside powers to build socialism on Korean soil. His party agreed. To an extent that rivaled the dimensions of Stalin's personality cult, the KWP credited him with every major achievement in contemporary North Korean history and glorified him as the "Great Sun," the "Shining Star," and the "Genius of Marxism-Leninism." He held all major party and state posts, including supreme command of the military. Confirming Kim's belief in this mythology, when he began to contemplate the implications of his mortality in the 1970s, he looked to his own bloodline, and not to the KWP, for a solution. Upon his death in July 1994, Kim was succeeded by his son, Kim Jong-il, who proclaimed his father Eternal President four years later.

THE TRIALS OF NORMALCY

Looking on, Brezhnev and his like-minded Eastern European colleagues must have felt as if they were viewing another world. Unlike their Romanian, Albanian, and North Korean contemporaries, they had grown weary of the confrontational ethos and violence that had suffused Leninist movements for more than half a century. Their parties' more pragmatic and predictable leadership styles and their disposition to reach decisions collectively provided them with something they had missed in their relations with both their followers and citizens. This was a sense of socialist normalcy.

Of course, normalcy is only an aspiration, never a sure thing. Everywhere in the 1970s, these parties' leaders encountered the expectation that they would live up to their promises. Their faith in the idea that the party of developed socialism could provide higher living standards was based on the conviction that command economies could be fine-tuned to become more productive and would grow through the infusion of new technologies. With the exception of Hungary, however, which experienced modest success in experimenting with price reforms and private enterprise, these regimes were both unwilling and unable to do anything more than tinker with the structure of centralized planning and their habitual reliance on labor-intensive industries. As a result, they could barely sustain the initial improvements in their population's quality of life, let alone provide them with new resources and opportunities. Making matters more difficult, as the 1970s progressed, additional problems—declining labor productivity, escalating production costs, and exploding levels of Eastern European indebtedness to Western banks and trading partners—drove overall growth rates downward.

Additionally, this harsh reality eroded the Soviet Union's willingness to make unconditional sacrifices for the common good. In the wake of the world energy crisis of 1973, Moscow raised the price of oil and natural gas exports to its energy-starved allies. In a private meeting with his Polish, Czechoslovak, Bulgarian, Hungarian, and German colleagues in Budapest on March 18, 1975, Brezhnev conceded that they were bearing a heavy burden. But he pointed out that his country, too, faced serious problems, a decreasing return on its investments, woefully insufficient financial and material resources, and uncertain international conditions. Thus, he did not have any easy solutions for their problems. "I came here," he advised, "with empty pockets." He added, "life is life." While they had all experienced difficult moments over the past thirty years (i.e., since the end of World War II), he noted that each had consistently found ways to overcome them, "moving ahead, not backward."[41]

Life may have been life, but this did not mean that there would be no consequences if these states failed to move forward. Once again, Poland provided a signal of trials to come. On June 24, 1976, Gierek's government responded to inflationary pressures and spreading food shortages by increasing the price of agricultural staples such as meat, sugar, and butter. The backlash was immediate. Convinced that Gierek had broken the party's social contract of 1971, enraged workers in the northern port cities again walked off their jobs and violent demonstrations spread throughout Poland. Faced with the prospect of a crippling nationwide strike, the government rescinded its decision less than twenty-four hours after its announcement. But the damage was done. This feeble gesture was not a solution, it was an indication that its relationship with its citizens had grown even worse.

Across the bloc, all of the communist regimes were further tested by an unintended consequence of Moscow's efforts to improve relations with the West. By the mid-1970s, Brezhnev's tentative steps toward resolving the question of Berlin's status through negotiations with the city's three Western occupying powers and improving ties with West Germany had evolved into a dense network of political, economic, and financial relationships with Western European states and the United States that transcended the ideological divide. In August 1975, what had begun as a risk for the Soviets culminated in an event that appeared to put the worst tensions of the Cold War to rest. Representatives of thirty-three European states, as well as the United States and Canada, met in Helsinki, Finland, to sign a comprehensive three-part agreement about the postwar order. The first two sections of the accord, or "baskets" as they were called, affirmed the two primary goals of Soviet foreign policy: the West's de facto recognition of the status quo in Eastern Europe and a broad opening to Western markets and capital. However, a third "basket," which formally bound the signatories to respect "civil, political, economic, social, cultural, and other rights and freedoms," proved to be an unwelcome challenge.[42] The recognition of social and economic rights was consonant with socialist principles. But otherwise, it is unlikely Moscow and its allies ever intended to accept the concepts of civil and political rights, at least as they were understood in the West. To do so would have been to call into question the concept of proletarian dictatorship. In the midst of the negotiations, Brezhnev assured his Eastern European partners that Soviet negotiators had already "repelled [the] excessive and obnoxious demands of some western countries."[43] Nevertheless, they had given their imprimatur to terms that could be taken quite literally by their citizens.

On May 12, 1976, a handful of outspoken scientists and writers held a press conference in the Moscow apartment of the dissident physicist Andrei Sakharov to announce the formation of a Helsinki Watch Group. Their straightforward goal was to monitor their government's observance of the Helsinki accords and call the world's attention to human rights violations. Predictably, the group's members immediately became targets of harassment by the Soviet security police, the KGB; many were jailed and others were forced into exile. But demonstrating that the letter of the Helsinki agreements was not as easily ignored, their example swiftly led to the formation of watch groups in other Soviet republics, including Ukraine, Lithuania, and Georgia. One year later, these developments were followed by an even more direct assault upon the party's authority in Czechoslovakia. Two prominent dissidents, Václav Havel and Pavel Kohout, published a document, soon to be known as Charter 77, which demanded that the regime abide by the legal protections of the country's constitution. Going beyond the unfulfilled aspirations of the Prague Spring, the authors appealed to their readers to imagine life in a country governed by the rule of law. In such a place, they contended, citizens would enjoy the right to "freedom without fear" and experience the personal fulfillment of "living within the truth."[44]

The organizers of both the Helsinki Watch Group and Charter 77 carefully skirted around the language of political engagement. For example, Havel and Kohout stressed that they had no intention of transforming Charter 77 into an organization. "It has no rules," they wrote, "permanent bodies or formal memberships." In their description, the Charter was simply a "free, informal, and open association of people of different convictions, different faiths, and different professions."[45] Still, it is unlikely that they truly believed that such assurances would allay their government's fears. Nor was this their primary intention. After all, they may have lacked formal organizations, but they sensed the opportunity to take the party to task for not living up to the promises of developed socialism.

The impact of these groups increased when they found common cause with other social actors. Here, again, Poland stood out. Some activists joined the Catholic Church in protesting constitutional amendments that would have further constricted civil and religious freedoms. Others formed an advocacy group, the Committee for the Defense of Workers, to pressure parliament to release workers who had been imprisoned during the 1976 strikes. Still other groups, both large and small, published underground newspapers and distributed anticommunist literature from abroad. One group even founded an independent "flying" university to provide alternative forms of education across the country.

For the time being, neither the Soviet Union nor most of its allies faced the prospect that these protests would coalesce with other sources of social disaffection to present a serious threat to public order. With the exception of Poland, the dissidents' numbers were too few and they were easily repressed. Nonetheless, the fact that these critics lacked an army to come to their defense did not make these regimes' claims to normalcy any more credible. Paradoxically, the more that the Brezhnevs, Honeckers, and Kádárs of the bloc maintained that the hard times of the class struggle and the clash with imperialism were on the decline, the more ordinary citizens were disposed to ask themselves a simple question: Was a Leninist dictatorship needed to achieve the goals of modest economic growth and national defense? As if to confirm that they had no ready answer to this question, several of these regimes took a step they would have barely considered necessary in earlier times. They finally got around to inserting references to the party's leading role into their constitutions. In 1976, the Polish parliament voted to describe the PUWP "as the leading political force at the time of socialist construction." In 1977, the Soviet parliament amended the USSR's constitution to proclaim the CPSU "the leading and guiding force of Soviet society and the nucleus of its political system."[46]

Of course, these ritualistic affirmations of an ambiguous principle would not have been satisfactory answers to any citizen who was dubious about the purpose of single-party rule. But as long as the number of those willing to challenge these regimes' authority was low, this weakness was inconsequential. The more important issue for party leaders was whether they had the support of that segment of the population whose loyalty mattered the most—their own members. As a result, from Moscow to East Berlin, Budapest, and Sofia, they turned their attention to rewarding their rank and file with the professional equivalent of eternal life.

This was no mean transition. In the days of Lenin's rule, at least according to the mythology, continued membership in the elite had to be earned through virtuous behavior and sacrifice for the common good. Six decades later, it appeared, one could earn the benefit of tenure simply by participating in the ritual of party leadership. At this juncture, Kádár's minimalist strategy of rewarding political compliance with social tolerance was supplemented with a new promise: to those to whom much had been given, even more would be given in return. At every level of the organizational hierarchy, inclusion meant privileged access to material goods and services that were unavailable to the uninitiated. Members could draw upon political connections to avail themselves of the second economy. Political, economic, and moral corruption became an accepted part of party life, both by those who benefited and by those who had simply come to expect it. Testifying to the seriousness with which these regimes pursued this strategy, party leaders in the USSR and throughout Eastern Europe attempted to buttress their authority by increasing the size of their ranks. For example, the CPSU had 11 million members when Brezhnev replaced Khrushchev in 1964, but by the time of his death in 1982, its size had nearly doubled to 19 million members.

There was, however, a potentially serious flaw to this strategy, especially within these parties' upper echelons. The low turnover rates throughout the Soviet bloc meant that their leaders were older than ever before. In 1980, their general secretaries had the features of a transnational gerontocracy. Brezhnev was 73; Gierek and Husák, 67; Honecker and Kádár, 68; Zhivkov, 69; and Tito, a death-defying 87. At 62, only the antireformer Ceauşescu was too young to have experienced the outbreak of the October Revolution. For this particular group of autocrats, all of whom had made their political fortunes under one or another form of Stalinism and had survived to play central roles in the construction of socialism, tenure seemed a just compensation for decades of devoted service. Yet for ambitious communists in the ranks below them who meaningfully constituted a post-Stalin generation, this circumstance was a cause for growing impatience. Although they were better educated, more attuned to the demands of modern society, and less burdened by the horrors of war and terror, they had the misfortune of having to wait for their elders' demise.

The Eclipse of Western Communism

For communists who still wanted to believe that the original ideas of Marxism were not universally fated to be reduced to the uninspiring dimensions of developed socialism, let alone be corrupted by personal despotism, the 1970s offered one major sign of hope—the specter of Eurocommunism. This reawakened the prospect that communist parties could come to power by peaceful means. On March 3, 1977, the leaders of the three most prominent Western European parties, Enrico Berlinguer of the Italian Communist Party (PCI), Georges Marchais of the French Communist Party (PCF), and Santiago Carrillo of the Spanish Communist Party (PCE), met in Madrid to affirm a position that had long ago seemed precluded by the October Revolution. A Marxist party, they maintained, could not only compete effectively in democratic elections; it could win broad popular support and form coalitions with bourgeois parties while simultaneously maintaining its core principles. This was a bold claim. Had the Eurocommunist parties' ambitions come to fruition, they might have vindicated the argument made by many Marxists that the deformation of socialist principles that began in the Soviet Union was not the inevitable result of communist dreams. In less than a decade, however, the grounds for optimism were gone. All three parties were fractured by internal divisions. Far from winning elections, their leaders' courtship of middle-of-the-road voters left them vulnerable to the appeal of moderate leftist politicians who bore neither the burden of close association with the Soviet Union nor the challenge of showing that the communist dream made sense in a modern democratic order.

The fate of the PCI was based on a gamble. For decades, the party had maintained its remarkable post–World War II record of success by winning sizeable shares of the vote at all levels of electoral competition. From 1948 to 1972, the PCI was Italy's second most popular party, averaging one-fourth of the vote in national parliamentary elections. What it lacked, however, was the ability to cross the threshold and enter a national government. In 1973, Berlinguer unveiled a strategy, dubbed the Historic Compromise, to surmount this barrier. Claiming to act in the spirit of Antonio Gramsci's encouragement of cross-class cooperation and to build on his predecessor Palmiro Togliatti's concept of the "historic bloc," Berlinguer maintained that the PCI could contribute to a renewal of Italian politics by forming a governing coalition with the majority Christian Democracy (DC) party, for which he had the support of its then leader Aldo Moro. To improve the PCI's bargaining position he sought to broaden the party's appeal by reaching out to traditional antagonists like the Catholic Church and the big state-directed industrial concerns. He assured business owners and the middle class that the PCI would foster social peace by reining in extremist elements in the trade unions. He also stressed the party's commitment to democratic values, agreed to parliamentary resolutions in support of European economic and political integration, and affirmed Italy's membership in NATO.

Berlinguer's advocacy of these positions was not based upon electoral calculations alone. Like many European communists, he had been shocked by the implications of the overthrow of the Chilean government's Marxist president, Salvador Allende, in September 1973. Because Allende had come into office with the support of the Chilean Communist Party, Berlinguer concluded that a leftist government in Europe would never survive without the approval of Italy's neighbors, even if it won a majority of the votes. Initially, Berlinguer's gamble was a stunning success. In the 1976 general elections, the PCI nearly overtook the

Christian Democrats, winning 34.37 percent of the votes compared to the latter's 38.71.[47] The DC held on to power, but only by aligning itself with a different party coalition. The PCI was nevertheless awarded prominent positions in the new parliament and gained a significant say in the government's decisions.

Yet, the ecstasy of electoral success was short-lived. Almost immediately, the PCI leadership was presented with agonizing blows to its credibility. In December, it proved incapable of living up to its promises to restrain the trade unions when huge demonstrations by metal workers shut down the streets of Rome. In March 1978, the party called for a vote of no confidence in the DC government but failed to get the needed support from other parliamentary delegations. At the same juncture, its reputation suffered when the extreme-leftist Red Brigades, which opposed the Historic Compromise, kidnapped and murdered Moro.

Ultimately, the PCI's trials were part of a deeper dilemma. By moving the party toward the middle of the political spectrum, Berlinguer inadvertently encouraged the party's voters to raise a troubling question. Why should one support a communist party when more moderate parties on the Left could be trusted to pursue similar objectives? Over the following decade, neither Berlinguer nor his two successors, Alessandro Natta and Achille Occhetto, were able to identify a satisfactory answer to this question. After 1977, although the PCI registered a strong showing in elections to the European Parliament, its share of the vote in the more consequential general elections consistently declined. Accordingly, its ability to shape government policy dwindled. Declaring that the PCI could no longer afford to isolate itself from Italian society, Occhetto attempted to convert its members to a "new course." He reached out to a variety of progressive social movements as well as to various Western European left-wing parties and advocated transforming the PCI's identity along social democratic lines. Then, in March 1989, more than a half year before the eruptions against communist rule in Eastern Europe, he shocked the PCI's radical wing by announcing the party's total break with Leninism. One year later, the PCI formally dissolved itself. It reappeared only as the much smaller, reformist Democratic Party of the Left, the first of many name changes.

The PCE would live on in name much longer than the PCI. But its decline as a substantial mass organization came much earlier and under even less forgiving circumstances. In many ways, this outcome was a shock to its leaders. The PCE enjoyed widespread sympathy even among noncommunists because of its long record of opposition to fascism. Until the early 1950s, thousands of communists had conducted guerrilla operations against the Franco dictatorship as members of the Spanish Maquis located in France. Thereafter, they made a calculated decision to infiltrate the government's official trade unions, eventually forming their own, illegal "workers commissions." In the process, the PCE became the strongest and best-organized of all of Spain's clandestine parties. As a result, when Franco died in 1975 and the party prepared for legalization, its general secretary, Carrillo, introduced a compelling picture of the PCE that equaled Berlinguer's ambitions for the PCI. In an evocative book, *Eurocommunism and the State*, he sought to overcome popular suspicions about his party's relationship with Moscow by excoriating the CPSU for losing touch with the ideals of its founders. He promised that the PCE would bring a "creative Marxism" to Spain, which would embrace democratic values and institutions. The PCE could only retain its identity as a vanguard party, Carrillo argued, by cooperating with other parties and nurturing the "political-social hegemony" of the working and intellectual classes.[48]

A skeptical reader of Carrillo's book might have wondered whether this redefinition of the vanguard role was anything more than word-play. When Spanish citizens went to the polls in Spain's first, free post-Franco elections in 1977, they showed that even a new and improved PCE was not enough to convince sufficient numbers of voters that it should hold office. Spain had changed over the thirty-six years of Franco's reign. Although the PCE was respected by many Spaniards, the promise of a middle-of-the-road course was a more credible way of ensuring their country's transition to democracy. As a result, the communists received a disappointingly small 9.4 percent of the vote while its seemingly weaker rival, the Spanish Socialist Workers' Party, received 29 percent. Confirming the electorate's message, the PCE fared only a little better in the next parliamentary elections in March 1979, garnering only 10.8 percent compared to the Socialists' 30.54 percent.[49]

What finally destroyed the PCE's chances of becoming a major political presence was not the Spanish voter. It was the party's return to the crippling infighting that had torn it apart during the Civil War. While Carrillo's doctrinal innovations were received with tepid enthusiasm by the electorate, they precipitated a bitter debate within the party. Carrillo's critics accused him of pursuing a flawed electoral strategy and being too open to compromise. As a result of these divisions, the party suffered a devastating defeat in the October 1982 parliamentary elections. Ironically, Carrillo, the reformer, tried to pull the PCE back from the abyss by demanding that its members exercise Leninist discipline in support of his position. But at this point, he was too seriously wounded to recover. In April 1985, only eight years after the PCE's return to legality, a less inspired coterie of leaders essentially conceded its lack of traction with the Spanish electorate by ousting Carrillo and his sympathizers from the Central Committee.

The PCF did not suffer the disastrous fates of the PCI and PCE. Not only did it survive the fall of Eastern European communism, it remained a viable force in local elections and maintained a modest presence in the National Assembly well into the 2000s. Still, it shared with both parties the unintended consequences of engagement in democratic politics. Like Berlinguer and Carrillo, the PCF's general secretary, Georges Marchais, made a show of reaching out to other leftist parties in the 1970s. In 1972, with Marchais's encouragement, the PCF approved a 185-page Common Program with France's reformed and renamed Socialist Party (PS) that led to the formation of an electoral coalition with the Socialists. This decision was not due to a newfound affection for the communists' longtime adversaries. Marchais's goal was to co-opt the smaller party before it had the chance to outflank the PCF. Also, in contrast to his counterparts in Italy and Spain, Marchais retained the stubbornly dogmatic posture that the party's founders had exhibited since the Congress of Tours in 1920. Notwithstanding his assurances of the PCF's commitment to democracy, the party remained defiantly anticapitalist and fixated on the class struggle.

At first, Marchais's strategy seemed to pay off. In the 1973 parliamentary elections, the PCF retained its leading position on the Left, winning 21.4 percent of the first ballots compared to 19.10 percent for the Socialists. In the 1974 presidential elections, Marchais sought to maintain his leverage by playing the role of kingmaker, instructing party members to support the popular Socialist politician, François Mitterrand. Thanks to this alliance of convenience, Mitterrand came within 1.6 percentage points of defeating the conservative candidate, Giscard d'Estaing, and bringing the Left coalition to power. Nevertheless, just as in Italy and France, the communists paid a steep price for their association with a moderate socialist party. Thanks to a superior political machine and the support of younger voters, Mitterrand put his party into the position to usurp the communists' long-held domination of the Left. Recognizing his party's diminishing leverage, Marchais defiantly withdrew his support for the Common Program. However, in the same way that the PCI and the PCE lost ground to the moderate socialists, the PCF was unable to regain its momentum. In the parliamentary elections in 1978, the Socialists established themselves for the first time since 1945 as the country's leading leftist party, besting the PCF by more than a half million votes in the first round and nearly two and a half million in the second round.[50]

This was not the last time the PS and the PCF would cooperate. When Mitterrand won the presidency in 1981, he assigned the PCF four minor cabinet positions. But even this unequal relationship was short-lived; the communist ministers left the government after three years of frustration. By continuing to tout fundamentalist principles, Marchais and his only somewhat less dogmatic successors excelled at the task of retaining the support of hard-core voters, just as they had through the century. Yet, the PCF's share of the total vote in the national elections rapidly declined and, with it, any realistic chance of winning high office.

Looking back on the PCF's struggles in the 1980s, as well as those of the PCI and the PCE, one is struck by how anticlimactic these events seemed. Although these parties' trials were the subject of deep consternation to the true believers within their respective ranks, a majority of French, Italian, and Spanish citizens barely noticed these developments. The success of middle-of-the-road, catchall parties in each country made the communists' flagging fortunes seem inconsequential.

From a historical standpoint, however, this perspective was misleading. The Eurocommunist parties' fate marked the end to the hopes, held by earlier generations of communists since the nineteenth century, that there was a chance of realizing any of Karl Marx's prophecies in Western Europe.

CHAPTER 12

The Party in Peril

In 1986, a catastrophic event demonstrated that there was a fatal flaw in the system of developed socialism. On April 26, Reactor No. 4 at the Chernobyl Nuclear Power Plant in the Ukrainian Soviet Republic exploded, raining massive amounts of radioactive particles over the surrounding area. In their long tradition of safeguarding socialism from adverse publicity, Soviet officials took two days before announcing in a brief press release that a nuclear accident had occurred; it took an additional two days before they admitted the gravity of the disaster. Even then, they assured their citizens that they had everything under control. The government would take immediate steps to contain the fallout from the reactor, move Chernobyl's citizens to safe ground, and cut off the city from the rest of the country and the neighboring Byelorussian Soviet Republic. Obligingly, Moscow's Eastern European allies followed suit in conveying this message to their own citizens.

The protective shield of dictatorship enabled the Soviets to act in this fashion. Had this tragedy occurred in a Western European democracy, the reaction would have been completely different. Given the free flow of information, it would have instantaneously precipitated panic in every household and workplace. Thereafter, public officials who could be tied to the disaster would have becomes targets of investigation and recrimination. Nevertheless, as I shall argue in this chapter, Moscow was vulnerable in a much more profound way. Because the party's central role was based on the viability of developed socialism, its leaders' elite status was at stake. The virtue of this set of tacit understandings was that when Soviet citizens' needs were fulfilled, the Communist Party of the Soviet Union (CPSU) could take credit for the success. Yet by the same logic, when times were bad, the party had to take responsibility for its failures as well.

It is hard to imagine a more tangible sign of failure than a nuclear cloud wafting over one's territory. By the time of the Chernobyl disaster, the idea of competent party leadership was already foundering throughout the USSR and Eastern Europe. The promise of what I have called the "Brezhnev consensus," upon which the Soviet Union and its allies had staked the organization's identity since the mid-1960s, was regularly undercut by the trials of daily existence, including food shortages, crumbling apartments, transportation failures, and environmental contamination. Furthermore, disgruntlement over the lifestyles of party members was rising. Soviet citizens had become deeply cynical about a system of governance that allowed the ruling elite to escape standard privations through access to Western consumer goods, exclusive restaurants, and dalliances abroad.

Even more significant, faith in the party's mission was eroding within the organization's ranks. Those members who still wanted to defend the merits of socialism over capitalism were discouraged by the steadily widening gulf between what they promised to achieve in their official capacities and what they could actually deliver. Additionally, their self-respect was challenged by the contradiction between the ritualistic slogans they were expected to mouth and the recognition that their compatriots took little of what they said seriously.

In these circumstances, communist rulers had a choice. They could stay the course, gambling that their economies could be set right and that they could simultaneously provide their cadres with additional incentives to ensure their commitment to the socialist project. The other possibility was to introduce serious reforms to the practice of developed socialism. At no time did the advocates of this position intend to compromise the party's leading role. To the contrary, their goal was to strengthen it.

Mikhail Gorbachev chose this latter, less traveled path. When he became general secretary of the CPSU on March 11, 1985, bringing the hopes and ideals of a rising generation of communists with him, he embraced the idea that the Soviet Union could do better. In a sensational step, he introduced a concept of economic reform, perestroika ("restructuring"), that was based upon fundamental changes to the system of centralized planning. Simultaneously, he advocated a new style of leadership, assuring the Soviet population that government and party officials would henceforth demonstrate a spirit of glasnost ("openness") in their behavior. As I shall argue, however, Gorbachev's most consequential innovation was one of which he was arguably least aware. Without recognizing the full implications of his decisions, he broke with the Leninist tradition of viewing the party as the unassailable font of truth and increasingly treated state institutions as equal to the task of leadership.

Predictably, this "new thinking," to use Gorbachev's terms, precipitated a rift in the communist world. Although for different reasons, Poland's and Hungary's leaders adopted and then moved beyond the precepts of Gorbachev's reforms. Other regimes, including those of East Germany, Bulgaria, and Czechoslovakia, fought back. Old-guard personalities like Erich Honecker, Todor Zhivkov, and Gustáv Husák, respectively, joined Gorbachev's critics within the CPSU Politburo, such as the Secretariat's chief of organizational affairs, Yegor Ligachev, in warning that the general secretary's focus on the role of the state would undermine the principle of single-party rule. Simultaneously, Romania's Nicolae Ceauşescu and Albania's Enver Hoxha fought to defend personal despotism.

Ironically, as we shall see, it turned out that Gorbachev's critics were absolutely right. Their general secretary's reforms were profoundly destabilizing. At the same time, however, their opportunities to make the case against precipitous change were running out. Unlike in the preceding decades of communist rule, when they could supplement a Marxist interpretation of their conditions with references to looming threats to national security, Cold War tensions, and economic perils, the credibility of these rationales had faded. This is not to say that opponents of significant change were equally disadvantaged in other parts of the communist world. In the case of China, which I shall highlight in this chapter, the regime managed to defend its rule. But China's leaders faced a different type of party crisis and responded with a different remedy—the use of brute force—that neither the Soviet Union's leader nor his Eastern European allies dared to implement. Otherwise, when Gorbachev gave in to pressures in March 1990 to remove the reference to the CPSU's leading role from the Soviet Constitution, the need for the vanguard that had made sense in its original European and Russian contexts vanished.

THE SHIFT TO THE STATE IN POLAND

It is not surprising that the impetus behind the transfer of political authority from the party to the state occurred first in Poland. The shift had already begun in the regime's response to the outbreak of massive strikes in the Baltic shipyards in 1970 and in the demonstrations and strikes in Radom, Ursus, and beyond in 1976. Although Poland's rulers justified their measures in terms of the restoration of the party's leading role, their actions were all about strengthening the state's hand in meeting economic targets. In 1970, they turned first to the army to restore order. But when this recourse failed, they accepted the workers' demands and assured them that they would find new ways to improve their well-being. In 1976, they simply gave the protestors what they wanted.

The difference between these conditions and the revolutionary developments in Poland at the end of the decade and into the 1980s is that the Polish United Workers' Party's (PUWP) reason for retaining a monopoly of power was undercut by a single event: the triumphant visit of a newly elected Polish pope, John Paul II, in 1979. When the pope made his first public appearance in Warsaw on June 2, 1979, he could have chosen, as his mentor Stefan Cardinal Wyszyński had done on countless occasions, to chastise the regime for refusing to grant construction permits for church buildings, practicing job discrimination against believers, and propagating atheism in schools. He could then have gone a step further by questioning the regime's credibility, broaching touchier, politically sensitive themes, such as the rights of workers to better conditions in the workplace. In fact, Edward Gierek and his coleaders would have welcomed such criticism. It would have allowed them to accuse the Vatican of interfering in the country's internal affairs and perhaps raised doubts among the PUWP's rank and file about the pontiff's intentions. Yet, John Paul II's public approach was more damaging. He acted as though the political realm, which the PUWP represented, was irrelevant to the true interests of his fellow Poles.

In front of hundreds of thousands of worshippers crowded into Warsaw's Victory Square, the pope used the power of the altar to speak for Poland itself. Why was it, he began, that "precisely in 1978, after so many centuries of well-established tradition in this field, a son of the Polish nation, of the land of Poland, was called to the chair of St. Peter?" This was a sign, he declared, of Poland's special responsibility to bear witness to the truth of the Gospel. Through centuries of suffering and torment, at the mercy of foreign invaders, behind the walls of the Warsaw ghetto, and amid the ruins of World War II, the Polish people's actions had consistently testified to the indomitable nature of the human spirit. These sacrifices were, in the pope's words, a "contribution to the development of man and humanity, to intellect, heart, and conscience."[1]

The significance of this statement is that John Paul II was not asking Poland's citizens to be anything more than servants of Christ. Standing before the tomb of the Unknown Soldier, he admonished the crowds that the history of the motherland was still being written. Every Pole would be called to do more for his or her nation. One form of sacrifice could be the "seed of the blood of a soldier shed on the battlefield." Others might be "the seed of hard daily toil . . . the love of parents . . . [or] the seed of creative work in the universities, the higher institutes, the libraries and the places where the national culture is built." Whatever Poles were called to do, their religious faith—and apparently not the PUWP—would sustain them.

For the Gierek regime, these words could not have been more unsettling. The mere presence of this self-described "son of Poland" called into question the fragile synthesis that Władysław Gomułka had aspired to build twenty-three years earlier between the PUWP's rule and the population's national identity. While the pontiff could speak of a heavenly reward for the pain that believers endured on earth, the country's secular representatives were reminded that they faced the more daunting challenge of competing for their citizens' national loyalties in the here and now. In the era of developed socialism, the absence of war and the diminution of Cold War tensions meant that Leninist appeals for heroic sacrifice and deferred gratification rang hollow.

The pope's awakening of doubts about the party's exclusive claim to speak for the Polish nation coincided with an array of secular developments that amplified the regime's failures. In summer 1980, labor strikes once more crisscrossed Poland. Initially, these protests looked much like their antecedents. In mid-July, the government announced once again that prices would be raised for certain foodstuffs—this time, it was meat—without a commensurate increase in wages. Workers stormed out of their factories in the vicinity of Warsaw, Lublin, and Wrocław. However, by the time these protests reached the northern shipyards of Gdańsk and Gdynia, the strikers had a new strategy. Rather than insisting that Gierek's government rescind its decision, they presented it with a list of twenty-one demands that marked a clear shift in their understanding of the standard demarcation between the state and society.

The strikers' demands, which became the basis for a historical agreement in Gdańsk on August 31 and the founding of a free trade union movement, Solidarity, on September 17, were shocking in their audacity. The first two demands—for the right to form independent trade unions and the right to strike—amounted to a flat rejection of the Leninist precept that only the party could represent the working class and act on the basis of the masses' true interests. Other demands on the list sounded less dramatic, such as an increase in monthly pay and in the commuter's allowance. Nonetheless, they showed that the strikers intended to treat the government as a conventional state institution that could be judged according to its performance.

Predictably, Gierek and his coleaders considered it preposterous that they should be bullied by what they believed was a handful of criminals. In fact, their allies in the Kremlin immediately let them know that it was their duty to crush the forces of counterrevolution, making veiled references to the possibility of Warsaw Pact intervention. But within days, the threat of greater labor unrest forced the leadership to recognize that the workers would not give in. After a week of negotiations with the strike coordinators, including the future head of Solidarity, Lech Wałęsa, they reached an agreement in Gdańsk and two other cities about the implementation of their twenty-one demands.

The accord's first article was as painful a blow as one could imagine to the principles that justified the regime's existence. In an expression of grassroots defiance that had not been seen in Eastern Europe since the Hungarian Revolution in 1956, the strike leaders challenged the party's proletarian credentials by underscoring the "expediency" of establishing "new, self-governing trade unions that will genuinely represent the working class." For the moment, the strikers moderated this shocking appropriation of the PUWP's foundations by insisting that they had no intention of forming political parties. Rhetorically, they affirmed the party's claim to play "the leading role in the state." Yet, these assurances were no more than words. Because their representatives reserved the right to require the state to meet their demands, it was hard to see how the PUWP would maintain this role.[2] What was a communist party to do if it could not reign supreme over the proletariat!

The founding of Solidarity brought the significance of these agreements into full relief, both for PUWP officials and union leaders. It is hard to determine whether figures like Wałęsa sincerely believed that they could square the circle between asserting Solidarity's independence and respecting the party's authority. They may have simply considered the issue irrelevant. One way or the other, the resultant clash of principles was virtually inevitable. Solidarity's rapid expansion into a national force was threatening because it signaled an unprecedented event—the birth of a counterparty. By December 1980, the union could claim nearly 9 million members, and an overwhelming majority of Poles regarded it as a legitimate representative of Polish society.

The PUWP's predicament was made even worse by becoming a major supplier of these enrollments. In a key tactical error, the party leadership encouraged its members to join the new trade union in order to dilute its ranks. In so doing, it vastly underestimated Solidarity's appeal. In the ensuing months, more than a million PUWP members joined the union. Of these numbers, a staggering 380,000 members, many of whom had been brought in during the recruiting drive of the second half of the 1970s, left the party for good. Between 60 and 72 percent came from working-class backgrounds.[3] Paradoxically, it may have been worse for the PUWP that other Solidarity sympathizers chose to remain. Their belief that they could live in both worlds proved that the party's claim to a special status was melting away. In a speech to the Central Committee Secretariat, Stanisław Kania, who replaced Gierek on September 6, admitted that precisely this issue was at hand: "We recommended to party members that they join the new trade unions. But a question arises, whether we have party members in Solidarity, or Solidarity members in the party."[4]

Under these circumstances, the regime had three options. For the old-line communists, the only acceptable course was to renege on the agreements, or at least make them so difficult to implement that Solidarity would give up its maximal demands. They used the court system to test this approach by refusing to register Solidarity. However, when the union responded with a warning strike, the regime backed down. In contrast, the least confrontational option, which was advanced by Kania and formed the basis for the two bodies' interactions over the coming year, was to continue negotiations on multiple fronts with the aim of co-opting the union leadership.

Behind the scenes, however, a third option was ever-present: to declare war on Polish society. As the strikes escalated, Moscow and Poland's socialist neighbors, Czechoslovakia and East Germany, repeatedly pressed Kania to quell the protests. None of these powers was oblivious to the risks of calling in Warsaw Pact troops to end the crisis. Even in the darkest days of the Cold War, Nikita Khrushchev had been unwilling to take such a risk with Poland. If anything, the danger had become even greater with the passage of time. As Kania frankly informed officials at the Ministry of Internal Affairs in January 1981, "Even if angels entered Poland, they would be treated as bloodthirsty vampires and the socialist ideas would be swimming in blood."[5]

This dilemma meant that if worse came to worst, the Poles would be required to use their own armed forces to restore order. For months, both the military command and the security forces were in accord that this option should be a last resort. It would risk sparking a civil war. In addition, they recognized that even if they could prevent this eventuality, the use of weapons against Polish citizens would destroy the regime's feeble chances of recouping the communist party's reputation. By early 1981, however, they concluded that this step was unavoidable.

One reason was that no matter what concessions the regime made to Solidarity, the trade union's opponents were determined to ensure that these agreements would never be implemented. Thus, every interaction between the regime and the opposition resulted in a battle within the PUWP. To placate these forces, as well as to mollify the Soviets, Kania signaled his endorsement of a tougher line by appointing his defense minister, Wojciech Jaruzelski, to be Poland's prime minister; he would later replace Kania as the PUWP's first secretary on October 18.

The other reason for this emerging consensus is that the regime could not count on Solidarity to fulfill its agreements. The larger the movement grew, the more unwieldy it became. In the organization's early months, Wałęsa and Solidarity's other founders held their followers together through persuasion, charisma, and the force of circumstances. Yet, a growing number of Solidarity activists were no longer willing to accept these calls for restraint. In their eyes, the greater danger was that the movement's leaders were bargaining away the union's achievements. They were convinced that Solidarity had won the requisite authority to dictate the regime's policies.

In a letter to the PUWP Secretariat on June 5, 1981, Soviet leaders expressed their displeasure with the worsening situation. They criticized both Kania and Jaruzelski by name. "Since the first days of the crisis," the letter stated, "we believed that it was a matter of importance that the party oppose in a determined manner any attempts by the enemies of socialism to take advantage of the difficulties which appeared to further their long-term aims." Instead, as a result of the two leaders' concessions, "the PUWP has been falling back step by step under the pressure of the internal counterrevolution." Worse still, the party had seemingly lost the ability to maintain order within its own ranks. The PUWP was scheduled to announce its long-term priorities at an impending party congress. Yet in the Soviet view, antisocialist forces were setting its agenda. "Time does not wait," the letter concluded ominously. "The party can and should find within itself the forces to reverse the course of events and to restore them to the right path even before the congress."[6]

The Soviet Union's leaders undoubtedly recognized that a viable party had practically ceased to exist. But all explanations aside, they instructed Jaruzelski that it was his responsibility to resolve the crisis. On December 5, 1981, the PUWP Politburo reached the fateful conclusion that order could only be reestablished through martial law. In the words of one member who would later become prime minister, Zbigniew Messner, "We cannot have delusions that society is ready to support us . . . we cannot passively watch the system fall apart because in a few weeks there will be nobody who can introduce martial law and nobody who might be interested in it." Jaruzelski agreed, conceding the bankruptcy of party leadership. "It is a horrible, monstrous shame for the party," he confessed, "that after 36 years in power it has to be defended by the police. But there is nothing left ahead of us. We need to be ready to make the decision that will allow us to save what is fundamental."[7]

In the face of a counterparty, Solidarity, the military was all that remained to hold Poland together. In this light, it is significant that when Jaruzelski declared Poland to be under a "state of war" on December 13, he did not speak to his fellow citizens in his capacity as PUWP first secretary. In fact, he did not mention the communist party at all. Instead, he presented himself "as a soldier and as the head of the Polish government." His heavy burden of responsibility, Jaruzelski explained, was to restore order to the country that "my generation fought for on all the fronts of the war and for which they sacrificed the best years of their life."[8] He stressed that the use of armed force was only a temporary measure. Military government would not solve Poland's deeper problems. But the possibility of restoring the regime's authority on the basis of single-party rule had disappeared.

GORBACHEV'S ALTERNATIVE COURSE

Scholars often assume that there is a direct relationship between the PUWP's loss of control in Poland and Gorbachev's readiness four years later to change the relationship between rulers and ruled in the Soviet Union.[9] Would it not have made sense for the Soviet leader to learn the lessons of Poland's crisis and apply them to his country? I am willing to accept the idea that the Solidarity period had an important atmospheric significance for global communism, not least as an indicator, in the communist party's earnest vocabulary, of the need for eternal vigilance to protect the achievements of socialism. However, there is no evidence that the Polish events played a major role in Gorbachev's decision to reform the Soviet system. Instead, the PUWP's perils in the early 1980s appeared to its allies to be what they had always been in the communist era. Poland was the special case, which required exceptional arrangements to defend socialism.

When Gorbachev became the CPSU's chief in March 1985, he did not require any Polish lessons to be persuaded to undertake a searching examination of the shortcomings of developed socialism. The Soviet regime, too, was burdened with serious difficulties. Like Poland, it was unable to meet its population's rising expectations. The country still suffered from an acute shortage of housing; its vaunted health care system was breaking down; and staples, like sugar and meat, were in short supply. At the same time, corruption had spread throughout the party establishment and state bureaucracies, fostering both disgruntlement and malaise. The first sentiment was driven by the injustice of a system that, despite its Marxist pretensions, appeared to benefit the few over the many; the second was due to the absence of realistic hopes that the situation would change for the better.

Unlike Poland, there were no significant autonomous challenges to the Soviet regime, let alone a powerful, independent movement like Solidarity. Moreover, there was no comparable social crisis. Instead, for party members who wanted their country to be perceived as the strategic equal of the United States and the sole legitimate leader of the global communist movement, the homeland of the October Revolution had lost its luster. Moscow's ill-fated invasion of Afghanistan exemplified this problem. When the Kremlin sent troops into the country in December 1979 to prop up the quasi-socialist Babrak Karmal regime, its pretext was nearly identical to that which it had used eleven years earlier to justify the suppression of the Prague Spring. In the CPSU's arcane phraseology, Moscow was doing nothing more than defending the international working class. However, despite their superior weaponry and training, Soviet forces were unable to defeat the roaming forces of the Mujahedeen.

This circumstance provides insight into the mentality that Gorbachev and the new cohort of Soviet policymakers evinced in confronting the system that led to such debacles. At a minimum, they had to be sufficiently idealistic about the possibility of reawakening a conception of leadership that had, in their view, once made socialism worth fighting for. By Soviet standards, these communists were relatively young. Born in the 1920s and 1930s, many had not served during World War II and lacked direct experience with the Terror. Their formative experiences in the party had been under Khrushchev and Brezhnev, not Stalin. Khrushchev's denunciations of the crimes of the Stalinist era left them entranced with the prospect of restoring the party's reputation by distinguishing its principles from the aberrant behavior of specific individuals. Furthermore, their experience under Brezhnev had provided them with the negative example of socialism in its least inspirational form. For them, the Afghanistan debacle was symptomatic of the rigid political culture that had shaped nearly every decision during these years. After Brezhnev's death in 1982, these concerns were not allayed by the Politburo's choice of two representatives of the old guard to succeed him. One was the chairman of the KGB, Yuri Andropov, who was thought by some to be a potential reformer. But he died after a mere one and a half years in power. The other was the much more conservative Konstantin Chernenko.

Against this background, we can appreciate what Gorbachev was seeking to accomplish in enunciating the concepts of perestroika and glasnost. In a speech on ideological questions on December 10, 1984, three months before his appointment as general secretary, he used these ideas to call attention to the "the problems of perfecting developed socialism." A restructuring of the system of planning and production was necessary to build an efficient and internationally competitive economy. Openness, about which he would elaborate later, meant that both party and government officials should secure the trust of citizens by speaking candidly about their activities.[10]

At first, Gorbachev consolidated his position the old-fashioned way. He removed his most likely opponents within the party bureaucracy. He then replaced them with more open-minded thinkers of his own background and political inclinations; many of his colleagues had previously been confined to lesser positions in the party. Gorbachev also showed appreciable skill in persuading his senior colleagues to shuffle the membership of the Politburo. One of his most notable successes was the appointment of Alexander Yakovlev, the so-called godfather of glasnost, as a candidate member of the Politburo in 1986. In an equally revealing development, the general secretary oversaw a substantial change in the composition of the Central Committee. At the CPSU's Twenty-Seventh Congress in February–March 1986, the body's turnover rate of 45 percent was the highest in twenty-five years.[11]

Gorbachev's greater challenge was to establish the processes according to which his policies would be implemented. As always, the default response was that the party was in charge. But as in times past, the decisive issue was what kind of party this would be: the party that had implemented the basic principles of the Brezhnev consensus or a party that somehow lived up to a higher ideal. During his first year in office, Gorbachev appears to have been torn over this question. After all, given the fact that he was still operating within Leninist parameters, how could the situation have been different?

Accordingly, when we examine Gorbachev's public statements immediately after his appointment, we encounter two seemingly contradictory images of party leadership. The first image is of a party suffused with the personality of the exuberant general secretary, the campaigner par excellence who can act upon the pent-up excitement and grievances of his generation. In a major address on the occasion of the CPSU's Twenty-Seventh Congress, Gorbachev is the grand master of perestroika, proclaiming that the rebuilding of the Soviet economy depends on the energy and initiative of party officials and managers. "Any restructuring of the economic mechanism," he lectures, "begins with a restructuring of types of thinking and practice, and a clear understanding of the new tasks." The country cannot continue to rely, he insists, on bureaucrats who "take a wait-and-see attitude or, like the Gogol character who organized all kinds of harebrained schemes, for all practical purposes do nothing and change nothing." "We and they," he emphasizes, "are simply not moving in the same direction."[12] Hence, this Gorbachev challenges the party to prove that it is capable of leading this transformation: "There is no vanguard role for the communists in the abstract; it is expressed in practical deeds."[13]

In contrast, Gorbachev's second image of the party is of an organization that will not lose sight of its special purpose. Interestingly, he justifies this stand in traditional Leninist terms. "Meaningful advances," he contends, can only unfold "in conditions of struggle, which is inevitable as long as exploitation and exploiter classes exist."[14] Accordingly, party members must adhere to the principles that make them uniquely suited for the battle against capitalism. "We must continue to improve the ideological upbringing of communists," he asserts, "and to increase demands on them for the observance of party discipline and for the unswerving fulfillment of statutory requirements."[15]

The great uncertainty, however, was how long the balance between these potentially contradictory images of leadership—one open and innovative, the other still disciplined and vigilant—could be sustained. One day after Gorbachev's address to the congress, Andrei Gromyko, the éminence grise of Soviet foreign policy, confirmed that internal battles were under way by explicitly denying their existence. Declaring the congress to be "striking evidence of the solidarity of the party's ranks and its ideological unity," Gromyko dared skeptics to prove otherwise. "No one should be allowed," he warned, "under the pretext of encouraging the healthy and necessary cause of criticism and self-criticism—and this cause should be law—to resort to fabrications alleging that there are rifts in our party and in Soviet society." Indeed, he concluded, "those who engage in this or who would engage in it should be put in their places—should get their just deserts."[16]

It would not take long before Gorbachev's desire to implement significant reforms would lead to intensified divisions. However, he initially attempted to hold them off by treating his reforms as a natural progression from the Soviet past. One finds a perfect example of this approach in his statements during the seventieth anniversary celebrations of the October Revolution on November 2, 1987. In defense of his proposals, Gorbachev invokes Lenin as a likely proponent of perestroika. In this portrayal, the father of the Revolution would have insisted that Marxism never be applied in a dogmatic or pedantic fashion. Quite the opposite: Lenin bequeathed to posterity "an instructive lesson in the living dialectics of revolutionary thought and action." The same wisdom, it seems, holds true for the present moment. "All of these things are not simply pages from the chronicle of the Great Revolution," Gorbachev emphasizes. "They are also a constant reminder to us, to those who are living today, of the communists' lofty duty to always be on the cutting edge of events, to be able to make bold decisions, to assume full responsibility for the present and the future."[17]

In addition, Gorbachev presents his listeners with an image of Lenin far removed from the combative tone of *What Is to Be Done?* His preference is for the mythologized late Lenin who supposedly showed flexibility in outlining a new way of organizing society. "We are now turning with increasing frequency to Ilyich's last works," he notes reverently, "to Lenin's ideas of the New Economic Policy [NEP]." Naturally, Gorbachev counters, one would not want to equate the NEP "with what we are doing at present, when we are in a fundamentally different stage of development." Still, in his view, the time has come to view Soviet history through a prism of missed opportunities. Notably, Gorbachev approvingly mentions Nikolai Bukharin's name in passing. However, he reserves his most effusive praise for Khrushchev, who evidently would also have been a perestroika supporter. Under Khrushchev's leadership, Gorbachev observes, "a wind of change swept through the country, and the people took heart, gained new life, and became more confident." Notwithstanding his failings, Khrushchev had the wisdom to campaign against "command-bureaucratic methods of management," to emphasize "humanistic ideals and values," and "to revive the creative spirit of Leninism in theory and practice."[18]

Conversely, Gorbachev directs his most pointed criticisms at two other periods in the Soviet past. One target is predictable—Stalin—whom he vilifies. The other is more provocative: Brezhnev. Gorbachev's critique of his predecessor does not amount to a blanket criticism. Brezhnev, we learn, played an important role in stabilizing the Soviet Union after Khrushchev's misadventures. But for Gorbachev, the last years of the Brezhnev era were the source of the CPSU's current travails. During "the latter years of L. I. Brezhnev's life and activity," he points out, "the search for paths of further progress [were] greatly impeded by an adherence to habitual formulas and patterns that did not reflect the new realities." As a result, the Soviet economy had been weakened, principles of social justice had been violated, and the country had been thrown into a "pre-crisis situation."[19] Now, the task is to resolve these problems.

Undoubtedly, Gorbachev would have liked to maintain this "Leninist" synthesis, assuring his doubters about his devotion to the party's traditions while at the same time calling for fundamental change. But in my view, the underlying problem with this balancing act is that it was an inherently contradictory enterprise. On the one hand, Gorbachev was seeking to overturn the preceding decades of economic inefficiency, bureaucratic retrenchment, and unreflective policymaking. On the other, he was putting this task into the hands of the organization, the party, that had created these problems in the first place. Thus, it soon became clear to him that he could not do both. He could either return to the conventions of communist party rule during the Brezhnev years or he could supplement the party's strengths with other institutions. He chose the latter course.

It makes sense that Gorbachev's transition first became evident in the area of foreign affairs. In a world in which the conflict among states had clearly ascended over the conflict between ideologies, Gorbachev embraced the opportunity to be a statesman, not an apparatchik. Additionally, perestroika provided him with an additional reason for distancing himself from the remaining strains of the class struggle. Because military spending was one of the heaviest burdens on the Soviet economy, he and advisers like Yakovlev were convinced that a reduction of international tensions through arms control agreements and other accords would make it easier to focus on domestic reform. Thus, by 1987, Gorbachev was preparing for agreements with the United States and other states that would have been inconceivable two years earlier when he came to power. In November 1987, he signed the Intermediate-Range Nuclear Forces Treaty with the United States. In February 1988, he announced the complete withdrawal of Soviet troops from Afghanistan. In July 1989, he presented himself as a European personality of the highest order, proclaiming a "common European home."

Predictably, Gorbachev's decision to accelerate the pace of change raised the anxieties of Politburo members who supported reform, but only on gradual terms. The most prominent figure was Yegor Ligachev, who despite being a Gorbachev protégé had become convinced that the party's leading role would not survive the shift away from its Leninist, revolutionary foundations. On March 13, 1988, Ligachev expressed his opposition in the same cryptic manner with which internal party struggles had been communicated for decades. The Moscow newspaper *Sovetskaya Rossiya* published a letter to the editor from a little-known chemistry teacher in Leningrad, Nina Andreyeva, that was unmistakably directed against Gorbachev's policies. In the letter, Andreyeva expressed dismay that her students' understanding of their country's history was being maliciously distorted by the proponents of what she called "some kind of left-liberal dilettantish socialism." It was urgent, she argued, that "young people learn the class vision of the world and gain an understanding of the connection between human and class interests." Presumably this was a reference to those party members, on the one hand, who stood on the side of the working class and those on the other, who apparently had doubts about the class struggle. It cannot be an accident that Andreyeva was directly quoting Ligachev.[20]

Whatever one thought about Andreyeva's and Ligachev's preferences, Gorbachev was indeed making a major change in course. As if to confirm their fears, on June 28, the general secretary convened a momentous party meeting, the Nineteenth All-Union CPSU Conference, at which he took the first steps toward formalizing an explicit division of labor between state and party power. In the spirit of giving Soviet citizens more influence over state policy, he proposed the creation of a new parliamentary body, the Congress of People's Deputies, which would elect a smaller but more powerful Supreme Soviet. Gorbachev's motives were transparent. Frankly admitting that perestroika was in danger, he aimed to use these state organs to increase the number of officials who were sympathetic to his policies and thereby acquire more power to muscle through his reforms. However, the means that he recommended for implementing this decision were extraordinary by Soviet standards. Under the rubric of "democratization," he pushed through a policy to allow for multicandidate elections to the Congress.

In no way was Gorbachev advocating Western parliamentary democracy. These would not be direct elections. Both the party leadership and officially sanctioned organizations, such as the All-Union
Central Council of Trade Unions and the Academy of Sciences, would
be guaranteed a fixed number of seats in the Congress. Still, Gorbachev
was treading on holy ground. From a philosophical standpoint, the
idea of enhancing the status of a legislative organ would have reminded
close observers of communist history of the ambiguities in Marx's and
Lenin's thinking about the relationship between party and state institutions. In the early 1920s, this issue had been decided in favor of the
former. On this occasion, however, Gorbachev's goal—to upgrade the
state as a mechanism for implementing perestroika—raised serious
questions about the definition of party leadership. Gorbachev assured
the conference participants that he was not calling this fundamental
tenet of Leninism into question. But more than any Soviet leader before him, he insisted upon a strict demarcation of functions: "The Central Committee and the Politburo are to act as agencies of political
leadership . . . [while] everything that the USSR Supreme Soviet and
the USSR Council of Ministers are supposed to do should be done by
them alone."[21]

On the surface, the fact that the selection of candidates to run for
seats in the Congress of People's Deputies was stacked in favor of the
CPSU seemed to guarantee that the party would retain its definitive
role. But there was an ambiguity to this strategy. What if the party
leadership's preferred candidates did not receive the number of votes
necessary to hold office? This problem would not have arisen if the
CPSU elite had been as united in practice as it was in theory. Yet, for
every passing day in the struggles over the Soviet Union's future, the
prospect appeared less realistic. On March 26, 1989, voters went to the
polls to take part in the first contested, multicandidate elections in
the country since voting in 1917 for the short-lived All-Russian Constituent Assembly. In a majority of cases, they supported the CPSU's
designated candidates. Nonetheless, when runoff elections were conducted in April and May, the Congress ended up with over 300 deputies who did not have the regime's endorsement. Instantly, the mythology of a unified vanguard was opened to doubt.

Poland and Hungary Do It Their Way

One can easily imagine why Gorbachev's willingness to look beyond the party's vanguard role would have a dramatic impact on the communist world. As I have shown throughout this book, Moscow's understanding of its role in the international movement was an almost perfect replication of the idea of party leadership, only on a global scale. Even a state like China, which had an antagonistic relationship with the USSR, was bound to be affected by a rethinking of the party's functions. For those in the Warsaw Pact, this issue also raised a practical question: To what extent should they reassess their own parties' purposes?

Earlier in this chapter, I noted that Brezhnev's Politburo decided in its final days that Poland's leaders, and not the USSR, should take responsibility for restoring order to their country. At the time, Moscow's allies could have interpreted this judgment in two ways. One possibility was that the Soviets expected Jaruzelski to resolve the crisis but would have reluctantly intervened had he failed. A contending interpretation is that they would have reflected on their perilous engagement in Afghanistan and done nothing. Because the first interpretation was, from the perspective of the early 1980s, as plausible as the second, the risk of testing the Soviets' intentions and being proven wrong was too great.

Gorbachev's foreign policy innovations resolved this uncertainty. As early as February 25, 1986, he hinted at a shift in his understanding of Moscow's leadership role by speaking approvingly about the "enormous diversity" of the communist movement and acknowledging that "there is not always total unanimity among the Communist Parties."[22] In his 1987 address on the October Revolution, he went a provocative step further, arguing that "the time of the Comintern and the Cominform is past." "We have also become convinced," he added, "that socialism does not and cannot have any 'model' that everyone must measure up to."[23] Behind the scenes, Soviet officials quietly informed their Eastern European counterparts that the obligatory features of proletarian internationalism were matters of the past. No longer bound together by a rigid ideology, these rulers were effectively cast adrift in a world of self-interested states.

The leaders of both Hungary and Poland had reason to regard this development as positive. In the first instance, János Kádár's regime was already far along the road toward fashioning a socialist alternative to the Soviet economic model. In the early 1980s, the general secretary had already begun to look for new ways of persuading the population that the Hungarian Socialist Workers' Party (HSWP) remained a source of enlightened leadership. The regime added to its record of reform by expanding the room for autonomous economic activity in small businesses, cooperatives, farms, and the manufacturing industry. In 1983, two years before Chernenko's death, the Hungarian government introduced an electoral law that actually *required* that at least two candidates run for every state office, with only a few exceptions. Party leaders made sure that they controlled this process by nominating ideologically and sometimes even professionally identical candidates ("two eggs," as they were known among the populace). Nonetheless, when the first multicandidate elections to the National Assembly took place in June 1985, the experiment backfired. In a demonstration of the shallowness of the pretense to party unity, some communists whose names had not been put up by the leadership won seats, while other, well-established figures were defeated.

For these reasons, Hungary's leaders hardly needed Gorbachev to teach them about reform. Quite the contrary, Budapest had been first to act. Nonetheless, by this time Kádár's reforms were almost entirely signs of the regime's weakness. The long-serving general secretary's bargain with his citizens was based upon the state's ability to keep up with their continually rising expectations. His government had managed to meet this demand in the late 1970s through heavy borrowing from Western lending institutions. However, this strategy all but collapsed at the turn of the decade when the regime was forced to adopt tough austerity measures in order to receive more loans. For the first time since the devastating events of fall 1956, citizens faced the prospect of losing their jobs, and some were threatened with impoverishment. At this juncture above all, Hungary's aged leader would have done well to acknowledge these problems. But in the imperious style to which he had grown accustomed in his later years, Kádár refused to admit their existence.

In contrast, Jaruzelski found himself in the classic position of any military commander who is able to use force but would prefer first to have maximal support from those around him. In the first year after the declaration of the state of war in Poland, the military government acted as one would have predicted. It banned Solidarity, arrested and imprisoned the union's members, and tightened its control over journalists. On the surface, these tactics seemed to work. Once Solidarity was decapitated, its leaders could no longer organize on a national scale. Nonetheless, this was a pyrrhic victory. Solidarity was not destroyed but only driven underground. Although the organization was weakened, its broadly dispersed structure made it harder for the regime to identify and apprehend its opponents. Furthermore, Jaruzelski recognized the difficulty of asking Polish soldiers once again to fire on their compatriots. As the economy deteriorated and Poles found themselves standing in food lines and struggling to survive on depressed incomes, the country's rulers became the logical explanation for every failure.

In earlier times, Jaruzelski would have turned to the PUWP rank and file for support. But in a demonstration that the prestige of the party was in free fall, 780,000 members left the party between its Ninth and Tenth Congresses (1981–1986). All told, since summer 1980, the PUWP lost 35 percent of its total membership.[24] Hence, Jaruzelski reached out to civil society. He offered the Catholic Church construction permits and access to the airwaves in exchange for its cooperation. He sought to lure prominent intellectuals away from Solidarity and its affiliated organizations by providing publication outlets. Like the Hungarian government, he also experimented with multicandidate elections at both the local level in 1984 and for the Sejm (parliament) in 1985. These contests were conducted on a much more restrictive basis than in Hungary, but they nonetheless attracted a high voter turnout. Possibly Jaruzelski's shrewdest public maneuver was his handling of the murder of the activist priest, Father Jerzy Popiełuszko, by state security officers in October 1984. Popiełuszko, who was widely hailed as the "chaplain of Solidarity," was an outspoken critic of the regime. When it became clear, however, that the authorities could not cover up the killing, Jaruzelski ordered the arrest and trial of the perpetrators.

Despite this cautiously conciliatory strategy, Jaruzelski's gestures could not eliminate the deeper sources of discontent that had produced the Polish crisis in the first place. In spring and summer 1988, a largely spontaneous wave of strikes swept across Poland in response to yet another reluctant decision by the government to raise food prices. This time, however, the strikers proceeded differently than in the past. Instead of pressing the government to rescind the price increases, they simply demanded that it raise their wages proportionately. They also insisted that the regime immediately recognize the legality of Solidarity.

These protests also took a new form. They were populated by younger, blue-collar workers who had less patience than their predecessors in negotiating with the state. In fact, the Solidarity old guard did not play a direct role in organizing these protests. Caught off guard by the strikes, Lech Wałęsa merely observed that he supported the workers' demands but was not personally on strike. For Jaruzelski, in contrast, this was a turning point. He had to face the fact that the only chance to win more time for his government was to accept Solidarity's legitimacy. On the principle that it was better to negotiate with an old enemy than an unfamiliar new one, on August 26 he directed his interior minister, Czesław Kiszczak, to invite Wałęsa to enter into "roundtable" talks about restoring harmonious relations, if such a quality had ever existed, among a majority of Poles.

By this point, the Hungarian regime as well was entering into negotiations with its adversaries. But this step took place under conditions in which the party itself, and not some noncommunist adversary, contributed to its own demise. In the mid-1980s, there was a superficial similarity between the HSWP leadership and Gorbachev's position. Hungary's old-guard leaders were being challenged by a generation of communists who had entered the party in the preceding decade and were acutely sensitive to the defects in the government's policies. They and key figures in the Politburo were united by one factor—the conviction that Kádár was the major impediment to Hungary's recovery and had to be removed. Unlike in the Soviet Union, however, there was a significant fissure in this alliance of convenience. One contingent, led by Kádár's protégé, Prime Minister Károly Grósz, focused on economic stabilization, fiscal discipline, and an overhaul of the planning system.

In opposition, a growing counterfaction contended that economic reform alone was insufficient. Under the leadership of Imre Pozsgay, the general secretary of the Patriotic Front, and spurred by a proliferation of informal "reform circles" in regional and municipal party organizations, this group's adherents were prepared to go further than ever in testing the fine boundary between developed socialism and social democracy. They promoted both inner-party democracy and, more provocatively, the participation of noncommunist groups in the public sphere. Accordingly, after the two factions briefly united to persuade Kádár to resign in May 1988 and Grósz stepped into his place, conflicts over the party's identity were unavoidable.

In my view, even a unified party would have been threatened by the fact that it faced a citizenry with a burgeoning sense of its own efficacy. Over the preceding decade, Kádár's policy of tolerating "those who are not against us" had given rise to a vibrant culture of independent thinking outside the party's ranks. Critics were emboldened to chastise the government for its mistakes and advance personal perspectives about enlivening socialism. In January 1987, three contributors to the samizdat journal *Beszélő* published a widely read statement that embodied this confrontational spirit. Declaring that it was time for the regime to create a "new social contract" with its citizens, they called for a mixed system of government in which executive and legislative functions would be divided between the party and the National Assembly, respectively. Much like the signatories of Charter 77, the writers argued that this demand was consistent with the country's constitution. They also professed to accept the HSWP's leading role. Their sole condition—a big one—was that the party sincerely observe the rule of law and respect the civil rights of its citizens.[25]

These were not the words of utopians. Well before Kádár's removal, civil society organizations and political forums were proliferating thanks to the government's efforts to curry the favor of its critics. As early as 1984, environmentalists were assembling to protest the planned construction of the Nagymaros Dam on the Danube River. In 1986, dissidents organized the first of many demonstrations over previously unmentionable dates in modern Hungarian history, including the revolutions of 1848 and 1956. In 1987, these groups evolved one step further. They assumed the characteristics of fledgling parties. The first significant indication of this shift came in September when a handful of dissident writers and regime critics gathered in the village of Lakitelek to coordinate their activities. The organizers made a point of inviting Pozsgay to take part, indicating their willingness to cooperate with the party. Pozsgay not only broke with party discipline by attending the meeting. By example, he showed that the party was coming apart from within. From this point, there was no turning back. In September 1988, several of the Lakitelek meeting's participants came together to transform one of their discussion circles, the Hungarian Democratic Forum, into a full-fledged political organization. Two months later, left-wing intellectuals, social scientists, and human rights advocates founded a similar organization, the Alliance of Free Democrats. Together with an association of university students, recent graduates, and lawyers known as the Alliance of Young Democrats, or Fidesz, these groups would soon become Hungary's major democratic parties.

Gorbachev's new policies accelerated the pace of these changes. Given the deep, collective memory of the bloody events of October 1956, the omnipresent shadow of the Soviet Union had been sufficient for decades to give the HSWP credit for doing its best to make the country's encounter with socialism livable. Yet once the CPSU chief began to question the "dignity of Lenin's Party," as he called it at the Nineteenth All-Union CPSU Conference, the basis for what I call the "Soviet excuse"—the threat of intervention—disappeared.[26]

In this context, the Hungarian regime gave up the ghost of party leadership. At first, Grósz tried to contain the new, noncommunist political organizations by pushing for legislation to contain their activities within narrow parameters. In a particularly strident address in fall 1988, he cryptically warned of the return of the "white terror," the period of uncontrolled violence and repression following the collapse of Béla Kun's Soviet Republic in 1919. When these tactics failed to repair the regime's diminishing authority, Grósz made a previously unthinkable decision. With surprisingly little opposition, he committed himself at a February 1989 Central Committee plenum to the formation of a multiparty system and agreed to remove references to the HSWP's leading role from the constitution. This descent into uncharted territory confirmed that Grósz and his supporters were grasping for political solutions. Since the HSWP could no longer prevent the formation of opposition groups, they gambled that it could instead ensnare them in a web of binding agreements and subordinate their members to the same core principles that governed the party. To this end, they followed Jaruzelski's example in Poland, proposing that their critics join them in roundtable talks in April.

This strategy had a major flaw. A year earlier, the Hungarian opposition was still weak enough that the regime could enforce the conditions under which these nascent parties participated in the new order; for example, each was required to affirm its loyalty to the socialist system. By this time, however, the leaders of these organizations recognized that they no longer needed to accept the communists' definition of legitimate political activity. In fact, they did not need to work with the regime at all. Thus, two weeks before the official roundtable talks were set to begin on April 8, 1989, an independent association of lawyers caught the government off guard by creating an alternate political forum, the Opposition Round Table, to unite the opposition groups against a common adversary.

At this juncture, the regime found itself in a race to find the support it needed to stay in power. Two of its steps could not have been more symbolically significant. On May 2, the Ministry of the Interior matter-of-factly announced that its border police would dismantle the fortifications along its western border with Austria. For the Hungarian people, this was a signal that their government had voluntarily seceded from the Cold War. In a second, even bolder stroke on June 16, the thirty-first anniversary of Imre Nagy's execution, the opposition organized the largest public demonstration since 1956. Although the HSWP's leading reformers, with Pozsgay at their head, took part, they were overshadowed by major opposition figures, such as Viktor Orbán, Fidesz's inspirational leader, who joined one-quarter of a million of their fellow citizens at Heroes' Square to witness the reburial of Nagy and four other victims of the Soviet invasion. In an electrifying speech, Orbán declared that the government could only fulfill the "will of the revolution" by putting an end to communist rule and demanding the removal of "Russian troops"—not *Soviet* troops—from Hungarian soil.[27]

Given the circumstances under which Nagy lost his life, many Hungarians undoubtedly appreciated the sweet irony of witnessing the communists take part in this politically charged event. But the solemnity of the moment raised a serious question. Even if the communists were sincere about changing their ways, why should one support a party at all that was responsible for these tragedies? In fact, many of the HSWP's members had come to this conclusion. By April 1989, the Young Communist League had lost half of its membership; by September, upward of 120,000 members had left the party.[28] Accordingly, when the HSWP's representatives resumed their talks with the opposition, this time including the Opposition Round Table, their monopoly on political power was gone. As a result, all conversation about what should be retained from the socialist system was replaced by negotiations over the construction of an authentic multiparty system.

In comparison, political developments were quite different in Poland, though they had a similar outcome. When Jaruzelski confronted Wałęsa with the offer to begin discussions about the legalization of Solidarity, the Polish government was weak. Yet, Wałęsa's ability to speak on behalf of the union was even more tenuous. Let us keep in mind that Solidarity had not existed as a cohesive national organization for seven years. Contacts among the organization's members were fragmented, and Wałęsa had no natural affinity with the activists in the Solidarity underground. Furthermore, he was fully aware of Jaruzelski's intentions. The negotiations were meant to compel Solidarity to share not only the privileges but also the burdens of national leadership. Accordingly, when Jaruzelski's and Wałęsa's representatives, as well as a host of other groups and mass organizations, met in February 1989, the trepidation was greatest on Solidarity's side of the table. For every gain the union made, it seemed, it faced the prospect that the negotiations would end up preserving the old order under a new name. Before the parliamentary elections of June 1989, this apprehension apparently prevented many of Solidarity's leaders, Wałęsa included, from appreciating that this was actually the PUWP's last stand. When the roundtable accords were finally signed on April 6, 1989, Poland was no longer a single-party state. Overnight, the country acquired the organs of democratic governance, including a bicameral legislature, which was divided between the Sejm and a restored version of the pre–World War II senate. Both bodies were given the responsibility to elect a president.

To be sure, Jaruzelski's negotiators did everything they could to safeguard the party's position in this agreement. While the Senate elections were open to equal competition, the PUWP reserved 65 percent of the seats in the Sejm for itself and its associated bloc parties. The opposition was allowed to contest the remaining 35 percent of the seats. With the mathematical advantage on the government's side and monopoly control of the mass media, the PUWP and its allies expected to win a majority in both houses and therefore be positioned to elect the president, presumably Jaruzelski. In the final weeks before the election, this optimism faded as support for Solidarity grew. Still, no one was prepared for the stunning outcome of the national vote. When Polish voters went to the polls on June 4 and in a runoff election on June 18, they cast their votes against the entire political system that had dominated their country since 1945. Incredibly, Solidarity won ninety-nine of the available one hundred seats in the Senate. It also won all of the seats that it was allowed to contest in the Sejm. Not a single PUWP candidate received majority support on the uncontested ballots. In the end, only one communist candidate was elected in the second vote, and the remainder of the seats went to Solidarity.

In a typically competitive parliamentary election in the West, Solidarity's demolition of its opponents would have been cause for celebration. But there was nothing routine about this transition from a single-party to a multiparty state. Wałęsa and other senior Solidarity members were so worried about their party's readiness to step into a political vacuum that they supported Jaruzelski's election as Poland's president. Yet, this was no victory for the general who had declared war on his own people. It was a colossal defeat for the system he sought to defend.

CHINA: A DIFFERENT TYPE OF CRISIS

On the surface, one might think that the instability that gripped China in the late 1980s was proof of a uniform, global crisis in communist party rule. But this assumption would be seriously misleading. True, there were widespread protests against the Chinese Communist

Party (CCP) in the second half of the decade that culminated, as on so many occasions over the twentieth century, in huge student demonstrations on Beijing's Tiananmen Square in spring 1989. Most prominently, on June 3–4 the government used military force to suppress the protests. Nevertheless, China's leaders faced a qualitatively different challenge than their European peers. Despite the discontent with the CCP's policies, the principle of party rule was not under siege. Instead, the crisis was created by divisions within the party leadership over how to restore control over an unruly public.

There are substantial reasons for the CCP's much stronger position. As I have shown in chapter 10, the CCP's rebirth as a viable institution in the 1970s was fueled by the trauma of the Great Proletarian Cultural Revolution. The universal agreement among the elite that they should prevent the country from slipping back into the "turmoil" (*dong luan*) of those years lent legitimacy to the party's aura as a force for stability. Under the pragmatic tutelage of Paramount Leader Deng Xiaoping, the organization earned the reputation for getting things done and doing so in a way that was compatible with "socialism with Chinese characteristics."

For this reason, in contrast to their peers in the Soviet Union and Eastern Europe, China's leaders entered the 1980s with a spirit of heightened expectations. With Deng's backing, modernizers like Zhao Ziyang, the premier and later CCP general secretary, began the decade by opening the door even wider to trade with the West, stimulating private economic ventures, and steering state and foreign investment toward coastal cities like Shanghai and Guangzhou. Along with these steps, the regime's endorsement of Western management styles and the promotion of performance-based standards of promotion had a positive impact on public attitudes. If, as Deng famously proclaimed, it no longer mattered "whether the cat is white or black, as long as it catches mice," citizens could expect to be hired and remunerated according to their skills and their labors. In theory, the more the Chinese economy flourished, the greater would be the benefit for everyone, even nonparty members.

The problem with rising expectations is that they can never be met for everyone equally, let alone permanently satisfied. In this case, the lot of many urban Chinese became worse during this period. While modernization allowed people with personal connections to make enormous fortunes in the 1980s, the living standards of many others were depressed. Jobs became harder to find for those who lacked the skills of an advanced economy. The nation's quantum leap in industrial production combined with the implementation of price reforms in spring 1988 spurred inflation and threatened to wipe out the savings of people on fixed incomes. When the regime responded to this adversity in fall and winter 1988–1989 by implementing austerity measures to cool the economy, inefficient factories that depended on state subsidies and cheap credit for their survival closed their doors and workers lost their jobs.

Amid these hardships, the CCP's reputation was tarnished by the quite accurate perception among the populace that China's economic boom had fostered rampant corruption. In the public mind, it was bad enough that their country's leaders were not living up to the centuries-old expectation that the powerful should provide for the welfare of those who served them. Ordinary citizens were enraged at the possibility that the principle of the "iron rice bowl" was being cast aside to enrich the lives of party functionaries' families and friends.

Just as in turn-of-the-century China, university students occupied a special place in this drama. In the short term, their ability to continue their studies was jeopardized by the impact of inflation on their stipends. The prospect that they might not find jobs that were equal to their social station was equally disquieting. In the early stages of Deng's reforms, it was widely assumed that admission to premier universities, such as Tsinghua University or Peking University, would guarantee a desirable position upon graduation. For the best and the brightest, this was the essence of a meritocracy. Because of these promises, many graduates were embittered when these expectations were unfulfilled.

The students' attitudes were also shaped by the expectation that a more open economy would be accompanied by a relaxation of state controls over culture and society. As we have seen, Deng's personal endorsement of the "seek truth from facts" campaigns had raised the hopes of the younger generation that free expression could be made compatible with the leading role of the CCP. In 1980 and again in

May 1986, on the thirtieth anniversary of the Hundred Flowers campaign, Deng added to this excitement by suggesting that political reforms were necessary for the party's success. They would strengthen the convictions of the party faithful and encourage cadres to establish closer bonds with the populace. In fact, in the early 1980s, some students had taken part in experiments with meaningful elections to county and district posts. By the mid-1980s, these circumstances, as well as increased access to information about the West and expanded opportunities to travel and study abroad, convinced them that China was at a crossroads. The question was which way their leaders would turn.

This atmosphere of escalating expectations and equally inflated anxieties cast a bright light on a widening gap between two major factions within the CCP leadership. Although this fissure bore a passing similarity to Gorbachev's first years in office, these differences cannot be reduced to a straightforward battle between the old and the new, reformers and reactionaries. No one wanted to risk a return to the chaos of the Cultural Revolution. Rather, the potential for a party split lay in competing interpretations of the lessons of that period. On one side, Zhao and the CCP general secretary, Hu Yaobang, embraced what they took to be Deng's central message: the only way to overcome the violent past was to accelerate China's transition to modernity. On the other side, critics, among whom Li Peng emerged as spokesperson, contended that the Cultural Revolution's real lesson was about the continuing threat of turmoil. Peng and his allies were not opposed to change itself, but instead to phenomena like "bourgeois liberalization" and "spiritual pollution" that would emerge as a result of moving too quickly.

It is conceivable that the conflict between these different currents could have been held in check were it not for the leadership's reaction to instances of renewed social protest. In December 1986, student demonstrations against the slow pace of reform broke out in several major cities. Although these protests were short-lived, they provided the Politburo's more risk-averse members with a pretext to call for a change of leadership. In January 1987, with Deng's approval, they perfunctorily removed Hu from his post. Zhao became the new general secretary and, later, Li succeeded him as premier.

The unintended consequence of this decision was increased unrest. As the leader of the party, Hu had been an unflinching campaigner against corruption and had a reputation for open-mindedness on questions of speech and expression. Thus, his fall became a rallying point for younger Chinese to express their grievances. When Hu died on April 15, 1989, students marched to Tiananmen Square to show support for his policies. On April 17, thousands more assembled before the Great Hall of the People to present a list of seven demands. Like the Polish workers' twenty-one demands of August 1980, these were hastily thrown together. Some were practical, such as increased state support for education. More ambitiously, the protestors demanded that the government affirm Hu's approval of looser political controls and publish the incomes of public officials and their families. By April 22, the day of Hu's funeral, these demonstrations escalated to the point where they involved hundreds of thousands of people, not only in Beijing but also Changsha, Tianjin, and Xi'an. Simultaneously, student leaders met at Peking University to coordinate their plans.[29]

Importantly, a majority of the protestors saw themselves as loyal patriots, not anticommunist radicals. After all, they were supporting the policies of a former CCP leader. Much like the youthful idealists of the precommunist New Culture and May Fourth Movements, they believed that they were acting in the nation's interests. They intended to persuade the country's rulers to remove corrupt officials and live up to the legal standards of the constitution. References to the former movement became a constant refrain in the protestors' speeches. In a demonstration on Tiananmen Square, one widely known activist, Wu'er Kaixi, read from a "New May Fourth Manifesto," describing the students as worthy defenders of a spirit that had begun seventy years earlier "to modernize an ancient and beleaguered China."[30]

In contrast, China's leaders took the opposite view. Looking abroad, they saw ominous similarities between these demonstrations and the systemic changes under way in Eastern Europe. In the words of one Politburo member, the Peking University students had "imitated Poland's Solidarity to form their own Solidarity Student Union."[31] Deng reportedly observed that the organizers, "who have been influenced by the free elements of Yugoslavia, Poland, Hungary, and the Soviet

Union, have reason to create turmoil." "Their motive," he added, not quite accurately, "is to overthrow the party."[32]

Deng's characterization of the protestors may have been hyperbole—but it was revealing hyperbole. His decision to take an uncompromising stand testifies to a problem we have encountered throughout this book. Even if the primary impetus to reform should come from within a communist party, it is difficult to convince all of the institution's leaders that significant change can be held in check. In fact, for many Politburo members, the demonstrations were reminders of the turmoil of the Cultural Revolution. On April 26, an editorial in the *People's Daily* entitled "It Is Necessary to Take a Clear-Cut Stand against Disturbances" provided the public with the first hint of the depth of this opposition. According to the editorial, an "extremely small number of people" were exploiting the students' grief to foment opposition to the CCP, "sow dissension among the people, plunge the whole country into chaos, and sabotage the political situation of stability and unity." Apparently, all of the achievements of the past decade were in jeopardy. For these reasons, the statement concluded, "all comrades in the party and the people throughout the country [needed to] soberly recognize the fact that our country will have no peaceful days if this disturbance is not checked resolutely."[33]

Interestingly, the *People's Daily* editorial appeared at a time when the strength of the demonstrations was abating and many students had returned to their classes. Yet instead of dampening their hopes, it had an incendiary impact. The protestors were enraged at finding that the regime did not take their demands seriously. Their perspective was shared by a growing number of citizens—blue-collar workers, teachers, and even low-level party officials—who concluded that their leaders had lost touch with their needs.

In this circumstance, the crisis convinced the opposing Politburo faction to speak up. It cannot have been a coincidence that Zhao used May 4 to defend the party in the name of enhancing its authority. In a speech to a delegation from the Asian Development Bank, he laid the blame for the current difficulties at the door of the leadership. The students did not oppose the socialist system, he insisted. They were "calling us to correct our mistakes and improve our work style." By "failing to take a stronger stand against corruption and practicing more openness and transparency," Zhao argued, officials had created the conditions under which the party's policies were misunderstood. Therefore, the regime's next step should be to address the students' grievances: "We should meet the students' reasonable demands through democracy and law, should be willing to reform, and should use rational and orderly methods."[34]

The extent of the party's split was reflected in a private conversation between Zhao and Li Peng after the speech. Zhao emphasized that the April 26 editorial had made the situation worse. It had wrongly "stigmatized" the students by failing to distinguish properly between the majority's legitimate complaints and the chicanery of a few troublemakers. For this reason, he proposed that the Politburo publish an additional editorial to underscore this difference. Li retorted that any modification of the message was impossible. It was not only he, Li added pointedly, but also Deng and the Elders, the most senior, retired party officials, who believed that the protestors were being manipulated by people who sought to destroy the party.[35]

At this point, we return to a familiar question: Who should be entitled to define what is good for the party? The answer would have been clear a decade earlier: Mao Zedong. However, this was no longer Mao's China. Thanks to the greater ease of access to information after Deng's opening to the West, word spread quickly of the leadership's divisions. Li later told his colleagues, accurately enough, that Zhao's speech had sown confusion in the party's ranks. In his description, "People were complaining, 'There are two different voices coming from the Center; which is right, which is wrong?'; others asked, 'You want us to maintain unanimity with the Center, but with which center?'"[36]

Taking advantage of the party's divisions, student leaders announced a hunger strike on May 13 to protest the regime's depiction of them as antisocialist and antipatriotic elements. Their timing was no accident. Gorbachev was scheduled to arrive in Beijing two days later to open a new chapter in Soviet-Chinese relations, symbolically reestablishing the link between Asian and European communism that had been broken nearly three decades earlier. Because Gorbachev's welcoming ceremony was to take place on Tiananmen Square, the students saw this as a chance to advocate an alternate definition of the public good.

In one respect, they were successful. As a result of their protests, Gorbachev's visit was transformed from a point of pride for Beijing into a source of humiliation. Throughout the visit, Zhao and his coleaders struggled in vain to prevent outside viewers from drawing undesirable connections between the presence of the father of glasnost and the strikers' demands. However, an unforeseen consequence of the students' actions was to strengthen the hands of those who argued for reunifying the party around the necessity of confrontation. When the Standing Committee of the Politburo met on May 17, Zhao was unable to convince his coleaders to give the students more time. Hence, he did not even attend the subsequent meeting at which the leadership agreed that there was no alternative to the use of force.

There is a revealing side story to this decision that led to the bloody clashes between People's Liberation Army (PLA) troops and unarmed protestors near Tiananmen Square and in western Beijing on June 3–4. After the first of these two meetings, Zhao repeatedly tried to resign from the Politburo, but his wishes were rebuffed by his colleagues. Their desire to keep him in his post cannot have been due to any lingering affection; they ridiculed him for days after the martial law decision. The only plausible explanation for delaying his demotion is one that we have encountered throughout this book. They had no other conception of political order aside from that which was based on the unity of the CCP. To repair the damage done to the party's standing before June 3, they needed to sustain the fiction of a united front. Interpreting the crisis after Hu Yaobang's ouster as proof of Zhao's failure to follow party rules, they convened a special Central Committee plenum in late June to announce that he was no longer general secretary.

In the meantime, on June 9 Deng presented a narrative about the preceding week in a speech to PLA units. Aside from his praise for the soldiers who participated in the crackdown, the speech is illuminating both for what it was and was not. On the one hand, there is Deng's justification for the government's actions. Notwithstanding his carefully nuanced observations throughout the 1980s about the complexity of China's leap into the modern world, Deng returned to the same

Maoist idiom of struggle that had motivated the CCP throughout its history. He observed that the April 26 editorial had correctly described the student protests. They were further evidence of "turmoil," which would have led inevitably to "a counterrevolutionary rebellion." It was a good thing, he stressed, that a large number of veteran comrades had been around because "they [had] experienced many storms and they [knew] what was at stake."[37] On the other hand, this was not Poland in 1981. Unlike in Poland where Jaruzelski's declaration of martial law confirmed the bankruptcy of the regime, the idea that the party was in charge of the gun was very much alive. As we shall see in chapter 13, the party's leading role would become more obscure over the next decade. But this development would happen for reasons that were significantly different from those in the Soviet Union and Eastern Europe.

THOSE WHO WAIT AND DO NOTHING

The final episode in the nearly perfect storm against party leadership in 1989 was played by the leaders of a group of states—the German Democratic Republic (GDR), Czechoslovakia, Bulgaria, Romania, and Albania—who responded to the changes around them by defiantly doing nothing. This is not to say they had many options. Given the tumult around them—Gorbachev's rush to implement reform and the rapid dissolution of political authority in Poland and Hungary—I believe it is highly unlikely that they could have done anything to preserve the mystique of single-party rule. At best, they could have postponed their fate, either through more accommodating policies or the use of brute force. For our purposes, however, the revealing aspect of these regimes' rejection of serious change is about how difficult it was for their leaders to justify the party's leading role in the later years of developed socialism.

No state better exemplifies this dilemma than the GDR. Since his appointment as general secretary in 1971, Erich Honecker appeared to have perfected the style of the Brezhnev consensus. In a careful balancing act, he attempted to preserve his citizens' loyalties by assuring them of continual improvements in the quality of life under "real existing socialism." At the same time, he used the tensions between East and

West Germany to underscore the irreconcilable conflict between social-ism and capitalism and demanded that Socialist Unity Party of Germany (SED) members exhibit unflinching devotion to the party line.

From the beginning, one could foresee that Honecker and Gor-bachev would be at odds over this formula for socialist stability. The two leaders came from distinctly different backgrounds. Honecker had been a member of the Communist Party of Germany since 1930 and, like Gustáv Husák in Prague, Nicolae Ceauşescu in Bucharest, and Todor Zhivkov in Sofia, had fought against fascism. He and his fellow com-munists from that era were still infused with the confidence that socialism would win the battle with capitalism. As a result, his en-counters with the Soviet general secretary were colored with the polite condescension of the older sibling who has already seen it all and has no need to learn anything new. In April 1986, when Gorbachev traveled to East Berlin to speak before the SED's Eleventh Congress and broached the possibility of introducing perestroika to the GDR, Honecker re-portedly reacted to his guest's words with amused disbelief: "The young man has been making policy for only a year, and already he wants to take on more than he can chew!"[38]

Nonetheless, the more Gorbachev pressed ahead, the greater was Honecker's inclination to question the wisdom of the time-honored slogan: "To learn from the Soviet Union is to learn to be victorious." Why, he and his colleagues wondered, should a state like the GDR, which had already experimented with economic reforms in the 1960s and registered some of the most impressive growth rates in the bloc, run the risk of large-scale reforms that suited the needs of another country? Or why should it undertake experiments in even more sensi-tive areas, such as greater political transparency, when the conditions along the border between socialism and capitalism proved that the class struggle was still raging?

Had Gorbachev's reform efforts stalled at this point, it is possible that East Berlin and Moscow could have found grounds for a modus vivendi. However, Gorbachev's triumphant moment at the Nineteenth All-Union CPSU Conference in 1988 made a confrontation unavoid-able. At first glance, the SED's oblique expressions of disdain for Gor-bachev's attempt to distinguish between state and party functions may seem petty and insignificant. Yet, by the standards of the Brezhnev years, they signaled a major breach over the nature of advanced socialism. To the surprise of even members of the SED Politburo—many of whom were kept in the dark due to their general secretary's restrictive definition of party discipline—Honecker contested the Kremlin's prerogative to shape the GDR's priorities. Issues of prominent Soviet publications, like *New Times* and *Ogonek*, were banned. Gorbachev's speeches were published in abbreviated form and often in tandem with articles questioning his strategies. For the first time, the East German media made thinly veiled references to the darker side of everyday socialism in the USSR, noting rising alcoholism, homelessness, and food shortages.

In December 1988, Honecker showed that he was still ensconced in the worldview of an earlier era. He introduced a belligerent idiom into his public references to Moscow that could, in part, have suited his exchanges with the capitalist world. In an acerbic report to the SED's Seventh Central Committee plenum, he co-opted the language of different paths to socialism to justify retrenchment, not reform. The GDR, Honecker stressed, was a sovereign state that was capable of making decisions itself. It was fine and good to speak about fraternal solidarity, but true cooperation meant accepting each party's "equality, independence, and autonomy." This entailed recognizing, Honecker added, that no model was universally applicable to all socialist states. It was up to the GDR, as was true of all of its Eastern European neighbors, to decide "its responsibility before its own people."[39]

To validate this stand domestically, Honecker and his coleaders attempted to breathe new life into the governing principle of developed socialism: fidelity to party rule would be repaid with continued improvements in living standards. In this spirit, Honecker initiated his own, highly circumscribed version of glasnost. Building on the rapprochement that had begun with the Evangelical Church in 1978, SED officials were instructed to provide pastors with greater leeway to raise sensitive topics, such as global disarmament and denuclearization, with their parishioners. Peace activists were allowed to take part in an officially sanctioned demonstration, the Olof Palme Peace March, and for the first time a debate was televised between East and West German politicians on the reduction of tensions between the superpower blocs. Within its own circles, the SED also awakened hopes for change, signing a joint declaration with West Germany's Social Democratic Party that endorsed a "culture of political argumentation" between the two long-alienated parties.

The regime matched these gestures with assurances that the relaxation of restrictions on West German travel to the GDR over the previous decade would be supplemented by even greater opportunities for East German citizens to travel to the Federal Republic. This was a gamble. The SED's leaders calculated that regular travel to the West would reduce the likelihood of their citizens leaving their homeland permanently. In the short term, this risk paid off handsomely. Bonn agreed to provide millions of deutschmarks in credits and bank loans in return for East Berlin's seemingly humanitarian largesse.

One decade earlier, this type of balancing act had largely worked. The trouble with these measures in the 1980s is that they were no longer sufficient to preserve the tacit understanding with the population about the payoff for dutiful acceptance of the status quo. Although most East Germans accepted the fact that their standard of living was unlikely to catch up with that of West Germany, they assumed that it would continue to improve. But this understanding was being undermined at precisely the moment Honecker was sparring with Gorbachev over the desirability of an East German perestroika. The SED regime could no longer afford the massive subsidies that were hidden behind Honecker's consumer-oriented policies. Overnight, the country's citizens had to confront trials, such as food shortages and deteriorating social services, which they associated only with the poorest socialist countries.

Additionally, the brief success of East Berlin's negotiations with Bonn did more than generate increased demand for travel to the West. As these pressures grew, they called renewed attention to the abnormality of Germany's division. Whether they meant to or not, Soviet officials added to these tensions. When Alexander Yakovlev was asked about the Berlin Wall during a press conference in Bonn in January 1989, he declared that the barrier's existence was no longer a concern for his government. "That isn't our wall," he observed. "We didn't build this wall. This is the GDR's affair."[40] East German officials were aghast at this complete denial of historical responsibility. True to the form of an old communist, Honecker responded by emphasizing the continuing battle with global capitalism, noting curtly that the Wall would "be around in 50 or even 100 years if the conditions for which it was constructed still existed."[41]

I am providing this background because it illustrates the tenuousness of the SED's effort to straddle the opposing realms of ideological fidelity and tactical flexibility. In this situation, the SED's leaders took two steps that some among them would later regret. The first was a seemingly low-risk response to popular demands that they emulate their counterparts in Poland, Hungary, and the USSR by experimenting with electoral reforms. Predictably, the Politburo rejected the idea of multicandidate elections outright. But to create the appearance of taking its citizens' wishes seriously, Honecker allowed church groups and other unofficial associations to monitor the statewide municipal elections of May 7, 1989. Naturally, the regime expected the elections to result in a resounding affirmation of its policies. However, it underestimated the radical shift in its citizens' mood. With their own exit polls in hand and Gorbachev's example to inspire them, the monitors pronounced the elections fraudulent. Although not a single East German voter would have been surprised by this revelation, the SED's failure to maintain the appearance of total domination was a galvanizing moment for citizens who had long regarded its grip on power as unassailable.

The regime's more profound error was to attempt to turn the Tiananmen tragedy into a didactic exercise in socialist obedience. Although East Berlin was not alone in supporting the CCP's action—the communist parties of Romania and Czechoslovakia commended Beijing for restoring order—it was the most fulsome in its praise. The state media congratulated Beijing for subduing a "counterrevolution." Honecker's presumed successor, Egon Krenz, declared that the Chinese government had acted in a perfectly normal manner. More ominously, Honecker's wife, Margot, the GDR's minister of education, declared that one should be prepared to defend socialism. For anyone who had grown up with the carefully formulated language of the East German press, the unmistakable message was that when all else failed, the GDR's rulers would use violence against their citizens to defend the socialist system.

Although it is unlikely that Honecker and his coleaders could have surmounted the challenges to their authority if they had handled the May 7 elections differently or, more importantly, refrained from praising Beijing's actions, they clearly hastened the regime's demise by confirming that they intended to stick with the old course. One result of their inaction might be called "willful depopulation." Beginning in May and June 1989, when a small stream of vacationers fled over the newly opened Hungarian border into Austria, thousands of East Germans voted with their feet against a government they perceived to have lost interest in their welfare. Honecker confirmed this impression on September 25, announcing through the Allgemeiner Deutscher Nachrichtendienst (German General News Service) that his government would not allow itself to be shaken by these events. There should be "no tears shed," he dictated, at the loss of people who had "trampled on the moral values [of socialism]" and chosen to "exclude themselves from our society."[42] The other result was the sudden emergence of an array of semiautonomous civil society organizations with lofty names like New Forum, Democratic Awakening, and United Left. Only a couple of years earlier, the threat of Soviet intervention would have deterred these protoparties from coming together. But perestroika and the gestation of noncommunist parties and organizations in Poland and Hungary nullified these concerns. Although a majority of the writers, pastors, and longtime dissidents who constituted these groups were not specifically focused on questioning the SED's authority, their existence alone signified the erosion of the party's credibility.

To understand these developments, one must take note of a crucial factor that is often left out of explanations of the GDR's demise. This was the deteriorating mood within the party itself.[43] Unlike the regimes in Warsaw, Budapest, and Moscow that were moving quickly to redefine their identities, the SED elite was frozen in time. There was no significant reformist wing within its uppermost ranks in the summer of 1989. Unlike in Poland and Hungary, there was no place for party factions within the organization's political culture. The expression of different views, even in the meetings of the Politburo, was inimical to the norm of "revolutionary discipline" that was supposedly required of a party that represented the weaker half of a divided nation.[44] Thus, even when senior SED members talked privately, few dared to bring up the subject of party reform. Their idea of a bold conversation was to speculate about when Honecker would retire—as if a change of leadership alone would rejuvenate the GDR.

The mood was different in the SED's lower ranks. For many members, there was increasingly no pride to be found in associating with the leaders of an organization who refused to acknowledge even the slightest shortcoming. If ever there was a time to learn from the Soviet Union, they thought, it was now. Instead of listening to their comrades in Moscow, however, Honecker and his associates were offering weary platitudes. Worse still, in the view of these members, the regime's intimations that it would turn its weapons against its own people threatened to make everyone in the party complicit in a national tragedy. Accordingly, with no Pozsgay-like faction to represent them, lower-level officials simply gave up the pretense that there was anything about the party still worth defending. Even officials in the Ministry of State Security concluded that the regime's policies had run their full course.

These elite attitudes not only illuminate why the GDR fell but why it collapsed so quickly. By early fall 1989, the as-yet unresolved question was what the GDR's leaders—as well as their Bulgarian, Czechoslovak, Romanian, and Albanian counterparts—would do to stem a growing tide of protest. Incredibly, this question was resolved in a mere three days in October. On October 7, Gorbachev arrived in East Berlin for what was supposed to be a joyous occasion, the fortieth anniversary of the GDR's founding. When he and Honecker met in the East German parliament building to celebrate the country's achievements, however, the two leaders were residing in different worlds. Honecker spoke—correctly, as it would turn out—as though everything the SED had accomplished was at stake. "Nothing, nothing at all," he declared, invoking the Leninist language of class struggle, "was given to us or put in our lap. We not only had more ruins to clear away than west of the Elbe and Werra but also obstacles that were put in our way. . . . It's no accident that our adversary now slanders us like never before. . . . This is because it can't stand the fact that German socialism has proven that the once exploited masses could determine their future by themselves without the help of capitalists."[45] In contrast, Gorbachev's comments about the GDR's achievements were restrained. Although he clearly disliked Honecker—he called him a "scumbag"—Gorbachev did not exactly criticize the East German regime.[46] Instead, he pressed for the adoption of an alternative path to socialism based on "democratization, openness, socialist legality, and the free development of all peoples and their inclusion in [their country's] affairs." Gorbachev also provided his host with a Marxist history lesson. "History has its own laws, tempo, and rhythm," he pointed out, "which is determined by the meaning of objective and subjective factors. To ignore this is to create new problems."[47]

By suggesting that Honecker was incapable of understanding his country's conditions, Gorbachev effectively told East Germany's citizens what they needed to know in order to take their bottled-up grievances into the streets. The USSR, the country that had given life to the GDR, would not intervene, as it had on Walter Ulbricht's behalf in June 1953. On the evening of October 7 and throughout the following day, mass demonstrations spontaneously broke out in cities across the country. Protestors were beaten and arrested by the police. But a day later, it became clear that the spirit of resignation that suffused the SED had spread throughout the party apparatus and the government ministries. No one had the will to defend what was already dissolving. On October 9, when 70,000 people streamed into the narrow streets surrounding Leipzig's St. Nicholas Church, party officials and the security police allowed the protests to continue.

The demonstrations that quickly engulfed the GDR and led to the opening of the Berlin Wall on November 9 allow for a revealing comparison with the student protests on Tiananmen Square five months earlier. First, there is the manifest difference: the former ended in liberation, the latter in tragedy. Second, there is a noteworthy similarity. The rulers of both countries were still locked into the same confrontational categories acquired along the journey to socialist power. They could not imagine a world in which they, as representatives of a historically validated organization and glorious international movement, were not paving the way toward the liberation of humanity.

On October 18, the SED Politburo finally forced Honecker out of office. If the GDR had been an ordinary country, one might imagine that the new general secretary, Krenz, would have quickly recognized that life could not go on as in the past. Although he publicly admitted that the old policies had failed, Krenz showed that he had nothing new to offer. Indeed, he could only look backward. At the Central Committee's plenum on November 8, Krenz was morose. "It is painful for all of us, Comrades," he observed, "that we are now coming under such criticism. It is even more painful for those who have put thousands of hours of their lives into serving the common interest over their personal interests. It is painful for all of our veterans who risked their lives in the antifascist opposition to create a better Germany. It is painful for the hundreds of thousands of comrades who on a daily basis and in many ways beyond the call of duty took responsibility for our country's progress. It is painful for us all."[48]

It is telling how little Krenz and his colleagues seem to have learned. Although the plenum released an Action Program that called for urgent changes, the one issue they refused to consider was the most important of all: the SED's leading role. Serious mistakes had been made, Krenz conceded, but it was people like Honecker and his associates, and not the system, who bore the responsibility. Now that these individuals were gone, it seemed, the party only needed to regain the trust of the people.[49] After the Wall was opened on the following day, Krenz and the remaining members of the party leadership finally learned something that they should have grasped months, if not years, earlier. The East German population no longer saw any reason to be led. As thousands of people streamed into West Berlin, Krenz made a frantic attempt to bolster the SED's image by forcing the old guard to resign and replacing them with putative reformers. But it was not only the party's survival that was at stake. It was the existence of the GDR. When the public mood shifted steadily toward the restoration of a unitary German state over the following month, the East German parliament voted on December 1 to divest itself of any further association with communism and removed the clause in the GDR's constitution that granted the SED its right to rule.

What Could No Longer Be Saved

From this point onward, we know that every subsequent effort to salvage the communist parties' claims to leadership in Eastern Europe and the USSR met with failure. Still, to stand in the shoes of the leaders who worked their way toward this conclusion between fall 1989 and fall 1990, we need to consider the sequencing of these events. For some, the party idea died despite their best efforts to save it. For others, its passing was at least in part the result of choices that could have been made differently.

One word sums up the mood of the Bulgarian, Czechoslovak, Romanian, and Albanian leaderships at this time—desperation. In all four states, the images of hundreds of thousands of people demonstrating against communist party rule in the GDR immediately brought their regimes' mortality to the fore. The Bulgarian government was the first to act. One day after the Wall's opening, a group of self-proclaimed "reform communists" removed Todor Zhivkov from power and promised to bring perestroika to the people. By early December, however, they realized that the only way they could remain in office was to abandon socialism. Hence, they promptly removed all references to the party's leading role in the constitution and called for democratic elections. In Czechoslovakia, the party's demise was just as quick, but it took place under circumstances that bore a closer resemblance to the GDR. When the communist regime failed to respond to massive demonstrations that engulfed the country from mid-November onward, opposition groups had to call for a general strike to force it to listen to their demands. Of its own accord, the Federal Assembly sought to save itself by revoking the party's leading role. But when the regime subsequently attempted to set up a new communist-dominated government, the opposition took its protests back to the streets and forced the end to forty-one years of communist party rule.

The fate of the Romanian Communist Party (RCP) was idiosyncratic. Here, there was no independent opposition to challenge the regime's policies because of Ceaușescu's success in atomizing Romanian society and exalting himself over every institution, including the RCP. Thus, when the protests finally came to Bucharest in mid-December 1989, they were spontaneous and violent. Still, the decisive factor behind the regime's quick collapse came from within. On December 22, under circumstances that remain cloudy, an organization composed largely of communist functionaries and calling itself the National Salvation Front (NSF) arose from nowhere to overthrow Ceaușescu. With no formal comment, the NSF simply abolished the communist party. More importantly, it obliterated the personality cult on which the regime's authority was based by subjecting the aged Conducător and his wife to a speedy trial and execution. As if to pierce the shroud of the dictator's immortality, the NSF promptly published photos of the two, bloodied bodies.

The dissolution of single-party rule would take longer in Albania, but nowhere were the conditions more treacherous. Since Enver Hoxha's death in 1985, his successor as head of the Albanian Party of Labor (APL), Ramiz Alia, had undertaken policies that oscillated between bouts of welcome conciliation (a break from Hoxha) and systematic repression (an affirmation of his predecessor's temperament). In the latter half of the 1980s, this strategy seemed to work. By continuing to propagate Hoxha's doctrine of self-reliance and cultivating national pride, Alia was able to insulate the country from the pressures for economic and social reform. However, beginning in early 1990, after the upheavals in Eastern Europe had peaked, these measures became unsustainable. In the face of a mounting economic crisis, an exodus of thousands of Albanian citizens to other countries, and the outbreak of massive antigovernment demonstrations that threatened to spill into civil war, Alia was forced to give in. On December 11, in a meeting with student demonstrators, he announced that the regime would begin preparations for multiparty elections, effectively putting an end to the APL.

In comparison with the fury of these changes, the fate of the Soviet communist party, as I have described in the opening pages of this book, seems oddly anticlimactic. When the Congress of People's Deputies voted on March 14, 1990, to amend Article 6 of the Soviet Constitution to relieve the ultimate representative of the October Revolution of the role it had exercised for nearly seventy-three years, the decision had a matter-of-fact quality. Notably, Gorbachev himself recommended this change to the Central Committee in February. Whereas two or three years earlier, he and his colleagues would have viewed this turn of events as a catastrophe, Gorbachev seems to have finally concluded that it was just one further step along the path to normalcy.

This is not to say that Gorbachev relished the decision to demote the party. In an ideal world, he would undoubtedly have preferred a system of dual rule. The CPSU would preside over strategic priorities and the state would take responsibility for the execution of the party's decisions. Yet, by 1989, both organs presented him with distinct challenges. Despite his efforts to contain the fierce infighting between the hardline opponents of change and the equally hard-line reformers, the CPSU was becoming an increasingly unmanageable body. At the same time, Gorbachev's supporters pressed him to follow the example of the Soviet Union's liberalizing neighbors in Eastern Europe.

Gorbachev must have sensed that the party had already lost its preeminent place in Soviet society, in fact if not in form. In 1989, 136,000 full and candidate CPSU members left the party, compared to 18,000 the year before. This dramatic exodus marked the first decline in total membership since 1954. In the first five months of 1990, they would be followed by 130,000 more.[50] From this point forward, the question was whether anything could be done to prevent the party from succumbing to the powerful political and social forces that Gorbachev had unleashed.

Notably, Gorbachev followed the precedent set by his predecessors by seeking to augment his political authority. His first step was to bind his position as CPSU general secretary to the Soviet Union's emerging center of political legitimacy, the Congress of People's Deputies, by consenting to his election to the new post of Soviet president. His second step was to present himself, in effect, as a post-Leninist theorist. In his keynote address at the CPSU's Twenty-Eighth Congress on July 2, 1990, he offered the delegates a distinction that, in his view, would keep the party alive. Because perestroika was advancing so quickly, he argued, it was no longer necessary for the party to claim a "leading role" in Soviet society. The organization could share that function with other institutions, even other parties. Furthermore, the CPSU was called upon to play the role of the true "vanguard" that it had never fully realized. Under this formulation, the party would *earn* the right to rule.

"We believe," Gorbachev averred, "that a vanguard role cannot be imposed on society, that it can only be won by an active struggle for the working people's interests, by practical deeds and by our whole political image."[51]

Gorbachev was not the first Soviet leader to suggest that the party should have to earn the support of the Soviet people. But no matter what the party did or did not do, the CPSU's leading role had never really been up for discussion. This was its function by virtue of being a Leninist organization. In the broad sweep of communist history, this perspective made sense. The party was either a vanguard or it was not. There could not be multiple vanguards. On some level, Gorbachev must have been aware that more than definitional issues were at stake. Even if he did not want to admit it, he was engaging in wishful thinking. His regime could no longer salvage the idea of a leading party when it had already pushed the institution aside.

CHAPTER 13

The Party Vanishes

In late February 1922, an aging Vladimir Ilyich Lenin penned an unusually thoughtful, even wistful essay, "Notes of a Publicist," in which he likened the communist party member to a mountain climber. Along the way, Lenin wrote, the man reaches a point at which he realizes that he can no longer continue along the same path. Naturally, he is discouraged, even to the point of despondency, at the prospect that he must look for another path to the peak. As he retraces his steps, he is certain to face new dangers. Meanwhile, down on the ground, people will be laughing and ridiculing him for his folly. Fortunately, he cannot hear them, for they would probably nauseate him—and, Lenin added, nausea prevents one from keeping a clear head, "particularly at high altitudes." Nonetheless, Lenin predicted that the climber would do what he must and find a new way to continue his arduous ascent to the summit.[1]

The occasion for Lenin's essay was the enactment of the New Economic Policy, when the Bolsheviks faced the difficult and immensely controversial prospect of having to recalibrate their approach to building socialism. Yet Lenin's emphasis, as he put it in the essay, on "soberly weighing up the situation" and avoiding the "waving of little red flags" is a theme we have encountered throughout this book. Global communism would not have survived for as long as it did and found traction among so many diverse peoples had the parties that espoused its ideas been unable or unwilling to adapt to their respective settings. Of course, force and dictatorship played major roles in the movement's longevity; the communist record is awash with violence and bloodshed. But, to use Lenin's analogy, the intrepid mountain climbers who embraced its ideals in scores of countries exhibited noteworthy dexterity in aligning the major categories of Marxism—the class struggle, the dictatorship of the proletariat, and the inevitability of the revolution—with the hopes and perceptions of those who came after them.

In this light, it is striking that the idea of a communist party as it developed from the 1840s onward evaporated after the 1980s. To be sure, Eastern European and Russian communists lost their monopoly on political power. Hence, they could no longer force their views on people who were now enthralled by the promise of democracy. Yet it is also true that a majority of the onetime leaders who had watched their regimes disintegrate were no longer interested in defending the institution that had long defined their political identity. As I shall show in this chapter by briefly describing the cases of the postcommunist parties of Hungary, Poland, Russia, Romania, and Yugoslavia, Marx and Lenin's ideas about the ineluctable march toward a just world had lost all credibility. At a juncture when hopeful populations perceived the Cold War to be over, politicians had little to gain by invoking the language of the class struggle, let alone the inevitability of revolution. By the same token, the former communists who wanted to remain engaged in political life recognized that they now had to play by the democratic rules of the game. As a result, when they reemerged in the 1990s, they came as representatives of renamed, leftist parties, espousing liberal democratic values and professing their confidence in open political competition. In fact, a majority of these new parties looked more like Western European social democratic parties than any other institutions. This was an epochal shift. The story of the European Left in the twentieth century had been dominated by the battle between radical and reformist conceptions of socialism. Now, the parties that the communists had consistently labeled "revisionist" and "counterrevolutionary" had won!

It is equally illuminating that, outside of Europe and Russia, the leaders of the socialist states that were not directly affected by the revolutions of 1989–1991 distanced themselves from their long-held assumptions about the functions of the communist party. Unlike the European and Russian ex-communists, they had the power to defend the political status quo. But, as I shall demonstrate by considering three of the most prominent cases—North Korea, China, and Cuba—they recognized that they, too, were no longer living in the world of Marx and Lenin. In different ways, each of these states drifted away from the different conceptions of single-party rule that we have encountered throughout this book. In North Korea, the break was complete. Under successive despots, Kim Il-sung, Kim Jong-il, and Kim Jong-un, the party's leading role was fully supplanted by the institution of dynastic rule. In China, the shift was gradual and less conspicuous. A new generation of leaders, represented by Jiang Zemin, Hu Jintao, and Xi Jinping, routinely invoked the principle of party rule to justify their policies. But they did not necessarily practice it. Indeed, by the 2000s, one was hard-pressed to say what specifically made the Chinese Communist Party (CCP) communist. Only Fidel Castro showed any consistency, but in a way that did not serve the party idea. Although he had two options to institutionalize his vision, the party and the military, he evidently remained convinced until his final days that he was the epicenter of his country's revolution.

In making these points, I do not mean to suggest that the break from communist party rule in Eastern Europe and the former Soviet Union or the institution's diminution in countries like China and Cuba was necessarily straightforward. In the former cases, as I shall contend, the leaders of some postcommunist parties, such as those in Hungary, Poland, Russia, and Romania, had the skills to benefit from their participation in democratic politics. In contrast, the transition to a new party system in Yugoslavia erupted into fratricidal war and genocide. Of the latter cases, China's leaders were adept at diluting the conventional Leninist justifications of single-party rule to serve their evolving goals. But in Cuba, after Castro's death in November 2016, the party's historically ambiguous status meant that it could not carry on the mystique of the Cuban Revolution. Overall, one point was certain: the leaders of these regimes, whether democratic or not, could move forward. But the vanishing idea of a vanguard party meant that there was no moving back.

THOSE WHO PART WAYS

In both Eastern Europe and Russia, it would have been surprising if the former communists had not taken quick steps to reinvent themselves in their democratizing countries. After all, the collapse of the

Soviet bloc presented those who wanted to form competitive party organizations with virtually no other choice. Thus, the same people who had once looked to the writings of Marx and Engels or the example of the Soviet Union for guidance now paid allegiance to democratic politics and the unfettered competition of ideas. The striking development was how successful most of them were in making this transition. Taking advantage of both the inexperience of the fledgling democratic parties that came to power in the early 1990s and their own administrative experience and personal networks, they built broad constituencies and, in many cases, won their way back to power.[2]

Of all the former bloc states, Hungary's communists made the transition to democracy the most efficiently. Thanks to János Kádár's moderate policies since the 1960s, they had the least antagonistic relationship with their citizens. The rise of the reformist wing of the Hungarian Socialist Workers' Party (HSWP) in 1988 and the party's early renunciation of dictatorship allowed them to participate in the National Round Table negotiations over the formation of a multiparty system. When their leaders met in October 1989 to adopt a new name, the Hungarian Socialist Party (HSP), they undoubtedly assumed that they would need to wait patiently for a return to prominence. In fact, in the first parliamentary elections in March and April 1990, they struggled under a cloud of anticommunist sentiment. The HSP came in fourth behind the omnibus Hungarian Democratic Forum, which formed the country's first, democratically elected coalition government in forty-three years. Nonetheless, the Socialists soon turned their opponents' lack of political experience to their advantage. Emphasizing their technocratic skills and moderately redistributionist policies, they built the HSP into a modern catchall party. In the general elections of May 1994, with the support of both workers and white-collar professionals, the postcommunists won a majority of the seats in parliament and joined their former adversaries in Fidesz in forming a left-center coalition government.

Under a new name, Social Democracy of the Republic of Poland (SDRP), Poland's communists underwent a similar transition. After the Polish United Workers' Party's unexpected defeat in the parliamentary elections of June 1989, their chances of returning to power looked bleak. But, paradoxically, this debacle was a blessing for the SDRP because it provided its moderate wing with the justification to build an electorally viable organization. The party's leaders professed their commitment to parliamentary democracy and cannily identified themselves with many of the same policies as their rivals—economic reform, the promotion of private enterprise, and privatization. As in Hungary, this strategy enabled them to take advantage of their opponents' weaknesses. While Solidarity showed that it was incapable of forming stable governments and splintered into competing parties, the former communists presented an image of competence and moderation. In a stunning turnaround, the party won a plurality of the vote in the September 1993 elections and, like the HSP, formed a left-center government.

Unlike the Hungarian and Polish parties, Russia's communist successor party, the Communist Party of the Russian Federation (CPRF), did not make a total break with the past. Popular sympathy with the ideals of the old Soviet Union was still sufficiently strong to make this step unnecessary. Nonetheless, the CPRF, too, adopted a catchall strategy to attract new voters. Led by a former official from the Communist Party of the Soviet Union's (CPSU) Ideology Department, Gennady Zyuganov, the party embraced democratic institutions and even aspects of the market system. Going one step further than its Polish and Hungarian peers, it simultaneously took advantage of public discontent over the USSR's collapse to cultivate nationalist and anti-Western constituencies. These appeals paid off in the elections of December 1993. Aided by its opponent's disarray over the handling of economic reform, the party won more than 10 percent of the seats in the lower house of the Federal Assembly, the State Duma. Two years later, in 1995, it won a plurality of the vote and was awarded more than one-third of the seats in the legislature.

Notwithstanding these successes, Russia's communists faced a hurdle that democratic credentials alone could not surmount. To a greater extent than in Hungary and Poland, the powers of the State Duma were severely constrained by the constitutional authority of the Russian presidency. Accordingly, the impact of the CPRF's victory was less than it seemed. In June–July 1996, Zyuganov came close to giving his party the chance to exercise power by running for president. Campaigning on a platform that combined the promise of a strong welfare state with nationalist appeals, he nearly defeated President Boris Yeltsin, a former Politburo member, in the first round of the election. But after Yeltsin's victory in the runoff election, the CPRF was unable to regain the momentum that had earlier made it Russia's dominant party.

The successors to the Romanian Communist Party (RCP) in the National Salvation Front (NSF) also portrayed themselves as converts to democracy. From the beginning, however, this commitment was ambiguous. Led by a former Central Committee member, Ion Iliescu, and dominated by second-echelon communist functionaries, the NSF quickly transformed itself into a full-fledged political party, blending promises of expanded welfare programs with populist and nationalist rhetoric. Thanks to its members' political experience and control of the communications media and other state institutions, the party easily outmuscled its opponents in the parliamentary elections of May 1990. Out of an extraordinary fifty-nine different parties that competed for seats in the Assembly of Deputies and sixty-nine for seats in the Senate, the NSF won huge majorities in both houses. In a separate election, Iliescu became the country's first freely elected president. For those Romanians, however, who hoped that the ex-communists' success would pressure them to commit themselves fully to liberal democracy, this was an occasion for disappointment. Despite Iliescu's expressions of interest in Scandinavian social democracy, the regime continued to exhibit many of the same paternalistic and chauvinistic characteristics of the Nicolae Ceauşescu era.

Finally, there is the tragedy of Yugoslavia. Josip Broz Tito's death in May 1980 had precisely the destabilizing effect that both he and the other leaders of the League of Communists of Yugoslavia (LCY) had long feared. After a decade of mounting tensions among the federal republics, Yugoslavia was engulfed in a cascade of insurgencies and genocidal wars that destroyed the idea of the unified South Slav state that had come into being after World War I. Yet, even Tito would have been surprised by the circumstances under which this conflagration came to pass. Rather than binding the disparate ethnic groups of the federation together as Tito had hoped, the republican parties became the vehicles for Yugoslavia's destruction.

The LCY's crisis had little to do with communism. It began in 1986, when the president of the federation's Serbian republic, Slobodan Milošević, rebuffed the demands of Albanians in the autonomous region of Kosovo for greater self-determination. Drawing upon the organizational power of the League of Communists of Serbia, Milošević whipped up nationalist and irredentist passions in the republic. When he subsequently attempted to impose Serbian control over the entire federation, the Slovenian and Croatian Leagues became agents of separatism. In January 1990, the two Leagues' delegates dramatically walked out of an emergency congress of the LCY, and the idea of a unified Yugoslav party was finished.

Like the postcommunist parties in other parts of Europe, the republican Leagues' transformation into new organizations was shaped by their different paths to democracy. The overwhelming presence of former communists in the new Socialist Party of Serbia and the eruption of ethnic hatred in other republics allowed Milošević to assume nearly dictatorial control of his party. In Slovenia, in contrast, the ex-communists were forced to adapt their policies to a fast-paced transition to democracy. The fact that the country's separatist movement had begun among popular noncommunist groups meant that the renamed Slovenian Party of Democratic Renewal could only compete for the population's support by endorsing the democratic process. The new Social Democratic Party of Croatia, too, embraced democratic principles. However, the outbreak of fighting between Serb and Croat forces infused the party with a hypernationalist spirit. There was, however, one thing that all of these parties shared in common. They bore little resemblance to the communist leagues of the Tito era.

DYNASTIC SOCIALISM IN NORTH KOREA

Not everyone in Russia and Eastern Europe was pleased to see the Leninist party disappear. For people who still harbored nostalgic feelings about the communist era, and there were many, the 1990s were deeply troubling times. Whatever its deficiencies, single-party rule had undergirded their faith in a system that supposedly put their welfare first. Nevertheless, we can learn a great deal about the fragility of the parties that once dominated their lives by recognizing that it would have done them no good to look elsewhere for evidence that the former political order could be brought back to life. Even the handful of social-ist states that did not experience democratic revolutions had ceased to be models of Leninism. From Pyongyang to Beijing and Havana, their leaders' commitment to their founding principles, which had already been weakened by the upheavals of 1989–1991, was steadily eroding.

North Korea is the easiest case to characterize. By the early 1990s, Kim Il-sung had already begun to transform the Korean Workers' Party (KWP) into an instrument of dynastic rule. The KWP had not held a congress for a decade. At that time, in October 1980, Kim had made lugubrious remarks about the party's function. He likened the KWP to "one's own mother" and declared that it moved "like an organ-ism according to the principle of democratic centralism."[3] But in his New Year's address in 1991, Kim's assessment was much less laudatory. He did not even make the standard reference to Marxism-Leninism.[4] One year later, he confirmed the KWP's demotion in a host of consti-tutional amendments. Whereas the North Korean constitution of 1972 had underscored "the creative application of Marxism-Leninism to the conditions of our country," the revised document replaced the concept of the dictatorship of the proletariat with an ambiguous reference to a "dictatorship of people's democracy."[5]

The upheaval in Eastern Europe, and especially Ceaușescu's execution at the hands of his citizens, played a decisive role in this new course. Thus, in 1990, Kim warned his population of the Western imperialists' intention to "blur the reason of the people of the world and achieve their aggressive and predatory ambitions."[6] Thanks to the specifically North Korean doctrine of *Juche*, he boasted a year later, the country's socialist system remained "unchanged, to the wonder and admiration of the entire world."[7] But Kim had an additional motivation that dis-tinguished North Korea from other socialist states. He was determined to ensure the seamless transfer of power to his elder son, Kim Jong-il. In 1980, the party congress had already taken steps to recognize the younger Kim as the heir apparent and appointed him to most of the regime's ruling bodies. Lest anyone misinterpret the significance of this development, the general secretary's deputies subsequently let it be known that this was not merely a family affair. Passing power to Kim Jong-il was an act of supreme love for the entire country. After the Great Leader's departure, the son would safeguard the purity of the North Korean revolution.

Despite the loving father's measures, North Korea was not immune to the challenges of succession that we have encountered throughout this book. When the state media sorrowfully announced on July 8, 1994, that the "great heart" of Kim Il-sung had stopped beating, Kim Jong-il apparently recognized that even good bloodlines do not make the transferral of charismatic authority automatic. As with other leaders of communist insurgent movements, his father's power had derived from the support of his fellow revolutionaries during the guerrilla struggle against Japan and the battles of the Korean War. Four decades later, Kim Jong-il did not have the benefit of association with these acts of heroism. Hence, he looked beyond the party to the Korean People's Army (KPA) for legitimacy. In this case, Kim probably benefited from the fact that it took time to build a patronage network. The delay relieved him of having to take full responsibility within the regime for one of the worst famines in modern times. From 1994 to 1998, more than a million people perished from starvation and disease. When the famine subsided, Kim showed that he was firmly in control by combining mythology with power. He promulgated a new constitution that literally proclaimed *itself* the "Kim Il-sung Constitution" and declared Kim's father, to whom it referred in the present tense, the "eternal president of the republic." Correspondingly, Kim appointed himself chairman of the National Defense Commission.

In retrospect, it is provocative that Kim's promotion was proposed by a moribund institution—the KWP. From this point onward, he put the party's fate in the hands of the military. On January 1, 1999, a joint editorial by the KPA, the KWP, and the Kim Il-sung Socialist Youth League announced that Kim had developed his own concept of leadership: "military first" (*songun*). Exactly one year later, a similar editorial used the expression "military-first politics" to confirm that this was a doctrinal change. "The Comrade Kim Jong-il's military-first politics," the writers stated, in a style previously reserved to describe the KWP's leading role, "depended on the People's Army as the pillar of our revolution, enabling the entire people, including workers and peasants, to wage their struggle armed with revolutionary army spirit."[8]

Importantly, "military first" did not mean that North Korea had become a military dictatorship. Until his death in December 2011, Kim proved to be a master manipulator of the KPA's command structure, making himself the sole adjudicator of disputes among the military's branches. Rather, "military first" was meant to strengthen his personality cult by replacing one form of militancy, the Marxist focus on class struggle, with another, the struggle for national glory.[9] In the early 2000s, Kim turned the KPA into an agent of mass mobilization, enlisting soldiers in planting crops and building roads and factories. In the second half of the decade, he took the doctrine one step further, invoking "military first" to justify a nuclear defense policy against imperialism. In defiance of international pressure, the regime conducted underground nuclear tests and embarked on the development of sophisticated missile technology.

When Kim's youngest son, Kim Jong-un, rose to power in 2011, he initially acted as though he would simply carry on the "military first" strategy; he declared the strengthening of the KPA his "first, second, and third" priorities.[10] But, two long steps removed from the charisma of his grandfather, Kim Jong-un faced an even greater succession challenge than his father. Showing that he could not take even the KPA's loyalty for granted, he neutralized the "military first" principle by purging anyone who could use the doctrine against him. Starting with his uncle and second-in-command, Jang Song-taek, he executed hundreds of military officers and senior officials. In a demonstration that only *he*, and not the military, could be first, Kim followed his grandfather's and father's examples by formulating his own doctrine, "parallel advance" (*byungjin*). One leg of the doctrine, the introduction of modest economic reforms, marked a departure from Kim Jong-il's Stalinist-style economic policies. However, the second, more prominent leg was one part policy and the other part political drama. Kim Jong-un not only poured more resources into his father's nuclear weapons program but did so with theatrical panache. Banging the drums of an imminent confrontation with South Korea and the United States, he attempted to divert his population's attention from the country's manifold problems.

CHINA'S MODERNIZING AUTOCRACY

In many respects, the differences between the North Korean and Chinese conceptions of single-party rule in the 1990s and 2000s could not have been greater. Whereas the KWP lost all meaningful decision-making authority in North Korea, the CCP officially remained China's premier political institution. Its leaders convened regular meetings, fostered informed debates, and professed to hold their members to the highest standards of accountability. Despite these differences, however, the idea of party leadership was undergoing profound changes in the PRC as well. In the aftermath of the Tiananmen crisis of June 1989, the primary issue on the minds of China's leaders was stability, not the inculcation of the revolutionary values that the party had cultivated during the Long March.

Like Kim Il-sung, Deng Xiaoping and other senior CCP leaders were distressed by communism's disintegration in Eastern Europe. But in their eyes, the Soviet Union's implosion was much worse because it grew out of Mikhail Gorbachev's reforms. One lesson that they drew from these events was that pluralism was a threat to stability. According to this interpretation, Gorbachev's mistake was to assume that he could revitalize the party by going beyond economic modernization to engage in political reform. In the CCP Politburo's view, Hu Yaobang and Zhao Ziyang had made the same error in the 1990s. By blurring the line between acceptable and unacceptable behavior, they had created unrealizable expectations and undermined the population's confidence in the party. Accordingly, Deng and his coleaders concluded that the party should convey a firm message that would prevent its authority from being tested. Chen Yun, one of the Eight Elders, imaginatively expressed this point of view with a "bird cage" theory of leadership. The party controlled the cage, he suggested, and was willing to enlarge it—but only if the bird's behavior justified it. If need be, the party was equally prepared to reduce the size of the cage, presumably to contain the bird's efforts to escape.[11]

A second lesson, which Deng personally endorsed, was that a dogmatic defense of the status quo would erode the party's credibility. In his eyes, the failure of Soviet and Eastern European communism was attributable to these parties' long-standing opposition to serious reforms. They might have been able to save themselves if they had acted earlier—interestingly, Deng singled out Khrushchev's policies as an option—but by Gorbachev's time, it was too late to change course.[12] For these reasons, Deng argued, the CCP should continue to do what it did best: it should build a vibrant economy.

There was nothing inherently contradictory about the twin mandates of political stability and economic growth. As the CCP leadership looked beyond the tumultuous events of spring and summer 1989, the key question was which of the two strategies the party should prioritize. Deng and his successors, Jiang Zemin and Hu Jintao, chose economic growth. In early 1992, the Paramount Leader emulated Mao's favorite technique for building support for his policies by traveling beyond Beijing's city limits. During his Southern Tour through Guangdong Province and Shanghai, he spoke in a direct and unrestrained fashion about China's needs. To leave the proper imprint on history, Deng observed, the CCP's leaders needed to take bolder and more courageous steps. "We should not act like women with bound feet," he lectured. It was necessary to experiment and forge new paths. Naturally, there could be no guarantees that all of the party's ventures would pay off. "Who dares to claim," Deng stressed, "that he is 100 percent sure of success and that he is taking no risks?" Yet China had no other choice. If the party leadership's current members were not up to this task, Deng added, they should step aside and let a younger generation take their place.[13]

Despite some initial concerns about the political risks of moving too quickly, Jiang Zemin endorsed Deng's stance at the CCP's Fourteenth Congress in October 1992. He enunciated a new concept, Deng Xiaoping Theory, that was based on the hallmarks of his mentor's post-Mao policies: economic modernization, the use of market mechanisms to guide investment, and closer relations with Western countries and international corporations. By all accounts, Jiang's decision to emulate Deng's example paid off. Over the following decade, China's economy expanded rapidly; state firms were broken into smaller, more efficient enterprises; and entrepreneurship proliferated. In the process, the country's educated, urban population experienced previously unthinkable gains in prosperity. When China was invited to join the World Trade

Organization in 2001, it seemed to Jiang and his supporters that their country had finally regained the international stature that had been lost under Mao's rule.

For our purposes, the most important development during Jiang's tenure was the reformulation of the CCP's identity. First, Jiang pressed for a streamlining of the organization's rules. The Fourteenth Congress abolished the Central Advisory Committee, the informal body that had allowed retired party leaders to interfere in the Politburo's operations. The CCP's leaders committed themselves to the principle of collective rule and promised to reach their decisions on the basis of consensus. They also eliminated the practice of making lifetime appointments. To bring new blood into the ruling circle, they required Politburo members to retire at the age of sixty-eight. These norms took hold quickly—at the Sixteenth Party Congress in November 2002, all eleven Politburo members who had reached the age of retirement relinquished their posts. Jiang himself turned over the general secretaryship to Hu Jintao, a representative of China's postrevolutionary generation. Although Jiang was criticized for not giving up his position as chair of the Central Military Commission, this was a signal event. Unlike so many other times in the history of global communism, the transfer of power had taken place on a truly voluntary basis.

Second, Jiang presided over a redefinition of the CCP's functions. In early 2000, eight years after Deng Xiaoping's Southern Tour, he made his own inspection tour of high-tech firms in Guangdong. At his stops, he characterized the party in purely utilitarian terms as the servant of rapid growth. To raise productivity, he emphasized, the regime would continue dismantling inefficient state-owned firms, even if these steps led to the dislocation of workers and unemployment. It would aggressively pursue foreign investment opportunities and further engagement in the world economy. Finally, the party would actively encourage the participation of every segment of society, including intellectuals, scientists, and entrepreneurs.

In an address on July 1, 2001, during the eightieth anniversary celebrations of the CCP's founding, Jiang confirmed that these were no mean changes.[14] To read his speech against the backdrop of more than one and a half centuries of the international communist movement is to find oneself in a new world. Although Jiang recounted the party's "torrential and anti-imperialist struggle" and its central role in the founding of the People's Republic of China, he did not refer at all to two major factors that distinguished Marxism and Leninism from other revolutionary movements: the class struggle and the dictatorship of the proletariat. In fact, he only used the word "revolution" once. In Jiang's depiction, the point of having a leading party was simply to make China modern. Accordingly, the institution needed to change with the times, promoting a "spirit of practicality, truth seeking, and truth in innovation." Jiang even came close to jettisoning the standard description of the party as a class-based organization. Although he stated that the party remained the vanguard of the working class, he broadened this function to make right thinking, and not class background, the criterion for membership. In a stunning departure from CCP orthodoxy, he announced that even private businesspersons should be invited to join the party.

From the standpoint of Marxist theory, we do not have to look far to see the problematic implications of this position. If capitalists can be included among the CCP's members, we have made an immense leap from Lenin's time when revolutionary heroes were trained in the "art of combat" and poised to go to war with anyone who stood in the way of the liberation of the proletariat. In addition, Jiang's revisions present the Marxist theorist with a related problem. If the profit-seeking activities of the party's capitalist members lead to greater inequalities in Chinese society, as surely they will, what are the chances of attaining the goal of communism? Jiang seemed to anticipate this question, but in a way that twentieth-century Marxists would have clearly found unsatisfactory. He declared that "human society [would] still inevitably move towards communism." But, he added, this goal could only be "realized on the basis of a fully developed and highly advanced socialist society." Therefore, Jiang insisted, the party needed to concentrate on the present: "To talk big about the lofty ideal without doing any practical work will get one divorced from reality."[15]

After Jiang stepped down as party chief in 2002, his successor, Hu Jintao, was no less committed to this growth-oriented strategy. His contribution was to emphasize that the party should pay greater attention to the adverse social effects of China's rapid modernization.[16] The situation changed, however, with Hu's successor, Xi Jinping. When Xi became general secretary in November 2012, he almost immediately swung the CCP to its other mandate: maintaining social and political order. In the process of establishing his authority, Xi launched a sweeping campaign against graft and corruption within party and state bodies. He instructed party officials to cull their ranks of dissenting members. Even more significant for our purposes, Xi sought to take control of the realm of ideas. He clamped down on the propagation of "Western values" and "wrong arguments," such as the advocacy of multiparty democracy and free self-expression. He also imposed new restrictions on the media, the Internet, and religious institutions.

In contrast to Jiang Zemin and Hu Jintao, Xi also showed his intention to leave a personal imprint on the political system by articulating a vision of the future that he called "the Chinese dream." One part of this amorphous concept was outwardly directed. According to Xi, China should play a greater role in fostering a "peaceful international environment." It could accomplish this task by contributing to a "shared destiny and the future of the world as a whole." Yet, Xi's domestic focus was more specific. China's citizens, he maintained, were required to invigorate their nation by building "an affluent, strong, civilized, harmonious, socialist modern society."[17]

The elements of Xi's dream were not new; they could all be found within the elastic realm of Deng Xiaoping Theory. However, Xi demonstrated that his understanding of this vision was as much backward-looking as forward-looking. Although he stressed that China would adhere to Deng's views about economic development, he devoted equal attention to China's pre-Marxist past. He visited Confucius's shrine and lauded the philosopher's teachings about social harmony and filial piety; he praised Legalist scholars for their ideas about maintaining public order; and he glorified generals from China's early dynasties as patriots and martyrs. Xi paid particular attention to precommunist revolutionaries, especially Sun Yat-sen, whom he lauded for offering a model of national rejuvenation.

To be sure, these appeals to earlier times did not prevent Xi from glorifying the CCP's Marxist credentials. In fact, in 2015 he ordered

Peking University to build a collection of Marxist writings that would exceed the size of its Confucius collection. Still, a building full of books and documents is no substitute for instilling ideological conviction. Nor is it a guarantee that a specific worldview will play a meaningful role in policymaking. Demonstrating that his idea of "the Chinese dream" was broader than the assortment of beliefs that had inspired communist heroes such as Mao Zedong and Zhou Enlai, Xi used the celebrations of the seventy-fifth anniversary of the CCP's founding to treat the party as the grand unifying element in Chinese history. The CCP, he asserted on July 1, 2016, had inspired the Chinese people "with more than 5,000 years of civilization and history [to] fully march toward modernization"; it had enabled "socialist views with their 500-year history to find a highly practical and workable correct path in the world's most populous country"; finally, it had made it possible for "a new China with its 60-year history to achieve results that have drawn the eyes of the world." This was high praise. Yet despite these grandiose claims, there was a glaring omission in Xi's address. He had almost nothing to say about whether it should matter that China was ruled by a specifically *communist* party and not some other autocratic organization. He could only declare, in the clichéd language of his predecessors, that the CCP's members should maintain the "fighting spirit" of the party's founders.[18]

Cuba's Charismatic Dictatorship

Cuba took a different course. At a time when North Korea's and China's leaders were either rejecting or substantially revising the idea of communist party rule, Fidel Castro was anxiously defending the vision of revolutionary struggle that he had cultivated since his days as a guerrilla fighter in the Sierra Maestra Mountains. Showing that his lifelong discomfort with organized parties was unchanged, he continued to emphasize the power of *communists* to sustain the Revolution. In an address at Havana's Karl Marx Theater on April 19, 1991, the anniversary of the Bay of Pigs Invasion, he applauded his *compañeros'* willingness to sacrifice everything for the cause. Just as true communists were "always heroic in the defense of their ideas and their cause," he proclaimed, summoning the examples of the Paris Commune, the Spanish Civil War, and the Battle of Stalingrad, so too would these heroes make history once again.[19]

Of course, Castro's understanding of how to serve the communist cause was quite different from the dreams of these early exemplars of revolution. Even after declining health forced him to turn over his position as first secretary of the Communist Party of Cuba (PCC) to his less charismatic, soberly minded brother Raúl in 2011, he still acted as though only a single person was capable of defending the Revolution: himself. In this light, when we look back at the PCC's role in Cuban politics over the preceding decades, it is not surprising that Castro's honeymoon with the party was short-lived. By the mid-1970s, his speeches about the PCC's leading role were pro forma at best. Indeed, in an interview for Soviet television on the sixtieth anniversary of the October Revolution in 1977, Castro mentioned the PCC only once and, even then, merely in reference to the first communist party's activities in the 1930s.[20]

In place of the PCC's support, Castro turned once again to the Cuban Revolutionary Armed Forces (FAR). In the aftermath of the failed sugarcane harvest of 1970, the Cuban government had become more dependent than ever on its Soviet and Eastern European allies for trade, financial and military assistance, and energy resources. Hence, Castro appealed to the military roots of the Revolution to show that he was still in command. In November 1975, he took even his Soviet benefactors by surprise by involving Cuba directly in the Angolan Civil War. This was an extraordinary way of reinforcing his authority given that the conflict was nearly 7,000 miles away. Yet by March 1976, roughly 20,000 Cuban soldiers were fighting alongside the army of the quasi-Marxist People's Movement for the Liberation of Angola.[21] Much closer to home, Castro also took a strong interest in the guerrilla struggles against Anastasio Somoza's government in Nicaragua. The leftist Sandinista National Liberation Front regarded both Castro and Che Guevara as quasi-deities. Hence, he reciprocated their adulation by sending them arms and military advisers.

This was vintage Fidel. In these battles and in other international engagements, he summoned the mythic elements of Cuba's age-old struggles against colonialism and imperialism. The Cuban people's willingness to sacrifice themselves for internationalist missions testified, in his words, to "our political culture, the complete victory of revolutionary ideals, the solidary [*sic*] communist blood that runs through the veins of men and women of our fatherland."[22] Predictably, Castro turned Washington's condemnations of these overseas adventures to his advantage at home, rallying the Cuban population again and again around the idea of national defense. In 1983, when US president Ronald Reagan sent troops to Grenada to topple the island's Marxist government, Castro ordered Cuban construction workers in the country to martyr themselves in combat with the invading army.

Nevertheless, it did not take long for the FAR to become just as problematic a partner in Castro's eyes as the PCC. The FAR was no longer the unkempt guerrilla army of the Sierra Maestra Mountains. Its officers had been well trained by their Soviet advisers and were battle-hardened. Moreover, they had won prestige both at home and throughout the developing world for defeating superior armies. Hence in the early 1980s, Castro indicated that his enthusiasm for the FAR was waning. Citing the strategic thinking of the North Vietnamese general Võ Nguyên Giáp, he introduced a new military doctrine, "the war of all the people," which emphasized the popular roots of the Revolution. At the PCC's Third Congress, he barely mentioned the FAR's ongoing fighting in Angola. The shocking culmination of this shift in Castro's thinking was to use force against those who had long supported him. In July 1989, he began with the arrest of the popular commander of Cuba's international forces, General Arnaldo Ochoa. Ochoa was subjected to a swift, Stalinist-style show trial and executed. The general was not alone; the minister of the interior was executed as well. Scores of high-ranking officers of the FAR and the Interior Ministry were imprisoned and thousands of others were relieved of their posts.[23]

There was no coincidence to the timing of Castro's crackdown. It took place amid the uncertainty surrounding Gorbachev's reforms and only a few weeks after Beijing's suppression of the Tiananmen demonstrations. A year earlier, in 1988, when he was asked about the possibility of a Cuban version of glasnost, Castro confidently remarked that the party had always supported this position: "There's no more self-critical party in the world than the PCC."[24] After the collapse of the Soviet bloc, however, Castro conceded that Cuban socialism was in trouble. In an interview with *El Nuevo Diario*, he emphasized that his government would do what it took to defend its precarious values "at a moment of confusion in the world." "The mere fact," Castro stressed, sounding a lot like Kim Jong-il, "that Cuba has decided to keep going forward and face the dangers and the challenges following the collapse of the socialist bloc and the disappearance of the USSR is a significant event in history."[25]

This was sheer bravado. Cuba would not be insulated from the consequences of the disappearance of its patron. After the USSR's demise, the country fell into a severe economic depression. As a result of the loss of billions of dollars in Soviet subsidies and the disappearance of major trading markets, exports and imports plummeted. In 1993, Cuba's GDP had fallen by 30 percent, and the regime was forced to confront food shortages and visible unemployment. For the first time in more than three decades, openly antigovernment street demonstrations and riots broke out in Havana and neighboring cities.

These trials illuminate the central flaw of all personality cults. Had Cuba been governed by the rule of law, Castro might have buttressed his authority by appealing to the legitimacy of the country's political institutions. Instead, he was left grasping for explanations for why Cuba should remain a revolutionary state. At first, he sought the answer in a romanticized version of the PCC's history, underscoring the party's roots in Latin American, rather than European, culture. According to his revisionist interpretation, José Martí, and not Marx, Engels, and Lenin, deserved full credit for the idea of the single-party system.[26] In 1992, this supposedly objective correction of the historical record found its way into a new constitution. The former constitution's reference to "the victorious doctrine of Marxism-Leninism" was replaced with a quotation from Martí: "I want the fundamental law of our republic to be the tribute of Cubans to the full dignity of man." Notably, the new body of laws changed the PCC's role. Instead of being the vanguard of the proletariat, it became the "vanguard of the Cuban nation."[27]

To stabilize the economy, however, Castro had no choice but to turn back to the FAR. Drawing upon the military's expertise and organizational efficiency, he introduced cautious reforms, including the partial legalization of the use of US currency, the opening of farmers' markets, selective inducements to foreign investment, and the promotion of tourism. As always, Castro had no intention of allowing the FAR to supplant his authority. On the most important questions, both the army and the PCC were only facilitators of the wishes of the legendary guerrilla fighter who had come to power with promises of national independence and popular democracy. As a result, when illness forced Castro to turn over his presidential duties to Raúl in 2006, followed by his leadership of the PCC in 2011, the Cuban regime entered unknown territory.

In his new positions, Raúl endeavored to emphasize two views simultaneously. He introduced moderate economic reforms, while simultaneously insisting that the regime would never compromise its commitment to socialism. He emphatically invoked the leading role of the PCC to back up this claim. However, this pro forma reference to an institution that had always been subordinated to its leader was not the same thing as devising an effective ruling formula. In fact, Raúl practically conceded that the regime was at a loss to find such a solution. In the Central Report to the PCC's Seventh Congress on April 16, 2016—"Year 58 of the Revolution"—he frankly admitted that "party membership has declined, impacted by the negative demographic trends affecting the country, a restrictive growth policy maintained since 2004, and shortcomings in efforts to train, retain, and motivate potential members." Looking for a sign of hope, Raúl could only add that "this trend has decelerated over recent years."[28] Against this somber background, an aged generation of *fidelistas* may have been heartened when Raúl's ninety-year-old brother surfaced three days later and proclaimed the eternal life of the Revolution. Every human being would perish one day, Fidel Castro emphasized, but "the ideas of Cuban communists will remain as proof on this planet that if they are worked at with fervor and dignity, they can produce the material and cultural goods that human beings need."[29] Nevertheless, Fidel's death seven months later in November 2016 testified to the drawback of associating a revolution with the personality of a single human being. Without his presence to embody these ideas, it was inconceivable that the Cuban people would want to continue this long journey.

THE PARTY WITHERS AWAY

The global demise of the distinctive concept of communist party rule by the 2000s provides us with an invaluable lesson about the centrality of ideas in sustaining institutions. The party of Lenin, Stalin, and Mao had all of the advantages of dictatorship. Seated at the pinnacle of political power, these states' leaders made decisions that affected the lives of millions. Thanks to their formidable resources, they launched massive industrialization campaigns, uprooted and transformed traditional societies, and extended their influence to every part of the world. But without the conviction that a single institution—the party—was capable of leading these revolutions, they would not have been able to recruit and then maintain the loyalties of the followers who put their visions into practice.

Over a relatively short period, the idea of the enlightened, disciplined, and virtuous communist party came to an end. For decades, the party's members had been like Lenin's mountaineer. Filled with the certainty of having justice on their side, they had begun their ascent with enthusiasm. They were the elect, chosen to be the vanguard in pursuit of a glorious cause. They enjoyed the gratification of belonging to a global movement, one that was certain to achieve its goal. Then, they reached an impasse—a crumbling economy, failed social policies, and popular disenchantment—at which point they were forced to retrace their steps. Yet, here the similarity with Lenin's dauntless climber breaks down. Instead of searching for a new path, the faithful left the mountain behind. After years of loyalty, they had lost the conviction that the party's demands were worth defending.

This decision was not automatic. Although communist leaders in the homeland of the Bolshevik Revolution, the Soviet Union, were fully aware of their diminishing credibility, there was a brief historical moment when a new party chief in Moscow, Mikhail Gorbachev, led many to hope that he could successfully breathe life into the preeminent institution of developed socialism. Since no one, neither leaders nor led, could have known in the 1980s that this system was so close to collapse, Gorbachev's supporters regarded his campaign for domestic reform as an enthralling alternative to the old ways of thinking and acting. In particular, the Soviet leader's buoyant optimism filled many communists, and especially those whose advancement had been held back for years, with anticipation at the possibility of reawakening their party's high ideals. In short, this was a time of great expectations. Yet for precisely this reason, these hopes came crashing down when it became clear that socialism could not be rescued from its manifold dysfunctions. In the end, no one was left to speak up for the party, not even the general secretary of the CPSU.

Gorbachev's central role in these events invites one of the most thought-provoking counterfactual exercises in the study of twentieth-century politics. What if, instead of Gorbachev, another figure had come to power in 1985, someone who embodied the highly risk-averse spirit of the Brezhnev generation and would therefore have been less inclined to experiment with the accepted model of developed socialism? Would the crisis of party leadership in the Soviet Union have taken place? In my view, it would have taken a few years longer. Given the organizational power of the general secretaryship, a conservative leader could have prevented his critics from building a coalition against him by securing the support of members of the inner circle who regarded any experimentation with the party's leading role as dangerous.

There is an even darker version of the counterfactual argument. In this case, one might assume that Gorbachev came to power but was much less flexible when confronted with the unintended consequences of his actions. For example, instead of criticizing Erich Honecker in October 1989 when the German Democratic Republic's (GDR) brittle social order was breaking apart, what if Gorbachev had given his blessing to his East German ally to use armed force to defend his regime? Such a response was not out of the question. On October 9, Honecker ordered the secret police to prepare to crush the protests in Leipzig.[30] Fortunately for the stability of Europe, Gorbachev chose prudence over intransigence. Rather than allowing the East German leader to risk the outbreak of civil war in the GDR and a possible confrontation with

NATO, he effectively gave Honecker's colleagues permission to remove him from power. From this point forward, Gorbachev's *inaction* was the key to the fall of communist rule.

Nevertheless, there are two reasons for thinking that the crisis of world communism would still have taken place within the coming decade. First, even before Gorbachev's rise, pressures for a reassessment of the party's role were growing in countries like Poland and Hungary. In this respect, even a conservative Gorbachev would eventually have been forced to take these demands seriously. Second, the opposition to Gorbachev's initiatives within the CPSU Politburo was never absolute. Critics like Yegor Ligachev agreed that gradual reforms were necessary. Even if they had moved more cautiously, the speed with which Gorbachev lost control of his reforms suggests that they would have been hard-pressed to contain the pent-up demands that suffused their society.

In claiming that the ideas that sustained communist party rule over the past century have vanished, I am not contending that the party's ideals have disappeared. Radical aspirations for economic justice and social equality are as alive in the twenty-first century as they were in 1848 when Karl Marx presented his *Manifesto of the Communist Party* to the Communist League. For example, when the socialist politician Hugo Chávez was elected president of Venezuela in 1999, he undertook a program of rapid social transformation that was reminiscent of Fidel Castro's policies in the 1960s. He instituted antipoverty programs, turned major industries into state enterprises, and experimented with self-governing communes. Yet the party that put Chávez into office was a mass organization that primarily served the populist and nationalist instincts of its leader. It had little in common with the institution that spurred Marx and Lenin's followers into action.

Of course, it would be unreasonable to expect that the rulers of any radical left-wing regime in the twenty-first century would embrace Leninism after the fate of communist regimes in 1989–1991. But this is precisely the point. The original idea of a revolutionary party and the organization into which it evolved made sense at specific times and in specific places. Over more than a century, communists in Germany, France, Russia, China, and many more countries and territories fought for their cause against a backdrop of social upheaval, civil and global wars, economic collapse, mass uprisings, and national humiliation. Although these revolutionaries were convinced that the evidence for the coming clash between the haves and the have-nots was incontrovertible, they had different views about the form this conflagration would take in their respective locations. Some espoused Marx's prediction about an imminent collision between the bourgeoisie and the proletariat; others anticipated that the proletariat would be joined by the peasantry; still others expected a confrontation between imperialism and the forces of national liberation. Nevertheless, the malleability of Marx and Lenin's ideas gave them confidence that they could realize their dreams. Thus, they all put their faith in the idea that the formation of the right kind of association—highly disciplined but discerning, dictatorial but self-sacrificing, uncompromising but virtuous—would ensure victory in the battle for a just world. Their conviction was so great that they were willing to sacrifice their lives—and the lives of others—to achieve this goal.

By the 1990s and 2000s, the factors that made this particular conception of revolutionary leadership compelling no longer existed. Still, we must be careful to keep this momentous development in perspective. The disappearance of the communist party should not be a cause for unreflective self-congratulation among those who championed the values of liberal democracy during the Cold War. Clearly, the West's military and economic superiority over the USSR played an important role in undermining the confidence of Soviet and Eastern European leaders that they could compete successfully with the capitalist world. But the primary cause of these regimes' collapse did not come from without. It came from a loss of faith among the communists themselves that the institution that had once ruled broad swaths of the globe was viable. The party was not defeated; it lost the will to stay alive.

Furthermore, the fate of the communist party has proved to have little to do with the vitality of democracy in the West. As the crisis of liberal democracy in Europe and the United States in the 2010s has shown, democratic institutions are only as strong as the will and determination of their citizens to defend the principles on which they are based. Democratic parties can provide effective mechanisms through which politicians infuse their societies with noble purpose. But there is no guarantee this will happen. Political parties can also be perverted into tools of unreason and extremism that tear societies apart. To an even greater extent than in the case of communist parties, which could always fall back on the use of violence to defend their political systems, liberal democratic states require good leaders to ensure that their parties serve the former purpose and not the latter.

PHOTO CREDITS

Plate 1. E. Capiro, *Karl Marx and Friedrich Engels, January 1, 1848* (1895). Credit: Universal History Archive / UIG / Bridgeman Images.

Plate 2. Johann Velten (1807–1883), *Eine Gefängnißscene* (Prison Scene) (1848); the painter is standing on the left. Credit: De Agostini Picture Library / A. Dagli Orti / Bridgeman Images.

Plate 3. Barricade at the Faubourg Saint-Antoine during the Commune, March 18, 1871. Credit: Bibliothèque Nationale / Bridgeman Images.

Plate 4. Rosa Luxemburg. Mary Evans Picture Library / Weimar Archive.

Plate 5. Vladimir Ilyich Lenin. Credit: Mary Evans Picture Library / Alexander Meledin Collection.

Plate 6. The Tours Congress, from *L'Humanité*, December 1920. Credit: Bibliothèque Nationale / Archives Charmet / Bridgeman Images.

Plate 7. Ernst Thälmann. Credit: Mary Evans Picture Library / SZ Photo / Scherl.

Plate 8. The Long March. Credit: Mondadori Portfolio / Bridgeman Images.

Plate 9. Joseph Stalin. Credit: Sputnik / Alamy Stock Photo.

Plate 10. The Spanish Civil War. Credit: Mary Evans Picture Library / Iberfoto.

Plate 11. Josip Broz Tito. Credit: Bridgeman Images.

Plate 12. World communist leaders at Lenin's grave. Credit: Bettman Collection / Getty Images.

Plate 13. Hungarian prime minister Imre Nagy and Mátyás Rákosi. Credit: Photo © PVDE / Bridgeman Images.

Plate 14. Khrushchev's "Secret Speech," 1956. Credit: Private collection / Sputnik / Bridgeman Images.

Plate 15. Fidel Castro. Credit: Roberto Salas / Mary Evans Picture Library / Salas Collection.

Plate 16. Red Guards with the "Little Red Book." Credit: Pictures from History / Bridgeman Images.

Plate 17. Communist party leaders in East Germany and Czechoslovakia. Credit: Rolls Press / Popperfoto / Getty Images.

Plate 18. Władysław Gomułka. Credit: Keystone Pictures USA / Alamy Stock Photo.

Plate 19. Leonid Brezhnev and Todor Zhivkov. Credit: TASS / UIG / Bridgeman Images.

Plate 20. Nicolae Ceauşescu. Credit: Patrick Robert / Corbis Getty Images.

Plate 21. Mikhail Gorbachev. Credit: TASS / UIG / Bridgeman Images.

Plate 22. Opening session of roundtable negotiations in Warsaw. Credit: Forum / Bridgeman Images.

Plate 23. Deng Xiaoping and Zhao Ziyang. Credit: John Giannini / AFP / Getty Images.

Plate 24. One hundred fiftieth anniversary of the birth of Sun Yat-sen. Credit: Étienne Oliveau / Getty Images.

Plate 25. Cubans say good-bye to Castro's remains as they travel across Cuba ahead of his burial. Credit: Chip Somodevilla / Getty Images / News Collection.

CHAPTER I. INTRODUCTION

1 See Article VI, "Constitution (Fundamental Law) of the Union of Soviet Socialist Republics," in *The Constitutions of the USSR and the Union Republics*, ed. F.J.M. Feldbrugge (Alphen an den Rijn, The Netherlands: Sijthoff and Noordhoff, 1979), pp. 77, 79.

2 *Pravda*, March 16, 1990.

3 *Los Angeles Times*, December 13, 1989.

4 These calculations are based on parties for which sufficient data is available. See Richard Starr, "Checklist of Communist Parties in 1985," *Problems of Communism* 35 (March–April 1986): 62–66, and the V-Dem (Varieties of Democracy) Dataset at https://v-dem.net/en/data/.

5 For comprehensive histories and theoretical accounts of world communism, see Archie Brown, *The Rise and Fall of Communism* (New York: HarperCollins, 2011); Ken Jowitt, *New World Disorder: The Leninist Extinction* (Berkeley: University of California Press, 1993); Gerd Koenen, *Was war der Kommunismus?* (Göttingen: Vandenhoeck und Ruprecht, 2010); Silvio Pons, *The Global Revolution: A History of International Communism 1917–1991* (Oxford: Oxford University Press, 2014); David Priestland, *The Red Flag: A History of Communism* (New York: Grove/Atlantic, 2016); and Robert Service, *Comrades! A History of World Communism* (Cambridge, MA: Harvard University Press, 2010).

6 On "family resemblances," see Ludwig Wittgenstein, *Philosophical Investigations*, 2nd ed. (New York: Blackwell, 1945), §§ 66–67, 31ᵉ–32ᵉ.

7 Ernest Hemingway, *For Whom the Bell Tolls* (New York: Scribner, 1968), p. 235.

8 Milovan Djilas, *Conversations with Stalin* (London: Penguin, 1962), p. 49.

9 In an interview conducted in December 1983, in Teresa Toranska, *"Them": Stalin's Polish Puppets*, trans. Agnieszka Kolakowska (New York: Harper and Row, 1987), p. 23.

10 Joseph Stalin, "On the Death of Lenin," delivered January 26, 1926, in *Works*, vol. 6 (Moscow: Foreign Languages Publishing House, 1953), p. 47.

[11] Karl Marx and Friedrich Engels, *Manifesto of the Communist Party*, in *The Marx-Engels Reader*, ed. Robert C. Tucker, 2nd ed. (New York: Norton, 1978), p. 500.

[12] "Fright at the Fall of the Old and the Fight for the New," first published in *Pravda*, January 22, 1921, reprinted in *The Lenin Anthology*, ed. Robert C. Tucker (New York: Norton, 1975), pp. 424–46.

[13] Leonid Brezhnev, "Fifty Years of Great Victories of Socialism," remarks on November 3, 1967, at a ceremonial session of the CPSU Central Committee, the Supreme Soviet of the USSR, and the Supreme Soviet of the Russian Republic, in *Current Digest of the Soviet Press* 19, no. 44 (November 22, 1967), p. 19.

[14] For representative views published before fall 1989, see Andrei Amalrik, *Will the Soviet Union Survive until 1984?* (New York: Harper Colophon Books, 1981); Carl Joachim Friedrich and Zbigniew K. Brzezinski, *Totalitarian Dictatorship and Autocracy* (Cambridge, MA: Harvard University Press, 1965); Zbigniew Brzezinski, *The Grand Failure: The Birth and Death of Communism in the Twentieth Century* (New York: Charles Scribner's Sons, 1989). For works after fall 1989, see François Furet, *The Passing of an Illusion: The Idea of Communism in the Twentieth Century* (Chicago: University of Chicago Press, 1999); Martin Malia, *The Soviet Tragedy: A History of Socialism in Russia, 1917–1991* (New York: Free Press, 1995); and Andrzej Walicki, *Marxism and the Leap to the Kingdom of Freedom: The Rise and Fall of the Communist Utopia* (Palo Alto, CA: Stanford University Press, 1997).

[15] For representative works published before fall 1989, see Seweryn Bialer, *Stalin's Successors: Leadership, Stability and Change in the Soviet Union* (New York: Cambridge University Press, 1982); George Breslauer, *Five Images of the Soviet Future: A Critical Review and Synthesis* (Berkeley, CA: Center for International Studies, 1978); Stephen F. Cohen, *Rethinking the Soviet Experience* (New York: Oxford University Press, 1986); and Robert C. Tucker, *The Marxian Revolutionary Idea* (New York: W. W. Norton, 1969). For examples after fall 1989, see Bruce Dickson, *The Dictator's Dilemma: The Chinese Communist Party's Strategy for Survival* (New York: Oxford University Press, 2016); Martin K. Dimitrov, ed., *Why Communism Did Not Collapse: Understanding Authoritarian Regime Resilience in Asia and Europe* (New York: Cambridge University Press, 2013); and Elizabeth Perry, *Anyuan: Mining China's Revolutionary Tradition* (Berkeley: University of California Press, 2012).

[16] On the role of leaders and their use of political institutions to their advantage, see Jörg Baberowski, *Scorched Earth: Stalin's Reign of Terror* (New Haven,

CT: Yale University Press, 2016); Archie Brown, *The Myth of the Strong Leader: Political Leadership in the Modern Age* (New York: Basic Books, 2014); Robert C. Tucker, *The Soviet Political Mind: Stalinism and Post-Stalin Change* (New York: W. W. Norton, 1972); Robert C. Tucker, *Political Culture and Leadership in Soviet Russia: From Lenin to Gorbachev* (New York: Norton, 1988); Andrew Walder, *China under Mao: A Revolution Derailed* (Cambridge, MA: Harvard University Press, 2015).

[17] The perils of overgeneralization are rampant in studies of modern dictatorship, especially those on communism. For a seminal example, consider Friedrich and Brzezinski, *Totalitarian Dictatorship and Autocracy.* For a recent example, see Martin Malia, "Foreword: The Uses of Atrocity," and Stéphane Courtois, "Introduction: The Crimes of Communism," in Stéphane Courtois, Nicolas Werth, Jean-Louis Panné, Andrzej Paczkowski, Karel Bartošek, and Jean-Louis Margolin, *The Black Book of Communism: Crimes, Terror, Repression,* ed. Mark Kramer, trans. Jonathan Murphy and Mark Kramer (Cambridge, MA: Harvard University Press, 1999), pp. ix–xx and 1–31.

[18] Consider Paul Hollander, ed., *From the Gulag to the Killing Fields: Personal Accounts of Political Violence and Repression in Communist States* (Wilmington, DE: ISI Books, 2006).

CHAPTER 2. A REVOLUTIONARY IDEA

[1] Karl Marx and Friedrich Engels, *Manifesto of the Communist Party,* in *The Marx-Engels Reader,* ed. Robert C. Tucker, 2nd ed. (New York: Norton, 1978), p. 483. I refer to Marx alone in my treatment of the *Manifesto* because he was the document's sole author.

[2] Ibid., pp. 483–84.

[3] Friedrich Engels, *The Condition of the Working Class in England* (London: Granada, 1969), p. 84.

[4] J. Walton, *Chartism* (London: Routledge, 1999), pp. 11, 27.

[5] Indeed, Proudhon, a critic, suggested that Cabet's "communists" numbered "one hundred thousand, perhaps two hundred." Cited in Christopher H. Johnson, *Utopian Communism in France: Cabet and the Icarians, 1839–1851* (Ithaca, NY: Cornell University Press, 1974), p. 145.

[6] Louis Auguste Blanqui, *Textes Choisis* (Paris: Les Éditions Sociales, 1971), pp. 64–69.

[7] Karl Marx, "Rules of the Communist League (1847)," in Michael Löwy, *The Theory of Revolution in the Young Marx* (Leiden: Brill, 2003), p. 132.

[8] Friedrich Engels, "Principles of Communism," in *Selected Works*, vol. 1 (Moscow: Progress Publishers, 1969), pp. 81–97.

[9] Marx and Engels, *Manifesto of the Communist Party*, pp. 476–77.

[10] Ibid., pp. 478–79.

[11] Ibid., pp. 481–83.

[12] Ibid., pp. 485–88. Compare with Engels, *Selected Works*, pp. 81–97.

[13] Marx and Engels, *Manifesto of the Communist Party*, p. 490.

[14] Ibid., pp. 491–99.

[15] Ibid., pp. 499–500.

[16] Karl Marx and Friedrich Engels, "Demands of the Communist Party in Germany," in *The Communist Manifesto: A Roadmap to History's Most Important Political Document*, ed. Phil Gasper (Chicago: Haymarket Books, 2005), pp. 153–55.

[17] Friedrich Engels, "The Assembly in Frankfurt," *Neue Rheinische Zeitung*, June 1, 1848, in *Karl Marx and Friedrich Engels: Collected Works* (hereafter *CW*), vol. 7 (London: Lawrence and Wishart, 1977), p. 16.

[18] Karl Marx and Friedrich Engels, "Address of the Central Committee to the Communist League," March 24, 1850, in Tucker, *The Marx-Engels Reader*, p. 511.

[19] Karl Marx, "Meeting of the Central Authority," September 15, 1850, *CW*, vol. 10 (1978), p. 626.

[20] Karl Marx, "Inaugural Address of the Workingmen's International Association," September 28, 1864, *CW*, vol. 20 (1985), pp. 5–13.

[21] Karl Marx, "Provisional Rules of the Association," October 1864, *CW*, vol. 20 (1985), pp. 14–16.

[22] Jacques Rougerie, *La Commune de 1871* (Paris: Presses Universitaires de France, 1988), p. 118.

[23] Karl Marx, "The Civil War in France," in Tucker, *The Marx-Engels Reader*, pp. 629–52.

[24] Ibid.

[25] Ferdinand Lassalle, *The Working Man's Program* (London: Modern Press, 1884), p. 56.

[26] Karl Marx, "The Socialist Program Issued at Gotha (1875)," in *Readings in European History*, ed. James Harvey Robinson (Boston: Ginn, 1906), pp. 617–19.

[27] Karl Marx, "Critique of the Gotha Program," in Tucker, *The Marx-Engels Reader*, p. 538.

[28] Statistics in Douglas A. Chambers, *The Social Democratic Party of Germany from Working-Class Movement to Modern Political Party* (New Haven, CT: Yale University Press, 1964), p. 5.

[29] In the words of the Labor politician Ernest Bevin, cited in Samuel Beer, *Modern British Politics* (New York: Norton, 1982), p. 113.

CHAPTER 3. A REVOLUTIONARY PARTY EMERGES

[1] V. I. Lenin, *What Is to Be Done?*, in *The Lenin Anthology*, ed. Robert C. Tucker (New York: Norton, 1975), pp. 76–78.

[2] Karl Marx, "The Proletarian Revolution and the Renegade Kautsky," in *The Marx-Engels Reader*, ed. Robert C. Tucker, 2nd ed. (New York: Norton, 1978), p. 472.

[3] Cited in Franco Venturi, *Roots of Revolution* (New York: Grosset and Dunlap, 1960), p. 416.

[4] Mikhail Bakunin, "Revolutionary Catechism," cited in Philip Pomper, *Sergei Nechaev* (New Brunswick, NJ: Rutgers University Press, 1979), p. 91.

[5] Ibid.

[6] According to Russia's first census of 1897; cf. Reginald Zelnik, "Russian Workers and Revolution," in *The Cambridge History of Russia*, ed. Dominic Lieven, vol. 2, *Imperial Russia, 1689–1917* (Cambridge: Cambridge University Press, 2006), p. 620.

[7] Georgi Plekhanov, "Our Differences," in *Selected Philosophical Works*, vol. 1 (Moscow: Progress Publishers, 1974), p. 341.

[8] Ibid., pp. 340–41.

[9] Lenin, *What Is to Be Done?*, pp. 48–49.

[10] Ibid., p. 24.

[11] Ibid., p. 27.

[12] Ibid., p. 24.

[13] Karl Marx and Friedrich Engels, *Manifesto of the Communist Party*, in *The Marx-Engels Reader*, ed. Robert C. Tucker, 2nd ed. (New York: Norton, 1978), p. 484.

[14] Lenin, *What Is to Be Done?*, pp. 32–33.

[15] See Brian Pearce, ed., *1903: Second Congress of the Russian Social Democratic Labour Party* (London: New Park, 1978).

[16] Robert C. Tucker, ed., *The Lenin Anthology* (New York: W. W. Norton, 1975), p. 119.

[17] Leon Trotsky, *Our Political Tasks* (1904; repr., London: New Park, 1979), p. 77.

[18] V. I. Lenin, "Two Tactics," in Tucker, *The Lenin Anthology*, pp. 130–41.

[19] V. I. Lenin, *Collected Works* (hereafter *CW*), vol. 22 (Moscow: Progress Publishers, 1963), pp. 185–304.

[20] V. I. Lenin, "Lecture on the 1905 Revolution," *CW*, vol. 23 (1964), p. 253.

[21] *CW*, vol. 24 (1964), pp. 21–22.

[22] Ibid., p. 24n2.

[23] V. I. Lenin, "Our Differences," in *Collected Works of V. I. Lenin*, ed. Alexander Trachtenberg (New York: International, 1929), pp. 380–81.

[24] Lenin's remarks can be found in "The Tasks of the Proletariat in Our Revolution," which he wrote on April 10, 1917, and shared with prominent Bolshevik leaders. The full document was not published until September; see *CW*, vol. 24 (1964), pp. 84–86.

[25] Tucker, *The Lenin Anthology*, p. 328.

[26] Ibid., p. 334.

[27] Ibid., p. 373.

[28] Ibid., p. 345.

[29] Ibid., pp. 374–75.

[30] Cited in Fischer, *Life of Lenin* (New York: Harper and Row, 1964), p. 141.

[31] V. I. Lenin, "Report on the Activities of the People's Commissars," *CW*, vol. 26 (1964), pp. 458–59.

[32] Richard Pipes, *The Unknown Lenin* (New Haven, CT: Yale University Press, 1996), p. 50.

[33] *CW*, vol. 24 (1964), pp. 593–99.

[34] *CW*, vol. 27 (1965), p. 110.

[35] *CW*, vol. 29 (1965), pp. 224–25.

CHAPTER 4. INTERNATIONALIZING THE PARTY IDEA

[1] V. I. Lenin, "Speech at the Opening Session of the Congress," March 2, 1919, in *Collected Works* (hereafter *CW*), vol. 28 (Moscow: Progress Publishers, 1965), pp. 455–56.

[2] Leon Trotsky, "Great Days," in *The First Five Years of the Communist International*, vol. 1 (New York: Pioneer, 1945), p. 48.

[3] Leon Trotsky, "Manifesto of the Communist International," in *Founding the Communist International*, ed. John Riddell (New York: Anchor Foundation, 1987), p. 222.

[4] V. I. Lenin, "Speech at the Closing Session of the Congress," March 6, 1919, *CW*, vol. 28 (1965), pp. 476–77.

[5] Statistics in Roger Chickering, *Imperial Germany and the Great War, 1914–1918* (New York: Cambridge University Press, 2004), p. 196.

[6] "Statutes of the Communist International," in Kevin McDermott and Jeremy Agnew, *The Comintern: A History of International Communism from Lenin to Stalin* (New York: St. Martin's Press, 1997), pp. 226–28.

[7] Hannah Arendt, *Men in Dark Times* (New York: Mariner Books, 1970), p. 52.

[8] Rosa Luxemburg, *"The Mass Strike, the Political Party and the Trade Unions" and "The Junius Pamphlet"* (New York: Harper and Row, 1971), pp. 16–17.

[9] Ibid., p. 54.

[10] Ibid., p. 66.

[11] Ibid., pp. 73–74.

[12] Ibid., pp. 76–77.

[13] Ibid., pp. 203–4.

[14] Ibid., p. 205.

[15] Statistics in Scott Stephenson, *The Final Battle: Soldiers of the Western Front and the German Revolution of 1918* (Cambridge: Cambridge University Press, 2009), p. 287.

[16] Rosa Luxemburg, "Our Program and the Political Situation," in *Selected Political Writings*, ed. Dick Howard (New York: Monthly Review Press, 1971), p. 385.

[17] Statistics in Mária Ormos, *Hungary in the Age of the Two World Wars: 1914–1945* (New York: Columbia University Press, 2007), p. 20.

[18] Ivan Berend, *History Derailed: Central and Eastern Europe in the Long Nineteenth Century* (Berkeley: University of California Press, 2005), pp. 110, 178.

[19] Statistics in Ormos, *Hungary in the Age of the Two World Wars*, pp. 82–84, 557, and Miklós Molnár, *From Béla Kun to János Kádár: Seventy Years of Hungarian Communism* (New York: Berg, 1990), p. 6.

[20] In Robert Daniels, ed., *Documentary History of Communism and the World* (Hanover, NH: University Press of New England, 1994), p. 27.

[21] György Borsányi, *The Life of a Communist Revolutionary, Béla Kun* (Boulder, CO: Social Science Monographs, 1993), pp. 142–43.

[22] György Lukács, "Party and Class," in *Tactics and Ethics* (New York: Harper and Row, 1972), pp. 28–36.

[23] Bennett Kovrig, *Communism in Hungary: From Kun to Kádár* (Stanford, CA: Hoover Institution Press, 1979), p. 77.

[24] Ibid., p. 62.

[25] Levi cited his observations from an article published three days after the Soviet's formation, in "The Lessons of the Hungarian Revolution," in *International Communism in the Era of Lenin*, ed. Helmut Gruber (New York: Anchor Books, 1972), pp. 143–52.

[26] Borsányi, *Life of a Communist Revolutionary*, p. 182.

[27] Ibid., p. 202; emphasis added.

[28] Chickering, *Imperial Germany and the Great War*, p. 195.

[29] *Report of the 13th Annual Conference of the Labour Party* (London: Labour Party, 1918), pp. 44–46.

[30] V. I. Lenin, "Reply to a Letter from the Joint Provisional Committee of the Communist Party of Britain," *CW*, vol. 31 (1966), p. 202.

[31] V. I. Lenin, *"Left-Wing" Communism, an Infantile Disorder* (Moscow: Progress Publishers, 1977), p. 73.

[32] Cited in Henry Pelling, *The British Communist Party: A Historical Profile* (New York: Macmillan, 1958), p. 13.

[33] Cited in Robert Wohl, *The French Communist Party in the Making* (Stanford, CA: Stanford University Press, 1966), p. 190.

[34] Cited in *Le Congrès de Tours, décembre 1920*, ed. Annie Kriegel (Paris: R. Julliard, 1964), pp. 49–50, 62, 72.

[35] Ibid., pp. 125–34.

[36] Ibid., p. 134.

[37] *Congress of the Peoples of the East, Baku, September 1920*, ed. and trans. Brian Pearce (London: New Park, 1977), p. 125.

[38] C. R. Bawden, *The Modern History of Mongolia* (New York: Praeger, 1968), pp. 209–10.

[39] Daniels, *Documentary History of Communism*, p. 39.

[40] V. I. Lenin, "Talk with a Delegation of the Mongolian People's Republic," *CW*, vol. 42 (1969), pp. 360–61.

CHAPTER 5. CREATING THE LENINIST PARTY

[1] Joseph Stalin, *Foundations of Leninism* (Moscow: Foreign Languages Press, 1970), chap. 8.

[2] Joseph Stalin, "On the Draft Constitution of the USSR," November 25, 1936, in *Works* (hereafter *W*), vol. 14 (London: Red Star Press, 1978), p. 164.

[3] Leon Trotsky, *My Life* (New York: Pathfinder Press, 1970), p. 334.

[4] Letter from Lenin to the Central Committee, written before July 3, 1919, in *Selected Works*, vol. 3 (New York: International, 1971), pp. 226–42.

[5] T. H. Rigby, *Lenin's Government: Sovnarkom 1917–1922* (Cambridge: Cambridge University Press, 1979), pp. 61–63.

[6] In a memorial article written on March 13, 1925, in *Fourth International* 7, no. 11 (1946): 327–30.

[7] Stephen Kotkin, *Stalin*, vol. 1, *Paradoxes of Power, 1878–1928* (New York: Penguin, 2014), p. 318.

[8] See Graeme Gill, *The Origins of the Stalinist Political System* (Cambridge: Cambridge University Press, 1990), chap. 2.

[9] V. I. Lenin, "Speech at the First All-Russia Congress of Workers in Education and Socialist Culture," on July 31, 1919, in *Collected Works* (hereafter *CW*), vol. 29 (Moscow: Progress Publishers, 1972), pp. 532–39.

[10] Donald V. Raleigh, "The Russian Civil War, 1917–1922," in *Cambridge History of Russia*, ed. Ronald G. Suny, vol. 3, *The Twentieth Century* (Cambridge: Cambridge University Press, 2006), p. 166.

[11] V. I. Lenin, "Preliminary Draft Resolution of the Tenth Congress of the R.C.P. on Party Unity," *CW*, vol. 32 (1960), p. 242.

[12] *CW*, vol. 33 (1965), pp. 21–29.

[13] Ibid., p. 29.

[14] Gill, *Origins*, pp. 61, 67.

[15] T. H. Rigby, *Political Elites in the USSR* (Cheltenham, UK: Edward Elgar, 1990), p. 84; Gill, *Origins*, p. 116.

[16] Stalin, *Foundations of Leninism*, p. 111.

[17] Gill, *Origins*, p. 16.

[18] Joint Meeting of the Politburo and the Presidium of the Central Control Committee, "On Building the Party," December 5, 1923, in *Documents of Soviet History*, ed. Rex Wade, vol. 3 (Gulf Breeze, FL: Academic International Press, 1995), pp. 82–88.

[19] Kotkin, *Stalin*, p. 425.

[20] Leon Trotsky, "The New Course (A Letter to Party Members)," December 8, 1923, in *Challenge of the Left Opposition 1923–1925*, vol. 1 (New York: Pathfinder Press, 1975), p. 127.

[21] Ibid.

[22] *Pravda*, December 30, 1923; *Pravda*, January 1, 1924.

[23] Boris Souvarine, *Stalin: A Critical Survey of Bolshevism* (New York: Longmans, Green, 1939), pp. 362–63.

[24] Leon Trotsky, *The Lessons of October*, trans. John G. Wright (New York: Pioneer, 1937), p. 5.

[25] L. Kamenev, "Speech by Kamenev," in G. E. Zinoviev, J. Stalin, and I. Kamenev, *Leninism or Trotskyism* (Chicago: Daily Worker, 1925), p. 70.

[26] Joseph Stalin, "Trotskyism or Leninism," in Zinoviev et al., *Leninism or Trotskyism*, p. 41.

[27] Nikolai Bukharin, "The Party and the Opposition Bloc," in *A Documentary History of Communism*, ed. Robert Daniels, rev. ed., vol. 1 (Hanover, NH: University Press of New England, 1984), pp. 290.

[28] Joseph Stalin, "The October Revolution and the Tactics of the Russian Communists," *W*, vol. 6 (Moscow: Foreign Languages Publishing House, 1953), pp. 419–20.

[29] *W*, vol. 11 (Moscow: Foreign Languages Publishing House, 1954), p. 209.

[30] Ibid., pp. 267–79.

[31] Nikolai Bukharin, "Notes of an Economist," in *A Documentary History of Communism*, ed. Robert Daniels, vol. 1 (New York: Vintage, 1960), pp. 313–17.

[32] Alex Cummins, ed., *Documents in Soviet History*, vol. 1 (Gulf Breeze, FL: Academic Press, 1991), pp. 302–3.

[33] Bukharin, "Notes of an Economist," pp. 204–6.

[34] Joseph Stalin, "The Right Deviation in the C.P.S.U. (B.), Speech Delivered at the Plenum of the Central Committee and the Central Control Commission of the C.P.S.U.(B.) in April 1929," *W*, vol. 11, p. 41.

[35] Joseph Stalin, "Speech on Agrarian Policy, December 27, 1929," *W*, vol. 12 (Moscow: Foreign Languages Publishing House, 1954), pp. 147–78.

[36] Joseph Stalin, "Speech on December 21, 1929," *W*, vol. 12, p. 146.

[37] *W*, vol. 13 (Moscow: Foreign Languages Publishing House, 1954), pp. 353–55.

[38] Statistics in George Liber, *Total War and the Making of Modern Ukraine, 1914–1954* (Toronto: University of Toronto Press, 2016), p. 248.

[39] Joseph Stalin, "The Tasks of Business Executives," February 4, 1931, *W*, vol. 13, p. 41.

[40] Ibid., pp. 40–44.

[41] Stalin, "On the Draft Constitution of the USSR," p. 160.

[42] See Oleg V. Khlevniuk, *The History of the Gulag* (New Haven, CT: Yale University Press, 2004), pp. 165–69.

[43] Nikita Khrushchev, "Report to the 20th Congress of the Communist Party of the Soviet Union," in *The Crimes of the Stalin Era* (New York: New Leader, 1962), pp. S20–S21.

[44] "Bukharin's Letter to Stalin," in *Crimes of the Stalin Era*, pp. 556–60.

[45] Joseph Stalin, "Constitution (Fundamental Law) of the Union of Soviet Socialist Republics," *W*, vol. 14, p. 199.

[46] Joseph Stalin, "Report on the Work of the Central Committee to the Eighteenth Congress of the C.P.S.U.," March 10, 1939, *W*, vol. 14, p. 418.

[47] David Brandenberger and N. V. Zelenov, eds., *The Short Course on the History of the All-Union Communist Party (Bolsheviks)* (New Haven, CT: Yale University Press, forthcoming).

[48] Robert C. Tucker, *Stalin in Power: The Revolution from Above, 1928–1941* (New York: W. W. Norton, 1992), p. 537.

[49] *Pravda*, December 20, 1939.

[50] Joseph Stalin, "Speech at the Red Army Parade," November 7, 1941, in *On the Great Patriotic War of the Soviet Union* (Moscow: Foreign Languages Publishing House, 1946), pp. 38–41.

[51] Yoram Gorlizki, "Ordinary Stalinism: The Council of Ministers and the Soviet Neo-Patrimonial State, 1946–1953," *Journal of Modern History* 74, no. 4 (December 2002): 699–736.

CHAPTER 6. A DIFFERENT TYPE OF PARTY

[1] "Report on an Investigation of the Peasant Movement in Hunan," in *Selected Readings from the Works of Mao Tse-Tung* (Peking: Foreign Languages Press, 1971), p. 24.

[2] Karl Marx and Friedrich Engels, *Manifesto of the Communist Party*, in *The Marx-Engels Reader*, ed. Robert C. Tucker, 2nd ed. (New York: Norton, 1978), p. 482.

[3] Mao, "Report on an Investigation," pp. 24, 28–29, 33.

[4] Cited in Michael Gasster, "The Republican Revolutionary Movement," in *Cambridge History of China*, ed. John King Fairbank and Kwang-Ching Liu, vol. 11, pt. 2 (Cambridge: Cambridge University Press, 1980), p. 481.

[5] In Pei-kai Cheng and Michael Lestz, eds., *The Search for Modern China: A Documentary Collection* (New York: Norton, 1999), pp. 198–202.

[6] *Min Bao*, August 25, 1905. (Translation by April Dan Feng.)

[7] "A Public Declaration," in Cheng and Lestz, *The Search for Modern China*, pp. 202–6.

[8] Vera Schwarcz, *The Chinese Enlightenment* (Berkeley: University of California Press, 1986), p. 6.

[9] Cited in Cheng and Lestz, *The Search for Modern China*, pp. 334–38.

[10] Ibid., p. 241.

[11] In Lee Faigon, *Chen Duxiu: Founder of the Chinese Communist Party* (Princeton, NJ: Princeton University Press, 1983), p. 152.

[12] "Program of the Chinese Communist Party," in *The Rise to Power of the Chinese Communist Party*, ed. Tony Saich and Benjamin Yang (Armonk, NY: M. E. Sharpe, 1995), Doc. A.3, pp. 16–17.

[13] "The First Congress of the CCP," in Saich and Yang, *The Rise to Power*, Doc. A.2, p. 14.

[14] Ibid., p. 157.

[15] Stanley Rosen, "The Chinese Communist Party and Chinese Society," *Australian Journal of Chinese Affairs* 24 (July 1990): 55.

[16] John Fitzgerald, *Awakening China: Politics, Culture, and Class in the Nationalist Revolution* (Stanford, CA: Stanford University Press, 1996), pp. 185–87; Jacques Guillermaz, *A History of the Chinese Communist Party* (New York: Random House, 1972), pp. 79–80.

[17] "Resolution concerning the Problem of Communist Party Work in the Guomindang," in Saich and Yang, *The Rise to Power*, Doc. B.1, p. 119.

[18] Hans Van den Ven, *From Friend to Comrade: The Founding of the Chinese Communist Party, 1920–1927* (Berkeley: University of California Press, 1993), pp. 180–81.

[19] See C. Martin Wilbur, "Politicization and Communist Penetration of the National Revolutionary Army," in *The Cambridge History of China*, ed. John K. Fairbank, vol. 12, pt. 1 (Cambridge: Cambridge University Press, 1983), pp. 561–63.

[20] "Resolution on the Question of Organization (1925)," in Saich and Yang, *The Rise to Power*, Doc. B.11, pp. 158–61.

[21] Van den Ven, *From Friend to Comrade*, p. 162; Rosen, "The Chinese Communist Party," p. 55.

[22] "Resolution on the Relations between the CCP and the GMD," in Saich and Yang, *The Rise to Power*, Doc. B.12, pp. 161–63.

[23] Mao Zedong, "Report on an Investigation of the Peasant Movement in Hunan," in *Selected Readings*, pp. 46–47.

[24] Van den Ven, *From Friend to Comrade*, p. 223.

[25] Mao Zedong, "The Struggle in the Chingkang Mountains," November 25, 1928, in *Selected Works of Mao Tse-tung* (hereafter *SW*), vol. 1 (Peking: Foreign Languages Press, 1965), pp. 82–83.

[26] Ibid.

[27] Mao Zedong, "A Single Spark Can Light a Prairie Fire," *SW*, vol. 1, pp. 117–28.

[28] "Tactics against Japanese Imperialism," *SW*, vol. 1, pp. 162–69.

[29] Ibid.

[30] Jerome Chen, "The Chinese Communist Movement to 1927," in Fairbank, *The Cambridge History of China*, vol. 12, pt. 1, pp. 620–21.

[31] Stuart Schram, ed., *The Political Thought of Mao Zedong* (New York: Praeger, 1969), pp. 171–74.

[32] I am focusing on chapter 2, the sole chapter that Mao personally authored. *The Chinese Revolution and the Chinese Communist Party* (Peking: Foreign Languages Press, 1954), pp. 24–56.

[33] Ibid., pp. 47–50.

[34] Mao Zedong, "Rectify the Party's Style of Work," *SW*, vol. 3 (Peking: Foreign Languages Press, 1965), pp. 35–36, 41–43, 49.

[35] Ibid., p. 49.

[36] Mao Zedong, "Some Questions concerning Methods of Leadership," *SW*, vol. 3, p. 119.

CHAPTER 7. MONOLITHIC SOCIALISM

[1] "Resolution of the ECCI Presidium Recommending the Dissolution of the Communist International," in *The Communist International, 1919–1943: Documents*, ed. Jane Degras, vol. 3 (London: Oxford University Press, 1965), pp. 476–79.

[2] The classic work is Zbigniew K. Brzezinski, *The Soviet Bloc: Unity and Conflict* (Cambridge, MA: Harvard University Press, 1967).

[3] Branko Lazitch, *Les partis communistes d'Europe: 1919–1955* (Paris: Les Iles d'Or, 1956), p. 225.

[4] "Theses on Tactics," in *Fifth Congress of the Communist International* (London: Communist Party of Great Britain, 1924), pp. 27–42.

[5] Ibid.

[6] Ibid.

[7] *Imprekor 77*, no. 80 (May 11, 1925): 1017–69.

[8] In Kevin McDermott and Jeremy Agnew, *The Comintern: A History of International Communism from Lenin to Stalin* (Basingstoke, UK: Palgrave Macmillan, 1996), pp. 234–35.

[9] Cited in Peter Huber, "The Central Bodies of the Comintern," in *Bolshevism, Stalinism, and the Comintern*, ed. N. LaPorte, K. Morgan, and M. Worley (New York: Palgrave Macmillan, 2008), p. 68.

[10] Joseph Stalin, *Works* (hereafter *W*), vol. 11 (Moscow: Foreign Languages Publishing House, 1954), p. 207.

[11] Statistics in Hermann Weber, "The Stalinization of the KPD," in LaPorte et al., *Bolshevism, Stalinism, and the Comintern*, pp. 32–33.

[12] Report of June 10, 1929, Twelfth Congress of the Communist Party of Germany, in *Reden und Aufsätze zur Geschichte der deutschen Arbeiterbewegung*, vol. 2 (Berlin: Dietz, 1956), pp. 44–49.

[13] Ted Moran, *A Covert Life: Jay Lovestone: Communist, Anti-Communist, and Spymaster* (New York: Random House, 1999), p. 99.

[14] Joan Barth Urban, *Moscow and the Italian Communist Party: From Togliatti to Berlinguer* (Ithaca, NY: Cornell University Press, 1986), p. 95.

[15] Ibid., p. 55.

[16] *W*, vol. 13 (Moscow: Foreign Languages Publishing House, 1954), pp. 299, 308.

[17] Cited in Edward Mortimer, *The Rise of the French Communist Party: 1920–1947* (New York: Faber and Faber, 1984), p. 228.

[18] Georgi Dimitrov, "Report before the Seventh World Congress of the Communist International," in *Selected Works*, vol. 2 (Sofia: Sofia Press, 1972), pp. 7–85.

[19] Ibid.

[20] Geoff Eley, *Forging Democracy: The History of the Left in Europe* (New York: Oxford University Press, 2002), p. 276.

[21] Rafael Cruz, *El Partido Communista de España en la Segunda República* (Madrid: Alianza Editorial, 1987), pp. 56–57, 304–5.

[22] Harvey Klehr, John Earl Haynes, and Friedrich Firsov, *The Secret World of American Communism* (New Haven, CT: Yale University Press, 1994).

[23] *W*, vol. 15 (London: Red Star Press, 1984), pp. 11–19.

[24] Wolfgang Leonhard, *Child of the Revolution* (Chicago: Henry Regnery, 1967), pp. 229–30.

[25] *History of the Communist Party of the Soviet Union (Bolsheviks): Short Course* (San Francisco: Proletarian Publishers, 1939), p. 346.

[26] Paolo Spriano, *Stalin and the European Communists* (New York: Verso, 1985), p. 79.

[27] McDermott and Agnew, *The Comintern*, p. 145.

[28] Timothy Snyder, *Bloodlands: Europe between Hitler and Stalin* (New York: Basic Books, 2010), p. 103.

[29] "The Dissolution of the Communist International—Answer to Reuters' Correspondent," *W*, vol. 15, pp. 114–15.

[30] Lazitch, *Les partis communistes d'Europe*, p. 193.

[31] In M. Adereth, *The French Communist Party: A Critical History* (Manchester: Manchester University Press, 1989), p. 135.

[32] Lazitch, *Les partis communistes d'Europe*, pp. 225–26.

[33] Dieter Nohlen and Philip Stöver, *Elections in Europe: A Data Handbook* (Baden-Baden: Nomos, 2010), p. 480.

[34] Leonhard, *Child of the Revolution*, p. 381.

[35] Norman Naimark, *The Russians in Germany: A History of the Soviet Zone of Occupation, 1945–1949* (Cambridge, MA: Harvard University Press, 1995), p. 329.

[36] Speech by Zhdanov on September 25, 1947, in *The Cominform: Minutes of the Three Conferences, 1947/1948/1949*, ed. Giuliano Procacci (Milan: Fundazioni Feltrinelli, 1994), pp. 219, 229, 231.

37 Ibid., p. 219.

38 Ibid., p. 251.

39 Cited in Leonid Gibianskii, "The Soviet-Yugoslav Split and the Cominform," in *The Soviet Union and the Establishment of the Communist Regimes in Eastern Europe, 1944–1954: A Documentary Collection*, ed. Leonid Gibianskii and Norman M. Naimark (Washington, DC: National Council for Eurasian and East European Research, 2004), p. 293.

40 Procacci, *The Cominform*, p. 525.

41 Bennett Kovrig, *Communism in Hungary: From Kun to Kadar* (Palo Alto, CA: Hoover Institution Press, 1979), p. 244.

CHAPTER 8. REDISCOVERING THE LENINIST IDEA

1 *Pravda*, March 6, 1953; *Izvestia*, March 6, 1953.

2 *Current Digest of the Soviet Press* (hereafter *CDSP*) 5, no. 7 (March 28, 1953), p. 8.

3 In the words of Beria's son, Sergo. In Sheila Fitzpatrick, *On Stalin's Team* (Princeton, NJ: Princeton University Press, 2015), p. 208.

4 Feodor Burlatsky, *Khrushchev and the First Russian Spring* (New York: Charles Scribner, 1988), p. 36.

5 In D. M. Stickle, *The Beria Affair: The Secret Transcripts of the Meetings Signaling the End of Stalinism* (New York: Nova Science, 1992), pp. 10–11.

6 Ibid., pp. 174–77.

7 Speech by Malenkov on August 8, 1953, *CDSP* 5, no. 30 (September 5, 1953), pp. 3–26.

8 Stickle, *The Beria Affair*, p. 17.

9 *CDSP* 5, no. 13 (May 9, 1953), pp. 3, 30.

10 *CDSP* 5, no. 39 (November 7, 1953), pp. 38–41.

11 Ibid.

12 "Uncorrected Transcript of a Meeting of the Party Group of the USSR Supreme Soviet, February 8, 1955," http://digitalarchive.wilsoncenter.org/document/113336.

13 Ibid.

14 See "Otto Grotewohl's Handwritten Notes of a SED CC Politburo Meeting, July 8, 1953," *Cold War International History Project Bulletin* (hereafter *CWIHPB*), no. 10 (March 1998), pp. 100–101.

15 "Transcript of the Conversation between the Soviet Leadership and a HUWP Delegation in Moscow on June 13, 1953," *CWIHPB*, no. 10 (March 1998), pp. 81–86.

[16] Ferenc Váli, *Rift and Revolt in Hungary: Communism versus Nationalism* (Cambridge, MA: Harvard University Press, 1961), pp. 120–28.

[17] Imre Nagy, *On Communism, in Defense of the New Course* (New York: Praeger, 1957), p. xxxvii.

[18] Dennison Rusinow, *The Yugoslav Experiment 1948–1974* (Berkeley: University of California Press, 1978), p. 75.

[19] Richard West, *Tito and the Rise and Fall of Yugoslavia* (London: Faber and Faber, 2009), p. 256. Also see Milovan Djilas, *Anatomy of a Moral* (New York: Praeger, 1959), p. 135.

[20] Cited in Rusinow, *The Yugoslav Experiment*, p. 89.

[21] Nikita Khrushchev, *Crimes of the Stalin Era: Special Report to the Twentieth Congress of the CPSU* (New York: New Leader, 1962), pp. S25–S29.

[22] Ibid., p. S41.

[23] Ibid., p. S19.

[24] Although Khrushchev's use of this document is significant, Stephen Kotkin questions its authenticity. See his *Stalin*, vol. 1, *Paradoxes of Power* (New York: Penguin, 2014), pp. 418–19.

[25] Khrushchev, *Crimes of the Stalin Era*, p. S9.

[26] Ibid., p. S18.

[27] Ibid., p. S42.

[28] *CDSP* 8, no. 4 (March 7, 1956), p. 11.

[29] "The Speech by Comrade Ulbricht at the Sixth PUWP Plenum, March 20, 1956," *CWIHPB*, no. 10 (March 1998), pp. 41–43.

[30] Jan B. De Weydenthal, *The Communists of Poland* (Palo Alto, CA: Hoover Institution Press, 1978), pp. 81–82.

[31] L. W. Gluchowcki, "Poland, 1956," *CWIHPB*, no. 5 (Spring 1995), p. 38.

[32] According to a record of Gomułka's private conversations with a visiting Chinese delegation, on January 1, 1957, in *CWIHPB*, no. 5 (Spring 1995), p. 44.

[33] Mark Kramer, "New Evidence on Soviet Decision-Making in the 1956 Polish and Hungarian Crises," *CWIHPB*, nos. 8–9 (Winter 1996/1997), p. 361.

[34] Paul Zinner, ed., *National Communism and Popular Revolt in Eastern Europe* (New York: Columbia University Press, 1956), pp. 206–8, 234.

[35] In Zinner, *National Communism*, pp. 274–75.

[36] Ibid., p. 406.

[37] "Report from Anastas Mikoyan on the Situation in the Hungarian Workers' Party, July 14, 1956," in *The 1956 Hungarian Revolution: A History in Documents*, ed. Malcolm Byrne (Washington, DC: National Security Archive, November 4, 2002), p. 4.

[38] Kramer, "New Evidence," p. 325.

[39] See Zinner, *National Communism*, p. 453.

[40] From the session on October 24, as quoted in the notes of Czechoslovak party leader Antonín Novotný, in *CWIHPB*, no. 5 (Spring 1995), p. 55.

[41] " 'The Malin Notes' on the Crisis in Hungary and Poland," trans. Mark Kramer, *CWIHPB*, nos. 8–9 (Winter 1996/1997), pp. 388–94.

[42] William Taubman, *Khrushchev: The Man and His Era* (New York: W. W. Norton, 2004), p. 296.

[43] Lin Yunhui, "The 20th Party Congress of the Soviet Union and Mao Zedong's Tortuous Path," in *Cold War History of Sino-Soviet Relations* (Zurich: Parallel History Project on Cooperative Security, June 2006), pp. 3–4.

[44] "New Evidence on North Korea 1956." Introduction by James Person, *CWIHPB*, no. 16 (Fall/Winter 2008), pp. 447–54, 496–500.

[45] Statistics in Tony Judt, *Postwar: A History of Europe since 1945* (New York: Penguin, 2006), p. 321.

[46] Robert V. Daniels, *Documentary History of Communism and the World* (Hanover: University of Vermont Press, 1994), pp. 164–66.

[47] Ibid.

[48] William J. Thompson, *Khrushchev: A Political Life* (Basingstoke, UK: Palgrave Macmillan, 1997), p. 180.

[49] *CWIHPB*, no. 10 (March 1988), pp. 55–56.

[50] *CDSP* 11, no. 5 (March 11, 1959), pp. 13, 17.

[51] *CDSP* 11, no. 5 (March 11, 1959), p. 7.

[52] George Breslauer, *Khrushchev and Stalin as Leaders: Building Authority in Soviet Politics* (London: Allen and Unwin, 1982), pp. 169–72.

[53] *CDSP* 11, no. 5 (March 11, 1959), pp. 18–20. Compare with Lenin's "Notes of a Publicist," in *Collected Works*, vol. 33 (Moscow: Progress Publishers, 1965), p. 204.

[54] *CDSP* 13, no. 44 (November 29, 1961), p. 7.

[55] *CDSP* 13, no. 45 (December 6, 1961), pp. 17–18.

[56] Ibid., p. 20.

[57] Ibid., p. 30.

[58] *CDSP* 16, no. 40 (October 28, 1964), p. 6.

CHAPTER 9. THE CHARISMATIC LEADER AND THE PARTY

[1] "Fidel Castro's Broadcast," Foreign Broadcast Information Service (FBIS), December 4, 1959, pp. 59–61.

[2] I am using CCP as the acronym of the earlier Communist Party of Cuba, instead of PCC, because the conventional acronym of the second party is PCC.

[3] Che Guevara, "Socialism and Man in Cuba," in *The Che Reader: Writings on Politics and Revolution*, ed. David Deutschmann (Melbourne, Australia: Ocean Press, 2003), p. 214.

[4] José Martí, "Our America," in *Our America: Writings on Latin America and the Struggle for Cuban Independence*, trans. Elinor Randall with additional trans. by Juan de Onis and Roslyn Held Foner, ed. Philip S. Foner (New York: Monthly Review Press, 1977), p. 84.

[5] José Martí and A. M. Fernández, *El Partido Revolucionario Cubano*, Colección Clásicos del 98, vol. 8 (Oviedo, Spain: Universidad de Oviedo, 1998), pp. 5–12.

[6] Cited in Richard Gott, *Cuba: A New History* (New Haven, CT: Yale University Press, 2004), p. 130.

[7] On the difficulty of counting the number of attendees, see Jorge García Montez, *Historia del Partido Communista de Cuba* (Miami: Ediciones Universal, 1970), p. 57.

[8] Cited in Hugh Thomas, *Cuba: The Pursuit of Freedom* (New York: Harper and Row, 1971), pp. 712–13.

[9] David Deutschmann and Deborah Shnookal, eds., *The Fidel Castro Reader* (Melbourne, Australia: Ocean Press, 2007), pp. 88–90.

[10] Ibid., p. 67.

[11] Ibid., pp. 52–53, 88–89, 104–5.

[12] *New York Times*, June 24, 1957.

[13] Cited in Herbert L. Matthews, *Revolution in Cuba: An Essay in Understanding* (New York: Charles Scribner's Sons, 1975), p. 50.

[14] Cited in Servando Gonzalez, *The Secret Fidel Castro: Deconstructing the Symbol* (Oakland, CA: Spooks Books, 2001), p. 246.

[15] Fidel Castro, "This Is Democracy," speech on May 1, 1960, in *Fidel Castro Speeches*, vol. 2, *Our Power Is That of the Working People*, ed. Michael Taber (New York: Pathfinder Press, 1983), p. 26.

[16] Che Guevara, *Guerrilla Warfare* (Washington, DC: Scholarly Resources, 1997), p. 50.

[17] Interview on February 1, 1961, in *Communism*, ed. Mark Sandle (Harlow, UK: Pearson Education, 2012), pp. 151–52.

[18] Fidel Castro, "Against Bureaucracy and Sectarianism," speech on March 26, 1962, in Tauber, *Fidel Castro Speeches*, vol. 2, pp. 47, 52–53.

[19] Guevara, "Socialism and Man in Cuba," p. 224.

[20] Ibid.

[21] "Fidel Castro's Broadcast," Foreign Broadcast Information Service (FBIS), October 4, 1959, p. 10.

[22] "Castro on the Selection of Members to the Party Central Committee," October 24, 1965, *LANIC*, http://lanic.utexas.edu/project/castro/db/1965 /19651024.html.

[23] Statistics in Robert Furtak, *Kuba unter Weltkommunismus* (Cologne: Westdeutscher, 1967), p. 96.

[24] Fidel Castro, *Speech Commemorating the XVII Anniversary of the Storming of the Moncada Barracks* (Washington, DC: Squirrel, 1970).

[25] Marifeli Perez-Stable, *The Cuban Revolution* (New York: Oxford University Press, 1994), pp. 142–48.

CHAPTER 10. THE REVOLUTION RETURNS

[1] Mao Zedong, "On the People's Democratic Dictatorship," January 30, 1949, in *Selected Works of Mao Tse-tung* (hereafter *SW*), vol. 4 (Peking: Foreign Languages Press, 1961), p. 411.

[2] Ibid., p. 422.

[3] Ibid., p. 412.

[4] Odd Arne Westad, Chen Jian, Stein Tønnesson, Nguyen Vu Tung, and James G. Hershberg, "77 Conversations between Chinese and Foreign Leaders on the Wars in Indochina, 1964–77," Cold War International History Project, Working Paper 22 (Washington, DC, 1998), p. 191.

[5] Cable from Kovalev to Stalin, May 17, 1949, Cold War International History Project, *Bulletin*, no. 16, p. 162.

[6] Shi Zhe, "The Path to Recovery," *Chinese Historians* 6, no. 1 (Spring 1992): 40.

[7] Cf. Andrew G. Walder, *China under Mao: A Revolution Derailed* (Cambridge, MA: Harvard University Press, 2015), p. 65; Frank Dikötter, *The Tragedy of Liberation: A History of the Chinese Revolution 1945–1957* (London: Bloomsbury, 2013), p. 100.

[8] Mao, "On the People's Democratic Dictatorship," p. 423.

[9] Quoted in Wilma Fairbank, *Liang and Lin: Partners in Exploring China's Architectural Past* (Philadelphia: University of Pennsylvania Press, 1994), p. 170.

[10] Mao Zedong, "On the Cooperative Transformation of Agriculture," July 31, 1955, *SW*, vol. 5 (1977), p. 184.

[11] Ibid, p. 185.

[12] Mao Zedong, "On the Ten Major Relationships," April 25, 1956, *SW*, vol. 5 (1977), p. 304.

[13] Mao Zedong, "Political Report of the Central Committee of the CCP," September 15, 1956, in *Communist China 1955–1959*, prepared at Harvard University under the joint auspices of the Center for International Affairs and the East Asian Research Center (Cambridge, MA: Harvard University Press, 1962), p. 199.

[14] Ibid., p. 200.

[15] Ibid., pp. 198–201.

[16] "Report on the Revisions of the Constitution of the Communist Party of China," September 16, 1956, in *Eighth National Congress of the Communist Party of China*, vol. 1 (Peking: Foreign Languages Press, 1956), pp. 199–200.

[17] Michael Schoenhals, "Original Contradictions—on the Unrevised Text of Mao Zedong's 'On the Correct Handling of Contradictions among the People,'" *Australian Journal of Chinese Affairs*, no. 16 (July 1968), p. 101.

[18] Ibid., p. 102.

[19] Ibid., p. 104.

[20] Ibid., p. 105.

[21] Ibid., pp. 106–7. Mao uses the word "*naoshi*" to convey an image of disorganized "disturbances" in contrast to "*dong luan*," a pejorative term for organized "disturbances." The latter term was used by Deng Xiaoping in the 1970s and 1980s to condemn both the Great Proletarian Cultural Revolution and the student protests of spring 1989. I am grateful to Flora Xiao Tang for clarifying this distinction for me.

[22] Cited in Walder, *China under Mao*, p. 150.

[23] Liu Shaoqi, "Report on the Work of the Central Committee of the CCP," in *Communist China 1955–1959*, pp. 416–38.

[24] Mao Zedong, "Talks at the Hangzhou Conference (Draft Transcript)," January 3, 1958, in *The Secret Speeches of Chairman Mao*, ed. Roderick MacFarquhar, Timothy Cheek, and Eugene Wu (Cambridge, MA: Harvard University Press, 1989), p. 38.

[25] Mao Zedong, "Sixty Points on Working Methods—A Draft Resolution from the Office of the Centre of the CPC," in *Mao's Papers*, ed. Jerome Ch'en (London: Oxford University Press, 1970), p. 62.

[26] Ibid., p. 64.

[27] Mao, "Talks at the Hangzhou Conference (Draft Transcript)," p. 381, and Mao, "Sixty Points on Working Methods," p. 66.

[28] Mao Zedong, "Talks at the Beidaihe Conference (Draft Transcript)," August 17, 1958, in MacFarquhar, Cheek, and Wu, *The Secret Speeches of Chairman Mao*, pp. 408, 418, 426, and 431.

29 Ibid., p. 414.

30 Declassified CIA intelligence report, "Factionalism in the Central Committee," POLO xviii, September 19, 1968, p. 22.

31 Mao Zedong, "Speech at the Lushan Conference," July 23, 1959, in *Chairman Mao Talks to the People*, ed. Stuart Schram (New York: Pantheon, 1974), p. 139.

32 Ibid., p. 145.

33 Compare Jasper Becker, *Hungry Ghosts: Mao's Secret Famine* (New York: Holt, 1998), p. 270, and Frank Dikötter, *Mao's Great Famine: The History of China's Most Devastating Catastrophe* (London: Walker Books, 2010), p. vii. On official Chinese estimates, see Becker, *Hungry Ghosts*, p. 270.

34 In Lowell Dittmer, *Liu Shaoqi and the Chinese Cultural Revolution* (Armonk, NY: M. E. Sharpe, 1998), p. 35.

35 Deng Xiaoping, "Speech Delivered at Enlarged Working Conference of the Party Central Committee," February 6, 1962, in *Selected Works of Deng Xiaoping*, vol. 1 (Beijing: Foreign Languages Press, 1984), p. 294.

36 Ibid., p. 295.

37 Ibid., p. 297; emphasis added.

38 Ibid., p. 308.

39 Ibid., p. 311.

40 Mao Zedong, "Talk on the Four Clean-Ups Movement," January 3, 1965, in *Miscellany of Mao Tse-tung Thought: 1949–1964*, pt. 2 (Arlington, VA: Joint Publications Research Service, 1974), p. 439.

41 Michael Schoenhals and Roderick MacFarquhar, *Mao's Last Revolution* (Cambridge, MA: Harvard University Press, 2006), p. 262.

42 *CCP Documents on the Great Proletarian Cultural Revolution* (Hong Kong: Union Research Institute, 1968), p. 47.

43 *Constitution of the Communist Party of China*, adopted at the Ninth National Congress of the Communist Party on April 14, 1964 (Peking: Foreign Languages Press, 1969), p. 439.

44 Lin Biao's report was given on April 9, 1969, and adopted on April 14, 1969, in *Report to the Ninth National Congress of the Communist Party of China* (Peking: Foreign Languages Press, 1969), p. 105.

45 "Chairman Mao Talks to the People," in Schram, *Chairman Mao Talks to the People*, p. 293.

46 Cited in Maurice Meisner, *Mao's China and After: A History of the People's Republic*, 3rd ed. (New York: Free Press, 1999), p. 404.

CHAPTER 11. THE PARTY COMES BACK

[1] *Current Digest of the Soviet Press* (hereafter *CDSP*) 19, no. 44 (December 6, 1967), pp. 3–20.

[2] Ibid.

[3] For example, Geoffrey Swain and Nigel Swain, *Eastern Europe since 1945* (New York: St. Martin's Press, 1993), p. 101.

[4] Bennett Kovrig, *Communism in Hungary: From Kun to Kádár* (Palo Alto, CA: Hoover Institution Press, 1979), p. 448.

[5] Cited in Roger Gough, *A Good Comrade: Janos Kádár, Communism, and Hungary* (London: I. B. Tauris, 2006), p. 113.

[6] Ibid., p. 117.

[7] Cited in Kovrig, *Communism in Hungary*, p. 50.

[8] Cited in George Mueller and Hermann Singer, "Can the New Course Survive?," *Problems of Communism* (January–February 1965): 33.

[9] In Kovrig, *Communism in Hungary*, p. 402.

[10] *CDSP* 16, no. 45 (December 2, 1964), p. 16.

[11] Speech by Brezhnev to the Moscow party organization on March 29, 1968, in *CDSP* 20, no. 13 (April 17, 1968), pp. 4–6.

[12] *CDSP* 18, no. 13 (April 20, 1966), p. 4.

[13] Turnover statistics reflect the percentage of Central Committee members who were not reelected. See Evan Mawdsley and Steven White, *The Soviet Elite from Lenin to Gorbachev: The Central Committee and Its Members, 1917–1991* (Oxford: Oxford University Press, 2000), pp. 167–71; Robert Blackwell Jr., "Cadres Policy in the Brezhnev Era," *Problems of Communism* 28, no. 2 (1979): 29–33.

[14] Stephen Hanson, "The Brezhnev Era," in *The Cambridge History of Russia*, vol. 3, *The Twentieth Century*, ed. Ronald Grigor Suny (New York: Cambridge University Press, 2015), pp. 301–5; George Breslauer, *Khrushchev and Brezhnev as Leaders* (London: Allen and Unwin, 1982), pp. 195–96.

[15] Cited in H. Gordon Skilling, *Czechoslovakia's Interrupted Revolution* (Princeton, NJ: Princeton University Press, 1976), p. 161.

[16] Jaromír Navrátil, ed., *The Prague Spring '68* (Budapest: Central European University Press, 1998), pp. 13–15.

[17] Ibid., p. 521.

[18] Cited in Robin Remington, *Winter in Prague* (Cambridge, MA: MIT Press, 1970), pp. 98–99.

[19] Ibid., pp. 103–4, 113–15, 130–31.

[20] Zdeněk Mlynář, *Nightfrost in Prague* (New York: Karc, 1980), pp. 83, 88.

21 See the editorials by Sergei Kovalev in *Pravda*, September 11, 1968, and *Pravda*, September 26, 1968.

22 *CDSP* 20, no. 46 (December 4, 1968), p. 4.

23 *CDSP* 23, no. 12 (April 20, 1971), p. 15.

24 *Neues Deutschland*, August 19, 1961.

25 A. James McAdams, *East Germany and Détente* (Cambridge: Cambridge University Press, 1985), p. 113.

26 *Neues Deutschland*, April 1, 1971.

27 *Reden und Aufsätze*, vol. 1 (Berlin: Dietz, 1975), pp. 64–65.

28 Gale Stokes, *The Walls Came Tumbling Down* (Oxford: Oxford University Press, 1993), pp. 17–18.

29 Vojislav Koštunica, "The Constitution of the Federal States," in *Yugoslavia, a Fractured Federalism*, ed. Dennison Rusinow (Washington, DC: Wilson Center Press, 1988), pp. 83–84.

30 Slobodan Stankovic, "Meaning of Tito's Rijeka Speech," Radio Free Europe, September 7, 1972, p. 2.

31 Ibid.

32 Deng Xiaoping, "Emancipate the Mind, Seek Truth from Facts and Unite as One in Looking to the Future," December 13, 1978, in *Selected Works of Deng Xiaoping, 1975–1982* (hereafter *SW*) (Beijing: Foreign Languages Press, 1984), pp. 153–56.

33 Ibid., p. 160.

34 Deng Xiaoping, "Uphold the Four Cardinal Principles," March 30, 1979, *SW*, p. 172.

35 Deng Xiaoping, "On the Reform of the System of Party and State Leadership," August 18, 1980, *SW*, pp. 318, 312.

36 Cited in Robert King, "The National Party Conference," Radio Free Europe, July 31, 1972, p. 18.

37 Interview with Henry Shapiro, United Press International, September 12, 1972.

38 Enver Hoxha, "The Demagogy of the Soviet Revisionists Cannot Conceal Their Traitorous Countenance," January 10, 1969, in *The Party of Labor of Albania in Battle with Modern Revisionism: Speeches and Articles* (Tirana, Albania: Naim Frasheri, 1972), p. 514.

39 Enver Hoxha, "Letter to Comrade Hysni Kapo," July 30, 1978, in *Albania Challenges Khrushchev Revisionism* (New York: Gamma, 1976), pp. 128–31.

40 Adrian Buzo, *The Guerilla Dynasty: Politics and Leadership in North Korea* (London: I. B. Tauris, 1999), pp. 64, 67, 72.

[41] "Record of Conversation of Cde. L. I. Brezhnev with Leaders of Fraternal Parties of Socialist Countries in Budapest," March 18, 1975, National Security Archive, George Washington University, http://nsarchive.gwu.edu /NSAEBB/NSAEBB191/1975-03-18%20Brezhnev%20memcon.pdf.

[42] "Conference on Security and Co-Operation in Europe: Final Act (Helsinki 1975)," Department of State Publication 8826, General Foreign Policy Series 298 (August 1975), p. 80.

[43] Ibid.

[44] H. Gordon Skilling, *Charter 77 and Human Rights in Czechoslovakia* (London: George Allen and Unwin, 1981), pp. 209–12.

[45] Ibid.

[46] Robert Sharlet, *The New Soviet Constitution of 1977: Analysis and Text* (Brunswick, OH: King's Court Communications, 1978), p. 78.

[47] Daniele Caramani, *Elections in Western Europe* (London: Macmillan Reference, 2000), p. 662.

[48] Santiago Carrillo, *Eurocommunism and the State* (London: Lawrence Wishart, 1977), p. 101.

[49] Caramani, *Elections in Western Europe*, pp. 841–43.

[50] Ibid., p. 358.

CHAPTER 12. THE PARTY IN PERIL

[1] John Paul II, "No One Can Exclude Christ from the History of Mankind," in *Pilgrim to Poland* (Boston: Daughters of St. Paul, 1979), p. 68.

[2] "Protocol of Agreement between the Government Commission and the Interfactory Strike Committee Concluded on August 31, 1980, Gdańsk Shipyard," in *Poland: Genesis of a Revolution*, ed. Abraham Brumberg (New York: Vintage Books, 1983), pp. 285–95.

[3] Statistics in David S. Mason, "Membership of the Polish United Workers Party," *Polish Review* 27, no. 3 (1982): 138–53, and Zvi Gitelman, "The Limits of Organization and Enthusiasm," in *When Parties Fail: Emerging Political Organizations*, ed. Kay Lawson and Peter Merkl (Princeton, NJ: Princeton University Press, 1988), p. 438.

[4] "Protocol of PUWP CC Secretariat Meeting," in *From Solidarity to Martial Law*, ed. Andrzej Paczkowski and Malcolm Byrne (Budapest: Central European University Press, 2007), p. 108.

[5] Cited in Andrzej Paczkowski and Malcolm Byrne, "The Polish Crisis: Internal and International Dimensions," in Paczkowski and Byrne, *From Solidarity to Martial Law*, p. 16.

[6] Ibid, pp. 295–96.

[7] Ibid., p. 443.

[8] Wojciech Jaruzelski, Declaration of a "State of War," December 13, 1980, in *From Stalinism to Pluralism: A Documentary History of Eastern Europe since 1945,* 2nd ed., ed. Gale Stokes (New York: Oxford University Press, 1996), pp. 214–215.

[9] For example, Richard Pipes, "Gorbachev's Russia: Breakdown or Crackdown?," *Commentary* 89, no. 3 (1990): 13.

[10] On this speech, see Archie Brown, *The Gorbachev Factor* (Oxford: Oxford University Press, 1996), pp. 79, 125, and Anatoly S. Chernyaev, in *My Six Years with Gorbachev,* trans. Robert D. English and Elizabeth Tucker (University Park: Pennsylvania State University Press, 2000).

[11] See comparative statistics in Evan Mawdsley and Stephen White, *The Soviet Elite from Lenin to Gorbachev: The Central Committee and Its Members 1917–1991* (London: Oxford University Press, 2000), p. 171.

[12] Speech by Gorbachev on February 25, 1986, in *Current Digest of the Soviet Press* (hereafter *CDSP*) 38, no. 8 (March 26, 1986), p. 17.

[13] Ibid., p. 33.

[14] Ibid., p. 5.

[15] Ibid., p. 34.

[16] Speech on February 26, 1986, in *CDSP* 38, no. 9 (April 2, 1986), p. 11.

[17] *CDSP* 39, no. 44 (December 2, 1987), pp. 2–3.

[18] Ibid., p. 8.

[19] Ibid., p. 9.

[20] *CDSP* 40, no. 13 (April 27, 1988), pp. 1–4.

[21] *CDSP* 40, no. 26 (July 27, 1988), p. 25.

[22] *CDSP* 38, no. 8 (March 26, 1986), p. 31.

[23] *CDSP* 39, no. 45 (December 9, 1987), p. 16.

[24] Antoni Sulek, "The Polish United Workers' Party: From Mobilization to Non-Representation," *Soviet Studies* 42 (July 1990): 499.

[25] János Kis, Ferenc Kőszeg, and Ottilia Solt, "A New Social Contract," in Stokes, *From Stalinism to Pluralism,* pp. 233–36.

[26] *CDSP* 40, no. 26 (July 27, 1988), p. 26.

[27] In *The Democracy Reader,* ed. Diane Ravitch and Abigail Thernstrom (New York: HarperCollins, 1992), p. 249.

[28] Statistics in Rudolf Tökés, *Hungary's Negotiated Revolution* (New York: Cambridge University Press, 1996), pp. 324, 332.

[29] Zhang Liang, comp., and Andrew Nathan and Perry Link, eds., *The Tiananmen Papers* (New York: PublicAffairs, 2001), p. 26; Zhao Ziyang, *Prisoner of the State* (New York: Simon and Schuster, 2009).

[30] See Robert Daniels, ed., *Documentary History of Communism and the World* (Hanover, NH: University Press of New England, 1994), p. 370.

[31] Liang et al., *The Tiananmen Papers*, p. 71.

[32] Cited in Merle Goldman, "Vengeance in China," *New York Review of Books*, November 9, 1989, p. 5.

[33] "It Is Necessary to Take a Clear-Cut Stand against Disturbances," editorial in *People's Daily*, April 26, 1989, in *Beijing Spring, 1989: Confrontation and Conflict, the Basic Documents*, ed. Michael Oksenberg, Lawrence Sullivan, and Marc Lambert (Armonk, NY: M. E. Sharpe, 1990), pp. 206–8.

[34] Liang et al., *The Tiananmen Papers*, pp. 115–16.

[35] Ibid., pp. 116–18.

[36] Ibid., p. 186.

[37] Deng Xiaoping, "June 9 Speech to Martial Law Units," in Oksenberg, Sullivan, and Lambert, *Beijing Spring, 1989*, p. 377.

[38] Günter Schabowski, *Das Politbüro* (Reinbeck bei Hamburg: Rowohlt, 1990), p. 34.

[39] *Neues Deutschland* (hereafter *ND*), December 2, 1988.

[40] *Frankfurter Allgemeine Zeitung*, January 10, 1989.

[41] *ND*, January 20, 1989.

[42] *ND*, October 2, 1989.

[43] See Heinrich Bortfeldt, *Von der SED zur PDS* (Bonn, Germany: Bouvier, 1992).

[44] Schabowski, *Das Politbüro*, p. 25.

[45] *ND*, October 9, 1989.

[46] Entry of October 11, 1989, in *The Diary of Anatoly S. Chernyaev 1989*, National Security Archive Electronic Briefing Book No. 275 (Washington, DC: George Washington University Press, 2009), p. 39.

[47] *ND*, October 9, 1989.

[48] *ND*, November 9, 1989.

[49] Ibid.

[50] Graeme Gill, *The Collapse of a Single-Party System: The Disintegration of the Communist Party of the Soviet Union* (Cambridge: Cambridge University Press, 1994), p. 101.

[51] *CDSP* 42, no. 27 (1990), p. 14.

CHAPTER 13. THE PARTY VANISHES

[1] V. I. Lenin, "Notes of a Publicist: On Ascending a High Mountain; the Harm of Despondency; the Utility of Trade, Attitude toward the Mensheviks, Etc.," in *Collected Works*, vol. 33 (Moscow: Progress Publishers, 1965), pp. 204–5.

[2] Anna Grzymala-Busse, *Redeeming the Communist Past* (New York: Cambridge University Press, 2002), pp. 1–30.

[3] Cited in Bruce Cummings, *Korea's Place in the Sun* (New York: W. W. Norton, 1997), p. 417.

[4] Rhee Sang-Woo, "North Korea in 1991," *Asian Survey* 32, no. 1 (1992): 56.

[5] For the 1972 constitution, see Dae-Sook Suh, *Korean Communism 1945–1980: A Reference Guide to the Political System* (Honolulu: University of Hawaii Press, 1981), p. 502. For the 1991 amended version, see https://www.constituteproject .org/constitution/Peoples_Republic_of_Korea_1998.pdf?lang=en.

[6] Rhee Sang-Woo, "North Korea in 1990," *Asian Survey* 31, no. 1 (1991): 71.

[7] Sang-Woo, "North Korea in 1991," 56.

[8] Byung Chul Koh, " 'Military-First Politics' and Building a 'Powerful and Prosperous Nation' in North Korea," in *IFES Forum* (Seoul: Kyungnam University, Institute of Far Eastern Studies, 2005).

[9] See Chris Monday, "Family Rule as the Highest Stage of Communism," *Asian Survey* 51, no. 5 (2011): 813, 818.

[10] Unofficial English translation at http://www.northkoreatech.org/2012/04/18 /english-transcript-of-kim-jong-uns-speech/.

[11] Steve Tsang, "Consultative Leninism: China's New Political Framework," *Journal of Contemporary China* 18, no. 62 (2009): 875.

[12] David Schambaugh, *China's Communist Party: Atrophy and Adaptation* (Berkeley: University of California Press, 2009), p. 67.

[13] Henry Kissinger, *On China* (New York: Penguin, 2011), p. 442.

[14] Jiang Zemin, "Speech at the Meeting Celebrating the 80th Anniversary of the Founding of the Communist Party of China," July 1, 2001, in *China President Jiang Zemin Handbook: Strategic Information and Materials* (Washington, DC: International Business Publications, 2011), p. 70.

[15] Ibid., p. 88.

[16] See John Lewis and Xue Litai, "Social Change and Political Reform in China," *China Quarterly*, no. 176 (December 2003): 936; Nora Sausmikat, "More Legitimacy for One-Party Rule?," *Asien* 99 (April 2006): 80.

[17] These quotations are paraphrases of Xi Jinping's "2049 China Modern Socialist Country" speech; see "Xinhua Insight: Xi's Worldwide Diplomacy Benefits China, the World," *Xinhuanet*, January 5, 2016, http://news.xinhua net.com/english/2016-01/05/c_134980392.htm.

[18] See "Celebration Speech at the 75th Anniversary of the Founding of the Chinese Communist Party," *Renmin Ribao*, July 2, 2016 (translation by Flora Xiao Tang).

[19] See "Castro Gives Speech on Bay of Pigs Anniversary," April 20, 1991, *LANIC*, http://lanic.utexas.edu/project/castro/db/1991/19910420.html.

[20] Interview with Soviet Television, November 7, 1977, *LANIC*, http://lanic
.utexas.edu/project/castro/db/1977/19771107.html.

[21] Rhoda Rabkin, *Cuban Politics: The Revolutionary Experiment* (New York:
Praeger, 1991), p. 157.

[22] See "Castro Addresses Rally on 26 July Anniversary," June 26, 1978, *LANIC*,
http://lanic.utexas.edu/project/castro/db/1978/19780626.html.

[23] See the analysis of the White House national intelligence officer, Brian Latell,
in his *After Fidel: Raul Castro and the Future of Cuba's Revolution* (New
York: Palgrave Macmillan, 2005), pp. 207–16.

[24] Fidel Castro, *An Interview for NBC, February 24, 1988* (Havana: Editora
Politica, 1988), p. 50.

[25] Interview with Tomas Borge, *El Nuevo Diario*, June 3, 1992, http://www
.marxists.org/history/cuba/archive/castro/1992/06/03.htm.

[26] See his interview with *Siempre*, June 8, 1991, *LANIC*, http://lanic.utexas.edu
/project/castro/db/1991/19910608.html.

[27] See "Constitution of the Republic of Cuba, 1992," *Cubanet*, http://www.cubanet
.org/htdocs/ref/dis/const_92_e.htm.

[28] See Raúl Castro Ruz, "The Development of the National Economy, along with
the Struggle for Peace, and Our Ideological Resolve, Constitute the Party's
Principal Missions," *Granma*, April 18, 2016, http://en.granma.cu/cuba/2016
-04-18/the-development-of-the-national-economy-along-with-the-struggle-for
-peace-and-our-ideological-resolve-constitute-the-partys-principal-missions.

[29] Reuters, April 19, 2016.

[30] Mary Elise Sarotte, *1989: The Struggle to Create Post–Cold War Europe*
(Princeton, NJ: Princeton University Press, 2011), pp. 205–6.

SUGGESTED READINGS (BOOKS IN ENGLISH)

CHAPTER I. INTRODUCTION

Borkenau, Franz. *World Communism: A History of the Communist International.* Ann Arbor: University of Michigan Press, 1962.

Brown, Archie. *The Rise and Fall of Communism.* New York: Ecco, 2011.

Cohen, Stephen F. *Rethinking the Soviet Experience: Politics and History since 1917.* New York: Oxford University Press, 1985.

Courtois, Stéphane, Nicolas Werth, Jean-Louis Panné, Andrzej Paczkowski, Karel Bartošek, and Jean-Louis Margolin, *The Black Book of Communism: Crimes, Terror, Repression.* Edited by Mark Kramer. Translated by Jonathan Murphy and Mark Kramer. Cambridge, MA: Harvard University Press, 1999.

Furet, François. *The Passing of an Illusion: The Idea of Communism in the Twentieth Century.* Chicago: University of Chicago Press, 1999.

Jowitt, Ken. *New World Disorder: The Leninist Extinction.* Berkeley: University of California Press, 1992.

Judt, Tony. *Postwar: A History of Europe since 1945.* New York: Penguin, 2005.

Lowenthal, Richard. *World Communism: The Disintegration of a Secular Faith.* New York: Oxford University Press, 1969.

Malia, Martin. *The Soviet Tragedy: A History of Socialism in Russia, 1917–1991.* New York: Free Press, 1994.

Mazower, Mark A. *Dark Continent: Europe's Twentieth Century.* London: Penguin, 1998.

Pons, Silvio. *The Global Revolution: A History of International Communism 1917–1991.* Oxford: Oxford University Press, 2014.

Priestland, David. *Red Flag: A History of Communism.* New York: Grove, 2009.

Rosenberg, William G., and Marilyn B. Young. *Transforming Russia and China: Revolutionary Struggles in the Twentieth Century.* New York: Oxford University Press, 1982.

Service, Robert. *Comrades! A History of World Communism.* Cambridge, MA: Harvard University Press, 2007.

Smith, Stephen A., ed. *The Oxford Handbook of the History of Communism.* Oxford: Oxford University Press, 2014.

Tucker, Robert C. *The Marxian Revolutionary Idea.* New York: W. W. Norton, 1969.

Walicki, Andrzej. *Marxism and the Leap to the Kingdom of Freedom: The Rise and Fall of the Communist Utopia.* Stanford, CA: Stanford University Press, 1995.

CHAPTER 2.   A REVOLUTIONARY IDEA

Anderson, Margaret Lavinia. *Practicing Democracy: Elections and Political Culture in Imperial Germany.* Princeton, NJ: Princeton University Press, 2000.

Barclay, David E., and Eric D. Weitz. *Between Reform and Revolution: German Socialism and Communism from 1840 to 1990.* New York: Berghahn Books, 1998.

Bevir, Mark. *The Making of British Socialism.* Princeton, NJ: Princeton University Press, 2011.

Cole, G.D.H. *The Second International 1889–1914.* London: Macmillan, 1956.

Eley, Geoff. *Forging Democracy: The History of the Left in Europe, 1850–2000.* Oxford: Oxford University Press, 2002.

Kolakowski, Leszek. *Main Currents of Marxism: The Founders—The Golden Age—The Breakdown.* New York: W. W. Norton, 2008.

Landauer, Carl. *European Socialism: A History of Ideas and Movements from the Industrial Revolution to Hitler's Seizure of Power.* Berkeley: University of California Press, 1959.

Lindemann, Albert S. *A History of European Socialism.* New Haven, CT: Yale University Press, 1983.

Sperber, Jonathan. *Karl Marx: A Nineteenth-Century Life.* New York: Liveright, 2014.

CHAPTER 3.   A REVOLUTIONARY PARTY EMERGES

Fitzpatrick, Sheila. *The Russian Revolution.* Oxford: Oxford University Press, 1982.

Fowkes, Ben. *Communism in Germany under the Weimar Republic.* New York: St. Martin's Press, 1984.

Gooding, John. *Socialism in Russia: Lenin and His Legacy, 1890–1991.* Houndsmills, UK: Palgrave, 2002.

Harding, Neil. *Leninism*. Durham, NC: Duke University Press, 1996.

Lih, Lars T. *Lenin Rediscovered: "What Is to Be Done?" in Context*. Boston: Brill, 2006.

Pipes, Richard. *Russia under the Old Regime*. New York: Charles Scribner's Sons, 1974.

Rigby, T. H. *Lenin's Government: Sovnarkom 1917–1922*. Cambridge: Cambridge University Press, 1979.

———. *Political Elites in the USSR: Central Leaders and Local Cadres from Lenin to Gorbachev*. Hants, UK: Edward Elgar, 1990.

Schapiro, Leonard. *The Communist Party of the Soviet Union*. New York: Random House, 1970.

Service, Robert. *The Bolshevik Party in Revolution: A Study in Organizational Change, 1917–1923*. New York: Barnes and Noble Books, 1979.

CHAPTER 4. INTERNATIONALIZING THE PARTY IDEA

Claudín, Fernando. *The Communist Movement: From Comintern to Cominform*. Vol. 2. New York: Monthly Review Press, 1975.

Degras, Jane, ed. *The Communist International 1919–1943*. Vol. 2. London: Oxford University Press, 1960.

Judt, Tony. *Marxism and the French Left*. Oxford: Clarendon Press, 1986.

Leonhard, Wolfgang. *Child of the Revolution*. Chicago: Henry Regnery, 1967.

Lindemann, Albert S. *The Red Years: European Socialism versus Bolshevism, 1919–1921*. Berkeley: University of California Press, 1974.

McDermott, Kevin, and Jeremy Agnew. *The Comintern: A History of International Communism from Lenin to Stalin*. New York: St. Martin's Press, 1997.

Müller, Jan-Werner. *Contesting Democracy: Political Ideas in Twentieth-Century Europe*. New Haven, CT: Yale University Press, 2011.

Rees, Tim, and Andrew Thorpe, eds. *International Communism and the Communist International 1919–43*. Manchester: Manchester University Press, 1998.

Torańska, Teresa. *"Them": Stalin's Polish Puppets*. Translated by Agnieszka Kołakowska. New York: HarperCollins, 1988.

Urban, Joan Barth. *Moscow and the Italian Communist Party: From Togliatti to Berlinguer*. Ithaca, NY: Cornell University Press, 1986.

Williams, Stuart. *Socialism in France: From Jaurès to Mitterrand*. New York: St. Martin's Press, 1983.

CHAPTER 5.   CREATING THE LENINIST PARTY

Baberowski, Jörg. *Scorched Earth: Stalin's Reign of Terror*. New Haven, CT: Yale University Press, 2016.

Cohen, Stephen F. *Bukharin and the Bolshevik Revolution: A Political Biography, 1888–1938*. Oxford: Oxford University Press, 1980.

Fitzpatrick, Sheila. *On Stalin's Team: The Years of Living Dangerously in Soviet Politics*. Princeton, NJ: Princeton University Press, 2015.

Gellately, Robert. *Lenin, Stalin, and Hitler: The Age of Social Catastrophe*. New York: Alfred A. Knopf, 2007.

Getty, J. Arch, Oleg V. Naumov, and Benjamin Sher, eds. *The Road to Terror: Stalin and the Self-Destruction of the Bolsheviks*. New Haven, CT: Yale University Press, 2010.

Gill, Graeme J. *The Origins of the Stalinist Political System*. New York: Cambridge University Press, 1990.

Gorlizki, Yoram, and Oleg Khlevniuk. *Cold Peace: Stalin and the Soviet Ruling Circle*. Oxford: Oxford University Press, 2005.

Hanson, Stephen E. *Time and Revolution: Marxism and the Design of Soviet Institutions*. Chapel Hill: University of North Carolina Press, 1997.

Hoffman, David. *Stalinist Values: The Cultural Norms of Soviet Modernity, 1917–1941*. Ithaca, NY: Cornell University Press, 2004.

Kotkin, Stephen. *Magnetic Mountain: Stalinism as a Civilization*. Berkeley: University of California Press, 1995.

———. *Stalin*. Vol. 1, *Paradoxes of Power, 1878–1928*. New York: Penguin, 2014.

Liber, George O. *Total Wars and the Making of Modern Ukraine, 1914–1954*. Toronto: University of Toronto Press, 2016.

Naimark, Norman M. *Fires of Hatred: Ethnic Cleansing in Twentieth-Century Europe*. Cambridge, MA: Harvard University Press, 2001.

Priestland, David. *Stalinism and the Politics of Mobilization: Ideas, Power, and Terror in Inter-war Russia*. Oxford: Oxford University Press, 2007.

Snyder, Timothy. *Bloodlands: Europe between Hitler and Stalin*. New York: Basic Books, 2010.

Tucker, Robert C. *Stalin in Power: The Revolution from Above, 1928–1941*. New York: W. W. Norton, 1990.

CHAPTER 6.   A DIFFERENT TYPE OF PARTY

Bergère, Marie-Claire. *Sun Yat-sen*. Palo Alto, CA: Stanford University Press, 1994.

Cheek, Timothy, ed. *A Critical Introduction to Mao*. New York: Cambridge University Press, 2010.

Guillermaz, Jacques. *A History of the Chinese Communist Party 1921–1949*. Translated by Anne Destenay. New York: Random House, 1972.

Ishikawa, Yoshihiro. *The Formation of the Chinese Communist Party*. New York: Columbia University Press, 2013.

Johnson, Chalmers. *Peasant Nationalism and Communist Power: The Emergence of Revolutionary China 1937–1945*. Stanford, CA: Stanford University Press, 1962.

Karl, Rebecca E. *Mao Zedong and China in the Twentieth-Century World: A Concise History*. Durham, NC: Duke University Press, 2010.

Knight, Nick. *Rethinking Mao: Explorations in Mao Zedong's Thought*. Lanham, MD: Lexington Books, 2007.

Perry, Elizabeth. *Anyuan: Mining China's Revolutionary Tradition*. Berkeley: University of California Press, 2012.

Rowe, William T. *China's Last Empire: The Great Qing*. Cambridge, MA: Belknap Press of Harvard University Press, 2012.

Schram, Stuart R. *The Political Thought of Mao Tse-tung*. New York: Praeger, 1969.

Spence, Jonathan D. *Mao Zedong*. New York: Penguin, 1999.

———. *The Search for Modern China*. 2nd ed. New York: Norton, 1990.

van de Ven, Hans J. *From Friend to Comrade: The Founding of the Chinese Communist Party, 1920–1927*. Berkeley: University of California Press, 1991.

Zhao, Suisheng. *A Nation-State by Construction: Dynamics of Modern Chinese Nationalism*. Palo Alto, CA: Stanford University Press, 2004.

CHAPTER 7. MONOLITHIC SOCIALISM

Applebaum, Anne. *Iron Curtain: The Crushing of Eastern Europe, 1944–1956*. New York: Doubleday, 2012.

Banac, Ivo. *The National Question in Yugoslavia: Origins, History, Politics*. Ithaca, NY: Cornell University Press, 1984.

Brzezinski, Zbigniew. *The Soviet Bloc: Unity and Conflict*. Cambridge, MA: Harvard University Press, 1967.

Connelly, John. *Captive University: The Sovietization of East German, Czech, and Polish Higher Education, 1945–1956*. Chapel Hill: University of North Carolina Press, 2000.

Cummings, Bruce. *Korea's Place in the Sun: A Modern History*. New York: W. W. Norton, 1997.

Djilas, Milovan. *Conversations with Stalin*. Harmondsworth, UK: Penguin, 1967.

Janos, Andrew C. *East Central Europe in the Modern World: The Politics of the Borderlands from Pre- to Post-communism*. Stanford, CA: Stanford University Press, 2000.

Rothschild, Joseph. *East Central Europe between the Two World Wars*. Seattle: University of Washington Press, 1983.

———. *Return to Diversity: A Political History of East Central Europe since World War II*. 2nd ed. New York: Oxford University Press, 1993.

Schöpflin, George. *Politics in Eastern Europe 1945–1992*. Oxford: Blackwell, 1993.

Seton-Watson, Hugh. *The East European Revolution*. New York: Praeger, 1962.

Snyder, Timothy, and Ray Brandon, eds. *Stalin and Europe: Imitation and Domination, 1928–1953*. New York: Oxford University Press, 2014.

Spriano, Paolo. *Stalin and the European Communists*. London: Verso, 1985.

West, Richard. *Tito and the Rise and Fall of Yugoslavia*. New York: Carroll and Graf, 1994.

CHAPTER 8.   REDISCOVERING THE LENINIST IDEA

Breslauer, George W. *Khrushchev and Brezhnev as Leaders: Building Authority in Soviet Politics*. London: George Allen and Unwin, 1982.

Fursenko, Aleksandr, and Timothy Naftali. *Khrushchev's Cold War*. New York: W. W. Norton, 2006.

Gati, Charles. *Hungary and the Soviet Bloc*. Durham, NC: Duke University Press, 1986.

Khrushchev, Sergei N. *Nikita Khrushchev and the Creation of a Superpower*. Translated by Shirley Benson. University Park: Pennsylvania State University Press, 2000.

Medvedev, Roy A., and Zhores A. Medvedev. *Khrushchev: The Years in Power*. Translated by Andrew R. Durkin. New York: W. W. Norton, 1978.

Taubman, William. *Khrushchev: The Man and His Era*. New York: W. W. Norton, 2003.

Taubman, William, Sergei Khrushchev, and Abbott Gleason, eds. *Nikita Khrushchev*. New Haven, CT: Yale University Press, 2000.

Tompson, William J. *Khrushchev: A Political Life*. New York: St. Martin's Press, 1995.

CHAPTER 9. THE CHARISMATIC LEADER AND THE PARTY

Colburn, Forrest D. *The Vogue of Revolution in Poor Countries.* Princeton, NJ: Princeton University Press, 1994.

Coltman, Leycester, and Julia Sweig. *The Real Fidel Castro.* New Haven, CT: Yale University Press, 2003.

Deutschmann, David, and Deborah Shnookal, eds. *Fidel Castro Reader.* Melbourne: Ocean Press, 2007.

Domínguez, Jorge I. *Cuba: Order and Revolution.* Cambridge, MA: Belknap Press of Harvard University Press, 1978.

Farber, Samuel. *The Origins of the Cuban Revolution Reconsidered.* Chapel Hill: University of North Carolina Press, 2006.

Gott, Richard. *Cuba: A New History.* New Haven, CT: Yale University Press, 2004.

Martínez-Fernández, Luis. *Revolutionary Cuba: A History.* Gainesville: University Press of Florida, 2014.

Pérez-Stable, Marifeli. *The Cuban Revolution: Origins, Course, and Legacy.* Oxford: Oxford University Press, 1993.

Rabkin, Rhoda P. *Cuban Politics: The Revolutionary Experiment.* New York: Praeger, 1991.

Sweig, Julia. *Inside the Cuban Revolution: Fidel Castro and the Urban Underground.* Cambridge, MA: Harvard University Press, 2002.

CHAPTER 10. THE REVOLUTION RETURNS

Dikötter, Frank. *Mao's Great Famine: The History of China's Most Devastating Catastrophe, 1958–1962.* New York: Walker, 2010.

Dittmer, Lowell. *Liu Shao-ch'i and the Chinese Cultural Revolution: The Politics of Mass Criticism.* Berkeley: University of California Press, 1974.

Lawrence, Alan. *China under Communism.* London: Routledge, 1998.

Li, Zhisui. *The Private Life of Chairman Mao: The Memoirs of Mao's Personal Physician.* Translated by Tai Hung-chao, with the editorial assistance of Anne F. Thurston. New York: Random House, 1994.

MacFarquhar, Roderick. *The Origins of the Cultural Revolution.* Oxford: Oxford University Press, 1997.

MacFarquhar, Roderick, Timothy Cheek, Eugene Wu, Merle Goldman, and Benjamin I. Schwartz, eds. *The Secret Speeches of Chairman Mao: From the Hundred Flowers to the Great Leap Forward.* Cambridge, MA: Council on East Asian Studies, Harvard University, 1989.

MacFarquhar, Roderick, and Michael Schoenhals. *Mao's Last Revolution.* Cambridge, MA: Belknap Press of Harvard University Press, 2006.

Meisner, Maurice. *Mao's China and After: A History of the People's Republic.* 3rd ed. New York: Free Press, 1999.

Saich, Tony, and Hans van de Ven, eds. *New Perspectives on the Chinese Communist Revolution.* Armonk, NY: M. E. Sharpe, 1995.

Schöpflin, George. *Politics in Eastern Europe.* Oxford: Blackwell, 1993.

Thaxton, Ralph A., Jr. *Catastrophe and Contention in Rural China: Mao's Great Leap Forward Famine and the Origins of Righteous Resistance in Da Fo Village.* New York: Cambridge University Press, 2008.

Walder, Andrew G. *China under Mao: A Revolution Derailed.* Cambridge, MA: Harvard University Press, 2015.

Yang, Dali L. *Calamity and Reform in China: State, Rural Society, and Institutional Change since the Great Leap Famine.* Stanford, CA: Stanford University Press, 1996.

CHAPTER 11. THE PARTY COMES BACK

Bialer, Seweryn. *Stalin's Successors: Leadership, Stability, and Change in the Soviet Union.* New York: Cambridge University Press, 1980.

De Weydenthal, Jan B. *The Communists of Poland: An Historical Outline.* Stanford, CA: Hoover Institution Press, 1978.

Dittmer, Lowell. *China's Continuous Revolution: The Post-liberation Epoch, 1949–1981.* Berkeley: University of California Press, 1987.

Ekiert, Grzegorz. *The State against Society: Political Crises and Their Aftermath in East Central Europe.* Princeton, NJ: Princeton University Press, 1996.

Kopstein, Jeffrey. *The Politics of Economic Decline in East Germany, 1945–1989.* Chapel Hill: University of North Carolina Press, 1997.

Kovrig, Bennett. *Communism in Hungary: From Kun to Kádár.* Stanford, CA: Hoover Institution Press, 1979.

Lendvai, Paul. *Hungary: Between Democracy and Authoritarianism.* New York: Columbia University Press, 2010.

McAdams, A. James. *East Germany and Détente.* Cambridge: Cambridge University Press, 1985.

———. *Germany Divided: From the Wall to Reunification.* Princeton, NJ: Princeton University Press, 1993.

Navrátil, Jaromire. *The Prague Spring 1968.* Budapest: Central European University Press, 1998.

Ramet, Sabrina P. *The Three Yugoslavias: State-Building and Legitimation 1918–2005*. Bloomington: Indiana University Press, 2006.

Rusinow, Dennison. *The Yugoslav Experiment 1948–1974*. Berkeley: University of California Press, 1978.

Smith, W. Rand. *Enemy Brothers: Socialists and Communists in France, Italy, and Spain*. Plymouth, UK: Rowman and Littlefield, 2012.

Teiwes, Frederick C., and Warren Sun. *The End of the Maoist Era: Chinese Politics during the Twilight of the Cultural Revolution, 1972–1976*. Armonk, NY: M. E. Sharpe, 2007.

Tismaneanu, Vladimir. *Stalinism for All Seasons: A Political History of Romanian Communism*. Berkeley: University of California Press, 2003.

CHAPTER 12. THE PARTY IN PERIL

Banac, Ivo, ed. *Eastern Europe in Revolution*. Ithaca, NY: Cornell University Press, 1992.

Brown, Archie. *The Gorbachev Factor*. Oxford: Oxford University Press, 1996.

Dimitrov, Martin. *Why Communism Did Not Collapse*. New York: Cambridge University Press, 2013.

English, Robert D. *Russia and the Idea of the West: Gorbachev, Intellectuals and the End of the Cold War*. New York: Columbia University Press, 2000.

Garton Ash, Timothy. *The Magic Lantern: The Revolution of '89 Witnessed in Warsaw, Budapest, Berlin, and Prague*. New York: Random House, 1990.

———. *The Polish Revolution: Solidarity, 1980–82*. New York: Scribner, 1984.

Ogushi, Atsushi. *The Demise of the Soviet Communist Party*. New York: Routledge, 2008.

O'Neill, Patrick H. *Revolution from Within: The Hungarian Socialist Workers' Party and the Collapse of Communism*. Cheltenham, UK: Edward Elgar, 1998.

Roeder, Philip G. *Red Sunset: The Failure of Soviet Politics*. Princeton, NJ: Princeton University Press, 1993.

Sarotte, Mary Elise. *1989: The Struggle to Create Post–Cold War Europe*. Princeton, NJ: Princeton University Press, 2011.

Stokes, Gale. *The Walls Came Tumbling Down: The Collapse of Communism in Eastern Europe*. New York: Oxford University Press, 1993.

Tismaneanu, Vladimir. *Reinventing Politics: From Stalin to Havel*. New York: Free Press, 1992.

Tőkés, Rudolf L. *Hungary's Negotiated Revolution: Economic Reform, Social Change, and Political Succession, 1957–1990.* Cambridge: Cambridge University Press, 1996.

Vogel, Ezra F. *Deng Xiaoping and the Transformation of China.* Cambridge, MA: Belknap Press of Harvard University Press, 2011.

Weston, Timothy, and Lionel Jensen. *China in and beyond the Headlines.* Lanham, MD: Rowman and Littlefield, 2012.

CHAPTER 13.   THE PARTY VANISHES

Bermeo, Nancy, ed. *Liberalization and Democratization: Change in the Soviet Union and Eastern Europe.* Baltimore, MD: Johns Hopkins University Press, 1992.

Bunce, Valerie. *Subversive Institutions: The Design and the Destruction of Socialism and the State.* New York: Cambridge University Press, 1999.

Dickson, Bruce J. *The Dictator's Dilemma: The Chinese Communist Party's Strategy for Survival.* New York: Oxford University Press, 2016.

Ekiert, Grzegorz, and Stephen E. Hanson, eds. *Capitalism and Democracy in Central and Eastern Europe: Assessing the Legacy of Communist Rule.* Cambridge: Cambridge University Press, 2003.

Fewsmith, Joseph. *China since Tiananmen: The Politics of Transition.* Cambridge: Cambridge University Press, 2001.

Fowkes, Ben. *The Post-Communist Era: Change and Continuity in Eastern Europe.* New York: St. Martin's Press, 1999.

Gill, Graeme. *Democracy and Post-Communism: Political Change in the Post-Communist World.* London: Routledge, 2002.

Grzymała-Busse, Anna Maria. *Redeeming the Communist Past: The Regeneration of Communist Parties in East Central Europe.* Cambridge: Cambridge University Press, 2002.

Holmes, Leslie. *Post-Communism: An Introduction.* Durham, NC: Duke University Press, 1997.

Ishiyama, John T., ed. *Communist Successor Parties in Post-Communist Politics.* Commack, NY: Nova Science Publishers, 1999.

McGregor, Richard. *The Party: The Secret World of China's Communist Rulers.* New York: Harper, 2010.

Pei, Minxin. *China's Trapped Transition: The Limits of Developmental Autocracy.* Cambridge, MA: Harvard University Press, 2006.

Shambaugh, David L. *China's Communist Party: Atrophy and Adaptation.* Berkeley: University of California Press, 2008.

Tismaneanu, Vladimir. *Fantasies of Salvation: Democracy, Nationalism, and Myth in Post-Communist Europe.* Princeton, NJ: Princeton University Press, 1998.

Way, Lucan. *Pluralism by Default: Weak Autocrats and the Rise of Competitive Politics.* Baltimore: Johns Hopkins University Press, 2015.

INDEX